CRC SERIES IN RADIOTRACERS IN BIOLOGY AND MEDICINE

Editor-in-Chief

Lelio G. Colombetti, Sc.D.
Loyola University
Stritch School of Medicine
Maywood, Illinois

STUDIES OF CELLULAR
FUNCTION USING
RADIOTRACERS
Mervyn W. Billinghurst, Ph.D.
Radiopharmacy
Health Sciences Center
Winnipeg, Manitoba, Canada

RECEPTOR-BINDING
RADIOTRACERS
William C. Eckelman, Ph.D.
Department of Radiology
George Washington University School
of Medicine
Washington, D.C.

GENERAL PROCESSES OF
RADIOTRACER LOCALIZATION
Leopold J. Anghileri, D.Sc.
Laboratory of Biophysics
University of Nancy
Nancy, France

BIOLOGIC APPLICATIONS OF
RADIOTRACERS
Howard J. Glenn, Ph.D.
University of Texas System Cancer
Center
M.D. Anderson Hospital and Tumor
Institute
Houston, Texas

RADIATION BIOLOGY
Donald Pizzarello, Ph.D.
Department of Radiology
New York University Medical Center
New York, New York

BIOLOGICAL TRANSPORT OF
RADIOTRACERS
Lelio G. Colombetti, Sc.D.
Loyola University
Stritch School of Medicine
Maywood, Illinois

RADIOTRACERS
FOR MEDICAL
APPLICATIONS
Garimella V. S. Rayudu, Ph.D
Nuclear Medicine Department
Rush University Medical Center
Presbyterian - St. Luke's Hospital
Chicago, Illinois

BASIC PHYSICS
W. Earl Barnes, Ph.D.
Nuclear Medicine Service
Edward Hines, Jr., Hospital
Hines, Illinois

RADIOBIOASSAYS
Fuad S. Ashkar, M.D.
Radioassay Laboratory
Jackson Memorial Medical Center
University of Miami School of Medicine
Miami, Florida

Biological Transport of Radiotracers

Editor

Lelio G. Colombetti, Sc.D.
Loyola University
Stritch School of Medicine
Maywood, Illinois

Editor-in-Chief
CRC Series in Radiotracers in Biology and Medicine

Lelio G. Colombetti, Sc.D.

CRC Press, Inc.
Boca Raton, Florida

Library of Congress Cataloging in Publication Data
Main entry under title:

Biological transport of radiotracers.

(CRC series in radiotracers in biology
and medicine)
Bibliography: p.
Includes index.
1. Radioactive tracers in biochemistry.
2. Biological transport. I. Colombetti,
Lelio G. II. Series.
QP519.9.R28B56   612'.01583   81-21569
ISBN 0-8493-6017-X   AACR2

Direct all inquiries to CRC Press, Inc., 2000 Corporate Blvd., N.W., Boca Raton, Florida, 33431.

© 1982 by CRC Press, Inc.

International Standard Book Number 0-8493-6017-X

Library of Congress Card Number 81-21569
Printed in the United States

FOREWORD

This series of books on Radiotracers in Biology and Medicine is on the one hand an unbelievably expansive enterprise and on the other hand, a most noble one as well. Tools to probe biology have developed at an accelerating rate. Hevesy pioneered the application of radioisotopes to the study of chemical processes, and since that time, radioisotopic methodology has probably contributed as much as any other methodology to the analysis of the fine structure of biologic systems. Radioisotopic methodologies represent powerful tools for the determination of virtually any process of biologic interest. It should not be surprising, therefore, that any effort to encompass all aspects of radiotracer methodology is both desirable in the extreme and doomed to at least some degree of inherent failure. The current series is assuredly a success relative to the breadth of topics which range from in depth treatise of fundamental science or abstract concepts to detailed and specific applications, such as those in medicine or even to the extreme of the methodology for sacrifice of animals as part of a radiotracer distribution study. The list of contributors is as impressive as is the task, so that one can be optimistic that the endeavor is likely to be as successful as efforts of this type can be expected to be. The prospects are further enhanced by the unbounded energy of the coordinating editor. The profligate expansion of application of radioisotopic methods relate to their inherent and exquisite sensitivity, ease of quantitation, specificity, and comparative simplicity, especially with modern instrumentation and reagents, both of which are now readily and universally available. It is now possible to make biological measurements which were otherwise difficult or impossible. These measurements allow us to begin to understand processes in depth in their unaltered state so that radioisotope methodology has proved to be a powerful probe for insight into the function and perturbations of the fine structure of biologic systems. Radioisotopic methodology has provided virtually all of the information now known about the physiology and pathophysiology of several organ systems and has been used abundantly for the development of information on every organ system and kinetic pathway in the plant and animal kingdoms. We all instinctively turn to the thyroid gland and its homeostatic interrelationships as an example, and an early one at that, of the use of radioactive tracers to elaborate normal and abnormal physiology and biochemistry, but this is but one of many suitable examples. Nor is the thyroid unique in the appreciation that a very major and important residua of diagnostic and therapeutic methods of clinical importance result from an even larger number of procedures used earlier for investigative purposes and, in some instances, procedures used earlier for investigative purposes and, in some instances, advocated for clinical use. The very ease and power of radioisotopic methodology tempts one to use these techniques without sufficient knowledge, preparation or care and with the potential for resulting disastrous misinformation. There are notable research and clinical illustrations of this problem, which serve to emphasize the importance of texts such as these to which one can turn for guidance in the proper use of these powerful methods. Radioisotopic methodology has already demonstrated its potential for opening new vistas in science and medicine. This series of texts, extensive though they be, yet must be incomplete in some respects. Multiple authorship always entails the danger of nonuniformity of quality, but the quality of authorship herein assembled makes this likely to be minimal. In any event, this series undoubtedly will serve an important role in the continued application of radioisotopic methodology to the exciting and unending, yet answerable, questions in science and medicine!

Gerald L. DeNardo, M.D.
Professor of Radiology, Medicine,
Pathology and Veterinary Radiology
University of California, Davis-
Sacramento Medical School
Director, Division of Nuclear Medicine

PREFACE

It has been said that life processes depend to some degree on biological transport. In effect, life itself could not exist without effective transport mechanisms, even in unicellular species, since nutrients must be transported into the cells and waste products, many of which are toxic, transported from them.

It was during the last few decades that this subject caught the attention of scientists trying to solve certain problems involved with life processes and disease. The need to understand how substances are brought together in the innermost part of cells, producing reactions that are in many cases completely incompatible with one another, and, at the same time, taking materials from the fluids surrounding the cells, secreting the products manufactured by cells, etc., created the need to develop new approaches to study these processes.

For our purpose we do not limit the problems of transport to determining the specific mode by which a solution or substrate passes from one side of the cell membrane to the other. It is not that we are trying to disregard the enormous role of transport in cellular function, but we recognize in addition that before a cell can incorporate a substance, this substance must be transported to the cell. This is quite a difficult problem in the human since body fluids are not only very complex in composition, but they may carry extraneous materials, such as drugs, which may influence chemically the substances introduced into the fluids through i.v. administration, intestinal absorption, etc.

This book attempts to explain many of these transport processes for radiolabeled tracers. We believe it is a timely topic since, in our need to know more about the behavior of radiotracers in the human body, transport is of prime importance in studying the disposition of these materials. It is our sincere hope that this book will stimulate scientists to study transport mechanisms of radiotracers as a means of creating more specific radiotracers which may be used in clinical diagnosis and therapy.

I acknowledge most gratefully the contributions of the authors and all those who inspired and encouraged the preparation of this book.

Lelio G. Colombetti

THE EDITOR-IN-CHIEF

Lelio G. Colombetti, Sc.D., is Professor of Pharmacology at Loyola University Stritch School of Medicine in Maywood, Ill. and a member of the Nuclear Medicine Division Staff at Michael Reese Hospital and Medical Center in Chicago, Ill.

Dr. Colombetti graduated from the Litoral University in his native Argentina with a Doctor in Sciences degree (summa cum laude), and obtained two fellowships for postgraduate studies from the Georgetown University in Washington, D.C., and from the M.I.T. in Cambridge, Mass. He has published more than 150 scientific papers and is the author of several book chapters. He has presented over 300 lectures both at meetings held in the U.S. and abroad. He organized the First International Symposium on Radiopharmacology, held in Innsbruck, Austria, in May 1978. He also organized the Second International Symposium on Radiopharmacology which took place in Chicago in September, 1981, with the active participation of more than 500 scientists, representing over 30 countries. He is a founding member of the International Association of Radiopharmacology, a nonprofit organization, which congregates scientists from many disciplines interested in the biological applications of radiotracers. He was its first President (1979/1981).

Dr. Colombetti is a member of various scientific societies, including the Society of Nuclear Medicine (U.S.) and the Gesellschaft für Nuklearmedizin (Europe), and is an honorary member of the Mexican Society of Nuclear Medicine. He is also a member of the Society of Experimental Medicine and Biology, the Coblenz Society, and the Sigma Xi. He is a member of the editorial boards of the journals *Nuklearmedizin* and *Research in Clinic and Laboratory.*

CONTRIBUTORS

Rene M. Babin, Sc.D., Pharm.D.
Honorary Professor of Chemical
  Pharmacy
Laboratory of Biochemistry
Cancer Center
Universite de Bordeaux
Bordeaux, France

James Bassingthwaighte, Ph.D.
Professor of Bioengineering and
  Biomathematics
University of Washington
Seattle, Washington

Paul Blanquet
Professor of Applied Nuclear Physics
  and Radiology
Universite de Bordeaux
Bordeaux, France

Robert E. Belliveau, M.D.
Nuclear Medicine and Pathology
  Departments
Salem Hospital
Salem, Massachusetts
Assistant Clinical Professor of Nuclear
  Medicine
University of Connecticut Health
  Center
Farmington, Connecticut

Robert Blumenthal, Ph.D.
Chief
Section on Membrane Structure and
  Function
Laboratory of Theoretical Biology
National Cancer Institute
National Institutes of Health
Bethesda, Maryland

Edward I. Cullen, M.S.
Department of Biological Chemistry
The University of Michigan Medical
  School
Ann Arbor, Michigan

David C. Dawson, Ph.D.
Associate Professor
Department of Physiology
The University of Michigan Medical
  School
Ann Arbor, Michigan

Rosa Ferraiuolo
Ricercatrice
Istituto di Chimica Biologica
Facolta di Medicina e Chirurgia
Universita di Napoli
Napoli, Italy

Brian M. Gallagher, Ph.D.
Section Leader
Pharmacological Sciences
Pharmaceutical Research
New England Nuclear Corporation
North Billerica, Massachusetts

Robert L. Hodges, Pharm.D.
Pharmacist
St. Joseph Memorial Hospital
Kokomo, Indiana

Luigi Mansi, M.D.
Assistente
Nuclear Medicine Section
Istituto Nazionale dei Tumori
Fondazione Pascale
Napoli, Italy

Fedor Medzihradsky, Ph.D.
Professor of Biological Chemistry and
  Pharmacology
Department of Biological Chemistry
The University of Michigan Medical
  School
Ann Arbor, Michigan

Gianni Morrone
Medical Student
Istituto di Chimica Biologica
Facolta di Medicina e Chirurgia
Universita di Napoli
Napoli, Italy

William M. Pardridge, M.D.
Associate Professor of Medicine
Department of Medicine/
  Endocrinology
School of Medicine
University of California at Los Angeles
Los Angeles, California

Marco Salvatore, M.D.
Chief
Section of Nuclear Medicine
Istituto Nazionale dei Tumori
Fondazione Pascale
Napoli, Italy

Howard S. Tager, Ph.D.
Associate Professor
Department of Biochemistry
The University of Chicago
Chicago, Illinois

Salvatore Venuta, M.D., Ph.D.
Professor
Istituto di Chimica Biologica
Facolta di Medicina e Chirurgia
Universita di Napoli
Napoli, Italy

Bernd Winkler, Ph.D.
Visiting Professor in Bioengineering
University of Washington
Seattle, Washington
Max Planck Institute for Physiological
  and Clinical Research
Bad Nauheim, West Germany

Yukio Yano
Senior Chemist
Donner Laboratory
Lawrence Berkeley Laboratory
University of California
Berkeley, California

TABLE OF CONTENTS

Chapter 1

BIOLOGICAL TRANSPORT: AN HISTORICAL VIEW

Lelio G. Colombetti

TABLE OF CONTENTS

I. INTRODUCTION

The Isua rocks of Greenland, which have been radiometrically dated as 3,800 million years old, contain carbon compounds in which the isotope ratios are similar to those resulting from the activity of living organisms. This finding is not, of course, an assurance that life existed that long ago, and the inference drawn by some investigators, that those rocks components are of biogenic origin has been challenged by others. There is no dispute, however, about the authenticity of fossilized cellular organisms present in Australian stromatolites 3,400 million years old. The species in the stromatolites appear to have mastered the metabolic trick of photosynthesis; by that time, then, life forms had become so complex that they depended absolutely upon transport, perhaps mechanistically simple, but efficient enough to enable the cells to capture the nutrients necessary to keep them alive. It seems quite safe to say that transport is by no means a new phenomenon.

By comparison, the scientific study of biological transport is of recent origin, and it is interesting to note that the first approaches to this discipline have been directed at the properties and functions of the cell membrane, not at how materials are transported to the boundary of the cell. We consider that it is important to know not only how a substrate is transported into the cell and how the products of metabolism are transported from the cell, but also how the substrates reach the immediate neighborhood of the cell. All transport functions in unicellular organisms depend on the cellular membrane, but for highly developed organisms the problem is much more complicated, since the substances to be transported to the interior of the cell have to be transported first to the cell in the biological fluids. It is very important, therefore, to examine the ways in which the transport mechanisms are influenced by variations in the composition of these fluids. In the case of man, the body fluids are highly complex. The principal fluid, the plasma, which is the liquid portion of circulating blood, contains several hundred different components,[1,2] the most important groups being (1) the proteins, including albumin, fibrinogen, and several globulins (α_1, α_2, β_1, β_2 γ); (2) nutrients, such as carbohydrates, amino acids, lipids, etc.; (3) inorganic salts, including chlorides, carbonates, sulfates, phosphates, etc., of sodium, potassium, calcium, magnesium, etc.; (4) gases, such as oxygen, nitrogen, carbon dioxide, etc.; (5) metabolic waste products; and (6) special substances such as hormones, enzymes, etc. It is not surprising, therefore, that this complex system may influence the transport of a tracer used to study the functions of the body.

In reviewing the development of the study of transport, it is convenient to divide the subject into two parts: transport into the cell and transport in body fluids.

II. TRANSPORT INTO CELLS

The study of mechanisms by which materials are transported into cells began with observations of the permeability of plant cell membranes in the mid-19th century by Naegely and Cramer.[3] These investigators found that the surfaces of plant cells were permeable to the pigments from cherry juice. In 1895, Overton demonstrated the selective permeability of plant cells to organic solutes,[4] later extending his original studies of plants to the permeability of muscle cells in animals.[5] About the same time, Nagano reported that pentoses are absorbed from the gut more slowly than hexoses, an unexpected phenomenon considering the molecular size of these compounds, suggesting that the difference in the speed of absorption was due to selective transport mechanisms.[6]

The classical work of Van Slyke and Meyer, done in 1913, showed that after an infusion of hydrolyzed casein into the bloodstream, the amino nitrogen level of several tissues became greater than that in the blood; in other words, the amino acids entered those tissues against the concentration gradient, indicating an active transport mechanism.[7] In 1916, Bang reported similar results upon infusing glycine or alanine solution in the dog, though infusion of lysine did not produce the effect, demonstrating that certain amino acids are selectively transported.[8] At the same time, Constantino demonstrated that red cells have a higher concentration of amino nitrogen than the serum, also indicating the existence of an active transport mechanism.[9] This phenomenon was later confirmed by other investigators, including Hamilton and Van Slyke,[10] Johnson and Bergeim,[11] Stein and Moore,[12] and Abderhanden and Kürten,[13] who suggested that the accumulation of amino acids in the red cells represented the binding of these amino acids to other cellular components. The accumulation and the state of free or bound amino acids in the red cells were debated for many years until Christensen showed that lysed erythrocytes of the duck did not bind alanine or glycine, even though these amino acids were concentrated to levels higher than those found in the cellular environment.[14] This conclusion was later revised by Christensen because, as he explained, the number of binding sites required to explain the high levels of amino acids found in the erythrocytes was in excess of any reasonable value.[15] Gorter and Grendel compared the surface of erythrocytes with a monomolecular film obtained by spreading the extracted total cellular lipids, creating the concept of a "cellular enclosing layer".[16] This idea was later modified into that of a cell membrane consisting of a double layer of lipid molecules with hydrophobic endings adhering back to back and hydrophilic endings facing the intra- and extracellular environments. This model of biological membranes later received strong support from electron microscopy.

The simplest transport process is diffusion through the cell membrane. Certain compounds and ions can engage in this process; special consideration should be given to solutes having a lipophilic nature. As shown by Collander, the lipophilic nature of some small organic molecules facilitates their entry into plant cells, with a rate of entry proportional to the partition coefficient between oil and water.[17]

In a second process, the entry of certain solutes into the cell has been found to be facilitated by a mediator, even though the solute does not become more concentrated inside the cell than outside. In the simple diffusion case, the rate of entry depends directly upon the concentration of solute outside the cells, while in the facilitated transport, a large concentration of solute could saturate the transport mediator and cause the proportionality to be broken. Some evidence of the facilitated transport mechanism was obtained by Ege and Cori.[18,19]

The intestinal absorption of some amino acids administered at the same time, such as alanine and glycine, is much lower than expected, as was demonstrated by Cori.[19] This fact could result from competition for absorption by a common transport mechanism, unless during these experiments the transport mediator was saturated, as was shown to occur during glucose resorption by the renal tubule in the dog.[20]

There is yet another mechanism of transport of solutes into cells, in which the solute reaches a larger concentration on one side of the cell membrane than the other. Since this higher concentration requires the expenditure of energy by the cells, it was called "active transport". The needed energy may derive from direct hydrolysis of a high energy compound, such as adenosine triphosphate (ATP), or from the coupled movement of another solute that has previously been concentrated against its electrochemical gradient. In the latter case, the second solute may be a metal ion, most frequently an alkali metal ion, as has been proved by Riggs et al.[21] for the uptake of sugars.

Several investigators [23-27] have reported that certain neutral depsipeptides (such as valinomycin), macrolide actins (such as nonactin), or polypeptides (such as gramicidin) induce the transport of alkali metal cations into the mitochondrial matrix against a concentration gradient at the expense of energy generated by electron transport or the hydrolysis of ATP. Coincident with this uptake there is an ejection of protons and a swelling of the particles due to a simultaneous uptake of water. On the other hand, the addition of some monocarboxylic polyethers (such as monensin, nigericin, or synthetic polyethers) induces permeability of cations, which then diffuse passively along the concentration gradient from the matrix to the outside. Coincident with this diffusion of alkali cations outward, there is a migration of protons inward and an extrusion of water.

Mechanisms for active transport of cations have been reviewed by Eiseman[28,29] and Pressman.[24,25] These investigators proposed four mechanisms by which such a selective permeation of cations may take place

1.   Coordination of a negatively charged ligand with the cation to form an ion pair that can cross the membrane
2.   Prior penetration of the ligand into the membrane, in this way permitting the cation to penetrate by ion exchange through fixed, negatively charged pores or channels
3.   Formation of a positively charged complex between a neutral, polar carrier that can surround the cation
4.   If the carrier molecule, as in (3), becomes fixed to the membrane by a mechanism similar to (2), one can visualize the permeation through a fixed, neutral polar pore.

Except for the expenditure of energy in the "active transport" mechanism, it can be accepted that "facilitated diffusion" and "active transport" are nearly the same. Osterhout,[30] and later Widdas and Rosenberg,[31,32] introduced the idea that a "mobile carrier" shuttles back and forth through the cell membrane, binding a solute molecule at the cell exterior and carrying it through the membrane to the interior of the cell, where the solute is released. Ussing proved experimentally the motility of the carrier as well as the phenomenon called "exchange diffusion".[33] During "exchange diffusion" the carrier works in both directions, translocating a solute molecule to the cell interior, where the solute is released and another molecule is bound. The carrier then diffuses back to the cell exterior carrying the second solute, which is then released. The process can now start again, since the carrier is not wasted, and will have the same chemical characteristics, at the end of the process. Different models have been proposed to explain how the mechanism works. Danielli proposed that the process was due to either the concentration of a protein or the rotation of a macromolecule,[34,35] while Patlak suggested that the translocation must be explained by a swinging effect of a gate, in which the external molecule causes the gate to swing inward, while another solute molecule will cause the opposite effect.[36]

The constancy of internal cellular composition, despite marked fluctuations in the concentration of solutes in the surrounding medium, is evidence that selective and active processes maintain the internal balance of cell composition. The observation that cells can regulate their internal solute concentrations was made in 1948 by Liebig. He noticed that muscle tissue contains a much higher concentration of potassium and much lower concentration of sodium than does the blood; this indicated that a selective transport mechanism for these two ions exists.

Mathematical techniques were first applied to the study of biological transport by Wilbrandt and Rosenberg[37] and by Widdas[38,39] in the early 1950s, and soon they became major contributions to the further description of the transport processes.[40]

The specificity and discrimination of transport system were recognized slowly. In the late 20s, Wilson reported that there was no difference in the rates of absorption of L-alanine and DL-alanine by the small intestine,[41] while Chase obtained similar results with D- and L-leucine, isoleucine, and valine.[42] Years later, Schofield reported that DL-serine was absorbed much faster that DL-isoserine, suggesting that the amino acid group must be on the α-carbon for an optimal rate of absorption, and that the small intestine maintains a degree of specificity for the transport of neutral amino acids.[43]

A general mechanism for amino acid transport into cells was proposed by Meister and co-workers.[44] Absorption of amino acids occurs chiefly in the small intestine and is an energy-requiring process. Several transport systems, with a high degree of specificity, function in the absorption of amino acids. The L-isomers are more rapidly absorbed than are the experimentally administered D-isomers. In general, the neutral and the more hydrophilic amino acids are more rapidly absorbed than are the basic and the more hydrophobic amino acids. Thus the absorption of leucine present in relatively high concentrations diminishes the absorption of isoleucine and valine, contradicting the results obtained by Chase in the middle 1940s. The mechanism for amino acid transport is quite complex, involving the action of few enzymes.[45]

The application of chemical and biological techniques to the study of transport permitted the identification of various membrane-bound proteins having the necessary characteristics to act as transport mediators. One of the biological techniques applied to these studies is the inhibition of B-galactoside transport in *Escherichia coli* by the sulfydryl reagent *N*-ethylmaleimide. By using a culture of this bacterium, which can duplicate in number every 20 min in a simple medium containing glucose and inorganic salts, these studies can be easily made. It was also found that in these cases, the transport substrate protected the cells from inactivation by the reagent.[46]

Another technique utilized to make these studies is to provoke the release of small groups of proteins from the bacteria, using a "cold osmotic shock technique" developed by Neu and Heppel in the middle 60s.[47,48] The microbial cells, suspended in a concentrated solution of glucose, are washed and rapidly resuspended in distilled water containing a magnesium salt. The cells loose proteins, some of which are involved in transport processes, while the cells remain viable. The treatment of *Escherichia coli* resulted in a loss of transport activity for some amino acids, including leucine and isoleucine.[49]

III. TRANSPORT IN BODY FLUIDS

The classical experiment in which Georg Hevesy, in the early 1920s, demonstrated the transport of radioactive lead in bean seedlings, was probably the first time in which a radioactive tracer was used to demonstrate transport in biology.[50] Similar experiments were later repeated by Hevesy in animals. In the mid-1920s, Yens, a physicist working in New York, used radiotracers to determine the blood circulation in humans, and to the best of our knowledge this is the first time in which a radiotracer was used to study transport in humans.[51]

The study of transport in body fluids using nonradioactive tracers is older. In effect, transport in body fluids was studied by the end of the last century by Steward, who used indicator dilution techniques to measure transit times and flow through the vascular system.[52-55] Chinard et al. established, in the middle 1950s, the multiple-tracer indicator-dilution techniques to study water and solute exchange in organs.[56-58]

The transport of radiotracers in body fluids may be affected by many factors, among them the route of administration, carrier concentrations, stimulation and depression of the transport system by disease or any other metabolic change, such as fasting, medication, etc. Most radiotracers are administered intravenously; therefore, the first consideration of transport is the binding of the radiotracer to blood components. Blood, like most of biological entities, is very complex in nature, having a large number of different types of components; some of these components are needed to maintain life, others are products of metabolism, waste materials in the process of being discarded. The concentration of these waste products in the blood may vary during disease states, together with the medication used to fight disease. All these components, the naturally occurring and those administered to a patient, may influence the transport of the radiotracers by modifying the radiotracer or by producing unexpected bindings.

Thyroid hormones enter the bloodstream and bind to thyroid-binding globulins (TBG), thyroid-binding prealbumin (TBPA), and thyroid-binding albumin (TBA).[59-60] The binding and debinding of thyroid hormones in plasma was studied by Hillier, who found that debinding is fast relative to the capillary transient time in the brain, as well as in the liver.[61-62] Pardridge found that there is a difference in transport depending on the type of binding: albumin-bound T_3 or T_4 is transported into the brain or the liver, while TBG-bound T_3 is transported only into the liver, and TBPA-bound T_4 is not transported to the liver.[63].

Metallic ions were introduced in nuclear diagnostic studies many years ago. In effect, the first studies in transport were done using radioisotopes of lead,[50] but these ions were not used widely until a few years ago. These ions do not remain free once they are introduced into the bloodstream, but bind immediately to plasma proteins. It was found that once injected,[67]Ga-citrate is bound to proteins, particularly transferrin, which not only plays an important role as a carrier for gallium in the plasma, but also appears to be essential for the incorporation of gallium into tumor cells.[64-68] Besides transferrin, gallium ions bind to at least three other iron-binding molecules: lactoferrin, ferritin, and siderophores. The relative affinity of gallium to ferritin is not known, but the relative affinity to lactoferrin was found to be higher than to transferrin.[68] Ferric ions easily displace gallium from its transferrin binding, and to a lesser extent from lactoferrin.[69] If large quantities of iron are administered before or coincident with ^{67}Ga-citrate, tumor localization of ^{67}Ga is inhibited, proving that transferrin plays an important role in the transport of gallium to the tumor cell.[70]

Radioindium ion was found to bind to transferrin when administered, becoming a blood pool label,[71] but it does not enter into a metabolic pathway as iron-labeled transferrin does. Indium ions have been used to label a series of compounds for medical applications; for example, ^{111}In was introduced as a label for bleomycin in nuclear diagnostic studies. After the labeled compound is introduced into the bloodstream, however, a competition occurs between the labeled bleomycin and free ions present in the plasma. Copper ions, for example, not bound to ceruloplasmin, remove indium from bleomycin, and indium ions becomes attached to beta-globulins.[72]

Pertechnetate is loosely bound to plasma proteins. This binding is affected by temperature and pH, and Hays et al. demonstrated that the binding may be reduced in disease states.[73] Since binding to proteins is weak, pertechnetate easily leaves the plasma compartment to cross the endothelium.

Radioiron ions are bound to transferrin, and may be transferred to intracellular ferritin via a collision mechanism occurring in the cell membrane.[74] After transferrin enters the cell and releases the iron ion, it returns across the cell membrane to the plasma and is ready to repeat the operation.[75]

Copper ions were found to label both ceruloplasmin and albumin,[76] preferentially ceruloplasmin, which is the specific binding material for copper ions. About 50% of the calcium ions circulate in the unbound state, while the other half are bound to proteins.[77]

Free fatty acids, when injected, are tightly bound to albumin, being distributed over multiple binding sites.[78] These sites of varying affinity probably favor the transport of fatty acids to different types of tissues. Cholesterol is bound by plasma lipoproteins.[79]

Steroid hormones are transported bound by albumin and also by specific globulins.[80,81] The sex hormone-binding globulin (SHBG) binds testosterone and estradiol; the corticoid-binding globulin (CBG) binds cortisol. The concentration of SHBG in serum is relatively low; therefore albumin competes with globulin, and as a result the steroids are distributed to both binding molecules.

Drug use may alter the plasma binding of some radiotracers and therefore alter their distribution. It was found that elevated plasma aluminum may alter the distribution of some radiotracers because of interactions of aluminum ions with the radiotracer; pertechnetate, for example, may remain in a vascular space during hyperaluminemia due to chronic use of aluminum antiacids.[82] Propanolol was found to bind to orosomucoid or α-acid glycoprotein[83] and also to albumin;[84] however, since the binding to the globulin is much stronger, most of the drug will be bound to it.

IV. CONCLUSION

The study of transport of radiotracers is indeed an important aspect in understanding the distribution and fixation of radiotracers in biological systems; therefore a better comprehension of the transport process will help to provide a basis for the development of more specific radiotracers to study the function and biochemical processes in vivo. We believe that a major effort in studying the transport mechanisms of radiotracers is amply justified.

Significant progress has been made already in the design of substrates to study the transport mechanisms and metabolic pathways of radiotracers. Christensen described the information that could be gained by modifying substrates structures.[85] These studies will undoubtedly contribute to the preparation of the radiotracers needed for diagnostic and therapeutic purposes.

REFERENCES

1. International Commission on Radiological Protection, *Reference Man*, ICRP Publ. Ser. No. 23, Pergamon Press, New York, 1975.
2. Diem, K. and Lentner, C., *Scientific Tables*, 7th ed., Geigy Pharmaceuticals, Ardsley, N.Y., 1974.
3. Naegely, G. and Cramer, K., *Pflanzenphysiologische Untersunchungen*, Schultess, Zurich, 1855.
4. Overton, E., *Naturforschhende Gesellschaft*, Vierteljahreschrift, Zurich, 40, 159, 1895.
5. Overton, E., *Pfluegers Arch. Gesamte Physiol. Menschen Tiere*, 92, 115, 1902.
6. Nagano, J., *Pfluegers Arch. Gesamte Physiol. Menschen Tiere*, 90, 389, 1902.
7. Van Slyke, D. D. and Meyer, G. M., *J. Biol. Chem.*, 16, 213, 1913.
8. Bang, I., *Biochem. Z.*, 74, 278, 1916.
9. Constantino, A., *Biochem. Z.*, 51, 91, 1913.
10. Hamilton, P. B. and Van Slyke, D. D., *J. Biol. Chem.*, 150, 213, 1943.
11. Johnson, C. A. and Bergeim, O., *J. Biol. Chem.*, 188, 833, 1951.
12. Stein, W. H. and Moore, S., *J. Biol. Chem.*, 211, 915, 1954.
13. Abderhanden, E. and Kürten, H., *Pfluegers Arch. Gesamte Physiol. Menschen Tiere*, 189, 311, 1921.
14. Christensen, H. N., Riggs, T. R., and Ray, N. E., *J. Biol. Chem.*, 194, 41, 1952.
15. Christensen, H. N. *A Symposium on Amino acid Metabolism*, McElroy, W. D. and Glass, H. B., Eds., Johns Hopkins Press, Baltimore, 1955, 63.
16. Gorter, E. and Grendel, F., *J. Exp. Med.*, 41, 439, 1925.
17. Collander, R., *Trans. Faraday Soc.*, 33, 985, 1937.
18. Ege, R., Gottlieb, E., and Rakestraw, N. W., *Am. J. Physiol.*, 72, 76, 1925.
19. Cori, C. F., *Proc. Soc. Exp. Biol. Med.*, 24, 125, 1926.
20. Shannon, J. A. and Fisher, S., *Am. J. Physiol.*, 122, 765, 1938.

21. Riggs, T. R., Walker, L. M., and Christensen, H. N., *J. Biol. Chem.*, 233, 1479, 1958.
22. Kleinzeller, A. and Kotyk, A., *Biochim. Biophys. Acta*, 54, 367, 1961.
23. Pressman, B. C., Harris, E. J., Jagger, W. S., et al., *Proc. Natl. Acad. Sci. U.S.A.*, 58, 1949, 1967.
24. Harris, E. J., Höferand, M. P., and Pressman, B. C., *Biochemistry*, 6, 1348, 1967.
25. Pressman, B. C., *Fed. Proc., Fed. Am. Soc. Exp. Biol.*, 27, 1283, 1968.
26. Haynes, D. H., Kowalsky, A., and Pressman, B. C., *J. Biol. Chem.*, 244, 502, 1969.
27. Lardy, H., *Fed. Proc., Fed. Am. Soc. Exp. Biol.*, 27, 1278, 1968.
28. Eisenman, G., *Fed. Proc., Fed. Am. Soc. Exp. Biol.*, 27, 1249, 1968.
29. Eisenman, G., Ciani, S. M., and Szabo, G., *Fed. Proc., Fed. Am. Soc. Exp. Biol.*, 27, 1289, 1968.
30. Osterhout, W. J., *Proc. Nat. Acad. Sci. U.S.A.*, 21, 125, 1935.
31. Widdas, W. F., *J. Physiol. (London)*, 118, 23, 1952.
32. Rosenberg, T. and Willbrandt, W., *Exp. Cell Res.*, 9, 49, 1955.
33. Ussing, H. H., *Physiol. Rev.*, 29, 127, 1949.
34. Danielli, J. F., *Symp. Soc. Exp. Biol.*, 6, 1, 1952.
35. Danielli, J. F., *Symp. Soc. Exp. Biol.*, 8, 505, 1954.
36. Patlak, C. S., *Bull. Math. Biophys.*, 19, 209, 1957.
37. Wilbrandt, W. and Rosenberg, T., *Helv. Physiol. Pharm. Acta*, 9, 86, 1951.
38. Widdas, W. F., *J. Physiol. (London)*, 115, 36, 1951.
39. Widdas, W. F., *J. Physiol. (London)*, 118, 23, 1952.
40. Heinz, E., *J. Biol. Chem.*, 211, 781, 1954.
41. Wilson, R. H. and Lewis, H. B., *J. Biol. Chem.*, 84, 511, 1929.
42. Chase, B. W. and Lewis, H. B., *J. Biol. Chem.*, 106, 315, 1934.
43. Schofield, F. A. and Lewis, H. B., *J. Biol. Chem.*, 168, 439, 1947.
44. Meister, A., *Science*, 180, 33, 1973.
45. White, A., Handler, P., and Smith, E. L., *Principles of Biochemistry*, 5th ed., McGraw-Hill, New York, 1973, 633.
46. Fox, C. F. and Kennedy, E. P., *Proc. Natl. Acad. Sci. U.S.A.*, 54, 891, 1965.
47. Neu, H. C. and Heppel, L. A., *Biochem. Biophys. Res. Commun.*, 14, 109, 1964.
48. Neu, H. C. and Heppel, L. A., *J. Biol. Chem.*, 240, 3685, 1965.
49. Piperno, J. R. and Oxender, D. L., *J. Biol. Chem.*, 241, 5732, 1966.
50. Hevesy, G., *Adventures in Radioisotope Research*, Pergamon Press, New York, 1962.
51. Chalmers, T. W., *Historical Researches in History of Physical and Chemical Discovery*, Morgan Brothers, London, 1949.
52. Steward, G. N., *J. Physiol. (London)*, 15, 30, 1894.
53. Steward, G. N., *J. Physiol. (London)*, 15, 31, 1894.
54. Steward, G. N., *J. Physiol. (London)*, 15, 73, 1894.
55. Steward, G. N., *J. Physiol. (London)*, 22, 159, 1897.
56. Chinard, F. P. and Enns, T., *Am. J. Physiol.*, 178, 202, 1954.
57. Chinard, F. P. and Flexner, L. B., *Proc. 19, Int. Cong. Physiol. Sci.* 1953, 267.
58. Chinard, F. P., Volsburg, G. J., and Enns, T., *Am. J. Physiol.*, 183, 221, 1955.
59. Rapoport, B. and De Groot, L. J., *Semin. Nucl. Med.*, 1, 265, 1971.
60. Lutz, J. H. and Gregerman, R. I., *J. Clin. Endocrinol.*, 29, 487, 1969.
61. Hillier, A. P., *Acta Endocrinol.*, 80, 49, 1975.
62. Hillier, A. P., *J. Physiol.*, 217, 625, 1971.
63. Pardridge, W. M. and Mietus, L. J., *J. Clin. Invest.*, 66, 1980.
64. Noujaim, A. A., Lebtle, B. C., Hill, J. R., et al., *Int. J. Nucl. Med. Biol.*, 6, 193, 1979.
65. Clausen, J., Edeling, C. J., and Fogh, J., *Cancer Res.*, 34, 1931, 1974.
66. Gunasekara, S., King, L. J., and Lavender, D. J., *Clin. Chim. Acta*, 39, 401, 1977.
67. Hara, T., *Int. J. Nucl. Med. Biol.*, 1, 152, 1974.
68. Weiner, R. E., Thakur, M. D., Goodman, M. M., et al., *Am. J. Roentgenol.*, 132, 489, 1979.
69. Hoffer, P. B., *J. Nucl. Med.*, 21, 282, 1980.
70. Oster, Z. H., Larson, S. M., and Wagner, H. J., *J. Nucl. Med.*, 17, 356, 1976.
71. Goodwin, D. A., Colombetti, L. G., De Nardo, G. L., et al., *Nucl. Med. Sess. San Francisco State*, Nov. 1967.
72. Fini, A., *Principles of Radiopharmacology*, Colombetti, L. G., Ed., CRC Press, Boca Raton, Fla., 1979, 243.
73. O'Flaherty, J. T., Showell, H. J., Becker, E. L., et al., *Am. J. Pathol.*, 92, 155, 1978.
74. Batey, R. G., Williams, K., and Milsom, J. P., *Am. J. Physiol.*, 238, 630, 1980.
75. Neville, D. M. and Chang, T. M., *Curr. Top. Membr. Trans.*, 9, 65, 1978.
76. Peters, T. and Reed, R. G., *Transport by Proteins*, Bauer, G. and Subd, H., Eds., W. deGruyter, 1978,.
77. Worstman, J. and Traycoff, R. B., *Am. J. Physiol.*, 238, 104, 1980.

78. Spector, A. A. and Fletcher, J. E., *Disturbances in Lipid and Lipoprotein Metabolism,* Dietschy, J. M., Gotto, A. M., and Antko, J. A., Eds., American Physiological Society, Washington, D.C., 1978.
79. Brunzel, J. D., Chait, A., and Bierman, E. L., *Metabolism,* 27, 1109, 1978.
80. Vermeulen, A., *Androgens and Antiandrogens,* Martini, L. and Motta, M., Eds., Raven Press, New York, 1977.
81. Rosenthal, H. E., Slaunwhite, W. R., and Sandberg, A. A., *J. Clin. Endocrinol.,* 29, 352, 1969.
82. Kaehny, W. D., Hegg, A. P., and Alfrey, A. C., *N. Engl. J. Med.,* 296, 1389, 1977.
83. Cooper, E. H. and Stone, J., *Adv. Cancer Res.,* 30, 1, 1979.
84. Evans, G. H., Nies, A. S., and Shand, D. G., *J. Pharm. Exp. Ther.,* 186, 114, 1973.
85. Christensen, H. N., *Biological Transport,* W. A. Benjamin, New York, 1975, 211.

Chapter 2

SOLUTE TRANSLOCATIONS; AN OVERVIEW OF BIOLOGICAL TRANSPORT

Howard S. Tager

TABLE OF CONTENTS

I. SCOPE OF BIOLOGICAL TRANSPORT

Biological transport, in its most complete sense, defines the flow of solutes (and solvent) in living systems. Study of these flows at any of several different levels leads us, as expressed by H.N. Christensen,[1] ". . . to understand how substances and reactions are segregated and brought together in the cell and in the organism." A careful reader of this statement will find much to explain both the fascination for transport and its importance in the biological context. The statement implies that biological transport is reversible (either in the true thermodynamic sense or in the sense that alternative routes can usually be found), that the *appropriate* bringing together or separation of biochemical substances (both organic and inorganic) is inherent to all life processes, and that a careful understanding requires consideration of these processes at the cellular, organ, and organismal levels. A broad view of solute translocation thus concerns itself not only with how a particular solute enters or exits a cell (biological transport with its truest meaning), but also with how the solute came in contact with the cell in the first place (perhaps by passage through the blood and subsequent diffusion) and even how the solute moves *within* the cell.

To emphasize the importance of solute translocation in biological systems is to imply the existence of barriers to flow and to the "correct" segregation of solute molecules. For the simplest case, this barrier is distance and the disciplines of physics and fluid dynamics serve important roles in helping us understand how a solute is moved from one *extracellular* location in the organism to another. For the more complex case, the barrier is a biological membrane (usually the plasma membrane) and the observer must rely on an interdisciplinary approach (one which includes the fields of biochemistry, physiology, biophysics, and cell biology and their subspecialties) to gain an understanding of solute flow. Although the membrane represents a barrier to the accumulation of cellular substrates and other components, it equally well represents a barrier to the loss of those components. Biological transport thus permits attainment of an instantaneous environment compatible with both generalized cellular function (e.g., respiration and protein synthesis) and specialized cellular function (e.g., neural transmission or muscle contraction). The constancy of the intracellular environment in the former case, and its often required changeability in the latter, reflect similar mechanisms: inward flow played against outward flow. When the two are balanced (possibly by equally *high* rates) the intracellular environment remains unchanged. When one exceeds the other, the intracellular steady-state is altered and the cell responds by appropriate biochemical and biophysical changes, both to account for specialized function and to readjust the rates of flow accordingly. The consistency of the internal environment within a single cell type and the variety of environments among different cell populations result in large part from sensitively counterbalanced transport processes.

The simple notion that solute translocation permits entry into the cell of biochemical nutrients and exit of cellular wastes defines only a portion of the biochemical and physiological impact of transport in eukaryotic, multicellular organisms. On one hand, the complete description requires consideration of membrane-enclosed, intracellular organelles and the roles they play in the segregation of biochemical solutes and reactions. On the other hand, the description requires consideration of solute translocation from one tissue or organ to another. Over all, solute transport maintains transmembrane and interorgan communication as well as the appropriate intracellular environment. An additional consideration in solute translocation relates to transport processes involving membrane flow. Although endocytosis (as it relates to cellular uptake) and exocytosis (as it relates to cellular secretion) do not represent mechanisms of biological transport in its usual — and most correct — sense, both processes reflect important mechanisms for the translocation of large solutes across cellular membranes. In the broadest sense, the scientist who studies transport, as the scientist who studies metabolism, must ultimately be concerned with mechanism, regulation, and the continuous interplay of parallel, sequential, and opposing phenomena. I will concentrate on simple aspects of transmembrane flow in this chapter, but will try not to neglect completely these other important aspects of solute translocation in complex organisms.

II. SOLUTE TRANSLOCATION

A. Flow in Free Solution

Although the investigator of solute translocation in biological systems is most interested in transmembrane flow, flows largely unrestricted by barrier intervention (i.e., within a single solvent phase) can influence presentation of the solute to the membrane in question. These flows are of two types, dynamic flow and diffusion. Both concern the extracellular movement of solute and both can influence the concentration of solute present at the cell surface as compared to that present in the bulk solution. To the extent that the bulk solution is well-mixed, dynamic flow presents little hindrance to the study of cellular transport. Incubation of a single cell suspension in a shaking incubator will accomplish the desired goal. Perfusion of an organ (either by the blood in vivo or by a defined medium in vitro), however, can lead to complications: layered or laminer flow through tubular vessels results in the more rapid movement of fluid down the center of the vessel than along its walls. When coupled to a secondary process, such as diffusion from the vessel, laminer flow may produce unexpected gradients of concentration. Although the circulation of fluid through an organ is seldom totally free from mixing due to turbulence, these uncertainties can complicate the kinetic analysis of solute flow through perfused tissues.

Unlike dynamic flow, diffusion plays an important role in solute translocation (in the biological context) only over relatively short distances. For a solute in free solution, Fick's first law of diffusion expresses the proportionality between the amount of solute (dS) moving during a period (dt) to the sectional area for movement (A) and the linear concentration gradient of the solute (dC/dx):

$$\frac{dS}{dt} = k_D A \left(\frac{dC}{dx}\right)$$

k_D is the diffusion coefficient, a proportionality term which is unique for each solute, and which is constant for that solute only under defined conditions of temperature, viscosity, and solvent composition. The coefficient is inversely proportional to molecular size, and its value varies over several orders of magnitude when progressing from very small (H_2O), to moderately sized (Na^+, glucose), to large molecules (peptides and proteins). The above equation holds for the movement of solutes through free solution, through a semipermeable membrane with pores or holes, and (in a way limited only to hydrophobic, lipid-soluble molecules) through the cellular plasma membrane. Although the last two subjects will be considered in later sections, it should be noted here that diffusion of a solute through the extracellular space represents a mechanism for solute translocation in this relatively static (from a fluid dynamic point of view) environment. The so-called "unstirred" layer of solvent which surrounds many cells represents another potential barrier overcome by diffusion. Delivery of solute *to* the membrane should not be confused with solvent movement *through* the membrane, however. The latter represents, in most cases, the biologically more important process.

B. Flow through Semipermeable Membranes

A solid sheet with holes or pores of defined dimension represents a semipermeable membrane. Objects (or molecules) smaller than the holes will pass through the membrane, whereas larger ones will not. The capillary wall behaves as a semipermeable membrane and as a barrier to the extent that, although it contains pores, these pores are rather small (about 35 Å in diameter). The capillary thus presents a barrier to the flow of large molecules (e.g., most of the plasma proteins), but not to the flow of smaller ones (e.g., glucose, amino acids, Na^+, and Cl^-). Although the barrier to large molecules, at least in nonpathological circumstances, is nearly complete, the passage of small molecules results from diffusion through the capillary pores. Fick's law of diffusion (presented earlier) expresses the movement of molecules in free solution through the semipermeable capillary wall. The only conditions are that the hydrated solute is much smaller than the pores and that the area considered is not the area of the wall, but the summed cross-sectional areas of the nonrestrictive pores.

The consequences of placing an impermeable solute on only one side of a semipermeable membrane extend beyond those described above. Water will move from the side without added solute (where the chemical activity of water is high) to the side containing the impermeable molecule (where the activity of water is low). In a completely open system, this process — called osmosis — results in dilution of the solute. In a system where the solute-containing compartment is closed, the process results in a pressure in the closed compartment. The osmotic pressure is defined practically as the pressure on the compartment containing the impermeable molecule required to prevent the flow of water. It is the semipermeable nature of biological membranes which results in the osmotic activity of cells. As the osmotic pressure depends on the concentration of the dissolved solute (and not on its chemical nature), the pressure can be maintained or modified by molecules as diverse as proteins, amino acids, and inorganic ions.

A related phenomenon, called the Gibbs-Donnan equilibrium, is best described by example. A semipermeable membrane (permeable to both Na^+ and Cl^-) divides an aqueous solution of Na^+Cl^-, and the sodium salt of an impermeable protein is added to one side. Since both compartments must maintain electrical neutrality, on one side the concentration of Na^+ will equal the concentration of Cl^-, whereas on the other, the concentration of Na^+ would equal the concentration of Cl^- plus the concentration of the protein anion times its net charge. At equilibrium, $[Na^+]_1 [Cl^-]_1 = [Na^+]_2 [Cl^-]_2$, but the distribution of the ions will be asymmetric across the membrane. It will appear that the ions have been concentrated against their electrochemical gradients (as indeed they have), but only because the impermeable anion has also been concentrated (by physical means) against its gradient.

C. Flow through Biological Membranes

Biological membranes (including the plasma membrane which encloses the intracellular constituents) are in every case semipermeable membranes which can restrict the flow of both high molecular weight and low molecular weight solutes. Since these membranes do not usually maintain pores, alternative and highly selective modes for solute translocation have evolved. Nevertheless, considerations of diffusion, osmotic pressure, and Gibbs-Donnan equilibrium have all played important roles in the recognition of cellular permeability. Indeed, the intracellular osmotic pressure induced by the selective uptake and concentration of solutes can alter cellular structure to an important extent. Not surprisingly, osmotic effects have been useful in the identification and quantitation of transmembrane biological transport into both eukaryotic[2] and prokaryotic[3] cells. The role of simple diffusion (i.e., diffusion through free solution), however, is limited to only one class of solutes. In 1933, Collander[4] showed that the permeability of plant cells to a great variety of organic solutes was directly proportional to their partition coefficients between olive oil and water. These results were

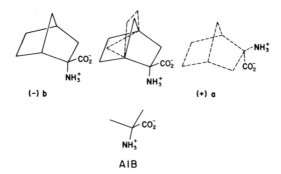

FIGURE 1. Attempted superposition of two isomers of an unnatural amino acid analogue. The upper drawings illustrate the analogue called BCH. The leftmost drawing shows the structure of the (−)b isomer and the rightmost, the structure of the (+)a isomer; the middle drawing shows the superposition of these two isomers in a way which permits superimposition of their amino and carboxyl groups. The lower drawing shows the structure of another, unrelated analogue called AIB. These analogues are discussed in the text.

consistent with the proposed lipophilic nature of the cell membrane and suggested a rate of transmembrane diffusion based simply on solute lipophilicity. Our current view of membranes as a "fluid mosaic"[5,6] (although not the view held at that time) easily accommodates the diffusion of lipophilic substances from the extracellular to the intracellular environment.

The biological transport of hydrophilic (or lipophobic) molecules presents a somewhat more difficult case. A very early test of sugar transport showed that pentoses are absorbed from the intestine of the dog more slowly than hexoses, but clearly the reverse should have been true if transport were mediated by simple diffusion. A great many subsequent studies of biological transport (as it relates to the transmembrane flow of hydrophilic solutes) have documented the exquisite specificities for cellular uptake of compounds as diverse as amino acids[7-15] and sugars[16,17] in cells as diverse as the erythrocyte,[7,8,14,17] the Erlich ascites tumor,[11-14] and the bacterium *Escherichia coli*.[9,10,15,16] The investigator of biological transport has often relied on the chemical synthesis of substrates with defined structure to probe the specificity of solute flow through cellular membranes. The outermost drawings in Figure 1 show the structures of two isomers of an unnatural amino acid called BCH;[18,19] the innermost drawing shows the superposition of those structures to permit alignment of their amino and carboxyl groups. Perhaps from the similarities between the two compounds (as shown in the middle drawing) it is not surprising that both isomers are transported by a similar route in the Erlich cell, *but* by a very different route than that serving for another amino acid analog called α-methyl-AIB.[18,19] In addition, *only* the isomer shown on the left of Figure 1 gains entry into *E. coli*. These examples, as well as the many alluded to earlier, emphasize the high structural specificity of membrane transport processes and their inconsistency with mediation by simple diffusion.

1. Mediation of Transport

The reliance of biological transport on solute structure suggests a strong requirement for solute recognition and an equally strong requirement for molecular mediation during the translocation event. Both predict the participation of membrane components and the dependence of transmembrane flow on solute concentration. If the membrane components were present in limiting amounts, increasing the concentration of solute would gradually saturate these surface participants and the velocity of cellular uptake would reach an apparent maximum. The saturation of membrane transport by increased solute concentrations was first described over 50 years ago, and it is now a well-accepted characteristic of transmembrane flow for a variety of hydrophilic biological constituents in a variety of both eukaryotic and prokaryotic cells. The nearly universal nature of transport saturation removes any doubt concerning the very restricted role of simple diffusion in biological transport: except at the very extremes of concentration (seldom encountered in biological systems), a diffusion-limited process would show a velocity of solute uptake proportional to solute concentration at any concentration chosen.

The essence of transport mediation requires consideration of neither the steady-state levels of solute reached during translocation nor the expenditure of metabolic energy. For the simplest case, called facilitated or mediated "diffusion", the solute gains entry into the cell with the help of a mediator, but the direction of solute movement is always *down* its electrochemical gradient. That is, the mediator facilitates the entry or exodus of solute (since translocation by simple diffusion is not permitted), but the steady-state position of the process is for practical purposes identical with its equilibrium position. The definition of a "mobile carrier" as the transport mediator[20,21] enhances a pictorial description of solute translocation. Although the carrier is usually viewed as molecule shuttling back and forth in the cell membrane, its mobility may equally well arise from rotation[22] or conformational change.[23] The uppermost drawing in Figure 2 illustrates in a simplistic way the biological transport of a solute *S* across a cell membrane by facilitated diffusion. The solute combines in a structurally specific way with the carrier on one side of the membrane, the complex changes its orientation so that it is available at the other side of the membrane, the solute dissociates from the carrier, and the carrier again changes orientation so that it is available at the first side. Note that the two compartments illustrated in the figure have not been identified. The one on the left could equally well represent the cytosol or the extracellular fluid, and the arrows indicating the direction of movement could equally well point in the opposite directions. These processes are completely reversible.

Determination of the molecular nature of the transport carrier represents one of the most intriguing and difficult problems available to the investigator of biological transport. That the carrier is — or is at least tightly associated with — a protein is most evident from considerations of solute specificity, the genetics of defective systems of transport,[24-26] and studies of the effects of protein-specific chemical reagents on transport processes. The periplasmic, solute-binding proteins of gram-negative bacteria undoubtedly provide an important degree of structural specificity for solute uptake,[27-29] but it is doubtful that they represent the carrier itself. During recent years, much attention has focused on the carrier in eukaryotic systems. A protein of the human erythrocyte membrane (Band 3) has been identified as the major anion carrier of that cell,[30,31] and considerable progress has been made in the isolation of the glucose carrier from the membrane of the rat adipocyte.[32,33] These important studies may soon result in a molecular description of mediated transport at the levels of both solute recognition and translocation per se.

2. Concentrative Transport

Although facilitated diffusion accounts for the specificity and saturation of transmembrane flow, it does not account for the widely observed phenomenon of transport of a solute against its electrochemical gradient. Concentrative uptake, a phenomenon first observed by Van Slyke and Meyer,[34] is usually described by the term "active transport". The term has a two-pronged meaning, however. On one hand it implies

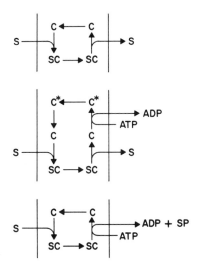

FIGURE 2. Models for translocation of a substrate across a biological membrane. The uppermost drawing illustrates *facilitated diffusion,* the middle drawing, *active transport* and the lowermost, *group translocation.* The substrate is indicated by *S* and the mobile carrier, by *C.* These models are discussed in the text.

uptake of a solute against its concentration gradient; on the other, it implies the expenditure of metabolic energy to achieve and maintain that gradient. The second of these is frequently easier to test (by the use of metabolic inhibitors) than the first. A question of great importance concerns the chemical and physical state of the solute in the more concentrated compartment. If the solute were bound to an impermeable molecule, the total concentration of the solute (in all its forms) could be greater than the concentration of the freely equilibrating solute. Just as in the case of the Gibbs-Donnan equilibrium, the solute would *appear* to have undergone concentrative uptake, but only because its electrochemical concentration is severely overestimated. Although the phenomenon described may complicate the measurement of biological transport, its real impact is less than theory would predict: in most cases a cell contains too few solute binding sites to account for the observed concentrative uptake.

The attainment of a transmembrane gradient by active transport inplies a mechanism by which the gradient can be driven or maintained. A purely hypothetical mechanism for the "activation" of a mediated transport process is presented in the middle drawing of Figure 2. The mechanism differs from that proposed in the uppermost drawing in only one regard, ATP (perhaps by transfer of its terminal phosphoryl group) modifies the carrier so that it *must* return to the other membrane surface uncomplexed with solute. At this surface the carrier reverts to its original state and active transport proceeds. This mechanism, in its general sense, need not depend on ATP (nor indeed on other potential phosphoryl group donors such as phosphoenolpyruvate). A direct coupling between the respiratory electron transfer chain of *Escherichia coli* and the lactose carrier may account for part of the concentrative transport of lactose into vesicles of bacterial membranes.[35,36] Furthermore, in the chemiosmotic hypothesis of Mitchell,[37] transfer of electrons along the respiratory chain of eukaryotic cells is seen to be tightly coupled to the active transport of protons across the inner mitochondrial membrane. The further coupling of this gradient to the phosphorylation of ADP is only one example of how a previously formed electrochemical gradient can be linked to a second process. Note that a related subject, coupled transport, will be discussed in a later section. The tightly coupled transport of one solute down its electrochemical gradient can drive the concentrative uptake of another. Thus, electrochemical gradients (produced by active transport) can be exchanged, one for the other.

3. Group Translocation

The criterion that a transported solute be in the same physical and chemical state on both sides of the dividing membrane is violated to an extent in considering transport by "group translocation". The term[38] implies that the solute appears on one side of the membrane in a form different from the other and that an enzyme has participated in the modification of its structure. The lowermost drawing in Figure 2 illustrates a hypothetical example. The substrate S is presented at one side of the membrane and transverses the barrier, but appears on the other side as its phosphorylated derivative. This illustration parallels the more complex phosphoenolpyruvate phosphotransferase system for the transport of some sugars into bacteria as described by Roseman and his co-workers.[39,40] (The complete model envisions the participation of at least four proteins.) The transport of lactose by this system results in its appearance in the cell interior as lactose phosphate (with phosphoenolpyruvate being the initial phosphoryl donor). An analogous coupling of amino acid transport to a series of enzymatic (but not phosphorylating) reactions in the mammalian kidney, called the γ-glutamyl transpeptidase system, may participate in amino acid resorption from the renal tubule.[41] In the latter example, the amino acid does not remain derivatized after translocation, but it nevertheless has undergone reactions forming and then cleaving a peptidyl bond with its α-amino group. Although these systems are of significant interest, transport by group translocation should not be confused with biological transport in its usual sense. Enzymatic manipulation of solute structure is not often a component part of solute translocation across biological membranes.

4. Coupled Transport

Mediated transport processes across biological membranes are frequently found to be tightly coupled to each other and the coupling can occur in two ways. The first, called cotransport, describes the carrier-mediated translocation of two components in the *same* direction. The second, called countertransport, describes the carrier-mediated translocation of two components in *opposite* directions. In each case, the carrier is viewed as a single molecular entity. Drawings illustrating these coupled transports are given in Figure 3. The upper drawing illustrates *cotransport* and formation of a ternary complex among the carrier and two substrates S and S' prior to the event which makes the complex available to the opposite membrane surface. The requirement for the ternary complex is easily tested in that, for a circumscribed route of entry, S will not be transported in the absence of S', and S' will not be transported in the absence of S. Systems for the cotransport of Na^+ and amino acids[42,43] and for the cotransport of Na^+ and sugars[44,45] have been well documented. It is clear from these studies that only the combination of the two substrates suffices for accommodation of either by the transport carrier and for initiation of the translocation event. The importance of cotransport, however, transcends what might seem to be a mere curiosity of solute specificity. The markedly elevated concentration of extracellular Na^+ relative to its intracellular concentration (a gradient itself produced by a separate process of active transport) can be seen to drive the intracellular accumulation of amino acids or glucose on the basis of simple mass action. Thus the translocation of Na^+ in a direction parallel to its electrochemical gradient can help to "activate" the process of solute translocation in a like direction.

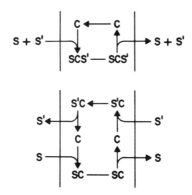

FIGURE 3. Models for coupled transport of solutes across a biological membrane. The upper drawing illustrates *cotransport* (coupled movement in the same direction) and the lower drawing illustrates *countertransport* (coupled movement in the opposite direction). Substrates are indicated by *S* and *S'* and the mobile carrier, by *C*. These models are discussed in the text.

The lower part of Figure 3 illustrates the process of countertransport. The solute *S* combines with the mobile carrier *C*, the complex transverses the membrane, and the solute dissociates from the carrier. Perhaps because of the immobility of the free carrier — or because of its predisposition to combine with the second substrate, *S'* associates with the carrier and is translocated to the opposite side of the membrane. This process, first described as "exchange diffusion" by Ussing,[46] emphasizes the character of the "mobile carrier". Many systems for the transport of solutes across both plasma and organellar membranes operate by compulsory exchange diffusion. That is, in the absence of an appropriate solute on one side of the membrane, transport of a second solute in the opposite direction will be slowed. Nevertheless, the consequences of countertransport, as those for cotransport, transcend the most obvious conclusion: the process also predicts that an asymmetric gradient of one solute can drive the transport of another in the *opposite* direction. If the concentration of solute *S'* in the lower part of Figure 3 were higher on the right side of the membrane than on the left (a condition possibly attained by a separate active transport), the transport of S' *down* its electrochemical gradient might well drive the countertransport of S *up* its electrochemical gradient. The phenomena of cotransport and countertransport should not be regarded as a way around the difficulties of active transport as such. Rather, they describe mechanisms for the exchange of one electrochemical gradient for another and, thus, for the active transport of a solute by a process which is distally — not immediately — dependent on either electron transfer or phosphoryl transfer reactions.

5. Transcellular Flow

Considerations of solute translocation across a single biological membrane do not describe completely the complement of transport processes available to or required of a living cell. For many solutes, transport through the plasma membrane represents only the first barrier crossed and subsequent events leading to transport into the many intracellular organelles (usually by mediated processes through semipermeable membranes) bring the solute to its ultimate or momentarily correct location. Indeed the inner mitochondrial membrane presents a barrier to the translocation of most solutes (both organic and inorganic), and multiple transport carriers (some single and some coupled) serve the complex function of maintaining the very special enironments of the intra- and extra-mitochondrial compartments. An additional fate of the transported solute concerns the possibility of its exodus from the cell. Random exodus through any portion of the cell membrane would yield no net change in cytoplasmic composition, nor likely in the composition of the "sink" of extracellular fluid. Vectorial exodus through a single surface of the membrane, however, leads to the processes of active absorption and secretion in epithelial tissues. These processes are essentially mirror images of each other and require only that one membrane surface on an appropriately oriented cell has the capacity for active transport. Uptake of solute through this surface will permit the vectorial discharge of solute through the opposing surface even if mediation of exodus is by facilitated diffusion. Although mediation of exodus might also occur by an active process, asymmetry in distribution of the transport apparatus may itself account for the flow of solute *across* a biologically active cell monolayer.

D. Secondary Interactions

As previously discussed, usual considerations of biological transport presume that a solute is present at the external surface of the cell in free solution and that it maintains its same physical state within the cell interior. Although these constraints hold more often than not, some solutes are presented to the cell exterior in partially bound form, are transported across the membrane as the free ligand, and are then bound again by intracellular components. A hypothetical, but plausible, model is presented in Figure 4. The substrate S is bound to a protein P_1 in the extracellular space, it is transported as S and is bound again by two proteins, P_2 and P_3. All of these components exist in the hypothetical living organism at a steady-state and the relative forward and reverse rate constants for the association of S with P_1, P_2, and P_3 determine the amount of free S available for membrane translocation and the electrochemical gradient of S across the cell membrane. Serum albumin is a good extracellular ligand binder and is known to bind compounds as diverse as fatty acids, bilirubin, and acetylsalicylic acid (aspirin), and thereby affect not only the transport of these components in free solution, but also their cellular uptake.

The complexity of Figure 4 is most applicable, however, to the translocation of inorganic cations. Thus, Fe^{++} circulates in the blood mainly in combination with the protein transferin, is transported as Fe^{++}, and is again bound in the cell interior by ferritin and as hemosiderin.[47] A similar mechanism holds for the transport of Ca^{++}. In the blood plasma Ca^{++} exists in both free and protein-bound forms.[48] Although it is transported as the free ion, it recombines with proteins such as calmodulin[48,49] and other proteins in the intracellular environment. In addition, Ca^{++} is markedly concentrated by the mitochondria of all cells and by the sarcoplasmic reticulum of muscle cells. The distribution of calcium between free and bound forms should not be regarded totally as a deterrent to the accurate measurement of Ca^{++} translocation across the plasma membrane. The interactions of Ca^{++} with extracellular and intracellular proteins (and its accumulation by intracellular organelles) allow a careful and timely control of intracellular concentrations of calcium ion. Such control permits the biologically important regulation of Ca^{++}-dependent processes as diverse as muscle contraction and hormone-stimulated metabolic reactions. The importance of secondary interaction is also emphasized by considerations of the mechanism for sterol hormone action.[50] These relatively hydrophobic effectors transverse the plasma membrane by lipophilic free diffusion, but combine with soluble cytoplasmic receptors for transport

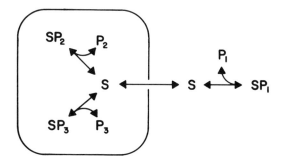

FIGURE 4. Model for the translocation of a substrate where the substrate binds reversibly to impermeable molecules in the extra- and intracellular spaces. The substrate is indicated by S, the extracellular binder by P_1 and the intracellular binders by P_1 and P_2. Use of the two-headed arrows allows the presentation of a formal mechanism for the overall process. Each binding event is of course governed by forward and reverse rate constants for binding. The model is discussed in the text.

into the nucleus where hormonal regulation of transcription takes place. In this special context, secondary interactions become a matter inherent to the process of solute translocation.

E. Multiple Entities for Mediation

Previous considerations of carrier-mediated transport have assumed solute translocation by a single mediating entity. As is frequently the case in biology, such simplicity rarely holds for the real situation. In many, perhaps even in most, cases the transmembrane flow of a solute is mediated by multiple carriers, each providing what is known as a transport system for the solute under study. These systems, all of which must show some degree of acceptance of the solute, vary, however, in terms of substrate specificity, rates of solute entry, ability to concentrate, and requirements for cotransport or countertransport. In the general and physiological sense, maintenance and modulation of appropriate transmembrane concentrations requires the simultaneous consideration of these and other possibilities.

Although the identification of individual systems for transport mediation requires time-consuming experimentation, Christensen has elegantly formulated methods for the assessment of transport heterogeneity.[51,52] These methods use transport inhibition by substrate analogues and kinetic analysis (in terms of both the completeness and the homogeneity of transport inhibition) to probe the simultaneous activity of multiple transport systems serving for a single substrate. Such analysis has allowed Christensen and his co-workers to define four separate systems for the transport of even uncharged amino acids into the Erlich ascites tumor cell.[13,53-55] These systems are identified as follows: (1) a system serving for β-amino acids, (2) a system called A serving mainly for small, apolar amino acids; (3) a system called ASC serving mainly for small, polar amino acids; and (4) a system called L serving mainly for large, apolar amino acids. Although model substrates can be designed so that entry is limited to only one of these routes (e.g., N-methylaminoisobutyric acid for system A and aminonorbornane carboxylic acid for system L), most natural amino acids will be transported by two or more separately mediated processes; that is, these transport systems retain substrate specificity, but this specificity is seldom absolute. Similar degrees of transport heterogeneity are known in bacteria, where, for example, as many as four systems serve for

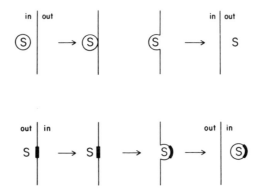

FIGURE 5. Simple pictorial representation of the processes for translocation of large molecules by membrane
flow. The upper series illustrates cellular exodus of a high
molecular weight solute by *exocytosis*, and the lower series,
cellular entry of a higher molecular solute by *receptor-mediated endocytosis*. In both cases, only the skeleton of the
model is given. Note that unlike the transport of low molecular weight solutes, the flow of membrane is required.
Note also that the sidedness of the membrane is reversed in
the upper and lower illustrations.

the transport of leucine alone,[19] and indeed in most other prokaryotic and eukaryotic
cells. It is of interest that during maturation of the reticulocyte to the erythrocyte,
some of the heterogeneity in amino acid transport described above is seen to decrease
as the cell undergoes degenerative differentiation.[56] Multiple transport mediation likely
represents a complex biological device to assure well-modulated entry and exodus of
solutes in cells of all types.

F. Membrane Flow

Although membrane-enclosed vesicles play no significant role in the translocation
of low molecular weight solutes, they are nevertheless important to considerations of
how peptides and proteins exit and enter cells. Proteins and peptides destined for secretion (including enzyme zymogens such as trypsinogen and chymotrypsinogen, blood
proteins such as albumin and the immunoglobulins, structural proteins such as colla-
gen and elastin, and hormones such as insulin and glucagon) all exit the cells where
they are made by a process known as exocytosis.[57,58] This process, in which intracellular, membrane-enclosed vesicles fuse with the plasma membrane and eventually expose
their contents to the extracellular compartment, permits translocation of components
too large for transport by both simple and mediated diffusion (see Figure 5.) The
further translocation of the peptide or protein then depends, in particular circumstances, on diffusion, flow through the blood, and possibly specific cellular uptake (see
later). Nevertheless, if the secreted protein was at one time surrounded by an intracellular membrane, one should wonder how the protein became segregated from other
cytoplasmic constituents. The problem is really separate from most considerations in
biological transport, but it deserves brief mention. Segregation of proteins from the
cytoplasm — whether considering those destined for disposition to secretion granules
or those destined for packaging into other intracellular organelles — occurs *during*
biosynthesis. Translocation across the membrane of the endoplasmic reticulum (a
process involving cleavage of a signal sequence as well as vectorial discharge) removes

the protein from the cytosolic compartment.[59,60] Subsequent events involving transfer to golgi or golgi-like structures and organelle formation eventually lead to the completed membrane-bound vesicle.

As mentioned before, membrane flow also plays a role in the cellular entry of large molecules such as peptides and proteins. Our view here, though, is mainly limited to bioactive molecules which participate in metabolic regulation. One example concerns the membrane-receptor-mediated action of peptide hormones. A current view holds that, subsequent to receptor recognition of the hormone and initiation of the biological response, the hormone and its receptor are internalized by a process known as receptor-mediated endocytosis.[61,62] The plasma membrane is thus seen to invaginate and surround that portion of the extracellular compartment subject to endocytosis. Fusion of the membrane then results in the formation of an intracellular, membrane-enclosed vesicle, as shown in Figure 5. A subsequent fusion of the vesicle with a lysosome could then lead to intracellular degradation of the peptide hormone. The elegant work of Brown and Goldstein on the cellular uptake of low-density lipoproteins emphasizes the impact of receptor-mediated endocytosis on metabolic regulation.[63] Endocytosis (via a specific low-density lipoprotein receptor) proceeds as briefly described above; the endocytotic vesicle then fuses with a primary lysosome, the components of the lipoprotein are metabolized and one of its components, cholesterol, is delivered to the smooth endoplasmic reticulum. At this site, cholesterol acts as an inhibitor of hydroxymethylglutaryl-coenzyme A reductase, the major controlling enzyme of sterol biosynthesis.

The above example yields an important solution to a difficult biological problem. Intuition suggests the logic of feedback inhibition of cholesterol biosynthesis, but two complicating factors arise. First, cholesterol is not very soluble in aqueous solutions. Second, cholesterol in high concentrations can disrupt membrane structure and can thus be considered cytotoxic. The circulation of cholesterol in the blood in combined form (i.e., as low-density lipoprotein) accommodates both of these considerations. Receptor-mediated endocytosis then allows the concentrated delivery of cholesterol to the appropriate intracellular site for metabolic regulation.

G. Intra- and Interorgan Flow

Biological transport within a single organ (intraorgan flow) can influence the delivery of solute to different portions of the tissue (through the formation of gradients in or opposite to the direction of vascular flow) and can provide communication among different cells comprising the tissue (through the selective secretion of effector molecules). As the former was discussed previously, only the latter will be considered here. Transmission of an electrical impulse (itself the result of alterations in Na^+ and K^+ flow across the axonal membrane) from one nerve cell to another proceeds by the vesicular secretion of a transmitter substance from an axonal end plate closely abutting a second neural cell.[65] Recognition of the neurotransmitter by a receptor on the second cell and degradation of the effector (in the case of acetylcholine), or carrier-mediated re-uptake of the effector (in the case of the amine transmitters) permit a rapid termination of the signaling event. Although the system is described here only very superficially, it illustrates how intercellular communication can result from vectorial, intraorgan flow. A different sort of communication concerns the local, sometimes called pericrine, action of the peptide somatostatin (secreted from D cells of the pancreatic islet) to inhibit the secretion of insulin from the B cells of *the same* islet organ.[66] The secretion of the effector by exocytosis and its diffusion through a very limited extracellular space provides specific control over the function of an adjacent or nearby cell. Similar secretory events (although not necessarily mediated only by vesicular transport) may play important roles in tissue differentiation and development. The recent demonstration of secretion of cyclic adenosine monophosphate as an external director of cellular migration in the development of the slime mold,[67] might presage findings implicating cellular secretion in the development of more complex organisms.

Solute flow between two organs (interorgan flow) might well be more familiar than that within a single organ. Its familiarity, however, should not detract from its importance in terms of solute translocation within complex eukaryotic systems. Processes of interorgan flow are crucial to the delivery of nutrients from one tissue to another, to the reutilization of both essential and nonessential metabolic products, and to the metabolic transformations of important biological effectors. Examples of these processes are numerous. One which is (or should be) readily recalled by the biochemist concerns the so-called Cori cycle. Actively contracting muscle can become relatively anaerobic, with the resulting slowing of the tricarboxylic acid cycle and accumulation of lactic acid. Such an occurrence would be unfortunate in two regards: first, the accumulation of an organic acid within the muscle cell produces difficulties in acid-base balance; second, the muscle does not utilize the full oxidative potential of the glucose molecule. The advanced organism has found a way around both problems. Lactate exits the muscle cell and is transported to the liver where it is converted to glucose. Glucose now exits the liver cell and is transported back to muscle where it can participate in anaerobic glycolysis. This scheme detracts little from the function of the liver (where neither oxygen nor phosphoryl donors are in short supply), but in essence permits functional survival of the oxygen-deficient muscle cell.

Mechanisms similar to the one described above also serve for the secretion of cholesterol and bilirubin into the bile, their flow to the intestinal lumen, and their reabsorption into the body (perhaps to the detriment of the organism). More clearly beneficial arrangements hold for the resorption of glucose, amino acids, and Na^+, as well as other solutes, from the renal filtrate and their delivery throughout the body. Although the Cori cycle represents an example of interorgan flow and metabolic transformation, the example is incomplete: the postulated transformations do not *absolutely* require the participation of specific organs. The interorgan distributions and metabolic transformations of vitamin D represent a more severe test of the same principle.[68,69] As illustrated in Figure 6, the biologically active forms of vitamin D_3 (those for example which stimulate Ca^{++} absorption across the intestinal mucosa) are produced from metabolic alterations of the precursor and these alterations occur in different tissues of the body. Thus, blood-borne vitamin D_3 is converted to the 25-hydroxy derivative in the liver, but this still inactive, potential effector must be transported to the kidney for further transformation. In the kidney, the 25-hydroxy derivative is converted to the biologically active 1,25-dihydroxy and 24,25-dihydroxy derivatives which are then capable of influencing Ca^{++} absorption. Although so complex an example of interorgan flow is somewhat unusual, similarly diverse flows and reactions undoubtedly play major roles in the synthesis, excretion, and absorption of both natural and unnatural effectors of important metabolic processes.

III. CONCLUDING REMARKS

The preceding review of processes associated with solute translocation in biological systems is both brief and personal. Some may be offended by my stress (or lack of it) and others, by my including (or excluding) certain topics in the framework of the discourse. As an investigator concerned with biological transport, I am frequently disturbed by the lack of respect often given the subject both within and without the laboratory. To study enzyme catalysis in an unmixed solution or in the presence of competing substrates would clearly be absurd. Yet, I have often seen a study involving tissue or cell incubation in which these points, as well as others directly concerned with

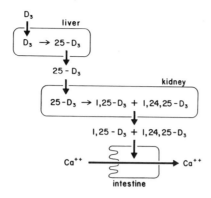

FIGURE 6. Interorgan translocations and transformations of vitamin D_3. The figure illustrates uptake of vitamin D_3 by the liver, its conversion to 25-hydroxy vitamin D_3 (cholecalciferol), exit of the derivative from the liver, uptake of the derivative by the kidney and conversion of 25-hydroxy vitamin D_3 to its 1,25-dihydroxy and 24,25-dihydroxy forms. These derivatives then exit the kidney and are taken up by cells of the intestinal mucosa where Ca^{++} absorption is stimulated.

biological transport, have been ill considered. My contribution to this book might best be thought of as a list of topics to be considered before embarking on an investigation requiring solute translocation across a biological membrane. These topics, as well as the important one of regulation of transmembrane flow by hormones and other effectors, represent a reasonably complete view of solute translocation in biological systems. To the novice, many of these considerations might seem hopelessly complex. The committed student of transport, however, will already know the enticement of the translocation event and the many remarkable ways in which soluble molecules of all kinds move from one place to another in the complex organism.

REFERENCES

1. Christensen, H. N., *Biological Transport,* 2nd ed., W. A. Benjamin, Reading, Mass., 1975, xvii.
2. Stein, W. D. and Danielli, J. F., Structure and function in red cell permeability, *Discuss. Faraday Soc.,* 21, 238, 1956.
3. Sistrom, W. R., On the physical state of the intracellulary accumulated substrates of β-galactoside-permease in *Escherichia coli, Biochim. Biophys. Acta,* 29, 579, 1958.
4. Collander, R., The permeability of plant protoplasts to non-electrolytes, *Trans. Faraday Soc.,* 33, 985, 1937.
5. Singer, S. J. and Nicolson, G. L., The fluid mosaic model of the structure of cell membranes, *Science,* 175, 720, 1972.
6. Singer, S. J., The molecular organization of membranes, *Annu. Rev. Biochem.,* 43, 805, 1974.
7. Christensen, H. N., Riggs, T. R., and Ray, N. E., Concentrative uptake of amino acids by erythrocytes *in vitro, J. Biol. Chem.,* 194, 41, 1952.
8. Beyer, K. H., Wright, L. D., Skeggs, H. R., Russo, H. F., and Shauer, G. A., Renal clearance of essential amino acids: their competition for resorption by the renal tubules, *Am. J. Physiol.,* 151, 202, 1947.

9. Cohen, G. N. and Rickenberg, H. V., Existence d'accepteurs specifique pour les amino acides chez *Eschericia coli*, *C. R. Acad. Sci.*, 240, 2086, 1955.
10. Cohen, G. N. and Rickenberg, H. V., Concentration specifique reversible des amino acides chez *Escherichia coli*, *Ann. Inst. Pasteur*, 91, 693, 1956.
11. Tennenhouse, A. and Quastel, J. H., Amino acid accumulation in Ehrlich ascites carcinoma cells, *Can. J. Biochem. Physiol.*, 38, 1311, 1960.
12. Oxender, D. L. and Christensen, H. N., Evidence for two types of mediation of neutral amino-acid transport in Ehrlich cells, *Nature (London)*, 197, 765, 1963.
13. Oxender, D. L. and Christensen, H. N., Distinct mediating systems for the transport of neutral amino acids by the Ehrlich cell, *J. Biol. Chem.*, 238, 3686, 1963.
14. Eavenson, E. and Christensen, H. N., Transport systems for neutral amino acids in the pigeon erythrocyte, *J. Biol. Chem.*, 242, 5386, 1967.
15. Piperno, J. R. and Oxender, D. L., Amino acid transport systems in Escherichia coli K12, *J. Biol. Chem.*, 243, 5914, 1968.
16. Rickenberg, H. V., Cohen, G. N., Buttin, G., and Monod, J., La galactoside-permease *d'Escherichia coli*, *Ann. Inst. Pasteur*, 91, 829, 1956.
17. LeFevre, P. G. and Marshall, J. K., Conformational specificity in a biological sugar transport system, *Am. J. Physiol.*, 194, 333, 1958.
18. Christensen, H. N., Handlogten, M. E., Lam, I., Tager, H. S., and Zand, R., A bicyclic amino acid to improve discrimination among transport systems, *J. Biol. Chem.*, 244, 1510, 1969.
19. Tager, H. S. and Christensen, H. N., Transport of the four isomers of 2-aminonorbornane-2-carboxylic acid in selected mammalian systems and in *Escherichia coli*, *J. Biol. Chem.*, 246, 7572, 1971.
20. Osterhout, W. J. V., How do electrolytes enter the cell, *Proc. Natl. Acad. Sci. U.S.A.*, 21, 125, 1935.
21. Rosenberg, T. and Wilbrandt, W., The kinetics of membrane transports involving chemical reactions, *Exp. Cell. Res.*, 9, 49, 1955.
22. Jarosch, R., On the behavior of rotating helices, in *Symposia of the International Society for Cell Biology*, Vol. 5, Warren, K. B., Ed., Academic Press, New York, 1966, 275.
23. Blumenthal, R. and Katchalsky, A., The effect of carrier association-dissociation rate on membrane permeation, *Biochim. Biophys. Acta*, 173, 357, 1969.
24. Dent, C. E. and Rose, G. A., Amino acid metabolism in cystinuria, *Q. J. Med.*, 20, 205, 1951.
25. Stanbury, J. B., Wyngaarden, J. B., and Fredrickson, D. S., *The Metabolic Basis of Inherited Disease*, 4th ed., (Part 11), McGraw-Hill, New York, 1978, 1526.
26. Oxender, D. L., Genetic approaches to the study of transport systems, in *Biological Transport*, 2nd ed., W. A. Benjamin, Reading, Mass., 1975, 214.
27. Pardee, A. B., Purification and properties of a sulfate-binding protein from *Salmonella typhimurium*, *J. Biol. Chem.*, 241, 5886, 1966.
28. Oxender, D. L., Membrane transport, *Annu. Rev. Biochem.*, 41, 777, 1972.
29. Boos, W., Bacterial transport, *Annu. Rev. Biochem.*, 43, 123, 1974.
30. Cabantchik, Z. I. and Rothstein, A., Membrane proteins related to anion permeability of human red blood cells, *J. Membr. Biol.*, 15, 207, 1974.
31. Steck, T. L., The band 3 protein of the human red cell membrane: a review, *J. Supramol. Struct.*, 8, 311, 1978.
32. Shanahan, M. F. and Czech, M. P., Partial purification of the D-glucose transport system in rat adipocyte plasma membranes, *J. Biol. Chem.*, 252, 6554, 1977.
33. Shanahan, M. F. and Czech, M. P., Purification and reconstitution of the adipocyte plasma membrane D-glucose transport system, *J. Biol. Chem.*, 252, 8341, 1977.
34. Van Slyke, D. D. and Meyer, G. M., The fate of protein digestion products in the body: the absorption of amino acids from the blood by the tissues, *J. Biol. Chem.*, 16, 197, 1913.
35. Kabach, H. R. and Barnes, E. M., Mechanisms of active transport in isolated membrane vesicles, *J. Biol. Chem.*, 246, 5523, 1971.
36. Simoni, R. D. and Postma, P. W., The energetics of bacterial active transport, *Annu. Rev. Biochem.*, 44, 523, 1975.
37. Mitchell, P., Vectorial chemiosmotic processes, *Annu. Rev. Biochem.*, 46, 996, 1977.
38. Mitchell, P. and Moyle, J., Group translocation: a consequence of enzyme-catalyzed group transfer, *Nature (London)*, 182, 372, 1958.
39. Kundig, W., Ghosh, S., and Roseman, S., Phosphate bound to histidine in a protein as an intermediate in a novel phosphotransferase system, *Proc. Nat. Acad. Sci. U.S.A.*, 52, 1067, 1964.
40. Simoni, R. D., Nakazawa, T., Hays, J. B., and Roseman, S., Sugar transport, *J. Biol. Chem.*, 248, 932, 1973.
41. Meister, A. and Tate, S. S., Glutathione and related γ-glutamyl compounds: biosynthesis and utilization, *Annu. Rev. Biochem.*, 45, 559, 1976.

42. Thomas, E. L., Shao, T.-C., and Christensen, H. N., Structural selectivity in interaction of neutral amino acids and alkali metal ions with a cationic amino acid transport system, *J. Biol. Chem.*, 246, 1682, 1971.

43. Thomas, E. L. and Christensen, H. N., Indicators of spatial relations among structures recognizing amino acids and Na^+ at a transport reception site, *Biochem. Biophys. Res. Commun.*, 40, 282, 1970.

44. Crane, R. K., Hypothesis of mechanism of intestinal active transport of sugars, *Fed. Proc., Fed. Am. Soc. Exp. Biol.*, 21, 891, 1962.

45. Goldner, A. M., Schultz, S. G., and Curran, P. F., Sodium and sugar fluxes across the mucosal border of rabbit illeum, *J. Gen. Physiol.*, 53, 362, 1969.

46. Ussing, H. H., Some aspects of the applicability of tracers in permeability studies, *Adv. Enzymol.*, 13, 21, 1952.

47. Aisen, P. and Listowsky, I., Iron transport and storage proteins, *Annu. Rev. Biochem.*, 49, 357, 1980.

48. Kretsinger, R. H., Calcium binding proteins, *Annu. Rev. Biochem.*, 45, 239, 1976.

49. Klee, C. B., Crouch, T. H., and Richman, P. G., Calmodulin, *Annu. Rev. Biochem.*, 49, 489, 1980.

50. Yamamoto, K. R. and Alberts, B. M., Steroid receptors: elements for modulation of eukaryotic transcription, *Annu. Rev. Biochem.*, 45, 721, 1976.

51. Christensen, H. N., Some special kinetic problems of transport, *Adv. Enzymol.*, 32, 1, 1969.

52. Christensen, H. N., *Biological Transport*, 2nd ed., W. A. Benjamin, Reading, Mass., 1975, 179.

53. Christensen, H. N., Relations in the transport of β-alanine and the α-amino acids in the Ehrlich cell, *J. Biol. Chem.*, 239, 3584, 1964.

54. Christensen, H. N., Liang, M., and Archer, E. G., A distinct Na^+ requiring transport system for alanine, serine, cysteine and similar amino acids, *J. Biol. Chem.*, 242, 5237, 1967.

55. Christensen, H. N. and Liang, M., An amino acid transport system of unassigned function in the Ehrlich ascites tumor cell, *J. Biol. Chem.*, 240, 3601, 1965.

56. Antonioli, J. A. and Christensen, H. N., Differences in schedules of regression of transport systems during reticulocyte maturation, *J. Biol. Chem.*, 244, 1505, 1969.

57. Jamieson, J. D. and Palade, G. E., Intracellular transport of secretory proteins, *J. Cell Biol.*, 34, 577, 1967.

58. Palade, G. E., Intracellular aspects of the process of protein synthesis, *Science*, 189, 347, 1975.

59. Blobel, G. and Dobberstein, B., Transfer of proteins across membranes, presence of proteolytically processed and unprocessed nascent immuno-globulin light chains on membrane-bound ribosomes of murine myeleoma, *J. Cell. Biol.*, 67, 835, 1975.

60. Blobel, G. and Dobberstein, B., Transfer of proteins across membranes, reconstitution of functional rough microsomes from heteralogous components, *J. Cell. Biol.*, 67, 852, 1975.

61. Silverstein, S. C., Steinman, R. M., and Zanvil, A., Endocytosis, *Annu. Rev. Biochem.*, 46, 669, 1977.

62. Ryser, H. J.-P., Uptake of protein by mammalian cell: an underdeveloped area, *Science*, 159, 390, 1968.

63. Goldstein, J. L. and Brown, M. S., The low-density lipoprotein pathway and its relation to athero-sclerosis, *Annu. Rev. Biochem.*, 46, 897, 1977.

64. Brown, M. S. and Goldstein, J. L., Receptor-mediated control of cholesterol metabolism, *Science*, 191, 150, 1976.

65. Barondes, S. H., Synaptic molecules: identification and metabolism, *Annu. Rev. Biochem.*, 43, 147, 1974.

66. Dubois, M. P., Presence of immunoreactive somatostatin in discrete cells of the endocrine pancreas, *Proc. Nat. Acad. Sci. U.S.A.*, 72, 1340, 1975.

67. Clark, R. L. and Steck, T. L., Morphogenesis in dictyostelium: an orbital hypothesis, *Science*, 204, 1163, 1979.

68. Hollick, M. F., Kleiner-Bossaller, A., Schnoes, H. K., Kasten, P. J., Boyle, I. T., and DeLuca, H. F., 1,24,25-Trihydroxyvitamin D_3: a metabolite of vitamin D_3 effective in intestine, *J. Biol. Chem.*, 248, 6691, 1973.

69. DeLuca, H. F. and Schnoes, H. K., Metabolism and mechanism of action of vitamin D, *Annu. Rev. Biochem.*, 45, 631, 1976.

Chapter 3

DYNAMIC ASPECTS OF CELL MEMBRANE STRUCTURE

Fedor Medzihradsky and Edward I. Cullen

A recent publication on the structure of cell membranes focused primarily on concepts regarding the organization of membrane components.[1] The aim of the present article is to discuss the dynamics of membrane constituents, and to describe some of the consequences of their mobility on membrane function. As reviewed in the previous paper, early evidence revealed lateral mobility of both proteins and lipids in the plane of cell membranes.[1] It was also shown that the catalytic function of certain membrane-bound enzymes is dependent on their interaction with surrounding lipid. Subsequently, processes restricting the lateral diffusion of intrinsic membrane proteins were described, e.g., the interaction between membrane spanning and cytoplasmic proteins such as glycophorin and spectrin in erythrocytes.[1,2] Recent research on the mobility of membrane components has been markedly facilitated by the introduction of the method of fluorescence recovery after photobleaching (FRAP). The procedure is based on the complete destruction of photosensitive, fluorescent tags on proteins in a small, discrete area of the membrane upon exposure to a highly focused laser beam. Recovery of specific fluorescence in the area of the bleached spot reflects lateral migration of other molecules of the protein back into the area under study. By applying this technique, the mobility of membrane proteins has been described in various cell lines.[3,4] In addition to supporting the general fluid-mosaic model of cell membranes, the results of these studies revealed that both the rate of protein migration and the amount returning were lower than theoretically expected.[5] The finding that the path of return was longer than expected for randomly "floating" molecules suggests the existence in the lipid bilayer of areas of exclusion due to structural organization and/or interaction between neighboring molecules of proteins and/or lipids. The results, in fact, imply that some fraction of the protein population has been immobilized, apparently by interaction with cytoskeletal structures underlying the plasma membrane.

Considering the lateral, temperature-dependent movement of lipid molecules, the membrane can be viewed as a fluid environment. However, due to interactions between neighboring lipid molecules, the fluidity is not uniform throughout the membrane, but increases towards the nonpolar hydrocarbon core.[6] The microviscosity, i.e., the reciprocal of fluidity, of cell membranes is a reflection of its chemical composition. Increased ratios of proteins to membrane lipids, of cholesterol to phospholipids, and of sphingomyelin to lecithin lead to higher microviscosity. In addition, elevated amounts of saturated fatty acids in the phospholipid moiety contribute to membrane rigidity. For example the replacement of stearic acid (18:0) with oleic acid (18:1) has been found to considerably increase membrane fluidity.[5]

Since the composition of cell membranes, including the ratio of saturated to unsaturated fatty acids, is influenced by metabolism, disturbances of the latter can be reflected in abnormal fluidity leading to specific deficiencies of membrane function.[7] For example, spur-cell anemia is characterized by the premature destruction of erythrocytes and platelets due to plasma membrane rigidity caused by an increased membrane content of cholesterol. This abnormality results from a disorder of plasma lipoprotein metabolism occurring in patients with severe liver disease. Erythrocytes of patients with abetalipoproteinemia have a similar fate. The plasma membranes of these cells are characterized by low deformability due to an increased ratio of sphingomyelin to lecithin. Furthermore, as a consequence of increased membrane cholesterol to phospholipid ratio, platelets of patients with Type IIa hyperlipoproteinemia exhibit increased sensitivity towards aggregation induced by adenosine diphosphate or epinephrine. Transport of neutral molecules and ions, occurring by diffusion as well as by carrier mediation, was inversely proportional to membrane fluidity altered either in vitro or as a consequence of pathogenesis.[7]

The dependence of the function of several membrane-bound enzymes on their lipid-phospholipid environment has been described. The activities of adenylate cyclase[8] and of Na,K-ATPase[8,9] were diminished as a result of increased cholesterol content in the plasma membranes. The effect on Na,K-ATPase was apparently due to altered V_{max}, whereas the K_m for ATP remained unchanged.[9] Sarcoplasmic ATPase, complexed with synthetic phospholipids, was completely inhibited below temperatures which corresponded to a phase transition of the lipid.[10] One of the most challenging questions facing investigators in this field is how, or indeed whether, cells regulate membrane properties like fluidity in order to achieve well-defined physiological goals. A possible link between membrane fluidity and lipid metabolism has recently been critically assessed.[11] The author found no firm evidence for the existence of adaptive mechanisms for altering the biosynthesis of unsaturated fatty acids in response to signals indicating inadequate membrane fluidity. His analysis suggests that reported cases of such corrective adaptations represent fortuitous rather than purposeful events.

Of considerable interest for understanding the events regulating membrane fluidity was the observation that enzymic methylation of phospholipids increases membrane fluidity.[12] This mechanism involves the successive, two-step methylation of phosphatidylethanolamine to phosphatidylcholine by two methyltransferases asymmetrically distributed in the membrane. The first methylation step occurs at the cytoplasmic side, the site for both methyltransferase I and its substrate, phosphatidylethanolamine. The methylated product is translocated to the external side of the plasma membrane, where it is further methylated to phosphatidylcholine by methyltransferase II. The first methylation and/or migration of the product leads to a significant decrease in membrane microviscosity. Further methylation of the monomethylated phosphatidylethanolamine apparently has no further effect on membrane fluidity. It was further shown that in reticulocytes and in HeLa cells, binding of agonists to the β-adrenergic receptor stimulated phospholipid methylation and the subsequent translocation of the monomethylated product from the cytoplasm to the external site.[13] As described above, these events decrease microviscosity and thus enhance the lateral mobility of the membrane receptor. Binding of β-adrenergic antagonists such as propranolol prevents the agonist-induced stimulation of phospholipid methylation and the concomitant increase of membrane fluidity. The causal relationship between microviscosity and membrane function was underlined by studies[14] in which membrane fluidity was experimentally altered by incubating erythrocyte plasma membranes with *cis* vaccenic acid ($\Delta 11$-12,18:1). Subsequently, the activation of adenylate cyclase by binding of agonist to the β-adrenergic receptor was investigated as a function of membrane fluidity. The results support the concept of membrane receptors which are, in part, mobile (Figure 1) and function after "collision coupling" with their effector, in this case adenylate cyclase.[15,16] The coupling process, involving the formation of a ternary complex between ligand, receptor, and effector,[17] and also requiring GTP and a protein coupling factor, is strongly influenced by membrane fluidity in accordance with the model of floating receptors.[18] Since mobility is a function of fluidity, the recently described effect of phospholipid methylation on microviscosity[12,13] suggests the following possible sequence of molecular events underlying the function of the membrane-bound β-adrenergic receptor (Figure 2): binding of agonist-ligand to receptor; stimulation of phospholipid methylation; decrease of microviscosity; enhanced lateral mobility of receptor and/or effector; collision coupling of receptor, effector, and coupling factor; activa-

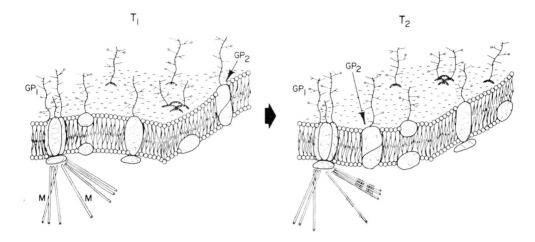

FIGURE 1. Modified version of the fluid mosaic model of membrane structure. T_1 and T_2 represent different points in time. Certain hypothetical integral membrane glycoprotein components (e.g., GP_2) are uncoupled and free to diffuse laterally in the membrane plane formed by a fluid bilayer matrix, while others such as the integral glycoprotein complex, GP_1, may be "anchored" or relatively impeded by a microfilament-microtubule cytoskeletal assemblage (M). (Modified from Nicolson, G. L., *Int. Rev. Cytol.,* 39, 89, 1974. With permission.)

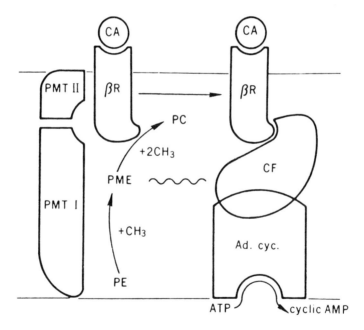

FIGURE 2.. Phospholipid methylation and β-adrenergic receptor coupling. When catecholamine (CA) binds to β-adrenergic receptor (βR), it stimulates phospholipid methyltransferase I (PMT I) and phospholipid methyltransferase II (PMT II). This increases the methylation of phosphatidylethanolamine (PE) to phosphatidyl-*N*-monomethylethanolamine (PME) and to phosphatidylcholine (PC). As the phospholipids are methylated they flip-flop and increase fluidity ($\sim$). This facilitates the lateral mobility of the β-adrenergic receptor to interact with the guanylnucleotide coupling factor (CF) and adenylate cyclase (Ad. cyc.) to generate cyclic AMP. (From Hirata, F. and Axelrod, J., *Science*, 209, 1082, 1980. Copyright 1980 by the American Association for the Advancement of Science. With permission.)

tion of adenylate cyclase and formation of cyclic AMP; hydrolysis of GTP and un-coupling of the complex. It should again be emphasized that the evidence for this hypothesis has been assembled primarily in studies on the β-adrenergic receptor. In contrast to that mechanism, the membrane-bound adenosine receptor appears to be permanently coupled to adenylate cyclase.[19,20]

Initial evidence for the relationship between membrane fluidity and transport func-tion was provided by studies of bacterial cells grown in the presence of various fatty acids. In these cells, the transport of β-galactoside displayed a characteristic tempera-ture dependence, reflecting the transition temperature for the fatty acid, i.e., the shift between a liquid-crystalline and a crystalline state of the lipid environment. In a given cell type identical temperature dependence was obtained, as assessed by corresponding Arrhenius plots,[21] for the uptake of β-glucosides and β-galactosides occurring by two independent transport systems.[22] These transport processes were also studied in a strain of *Escherichia coli* requiring unsaturated fatty acids for growth. By inclusion of spe-cific unsaturated fatty acids, the membrane fluidity of these cells was altered. The results indicated partitioning of the transport proteins between ordered and fluid do-mains in the membrane by lateral migration.[23] The partition was dependent on the lipid composition of the membrane and on the transport protein, the latter displaying a strong preference for diffusing into fluid parts of the membrane.

Appreciable differences in the transport of methotrexate were described in L 1210 mouse leukemia cells after altering the fatty acid composition of the plasma membrane by feeding diets rich in saturated or polyunsaturated oils.[24] Using fatty acids tagged with the nitroxide group, detectable by electron spin resonance spectroscopy, a corre-lation between increased membrane fluidity and an elevated content of unsaturated fatty acid was described. In the cells harvested after unsaturated fatty acid diet, the K_m for methotrexate transport was 2.9 μM in contrast to the value of 4.1 μM found in cells obtained after feeding saturated fatty acids. These results indicate that drug up-take, and thus its effectiveness, can be affected by the diet-related composition of the plasma membrane.

Interesting evidence for the relationship between transport function and membrane fluidity was provided by recent studies on the uptake of D-glucose. In reconstituted phospholipid vesicles containing phosphatidylcholine and phosphatidylethanolamine the membrane bilayer melted at $-15°$ and was fully fluid at $17°$.[25] Whereas at $0°$, mediated transport of D-glucose was undetectable, its rate with temperature increased markedly up to $17°$, representing the completion of phase transition into the fluid state of membrane phospholipids. The subsequent temperature dependence of glucose trans-port was considerably smaller. If an appreciable concentration of cholesterol was in-corporated into the vesicles, the rate of carrier-mediated glucose transport was de-creased, reflecting impaired mobility of the carrier in the state of decreased fluidity induced by the sterol. On the other hand, transport of glucose by passive diffusion was independent of changing membrane fluidity, indicating that this form of glucose transport occurred through relatively rigid channel-like structures. Of particular inter-est was the observed analogous effect of membrane fluidity and insulin on glucose transport.[26] In adipocytes, with decreased membrane microviscosity due to the incor-poration of unsaturated fatty acids, the carrier mediated uptake of glucose was en-hanced to the level achieved by insulin in untreated vesicles. In the treated adipocytes insulin had no additional effect.

A recent experimental and theoretical analysis of the relationship between membrane fluidity and the transport of glucose in erythrocytes and fibroblasts revealed two coun-teracting phenomena.[27] Limited increase of microviscosity (10 to 20%), caused by the incorporation of cholesterol or one of its hydrophilic esters, resulted in enhanced rate of transport. However, further increase in membrane microviscosity progressively re-

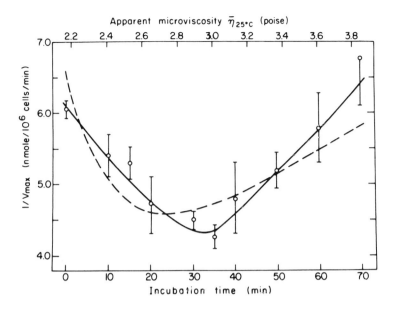

FIGURE 3. Effect of incorporated cholesteryl hemisuccinate (CHS) (presented in a scale of incubation time) on the uptake of 2-deoxy-d-[^{3}H]glucose in monolayers of 3T3 mouse fibroblasts. The experimental points represent the mean and the standard deviation of six to nine independent measurements. The solid line represents the experimental pattern, and the dashed line was computed for data fitting according to Equation 14. (From Yuli, I., Wilbrandt, W., and Shinitzky, M., *Biochemistry*, 20, 4250, 1981. With permission.)

duced the V_{max} of glucose uptake (Figure 3) and efflux (Figure 4). These findings correlated well with theoretical data computed on the basis of the expected dependence of carrier mediated transport on membrane fluidity. A slight increase in membrane microviscosity apparently exposed additional, previously dormant, carrier sites. With further decreasing fluidity, the translocation of carrier sites became progressively hindered. According to earlier forwarded models, the rate of glucose transport was expected to decrease proportionally with increased membrane microviscosity.[28]

The examples described here illustrate consequences on cell membrane function of the dynamics of its major constituents, proteins and lipids. Thus, in investigating membrane phenomena such as receptor mechanisms, transport, and enzyme properties, their dependence on membrane microviscosity should be assessed. Concurrently, it should be considered that membrane fluidity is influenced by manifold factors such as nutrition, pathogenesis, and hormonal stimulation. It is expected that future work in this area will reveal additional pertinent correlations of great biological interest.

ACKNOWLEDGMENTS

This work was supported in part by USPHS Grants GM 27028 and EY 02450.

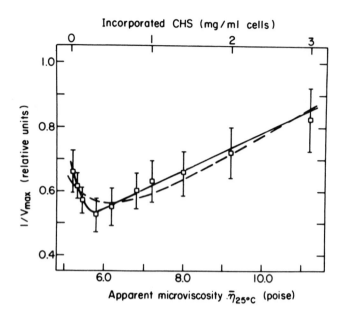

FIGURE 4.   Effect of apparent microviscosity, modulated by incorporation of cholesteryl hemisuccinate (CHS), on the reciprocal
maximal rate of glucose efflux ($1/V_{max}$) in human erythrocytes at
37°C. The squares represent the mean of six to nine independent
experiments, and the bars indicate their standard deviation. The
experimental pattern is given by the solid line, whereas the dashed
line was computed for data fitting according to Equation 14.
(From Yuli, I., Wilbrandt, W., and Shinitzky, M., *Biochemistry*,
20, 4250, 1981. With permission.)

REFERENCES

1. **Medzihradsky, F.,** Structure and function of cell membranes, and cellular transport of drugs, in *Principles of Radiopharmacology*, Colombetti, L. G., Ed., CRC Press, Boca Raton, Fla., 1979, 197.
2. **Nicolson, G. L. and Painter, R. G.,** Anionic sites of human erythrocyte membranes. II. Antispectrin-induced transmembrane aggregation of the binding sites for positively charged colloidal particles, *J. Cell. Biol.,* 59, 395, 1973.
3. **Zagyansky, J. and Edidin, M.,** Lateral diffusion of concanavalin A receptors in the plasma membrane of mouse fibroblasts, *Biochim. Biophys. Acta,* 433, 209, 1976.
4. **Axelrod, D., Koppel, D. E., Schlessinger, J. E., Elson, E., and Webb, W. W.,** Mobility measurement by analysis of fluorescence photobleaching recovery kinetics, *Biophys. J.,* 16, 1055, 1976.
5. **Shinitzky, M. and Henkart, P.,** Fluidity of cell membranes - current concepts and trends, *Intern. Rev. Cytol.,* 60, 121, 1979.
6. **Seelig, A. and Seelig, J.,** The dynamic structure of fatty acyl chains in a phospholipid bilayer measured by deuterium magnetic resonance, *Biochemistry,* 13, 4839, 1974.
7. **Cooper, R. A.,** Abnormalities of cell-membrane fluidity in the pathogenesis of disease, *N. Engl. J. Med.,* 297, 371, 1977.
8. **Lands, W. E. M.,** Dialogue between membranes and their lipid-metabolizing enzymes, *Biochem. Soc. Trans. (London),* 8, 25, 1979.
9. **Klein, I., Moore, L., and Pastan, I.,** Effect of liposomes containing cholesterol on adenylate cyclase activity of cultured mammalian fibroblasts, *Biochim. Biophys. Acta,* 506, 42, 1978.
10. **Kimmelberg, H. K.,** Alterations in phospholipid-dependent ($Na^+ + K^+$)-ATPase activity due to lipid fluidity. Effects of cholesterol and Mg^{2+}, *Biochim. Biophys. Acta,* 413, 143, 1975.

11. Warren, G. B., Toon, P. A., Birdsall, N. J. M., Lee, A. G., and Metcalfe, J. C., Reversible lipid titrations of the activity of pure adenosine triphosphatase-lipid complexes, *Biochemistry*, 13, 5501, 1974.

12. Hirata, F. and Axelrod, J., Enzymatic methylation of phosphatidylethanolamine increases erythrocyte membrane fluidity, *Nature (London)*, 275, 219, 1978.

13. Hirata, F. and Axelrod, J., Phospholipid methylation and biological signal transmission, *Science*, 209, 1082, 1980.

14. Rimon, G., Hanski, E., Braun, S., and Levitzki, A., Mode of coupling between hormone receptors and adenylate cyclase elucidated by modulation of membrane fluidity, *Nature (London)*, 276, 394, 1978.

15. Tolkovsky, A. M. and Levitzki, A., Mode of coupling between the β-adrenergic receptor and adenylate cyclase on turkey erythrocytes, *Biochemistry*, 17, 3795, 1978.

16. Hanski, E., Rimon, G., and Levitzki, A., Adenylate cyclase activation by the β-adrenergic receptors as a diffusion-controlled process, *Biochemistry*, 18, 846, 1979.

17. De Lean, A., Stadel, J. M., and Lefkowitz, R. J., A ternary complex model explains the agonist-specific binding properties of the adenylate cyclase-coupled β-adrenergic receptor, *J. Biol. Chem.*, 255, 7108, 1980.

18. De Haën, C., The non-stoichiometric floating receptor model for hormone sensitive adenylyl cyclase, *J. Theor. Biol.*, 58, 383, 1976.

19. Tolkovsky, A. M. and Levitzki, A., Coupling of a single adenylate cyclase to two receptors: adenosine and catecholamine, *Biochemistry*, 17, 3811, 1978.

20. Braun, A. and Levitzki, A., Adenosine receptor permanently coupled to turkey erythrocyte adenylate cyclase, *Biochemistry*, 18, 2134, 1979.

21. Medzihradsky, F., Transmembrane transport as the rate-limiting phenomenon in the distribution of pharmacological agents, in *Biological Transport of Radiotracers*, Colombetti, L. G., Ed., CRC Press, Boca Raton, 1982, chap. 4.

22. Wilson, G., Rose, S. P., and Fox, C. F., The effect of membrane lipid unsaturation on glycoside transport, *Biochem. Biophys. Res. Commun.*, 38, 617, 1970.

23. Thilo, L., Träuble, M., and Overath, P., Mechanistic interpretations of the influence of lipid phase transitions on transport functions, *Biochemistry*, 16, 1283, 1977.

24. Burns, P. C., Luttenegger, D. G., Dudley, D. T., Buettner, G. R., and Spector, A. A., Effect of modification of plasma membrane fatty acid composition on fluidity and methotrexate transport in L 1210 murine leukemia cells, *Cancer Res.*, 39, 1726, 1979.

25. Melchior, D. L. and Czech, M. P., Sensitivity of the adipocyte D-glucose transport system to membrane fluidity in reconstituted vesicles, *J. Biol. Chem.*, 254, 8744, 1979.

26. Pilch, P. F., Thompson, P. A., and Czech, M. P., Coordinate modulation of D-glucose transport activity and bilayer fluidity in plasma membranes derived from control and insulin-treated adipocytes, *Proc. Natl. Acad. Sci. U.S.A.*, 77, 915, 1980.

27. Yuli, I., Wilbrandt, W., and Shinitzky, M., Glucose transport through cell membranes of modified lipid fluidity, *Biochemistry*, 20, 4250, 1981.

28. Janacek, K. and Kotyk, A., in *Cell Membrane Transport; Principles and Techniques*, Kotyk, C. and Janacek, K., Eds., Plenum Press, New York, 1969, 57.

Chapter 4

TRANSMEMBRANE TRANSPORT AS THE RATE-LIMITING PHENOMENON IN THE DISTRIBUTION OF PHARMACOLOGICAL AGENTS

Fedor Medzihradsky

The aim of this article is to review the experimental conditions and criteria applied in characterizing the transmembrane transport of pharmacological agents, amid other forms of drug-tissue associations often described by the general term "uptake". For example, a large number of neuroactive drugs are basic and thus display considerable binding liability to negatively charged proteinaceous sites abundantly present in cellular preparations but unrelated to transport.[1] The resulting accumulation of these compounds in tissue then falsely indicates active transport as the underlying mechanism. While the terminology, definitions, and basic aspects of biological transport have been comprehensively reviewed,[2] the properties of pharmacological agents justify a critical assessment of specific conditions suitable to resolve the multiplicity of their interactions with biologic material, including membrane transport. Biological transport is identified as a process by which a solute, representing a given compound in solution, is transferred from one phase to another, whereby it remains in identical states in the two phases.[2] This definition thus excludes unequal distribution of compounds due to phenomena such as extracellular and intracellular binding, ionization, or metabolism. The investigator is faced with the burden to design experimental conditions under which membrane transport can be studied with minimal interference by the above-listed processes, or which allow their contribution to the observed cellular uptake to be quantified and corrected for.

The frequently applied approach of using radiolabeled compounds to study transport phenomena can give rise to artifacts related to the localization and stability of the radiolabel. In addition to the obligation to determine the radiochemical purity of the employed radioactive compound, e.g., by thin-layer chromatography in at least two different solvent systems, the association of the radiolabel with the initial parent form of the compound for the duration of the particular experiment has to be ascertained. Assessing possible chemical changes of the investigated solute is of particular importance in intact cellular preparations, or tissue homogenates, due to the likely presence of endogenous metabolizing systems. Interference by metabolism, or chemical instability of the solute, can be evaluated by determining the cellular uptake using two different methodological approaches. Identical uptake kinetics, e.g., time dependence of the uptake, established by measuring radioactivity of the solute and by its chemical determination, e.g., gas-liquid or high-pressure chromatography, indicate that under the given experimental conditions the radiolabel is associated with the initial chemical structure of the investigated solute. Such conclusion then justifies using measurements of radioactivity as a sensitive and convenient method of quantifying the transport process.[3,4] Information on the stability of radiolabel can also be obtained by homogenizing the biologic material subsequent to the uptake experiment, extracting the solute under investigation, and subjecting it to cochromatography with a pure sample on thin-layer plates.

An initial approach in distinguishing between the binding of a solute to a transport carrier and its interaction with other extracellular sites on the plasma membrane is to investigate the uptake under conditions of intact cellular morphology and also subsequent to perturbation of the plasma membrane. Assuming the existence of a pertinent transport process, the characteristics of solute-tissue association, e.g., affinity and extent binding, temperature and pH dependence, energetics of binding, are likely to be altered after abolishing the vesicular structure of the cells.[4-6] The latter can be accomplished by gentle perturbation of the plasma membrane, e.g., by freezing at $-70°C$ and thawing to room temperature. Such process eliminates the barrier between the extra- and intracellular compartments, but should not significantly impair binding of the solute to membrane sites unrelated to transport. However, altered binding under conditions of abolished plasma membrane integrity should be interpreted with caution and investigated by additional criteria. The perturbation exposes possible intracellular particulate binding sites not accessible to the solute facing intact cells. On the other hand, the effect of such treatment on extracellular binding sites unrelated to transport cannot be excluded. Certainly, abolishment of plasma membrane integrity should be undertaken by more than one method, e.g., by exposing cells to the freeze-thaw cycle, to osmotic changes, or to metabolic inhibitors.[7] The degree of perturbation can be assessed by the cellular contents of K^+ and Na^+, conveniently determined by flame photometry, which represent sensitive indicators of plasma membrane permeability.[7]

Among the kinetic approaches distinguishing between the binding of a solute to a transport carrier and to immobile ("fixed") sites in the membrane, the demonstration of a transmembrane phenomenon, e.g., countertransport, represents a stringent criterion.[8-10] In a simple illustration of this principle, the cellular uptake of the radiolabeled solute is determined under two different experimental conditions. One aliquot of the cells is initially incubated with the unlabeled form of the solute to reach equilibrium in uptake, while the other is kept for the same length of time in buffer alone (control). Subsequently, the radiolabeled solute is added to both aliquots of cells and the initial rate of uptake is determined, for example, by quickly filtering the cells after a predetermined incubation time. The concentration of the radiolabeled solute in the medium is kept well below that of the unlabeled solute employed to preload the cells. Binding of the solute to a transport carrier, i.e., a mobile site involved in a translocation across the plasma membrane, will be indicated by the enhanced rate of uptake into the preloaded cells (Figure 1). Solute binding to a membrane site unrelated to transport will not yield such kinetics, nor would uptake by a nonmediated process.[8] The phenomenon of countertransport is based on stimulation of the cellular uptake of the radiolabeled solute by its unlabeled form present intracellularly. The effect is explained by the slower migration of the empty carrier site relative to that occupied by a molecule of the transported solute. Hence, in the here-described case, fewer carrier binding sites will be available in a given time period on the extracellular surface for interacting with the radiolabeled solute. It should be emphasized that countertransport does not affect the position of the equilibrium and the final distribution of the solute, i.e., it does not result in net transport.[2]

Assuming bidirectional mediation by the carrier, the phenomenon of countertransport can also be examined during efflux.[4-6,8] In such experiments the cells are incubated with the radiolabeled solute to reach equilibrium, and are then rapidly diluted with buffer medium containing relatively high concentrations of the unlabeled solute. At various times after the dilution, the cellular material is quickly filtered or centrifuged and its radioactivity determined. Again, the concentration of the added radiolabeled solute represents a small fraction of that of the unlabeled solute in the diluting media[4-6] Mediation during efflux will be indicated by enhanced rates of exodus into the media containing increasing concentrations of the unlabeled solute (Figure 1).

Transacceleration of transport thus serves as a useful criterion in revealing solute binding to a mobile (carrier) site, whereby mobility is defined in a wider sense and includes changes in site orientation, e.g., by altered conformation.[2] The criterion also differentiates between mediated transport and nonsaturable translocation, although these processes should be distinguishable by their respective uptake kinetics.

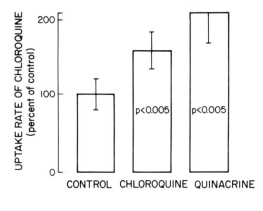 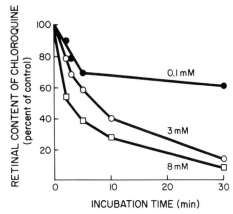

FIGURE 1. Transacceleration of ³H-chloroquine transport in the isolated rat retina. Retinae were incubated for 30 min in buffer alone (control), or in the presence of 8 mM chloroquine or 8 mM quinacrine, a structural analogue (left graph). Then, radiolabeled chloroquine was added and after 3 min the tissue was rapidly filtered through disks of nylon screen, washed, and freeze-dried. The weighed tissue was digested and subjected to liquid scintillation counting. The concentration of radiolabeled chloroquine in the medium was less than 5% of that of the unlabeled drug present during the initial incubation of tissue. In computing the results, the diffusional component of chloroquine uptake was subtracted from total drug uptake. In other experiments (right graph) the tissue was incubated for 30 min with 1 mM radiolabeled chloroquine. The samples were rapidly diluted ninefold with the buffer medium containing unlabeled chloroquine at concentrations as listed. At the times indicated, the retinal content of radiolabeled drug was determined after rapid filtration of the tissue as described above. (From Bednarczyk, D. J. and Medzihradsky, F., *Mol. Pharmacol.*, 13, 99, 1977. With permission.)

In characterizing the accumulation of pharmacological agents, described in various tissue,[11] additional criteria have to be considered. Accumulative or "active" transport is dependent on metabolic energy, e.g., the uptake correlates with cellular ATP levels,[4] and thus is sensitive to the action of metabolic inhibitors. These agents diminish the observed cellular accumulation of the solute, displaying thereby noncompetitive inhibition kinetics.[4] The use of either aerobic or anaerobic inhibitors is suggested by the predominant dependence of the investigated cells on oxidative or glycolytic energy generation. Hence in leukocytes,[4] but not in synaptosomes,[6] glycolytic poisons were more potent in inhibiting drug accumulation than were inhibitors of electron transport or uncouplers of oxidative phosphorylation (Figure 2).

Temperature dependence represents a supportive criterion in distinguishing active transport from other forms of solute translocation. Reflecting solute interactions with membrane components, and/or dependence of cellular accumulation on metabolic energy generated by enzyme catalysis, the temperature dependence of active transport frequently displays Q_{10} values approximating 2.[6,12] Lower values are obtained for processes of facilitated diffusion and nonmediated transport. The Q_{10} values are estimated from Arrhenius plots of the uptake data, generated at three or more different temperatures (Figure 3).

Mediated transport of a solute, both equilibrating and accumulative, is competitively inhibited by its structural analogues. Such interactions, assessed by Lineweaver-Burk plots of the uptake data (Figure 4), represent an important experimental approach in characterizing carrier-mediated transport processes.[5,13] In addition to Lineweaver-Burk analysis, plotting the data on transport inhibition according to Dixon[5,6,14] will yield the K_i values for various structural analogues (Figure 5).

Processes other than active transport can account for the accumulation of compounds in tissue. In the case of weak acids or bases, such distribution can be the result

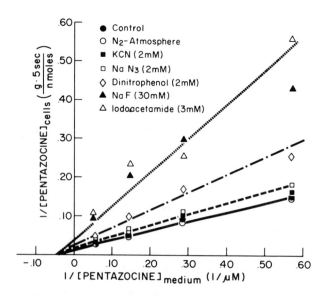

FIGURE 2.   Effect of metabolic inhibitors on the uptake of ^{3}H-pentazocine in rat leukocytes. Suspensions of leukocytes in the buffer medium were incubated at 37°C in the presence of 2 mM each of either KCN, NaN₃, or dinitrophenol; 3 mM iodoacetamide, or 30 mM NaF. The osmolarity of the incubation medium was maintained constant by decreasing the concentration of NaCl equivalently. In separate experiments, suspensions of the cells were incubated for 60 min in a nitrogen atmosphere. After these treatments, the cells were exposed to radioactive pentazocine for 5 sec. The separation of the cells occurred by rapid filtration, and the drug was quantitated by liquid scintillation counting. (From Marks, M. J. and Medzihradsky, F., *Mol. Pharmacol.*, 10, 837, 1974. With permission.)

of different pH in the extracellular and intracellular compartments. Following ionization in the extracellular compartment according to the respective values of pKa and pH, the undissociated form of these solutes can penetrate cell membrane on the basis of its lipid solubility.[15,16] Assuming a different intracellular pH favoring a greater extent of ionization, a sink ("ion trap") for the undissociated form of the solute will be provided (Figure 6). Such pH-dependent partition[17] mimics active transport, although membrane translocation of the solute occurs by diffusion rather than by carrier-mediation.

In the course of investigating the distribution of compounds with structure-related liability for interacting with proteinaceous material,[11] it is of considerable interest to assess intracellular binding as a possible contributing factor. Binding of the solute to particulate intracellular sites can be studied in membrane fractions prepared from intact cellular material by suitable homogenization procedures. However, according to the protagonists of the sorption theory of transport,[18,19] intracellular binding to cytoplasmic coacervates of high molecular weight can result in cellular accumulation of solutes, thus mimicking active transport. Ongoing work in our laboratory is committed to assess the role of intracellular binding in the transmembrane distribution of pharmacological agents.

Frequently the cellular uptake of a compound occurs by more than one transport process, and the investigator is faced with the resolution of these multiple systems. The biological transport of many drugs involves diffusion, in addition to a saturable process.[5,6] The resolution of the latter two components is based on the assumption

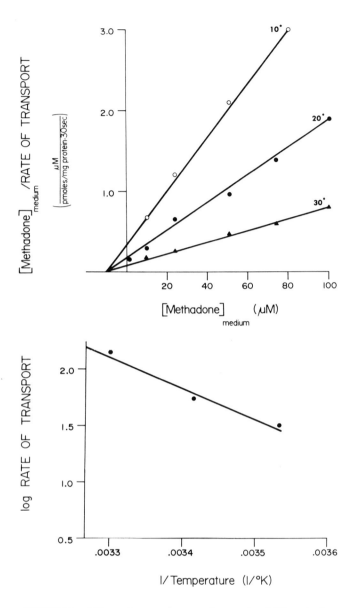

FIGURE 3. Effect of temperature on the uptake of ^{3}H-methadone in synaptosomes from rat brain. Aliquots of the synaptosomal fraction were incubated for 5 min at the indicated temperature and then quickly filtered. The data, representing initial rates of drug uptake, were plotted according to Lineweaver-Burk (upper graph). The values for V_{max} were used to obtain the Arrhenius plot shown in the lower graph. The slope of the line in the latter plot corresponded to a Q_{10} of 1.99. (From Cahill, A. L., Hoornstra, M. P., and Medzihradsky, F., *Mol. Pharmacol.*, 16, 587, 1979. With permission.)

that at sufficiently high concentrations of the solute its uptake will occur predominantly by diffusion. From the uptake data obtained under such experimental conditions, a diffusion constant is determined. The latter is used to subtract the diffusional component from total uptake, assessed at various concentrations of the solute.[5,6,20] This computation then reveals the mediated uptake component (Figure 7). The importance of such resolution is illustrated by characteristics of the recently described syn-

EFFECT OF A COMPETITIVE INHIBITOR (CYCLAZOCINE) ON
PENTAZOCINE UPTAKE

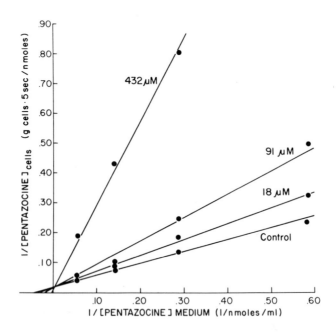

FIGURE 4.   Competitive inhibition of ³H-pentazocine uptake in
leukocytes by structural analogues. Shown is a Lineweaver-Burk
plot of the uptake in the presence of cyclazocine, a benzomorphan
analogue. Leukocytes were incubated simultaneously with pentazocine and cyclazocine at concentrations as indicated. (From Medzihradsky, F., Marks, M. J., and Metcalfe, J. I., *Adv. Biochem.
Psychopharmacol.*, 8, 537, 1974. With permission of Raven Press,
New York.)

aptosomal transport of methadone.[6] The dependence of the accumulative drug uptake
on metabolic energy was revealed only after resolution of the saturable component
from total uptake as described above (Figure 8). In this particular case, the enhancement of diffusional transport by 2,4-dinitrophenol, the employed inhibitor of ATP
generation, created an additional complication in the kinetic resolution.

Transport of a compound by two mediated processes can be detected by appropriate
Lineweaver-Burk analysis.[2,21] The determination of accurate kinetic parameters (K_m,
V_{max}) for the concurrently operating mediated transport processes requires that their
mutual interference be considered and mathematically resolved. Simple extension of
the biphasic double reciprocal plots to the corresponding intercepts at the coordinates
can lead to markedly distorted values for the kinetic constants.[21] The resolution is
based on different affinities of the two transport processes. Since at very low and high
concentrations of the solute its uptake will occur predominantly by the high and low
affinity process, respectively, kinetic constants under such experimental conditions are
determined and used to alternatively correct the kinetics of each process. This procedure is applied repeatedly until constant values for K_m and V_{max} are obtained.[2] Such
mathematical treatment of the data is conveniently accomplished by computer analysis
according to published programs.[22]

In characterizing the cellular transport of a compound, it is of importance to examine the kinetics of its efflux.[4] Multiphasic cellular exodus (Figure 9) can be kinetically

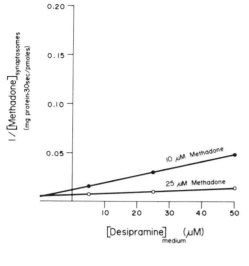

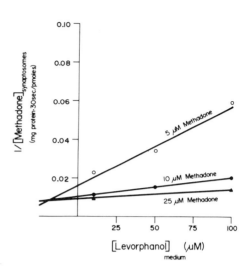

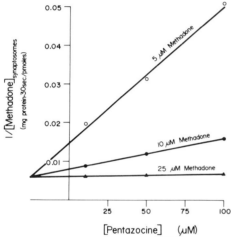

FIGURE 5. Inhibition of synaptosomal uptake of ³H-methadone by CNS acting drugs. Aliquots of the synaptosomal fraction were incubated for 5 min at 20°C in the standard buffer containing various concentrations of desipramine, levorphanol, or pentazocine. The initial rate of ³H-methadone uptake was determined at three concentrations of the drug. Transport due to diffusion was subtracted from total uptake (see Figure 8), and the reciprocal of the initial rate of saturable transport was plotted against inhibitor concentration in the medium according to Dixon.[14] (From Cahill, A. L., Hoornstra, M. P., and Medzihradsky, F., *Mol. Pharmacol.*, 16, 587, 1979. With permission.)

resolved,[23] and the properties of the separated components (e.g., rate constants, temperature dependence, transacceleration by external drug) compared to those of the uptake process.

ACKNOWLEDGMENTS

This work was supported in part by USPHS Grants GM 27028 and EY 02450.

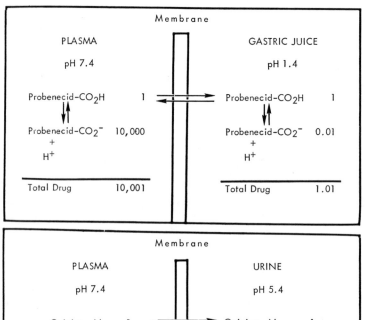

FIGURE 6.   The pH-dependent distribution of weak acids and bases across biological membranes. The listed concentrations represent theoretical equilibrium values. (From Cohn, V. H., Transmembrane movement of drug molecules, in *Fundamentals of Drug Metabolism and Drug Disposition,* LaDu, B. N., Mandel, H. G., and Way, E. L., Eds., Williams & Wilkins, Baltimore, 1972, 3. With permission.)

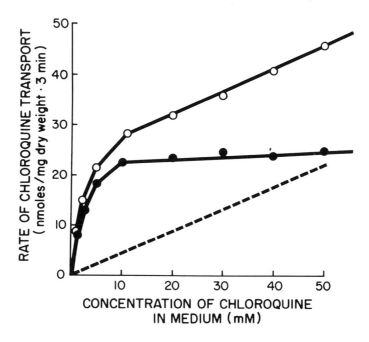

FIGURE 7.   Resolution of ^{3}H-chloroquine uptake in the isolated retina. The initial rate of ^{3}H-chloroquine uptake was determined at various concentrations of the drug in the medium. Plotted are total uptake (O——O) and uptake by the saturable (●——●) and nonsaturable (−−−) transport components. From the linear portion of uptake, obtained at high concentrations of drug in the medium, a kinetic constant for the nonsaturable component of the process was calculated. Correcting the total uptake by this factor (0.42 nmol/3 min/mg, dry weight) resulted in plots representing diffusion and the saturable component of the transport system. The latter displayed an apparent K_m and V_{max} of 2.4 mM and 8 nmol/min/ mg, dry weight. (From Bednarczyk, D. J. and Medzihradsky, F., *Mol. Pharmacol.*, 13, 99, 1977. With permission.)

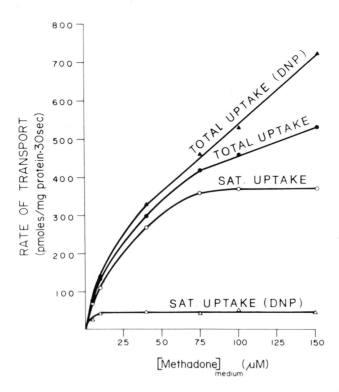

FIGURE 8.   Effect of metabolic poisons on the uptake of ³H-methadone in synaptosomes. Aliquots of the synaptosomal fraction were incubated for 5 min at 20° in the standard buffer medium, or in buffer medium containing 2 m*M* 2,4-dinitrophenol (DNP). Subsequently, the initial rate of uptake of ³H-methadone was determined at various concentrations of the drug. Plotted are total uptake in absence (●) and presence (▲) of DNP, and the saturable uptake component in absence (○) and presence (△) of the inhibitor. The resolution of mediated transport from total drug uptake was carried out by subtracting the diffusional constant, corresponding to the slope of the linear portion of total methadone uptake, obtained at high concentrations (> 100 μ*M*) of the drug. In the presence of DNP, the diffusional constant increased 5-fold relative to control, and saturable methadone transport was inhibited 93%. (From Cahill, A. L., Hoornstra, M. P., and Medzihradsky, F., *Mol. Pharmacol.*, 16, 587, 1979. With permission.)

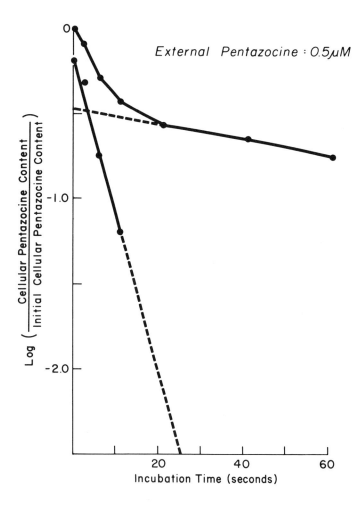

FIGURE 9. Resolution of the efflux of ³H-pentazocine from leukocytes. Analyzed, according to Robertson,[23] are the data from an experiment in which the efflux from leukocytes was determined at 17°C.
Previously the cells had been loaded with pentazocine by incubation
with 5 μM drug for 8 sec. Up to 60 sec after dilution, the cell content
at any time can be calculated as the sum of 2 first-order processes:

$$C_t = C_0[f_1 e^{-k_1 t} + (1 - f_1)e^{-k_2 t}]$$

where C_t and C_0 are the cellular concentrations of the compound at
times t and 0, f_1 is the fraction of the efflux accounted for by the
process with a rate constant k_1, and $(1 - f_1)$ is the remaining fraction
of the efflux occurring with a rate constant k_2. As shown, this analysis
indicates the intervention during the efflux of pentazocine of two
processes with considerably different rate constants. (From Marks,
M. J. and Medzihradsky, F., *Mol. Pharmacol.,* 10, 837, 1974. With
permission.)

REFERENCES

1. **Medzihradsky, F.,** Structure and function of cell membranes, and cellular transport of drugs, in *Principles of Radiopharmacology,* Colombetti, L. G., Ed., CRC Press, Boca Raton, Fla., 1979, 197.
2. **Christensen, H. N.,** *Biological Transport,* W. A. Benjamin, Reading, Mass., 1975.
3. **Medzihradsky, F., Marks, M. J., and Carr, E. A., Jr.,** Energy-dependent uptake of benzomorphans by leukocytes, *Biochem. Pharmacol.,* 21, 1625, 1972.
4. **Marks, M. J. and Medzihradsky, F.,** Characterization of the transport system for benzomorphans in leukocytes, *Mol. Pharmacol.,* 10, 837, 1974.
5. **Bednarczyk, D. J. and Medzihradsky, F.,** Mechanism of chloroquine transport in the isolated retina, *Mol. Pharmacol.,* 13, 99, 1977.
6. **Cahill, A. L., Hoornstra, M. P., and Medzihradsky, F.,** Active transport of methadone in synaptosomes, *Mol. Pharmacol.,* 16, 587, 1979.
7. **Medzihradsky, F. and Marks, M. J.,** Measures of viability in isolated cells, *Biochem. Med.,* 13, 164, 1975.
8. **Wilbrandt, W. and Rosenberg, T.,** The concept of carrier transport and its corollaries in pharmacology, *Pharmacol. Rev.,* 13, 109, 1961.
9. **Wilbrandt, W.,** Recent trends in membrane transport research, *Life Sci.,* 16, 201, 1975.
10. **Wilbrandt, W.,** Coupling between simultaneous movements of carrier substrates, *J. Membr. Biol.,* 10, 357, 1972.
11. **Schanker, L. S.,** Transport of drugs, in *Metabolic Transport,* Hokin, L. E., Ed., Academic Press, New York, 1972, chap. 14.
12. **Marks, M. J. and Medzihradsky, F.,** Transport and interaction of drugs in leukocytes, *Biochem. Pharmacol.,* 23, 2951, 1974.
13. **Medzihradsky, F., Marks, M. J., and Metcalfe, J. I.,** Cellular transport of CNS drugs in leukocytes, *Adv. Biochem. Psychopharmacol.,* 8, 537, 1974.
14. **Dixon, M.,** *Enzymes,* Academic Press, New York, 1964, 327.
15. **Schanker, L. S., Nafpliotis, P. A., and Johnson, J. M.,** Passage of organic bases into human red cells, *J. Pharmacol. Exp. Ther.,* 133, 325, 1961.
16. **Brodie, B. B., Kurz, H., and Schanker, L. S.,** The importance of dissociation constant and lipid-solubility in influencing the passage of drugs into the cerebrospinal fluid, *J. Pharmacol. Exp. Ther.,* 130, 20, 1960.
17. **Jollow, D. J. and Brodie, B. B.,** Mechanism of drug absorption and of drug solution, *Pharmacology,* 8, 21, 1972.
18. **Troshin, A. S.,** *Problems of Cell Permeability,* Pergamon Press, Elmsford, New York, 1966.
19. **Ling, G. N.,** The membrane theory and other views for solute permeability, distribution, and transport in living cells, *Perspect. Biol. Med.,* 9, 87, 1966.
20. **Akedo, H. and Christensen, H. N.,** Nature of insulin action on amino acid uptake by the isolated diaphragm, *J. Biol. Chem.,* 237, 118, 1962.
21. **Cahill, A. L. and Medzihradsky, F.,** Interaction of central nervous system drugs with synaptosomal transport processes, *Biochem. Pharmacol.,* 25, 2257, 1976.
22. **Neal, J. L.,** Analysis of Michaelis kinetics for two independent, saturable membrane transport functions, *J. Theor. Biol.,* 35, 113, 1972.
23. **Robertson, J. S.,** Theory and use of tracers in determining transfer rates in biological systems, *Physiol. Rev.,* 37, 133, 1957.

Chapter 5

MEMBRANE TRANSPORT

Robert Blumenthal

TABLE OF CONTENTS

I. INTRODUCTION

Molecules are transported into and out of cells in a variety of ways: passive diffusion, facilitated diffusion, active transport, and endocytosis. I will first discuss the salient features of the various modes of transport and then discuss the use of radiotracers in the study of transport. The radiotracers could pose a problem in the interpretation of transport data, but could, on the other hand, help elucidate mechanisms of transport. In this chapter, I will not focus on any particular transport system, but outline the general concepts involved in understanding how molecules cross membranes.

The study of membrane permeability has for a long time been of wide interest because (1) it might lead to an understanding of ways particular substances are moved into or out of the cell, and (2) it could provide information about membrane structure and function. In the beginning of this century, Overton[1] observed a correlation between the hydrophobicity of a compound (that is, its ability to partition into an organic phase) and its cell permeability. His observation that the more polar molecules permeate the membrane less rapidly led to the conclusion that the cell membrane is "lipoid" in nature. The tradition of probing membrane structure by the permeability of molecules with varying hydrophobicity has been followed up by many investigators.

An extensive series of measurements on the permeability of plant cells was carried out by Collander and Barlund.[2] They essentially showed that a number of small polar substances (H_2O, urea) did not follow the hydrophobicity-permeability correlation developed by Overton. This observation led to the concept of a mosaic membrane of hydrophobic and polar pathways for permeation. The polar pathways were identified as transport entities either in the form of carriers or channels.[3] Transport which operates faster than predicted from the hydrophobicity-permeability correlation, but in which the movement of the molecules is determined by its (electro) chemical potential difference across the membrane, is called facilitated diffusion. With facilitated diffusion, the concentration of molecules will eventually (when equilibrium is reached) be distributed according to its electrochemical potential.

Many substances are not distributed between cells and their surroundings according to their electrochemical potential. For instance, many cells extrude sodium ions and concentrate potassium ions. This could in principle occur by coupled transport; that is, a gradient of one type of ion (for instance, protons) could drive the movement of another ion species (for instance, sodium) against its gradient. When there is direct coupling between movement of a substance and a metabolic reaction (mostly the breakdown of ATP) the process is called active transport.[4]

Finally, some cells seem to take up nutrients by endocytosing the media they are in. This mode of transport is generally not very specific. It would not account for an unequal distribution of K^+ and Na^+. However, recently, there has been interest in specific receptor-mediated endocytosis mechanism for hormones, lysosomal enzymes, serum lipoproteins, and asialoglycoproteins.[5] Since those systems have only been described on a phenomenological level, I will not discuss them in this chapter.

II. PASSIVE DIFFUSION — NONELECTROLYTES

A. The Continuum Model

A representation of this model is shown in Figure 1. The electrochemical potentials (μ_1 and μ_2) of the molecule on both sides of the membrane are well defined. Inside the membrane there is a different standard chemical potential μ_m^{o} [1] because the molecule is partitioned into a different phase. At equilibrium, the ratio of the concentration of the molecule in the aqueous phase and in the lipid phase is given by the partition

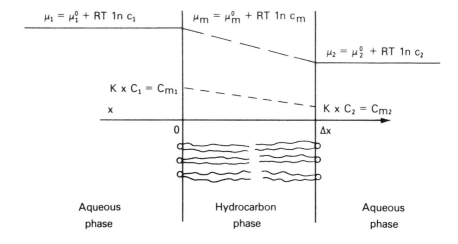

FIGURE 1. Continuum model for passive diffusion of nonelectrolytes across a bilayer membrane. The μs are chemical potentials, the Cs are concentrations and the subscripts 1,2 and m refer to sides 1,2 and the membrane phase, respectively. K is the partition coefficient.

coefficient (see below). One of the assumptions of this system is that there is quasi-equilibrium between the molecules in medium and on the surface of the membrane. The assumption hinges on the question whether adsorption-desorption to the interface, or diffusion across the membrane, is the rate-limiting step in transport. As we shall see below, this seems to be quite an unwarranted assumption.

To calculate the relationship between the flow and concentration difference of the transported species, we first set up the continuum equation for flow (in one dimension) in the membrane phase, which is given by Fick's law.

$$J = -D \frac{dc_m}{dx} \tag{1}$$

D is the diffusion coefficient, and c_m the concentration in the membrane. Since there is no accumulation in the small volume of the membrane, we assume J = constant and set up the integral equation between 0 and Δx

$$\int_0^{\Delta x} J \, dx = \int_{c_{m1}}^{c_{m2}} -D \, dc_m \tag{2}$$

Assuming that the diffusion coefficient is independent of concentration and position, we perform the integration:

$$J = \frac{D}{\Delta x} \left(c_{m1} - c_{m2} \right) \tag{3}$$

In this derivation, the rate-limiting step is assumed to be transfer across the membrane. Accordingly, there is an assumption of "instant equilibrium" between the membrane surface ($\mu_1 = \mu_{m1}$, and $\mu_2 = \mu_{m2}$), and the concentrations at the two surfaces are given by:

$$c_{m1} = K c_1$$

$$c_{m2} = K c_2 \tag{4}$$

where K is the partition coefficient. Substituting Equation 4 into Equation 3 yields

$$J = P (c_1 - c_2) \qquad (5)$$

where P is the permeability coefficient given by

$$P = \frac{DK}{\Delta x} \qquad (6)$$

Equation 6 shows a clear relationship between the permeability and partition coefficient inherent in the measurements by Overton and others.

B. The Eyring Model

The assumption of instantaneous partitioning is not necessarily a very good one: The main barrier for a relatively polar substance partitioning into a nonpolar environment is breaking hydrogen bonds. A treatment based on Eyring's absolute reaction theory[6], involving the kinetics of partitioning and transfer through the membrane, is more applicable to membrane transport. According to this model, the flow of molecules through the membrane is viewed as a series of m successive molecular jumps of length λ from one energy minimum to another. The rate constants for adsorption and desorption on the surface are k_{sm} and k_{ms}, respectively, and the rate constant for diffusion in the membrane is k_m. By setting up a series of steady-state equations for the flow across each barrier and assuming that those flows are equal (since there is no accumulation in the membrane), one can solve for the permeability coefficient:

$$\frac{1}{P} = \frac{2}{k_{sm}\lambda} + \frac{mk_{ms}}{k_{sm}k_m\lambda} \qquad (7)$$

If we set the rate constant for adsorption $k_{sm}\lambda = k_a$, the membrane thickness $\Delta x = m\lambda$, the diffusion coefficient $D = k_m/\lambda_2$, and the partition coefficient $K = k_{sm}/k_{ms}$, we get:

$$\frac{1}{P} = \frac{2}{k_a} + \frac{\Delta x}{KD} \qquad (8)$$

If diffusion across the membrane is rate-limiting $[(2/k_a) \ll (\Delta x/KD)]$, Equation 8 reduces to Equation 6. If, on the other hand, adsorption is limiting $2/k_a \gg \Delta x/KD$ then we have

$$\frac{1}{P} = \frac{2}{k_a} \qquad (9)$$

or permeability is equal to the rate of adsorption to the membrane. The apparent proportionality between partition and permeability initially found by Overton[1] indicates that the same forces which determine the rate of adsorption to the membrane also determine partitioning into the membrane phase.

C. The Interface or Interior as the Rate-Limiting Step

Since permeabilities of the interface and the hydrophobic region are in series we could write for the total permeability (P)

$$\frac{1}{P} = \frac{1}{P_{int}} + \frac{1}{P_{hc}} \qquad (10)$$

where P_{int} is the permeability across the interface and P_{hc} the permeability across the hydrophobic region, given by Equation 6 ($P_{hc} = Dk/\Delta x$).

If diffusion across the membrane is rate-limiting ($1/P_{int} \ll 1/P_{hc}$), then we have $P \approx P_{hc}$.

Table 1 (taken from Finkelstein[7]) shows calculated values for P_{hc}, as well as observed values for the permeability of a number of nonelectrolytes across a bilayer. It shows that only for H_2O in phosphatidylcholine bilayers the equality holds. The difficulty in determining the rate-limiting step hinges, however, on the measurement of the partition coefficient. Does partitioning mean that the molecule is at the relatively polar interface, or in the more hydrophobic portion of the membrane, or somewhere in between? The experiment to answer the question which step is rate-limiting would be to study permeability as a function of the thickness of the membrane. Since the thickness is proportional to $1/P_{hc}$, extrapolating to zero thickness would yield $1/P_{int}$. The thickness can be varied by taking membranes with organic solvents in between. Such an experiment was carried out by Tosteson and his co-workers[7a] on transport of potassium in the presence and absence of an ionophore across membranes of different widths. Those experiments showed that the major barrier for movement of K^+ was the interface, and that valinomycin lowered this "interfacial resistance."

D. The Unstirred Layer

One of the potential problems in measuring permeabilities is the unstirred layer. This derives from the fact that with laminar flow the velocity next to a surface is zero. In the diagram shown in Figure 2, the concentration c and the flow rate are plotted as a function of distance x from a planar surface. Δx_u is the thickness of the unstirred layer. The magnitude of Δx_u can be calculated by taking a permeant for which the membrane is not rate-limiting.[8] Total permeability (P_{tot}) is given by

$$\frac{1}{P_{tot}} = \frac{1}{P} + \frac{1}{P_{unst}}$$ (11)

where the permeability of the unstirred layer (P_{unst}) is given by:

$$P_{unst} = \frac{D}{\Delta x_u}$$ (12)

For instance, Holz and Finkelstein[8] measured the permeability of butanol across a planar bilayer membrane and found: $P_{tot} = P_{unst} = 6 \cdot 10^{-4}$ cm $\cdot$ sec^{-1} (assuming $1/P \approx 0$), $D = 10^{-5}$ cm$^2 \cdot$ sec^{-1}, so that $\Delta x = 0.017$ cm for the unstirred layer thickness.

Since P_{unst} is usually about 10^{-2} cm $\cdot$ sec^{-1}, it should be pointed out that the unstirred layer only becomes significant at high permeabilities. For instance for H_2O, when $P \sim 10^{-3}$ cm $\cdot$ sec^{-1}. Even for such a fast system as chloride exchange in red cells[9] ($P \sim 10^{-4}$ cm $\cdot$ sec^{-1}), the unstirred layer correction is insignificant. Moreover, in red cells, the thickness has been calculated[10] to be 5.5 μm, so that P_{unst} is about 10 cm $\cdot$ sec^{-1}.

E. Methodologies

Membrane transport is in principle simple to measure. The transported molecule is incubated with a cell and the amount taken up after a certain time is measured. The rate-constant for influx or efflux can be related to the permeability the following way:

The flow across the membrane is given by

$$J = \frac{1}{A} \frac{dn}{dt} = P\left(C_o - C_i\right)$$ (13)

Table 1

PERMEABILITY COEFFICIENTS (P_ds) OF WATER AND NONELECTROLYTES
THROUGH LIPID BILAYER MEMBRANES OF VARYING COMPOSITION

Molecule	$10^6 K_{hc}$	$10^5 D$	$10^7 P_d$				$P_d(L)/$ $(DK_{hc}/\Delta x)$	$P_d(LC)/$ $(DK_{hc}/\Delta x)$	$P_d(SC)/$ $(DK_{hc}/\Delta x)$
			L	LC	SC	SC, 14.5°			
		cm²/sec	cm/sec						
1,6 Hexanediol	540	0.9	—	2,250	450	—	—	0.023	0.0046
Isobutyramide	370	1.02	—	1,980	118	—	—	0.026	0.0016
n-Butyramide	360	1.07	—	3,000	288	51	—	0.039	0.0038
1,4 Butanediol	43	1.0	2,600	200	30	—	0.30	0.023	0.0035
H₂O	42	2.44	22,000	5,730	810	210	1.08	0.28	0.040
Acetamide	21	1.32	1,650	196	21	—	0.30	0.035	0.0038
Formamide	7.9	1.7	1,030	269	25	—	0.38	0.10	0.0093
Urea	3.5	1.38	40	6.1	—	—	0.042	0.006	—

Note: L = lecithin; LC = lecithinolesterol = 1:2; SC = sphingomyelinolesterol = 1:2. K_{hc} = partition coefficient in hexadecane, D = diffusion coefficient, Δx = 50 Å.

From Finkelstein, A., *J. Gen. Physiol.*, 68, 127, 1976. With permission.

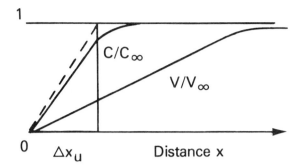

FIGURE 2.   The unstirred layer model. Hypothetical profiles for volume flow and concentration as a function of
distance from a surface. Δx_u is the thickness of the unstirred
layer.

where C_i and C_o are internal and external concentrations, n the number of molecules
in the cell, and A the area.

Since $C_i = n_i/V_i$ where V_i is the volume of the cell, this equation can readily be
integrated. The time course for influx is then given by

$$C_i = C_o \left(1 - e^{-kt}\right) \tag{14}$$

where

$$k = \frac{PA}{V_i} \tag{15}$$

The conclusion is that the rate of movement of molecules increases with surface to
volume ratio. If we have, for instance, a round cell of 1 μm radius and break it up
into vesicles with average radius of 0.01 μM, the rate of equilibration of a transported
molecule will be enhanced 100-fold.

Permeability can also be measured in an efflux experiment. The cells are preloaded
with the transported species and the decrease followed as a function of time is given by

$$C_i = C_i (o) e^{-kt} \tag{16}$$

where $C_i(o)$ is the initial concentration and k is given by Equation 15.

Lipid vesicles or liposomes have been used effectively to assay and characterize
transport. They are either made of pure lipid and the effect of lipid structure and
composition on transport through the bilayer is assessed, or certain transport systems
are reconstituted in liposomes and studied separated from other components present
in the cell membrane.

Liposomes are structures which form spontaneously when a lipid is dispersed in an
aqueous solution. The first to recognize these as closed structures was Bangham.[11]
Those spontaneous structures are multilamellar, often called "Bangosomes." Upon
sonication of those structures, a population of small unilamellar vesicles (SUV) is obtained whose size can by characterized by gel chromatography. The vesicles are made
in the solution to be encapsulated and the encapsulated vesicles are separated from the
free material either by dialysis or by gel chromatography.

Another version of the lipid model membrane is the black lipid membrane (BLM), developed by Mueller and Rudin.[12] Here, a lipid dissolved in an organic solvent is spread across a hole in a hydrophobic partition. The membrane spontaneously thins to form a bilayer with properties very similar to the lipid portion of cell membranes. Electrodes are present on the two sides, and changes in permeability are measured with exquisite sensitivity.

Both systems have their advantages and disadvantages. The lipid vesicles, with their high surface to volume ratios, allow convenient measurements of fluxes of molecules. There is, however, no convenient accessibility to inner compartments in that system, and it is not very feasible to make electrical measurements in that system. The BLM does have the advantage of electrical measurements and of accessibility to both compartments. Its small area to volume ratio, however, does not readily allow measurement of ion fluxes.

F. Water Transport

Water will either cross the membrane by dissolving into the bilayer and diffusing across, or by moving in bulk through a pore. Radioactive tracers have helped elucidate which of the two mechanisms is operative. Two types of measurements are carried out to assess water permeability. A diffusive permeability coefficient (P_d) is measured with ^3HHO:

$$P_d = J^*/C^* \tag{17}$$

where J^* is the flow of tritium (the number of tritium molecules passing the membrane per unit area per unit time) and C^* is the concentration of tritium on the side of origin.

A hydrolic permeability is measured by assessing the volume flow dV/dt per unit area (A), driven by a hydrostatic or osmotic gradient ($\Delta\pi$)

$$P_f = \frac{1}{A}\frac{dV}{dt} \bigg/ \frac{\Delta\pi}{RT} \tag{18}$$

If $P_f/P_d = 1$, there is no coupling between bulk water movement and diffusion of ^3HHO, and therefore H_2O permeates according to the solubility mechanism. If $P_f/P_d > 1$, however, interaction between H_2O molecules is suggested and therefore pores might be present in the membrane. With the introduction of lipid model membranes, an unambiguous test could be made for such considerations. The first measurements of P_f/P_d in lipid bilayers yielded values larger than one. However, with the appropriate correction for the unstirred layer, Finkelstein and his co-workers showed that for pure bilayers, $P_f/P_d = 1$.[8] Moreover, when pores were induced in the BLM by the polyene antibiotic amphotericin B, the value of P_f/P_d increased, showing that pores indeed changed the ratio.

G. The Reflection Coefficient

The previous section dealt with the relatively simple system of water and membrane. When dealing with water, solutes, and membrane the situation becomes more complex. The rate of volume flow is given by[13]

$$\frac{1}{A}\frac{dV}{dt} = L_p\left(\Delta\pi_i - \sigma\,\Delta\pi_S\right) \tag{19}$$

where L_p ($= P_f \times RT$) is the hydrolic coefficient, $\Delta\pi_i$ and $\Delta\pi_s$ are osmotic pressure differences of "impermeant" and "permeant" species and σ the reflection coefficient.[14] The reflection coefficient essentially gives the contribution of a given "permeant" species to the overall osmotic pressure difference.

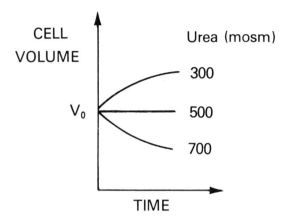

FIGURE 3. Hypothetical volume changes of cell in the presence of a partial permeable solute (urea) at different osmotic pressures.

There are two ways to measure reflection coefficients. One is to observe at what concentration of permeant the volume flow becomes zero. For instance, in red blood cells when isotonic saline is replaced by isoosmotic urea (300 mosmol) the cells will swell (Figure 3). Only when the isotonic saline is replaced by 500 mosmol urea they will not swell. The reflection coefficient for urea in these cells[10] is therefore 300/500 = 0.6. The other way to measure reflection coefficients is to consider the volume flow for an impermeable species and replace it by a partially permeable one using the same osmotic gradient in the two cases. The reflection coefficient is then given by

$$\sigma = \left(J_V\right)_{\text{perm}} / \left(J_V\right)_{\text{imperm}} \tag{20}$$

If the molecules are partially permeant, they flow with the water into the cells according to[13]

$$J_S = \left(1 - \sigma\right) C_S J_V + P_d \triangle C_S \tag{21}$$

where J_s = solute flow, C_s = the average concentration of solute between the two sides of the membrane, and J_v = the volume flow.

Equation 21 explains the "overshoot" in cell volume as a function of time, when cells in isotonic buffer are challenged (Figure 4) with a hyperosmotic concentration of solute. If the solute is as permeable as H_2O (for instance D_2O), nothing will happen. If the solute is impermeable, the cell will shrink to a smaller volume. In that case $P_d \approx 0$ and $\sigma \approx 1$ and there is no flow of solute. If the solute is less permeable than water ($0 < \sigma < 1$), then the cell will initially shrink according to Equation 19. Solute will move in with the water in a ratio $J_s/J_v = (1 - \sigma) C_s$ and, after achieving a maximum shrinkage, the solute will diffuse out again according to $P_d \Delta C_s$ and finally achieve equilibrium.

An empirical relationship between P_d and σ has been described by Diamond and Wright.[15] They measured σ in rat bladder for a wide range of compounds and took P_d values for the same compounds measured in giant algae by Collander and Barlund[2] (see Figure 5). It is clear from the definition that $\sigma \rightarrow 1$ as $P_d = 0$ and $\sigma \rightarrow 0$ for large P_d values. Kedem and Katchalsky[13] derived the relationship

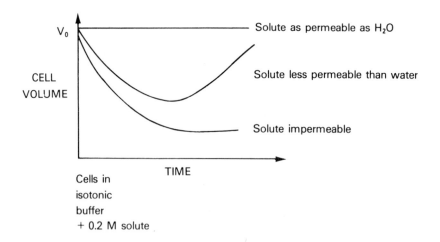

FIGURE 4.   Hypothetical volume changes of a cell in the presence of a hyperosmotic concentration of solutes with different reflection coefficients.

$$\sigma \leqslant 1 - \overline{V}_S P_S / P_f \tag{22}$$

where $\overline{V}_s$ is the partial specific volume of the solute. When the equality Equation 22 obtains, permeability occurs according to a solubility mechanism. Inequality is an indicator of "solvent drag" that is the presence of possible pores in the membrane. The relationship has been tested in red blood cells for a number of polar substances by Sha'afi and Gary-Bobo.[10]

H. Osmotic Lysis

We consider this topic here because (1) the mechanism is commonly misunderstood and (2) the principles of water and solute transport outlined in the previous sections readily explain the phenomenon. Cells are lysed by immune cytotoxic mechanisms or by toxins. The complement system kills cells by colloid osmotic lysis:[16] (1) the large molecules leave the cell at a different rate than the small ones and (2) the lysis can be protected by adding large molecular weight compounds on the outside. The general feature is described by Equation 19. In that equation $\Delta\pi_i$ is the osmotic pressure of the impermeant colloid, $\Delta\pi_s$ is that of the balancing saline. Initially the cell membrane is impermeant to the saline. However, when the permeability to small ions is changed, σ changes from 1 to 0, and the volume flow becomes

$$dV/dt = L_p \Delta\pi_i \tag{23}$$

The cell starts to swell. If the salt influx is fast enough to stop the cell from lysing, then an overshoot in volume can occur. The cell will then shrink somewhat. A common misunderstanding about colloid osmotic lysis is that the swelling is caused by influx of salt as the primary event. The primary event is the influx of water.

An example of lysis caused by a *diffusional* process is the killing of red blood cells by $NH_4^+Cl^-$ according to Figure 6:[17] On the outside, NH_4^+ dissociates to $NH_3 + H^+$; the NH_3 freely permeates the membrane. The outside Cl^- moves in through the carrier to be exchanged by an internal OH^-. This combines with the H^+ liberated from outside NH_4^+ to form H_2O. The OH^- inside leaves an H^+ behind which recombines with NH_3 inside to form NH_4Cl in the cell. The NH_4Cl is in fact accumulated in the cell. This system only lyses cells which have the anion transporting system: Cl^- for OH^-. It will

59

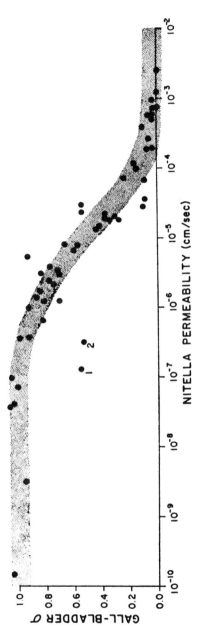

FIGURE 5. Ordinate, reflection coefficients (σs) of nonelectrolyte measured in rabbit gall bladder epithelium. Abscissa, permeability coefficients of the same nonelectrolytes measured in the alga *Nitella mucronata*. The two deviant points are urea (1) and methyl urea (2). Except for these two solutes, gall bladder σs decrease closely in parallel with increasing permeability in Nitella, showing that the two systems have essentially the same permeability pattern. The shaded band is drawn to indicate the general trend of the points and has no theoretical significance. (Reproduced, with permission, from the *Annual Review of Physiology*, Volume 31. © 1969 by Annual Reviews, Inc.)

medium   membrane   cell

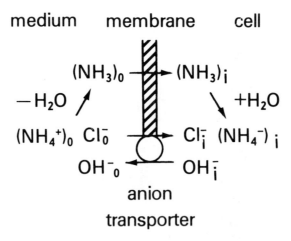

FIGURE 6.   Lysis of red blood cells by NH₄ Cl⁻. Ammonium enters as NH, chloride enters via the anion transport system. NH₄⁺ + Cl⁺ accumulates in the cell, and gives rise to an osmotic pressure gradient.

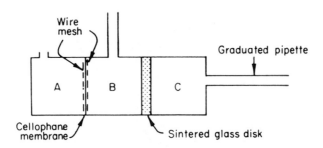

FIGURE 7.   A model system for biological water transport. The solution in compartment A contains various concentrations of sucrose in water. Compartment B contains 0.5 M sucrose, compartment C initially contains distilled water. Between A and B is a cellophane membrane of low porosity, between B and C is a sintered glass disk of high porosity. Water flows from A to C against the prevailing osmotic pressure gradient. (Reprinted with permission from Curran, P. F. and McIntosh, J. R., *Nature (London)*, 193, 347, 1962. Copyright (©) 1962. MacMillan Journals Limited.)

therefore kill red blood cells but not lymphocytes. This turns out to be the way to remove red blood cells from lymphocytes by a "lysing" buffer which contains NH_4Cl.

I. Volume Flow in Epithelia

An apparent paradox in epithelial transport was that volume flow could take place against an apparent osmotic pressure gradient. As shown by Curran and McIntosh,[18] this could be achieved by two membranes in series with different σ. They simulated this situation by constructing two artificial membranes in series (Figure 7).

The first membrane was a semipermeable cellulose acetate membrane. Due to the osmotic pressure difference, a large volume flow takes place to the second compartment. Hydrostatic pressure is then built up in the second compartment. The low sigma of the second (sintered glass disc) membrane does not allow back volume flow. There is therefore a net volume flow against the osmotic gradient. To sustain such an energetically unpromising situation, salt continuously has to be added to the second compartment. Otherwise, the process will stop fairly rapidly. In the artificial system this is achieved by dripping salt into the second compartment. In an epithelial system, active water transport is considered to occur by means of a "standing gradient flow system."[19] Epithelia are sheets of cells separated by long and narrow lateral intercellular spaces terminated at one end by so-called tight junctions. Solute is actively transported into these intercellular spaces, making the fluid there hypertonic. According to the Curran and McIntosh[18] analogue, the cell membrane equals the cellulose acetate membrane, the intercellular space equals the second compartment, and the interface between intercellular space and medium equals the sintered glass disc.

III. PASSIVE DIFFUSION — ELECTROLYTES

A. Electroneutrality

One of the strongest constraints on electrolyte transport is electroneutrality. If electroneutrality is violated, separation of charges will build up a significant amount of energy, enough to move a battleship. This can be calculated the following way: The potential on a sphere is given by

$$\Psi = Q/\epsilon_0 r \tag{24}$$

where Q is the charge, ϵ_0 the permittivity, and r the radius of the sphere. If we separate 10^{-10} equivalents of charge (which is not measurable chemically) corresponding to 10^{-5} coulomb, over a distance of $10\ \mu = 10^{-5}$ m, in a medium with permittivity of 10^{-10} (coulomb × meter)/volt we get, according to Equation 24, a potential of 10^{10} volt. That is, if we separate charges in quantities not measurable chemically in an area of the order magnitude of the cell, we will generate enormous potentials. Reasonable potentials can occur if only a very low (molecules rather than moles) amount of charge is separated. When 10^{-21} equivalents ($= 600$ ions) are separated over the same distance, a "reasonable" potential of 100 mV is generated.

B. Diffusion Potentials

The thermodynamic description of the state of an ion in a given phase is the electrochemical potential given by:

$$\tilde{\mu} = \mu_0 + RT \ln a + zF \Psi + p\overline{V} \tag{25}$$

where μ_0 is the standard chemical potential, a the activity of the ion, z the charge, F the Faraday constant, p the pressure, and $\overline{V}$ the partial molar volume.

The driving force for movement of ions across membranes is given by the difference in the electrochemical potential between the two sides, $\Delta\tilde{\mu}$. For an ion in equilibrium between the two sides of the membrane the electrochemical difference is given by (ignoring the pressure difference):

$$\Delta\tilde{\mu} = 0 = RT \ln(a_1/a_2) + zF \Delta\Psi \tag{26}$$

where a_1 and a_2 are activities on the two sides of the membrane, and $\Delta\Psi$ the membrane potential.

Rearranging Equation 26 yields

$$\Delta\Psi = \frac{RT}{zF} \ln(a_1/a_2) = -2.3 \frac{RT}{zF} \log(a_1/a_2) = -\frac{59}{z} \log(a_1/a_2) \tag{27}$$

In Equation 27 we have incorporated the fact that at room temperature $RT/F \sim 25$ mV. If a membrane is perfectly selective for a positive monovalent ion with $z = 1$, then the membrane potential will be −59 mV per decade activity ratio. The potential will be negative at the concentrated side of the ion. For a divalent positive ion, the membrane potential will be −28.5 mV for a 10-fold concentration ratio. If the membrane is, however, permselective for negative ions, then the potential will be $+59$ mV/decade. The potential will then be positive at the side of highest concentration. One way of rationalizing this is to envisage the positive ion tending to diffuse across the membrane, but being held back by the stringency of electroneutrality. This will leave a small (δ^-) negative charge on the concentrated side. With a negative permselective membrane, the situation is exactly opposite.

The potential difference created by an ion gradient has a variety of nomenclatures: the diffusion potential, the Nernst potential, the equilibrium potential, or, in nerve physiology, the reversal potential. The current (I) passing across a membrane of given ion with conductance (g) is given by:

$$I = g(E - \triangle\Psi) \tag{28}$$

where

$$E = -\frac{RT}{zF} \ln(a_1/a_2)$$

If a membrane is not perfectly permselective but permeable to other ions with conductance g_i, the current carried by each ion is given by:

$$I_i = g_i (E_i - \triangle\Psi) \tag{29}$$

An equivalent circuit can be drawn for each ion assumed to flow across the membrane independently. At equilibrium ($\Sigma I_i = 0$) the membrane potential is then given by:

$$\triangle\Psi = \Sigma_i t_i E_i \tag{30}$$

where t_i is the transference number of the ith ion. It is the relative contribution of the particular ion to total conductance ($t_i = g_i/g$). For instance, if a given membrane has a membrane potential of 40 mV per decade in the presence of a monovalent salt, the transference numbers are

$$40 = (t_+ - t_-) \times 59 \qquad t_+ = 0.83$$

$$t_+ + t_- = 1 \qquad t_- = 0.17 \tag{31}$$

In some cells the potential is given by a Donnan potential and the distribution of ions by a Donnan ratio: the counter ions of polyelectrolytes enclosed by a membrane permeable to ions are not free to move because they have to provide electroneutrality for the charges on the polyelectrolytes. The counter ions and coions are, however, in equilibrium between the two sides and the electrochemical potentials between two sides of the membrane are zero ($\Delta\tilde{\mu} = 0$).

For instance for NaCl:

$$\triangle\tilde{\mu}_{Na} = 0 = RT \ln Na_i/Na_o + \triangle\Psi$$

$$\triangle\tilde{\mu}_{Cl} = 0 = RT \ln Cl_i/Cl_o - \triangle\Psi \tag{32}$$

so that $e^{\Delta\Psi/RT} = Na_i/Na_o = Cl_o/Cl_i = r$, and $Na_oCl_o = Na_iCl_i$, where r is called the Donnan ratio.

In red blood cells, the Donnan ratios of H^+ and Cl^- were found to be equal,[20] and in lysosomes, Donnan ratios for H^+, K^+, and Cl^- were equal.[21] In both cases the membrane potential was considered to be determined by a Donnan potential.

C. Born Charging Energy

According to the solubility-permeability paradigm, ions have to partition in the bilayer in order to get across. The energy required for moving an ion into a medium with low dielectric constant is given by the Born charging energy: The energy for partitioning an uncharged atom (for instance, a noble gas) is negligible. The energy eu(r) required for turning this uncharged atom into a monovalent cation in the low dielectric medium is given by[22]

$$u(r) = \frac{q^2}{r}\left(\frac{1}{\epsilon_1} - \frac{1}{\epsilon_2}\right) \tag{33}$$

where q is the charge on the ion, r its radius, and $\epsilon_1 = 2$, the dielectric constant in the hydrophobic medium, and $\epsilon_2 = 80$, the dielectric constant of water. For $r \sim 2\,\text{Å}$, u(r) $= 1.5\,eV = 44\,kcal \cdot mole^{-1}$. The "partition" coefficient is given by Equation 4

$$K = \frac{c_m}{c_w} = e^{-u(r)/RT} \tag{34}$$

For the 2 Å radius ions this turns out to be 10^{-26}. If we then calculate the permeability across a bilayer according to Equation 6, we get $P = DK/d = 10^{-25}\,cm \cdot sec^{-1}$. The permeability for Na^+ across bilayer vesicles has been found to be $\sim 10^{-15}$ $cm \cdot sec^{-1}$.[23] It could be that the permeability is somewhat lowered by charge neutralization with Cl^-, or the higher apparent permeability could be due to vesicle disruption. When the ion radius is increased, the partition coefficient is considerably lowered. For instance, for $r = 6\,\text{Å}$, $u = 0.3\,eV$, and $K = 5 \times 10^{-4}$. Thus by charge delocalization, larger ions or ion-ionophore complexes become more permeable to lipid bilayers.

D. Ion Flows

The "equivalent circuit" assumption used to calculate relative ion permeabilities, Equation 30, is not strictly correct because the flows depend in a more complex way on concentrations and potentials. The general formulation is

$$\text{flow} = \text{mobility} \times \text{concentration} \times \text{driving force}$$

or

$$j = u \times c \times (-d\tilde{\mu}/dx) \tag{35}$$

developing $\tilde{\mu}$ according to Equation 25 yields

$$j = -\left(u\,RT\,\frac{dc}{dx} + uczF\,d\Psi/dx\right) \tag{36}$$

Since $uRT = D$, the diffusion coefficient, the first part of the right side of this equation is a reformulation of Fick's law. Assuming a constant field ($d\psi/dx = $ constant), Equation 36 can be integrated to yield[24]

$$j = \frac{uzF\triangle\Psi}{\triangle x} \frac{(c_1 e^{zF\triangle\Psi/RT} - c_2)}{(e^{zF\triangle\Psi/RT} - 1)} \qquad (37)$$

This is the Goldman-Hodgkin-Katz constant field equation. In the absence of an ion gradient ($c_1 = c_2$) it reduces to Ohm's law for the relation between ion flow and electrical potential

$$I = jF = \frac{uzF^2}{\triangle x} \triangle \Psi \qquad (38)$$

In the presence of an ion gradient, the relation between flow and membrane potential will become significantly nonlinear. Using a discontinuous "Eyring model", a similar formulation for the flow of ions as a function of membrane potential can be developed. The curve has the form of a hyperbolic sine function: At high voltages the current will bend over towards the voltage axis. The contribution of the voltage to the energy necessary to move a charged ion across a membrane is $zF\triangle\Psi$.

Using either the constant field equation or the Eyring model, an expression can be derived for the relationship between the membrane potential, ion permeabilities, and ion concentrations. For Na^+, K^+, and Cl^- as permeable ion this is

$$\triangle\Psi = -[RT/F]\ln \frac{P_K K_i + P_{Na} Na_i + P_{Cl} Cl_o}{P_K K_o + P_{Na} Na_o + P_{Cl} Cl_i} \qquad (39)$$

where P_K, P_{Na}, P_{Cl} are the ion permeabilities and the subscripts i and o denote inside and outside concentrations. Equation 39 is known as the Goldman equation.[25]

Relative selectivity between the ions can be obtained by measuring $\triangle\Psi$ as a function of salt concentrations and fitting to Equation 39. Hodgkin and Katz used the equation to determine the relative permeabilities of the ions in nerve at rest, during an action potential, and in the refractory period. Although some of the assumptions used to derive the Goldman equation are not totally justified, it is used empirically to determine relative permeabilities of ions.

Membrane potentials are measured by applying electrodes to both sides of the membrane. This can easily be achieved in large cells such as nerve cells using microelectrodes, or across a BLM. However, for small cells and vesicles whose internal compartments are not readily accessible to microelectrodes, other techniques have been devised based on potential sensitive fluorescent dyes[26] or radiolabeled lipid soluble ions[27] which distribute across the membrane according to their equilibrium potential (see Equation 32).

IV. FACILITATED DIFFUSION

A. Carriers — General Schemes

We have shown in the previous section that there are certain substances which permeate cell membranes at rates significantly faster than predicted from their oil-water partition coefficients. Such permeation is commonly categorized under the term "facilitated diffusion." There are two categories of facilitated diffusion, operationally defined as carrier or channel mechanisms. About a decade ago, it seemed to be very important to distinguish between carrier and channel mechanisms. Those distinctions have been blurred in the past years with the introduction of "gated channels" which are a hybrid carrier-channels. The attributes of facilitated diffusion are the following:

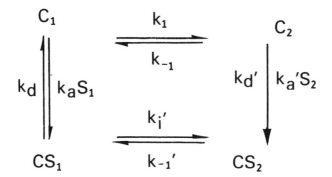

FIGURE 8. Model for carrier-mediated transport. The symbols are defined in the text.

1. The permeant moves according to its gradient of electrochemical potential.
2. Its permeability is unrelated to its oil-water partition coefficient.
3. Its permeability is "specific," i.e., small changes in its structure will dramatically alter permeability.
4. Its permeation does not obey Fick's law, but saturates as a function of concentration.
5. Its permeation is inhibited by competitive inhibitors.
6. Measurement of permeability by unidirectional fluxes with isotypes will be different from the permeability measured from the net flux.
7. Its transport might be enhanced by counter transport or diminished by cotransport of another permeant.
8. The temperature and pH dependence of permeability will be different than expected from solubilization into a lipid bilayer.

The general scheme for a carrier-type facilitated diffusion mechanism is shown in Figure 8. k_a and k_d are rate constants for association and dissociation of the substrate (S) to the carrier (C) and k_1 and k_{-1} rate constants for translocation of the carrier across the membrane. The primes refer to the loaded carrier (for translocation) or to the carrier on side 2 (for association and dissociation). According to this scheme, the substrate (S) binds to the carrier (C_1) on side 1 to form the complex CS_1. The complex is translocated to side 2 (CS_2). The substrate dissociates on side 2 to form the free carrier (C_2), which returns back to side 1 to pick up a new molecule. This process will continue until equilibrium ($S_1 = S_2$) is reached.

Figure 8 applies to an asymmetrical system. For a symmetrical carrier the primed rate constants are equal to the unprimed ones. In any event, the principle of detailed balance or microscopic reversibility[28] must hold for this system:

$$k_1 k_a' k_{-1}' k_d = k_{-1} k_d' k_1' k_a$$

or

$$k_1 / k_{-1} K_d = k_1' / k_{-1}' K_d' \tag{40}$$

where $K_d = k_d / k_a$ is the dissociation constant of the carrier complex.

The rate of carrier-mediated transport is given by:

$$J = k_1' CS_1 - k_{-1}' CS_2 \tag{41}$$

a) zero trans.

b) equilibrium exchange

c) infinite cis

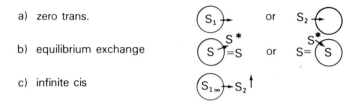

FIGURE 9.   Experimental design to determine rate constants for carrier-mediated transport. S* is radiolabeled substrate.

A diagram method developed by Hill[29] for calculation of fluxes across membranes yields an immediate solution for this system

$$J \propto k_1 k_{-1}' k_a' k_d (S_1 - S_2) \tag{41a}$$

The proportionality constant is, however, derived from steady-state kinetics by setting

$$\frac{dCS_1}{dt} = 0, \quad \frac{dCS_2}{dt} = 0, \quad \frac{dC_1}{dt} = 0$$

(no accumulation of carrier "states" in the membrane) and the mass balance $C_1 + C_2 + CS_1 + CS_2 = C_t$. where C_t is the total carrier concentration.

The solution, assuming that transfer is the rate-limiting step, is given by

$$J = \frac{k_1' k_{-1} C_t (S_1 - S_2)}{(K_D + S_1)(k_{-1} + k_{-1}' S_2/K_D') + (k_1 K_D + k_1' S_1)(1 + S_2/K_D)} \tag{42}$$

It is clear from Equation 42 that different $K_{1/2}$ (concentration at half maximal saturation) will be obtained, whether the substrate concentration is changed from side 1 or from side 2. There are a number of experiments to assess whether the carrier is symmetrical or not. The experiments[30] shown in Figure 9 should give the same $K_{1/2}$ and V_{max} for a symmetrical carrier, or should provide a way to obtain the relevant parameters for an asymmetrical carrier. S* represents radiolabeled substrate.

The classical way the carrier has been thought to negotiate passage of its substrate is by "shuttle diplomacy." That is, the carrier moves back and forth across the membrane as if it were a ferry boat. This representation was thought to be thermodynamically implausible because of the energy required to move a membrane protein across a hydrophobic membrane. However, it is not at all necessary to postulate a "diffusive" type of carrier. The same type of kinetics can be obtained by postulating a "gate" opening or closing. Such a model had been postulated many years ago by Patlak[31] and has been amplified upon by many others. It is clear that a carrier mechanism indicated by the scheme outlined in Figure 8 will cover a large realm of mechanisms and has all the attributes discussed in Section IV.A.

B. Ionophores

A variety of agents have been studied which modify bilayer permeability as measured by conductance changes in BLMs. One class is lipid-soluble ions which have lowered partition coefficients in bilayers due to charge delocalization (as discussed previously).

Examples are the negatively charged tetraphenylboride and the positively charged tetraphenylphosphonium.[31] They are, in fact, only carriers of charge. They have been found to be useful to:

1.   Analyze potential energy barriers across membranes
2.   Analyze surface charges and dipole potentials in membranes
3.   Probes for membrane potential

One of the first in the category of ionophores is the iodine-iodide carrier system. It turned out that in the presence of I_2 there was a significant contribution of conductance which was anion selective. According to Finkelstein and Cass,[33] charge delocalization was achieved by polyiodide complexes I_5^-, I_8^-.

A second class of ionophore is the proton carrier, which turns out to be an uncoupler of oxidative phosphorylation, presumably by dissipating a Mitchell type of proton gradient, which is used to synthesize ATP or to transport ions. Proton carriers include TTFB, FCCP, CCCP, and TNP, abbreviations for tetrachloro-2-trifluoromethylbenz-imidazole, carbonylcyanide-p-trifluoromethoxyphenylhydrazone, carbonylcyanide-m-chlorophenylhydrazone, and 2,4 dinitrophenol, respectively.[32] Evidence based on pH dependence of permeability suggests that the proton permeation occurs by forming a sandwich of two uncouplers per proton.[34]

A third class is the neutral carrier.[35] It acts by replacing the hydration shell or an ion by a solvation shell consisting either of carbonyl or ether oxygens, transporting the ion through the bilayer, dissociating the ion from its complex, and then returning empty to pick up a new ion. This class of carrier acts as a shuttle; it presumably enters and leaves the membrane. An extensively studied example in this class is valinomycin, a carrier with high selectivity for K^+. Its structure has been determined by X-ray diffraction, and the dynamics of its interaction with ions and membranes by a variety of spectroscopic techniques including NMR, CD, and laser Raman spectroscopy. Eigen and Winkler[36] carried out experiments on the kinetics of complexation of Na^+ with monactin, using murexide as a probe. They obtained the following constants: $K_{diss} = 2 \times 10^{-3}$ M, $k_a = 3 \times 10^8$ M^{-1} sec^{-1}, and $1/k_D = 1.5$ μsec. Each oxygen substitutes the solvation shell in 10^{-9} sec. It is important that the dissociation be relatively fast because otherwise the carrier will not deliver its ion and go back empty-shelled. For instance, a very sodium-selective muscle toxin, antamide, complexes Na^+ with exquisite selectivity, but cannot act as an ionophore because of its inability to dissociate.

The valinomycin-K^+ system has a turnover number of 2×10^4 ions per sec. Stein[37] analyzed data in the literature for turnover numbers of biological carriers (30 to 100 for the cation pump in red cells, 20 to 200 for the β-galactosidase permease system in *Escherichia coli*, 2 to 3×10^4 for Cl^- transport in red cells) and came to the conclusion that those transport systems must also be carriers.

A channel can be shown to have a turnover number of the order of 10^8 ions per second (see below). Complexation and decomplexation do not necessarily limit the rate of carrier-mediated transport: for instance, using Eigen's numbers[36] for Na^+-monactin with 0.1 M salt, the association turnover number is $k_R \times$ concentration $= 3 \times 10^7/sec^{-1}$. Neither should transfer across the membrane be limiting. It is of the order of D/d^2; with a diffusion coefficient of 10^{-6} cm^2/sec^{-1} and a thickness of 3×10^{-7} cm, this comes out to be $10^7/sec^{-1}$. The limiting step is probably crossing the barrier between an aqueous environment and the hydrophobic milieu of the membrane. If the carrier would sit in the mouth of a channel there would be no problem with turning over 10^7 to 10^8 molecules per second.

The fourth type of ionophoric carrier is the charged carrier which has the property that it can form a complexation structure around an ion.[38] These carriers are electrically silent and therefore will not show manifestations of ion transport in BLMs. A system to measure transport properties of charged ionophores is the Pressman cell.[38] Two aqueous compartments are separated by a layer of organic solvent, a radioactive ion is added to one compartment and the appearance of radioactivity in the second

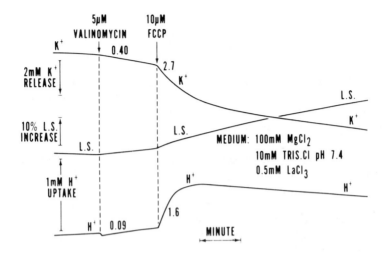

FIGURE 10.   Release of K⁺ from human erythrocyte ghosts resealed with KCl. The numerical values on the K⁺ and H⁺ curves are the rates of K⁺ release and H⁺ uptake in millimolars per minute (cells equivalent to a packed volume of 10%). The addition of FCCP (trifluormethyoxycarbonylcyanide phenyl-hydrazone) without valinomycin produced no discernible K⁺ release. L.S. = light scattering. (From Pressman, B. C., *Fed. Proc., Fed. Am. Soc. Exp. Biol.*, 32, 335, 1973. With permission.)

compartment in the presence or absence of ionophore is measured. Complexation is also studied by solvent extraction, pH titration, and spectroscopic methods. The best known in this series of charged carriers are monensin, nigericin X537A, and the Ca^{2+} ionophore A23187.[38]

These ionophores have also been shown to exchange ions in biological systems. In red cells, the use of ionophores indicated that Cl^- transport occurs according to a "silent" mechanism (see below). K⁺ release from red cells is measured (see Figure 10). Adding valinomycin did not significantly speed up K⁺ flux, because there was no net Cl^- efflux to provide electroneutrality. Adding the proton carrier FCCP did enhance K⁺ efflux because K⁺ could be exchanged for protons. Adding nigericin instead did the same as the combination of valinomycin and FCCP because nigericin by itself can act as a K^+-H^+ exchange carrier.

Apart from their ability to serve as models for transport systems (both electrogenic and silent mechanisms have been described), the ionophores also proved useful in perturbing biological systems in such a way that something can be learned about triggering mechanisms. For instance, the Ca^{2+} ionophore A23187 has been shown to mimic triggering events in a great number of systems where calcium has been postulated to be the trigger signal. These include muscle contraction, heart beat, excitation-secretion coupling, transmitter release, and activation of mast cells and lymphocytes. The ionophore X537A has been sbown to be able to serve as a carrier of biological amines.

C. Channels

Pores in membranes had been postulated quite a while ago to account for the observation that small molecules (H_2O, urea, formamide, K⁺, Na⁺) move across membrane at rates faster than predicted from oil-water partition coefficients. In principle, one can calculate the conductance (g) of a single channel from

$$g = \frac{\pi r^2 \Lambda c}{d} \tag{43}$$

where r is the radius, d the length of the channel, Λ is the equivalent conductivity of the channel, and c is the ion concentration in the medium. An equivalent conductance of 129 Ω^{-1} cm$^2\cdot$mol^{-1}, and an ion concentration of 0.1 M yields g = 10^{-10} Ω. The current across such a channel is given by:

$$I = gV \qquad\qquad (44)$$

With an imposed potential of 0.1 V, the current is 10^{-11} A. To convert this into ions per second we make the following calculation: 10^{-11}A $\rightarrow$ 10^{-11} coulomb$\cdot$sec^{-1} $\rightarrow$ 10^{-16} ion-equivalents per second $\rightarrow$ 6 $\times$ 10^7 ions per second.

In the previous section we had seen that carriers turn over about 3 $\times$ 10^4 ions per second. This would give rise to a current of 0.5 $\times$ 10^{-14} A. Current jumps of pA are easily detectable in a BLM system and have also recently been demonstrated in biological systems (acetylcholine receptor-associated channels in postsynaptic membranes[34] and excitable Na$^+$ and K$^+$ channels in squid axons).[40] The single carrier events are, however, beyond detection. The channel-forming ionophores such as gramicidine, nystatin, alamethicin, EIM can be distinguished from carriers in artificial systems by a number of criteria. Carriers form stable complexes with ions, can dissolve them in organic solvents, conduct ions through thick membranes, and often show exquisite selectivities between ions. Channels will only act in thin films, show discrete conductance jumps, often have a different stoichiometry or temperature dependence, and support nonelectrolyte transport. It is very hard, however, to distinguish between a bona fide channel or a lipid perturbation. For more refined distinctions among carriers, channels, and lipid perturbing agents the reader is advised to consult recent reviews.[41]

V. ACTIVE TRANSPORT

A. Coupling Mechanisms

Active transport has similar characteristics to facilitated diffusion. There is, however, one important difference: the molecules are transported against their gradient of electrochemical potential. There are a variety of ways molecules can be transported against their gradient. Active transport is, however, defined for the case in which direct coupling between transport and a metabolic reaction can be demonstrated.

An example of a concentrative mechanism involves coupling of fluxes mediated by carriers. For instance, K$^+$ can be transported against its gradient, driven by a gradient of protons. This situation can be modeled in an artificial system: a pH gradient is imposed across a vesicle membrane, and in the presence of the ionophore nigericin or valinomycin + FCCP in combination, K$^+$ is actively taken up into vesicles. Osterhout[42] carried out such an experiment about 45 years ago moving K$^+$ across an oil layer carried by guaiacol (an expectorant) in the presence of an H$^+$ gradient. Such a carrier scheme is given by Figure 11.

According to the diagram method,[29] the flow is given by

$$j_k \propto H_1^+ K_2^+ - K_1^+ H_2^+$$

At equilibrium $j_K = 0$ and therefore $H_1^+/H_2^+ = K_1^+/K_2^+$.

Provided that the H$^+$ gradient is maintained, the system will transport K$^+$ until its gradient equals the H$^+$ gradient.

Another case of "pseudo" active transport is the movement of a molecule into a cell by facilitated diffusion and subsequent conversion of that molecule to a product which cannot leak out. An example is the carrier-mediated movement of glucose, and subsequent conversion into glucose-6-phosphate. We shall discuss a case of real "vectorial" phosphorylation.

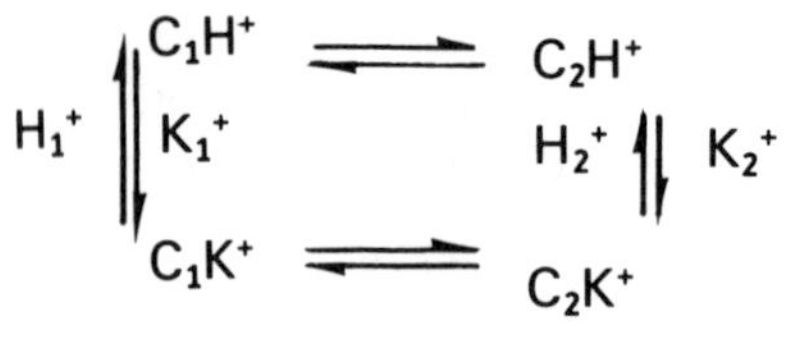

FIGURE 11.   Model for an H^+ - K^+ exchange carrier.

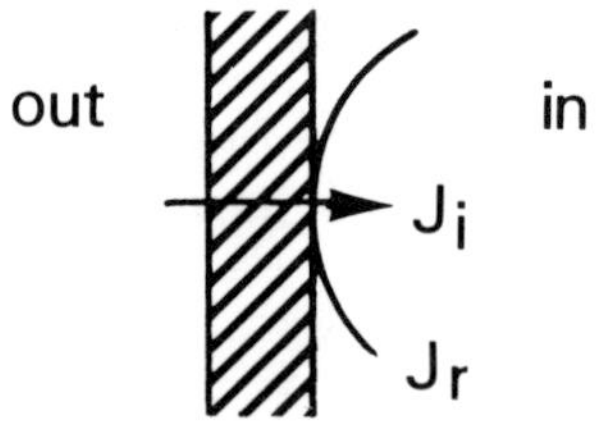

FIGURE 12.   Schematic diagram of active transport. The striped pattern represents the membrane, J_i is the rate of solute transport, J_r is rate of metabolic reaction driving the transport.

B. Definition of Active Transport

Active transport involves primary coupling between transport and metabolism without conversion of the transported species. A general scheme is shown in the diagram in Figure 12.

J_i and J_r are the flows of molecules and metabolism, respectively. With active transport, a flow of molecules ($J_i > 0$) occurs against an electrochemical potential difference ($\Delta\mu_i < 0$). The product of J_i and $\Delta\mu_i$ is the rate of entropy production, which, according to the second law of thermodynamics, must be positive. Only if the process is coupled to a metabolic reaction with $J_r > 0$ and the "affinity" of the metabolic reaction $\Delta\mu_r > 0$, can the negative contribution to entropy production be overridden. Kedem[4] defined active transport in terms of a non-negative coupling coefficient (R_{ir}) between transport and metabolism.

C. Demonstration of Direct Coupling

It is not so easy to disentangle *direct* coupling between transport and metabolism from cases where other mechanisms contribute to transport. In a few instances, however, demonstration of true active transport is relatively clear: a classic example is active transport of Na^+ across the frog skin studied by Ussing.[43]

The frog skin is clamped in an "Ussing" chamber (Figure 13) with identical electrodes on both sides of the membrane system inserted into identical solutions. Ussing found that with $\Delta\tilde{\mu}_{Na} = 0$ or even $\Delta\tilde{\mu}_{Na} < 0$ he could measure a short circuit current with $J_{Na^+} > 0$. This was an important result because it had been claimed that active transport occurs through binding of the transported molecules to the intracellular matrix. There are indeed some systems where binding can contribute to concentration of molecules in cells or organelles: for instance, Ca^{2+} in the sarcoplasmic reticulum is bound by binding proteins such as calsequestrin; or methotrexate in leukemia cells is bound by the enzyme, dihydrofolate reductase. Even in those cases, however, bona fide active transport system has been demonstrated over and above the binding capacity of the proteins.

Another classical demonstration of active transport is Na^+ and K^+ transport in resealed red cell ghosts. In that system, the two sides of the membrane are also accessible to well-defined electrochemical potentials. Maizels[44] did the experiment shown in Figure 14. He resealed red cell ghosts at 4°C with the gradients indicated in Figure 14A. After 24 hr at 37°C he found buildup of the following gradients shown in Figure 14B. Both Na^+ and K^+ had moved against their electrochemical gradient, so this is clearly not a case of coupled transport.

Another clear example of coupling between ion transport and metabolism is active Na^+ flux in perfused squid axon.[45] In this system, both sides of the membrane are

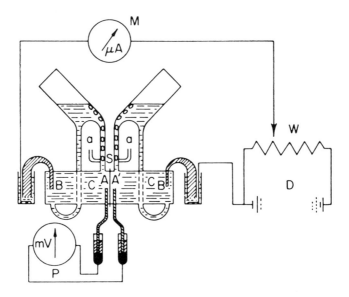

FIGURE 13. Apparatus used for determining Na flux and short-circuit current, where C is the celluloid chamber holding the frog skin S, A,A′ are agar-Ringer bridges to calomel electrodes and potentiometer P, and B,B′ are agar-Ringer bridges to outside emf from battery D. (From Ussing, H. H., *Acta Physiol. Scand.*, 19, 43, 1949. With permission.)

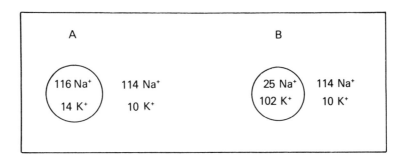

FIGURE 14. Experimental design for showing active transport of Na⁺ and K⁺ in red blood cell ghosts.

accessible and can electrochemically be defined. Na⁺ is shown to be actively extruded from the inside (Figure 15). This extrusion is blocked by poisoning the energy sources and is resumed by adding ATP to the inside solution.

Stoichiometry of reaction and transport has been measured extensively. Fixed stoichiometries are obtained when transport and ATP breakdown are fully coupled; stoichiometries will depend on the experimental conditions (Js, $\Delta\mu$s) when there is loose coupling between the two.[45a]

The exquisite coupling between Na⁺ and K⁺ movements, on the one hand, and metabolism, on the other hand, predicts that reverse gradients of Na⁺ and K⁺ would induce synthesis of ATP. This has indeed found experimental confirmation in an experiment performed by Glynn and his co-workers.[45b] Under conditions of high Na⁺ gradients out vs. in, and K⁺ gradients in vs. out, it can indeed be demonstrated that the pump can be driven back to get ATP synthesis.

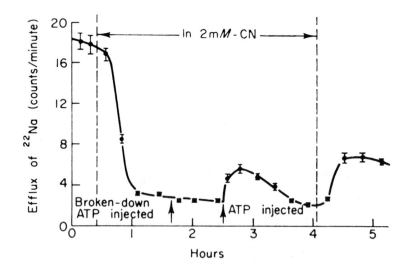

FIGURE 15.   The effect of the microinjection of high-energy phosphate compounds on the sodium efflux from cyanide-poisoned squid axon. The microinjection of a boiled ATP solution and of ATP itself is shown. (From Keynes, R. D., in *Membrane Transport and Metabolism,* Kleinzeller, A. and Kotyk, A., Eds., Academic Press, New York, 1961, 131. With permission.)

D. Vectorial Phosphorylation

An example of vectorial transport is the P-enol pyruvate system developed by Roseman and his co-workers,[46] and later by Kaback.[47] According to this system, glucose is transported but enters the cell as a glucose-6-phosphate. Two possible modes of transport could account for this situation: (1) phosphorylation takes place after transport, and (2) "vectorial" phosphorylation (during transport) takes place. Kaback[47] demonstrated the second possibility by carrying out an experiment with *Escherichia coli* vesicles. The system had ^{14}C glucose encapsulated in the vesicles and ^{3}H glucose was on the outside. In the presence of ^{31}P, transport was allowed to take place and the product assessed.

It was shown that only the tritiated glucose was phosphorylated, indicating that vectorial phosphorylation takes place during transport.

VI. ISOTOPE INTERACTION

A. Introduction

The measurement of permeability by assessing net flows of unlabeled compounds or by assessing isotope fluxes of labeled compounds need not always yield the same result. We have already seen that in many systems water permeability, as measured by bulk flow, is different from water transport as measured by tritium-labeled water. The difference appears when there are pores in the membrane, and this information was used as an important piece of evidence that there are water-filled pores in membranes. Thus, the use of isotopes can reveal certain features about membrane structure and function. Isotope interaction does not mean that isotopes interact directly to produce erroneous results in the measurement, but that the abundant species interacts with a membrane structure in such a way as to effect the movement of the isotope. Two well-known examples of isotope interaction are exchange diffusion and single file diffusion. In the following, we will present models for those cases and show how permeabilities will be effected.

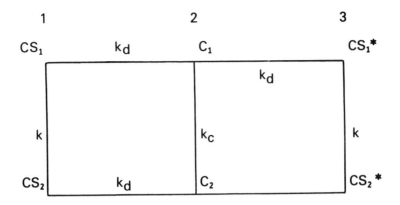

FIGURE 16.   Carrier-mediated transport of abundant (S) and radiolabeled (S*) substrate. The symbols are defined in the text.

B. Exchange Diffusion

This case is again well represented by the diagram method (Figure 16).

This is a similar scheme as that shown in Figure 8, but with the extra two states of the carrier complexed with the isotope on the two sides of the membrane (CS_1^*, CS_2^*). In analyzing this problem, we assume a symmetrical system, but with different rate constants for free carrier (k_c) or carrier complex (k) translocation.

Essig, Kedem, and Hill[48] calculated the relationship between permeability as measured by isotopes or as measured by net flux for this system. The result is

$$\frac{P^*}{P} = 1 + \left(\frac{S}{K}\right)\left(\frac{k}{k_c}\right) / \left(1 + \frac{2k}{k_d}\right) \tag{45}$$

where P^* is permeability as measured by isotopes.

No isotope interaction will occur ($P^*/P \to 1$) if $S \ll K$, $k \ll k_c$, and $k_d \gg k$. These conditions are intuitively clear: there are three cycles. If the rate of movement of the loaded carrier is more rapid than that of the empty carrier, the exchange pathway $1 \to 2 \to 3 \to 4 \to 5 \to 6 \to 1$ will be used and exchange diffusion will take place. If, on the other hand, the empty carrier moves more rapidly, the pathway $1 \to 2 \to 5 \to 6 \to 1$ will shunt out the exchange pathway and no exchange diffusion will occur. High substrate concentration will also favor the exchange pathway, so that if $S/K \ll 1$ there will be less isotope interaction. Finally, if dissociation is fast as compared to carrier movement, the shunt path will also override the exchange path and there will be less isotope interaction.

C. Single File Diffusion

A channel with sites for a permeant species will give rise to isotopic interaction because abundant species will block the flow of the isotope species. The channel will have the states (O indicates empty sites) shown in Figure 17:

The following constants are defined: the dissociation constant (K) for the site, the dissociation rate constant (k_d), and the rate constant for translocation (k) between the sites. It is evident from the model that presence of abundant species S will lead to blocking of S_1^*, S_2^* permeation especially in states 9 and 10.

Essig, Kedem, and Hill[48] solved the isotope problem for this system and derived the following equation for the relation between isotope permeability and net permeability:

$$\frac{P^*}{P} = 1 - \frac{2(S/K)\,(k/k_d)}{(1 + S/K)\,(2 + S/K + 4\,k/k_d)} \tag{46}$$

0	S_1	0	S_1	S_1*	0	S_1*	S_1*	S_1
0	0	S_2	S_2	0	S_2*	S_2*	S_2	S_2*
1	2	3	4	5	6	8	9	10

FIGURE 17.   A two-site channel model for transport of abundant (S) and radiolabeled (S*) substrate. 0 denotes an empty site.

According to this equation, P*/P will always be less than one. It will, however,
approach unity (no isotope interaction) at low S/K (there will be enough empty sites
so that there will be no interference between abundant species and isotope), and if k
$\ll k_d$; that is, if the rate constant for dissociation is rapid as compared to the rate
constant for translocation.

D. Flux Ratios

Although P*/P seems to be the most straightforward way to look at isotope interaction, historically the "flux ratios" have been considered: isotope is added to side 1
of the membrane and appearance of radioactivity is measured on side 2 (influx), and
conversely, another isotope is added to side 2 and appearance of radioactivity on side
1 (efflux) is measured. The experiment can be carried out simultaneously on the same
membrane system if there are two different isotopes of the same species. The relationship between isotope fluxes and net flux is given by:[43]

$$\text{net flux} = \text{influx} - \text{efflux} \tag{47}$$

The net flux is assessed by measuring the flux of unlabeled species. The ratio between
influx and efflux (the flux ratio) has been considered as a measure of the driving force
for transport. A simplified derivation of the relationship between the flux ratio and
driving forces is given by starting with the Goldman-Hodgkin-Katz equation for a
single ion (see Equation 37):

$$\text{influx:} \quad j_1 = \alpha c_1 e^{zF\Delta\Psi/RT} \tag{48}$$

$$\text{efflux:} \quad j_2 = \alpha c_2$$

where

$$\alpha = uzF\Delta\Psi (e^{zF\Delta\Psi/RT} - 1)^{-1} \tag{49}$$

so that

$$j_1/j_2 = (c_1/c_2) e^{zF\Delta\Psi/RT}$$

or

$$RT \ln j_1/j_2 = RT \ln c_1/c_2 + zF\Delta\Psi = \Delta\tilde{\mu}$$

According to this equation, the membrane potential can be assessed by measuring
flux ratios in the absence of isotope interaction. Kedem and Essig[49] have presented a
thermodynamically based derivation of the flux ratio equation, which includes the
presence of isotope interaction. Their result is

$$RT \ln j_1/j_2 = \frac{P*}{P} \Delta\tilde{\mu} \tag{50}$$

Hodgkin and Keynes measured the flux ratio of K^+ in squid and the electrochemical potential and their result indicated that

$$n \, RT \ln j_1/j_2 = \Delta\tilde{\mu} \tag{51}$$

with $n \simeq 4$. This result was interpreted in terms of a 4-site model in the K^+ channel. Hodgkin and Keynes stimulated their result on abnormal flux ratios with a mechanical model. The assumption was that K^+ ions move through the membrane in narrow channels. The essential feature is that ions are constrained to move in single file and that on the average there sbould be several ions in the channel. The model consisted of two flat compartments joined by a short gap or by a long gap. One hundred blue balls were put in the left compartment, 50 silver balls in the right. The model was then shaken and the number of blue balls moved to the right was compared with the number of silver ones to the left during the same interval. The experiment was repeated with the opposite configuration (silver right, blue left). With a short gap the prediction was that the number of balls leaving the side with 100 would be twice as great as the number leaving the side with 50. The experimental ratio was 2.7 ± 0.2. With the long channel, the ratio was 18 ± 4. In this model for isotope interaction a number of sites in the long channel gives rise to the abnormal flux ratios.

In the case of electrical measurements, the conductance determined from isotope measurements is given by:

$$g = j \, F^2/RT \tag{52}$$

whereas conductance measured electrically is given by $g = \Delta I/\Delta V$. Pagano and Thompson[51] measured conductance of Cl^- ions isotopically and electrically in large bilayer membranes. They came to the surprising result that isotope flux of Cl^- ions is 10^3 faster than "electrogenic" Cl^- movement. The interpretation of those results is still unclear, but can be reconciled with a lipid exchange carrier for Cl^- ions. This "carrier" is, however, still about 10^5 times slower than the exchange carrier of erythrocytes.

Net and exchange conductances of Cl^+ in red cells were indirectly measured by Tosteson and his co-workers.[52] In the presence of valinomycin, net K^+ transport is measured which should equal net Cl^- transport, The exchange diffusion of Cl^- was measured using ^{36}Cl. They found a $P*/P \gg 1$, clearly indicating the presence of exchange carrier for Cl^- in red cells.

E. Flux Ratios and Active Transport

Ussing[43] has shown that the flux ratio could be a measure for the driving force for active transport in the absence of all other driving forces. In frog skin, this situation can be attained: the skin is bathed between two identical solutions and the transmembrane potential is short-circuited. The application of this idea is not very feasible for many systems, since it is not possible to keep other (nonmetabolic) driving forces constant. Moreover, in the presence of isotope interaction, and if transport and metabolism are not tightly coupled, this relationship does not hold. Blumenthal and Kedem[53] examined the relationships between flux ratios, driving forces, and the free energy of active transport in a model for active transport. They showed under which conditions the Ussing relationship would hold, and how deviation from this relationship can give an insight into the mechanism of active transport.

REFERENCES

1. Overton, E., Ueber die allgemeinen osmotischen Eigenschaften der Zelle, ihre vermutlichen Ursachen and ihre Bedeutung fur die Physiologie, *Vierteljahresschr. Naturforsch. Ges. Zeurich*, 44, 88, 1899.
2. Collander, R. and Barlund, M., Permeabilitats-studien an *Chara ceratophylla, Acta Bot. Fenn.*, 11, 1, 1933.
3. Shamoo, A. E., Ed., Carriers and channels in biological systems, *Ann. N.Y. Acad. Sci.*, 264, 1, 1975.
4. Kedem, O., Criteria for active transport, in *Membrane Transport and Metabolism*, Kleinzeller, A. and Kotyk, A., Eds., Academic Press, New York, 1961, 87.
5. Goldstein, J. L., Anderson, R. G. W., and Brown, M. S., Coated pits, coated vesicles, and receptor-mediated endocytosis, *Nature (London)*, 279, 679, 1979.
6. Zwolinsky, B. J., Eyring, H., and Reese, C. E., Diffusion and membrane permeability, *J. Phys. Colloid Chem.*, 53, 1426, 1949.
7. Finkelstein, A., Water and non-electrolyte permeability of lipid bilayer membranes, *J. Gen. Physiol.*, 68, 127, 1976.
7a. Tosteson, D. C., Macrocyclic compounds and ionic movement through lipid membranes, *Neurosci. Res. Prog. Bull.*, 9, 339, 1971.
8. Holz, R. and Finkelstein, A., The water and nonelectrolyte permeability induced in thin lipid membranes by the polyene antibiotics nystatin and amphotericin B, *J. Gen. Physiol.*, 56, 125, 1970.
9. Cabantchik, Z. I., Knauf, Ph. A., and Rothstein, A., The anion transport system of the red blood cell, *Biochim. Biophys. Acta*, 515, 239, 1978.
10. Sha'afi, R. I., and Gary-Bobo, C. M., Water and non-electrolyter permeability in mammalian red cell membranes, *Prog. Biophys. Mol. Biol.*, 26, 103, 1972.
11. Bangham, Lipid bilayers and biomembranes, *Ann. Rev. Biochem.*, 41, 753, 1972.
12. Mueller, P. and Rudin, D. O., Translocators in bimolecular lipid membranes, *Curr. Top. Bioenergetics*, 3, 157, 1969.
13. Kedem, O. and Katchalsky, A., Thermodynamic analysis of the permeability of biological membranes to non-electrolytes, *Biochim. Biophys. Acta*, 27, 229, 1958.
14. Staverman, A. J., The theory of measurement of osmotic pressure, *Rec. Trav. Chim. Pay-Bas*, 70, 344, 1951.
15. Diamond, J. M. and Wright, E. M., Biological membranes: the physical basis of ion and non-electrolyte selectivity, *Annu. Rev. Physiol.*, 31, 581, 1969.
16. Blumenthal, R., Weinstein, J. N., and Henkart, P., Lipid model membrane studies on immune cytotoxic mechanisms, in *Membrane Toxicity*, Miller, M. W. and Shamoo, A. E., Eds., Plenum Press, New York, 1977, 495.
17. Jacobs, M. H., Some aspects of cell permeability to weak electrolytes, *Cold Spring Harbor Symp. Quant. Biol.*, 8, 30, 1940.
18. Curran, P. F. and McIntosh, J. R., A model system for biological water transport, *Nature (London)*, 193, 347, 1962.
19. Diamond, J. M. and Bossert, W. H., Functional consequences of ultrastructural geometry in "backwards" fluid-transporting epithelia, *J. Cell Biol.*, 37, 694, 1968.
20. Funder, J. and Wieth, J. O., Chloride and hydrogen ion distribution between human red cells and plasma, *Acta Physiol. Scand.*, 68, 234, 1966.
21. Goldman, R. and Rottenberg, H., Ion distribution in lysosomal suspensions, *FEBS Lett.*, 33, 233, 1973.
22. Parsegian, A., Energy of an ion crossing a low dielectric membrane: solutions to four relevant electrostatic problems, *Nature (London)*, 221, 844.
23. Hauser, H., Oldani, D., and Philips, M. C., Mechanism of ion escape from phosphatidylcholine and phosphatidylserine single bilayer vesicles, *Biochemistry*, 12, 4507, 1973.
24. Hodgkin, A. L. and Katz, B., The effect of sodium ions on the electrical activity of the giant axon of the squid, *J. Physiol. (London)*, 108, 37, 1949.
25. Goldman, D. E., Potential, impedance and rectification in membranes, *J. Gen. Physiol.*, 27, 37, 1943.
26. Hoffman, J. F. and Lavis, P. C., Determination of membrane potentials in human and amphiuma red blood cells by means of a fluorescent probe, *J. Physiol. (London)*, 239, 519, 1974.
27. Schuldiner, S. and Kaback, H. R., Membrane potential and active transport in membrane vesicles from *Escherichia coli, Biochemistry*, 14, 5451, 1975.
28. Hill, T. L. and Kedem, O., Studies in irreversible thermodynamics. III. Models for steady-state and active transport across membranes, *J. Theoret. Biol.*, 10, 399, 1966.

29. **Hill, T. L.**, Studies in irreversible thermodynamics. IV. Diagrammatic representation of steady state fluxes for unimolecular systems, *J. Theoret. Biol.*, 10, 442, 1966.

30. **Miller, D. M.**, The kinetics of selective biological transport. IV. Assessment of three carrier systems using the erythrocyte-monosaccharide transport data, *Biophys. J.*, 8, 1339, 1968.

31. **Patlak, C. S.**, Contributions to the theory of active transport. II. The gate type non-carrier mechanism and generalisations concerning tracer flow, efficiency, and measurement of energy expenditure, *Bull. Math. Biophys.*, 19, 209, 1957.

32. **Haydon, D. A. and Hladky, S. B.**, Ion transport across thin lipid membranes: a critical discussion of mechanisms in selected systems, *Q. Rev. Biophys.*, 5, 187, 1972.

33. **Finkelstein, A. and Cass, A.**, Permeability and electrical properties of thin lipid membranes, *J. Gen. Physiol.*, 52, 145S, 1968.

34. **Finkelstein, A.**, Weak-acid uncouplers of oxidative phosphorylation. Mechanism of action on thin lipid membranes, *Biochim. Biophys. Acta*, 205, 1, 1970.

35. **Mueller, P. and Rudin, D. O.**, Development of K^+-Na^+ discrimination in experimental biomolecular lipid membranes by macrocyclic antibiotics, *Biochem. Biophys. Res. Commun.*, 26, 398, 1967.

36. **Eigen, M. and Winkler, R.**, Alkali ion carriers: specificity, architecture and mechanisms, *Neurosci. Res. Prog. Bull.*, 9, 330, 1971.

37. **Stein, W. F.**, Turnover numbers of membrane carriers and the action of the polypeptide antibiotics, *Nature (London)*, 218, 570, 1968.

38. **Pressman, B. C.**, Properties of ionophores with broad range cation selectivity, *Fed. Proc., Fed. Am. Soc. Exp. Biol.*, 32, 335, 1973.

39. **Neher, E., Sakmann, B., and Steinbach, J. H.**, The extracellular patch clamp: a method for resolving currents through individual open channels in biological membranes, *Pflugers Arch. Gesamte Physiol. Menschen Tiere*, 375, 219, 1978.

40. **Conti, F. and Neher, E.**, Single channel recordings of K^+ currents in squid axons, *Nature (London)*, 285, 140, 1980.

41. **Blumenthal, R. and Shamoo, E. A.**, in *The Receptors. A Comprehensive Treatise, Vol. 1*, O'Brien, R. D., Ed., Plenum Press, New York, 1979, 215.

42. **Osterhout, W. J. V. and Stanley, W. M.**, The accumulation of electrolytes. V. Models showing accumulation and a steady state, *J. Gen. Physiol.*, 15, 667, 1932.

43. **Ussing, H. H.**, The distinction by means of tracers between active transport and diffusion, *Acta Physiol. Scand.*, 19, 43, 1949.

44. **Maizels, M.**, Cation transfer in human red cells, in *Membrane Transport and Metabolism*, Kleinzeller, A. and Kotyk, A., Eds., Academic Press, New York, 1961, 256.

45. **Keynes, R. D.**, The energy source for active transport in nerve and muscle, in *Membrane Transport and Metabolism*, Kleinzeller, A. and Kotyk, A., Eds., Academic Press, New York, 1961, 131.

45a. **Caplan, S. R.**, Nonequilibrium thermodynamics and its application to bioenergetics, *Curr. Top. Bioenergetics*, 4, 1, 1971.

45b. **Glynn, I. M. and Karlish, S. J. O.**, The sodium pump, *Ann. Rev. Physiol.*, 37, 13, 1975.

46. **Roseman, S.**, The transport of carbohydrates by a bacterial phosphotransferase system, *J. Gen. Physiol.*, 54, 138S, 1969.

47. **Kaback, H. R.**, The role of the phosphoenol pyruvate-phosphotransferase system in the transport of sugars by isolated membrane preparations of *Escherichia coli*, *J. Biol. Chem.*, 243, 3711, 1968.

48. **Essig, A., Kedem, O., and Hill, T. L.**, Net flow and tracer flow in lattice and carrier models, *J. Theoret. Biol.*, 13, 72, 1966.

49. **Kedem, O. and Essig, A.**, Isotope flows and flux ratios in biological membranes, *J. Gen. Physiol.*, 48, 1047, 1965.

50. **Hodgkin, A. L. and Keynes, R. D.**, The potassium permeability of a giant nerve fibre, *J. Physiol. (London)*, 128, 61, 1955.

51. **Pagano, R. and Thompson, T. E.**, Spherical lipid bilayer membranes: electrical and isotopic studies of ion permeability, *J. Mol. Biol.*, 38, 41, 1968.

52. **Tosteson, D. C., Gunn, R. B., and Wieth, J. O.**, Chloride and hydroxyl ion conductance of sheep red cell membrane, in *Erythrocytes, Thrombocytes and Leukocytes*, Gerlach, E., Moser, K., Deutsch, E., and Wilmanns, W., Eds., Georg Thieme Verlag, Stuttgart, 1972, 62.

53. **Blumenthal, R. and Kedem, O.**, Flux ratios and driving forces in a model for active transport, *Biophys. J.*, 9, 432, 1969.

Chapter 6

THERMODYNAMIC ASPECTS OF RADIOTRACER FLOW

David C. Dawson

TABLE OF CONTENTS

I. INTRODUCTION

The ease and accuracy with which radioactivity can be detected renders radio tracer flow the most precise method for quantifying transport rates; and radiotracers have been of inestimable value in the study of the *kinetics* of transport processes. It is less obvious, perhaps, that the measurement of tracer flows can provide information about the *energetics* of a transport process. The purpose of this chapter is to review the concepts which lead to the use of radio tracer flows to define the driving forces for a transport process. Although the modern history of this idea begins with Ussing's classic paper in 1949,[21] the concepts involved can be traced to developments in physical chemistry in the late 1800s.

The concept of "unidirectional rate" was introduced into the theory of chemical reactions in the late 19th century in connection with the emerging view of chemical equilibrium as a dynamic state. (See Glasstone[6] for a concise history.) For a process of the type

$$A_1 \rightleftarrows A_2$$

where A_1 and A_2 might represent two states of a unimolecular reaction or the movement of a substance across a membrane, it was recognized that equilibrium did not represent a cessation of all molecular transitions. Rather, equilibrium was viewed as a state in which the *net* progress of the reaction or transport process was zero because the *unidirectional rates* for the forward and backward reactions were equal. Formally this was expressed by defining the rate coefficients for the forward and reverse process so that

$$v_{12} = k_{12}[A]_1 \qquad\qquad v_{21} = k_{21}[A]_2$$

where v_{12} and v_{21} are the forward and reverse reaction rates and k_{12} and k_{21} are the respective rate coefficients. For a transport process we may define by analogy the *unidirectional fluxes* J_{12} and J_{21} such that

$$J_{12} = \lambda_{12}[A]_1 \qquad\qquad J_{21} = \lambda_{21}[A]_2$$

where λ_{12} and λ_{21} are the rate coefficients for the forward and reverse transport steps.

The enormous value of radiotracers in studies of membrane transport processes derives in large part from the fact that they permit the measurement of unidirectional rates under a wide variety of conditions.

The relation between the equilibrium constant and the free energy of a reaction established a link between the thermodynamic and kinetic descriptions of the *equilibrium state*.[6] The concept of dynamic equilibrium required that at equilibrium

$$v_{12} = k_{12}[A]_1 = v_{21} = k_{21}[A]_2$$

so that the equilibrium constant, K_{eq}, could be defined

$$K_{eq} \equiv ([A]_2/[A]_1)_{equil} = (k_{12}/k_{21})_{equil}$$

Equating this with the thermodynamic expression for the equilibrium ratio of products to reactants we obtain the familiar relation for the equilibrium state:

$$(k_{12}/k_{21})_{equil} = (-\Delta G^o/RT)$$

where ΔG^o is the standard Gibbs Free Energy.

Ussing[21] first showed that the kinetic and thermodynamic descriptions of mass transport were related under *nonequilibrium* conditions, and proposed that the *ratio* of unidirectional fluxes, J_{12}/J_{21}, for a transport process was a measure of the total driving force for that process.[22] Patlak, Pettigrew, and Rapoport have recently considered the use of flux-ratios to obtain free energy changes of chemical reactions in the nonequilibrium steady-state.[14]

In this chapter we will examine several cases where flux-ratios may be predicted on the basis of energetic considerations alone. These predictions arise from a consideration of coupling between tracer flow and the flow of the parent species. Because of the emphasis on coupled flows, the equations of irreversible thermodynamics provide a convenient starting point.

II. PHENOMENOLOGICAL DESCRIPTION OF TRACER FLOW

The phenomenological equations of nonequilibrium thermodynamics[9,10] provide a convenient "bookkeeping" system which can be employed to specify the forces which may contribute to tracer flow. Consider a membrane system in which there are n flows of matter. The term "flow" is used here in the general sense to encompass vectorial movement of matter *across* the membrane as well as the scalar progress of chemical reactions *within* the membrane. In a system of n flows, one limiting case is that in which no interaction (or coupling) exists between any of the individual flows. In this case the phenomenological equations assume their simplest form, i.e., n equations of the form:

$$J_i = L_{ii}X_i \tag{1}$$

where J_i is the i th flow, X_i is the "conjugate force", and L_{ii} is a phenomenological coefficient. The flow of a tracer across the membrane, J^*, would be written as

$$J^* = L_{**} X_* \tag{2}$$

In the present analysis, the linearity or nonlinearity of this equation is of no consequence. The equation states concisely that when X_* is zero, J^* is also zero.

In the absence of temperature and pressure gradients across a membrane bathed by aqueous solutions, X_* is equated with the negative of the difference in electrochemical potential, $-\Delta\tilde{\mu}_*$, where

$$\Delta\tilde{\mu}_* = RT\ln(a_1^*/a_2^*) + zF(\psi_1 - \psi_2) \tag{3}$$

a_1^*, a_2^* are the tracer activities on the two sides of the membrane, and $\psi_1 - \psi_2$ is the electrical potential difference across the membrane, and R, T, z, and F have their usual significance.

In the most general case, where we allow for the coupling of any one flow to all other flows, the phenomenological equations have the form:

$$J_i = L_{ii} X_i + L_{ij} X_j + \ldots + L_{in} X_n$$
$$J_j = L_{ji} X_i + L_{jj} X_j + \ldots + L_{jn} X_n$$
$$J_n = L_{ni} X_i + L_{nj} X_j + \ldots + L_{nn} X_n \tag{4}$$

which is written concisely as

$$J_i = L_{ii} X_i + \sum_{\substack{j=1 \\ j \neq i}}^{n} L_{ij} X_j \qquad (5)$$

Here, in addition to the "straight coefficients which relate the flow of i to its "conjugate force", X_i, we have introduced "cross coefficients", L_{ij}, which describe the coupling between the flow of i and other flows of matter. Again the importance of this description in the present case is primarily one of bookkeeping. Equation 5 accounts explicitly for the fact that, in the presence of coupled processes, J_i may be nonzero despite the fact that its conjugate force, X_i, is zero.

We have employed phenomenological equations written in the form of "conductance coefficients". Alternatively, we may express the forces as a function of the flows using "resistance" coefficients,[9] i.e., in the absence of coupled processes

$$X_i = R_{ii} J_i \qquad (6)$$

Or for the system of coupled flows

$$X_i = R_{ii} J_i + R_{ij} J_j + \cdots R_{in} J_n$$

$$X_j = R_{ji} J_i + R_{jj} J_j + \cdots R_{jn} J_n$$

$$X_n = R_{ni} J_i + R_{nj} J_j + \cdots R_{nn} J_n \qquad (7)$$

or

$$X_i = R_{ii} J_i + \sum_{\substack{j=1 \\ j \neq i}}^{n} (R_{ij} J_j) \qquad (8)$$

Kedem obtained a particularly useful form of these equations by solving Equation 8 for J_i to obtain:

$$J_i = X_i/R_{ii} - \sum_{\substack{j=1 \\ j \neq i}}^{n} (R_{ij}/R_{ii}) J_j$$

Now, for a transmembrane flow of tracer $J_i = J^*$ and the conjugate force X_i is $-\Delta\tilde{\mu}_*$. In addition we consider explicitly two classes of coupled flows; a chemical reaction, J_r, and other transmembrane flows of matter, J_k, and obtain

$$J^*_{net} = -\Delta\tilde{\mu}_*/R_{ii} - \sum_{\substack{k=1 \\ k \neq i}}^{n} (R_{ik}/R_{ii}) J_k - (R_{ir}/R_{ii}) J_r \qquad (9)$$

Equation 9 identifies the three classes of forces which may contribute to the flow J^*: the conjugate force, $\Delta\tilde{\mu}_*$; other transmembrane flows of matter, J_k; and the flow of a chemical reaction, J_r. It is useful at this point to call attention to the fact that in a case where the flow of interest is that of a radiotracer, the summation over other coupled flows, J_k, must be taken to include the flow of the abundant (nonradioactive) isotope of the tracer species. It is the analysis of coupling between tracer and abundant isotopes of a single species which is the basis for a major portion of flux-ratio analysis presented here.

III. THE UNIQUE NATURE OF THE TRACER RATE COEFFICIENT

The unique contribution of radiotracer analysis to the study of mass transport is a direct result of the fact that tracer flow may be measured by introducing a vanishingly small perturbation into the system of interest. As an example, consider a particularly simple experimental setting, a membrane of arbitrary geometry and properties which separates two well-stirred solutions. Tracer is introduced into one bathing solution and tracer flow is monitored by measuring tracer appearance on the opposite or "trans" side. The parameter of interest is the "unidirectional rate coefficient". In general the rate coefficient(s) may be obtained by analyzing the time course of tracer flow using differential equations associated with compartmental analysis, or by rigging the conditions so that the "unidirectional rate" is measured directly. In the latter case we add radioisotope to the "hot side", and sample the solution on the "cold side" under conditions where a very small amount of isotope accumulates on the cold side. Under these conditions the operational definition of the "unidirectional" tracer flux from side 1 to side 2 is given by

$$J_{12}^* = V_2 \{ C_2^*(t_2) - C_2^*(t_1) \} / \Delta t$$

where $C_2^*(t_1)$ is the concentration of tracer on side 2 at time t_1 in counts per minute per milliliter, $C_2^*(t_2)$ is the tracer concentration on side 2 at time t_2, Δt is the time interval $t_2 - t_1$, V_2 is the volume of the bathing solution, and J_{12}^* is the flow of tracer from side 1 to side 2 in cpm min^{-1}. Experimental design, say in the measurement of tracer flow across isolated epithelial sheets, is typically such that during the interval Δt, $C_2^* \ll C_1^*$ and $\partial C_1^* / \partial t \simeq 0$, so that the undirectional tracer rate coefficient, λ_{12}^*, is defined as

$$\lambda_{12}^* = J_{12}^* / C_1^* \tag{10}$$

If λ_{12}^* is to provide a measure of the transport properties of the membrane, at least two conditions must obtain:

1.   The properties of the membrane must be time-invariant.
2.   The addition of tracer to the system must not alter the properties of the membrane.

If the flow J_{12}^* is to provide a measure of a particular transport property of a membrane, it is axiomatic that the properties of the membrane must not change appreciably over the time required to measure tracer flow, i.e., the system should be in a "stationary" or "steady-state".[20] It is the possibility of meeting condition 2, however, which confers enormous value on the tracer rate coefficient. Because radiotracers may be obtained in high specific activity (many counts per minute per mole), we can add an amount of tracer which is readily detectable due to its radioactivity, but which represents a negligible addition on a molar basis. A large gradient of counts may be introduced without perturbing the steady-state. This is particularly important in the case of nondiffusional transport systems in which the properties of the transport mechanism may be a strong function of the concentration of the transported species.

A pertinent example is the nonlinear dependence of transport rate on concentration in so-called "facilitated" transport systems which exhibit "saturation kinetics" where the unidirectional flux of a species i is given by an expression of the form

$$J_{12}^i = \frac{J^m [i]_1}{K_T + [i]_1}$$

where J^m is the maximal flux, and K_T is the apparent Michaelis constant.

Note that the expression can also be written

$$J_{12}^i = \lambda_{12}^i [i]_1$$

where λ_{12} is the unidirectional rate coefficient.

The *tracer* rate coefficient (the measured quantity) is assumed to be equal to the rate coefficient for the abundant isotope and is given by

$$\lambda_{12}^* = \lambda_{12}^i = J^m/(K_T + [i]_1)$$

In this case, the rate coefficient is a strong function of the concentration of the abundant isotope, presumably because tracer and abundant "compete" for the transport site. To determine the kinetic behavior of the transport system, we set the operating point by setting the concentration of the abundant isotope, then the rate coefficient is determined by adding an amount of tracer which is so small on a molar basis that it has no effect on the rate coefficient. We add many counts and few moles. Under these conditions, we can make the important assumption that the rate coefficient for tracer flow is independent of tracer concentration. Alternatively, we may say that the rate coefficients for tracer flow are independent of tracer distribution. *This means that the rate equations for tracer flow are first order regardless of the intrinsic kinetic order of the transport process.*[15,20] Consider the flow of tracer in a two-compartment system after tracer is initially added to compartment one. The tracer rate coefficient may in general be a function of membrane potential, the concentration of the abundant isotope, or other variables, but as long as the system is truly in a stationary state these parameters will be constant and the redistribution of tracer will be a first order relaxation process.†

The determination of the tracer rate coefficient bears a direct relation to the determination of small signal conductance in nonlinear electrical systems. In an electrical system in which the I-V relation is nonlinear, the conductance is a function of the operating point, for instance, a dissipative element for which the resistance (or conductance) is a function of the applied voltage. In such a system the behavior of the conductance (g) as a function of voltage might be determined by setting the operating point at some I,V and then making a small perturbation around that operating point, i.e.,

$$g = (\delta I/\delta V)_{\delta V \to 0}$$

---

† In practice, the validity of this assumption cannot be presumed, but must be established for each isotope and experimental paradigm. Clearly the applicability of this assumption will be favored by high isotope-specific activity and large bath volumes as in, for instance, the use of "carrier-free" ^{22}Na in Ussing-chamber experiments on isolated epithelial sheets. Conversely, the use of low specific activity isotopes (i.e., ^{36}Cl, for instance) accumulating in a small volume, like a membrane vesicle, could easily invalidate the assumption of negligible molar concentration of tracer.

Similarly, in a system in which mass flow is a nonlinear function of concentration the measurement of tracer flow, in Ussing's words, provides "unique information"[23] because the tracer rate coefficient can be measured by introducing a vanishingly small perturbation into the system.

IV. FLUX-RATIO ANALYSIS

In this section we will consider several situations where flux-ratios may be analyzed in light of the thermodynamic constraints on tracer flow in order to provide information about the mechanism of mass transport. We will specify the physical situation as a membrane separating two well-stirred solutions. Regardless of the presence or absence of unstirred layers, the values of concentration and electrical potential are well defined in the bulk solutions. We will consider four more or less specific transport mechanisms: simple diffusion, coupled transport in general, obligate exchange transport, and single-file transport. In each case we will analyze the transport process using a method first employed by Britton[1-3] and more recently by Dawson,[4] in which coupling between the flow of tracer and some other flow of matter or a chemical reaction is considered in terms of the flux-ratio. By combining the kinetic assumptions regarding tracer flow with the specific thermodynamic constraints on the flow of tracer, we will arrive at a prediction for the flux-ratio.

In every case we will utilize the central assumption of tracer analysis, i.e., that the rate coefficient for tracer flow is independent of tracer concentration. In the simple physical situation specified above, we may express this assumption concisely by requiring that the ratio of the unidirectional *tracer* rate coefficients for the species of interest, $\lambda_{12}^* / \lambda_{21}^*$, be independent of the ratio of *tracer* concentrations, C_1^* / C_2^*. This means that if a relation between the tracer rate coefficients can be specified at any *particular* tracer distribution, then this relation must apply for *all* tracer distributions, i.e., if we can specify $\lambda_{12}^* / \lambda_{21}^*$ for *any* single value of C_1^* / C_2^*, then it is specified for *all* values of C_1^* / C_2^*.

In general the flux-ratio is defined as:

$$J_{12}^* / J_{21}^* = (C_1^*/C_2^*) \ (\lambda_{12}^*/\lambda_{21}^*) \tag{11}$$

So that the ratio of the tracer rate coefficients can be written as

$$\lambda_{12}^*/\lambda_{21}^* = (J_{12}^*/J_{21}^*) \ C_2^*/C_1^* \tag{12}$$

In each of the following examples, we will apply simple thermodynamic arguments to obtain an explicit expression for the ratio of tracer rate coefficients for one of two particular tracer distributions; equilibrium or a nonequilibrium, steady-state. For these two situations, the *net* flow of tracer vanishes, i.e., $J_{12} = J_{21}$, and the ratio of the tracer rate coefficients can be equated with the tracer distribution ratio.

V. SIMPLE DIFFUSION

In his classic paper, Ussing[21] demonstrated that for a substance which traverses a membrane by simple diffusion the tracer flux-ratio is given by

$$J_{12}^* / J_{21}^* = (\gamma_1^* C_1^* / \gamma_2^* C_2^*) \ \exp \left\{ \frac{z F}{RT} \ (\psi_1 - \psi_2) \right\} \tag{13}$$

where J_{12}^*, J_{21}^*, C_1^*, and C_2^* are unidirectional tracer flows and tracer concentrations; γ_1^* and γ_2^* are the tracer activity coefficients; $\psi_1 - \psi_2$ is the electrical potential difference across the membrane, and z, F, R, T have their usual significance. Ussing arrived at this result by using the Nernst-Planck equation to describe simple diffusional flow at any point in the membrane. By taking the *ratio* of the two unidirectional fluxes and integrating for the case of steady tracer flow, he obtained the result that, for simple diffusional flow, the tracer flux-ratio depends *only* on the activities of tracer in the bathing solutions and the electrical potential across the membrane. Subsequently, several papers examined the theoretical foundations of the flux-ratio equation in an effort to generalize the relation to include the effects of coupled processes and membrane inhomogeneity.[8,12,19] These treatments also proceeded from a local description of flows and forces to a global flux-ratio equation.

An alternative approach to this problem was developed by Britton,[1-3] and independently by Dawson.[4] In this method simple diffusion is specified using a macroscopic thermodynamic criterion, and this, combined with the standard assumptions regarding tracer kinetics, leads directly to the flux-ratio equation without resort to a local description of tracer flow. We define simple diffusional flow by requiring that the flow of tracer is not coupled to any other flow of matter across the membrane (including the abundant isotope of the tracer species) or to any chemical reaction in the membrane. According to Equation 9, this is tantamount to the assumption that in simple diffusional flow the only *driving force* for tracer movement is the conjugate force, $\Delta\tilde{\mu}_*$. Thus, for a substance which traverses a membrane only by simple diffusion it *must be possible for the tracer to attain thermodynamic equilibrium,* regardless of the state or distribution of other species, *including the abundant isotope.*

According to Equation 12, the ratio of the rate coefficients for tracer flow is given by:

$$\lambda_{12}^*/\lambda_{21}^* = (J_{12}^*/C_1^*)/(J_{21}^*/C_2^*)$$

We can specify the relation between the tracer rate coefficients by noting that at tracer equilibrium the electrochemical potential difference for tracer, $\Delta\tilde{\mu}_*$, must be zero and:

$$\gamma_1^*C_1^*/\gamma_2^*C_2^* = \exp\left\{\frac{zF}{RT}(\psi_2 - \psi_1)\right\} \qquad (14)$$

In addition, at equilibrium the unidirectional tracer fluxes must be equal so that we obtain for the ratio of the tracer rate coefficients at *tracer equilibrium*:

$$(\lambda_{12}^*/\lambda_{21}^*)_{equil} = (\gamma_1^*/\gamma_2^*)\exp\left\{\frac{zF}{RT}(\psi_1 - \psi_2)\right\} \qquad (15)$$

This relation was derived for the particular case of *equilibrium* tracer distribution where, of course, net tracer flow would vanish. Clearly, the rate coefficients cannot be *measured* at tracer equilibrium. Our assumptions about tracer behavior, however, require that the tracer rate coefficients and their ratio, $\lambda_{12}^*/\lambda_{21}^*$, be independent of the distribution of tracer, C_1^*/C_2^*. Thus, the rate coefficients measured in unidirectional flux paradigms, i.e., with tracer far from equilibrium must also conform to this relation (Equation 15).

Inserting this relation into the general expression for the flux-ratio (Equation 11), we obtain the well-known flux-ratio equation for simple diffusion in the form originally given by Ussing.[21]

$$J_{12}^*/J_{21}^* = (\gamma_1^* C_1^*/\gamma_2^* C_2^*) \exp \left\{ \frac{zF}{RT} (\psi_1 - \psi_2) \right\} \tag{13}$$

Thus, from a purely phenomenologic viewpoint, the flux-ratio for simple diffusion arises from the general first-order nature of the tracer rate coefficient and the stipulation that, if tracer moves by simple diffusion, the labeled molecule must be able to attain thermodynamic equilibrium.

In this light, Ussing's flux-ratio is seen as a *thermodynamic* criterion for simple diffusion. A nondiffusional flux-ratio implies that there is a net force, in addition to $\Delta\tilde{\mu}_*$ which drives tracer flow. The flux-ratio equation can be cast in a somewhat more general form by introducing the additional assumption that the tracer is identical to the parent isotope in all of its thermodynamic and kinetic properties. Thus, we may equate the *activity coefficients* for tracer and abundant, i.e.,

$$\gamma_1^* = \gamma_1^i = a_1^i/C_1^i \qquad \gamma_2^* = \gamma_2^i = a_2^i/C_2^i \tag{16}$$

where γ_1^i and γ_2^i, a_1^i and a_2^i, and C_1^i and C_2^i represent the activity coefficients, the activities, and the concentrations of the abundant isotope of the tracer species. Inserting these relations into Equation 13 we obtain the practical form of the flux-ratio equation:

$$\frac{J_{12}^*/\rho_1}{J_{21}^*/\rho_2} = \frac{a_1^i}{a_2^i} \exp \left\{ \frac{zF}{RT} (\psi_1 - \psi_2) \right\} \tag{17}$$

which can be written concisely as;

$$\frac{J_{12}^*/\rho_1}{J_{21}^*/\rho_2} = \exp \left\{ \frac{\Delta\tilde{\mu}_i}{RT} \right\} \tag{18}$$

where $\Delta\tilde{\mu}_i$ is the electrochemical potential difference for the abundant isotope of the tracer species and ϱ_1 and ϱ_2 are the *specific activities* of tracer on side 1 and side 2, i.e.,

$$\rho_1 = C_1^*/C_1^i \qquad \rho_2 = C_2^*/C_2^i \tag{19}$$

It is useful to examine the quantity J_{12}^*/ϱ_1. Since J_{12}^* can be expressed as $\lambda_{12}^* C_1^*$ if we insert the definition of ϱ_1 we obtain

$$J_{12}^*/\rho_1 = \frac{\lambda_{12}^* C_1^*}{C_1^*/C_1^i} = C_1^i \lambda_{12}^* \equiv J_{12}^i \tag{20}$$

The quantity $C_1^i \lambda_{12}^*$ has units of the unidirectional flux of the *abundant species,* and it is this quantity which is often reported in the literature. This form is convenient because it can be directly converted to *net* flow if *both* unidirectional flows are known. This should not obscure the fact, however, that the quantity J_{12}^i is a *derived* quantity, the physical significance of which derives completely from J_{12}^*, the flow of tracer, which is the measured parameter.

VI. COUPLED FLOWS: A GENERAL APPROACH

In this section we consider a general approach to the form of the flux-ratio in the presence of coupled flows. Recalling Equation 9 we write in general for the *net* flow of tracer:

$$J^*_{net} = -\Delta\tilde{\mu}_*/R_* - \sum_{k=1}^{n} (R_{*k}/R_*) J_k - (R_{*r}/R_*) J_r \qquad (9)$$

To obtain a general relation between the tracer rate coefficients, consider the condition of true tracer steady-state, i.e., zero *net* tracer flow. At tracer steady-state utilizing Equation 9 we obtain for $\Delta\tilde{\mu}_*$.

$$\Delta\tilde{\mu}_* = - \sum_{k=1}^{n} (R_{*k} J_k) - R_{*r} J_r$$

Proceeding as indicated previously, and substituting into Equation 12, we obtain a relation for the ratio of tracer rate coefficients at tracer steady-state

$$(\lambda^*_{12}/\lambda^*_{21})_{s.s.} = (\gamma^*_1/\gamma^*_2) \exp\left\{ \frac{zF(\psi_1 - \psi_2) + \sum_{k=1}^{n} (R_{*k} J_k) + R_{*r} J_r}{RT} \right\}$$

Again noting that $\lambda^*_{12}/\lambda^*_{21}$ is independent of C^*_1/C^*_2 and invoking the postulate that the tracer and abundant have identical physical properties, we obtain the most general form of the flux-ratio equation

$$\frac{J^*_{12}/\rho_1}{J^*_{21}/\rho_2} = \exp\left\{ \frac{\Delta\tilde{\mu}_i + \sum_{k=1}^{n} (R_{*k} J_k) + R_{*r} J_r}{RT} \right\} \qquad (22)$$

This expression shows clearly that the flux-ratio provides a measure of the total effective driving force for *tracer flow*, and is similar to an expression previously derived by Kedem and Essig.[†][12] The three possible contributions to the driving force for tracer flow appear in the argument of the exponential: the conjugate force, $\Delta\tilde{\mu}_i$, other transmembrane mass flows, j_k, and a chemical reaction, J_r.

In the absence of direct coupling to a metabolic reaction (an ATPase, for instance) tracer flow can be driven by coupling to other transmembrane flows of matter. In this regard, it is important to recognize that the summation over J_k must be taken to include the abundant isotope of the tracer species. As shown below, nondiffusional flux-ratios can arise directly from coupling between the flows of the tracer and *abundant* isotopes of a single species.

In the absence of all coupled flows, i.e., J_r, $J_k = 0$, Equation 22 reduces to that obtained in the previous section for the special case of simple diffusion. In the case of an isolated epithelium where the conjugate force, $\Delta\tilde{\mu}_i$, may be conveniently reduced to zero, a nonunity flux-ratio is a direct indication of the coupling of other flows to the

† Equation 29 of Kedem and Essig[12] differs *formally* from Equation 22 of the present development in that the effect of coupling between the flow of the radioactive and nonradioactive isotopes of a given species is expressed by Kedem and Essig in terms of a ratio, R^x/R, which represents the effects of isotope interaction.

flow of i. In principle, the flux-ratio provides a measure of the apparent driving force due to these coupled flows. In practice, however, this simple interpretation can be compromised by the presence of parallel pathways for transmembrane flow (see Kedem and Essig[12]).

VII. TRANSPORT MECHANISMS AND COUPLING OF TRACER AND ABUNDANT

In principle, any transport system in which tracer and abundant species "interact" will produce coupling of the flow of tracer to the flow of the abundant species, and, hence, a nondiffusional flux-ratio. Perhaps the simplest form of such interaction would be competition for a transport site, such as would be expected from a simple "mobile carrier" model. It has been pointed out that such competition can give rise to a counter-flow type interaction, i.e., net flow of tracer driven by a flow of abundant.[1,18] Similarly, a co-transport type of interaction between tracer and abundant can be envisioned if the interaction between tracer and abundant is cooperative.

A simple analysis of the energetics of tracer flow, however, will yield an explicit prediction for the flux-ratio *only* if the stoichiometry of the process is fixed. In a simple, mobile carrier model, for instance, the nature and degree of coupling will be governed by kinetic considerations. The following analysis considers two transport mechanisms which are characterized by fixed stoichiometric coupling and for which energetic considerations lead directly to a prediction for the tracer flux-ratio: obligatory exchange flow and simple, knock-on, single file transport.

VIII. 1:1 EXCHANGE FLOW

Consider a one-for-one exchange transport mechanism. It is axiomatic that in the presence of one transported substrate the flux-ratio must be *unity* regardless of the distribution of the transported species. It is useful, however, to examine the origin of this unity flux ratio from the standpoint of the interaction of tracer and abundant. Consider a membrane containing as its only transport path a one-for-one exchanger for the substrate, i. Let the solutions contain only one transportable substrate, i, and a tracer for i; i*, the concentration of each being denoted by C^i and C^*, respectively. As before, we obtain the *tracer* flux-ratio by considering a particular tracer distribution for which the ratio of tracer rate coefficients is well defined. In the situation outlined above, we note that, due to the obligatory exchange net, mass flow *only* occurs if tracer is exchanged for abundant. Since only the *exchange* of tracer for abundant results in a change in composition of the bathing solutions, this exchange process is the only relevant event thermodynamically. As a consequence of the coupling, we cannot treat the equilibrium of the individual species (tracer and abundant), but only the equilibrium for the *exchange process* which is specified as:

$$\sum \mu_j \, dn_j = 0 \qquad (23)$$

Since $dn^* = -dn^i$, the exchange of tracer and abundant is at equilibrium if

$$\Delta\mu_* = \Delta\mu_i$$

$$\Delta = (\;)_1 - (\;)_2$$

Thus, for any value of $\Delta\mu_i$, we can choose a value of $\Delta\tilde{\mu}_*$ which will bring the exchange to equilibrium. Since at equilibrium the *net* tracer flow must vanish, we can, as in the simple diffusion case, obtain the ratio of the tracer rate coefficients from the equilibrium tracer distribution, i.e.,

$$\lambda^*_{12}/\lambda^*_{21} = (C^*_2/C^*_1)_{eq} = (\gamma^*_1/\gamma^*_2) \exp \left\{ \frac{-\Delta\mu_i}{RT} \right\} \tag{24}$$

so that the *tracer* flux-ratio is given by

$$J^*_{12}/J^*_{21} = (\gamma^*_1 C^*_1/\gamma^*_2 C^*_2) \exp \left\{ -\Delta\mu_i/RT \right\} \tag{25}$$

or

$$J^*_{12}/J^*_{21} = \exp \left\{ \frac{\Delta\mu_* - \Delta\mu_i}{RT} \right\} \tag{26}$$

This expression for the tracer flux-ratio shows that in a simple 1:1 exchanger there are *two* driving forces for tracer flow: the chemical potential gradient of the tracer (conjugate force) and the chemical potential gradient of the abundant isotope which drives the tracer by counter flow.

Note, however, that if we convert from units of tracer flow to units of abundant isotope flow by equating the activity coefficients, we obtain

$$\frac{(J^*_{12}/\rho_1)}{(J^*_{21}/\rho_2)} = (a^i_1/a^i_2) \exp \left\{ \frac{-\Delta\mu_i}{RT} \right\} = 1.0 \tag{27}$$

Thus, by viewing the exchange process from the standpoint of the behavior of the *tracer* flow we arrive at the required value of unity for the flux-ratio, but we have shown how this flux-ratio emerges from the obligatory coupling of tracer and abundant.

IX. SINGLE-FILE TRANSPORT

A. Ions

Hodgkin and Keynes[7] invoked the concept of a "single-file" channel to account for nondiffusional potassium flux-ratios across the membrane of the squid giant axon. They analyzed a pore which was always maximally occupied by N_K potassium ions and found that if translocation was due to a simple "knock-on" mechanism, the expected flux-ratio was

$$J^K_{12}/J^K_{21} = \left[([K]_1/[K]_2) \exp \left\{ \frac{F\Delta\psi}{RT} \right\} \right]^{(N_K + 1)} \tag{28}$$

where J^K_{12}, J^K_{21}, $[K]_1$ and $[K]_2$ are the potassium fluxes and concentrations.

Recently Levitt[13] pointed out that the "no-pass" condition produces an obligatory coupling between permeable species (see also Rosenberg and Finkelstein[16,17]). For a simple knock-on transfer, this condition leads directly to a prediction for the tracer flux ratio. Consider a no-pass pore through which an ion, i, moves by a strict knock-on mechanism, i.e., an ion only leaves the pore if it is displaced by an ion entering. Let the pore always contain N_i ions. Now consider the process by which a tracer ion moves from side 1 to side 2. We assume that due to the low molar abundance of the tracer the channel will never contain more than one labeled ion. Thus the translocation of one tracer ion in either direction must be accompanied by the obligatory transfer of N_i abundant ions, i.e., the entire contents of a filled pore must be displaced. As before, we obtain the ratio of the tracer rate coefficients by examining an equilibrium condition. We note that for any value of $\Delta\tilde{\mu}_i$ we may choose a value of $\Delta\tilde{\mu}_*$ which will abolish net tracer flow. Due to the obligatory coupling specified by the no-pass condition, equilibrium for a pore containing one tracer ion is written:

$$\Delta\tilde{\mu}_* + N_i\,\Delta\tilde{\mu}_i = 0$$

This situation is depicted (see Rosenberg and Finkelstein[5,16,17]) as one in which the species which is formally in equilibrium is the tracer ion plus N_i abundant ions. Note that this does *not* imply that the flow of the abundant is zero. The equilibrium applies only to those pores which contain a tracer ion.

This expression yields the ratio of the tracer rate coefficients for any value of $\Delta\tilde{\mu}_i$, i.e.,

$$\lambda_{12}^*/\lambda_{21}^* = (C_2^*/C_1^*)_{equil}$$

$$= \exp\left\{\frac{N_i\Delta\tilde{\mu}_i + F\Delta\psi}{RT}\right\} \tag{29}$$

The *tracer* flux-ratio is then

$$J_{12}^*/J_{21}^* \quad (\gamma_1^*C_1^*/\gamma_2^*C_2^*)\ \exp\left\{\frac{F\Delta\psi + N_i\Delta\tilde{\mu}_i}{RT}\right\} \tag{30}$$

which can also be written as

$$J_{12}^*/J_{21}^* = \exp\left\{\frac{\Delta\tilde{\mu}_* + N_i\,\Delta\tilde{\mu}_i}{RT}\right\} \tag{31}$$

The argument of the exponential reflects the two driving forces for tracer flow: the conjugate force, $\Delta\tilde{\mu}_*$, and the electrochemical potential of the abundant species, $\Delta\tilde{\mu}_i$ which is coupled to the tracer flow with a stoichiometric coefficient of N_i.

Equating the activity coefficients of tracer and abundant, and substituting in equation 30, we obtain the flux ratio equation for the "knock-on" channel.

$$\frac{J_{12}^*/\rho_1}{J_{21}^*/\rho_2} = \exp\left\{\frac{(N_i+1)\Delta\tilde{\mu}_i}{RT}\right\}$$

$$= \left[(a_1^i/a_2^i)\exp\left\{\frac{F\Delta\psi}{RT}\right\}\right]^{(N_i+1)} \tag{32}$$

B. Water

Levitt[13] and Rosenberg and Finkelstein[5,16,17] have considered in detail the behavior of water flows in channels (such as gramicidin) where the no pass condition obtains. The fact that water and its tracer cannot pass in the channel produces an obligatory coupling between the two flows which would be reflected in an anomalous tracer flux-ratio. We consider this situation because the flux-ratio approach leads rather directly to the derivation of a quantity of some experimental significance, namely the ratio of the *osmotic* water permeability to the *tracer* water permeability, P_f/P_d.

Consider a channel permeable only to water, and let the solutions contain some osmoticant (say sucrose) and tracer water. We assume knock-on kinetics where the pore is always occupied by N_w water molecules and where never more than one is a tracer. As in the previous example, we obtain the tracer flux-ratio by noting that for any value of the chemical potential gradient of abundant water, $\Delta\mu_w$ (produced by adding osmoticant to one side of the membrane) we may choose a value of $\Delta\mu_*$, the chemical potential gradient of labeled water, which will result in zero net tracer flow. The obligatory coupling requires that the equilibrium for channels containing tracer be written

$$\Delta\mu_* + N_W \, \Delta\mu_W = 0$$

where N_w is the total number of water molecules which may occupy a channel.

The *tracer* flux-ratio is then obtained directly as

$$J^*_{12}/J^*_{21} = (\gamma^*_1 C^*_1/\gamma^*_2 C^*_2) \, \exp \left\{ \frac{N_W \Delta\mu_W}{RT} \right\} \tag{33}$$

or

$$J^*_{12}/J^*_{21} = \exp \left\{ \frac{\Delta\mu_* + N_W \Delta\mu_W}{RT} \right\} \tag{34}$$

This is the expected result, namely that there are *two* driving forces for tracer water flow through the no pass pore, the chemical potential of labeled water and the chemical potential of the abundant water.

To obtain the ratio of the unidirectional fluxes of abundant water, we again assume that the activity coefficients for the labeled and unlabeled molecule are identical, i.e.,

$$\gamma^* = \gamma^W$$

or

$$a^*/C^* = a^W/C^W$$

Note that this is not equivalent to the conventional definition of water activity in terms of mole fraction but is the appropriate convention when comparing tracer and abundant.

Substituting in Equation 34 and introducing the specific activities, we obtain the flux ratio of the *abundant* water as

$$J^W_{12}/J^W_{21} = (a^W_1/a^W_2) \, \exp \left\{ \frac{N_W \Delta\mu_W}{RT} \right\} \tag{35a}$$

which may be written

$$J^W_{12}/J^W_{21} = \exp \left\{ \frac{(N_W + 1) \, \Delta\mu_W}{RT} \right\} \tag{35b}$$

The chemical potential difference of water, $\Delta\mu_w$, may be expressed in terms of the difference in osmotic pressure, $\Delta\pi$, i.e.,

$$\Delta\mu_w = -\overline{V}_w\Delta\pi$$

where $\overline{V}_w$ is the partial molar volume of water, and $\Delta\pi$ is the osmotic pressure difference, which yields for the flux-ratio:

$$J_{12}^W/J_{21}^W = \exp\left\{\frac{-(N_w + 1)\,\overline{V}_w\Delta\pi}{RT}\right\} \tag{36}$$

Now, consider the definition of the osmotic water permeability, P_f.

$$P_f = (RT/\overline{V}_w)\,L_p = -J_{net}^W/(\Delta\pi/RT) \tag{37}$$

where L_p is the hydraulic conductivity and J_{net}^w is the net molar water flow. If J_{net}^w is expressed in terms of the quantities in the flux-ratio equation (Equation 36), we obtain for P_f

$$P_f = \frac{-J_{21}^W\left(\exp\left\{\frac{-(N_w + 1)\,\overline{V}_w\Delta\pi}{RT}\right\} - 1\right)}{\Delta\pi/RT} \tag{38}$$

Taking the limit of P_f as $\Delta\pi$ approaches zero, we obtain the value of P_f in the limit of zero osmotic pressure.

$$\lim_{\Delta\pi \to 0} P_f = \lim_{\Delta\pi \to 0} \frac{-J_{21}^W\left(\exp\{-(N_w + 1)\,\overline{V}_w\Delta\pi/RT\} - 1\right)}{\Delta\pi/RT} \tag{39}$$

$$= {}_oJ_{21}^W\,(N_w + 1)\,\overline{V}_w \tag{40}$$

Recall, however, that the diffusional water permeability, P_d, measured when $\Delta\pi = 0$ is defined as

$$P_d = {}_oJ_{21}^W/C_2^W = J_{21}^*/C_2^* \tag{41}$$

where ${}_oJ_{21}^w$ is the unidirectional water flow when $\Delta\pi = 0$ (corrected for unstirred layer effects).

But for dilute solutions, in the limit of zero osmotic pressure difference, the water concentration difference may be approximated as

$$C_2^W = C_1^W \simeq 1/\overline{V}_w \tag{42}$$

Inserting these relations in Equation 40, we obtain the ratio for P_f/P_d as

$$P_f/P_d = N_w + 1 \tag{43}$$

Levitt showed that the obligatory coupling between water molecules in a no-pass channel leads to a fixed relation between diffusional and osmotic permeabilities, and that the ratio is a measure of the number of water molecules in the channel. Using a frictional approach to obtain values for P_f and P_d, Levitt obtained a predicted value for

P_f/P_d of N_w (see also Finkelstein and Rosenberg[5]), whereas the flux-ratio approach, which assumes a knock-on mechanism of transfer, yields $N_w + 1$ for the ratio. Both approaches, however, arrive at the same qualitative conclusion, that fixed ratio of coupling between the flow of tracer and abundant leads to a fixed ratio of P_f to P_d, which is related to the number of water molecules which may occupy a channel.

X. CAVEATS

The purpose of this review has been to point out that tracer flux-ratios are a measure of the total free energy involved in the tracer transport process and to emphasize that the form of the flux-ratio equations depends on the presence or absence of coupling between tracer flow and the flows of other species. In several instances, as shown above, specific transport mechanisms yield tracer flux-ratios which, apart from measuring the driving force for the transport process, also offer a diagnostic test for the existence of the particular type of transport mechanism in the membrane. In all of these cases, however, we have simplified the analysis enormously by considering a single transport path. It is likely that in most experimental systems, parallel paths for tracer flow will exist. Clearly, as discussed by Kedem and Essig,[12] the presence of parallel paths complicates the analysis. Thus, the challenge to the experimentalist is to design experiments in which the tracer fluxes and flux-ratio pertaining to one transport path can be resolved.

ACKNOWLEDGMENTS

I am grateful to my colleagues for their help with this chapter. Michael Jennings, Jack Kaplan, Dan Halm, and Kevin Kirk grappled with the first draft; Qais Al-Awqati, Alvin Essig, and John Jacquez provided valuable comments on the final version, and David Levitt and Alan Finkelstein reviewed the section on single-filing. Bill Germann and Joe Cannon proofed the final version. Special thanks also to Catherine Corson who fought her way through pages of scribbled equations to type the final draft. The writing of this article was supported by a grant from the National Institute for Arthritis and Metabolic Diseases (AM 29786). The author was a recipient of a Research Career Development Award (AM00994) from NIAMD.

REFERENCES

1. Britton, H. G., Induced uphill and downhill transport: relationship to the Ussing criterion *Nature (London)*, 198, 190, 1963.
2. Britton, H. G., The Ussing relationship and chemical reactions: possible applications to enzymatic investigations, *Nature (London)*, 205, 1323, 1965.
3. Britton, H. G., Relationship between the number of interacting particles and flux-ratio, *Nature (London)*, 209, 296, 1966.
4. Dawson, D. C., Tracer flux ratios: a phenomenological approach, *J. Membr. Biol.*, 31, 351, 1977.
5. Finkelstein, A. and Rosenberg, P. A., Single-file transport: implications for ion and water movement through gramicidin A channels, *Membrane Transport Processes*, Vol. 3, Stevens, C. F. and Tsien, R. W., Eds., Raven Press, New York, 1979.
6. Glasstone, S., *Textbook of Physical Chemistry*, Van Nostrand, New York, 1940.
7. Hodgkin, A. L. and Keynes, R. D., The potassium permeability of a giant nerve fiber, *J. Physiol. (London)*, 128, 61, 1955.
8. Hoshiko, T. and Lindley, B. D., The relationship of Ussing's flux-ratio equation to the thermodynamic description of membrane permeability, *Biochim. Biophys. Acta*, 79, 301, 1964.

9. Katchalsky, A. and Curran, P. F., *Nonequilibrium Thermodynamics in Biophysics,* Harvard University Press, Cambridge, 1967.
10. Katchalsky, A. and Kedem, O., Thermodynamics of flow processes in biological systems, *Biophys. J.,* 2, 53, 1962.
11. Kedem, O., Criteria of active transport, in *Membrane Transport and Metabolism,* Kleinzeller, A. and Kotyk, A., Eds., Academic Press, New York, 1961, 87.
12. Kedem, O. and Essig, A., Isotope flows and flux ratios in biological membranes, *J. Gen. Physiol.,* 48, 1047, 1965.
13. Levitt, D. G., A new theory of transport for cell membrane pores. I. General theory and application to red cell, *Biochim. Biophys. Acta,* 373, 115, 1974.
14. Patlak, C. S., Pettigrew, K. D., and Rapoport, S. I., Use of transient and steady-state measurements for the determination of the free energy change of chemical reactions and active transport systems, *Bull. Math. Biol.,* 42, 529, 1980.
15. Robertson, J. S., Theory and use of tracers in determining transfer rates in biological systems, *Physiol. Rev.,* 37, 133, 1957.
16. Rosenberg, P. A. and Finkelstein, A., Interaction of ions and water in gramicidin A channels, *J. Gen. Physiol.,* 72, 327, 1978.
17. Rosenberg, P. A. and Finkelstein, A., Water permeability of gramicidin A-treated lipid bilayer membranes, *J. Gen. Physiol.,* 72, 341, 1978.
18. Rosenberg, T. and Wilbrandt, W., Uphill transport induced by counter flow, *J. Gen. Physiol.,* 41, 289, 1957.
19. Schwartz, T. L., The validity of the Ussing flux-ratio equation in a three dimensionally inhomogeneous membrane, *Biophys. J.,* 11, 596, 1971.
20. Solomon, A. K., Compartmental methods of kinetc analysis *Mineral Metabolism I,* Comar, C. L. and Bronner, F., Eds., Academic Press, New York, 1960, 119.
21. Ussing, H. H., The distinction by means of tracers between active transport and diffusion, *Acta Physiol. Scand.,* 19, 43, 1949.
22. Ussing, H. H. and Zerahn, K., Active transport of sodium as the source of electric current in the short circuited isolated frog skin, *Acta Physiol. Scand.,* 23, 110, 1951.
23. Ussing, H. H., Some aspects of the application of tracers in permeability studies, *Adv. Enzymol.,* 13, 31, 1952.

Chapter 7

KINETICS OF BLOOD TO CELL UPTAKE OF RADIOTRACERS*

James B. Bassingthwaighte and Bernd Winkle

TABLE OF CONTENTS

*   Supported by research grants from the National Institutes of Health (HL 19139, HL 19135), Reynolds
    Industries, and the Max Planck Institute for Physiological and Clinical Research, Department for Ex-
    perimental Cardiology, Bad Nauheim.

INTRODUCTION

The objective of the techniques and studies to be discussed in this chapter is to provide some understanding of the kinetics of exchange in intact systems in the body. We wish to emphasize in vivo studies because in many aspects of physiology and biochemistry it has been learned through long experience that the behavior of a system in vivo is often dramatically different from that observed in vitro. The problems of examining in vivo systems are that they are technically more difficult and usually more complex, and commonly it is difficult or impossible to control the conditions of a particular experiment as well as one can with a patient or animal under anesthesia and an organ exposed, or with the organ removed from the body and perfused, or with isolated cells or subcellular organelles. Thus, it is timely to attempt to establish techniques which can be used with the organ or system in the most normal state that one can approach.

The development of techniques for obtaining information noninvasively or with minimal invasion in patients and animals has undergone a great surge in the last 3 decades with the advent of cardiac catheterization and in the past few years with imaging techniques. A major virtue of using noninvasive techniques, and of using information from implanted transducers in awake normal animals, is that the observations can be made repeatedly under a variety of physiological circumstances. It also means that studies can be done in chronic disorders or for the assessment of improvement in pathophysiological state with time or with pharmacologic intervention.

The techniques that we emphasize for the estimation of rates of exchange between the blood and tissue are those which will provide the fundamental information for understanding the pharmacokinetics of ions, substrates, and drugs of interest. Much work that has been done over the years with pharmaceutical agents or inert tracers and with tracer-labeled normal body constituents (e.g., ions and substrates of metabolism) has been based on making an injection of the tracer-labeled substance into the plasma and observing the plasma disappearance curves over a period of time.

A common approach to the analyses of such plasma disappearance curves was to use multiexponential analysis, that is, to fit the observed diminishing concentration-time curve in the plasma with a sum of exponentials or other composites of exponential expressions. While these expressions could fit the curves quite well, such compartmental analyses usually seemed somewhat unsatisfactory to us in the sense that the conductances or exchange rates and the volumes used in the analysis did not reflect the true physiological system. The mathematical expressions therefore represented composites of many processes which could be occurring in any of many organs of the body, so that distinguishing the role of particular organs was impossible. Further developments of these techniques occurred when information was taken from more than one part of the body, for example, from urine or bile or expired air, simultaneously with the plasma concentrations. This was very useful for identifying the influences of the excretory process on the plasma disappearance curves; for the most part, however, compartmental analysis still did not lend itself to defining the processes of binding or transformation of tracer within specific nonexcretory organs.

The indicator dilution technique, developed by Stewart[98-101] for the measurement of transit times and flow through the vascular system, turned out to be invaluable for the study of rapid kinetics of exchange in individual organs. The early experiments of Flexner, Cowie, and Vosburgh,[30] and Chinard and Flexner[19] led to the establishment of the multiple tracer indicator dilution technique, e.g., the studies of water exchange by Chinard and Enns,[18] and Chinard, Vosburgh, and Enns,[20] and of solute exchange in the liver by Goresky.[31]

The approach was extended by Crone,[22] who demonstrated the use of a pair of tracers simultaneously to obtain estimates of capillary permeability in the brain. The technique was to use an intravascular tracer, ^{131}I-albumin, which did not escape across a capillary membrane, and a permeating tracer, in his case ^{3}H-glucose, which was taken up by the brain. These were injected into the arterial inflow, the carotid artery, and the outflow concentration-time curves were recorded from the venous outflow, the sagittal sinus. Recognizing that the escape of glucose from the blood aross the capillary membrane would lead to fractional decrements in intravascular glucose concentration for each fraction of the length of the capillary, Crone saw that this gave an exponential decrease in intravascular concentration with the distance along the capillary. With this in mind, he formulated the equation for the capillary permeability-surface area product, PS_c, as a function of the flow F_s of solute-containing mother fluid, and an observed extraction, E or maximal extraction E_{max}:

$$PS_c = F_s \log_e(1 - E_{max}) \qquad (1)$$

This equation has a long history going back to Christian Bohr,[16] and was also redeveloped by Renkin[81,82] for the analysis of constant infusion experiments in skeletal muscle. In any case, while Chinard had demonstrated the use of multiple tracers for assessing relative volumes of distribution within an organ for tracers which were exchangeable at very high rates between the blood and tissue (flow-limited tracers, as we shall discuss later), Crone[22] and Martin and Yudilevich[71] now had demonstrated its applicability to the estimation of a rate of transport across the capillary membrane. In 1965, Crone[23] also demonstrated that the mechanism for glucose transport across the brain capillary membrane was a carrier-facilitated process. The identification of capillary and cellular rates separately should be attributed to Goresky, Ziegler, and Bach.[37]

The extension of this multiple tracer technique is the main focus of our presentation. By using several different tracers simultaneously, one can isolate the information on the transport rate for a particular solute by comparing it with others serving as controls. An example of this is the use of a set of tracers to isolate the rate of cellular uptake of glucose in the myocardium: for this, we have used albumin for the intravascular reference tracer, L-glucose for capillary permeation and distribution throughout the interstitial fluid region, 2-deoxy-D-glucose as one that is taken up across the cell wall but not metabolized and not released from the cell, all of which serve as references for D-glucose in different ways and serving to identify the cellular uptake of D-glucose.[58]

The key to the understanding of whole body exchange and regulation is having sets of studies on individual organs. When rates of exchange in each of several organs have been estimated, the simplified models of the total circulation can give an integrated description of the events governing the plasma disappearance of a particular tracer and of the rate constants for transmembrane exchange and circulatory mass transport.

These processes may be just as important in delaying excretion as the excretory process in the kidney or liver. The great advantage of individual organ studies is that through these studies one can obtain an intimate idea of the relationships between the anatomy, the physiology, and the kinetics of the tracer exchange in that single organ.

Currently, there are techniques available for measuring the following:

1. Intravascular transport and dispersion from inflow to outflow of an organ
2. The capillary permeability-surface area product, PS_c
3. The interstitial volume of distribution for tracers which do not enter cells, V_I
4. The cellular uptake rates for those tracers which do enter the parenchymal cells of an organ, PS_M
5. The volume of distribution of the tracer within the cells, V_M, which is a measure of the cell's retention of the tracer

In some instances, one can also obtain estimates of the metabolic rate. For the most part, the processes of exchange across the capillary membrane and into the interstitium are passive (the exception being the transport of certain sugars across brain capillaries), so that these techniques allow the investigation of carrier-mediated or energetically coupled transport processes at the cell walls, and perhaps intracellular metabolic rates.

The relationship of data obtained by in vivo experiments to data from in vitro experiments is something on which, in general, we have relatively little information. Hopefully, the in vivo techniques will confirm the information obtained from in vitro experiments. However, this is by no means guaranteed; for example, the rates of calcium uptake by isolated vesicles of sarcoplasmic reticulum estimated in many laboratories over the past 2 decades have been orders of magnitude too low to account for the observed rates of relaxation of muscle after a contraction. Only with the recent development of rapid reaction apparatus, for example, by Inesi,[50,108] were rates of uptake of calcium by the sarcoplasmic reticulum shown to be compatible with what was needed for their biological function.

A trend in modern quantitative physiology, pharmacology, and biochemistry is to formulate mathematical descriptions of integrated systems. This is an efficient way of describing systems, since a careful formulation from known observations greatly reduces the degrees of freedom in a mathematical model and thereby enhances the accuracy. This contributes greatly to their use in predicting the behavior of components which are unknown, or in devising experiments to elucidate the rate parameters for those parts of the system which are least known. A further advantage of looking at the observed whole organ data with integrated analysis is that one is forced to consider all of the physical and chemical approaches that are related to the transport of the tracer of interest. Some of these may simply be passive processes such as diffusive permeation across the capillary or diffusion through interstitial ground substance in which there may or may not be binding sites, but the analyses might reveal that these essential components of an in vivo system are rate limiting in some fashion, which would not be guessed by simply looking at the rate of exchange in isolated cell systems. Another virtue is that such studies may reveal the presence of activators or inhibitors of transport which might not be observable in the studies of isolated cells or cell fragments.

A. Studies in Single Organs or Tissues
1. General Approaches to the Experimentation and Analysis
a. Input-Output Relationships

In the studies of single organs, the phrase, input-output relationships, generally implies the defining of a system with an arterial inflow and a venous outflow.

The movement of a substance through a system can be made evident by the introduction of a radioactive substance which "traces" the behavior of the chemically identical "mother" substance, or by the use of foreign indicators, which may or may not be radioactive. Such foreign indicators are usually chosen for their similarity to some naturally occurring substance, e.g., L-glucose for D-glucose or Evans blue dye to label plasma proteins. The underlying physical principle in all exchange processes is the mass balance of the substance under consideration.

Input-output relationships for flowing systems have been well defined by Zierler[119,121] and Meier and Zierler.[73] These have been summarized nicely by Lassen and Perl.[62] We utilize the nomenclature approved by a committee, Bassingthwaighte et al.[9] Bassingthwaighte's reviews covered intravascular transport[5] and transport of highly diffusible substances.[7] Our considerations include bolus injections and constant infusion techniques. In this section we will summarize the principles on which experimental approaches are based.

After a bolus impulse injection of an indicator, ideally represented as a delta function, $\delta(t)$, the outflow concentration-time curve $C_o(t)$ is given by:

$$C_o(t) = q_0 h(t)/F_B \tag{2}$$

where F_B is the blood flow, q_0 is the injected indicator amount and $h(t)$ is the transport function, the frequency function, or the probability density function of transit times, as defined by Zierler.[73] The area under $h(t)$, the integral up to infinite time, is unity; that is, all material which has entered the organ finally exits. For general input concentration-time curve $C_i(t)$ the output curve $C_o(t)$ is completely defined by $h(t)$ and by the convolution integral, assuming linearity and stationarity of the system:

$$C_o(t) = \int_0^t h(t - t') C_i(t') \, dt' \tag{3}$$

The transport function $h(t)$ is the impulse response of a linear system. As such, it describes the transformation of any input function, $C_i(t)$, into the corresponding output function, $C_o(t)$; i.e., $h(t)$ determines the system completely.

Harris and Newman[43] have summarized a variety of mathematical models representing the transport function, $h(t)$, for intravascular markers. Different models of a stochastic nature work more or less equally well, e.g., the random walk with a first traversal,[92] a gamma-variate model,[106] a lagged normal density curve,[8] and a log-normal curve.[102] For intravascular indicators, a minimum of four parameters are usually necessary to describe the transport function, $h(t)$. These parameters are usually algebraically translatable to: (1) a scaling factor (the area is unity if no material is gained or lost), (2) the mean transit time, (3) the dispersion, and (4) the skewness. Related models that are adequate descriptors are sets of mixing chambers in series,[90] or in series-parallel arrangements.[57] The mean transit time $\bar{t}$, is defined as the first moment of the "frequency function of transit times" using Zierler's notation

$$\bar{t} = \int_0^\infty t h(t) \, dt \Big/ \int_0^\infty h(t) \, dt \tag{4}$$

Dispersion and skewness are related to the second and third moments. The product of the mean transit time times flow in the steady-state gives the volume of distribution indicator, which is merely an expression of conservation of material:

$$V = F \cdot \bar{t} \tag{5}$$

The cumulative residence time distribution H(t) is the fraction of indicator collected by time t at the output and is the integral of h(t):

$$H(t) = \int_0^t h(t')\, dt' \tag{6}$$

H(t) is the complementary function to the organ's fractional residual content, the residue function:

$$R(t) = 1 - H(t) \tag{7}$$

R(t) is the fraction of material introduced into the system at time zero which is still remaining in the system at time t. The rate of escape of material from the system after an impulse injection is termed the specific fractional escape rate, $\eta(t)$, or the emergence function:

$$\eta(t) = h(t)/R(t) \tag{8}$$

The different equations are explained in detail by Bassingthwaighte.[7] Equation 8 is the special case for fractional escape rate, FER, when the material is all suddenly introduced into the entrance of the system at t = 0. The general case for FER is rate of loss, -dq/dt, of material per unit time as a fraction of that present at each moment, q(t):

$$FER = -(dq/dt)\,/\,q(t) \tag{9}$$

b. Multiple Indicator Dilution Pulse Injection Technique

The multiple indicator dilution technique is a method to study transcapillary exchange processes. Following the method of Chinard and Enns,[18] the transcapillary movement of a diffusible indicator can be estimated if it is injected intra-arterially together with an intrasvascular indicator, a reference tracer. The paired (or more) venous outflow dilution curves are each normalized to h(t) by applying Equation 2, $h(t) = F_B C(t)/q_0$, to obtain $h_R(t)$ for the reference tracer and $h_D(t)$ for the permeating or diffusible tracer. The instantaneous apparent fractional extraction E(t), is

$$E(t) = [\,h_R(t) - h_D(t)\,]/h_R(t) \tag{10}$$

The choice of reference tracer depends on the situation, absence of permeation and ease of measurement being key considerations. T-1824 (Evans blue) labeled-albumin or indocyanine green-labeled albumin can be used as intravascular reference molecules. Generally, radioactive indicators such as ^{125}I- or ^{131}I-labeled serum albumin are preferred for the intravascular plasma space. Red blood cells labeled with ^{59}Fe, ^{51}Cr, or ^{99m}Tc, can also be used as an intravascular reference tracer, but it should be recalled that erythrocytes have higher intracapillary velocities than does plasma because red blood cells travel in the faster central streams.[35] Also, 3 μm diameter tracer microspheres can be used in animal experiments, since they have velocities similar to red blood cells.[111]

We like to distinguish four terms with respect to the indicator dilution technique:

1. "Label", a radioactive or stable moiety which is attached to a molecule
2. "Tracer", a substance having special characteristics allowing it to be measured in low concentration and which travels in a fashion more or less identical to that

of a normal body constituent in relatively high concentrations (the mother substance)

3. "Mother substance", or tracee
4. "Indicator", a substance for which there may or may not be a mother substance

Diffusible indicators leave the vascular bed to enter the interstitial space: some of these penetrate the membranes of the parenchymal cells. For this reason indicators may be divided with respect to their volumes of distribution as:

1. Vascular indicators (which penetrate capillary membranes not at all or very slowly)
2. Interstitial indicators (which remain extracellular)
3. Indicators which enter cells

Useful interstitial indicators are small inert hydrophilic molecules, such as cobaltic ^{57}CoEDTA, ^{14}C-sucrose, ^{32}SO$_4$, and ^{14}C-inulin.

Inert nonmetabolized tracers which can enter cells are surprisingly uncommon. ^{3}HHO (tritiated water) and D$_2$O (heavy water) have stood the test of time as water indicators. Urea and antipyrine also provide reasonably good measures of water space; the former is polar but small, and the latter is moderately lipid soluble and has a tissue/plasma solubility ratio close to unity. Iodo-antipyrine is more lipid soluble than antipyrine,[80,112] but both are metabolized in the liver.[96]

Ions and other elements label any compound into which they can be incorporated, but it is usual to think of the akali metal ions as a unique species existing part free and part bound, the free form being in equilibrium with ions attached to miscellaneous binding sites. In studies of potassium, the use of ^{42}K or ^{43}K has not been supplanted by the use of the analogues ^{86}Rb, ^{137}Cs, or ^{201}Tl since their transmembrane kinetics and diffusion rates are not the same.

The growing emphasis is on the study of tracers involved in cellular metabolism. The cellular uptake rates of the standard substrates, glucose and fatty acids, can now be examined using the multiple indicator dilution technique. Kuikka et al.[58] examined D-, L-, and 2-deoxy-D-glucose uptake by myocardial cells. Goresky and colleagues studied the myocardial uptake of ^{14}C-palmitic acid[86] and have demonstrated competition for binding sites for fatty acids[36] and alcohols[32] in the liver. The rates of amino acid transfer in the brain were estimated by Yudilevich, De Rose, and Sepulveda[115] and more recently in the salivary glands and pancreas.[69,70]

Indicator outflow curves from the heart are presented in Figure 1. They were obtained by collecting the coronary sinus outflow as a series of samples after a bolus containing the tracers was injected into the inflow line of an isolated dog-heart preparation. All the indicators were dispersed equally within the vascular bed, and the two permeating tracers, Na$^+$ and iodo-antipyrine, were further delayed and dispersed by their transport through the extravascular region, causing their corresponding outflow curves to be lower and broader than that of the reference tracer. In the upslope region of the curves, the apparent extraction E(t) is larger for antipyrine than for sodium, indicating a higher permeability of the capillary membrane. The volume of distribution of antipyrine spreads it out further throughout the remainder of the curve. The sodium is restricted mainly to the interstitial and vascular space because of its slow entry to the cell and its extrusion via the Na-K-ATPase. All the indicator curves would have the same area if all the material emerges so that the crossing of the diffusible tracer with the reference indicator indicates return flow (back diffusion) of the diffusible substance from the interstitial into the intravascular space.

In the right panel, the reference tracer is ^{131}I-albumin and the permeating indicators

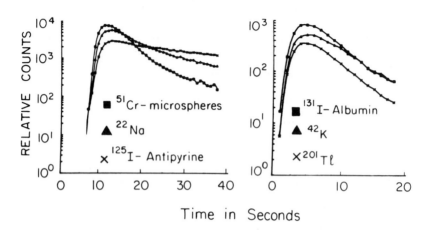

FIGURE 1.   Indicator dilution curves obtained from isolated blood-perfused (Langendorff) dog hearts without recirculation. Left panel: the reference tracer, highest peaked curve, was ^{51}Cr-labeled microspheres (diameter of 3 μm). The permeating indicators were ^{22}NaCl and ^{125}I-antipyrine. Myocardial plasma flow, F_s, was 1.2 mℓ g^{-1} min^{-1}. Right panel: ^{131}Tl-albumin is the reference tracer; ^{201}Tl and ^{42}K were injected as the chloride salts; F_s = 1.45 mℓ g^{-1} min^{-1}. Adenosine infusion to produce maximal vasodilatation was at 3.7 μmol/min or an inflow concentration of about 1.4 × 10^{-5} M adenosine.

are ^{42}K and ^{201}Tl, both of which enter myocytes. In this preparation vasodilated with adenosine (concentration 10^{-5} M), return flow (back diffusion) leads to early crossover of the ^{42}K and albumin curves. In contrast, the thallium is extracted during the whole 18-sec period of observation and the crossover occurs at an unknown later time. Undoubtedly, the back diffusion of thallium into the intravascular space has been lowered by uptake into the cell. Strauss et al.[104] showed in addition that the washout of ^{201}Tl was much slower than had been observed for potassium by Tancredi, Yipintsoi, and Bassingthwaighte.[105] From this and their own observations, Winkler and Schaper[110,111] concluded that there is likely to be substantial intracellular binding of thallium.

The methods of analysis of such dilution curves for the estimation of capillary and cell permeabilities are to be provided in later sections.

c. Continuous Infusion Method for the Estimation of Cellular Uptake

With a constant infusion rate, the input into the arterial inflow to the organ is a step function, rather than a bolus input. The output concentration, when there is no consumption, after some delay, rises to have the same concentration as the input; the form of the rise is H(t), the integral of the impulse response. Prolonged steady input to the organ of a nonconsumed indicator leads to a prolonged, nearly steady A-V difference (pseudo steady-state) in the circumstance where there is a large and continued rate of uptake into a large cellular sink (e.g., for potassium or thallium). Sequential venous outflow samples can be collected, but a useful alternative technique is continuous monitoring of gamma activity in the outflow, H(t), as was used by Renkin,[81] and by Guller et al.[41] for the pulse injection technique.

The venous outflow curves from such an experiment using ^{42}K show an initial transient period followed by a slowly rising pseudo-plateau. As pointed out by Sheehan and Renkin,[91] the transient part is mainly due to exchange at the capillary wall, but the plateau, representing the pseudo steady-state, reflects net transfer across both capillary and cell membranes. Therefore, interventions at the cellular membrane should be observed during this pseudo steady-state.

In experiments by Yudilevich et al.[116] and Sheehan and Renkin,[91] both methods were combined. Data from the rising transient state of the constant infusion curve, which is analogous to the upslope and peak portions of the bolus injection indicator-dilution curve, gives an estimate of the permeability-surface area product of the capillary membrane by comparison with an intravascular reference. The continuous infusion technique can be applied without injecting a reference indicator, in which case the venous outflow concentrations are considered as a fraction of the arterial concentration.

Sheehan and Renkin[91] considered the blood-tissue transport in terms of a series of resistances across the capillary membrane, $1/PS_C$, the interstitial space, $1/PS_I$, and the cell membrane, $1/PS_M$. Each of these resistances is the reciprocal of the permeability-surface area product, PS, for the barrier. The total resistance from blood into cell is the sum:

$$\frac{1}{PS_T} = \frac{1}{PS_c} + \frac{1}{PS_I} + \frac{1}{PS_M} \tag{11}$$

Rearranging to obtain PS_M:

$$PS_M = \frac{PS_T \cdot PS_c \cdot PS_I}{PS_c \cdot PS_I - PS_T(PS_I + PS_c)} \tag{12}$$

Sheehan and Renkin estimated PS_T for ^{86}Rb and ^{42}K from plateau extractions in their constant infusion experiments from the same equation used by Renkin[81,82] and Crone:[22]

$$PS_T = F_s \cdot \log_e(1 - E) \tag{13}$$

where F_s is the plasma flow, and the extraction E was derived from the net arteriovenous concentration difference, $C_A - C_V$, during the psuedo steady-state of nearly constant extraction:

$$E = \frac{C_A - C_V}{C_V} \tag{14}$$

The capillary PS_C was evaluated from the initial extraction values in single bolus injection experiments, or from the transient state in the constant infusion experiments as described by Martin and Yudilevich.[71] The resistance at the interstitial barrier, $1/PS_I$, was estimated by Sheehan and Renkin, on the basis of a geometric model of the skeletal muscle capillary-tissue space, to be less than 5% of the total resistance. Considering a model similar to that in Figure 2, they made the following assumptions:

1. Intracellular indicators permeate through the capillary wall into interstitial space and diffuse across the ISF to the cell wall and permeate it to enter the cellular pool from which there is no return.
2. All capillaries are identical and are perfused in parallel.
3. Radial concentration gradients within the capillary are negligible.
4. Longitudinal diffusion in the extravascular space is negligible.
5. No material transfer occurs across the ends of the interstitial cylinder associated with each capillary.

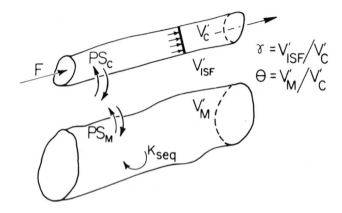

FIGURE 2.   Capillary ISF-cell model with barriers in series. This
is the conceptual model used by Sheehan and Renkin[91] for analyzing the uptake of K[+] by skeletal muscle after calculating that the
ISF resistance was negligible, and is the model used by Tancredi
et al.[105] for analyzing potassium washout from the heart. For potassium, the cell sequestration (or metabolic) rate, K_{seq}, is zero.
Sheehan and Renkin considered efflux from the cell to be zero in
their uptake experiments. Similarly, Tancredi et al. considered the
reuptake into the cell to be negligible in their washout experiments.

6.   Concentrations of indicator in the capillary lumen, interstitial space, and intracellular space are in a steady-state during the "plateau" phase of the continuous
infusion experiments.

The analysis demonstrating that $1/PS_I$ was small, as was also shown for the heart by
Tancredi et al.,[105] led to the practical equation:

$$\frac{1}{PS_T} = \frac{1}{PS_c} + \frac{1}{PS_M} \tag{15}$$

or to calculate PS_M,

$$PS_M = \frac{PS_c \cdot PS_T}{PS_c - PS_T} \tag{16}$$

Sheehan and Renkin estimated from their experiments that the capillary wall presents
69% of the total resistance and 31% comes from the skeletal muscle cell membrane
for potassium. For rubidium, the sarcolemmal resistance was higher, so that 47% was
at the capillary and 53% at the cell membrane.

   The essential condition in the Sheehan-Renkin approach is the pseudo steady-state,
which is obtainable with an isolated organ without recirculation. Achieving such experimental conditions in vivo is extremely difficult since one would have to infuse the
radioactive substance at a continuously variable rate, matching it to the concentration
in the recirculating blood to obtain a constant inflow concentration. Although we have
done this with [24]Na in a fashion similar to that used for creatinine by Heppner, Harvey,
and Bassingthwaighte,[45] it is too difficult to be very practical.

   It may be seen from this approach that the analysis was dependent on the choice of
a model for the organ (parallel, independent, uniform capillary-tissue units), even
though no complex formulations were needed for its presentation here. Both the Ren-

kin-Crone formula, $PS_C = -F_s\log_e(1 - E)$, and the Renkin-Sheehan-Tancredi analyses depended on the assumption of the absence of return flux of tracer. This assumption is not wholly valid, so more complex approaches to the analysis must be considered in the later sections. The earliest analyses, taking into account both the observations in the transient state and the back diffusion, were those of Conn and Robertson, who used a compartmental analysis.[21]

d. Tracer Washout or Clearance from an Organ

For our purposes, we consider the washout of tracer following introduction into the inflow at t = 0, rather than, for example, washout after complete equilibration or some intermediate state. Clearance is then defined as the equivalent flow per unit volume or mass of tissue of the effluent perfusate in which the concentration is equal to the average concentration in the system.[7] If there is instantaneous complete mixing of indicator throughout the organ from inflow to outflow at every instant, then the clearance equals the flow. However, in mammalian systems, long diffusion distances inside and outside the bloodstream and relatively impermeable membranes prevent such instantaneous mixing. Even the highly diffusible inert gases, xenon, krypton, and argon, fail to show monoexponential washout even though their washout is limited mainly by the flow.[12,72]

The washout time course may be observed by collecting outflow samples, or by using residue detection of gamma emitters via an external detector. The latter method is commonly used in clinical cardiology to estimate myocardial blood flow: a small bolus of an indicator, e.g., ^{133}Xe, is injected into the coronary arterial inflow and the residue observed via a detector placed over the chest. Although washout curves have often been analyzed in terms of sets of exponential processes in parallel, on the assumption that there is instantaneous mixing throughout each region, this may lead to incorrect interpretations. For example, although it is common to treat brain washout as a two-exponential process, one for grey matter and one for white matter, it is virtually assured that either one of these alone will exhibit a multiexponential washout.

Direct intra-tissue injection is an alternative to intra-arterial injection. If there were complete instantaneous equilibration, the two techniques would yield identical washout curves. That they do not, as shown for example, by Bassingthwaighte, Strandell, and Donald,[12] is not surprising in a system where inflow and outflow are linked through a distributed network with capillaries that are long compared to the distances over which diffusion can occur during a capillary transit time. Although washout curves have been treated fairly extensively,[7,121] washout from nonequilibrating depot injections cannot be confidently treated theoretically since the degree of local equilibration cannot be measured.

Nevertheless, washout of extracellular tracers has been used to estimate capillary PS_C, from Equation 1, when flow is known.[38,103] Similarly, when the tracer has entered a cellular pool and its washout is limited by cell and capillary membranes in series, then PS_M can be estimated. The washout of ^{42}K from myocardium was analyzed in this way by Tancredi, Yipintsoi, and Bassingthwaighte,[105] using Equation 16.

e. Extraction During Transcapillary Passage

Chinard[20] proposed estimating the permeability across the capillary wall by relating the normalized outflow concentration of a reference substance $h_R(t)$ to the concentration of a test substance $h_D(t)$ after a bolus injection. Guller et al.[41] demonstrated the application of different methods of calculating six versions of moment-to-moment estimation of extraction for the assessment of capillary permeability. These extractions were calculated from the normalized venous outflow dilution curves, $h(t)$, and from the residue functions, $R(t)$.

In 1963, Zierler[120] proposed an integral extraction, which is a measure of the fractional retention of the permeant tracer in the organ:

$$E_{int}(t) = \int_0^t [h_R(t') - h_D(t')]\,dt' \tag{17}$$

The analogous extraction obtained from externally monitored residue functions $R_R(t)$ and $R_D(t)$ is a direct calculation yielding E'_{int} which is theoretically identical to E_{int}:

$$E'_{int}(t) = R_D(t) - R_R(t) \tag{18}$$

The usual extraction is the instantaneous extraction proposed by Crone.[22]

$$E(t) = [h_R(t) - h_D(t)]/h_R(t) = 1 - h_D(t)/h_R(t) \tag{19}$$

The analogous calculation from residue functions is

$$E'(t) = 1 - dR_D(t)/dR_R(t) \tag{20}$$

Lassen and Crone[61] introducd an averaged version of this extraction:

$$E_{net}(t) = \int_0^t [h_R(t') - h_D(t')]\,dt' \Big/ \int_0^t h_R(t')\,dt' \tag{21}$$

From the residue detection curves, this is

$$E'_{net}(t) = \frac{R_D(t) - R_R(t)}{1 - R_R(t)} \tag{22}$$

These net extractions are close to the instantaneous extraction E(t), Equation 19, only in the earliest moments, and are thereafter always more because of the back diffusion of the diffusible tracer as can be seen from Figure 3.

The idea was that the integration might go up to the time of the peak of $h_R(t)$ or to the steepest part of $R_R(t)$ on the basis that this would average over some heterogeneity of flows and transit times. This integration method has the advantage of reducing the effects of noise on upslope. It was also assumed that back diffusion does not occur up to the time, t_p, when the reference curve, $h_R(t)$, achieves its maximal value. Guller et al.[41] found that similar results were obtained with the second and the third method, and that E_{int} was not useful in calculating a permeability surface product. Martin and Yudilevich[71] considered back diffusion from extravascular space into the capillary by extrapolating the indicator outflow concentrations back to the appearance time:

$$E(0) = \lim_{t \to t_a} (1 - C_D(t)/C_R(t)) \tag{23}$$

where t_a is the time of appearance of the tracers in the outflow. This does not directly account for the back diffusion process, but does introduce smoothing by extending a line through the early data points. They also suggested using the area between h_R and h_D to account for the rising concentration of permeant tracer in the ISF volume of distribution, V_I:

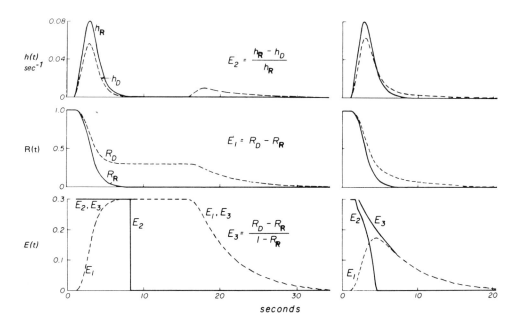

FIGURE 3. Methods of estimating extractions, E. Broken lines = diffusible indicator (subscript D) and solid lines = reference indicator (subscript R). Left: The transport function $h_D(t)$, the probability density component which has a shape similar to the transport function for a nonpermeating reference tracer, $h_R(t)$, and, in this unphysiological example, a temporally separated second component representing tracer which enters the tissue, later returns to the blood, and is washed out. The basic definitions are given for the integral extraction, E_1 or E_{int}, for the instantaneous extraction E_2 or $E(t)$, and for the area-weighted mean extraction, E_3 or E_{net}; all have similar maximums when the extravascular component returns very late, starting at 16 sec in the diagram. Right: the normal situation is that the two components overlap; the back diffusion of the extracted component begins at about 2 sec and has a shape identical to that in the left of the figure. In this case, the maximum E, is less than for E_2 or E_3. The diagram is oversimplified in that E_2 and E_3 are identical in the first seconds, which only occurs so long as $E_2(t)$ is constant.

$$\lim_{t \to t_a} \frac{K \int_0^t [h_R(t) - h_D(t)]\,dt}{h_R(t)} - \frac{h_D(t)}{h_R(t)} = E - 1 \qquad (24)$$

where $1/k$ is the slope of the plot of the first term against the second. K was interpreted to be $E \cdot F_s/V_I$, so that V_I was also estimated from the data. This really considers the ISF to be a mixing chamber from which reflux into the capillary occurs; this was an important conceptual approach to correcting for the return flux (or back diffusion). It did not account for axial gradients in concentrations in the ISF, and has been superseded by the use of the spatially distributed Krogh cylinder models.

f. Capillary Permeability-Surface Area Products

In Table 1 are summarized permeability-surface area products PS_c in the heart for different indicators. These estimates were obtained mainly with the multiple indicator single bolus injection technique, and those of Renkin and collaborators with the continuous infusion technique. PS_c was calculated usually with the Crone-Renkin equation (Equation 1), but Ziegler and Goresky,[117-118] Guller et al.,[41] and Rose and Goresky[86] obtained the estimates by fitting with the more fully developed models which are described under Krogh-cylinder analysis.

Values of PS_c for skeletal muscle are substantially lower than for the heart. This is to be expected, since the capillary surface area is much less: about 50 to 150 cm²/g for skeletal muscle[39] and 500 cm²/g for heart.[13]

Table 1
TRACER DIFFUSION COEFFICIENTS AND ESTIMATED PS$_C$

Organ	Indicator	Molecular or atomic weight	Molecular or ionic radii[Å]	Diffusion coefficient 25°C × 10^5	PS$_C$ (mℓ min^{-1} g^{-1})	Ref.
Heart	NaCl	58.5	0.95[Na +](83)	1.48(2)	0.3—1.0	113
					0.082—0.163	118
					0.29—1.37	27
					0.88—1.01	41
					0.26—0.47	44
	Cl	35.5	1.81(83)		0.35—2.04	1
	RbCl	120	1.48[Rb +](83)	1.9	0.28—1.43	1
					0.11—0.28	118
	KCl	74.5	1.33[K +](83)	1.84(2)	0.9	105
					0.48—1.3	111
	TlCl	236	1.44[Tl +](83)		0.48—2.3	111
	Urea	60	2.6(78)	1.38(2)	0.71—0.92	1
	Thiourea	76			0.3—2.0	113
	Glucose	180	3.6(2)	0.67(2)	0.26—0.13	1
					0.092—0.71	27
	Sucrose	342	5.2(2)	0.52(2)	0.16—0.24	1
					0.076—0.121	118
					0.9	85
					0.26	44
	Inulin	5000	10-15(107)	0.72(78)	0.076—0.08	1
Skeletal	NaCl	58.5	0.95[Na +](83)	1.48	0.024—0.117	116
Muscle	KCl	74.5	1.33[K +](83)	1.84	0.04—0.1	82
					0.021—0.042	91
	RbCl	120	1.48[Rb +](83)	1.9	0.019—0.148	116
					0.016—0.036	91

The large range of estimates of PS$_c$ reflects in part significant differences between experimental preparations; for example, those of Goresky and colleagues[86,118] were innervated hearts in vivo and were partially vasoconstricted, and therefore probably had less capillary surface area than the nearly maximally vasodilated isolated hearts. The permeability and the surface area together govern the exchange rate in indicator dilution experiments, so lower values of PS$_C$ are more likely explained in vasoconstricted states by a smaller surface area than by a smaller permeability.

The values of PS$_C$ for hydrophilic molecules are inversely related to the effective hydrated molecular diameters, and, over a limited range of small molecules, are nearly proportional to the free diffusion coefficients. Larger molecules such as protein are relatively more impeded in organs with closed capillary endothelial membranes, so that in heart and skeletal muscle, the routes of penetration through endothelial clefts or pores have the equivalent radii of about 100 Å. Organs such as pancreas, salivary glands, and especially the liver, have open capillaries with relatively high permeabilities.[31,69,70] The brain has tightly closed capillaries with very low permeability to hydrophilic molecules except those such as glucose, for which there are facilitated transport mechanisms.[23,114,115]

2. Krogh Capillary-Tissue Approaches to the Analysis
a. Sequential Development of Models for Capillary and Cell PS

Krogh cylinder analysis is designed for the analysis of organs composed of parallel arrays of long capillaries having steady flows with the same velocities in neighboring capillaries so that there are no exchanges of tracer material between neighboring capillaries. Such a system is diagrammed in Figure 4.

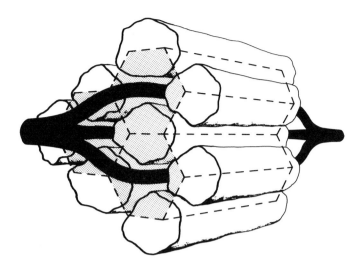

FIGURE 4. Krogh capillary-tissue hexagons with uniform dimensions and flows. Exchange occurs only in the capillary-tissue regions and not in the large vessels. A fundamental prerequisite is that flows in the adjacent capillaries are similar and the volumes in adjacent capillary tissue regions are similar so that although there are concentration gradients both radially and longitudinally in the tissue, there will be no gradients across the interface between regions. In such a circumstance, all the region can be modeled as a composite of capillaries all having identical behavior.

Organs having flows and geometries highly suitable for Krogh cylinder analysis are few. The best are the heart and the liver. Skeletal muscle has long capillaries, but it appears that the variation in intercapillary distance and the fluctuations and flows in skeletal muscle are likely to cause more intercapillary variations or heterogeneity than will occur in the more compact organs.

There is a dearth of suitable models for other organs, which has led to the utilization of the Krogh cylinder models for many other organs. Their degree of suitability is not really known, but Crone[22] used the Krogh cylinder analysis for the brain, Mann et al. for the salivary glands,[69,70] and Kelly et al. for bone studies.[53,54] Grunewald[40] and Metzger[74] have developed multicapillary rectangular and tetrahedral models which would predict more or less flat oxygen profiles of capillary tissue regions in the brain, demonstrating their recognition that Krogh cylinder models are not always suitable, but in general other types of geometric models have not been sought for individual organs. This should be considered as a future area of research.

A diagram of selected steps in the process of Krogh cylinder model development is shown in Figure 5. These all are distributed models, in which axial concentration gradients are accounted for. For simplicity of computation, it is assumed that the intracapillary velocity profile is flat and that there is no axial dispersion due to axial diffusion (or turbulence) or to a nonuniform velocity profile. This means that an impulse input, a spike in tracer concentration at the inflow, appears at the outflow as a delayed spike. That is, that for the intravascular, the response to a Dirac delta function input $\delta(t)$ is simply $\delta(t - \tau)$, where τ is the capillary transit time. The normalized outflow concentration $h_D(t)$ of a tracer which permeates through the capillary wall can be divided into two components: (1) a component of the input impulse which is diminished by the amount permeating into the extravascular space and which appears first; and (2) a component which is the tracer returning into capillaries after extravascular permeation (back diffusion). The first component can be expressed in mathematical form as $\delta(t - \tau) \cdot e^{-PS_c/F_s}$, which is just the impulse response reduced by permeation and

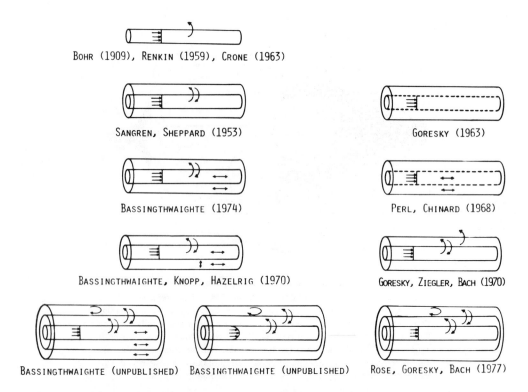

BOHR (1909), RENKIN (1959), CRONE (1963)

SANGREN, SHEPPARD (1953)

GORESKY (1963)

BASSINGTHWAIGHTE (1974)

PERL, CHINARD (1968)

BASSINGTHWAIGHTE, KNOPP, HAZELRIG (1970)

GORESKY, ZIEGLER, BACH (1970)

BASSINGTHWAIGHTE (UNPUBLISHED)   BASSINGTHWAIGHTE (UNPUBLISHED)   ROSE, GORESKY, BACH (1977)

FIGURE 5.   Evolution of Krogh-cylinder type models for blood-tissue exchange.

which is derived in the next section. The mathematical description of the second component will be discussed in the following section.

As for the first component, one can see that the larger the PS_C/F_S, the smaller the nonextracted component, and the larger the F_s, the larger is this transmitted or throughout component. A large F_s reduces the contact time or the capillary transit time so that the time available for permeation is less. This concept was summarized by Perl, where the frequency function of transit times for the diffusible indicator is written as a sum of a transmitted fraction, T, traveling with the nonpermeating reference tracer, $h_R(t)$; and an exchanging fraction, E, which escapes and returns; a "tail function" having the form $h_E(t)$:

$$h_D(t) = T \cdot h_R(t) + E \cdot h_E(t) \tag{25}$$

where $T + E = 1.0$. Focusing on the transmitted fraction of the permeating tracer, which has the same shape of dilution curve as does the reference tracer, and ignoring the returning fraction, we have:

$$h_D(t) = T \cdot h_R(t) \tag{26}$$

or

$$1 - E = \frac{h_D(t)}{h_R(t)}$$

but $h_D(t)/h_R(t)$ is given by e^{-PS_C/F_S}, so that

$$1 - E = e^{-PS_c/F_s}$$

or

$$PS_c = -F_s \ln(1 - E) \tag{27}$$

as described by Bohr,[16] Renkin,[82] and Crone.[22]

As one can see, this computation of this extraction accounts for only unidirectional loss of tracer from blood across the capillary membrane, and the calculation of PS_c implicitly assumes that there is no return of tracer from an extravascular space back into the blood. It turns out that this is a fairly reasonable viewpoint when PS_c is small, i.e., when the extraction is small. One can see that when the fraction of tracer escaping from the blood is small, the likelihood of its return must also be small. In fact, the rate of return will be even smaller than the rate of loss, since the volume of the interstitial fluid is ordinarily larger than that of the capillary, i.e., $PS_c/V_I' < PS_c/V_c'$.

The rest of Figure 5 emphasizes the development occurring in our lab and in Goresky's laboratory for accounting for interstitial volumes and cell uptake and return of tracer from cell to ISF to blood. These will be discussed in detail in the later sections as we go into the mathematical aspects of these more complex models.

Another phenomenon not represented in the figure, but which is quite important for lipophilic tracers in vivo in the presence of red cells, is the "red cell carriage phenomenon". During transcapillary passage, tracer exchanges occur not only between plasma and ISF across the capillary membrane, but also between plasma and red cells. If this exchange is extremely rapid, then F_s is the sum of plasma flow plus red cell flow. However, if the time for complete exchange is nearly the same order of magnitude as the capillary transit time, the red cell exchange will influence the transcapillary exchange and the estimate of PS_c. A very nice analytical model describing this process was developed by Goresky, Bach, and Nadeau.[35] The effect of red cell carriage is twofold, first to sequester tracer within the red cells so it is not available for transport across the capillary membrane, and secondly to transport tracer more rapidly through the capillary than it would be if it were carried in the plasma alone. This second phenomenon of red cell trapping increasing the tracer velocity is due to the fact that red cells have higher velocities than does plasma simply because they lie more centrally in the flowing stream. (This observation serves also to remind us that the most simple Krogh cylinder analysis assuming plug flow is incorrect, that is, there is some velocity profile causing dispersion.) Roselli and Harris[88] have developed a numerical model which includes the red cell transport as well as the capillary and cell membrane transport. In general, the effects of red cell carriage have been ignored, and so we issue a plea for their consideration, especially with lipophilic substances and gases.

b. Interstitial Volume, V_I, and the Influence of "Back Diffusion" from ISF to Capillary on the Estimation of PS_c

Sangren and Sheppard[89] formulated a Krogh cylinder model that was complete in the sense that it accounted for the conservation of material passing through the unit. This is described by a pair of partial differential equations, one for the capillary:

$$\frac{\partial C_c}{\partial t} = \frac{-PS_c}{v_c V_c} (C_c - C_I) - \frac{F_s}{v_c V_c} \frac{\partial C_c}{\partial x'} \tag{28}$$

where x' is the fractional distance along the capillary ($x' = x/L$ dimensionless, where L is the capillary length), and one for the interstitial fluid region:

$$\frac{\partial C_I}{\partial t} = \frac{+PS_c}{v_I V_I} (C_c - C_I) \tag{29}$$

V_c and V_I are the total volumes (mℓ/g tissue) of the capillary and ISF and v_c and v_I are the fractional volumes (mℓ/mℓ) accessible to the solute in each region. The ratio of these volumes of distribution is γ:

$$\gamma = \frac{v_I V_I}{v_c V_c} = \frac{V_I'}{V_c'} \tag{30}$$

and V_I' and V_c' are the effective volumes of distribution. The conservation equation is written by substituting for $PS_c(C_c - C_I)$ in Equation 28 using Equation 29:

$$\frac{\partial C_c}{\partial t} + \frac{F_s}{v_c V_c} \frac{\partial C}{\partial x'} + \frac{\gamma \partial C_I}{\partial t} = 0 \tag{31}$$

$C_c = C_c(x',t)$ and $C_I = C_I(x',t)$ are the position- and time-dependent concentrations in the capillary and ISF. In a Krogh capillary-ISF unit in a hexagonal column configuration within an organ, the velocity per capillary length is

$$\frac{F_s}{v_c V_c} = \frac{F_B \rho 2\sqrt{3} R^2}{W(1 - v_v)\pi R_c^2} \tag{32}$$

F_B is total flow of blood, mℓ/sec, W is organ weight, g; ϱ is the specific gravity, g/mℓ, of the whole organ; R is the half-intercapillary distance, cm; v_v is the fractional volume of nonexchanging vessels in the organ, dimensionless; R_c is capillary radius, cm. The fractional volume of capillary available to solute is

$$v_c = (1 - Hct) + v_{rbc} \cdot Hct \tag{33}$$

and

$$F_s = v_c F_B / [W(1 - v_V)] \tag{34}$$

F_s is the flow of solute containing mother fluid per gram tissue excluding large vessels. Hct is the hematocrit (milliliter erythrocytes per milliliter blood), v_{rbc} is the fractional volume of erythrocytes freely accessible to solute (and with instantaneous equilibration with plasma), and v_c is the plasma fraction, $1 - Hct$, if $v_{rbc} = 0$. The velocity per unit length is the reciprocal of the capillary transit time τ:

$$\tau = \frac{v_c V_c}{F_s} \tag{35}$$

These equations are written in rather detailed form in order to emphasize two things: namely that most of the variables are measurable from experiments separate from the indicator dilution experiments, and secondly, that there are quite a few little things, such as the fractional volumes of distribution, which need to be taken into account in order to use the expressions precisely.

With the normalized outflow concentration-time curve

$$h_D(t) = \frac{F_s}{q_0} C(x' = 1) \tag{36}$$

the solution of Equation 31 is

$$h_D(t) = \delta(t - \tau_c)\, e^{-PS_c/F_s}$$

$$+ \exp\left(-\frac{PS_c}{F_s}\frac{t}{\gamma\tau_c}\right) \exp\left(-\frac{PS_c}{F_s}\left(1 - \frac{1}{\gamma}\right)\right) \sqrt{\frac{\left(\frac{PS_c}{F_s}\right)^2 \frac{1}{\gamma\tau_c}}{t - \tau_c}}\; I_1(\beta) \tag{37}$$

where

$$\gamma = v_I V_I / v_c V_c$$

and

$$\beta = 2\,\frac{PS_c}{F_s}\left(\frac{1}{\gamma}\left(t/\tau_c - 1\right)\right)^{1/2}$$

where $I_1(\beta)$ is a first order modified Bessel function. This is given in slightly different notation by Sheppard[93] and by Goresky, Ziegler, and Bach,[37] who give a complete derivation.

What the model does, as can be seen from the solution in Equation 37 is to consider the outflow to consist of two portions, an impulse delayed from the input by one capillary transit time and scaled in proportion to the nonexchanging fraction, and a tail portion which represents tracer which has escaped from the capillary into the interstitial space and returned from the ISF. The forms of these "tails" have been diagramed well by Goresky, Ziegler, and Bach.[37] When the permeability surface area product is small, then the earliest values of E(t) are small and the tail function is very close to being a single exponential with time constant equal to $v_I V_I/PS_c$. At higher values of PS_c, the initial E(t) is larger and the returning tracer comes out as a trailing wave. At all PS_c values the mean transit time for the permeating tracer is the flow divided by the volume of distribution, $V_c' + V_I'$. At the highest values of PS_c, the outflow $h_D(t)$ is a wave centered almost symmetrically around this mean transit time. In an isolated capillary-tissue unit, one could estimate the capillary volume and the interstitial volume by using two tracers simultaneously and observing each of their mean transit times. When one observes the outflow from a whole organ, then the observed total transit time is the sum of the transit times in large vessels of the capillary and the interstitial space, and ordinarily we do not have sufficient information to separate each of these components cleanly.

The Sangren-Sheppard equation reduces exactly to the Bohr-Renkin-Crone expression (Equation 1) when V_I is infinitely large. This can be seen from Equation 37 when the tail portion of the equation simply vanishes. Despite this nice development by Sangren and Sheppard,[89] the virtues of the equation were not generally appreciated, and the expression was not used in the early years of the multiple indicator dilution technique. Nevertheless, it was appreciated that some correction for back diffusion from ISF to capillary was needed. Martin and Yudilevich[71] worked out an approach which had the same basic ideas as is contained in the Sangren-Sheppard expression, but with one further assumption. Instead of assuming that the capillaries were long and therefore that there would be gradients within the capillary and the interstitial fluid, they made an assumption that the interstitial fluid region would be more or less uniform in concentration and that the back diffusion would be proportional to this average concentration in the ISF. They reasoned further that the back diffusion would be greater at longer times after the initial appearance of the indicator in the outflow, and therefore derived an integral expression which accounted for this accumulation in the ISF. They extrapolated the observed data points linearly back to the time of initial appearance in order to estimate an initial extraction which was assumed to be nearly independent of any back diffusion and from which PS_C was calculated.

The fundamental assumption of the Yudilevich correction for tracer-return is that the interstitial space is a mixing chamber, which does not account for spatial gradients in concentration, but the error due to this assumption probably caused errors in PS_C estimates of less than 20% compared with the Sangren-Sheppard equation, of which they were apparently unaware.

Ziegler and Goresky[117,118] took the development to the next stage beyond that of Sangren and Sheppard. In their model they accounted for F_S, the flow along the capillary, PS_C, V'_i, and PS_M the permeability-surface area product defining unidirectional flux from ISF into cell, but did not account for return of tracer from the cell. This model, like the Sangren-Sheppard model, is distributed in space along the capillary length and when PS_M was set to 0, it becomes exactly the Sangren-Sheppard expression, without axial diffusion.

They fitted the model to curves for albumin and rubidium injected simultaneously into the inflow of the dog heart and obtained estimates of PS_C, V'_i/V'_c as a ratio and of PS_M. One of their published figures is shown reproduced in Figure 6. The fitting of the model to the data automatically provides a back diffusion correction. One of the limitations to the model is that it accounts for the tracer flux into the cell but not for its return, so that it does not account for mass balance. It also had the virtue providing estimates of PS_C and of V'_i which were not dependent solely on the initial values, but rather based on fitting the whole of the curve. Since the tracers used were not the same ones as had been used by Yudilevich et al.,[1,113,116] it is not practical to attempt to compare the estimates by the two techniques, and such a comparison was not made by Ziegler and Goresky.

The 1970 model developed by Bassingthwaighte, Knopp, and Hazelrig[11] was mass-conservative and accounted for back diffusion, but was so tedious to compute that it was not very practical for analyzing data. Therefore, a simplified model, eliminating the radial diffusion terms, was derived from it. This model provides outflow concentration-time curves for different input functions: impulse-injection, continuous infusion, and experimental driven input functions. Within the capillary-tissue region is assumed:

1. Plug flow, finite axial diffusion (different for the individual indicators), and instantaneous radial diffusion in the capillary
2. An endothelial barrier with finite permeability which can vary along the length of the capillary
3. A stagnant extravascular region with finite axial and infinite radial diffusion
4. Explicit definitions of distribution volumes of the indicators accounting for volume exclusion and apparent solubilities in the separate regions

The geometrical representation of the model is as diagramed in Figure 4. One-dimensional diffusion equations were solved for the concentrations in the capillary and in the extravascular region using a finite difference technique. The parameters of the model were controlled and modified by the interactive simulation program SIMCON.[3] The model was extended in 1978[48] to a complete description of the concentration within the capillary, interstitial, and cellular spaces.

The cellular uptake of glucose and rubidium was estimated by Goresky et al.[33] for

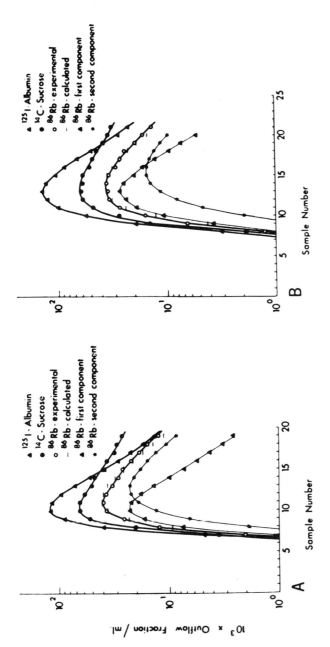

FIGURE 6. Experimental and calculated ^{86}Rb curves. The ordinate on this illustration is logarithmic. In each instance the curves have been resolved into throughput (the first component) and exchanging indicator (the second component). The latter corresponds to that indicator which has left the vascular space, which has not been taken up by the muscle cells, and which has then returned to the vascular space. It should be noted that the calculated first component of the ^{86}Rb curve, derived by use of the present modeling, is identical in shape to that of the vascular reference curve. (From Ziegler, W. H. and Goresky, C. A., *Circ. Res.*, 29, 208, 1971b. With permission of the American Heart Association.)

the liver. A model of the special anatomical situation of a single sinusoid was formulated: the blood flows through the sinusoid which is surrounded by the extracellular space of Disse. The extracellular space is freely accessible to solutes through the fenestrated sinusoidal endothelium which means that exchange is only limited by flow. The barrier limitation for Rb and glucose occurs at the hepatocyte membrane. The conservation equation was solved for the solute concentration in the sinusoid and in the cell for unsequestered material. The extracellular concentration equals the sinusoid concentration multiplied by the partition coefficient of the substance in the space of Disse. An analytical solution was obtained for the Dirac delta function as impulse input by applying the Laplace transformation.

The complete description of the capillary-interstitial-cellular exchange was accomplished by Rose, Goresky, and Bach.[87] Their model was formulated for barrier limitations at both the capillary wall and at the cellular membrane and added the expression for irreversible sequestration within the intracellular space, as diagrammed in Figure 2.

The following assumptions must be considered to solve the set of differential equations:

1. There is no concentration gradient perpendicular to the capillary in the extracellular or cellular space (as with earlier models)
2. Diffusion parallel to the capillary is zero
3. There is plug flow in the capillary

The concentrations of the substance under consideration are $C_c(x,t)$ $C_I(x,t)$, $C_M(x,t)$ in the capillary, extracellular, and intracellular spaces, being one-dimensional in space in accordance with the assumptions. With F_s/v_cV_c as the velocity of blood flow in the capillary and γ and θ as the relative distribution spaces, extracellular and intracellular, as defined in Figure 2, then three partial differential equations can be formulated:

1. Equation for conservation of matter:

$$\frac{\delta C_c}{\delta t} + \frac{F_s L}{v_c V_c} \frac{\delta C_c}{\delta x} + \gamma \frac{\delta C_I}{\delta t} + \theta \frac{\delta C_M}{\delta t} + K_{seq} \theta C_M = 0 \qquad (38)$$

2. Rate equation for accumulation in the extracellular space

$$\frac{v_I' \delta C_I}{\delta t} = P_{c1} S_c C_c - P_{c2} S_c C_I - P_{M3} S_M C_I + P_{M4} S_M C_M \qquad (39)$$

3. Rate equation for accumulation in the intracellular space

$$\frac{v_M' \delta C_M}{\delta t} = P_{M3} S_M C_I - P_{M4} S_M C_M - K_{seq} v_M' C_M \qquad (40)$$

where P_{c1} and P_{c2} are capillary permeability coefficients from plasma to ISF and vice versa, and P_{M3} and P_{M4} are the permeability coefficients for transfer into and out of the cell, and S_c and S_M are the capillary and cell surface areas, cm²/g.

These three partial differential equations have to be solved simultaneously. Rose, Goresky, and Bach used the Laplace transformation to obtain a solution for a bolus-input approximated by a δ-function in a capillary of length L. The initial conditions are that the concentrations everywhere are zero except that an impulse input of mass q_0 is introduced into the capillary entrance at $t = 0$.

The solution at the outflow end, $x = L$, of a single capillary is given by:

$$C_c(L, t) = \frac{q_0}{F_c} e^{-k_1 \gamma \tau} \delta(t - \tau) + \frac{q_0}{F_c} e^{-k_1 \gamma \tau}$$

$$\times \left[\left\{ e^{d(t-\tau)} \sqrt{\gamma k_1 k_2 \tau A'/(t - \tau)} \; I_1 [2\sqrt{\gamma k_1 k_2 \tau A'(t - \tau)}] \right. \right.$$

$$\left. + e^{f(t-\tau)} \sqrt{\gamma k_1 k_2 \tau B'/(t - \tau)} \; I_1 [2\sqrt{\gamma k_1 k_2 \tau B'(t - \tau)}] \right\} S(t - \tau)$$

$$+ \int_\tau^t e^{d(\lambda-\tau)} \sqrt{\gamma k_1 k_2 \tau A'/(\lambda - \tau)} \; I_1 [2\sqrt{\gamma k_1 k_2 \tau A'(\lambda - \tau)}]$$

$$\left. \times \; e^{f(t-\lambda)} \sqrt{\gamma k_1 k_2 \tau B'/(t - \lambda)} \; I_1 [2\sqrt{\gamma k_1 k_2 \tau B'(t - \lambda)}] \; d\lambda \right] \tag{41}$$

where $K_1 = P_{c1}S_c/V_I'$, $K_2 = P_{c2}S_c/V_I'$, $K_3 = P_{M3}S_M/V_I'$, $K_4 = P_{M4}S_M/V_I'$, $K_5 = K_{SEQ}$, and where $I_1[r]$ is a first order modified Bessel function with argument r and where d and f are the roots of the quadratic equation,

$$s^2 + [k_2 + k_3 + (\gamma/\vartheta)k_4 + k_5]s + ((\gamma/\theta))k_2 k_4 + k_2 k_5 + k_3 k_5 = 0$$

$$A' = \frac{d + (\gamma/\theta)k_4 + k_5}{d - f}$$

$$B' = \frac{f + (\gamma/\theta)k_4 + k_5}{f - d}$$

$\delta(t-\tau)$ is the Dirac delta function delayed 1 capillary transit time, $S(t - \tau)$ is the unit step function starting at $t = \tau$ and being zero previously, and λ is a dummy variable of integration, in the integral concerning the intracellular accumulation, and where τ is the transit time, V_c'/F_s. This equation represents the solution for a single capillary. Multicapillary approaches are discussed later.

A different approach for the solution of the three partial differential equations was used by Holloway, Williams, and Levin,[48] applying the finite difference technique of Bassingthwaighte.[6] With the numerical technique, the permeability could be varied with position along the capillary. This procedure also enabled the incorporation of the axial diffusion, but its contribution was, for most substances, small.

A definitive attempt to provide a simple expression for correcting for back diffusion was presented by Guller et al.[41] In this study, they used the Krogh capillary-ISF model developed by Bassingthwaighte[6] which included axial diffusion, but which was otherwise similar to that of Sangren and Sheppard.[89] They fitted observed pairs of albumin and ^{24}Na outflow dilution curves from the dog heart to solutions from the model. The model utilized the observed albumin dilution curve shifted to the left in time by one capillary transit time as the input function to the model for the sodium which permeated the capillary membrane. It was assumed that there was no cellular uptake, so that the model was complete and self-sufficient without a cellular component. It was found that the estimates of PS_c obtained via fitting the model to the data were universally higher than those obtained using the Crone expression. An empirical graphical relationship was developed between the observations of one minus the extraction at the time of the peak of the albumin curve, and of the value for PS_c/F_s obtained via the model fitting. From the set of data for the sodium dilution curves, it was observed that the data deviated from the Renkin-Crone expression, Equation 1, in a direction and by an amount best described by back diffusion from an extravascular volume of distribution of 0.21 mℓ/g. Linearization of this plot led to a modified equation which gives a back diffusion correction for the estimate of PS for sodium:

$$PS'_c = -F_s \log(1 - 1.14E) \qquad (42)$$

where E is the peak value of E(t) as defined by Equation 19. Thus, for the observed extractions of sodium ranging from 30 to 70%, this expression gave estimates of PS_c essentially compatible with those given by the model fitted to the data, shown in Figure 7, but without requiring the extensive computer work for fitting model to data. Equation 42 is therefore adequate for sodium in the heart, and it is reasonable to search for similar simple analyses for other solutes in the heart and other organs.

3. Multicapillary Analysis
a. Heterogeneity of Flows

The heart is a compact organ, more or less uniform in function and in its anatomy, nevertheless, there is marked heterogeneity of regional flows. This is illustrated in Figure 8, which shows a rather symmetrical probability density function of local regional blood flows relative to the average blood flow for the heart. The standard deviation divided by the mean flow was 0.4, calculated on the dividing of the heart into about 200 pieces (168 LV, and about 27 RV and 14 atrial), which, for a 60-g heart, meant that the average piece weighed about 0.3 g. Must one account for this known, and consistently measurable, heterogeneity in order to obtain accurate, unbiased estimates of the exchange coefficients? The answer is yes.

b. Errors in Estimation of PS$_C$ Due to Heterogeneity of Flow

Clearly, the local value for F_S, mℓ g^{-1} min, influences the exchange and therefore the estimation of PS_c in each region; this can be seen directly from the simplest equation for estimating $PS_C = -F_s \log_E (1 - E)$, as described above. The relationship between E, F_s, and PS_C is nonlinear such that the extraction is more sensitive to flow at low F_s than at high F_s, as seen in Figure 9. Because of the nonlinearity, the presence of heterogeneity leads to estimates of PS_C biased downward erroneously.

A numerical test of this idea can be constructed as in Figure 10 using the Crone-Renkin equation (Equation 1) to calculate the expected values of extraction, E_i in each of 7 independent parallel pathways. The approximately weighted flow average of the E_i is given by $\overline{E} = \Sigma w_i f_i E_i = 0.611$, which is smaller than the extraction at the mean flow (at $f_i = 1.0$), which was 0.632. The estimate of PS'_c from this "observed" E = 0.611 gives $PS'_c = 0.945$. The direction of the error, underestimation by 5.5%, is in the expected direction but could hardly be termed large. However, the "model" used for this test is inadequate, not accounting for back diffusion, and, therefore, this result should ideally be backed up by a more definitive test using more reasonable models. Furthermore, this test is of no value in assessing the degree of error in the cell uptake rate PS_M. Such tests require formulation of multicapillary models in which each capillary is complete, accounting not only for PS_C, but also back diffusion and cellular uptake.

c. Models for Heterogeneity of Flow

A model for heterogeneous flow is shown in Figure 11. The principle is that dispersion and delay in the arterial and venous components of the organs' vasculature are completely independent of the transit time through the individual capillary. The rationalization is based on our observations (implied in the figures of Bassingthwaigthte, Yipintsoi, and Harvey[3]) that intercapillary distances and lengths appear to be similar

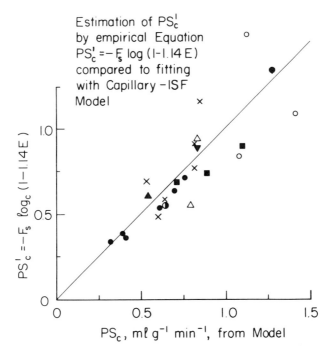

FIGURE 7. Comparison of estimates of PS_c obtained from the expression $PS'_c = F_s \log_e(1 - 1.14E)$ with the values of PS_c obtained by fitting a capillary-ISF Krogh cylinder type model to the observed indicator dilution curve. Data were obtained from isolated blood-perfused dog hearts and are from Table 2 of Guller et al.,[41] columns 17 and 18.

in regions at the base and the apex of the heart, i.e., whether linked to short or long arterial vessels, and that flows per gram tissue in the various regions are not dependent on the length of the supplying arteries. An additional factor making this a good approximation in the heart is that regions with long arterial inflows have relatively short venous outflows, and vice versa, so that the total large vessel transport functions may be reasonably similar for all capillary-tissue regions.

This is model I, with independence of h_A, h_v, and h_C. Because of this independence, convolution of the transport processes of the separate axial segments of the system is appropriate. For the total transport function,

$$h(t) = h_A(t) * \left[\sum_{i=1}^{N} w_i \, f_i \, h_{c_i}(t) \right] * h_v(t) \tag{43}$$

For large vessels, since convolution is commutative (the sequence of operations can be taken in any order),

$$h_{LV}(t) = h_A(t) * h_v(t) \tag{44}$$

The transport function of the set of capillaries in parallel is the sum of their individual transport function, weighted by the relative amount of flow through each type of pathway:

$$h_c(t) = \sum_{i=1}^{N} w_i \, f_i \, h_{c_i}(t) \tag{45}$$

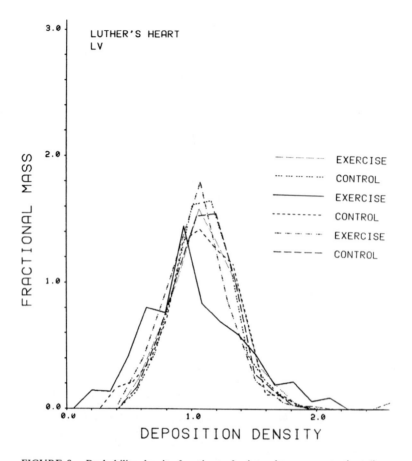

FIGURE 8.   Probability density functions of microsphere concentrations (indicating relative regional flows) in the left ventricular myocardium in an awake baboon at rest and during leg bicycle exercise. The abscissa is density of deposition relative to the mean density and is interpreted as regional flow divided by the mean flow: the ordinate gives the fraction of the left ventricular mass with a specified flow. The distributions are spread fairly symmetrically, with standard deviations of about 35%. The exercise levels were not very strenuous so that the coronary flows only doubled at the highest exercise levels.

When $h_C(t)$ is for a single capillary, which in our model has no dispersion, then $h_{LV}(t)$ is the shape of the reference concentration-time curve $h_R(t)$ shifted to the left by one capillary transit time, that is, $h_{LV}(t) = h_R(t + \tau)$. For the multicapillary situation each element of the $h_{LV}(t)$ can be defined by a similar time shift:

$$w_i\, f_i\, h_{LV_i}(t) = w_i\, f_i\, h_R(t + \tau_i) \qquad (46)$$

where the $w_i f_i$ is used to emphasize that each fraction of the tracer is so shifted. From this, the expression for any permeating or nonpermeating tracer is

$$h(t) = \sum_i h_{LV_i} * w_i\, f_i\, h_{c_i}(t) \qquad (47)$$

To demonstrate the applicability of this to the reference tracer, we substitute the definition from Equation 46 and use the knowledge that the capillary impulse response $h_{c_i}(t)$ for an intravascular tracer is $\delta(t - \tau_i)$,

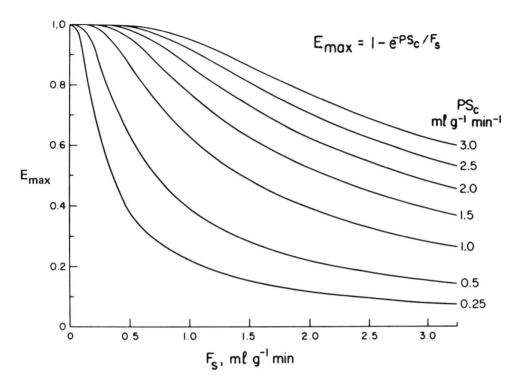

FIGURE 9. The effect of flow and permeability on extraction during transcapillary passage in a system in which there is no return of tracer from the ISF to the effluent blood. E_{max} is the same as E in Equation 1, the peak of E(t) of Equation 19.

Computation of Error in PS_c Estimation Due to Heterogeneity of Flow (No back diffusion; $PS_c = -F_s \log_e (1-E)$)

$\Delta f_i = 0.2$

fractional mass per 0.2 $\bar{f}$

$w_i = w'_i \cdot \Delta f_i$

f_i	w_i	$w_i f_i$	E_i	$w_i f_i E_i$
0.4	0.0625	0.025	0.92	0.023
0.6	0.125	0.075	0.81	0.061
0.8	0.1875	0.150	0.71	0.107
1.0	0.250	0.250	0.63	0.158
1.2	0.1875	0.225	0.57	0.127
1.4	0.125	0.175	0.51	0.089
1.6	0.0625	0.100	0.46	0.046
$\Sigma =$	1.0	1.0		$\bar{E} = 0.611$

f_i, relative flow in region i

Actual $PS_c / \bar{F}_s = 1.0$; Relative Dispersion of f_i's = 33%

Calculated $PS'_c / \bar{F}_s = -\ln(1-\bar{E}) = -\ln(1-0.611) = 0.945$

i.e. Error = -5.5%

FIGURE 10. Computation of error in PS_c estimation due to heterogeneity of flow using the Renkin-Crone equation $PS_c = -F_s \log_e (1 - \bar{E})$, where $\bar{E}$ is the "observed" average extraction. The E_i are calculated from the equation for each of the regional flows, F_i, for the specific case where $PS_c/F_s = 1.0$. The probability density function of regional flows is w'(f), or $W'_i(f_i)$ in finite histogram form, and $w_i = w'_i \Delta f_i$.

Capillary – Tissue Transport Model: Transport Functions in Capillaries and Large Vessels Independent

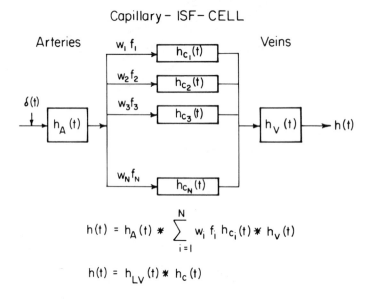

Capillary – ISF – CELL

$$h(t) = h_A(t) * \sum_{i=1}^{N} w_i f_i h_{c_i}(t) * h_V(t)$$

$$h(t) = h_{LV}(t) * h_c(t)$$

FIGURE 11. Model for exchange in an organ in which the transport functions of the arteries and veins, $h_A(t)$ and $h_V(t)$, are independent of those in a set of capillary-tissue regions, the $h_{c_i}(t)$s. The capillary-tissue regions are considered to be alike except for their relative flows, the f_is; the fraction of the organ mass having flow f_i is w_i is that the fraction of tracer traversing a region with flow f_i is $w_i f_i$. The asterisk denotes the process of convolution. The large vessel transport function $h_{LV}(t)$ is $h_A(t)*h_V(t)$. This is model I, Equation 48.

$$h_R(t) = \sum_i \left[h_R(t + \tau_i) * \left(w_i f_i \, \delta(t - \tau_i) \right) \right]$$

$$= \sum_i w_i f_i h_R(t + \tau_i) * \delta(t - \tau_i)$$

$$= \sum_i w_i f_i h_R(t)$$

$$= h_R(t)$$

An equally reasonable alternative to defining the input to each capillary separately is to deconvolute the observed $h_R(t)$ with the reference capillary transport function, $\sum_i w_i f_w \delta(t - \tau_i)$. To obtain a single input function $h_{LV}(t)$ which enters all capillaries. In this case, this $h_{LV}(t)$ is less dispersed than $h_R(t)$; it gives rise to the equations in Figure 11, so that as an alternative to Equation 47 we have the expression for model 1

$$h(t) = h_{LV}(t)*h_c(t) \qquad (48)$$

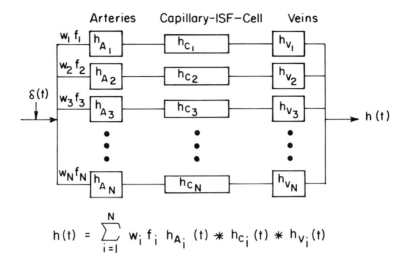

$$h(t) = \sum_{i=1}^{N} w_i \, f_i \, h_{A_i}(t) * h_{c_i}(t) * h_{v_i}(t)$$

FIGURE 12. Capillary-tissue transport model with linear relationship between transit times in large vessels and in capillaries. In the special case of this model used by Rose and Goresky (1976 and their subsequent papers), they considered all vascular pathways to be nondispersive so that $h_i(t) = \delta(t - \tau_{Lv_i} - \tau_{c_i})$, where τ_{Lv_i} is the sum of the arterial and venous transit times through pathway i. Our more general form as in Equation 49, would allow for any form of h_A, h_c, or h_v that is linear, stationary, and mass conservative; this is model II.

Model II, shown in Figure 12, is different from model I in that that there is an individual large vessel pathway associated with each type of capillary pathway, as was the case in Equation 47:

$$h(t) = \sum w_i f_i \, h_{A_i}(t) * h_{c_i}(t) * h_{v_i}(t) \tag{49}$$

The idea is that each capillary-tissue region with a mean intracapillary transit time τ_{c_i}, is associated uniquely with a specific mean transit time through large vessels, $\tau_{L_{v_i}}$ such that the slower flowing capillaries are supplied and drained by arteries and veins with longer transit times. That is to say, there is a precisely ordered association of long LV transit times with long capillary transit times, and of short LV times with short capillary times. The components of this model may be dispersive (with variation in transit times around the mean) or nondispersive (piston or plug flow). The nondispersive case has been thoroughly described for fitting transcoronary transport functions by Rose and Goresky,[85] making the explicit assumption that there is no axial dispersion in large vessels or capillaries. We consider this assumption to be an undesirable complicating factor because it is contrary to one's notions and observations with respect to axial dispersion via diffusion, red cell rotation, velocity profiles, eddies at branches, etc., but we recognize the mathematical simplicity which is allowed by having a single transit time in each pathway. As they define it, the observed albumin (the nonpermeating reference) outflow dilution curve at any time, t, is the result of transit through a parallel set of nondispersive large vessels and capillaries in series. For each pathway, the total transit time, τ_i, is the sum of the large vessel and capillary transit times:

$$\tau_i = \tau_{c_i} + \tau_{LV_i}$$

or in general

$$\tau = \tau_c(t) + \tau_{LV}(t) = t \tag{50}$$

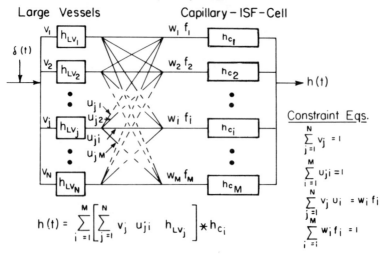

FIGURE 13.   Capillary - tissue transport model III with variable degree of association between transport functions of large vessels and capillaries. The large vessel transit times may be nondispersive, $h_{LV_i}(t) = \delta(t - \tau_{LV_i})$, or dispersive. When they are nondispersive, when N = M, and u_{ji} = 1.0 for all j = i and u_{ji} = 0 for all j ≠ i, then this model is identical to Model II, that of Rose and Goresky.[85] When all $h_{LV_i}(t)$ are dispersive and identical, then the model is the same as that in Figure 11, model I.

where τ_C and τ_{LV} are both linearly increasing functions and their sum is the observation time t. The next condition is that the relation between them is given by:

$$\tau_c(t) = \underline{a} + \underline{b}t \text{ for } t > t_{min} \tag{51}$$

The values for $\underline{a}$ and $\underline{b}$ were found by Rose and Goresky by fitting sucrose outflow dilution curves with the model of Figure 12 using as input to each capillary a Dirac delta function (unit impulse) at $t' = t - \tau_c(t)$ weighted by the value of $h_R(t)$ at that time, t. Their success in fitting the curves was well demonstrated, an experience which we have reproduced with their program on our computer using our data. A nagging problem with this model, in addition to the unrealistic assumption of nondispersive velocity profiles, is that some of the estimates of minimum capillary transit times appear impossibly long. For example, from their data (Table using their third model with parameter $K_1\gamma$ = 0.1 sec^{-1} and calculating a minimum $\tau_c = \underline{a}/K_1\gamma$) we calculate that in two cases their minimum $\tau_c s$ were 3 and 7 sec. Since all the rest of the capillary transit times were longer than these, these times seem unreasonably long, especially compared to the *average* capillary transit time, calculated according to Equation 35.

We look upon the models of Figures 11 and 12 as being at opposite ends of a spectrum of models having varying degrees of interdependence of large vessel and capillary transit times and a considerable range of possible values for intravascular dispersion. A more general formulation is given in Figure 13. Because of lack of detailed information on intra-organ dispersion, this model can only be used by making certain assumptions about either the forms of the large vessel transport functions, $h_{LV_i}(t)$, and their relationship to each other, or of the probability density functions for the distri-

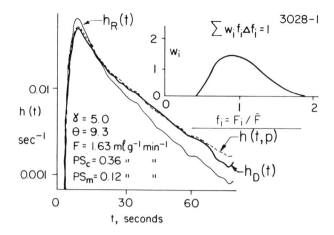

FIGURE 14.   Transcoronary transport functions for albumin, $h_R(t)$, and 2-deoxy-D-glucose, $h_D(t)$ in an isolated perfused heart. The spline-smoothed microsphere deposition density function, $w_i(f_i)$, giving the relative regional flows, f_i, and the fraction of total flow to each type of region, $w_i f_i$, (comparable to Figure 8), is shown in the insert. The mean F_s was 1.63 mℓ g^{-1} min^{-1}, hematocrit 16%, and there was no vasodilator. The relative dispersion of the f_ss was 0.31. Parameter values for this fit were $PS_C = 0.36$ mℓ g^{-1} min^{-1}, $V_I'/V_C' = 5.0$, $PS_M = 0.12$ mℓ g^{-1} min^{-1}, and the coefficient variation of the fit was 0.067.

bution from each of the $h_{LV_j}(t)$s to the $h_{c_i}(t)$s (js and is are used for large vessel and capillary indexes).

Thus we have three possible general types of heterogeneity models, the latter of which really includes the first two and which has not been defined in a very specific fashion. This is a field for further research.

Each of these models of heterogeneity should be compared with observed data, preferably multiple indicator dilution curves with simultaneously obtained microsphere distribution profiles, in order to determine which might be more realistic. The use of microspheres in such experiments is not yet general, but our first results using model I are shown in Figure 14.

In order to test the influence of heterogeneity on the estimate of PS_C provided via each of these models, Levin generated a pseudo-Gaussian distribution function (Gaussian with 7 class sized) in flows and generated model indicator dilution curves with constant PS_C but with the variation in regional flows, f_is with relative dispersions (SD/mean) from 0 up to 50%. Using model I as a test case, the best fits of a single capillary model to the test curves were obtained for two situations, one with V_I'/V_C' fixed at the same value used to generate the heterogeneous test curves, and the other with V_I'/V_C' as a free parameter. For this test $PS_M = 0$. The results are shown in Figure 15.

It is evident that PS_C is underestimated by using the single capillary model to fit the multicapillary data, and that the error is increased with greater heterogeneity. The error, with $PS_C/F_s = 1$, is 16% with a relative dispersion of f_i of 30%, which is about the physiological range. Since this test is on virtually noise-free "data" generated from a seven-pathway model, the error on actual data will presumably be greater.

When both PS_C and V_I'/V_C' are free to be varied in the fitting procedure, the fitting is improved, the coefficient of variation between $h_D'(t)$ and $h_D(t)$ is reduced. This is the mathematical expectation, namely that increasing the degrees of freedom in a model allows for a better fit. Note that values of PS_C are only very slightly improved with V_I'/V_C' free to vary, indicating that the dominant sensitivity is to PS_C.

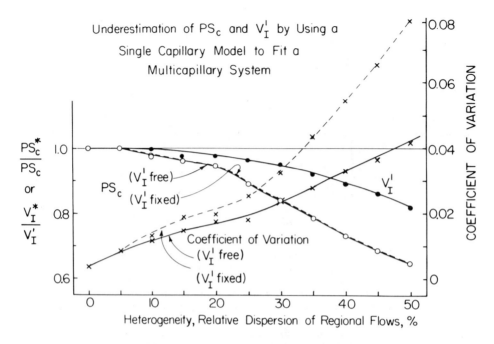

FIGURE 15.   Underestimation of PS_C and V'_I by failure to account for heterogeneity of regional flows. Estimates of PS_C were obtained using a single capillary model to fit to "observed" concentration-time curves which had been generated from a multicapillary model with fixed PS_C and V'_I, but with heterogeneity of regional flows. The abscissa is the relative dispersion of the flows, the standard deviation of a Gaussian distribution of regional flows (partitioned into 7 regions) divided by the mean flow. The single capillary-ISF-cell equation is that of Rose, Goresky, and Bach,[86] our Equation 41 with PS_C of 1.0 ml g^{-1} min^{-1}, V'_I/V'_c of 5.0, PS_M or zero. The heterogeneity model is Model I, with parallel noninteractive capillary units of varied flows all having the same large vessel transport functions, as diagrammed in Figure 11. The input function defining the large vessel transport function $h_{LV}(t)$, was a lagged normal density curve with $\sigma = 1.0$, $\tau = 1.5$ and $t_c = 8.5$ sec in the terminology of Bassingthwaighte, Ackerman, and Wood.[8]

The main point of this section is that taking the heterogeneity into account is important in analyzing multiple indicator dilution curves. The difficulties remaining are in assessing the heterogeneity and using it in estimating the permeabilities and volumes.

Levin et al.[65] performed another test on a set of multiple indicator dilution curves obtained from an isolated dog heart. The permeant tracer was sucrose, assumed not to enter myocytes, so that $PS_M = 0$. The degree of heterogeneity was treated as an unknown parameter, along with PS_C and V'_I/V'_c. The results in Figure 16 show that the best fit was obtained with a relative dispersion of regional flows of 25%. In this particular experiment, no microsphere data were available for a direct comparison with the computed best fit, but since heterogeneity of microsphere densities in these hearts is 30 to 35%, it would appear that the estimate of 25% is reasonable. This introduces the possibility of estimating it routinely from the outflow dilution curves; if this could be done with sufficient accuracy in the estimates of the parameters of interest, particularly PS_C, V'_I/V'_c, and PS_M, then the multiple indicator dilution technique could be used for repeated assessment of heterogeneity as well as of other parameters without resorting to the destructive technique of measuring the deposition densities of microspheres. At this time, this should be considered merely as a hope, but the initial result shown in Figure 16 at least points out that the procedure should be investigated.

The error in PS_C over the physiological range of interest is approximately constant, as shown in Figure 17. The degree of heterogeneity (at 30%) V'_I/V'_c (at 5.0) was held

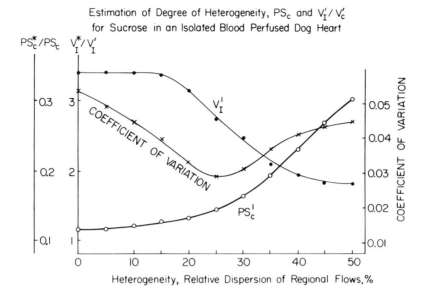

FIGURE 16. Estimation of degree of heterogeneity and of other parameters, PS_c and V'_i / V'_c, for the best fit of a multicapillary model to a coronary outflow dilution curve from a dog heart. The best estimates are: heterogeneity of 25%, $PS_c = 0.15$ mℓ g^{-1} min^{-1}, and V'_i / V'_c or $\gamma = 2.8$.

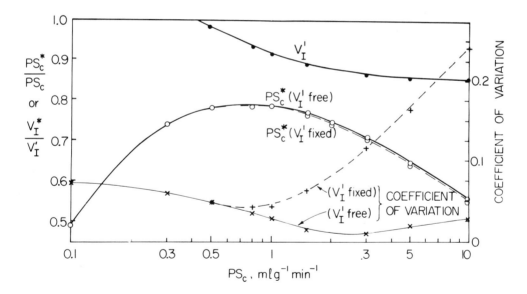

FIGURE 17. Constancy of error in estimation of PS_c when using a single capillary model to fit multicapillary data. The multicapillary test data were generated using Model I with a relative dispersion of regional flows of 35%, $F_s = 1$ mℓ g^{-1} min^{-1}, $V'_i / V'_c = 5.0$, and PS_c different for each case. Although the single capillary model fits the test data better when V'_i is free, the improvement is slight. The error in PS'_c is approximately 23% over the range of true PS_c from 0.5 to 2.0 mℓ g^{-1} min^{-1}.

constant while the true PS_c was varied in generating the sets of test curves. As before, a single capillary model was fitted to each of the multicapillary sets of test curves by adjusting parameters. As in Figure 15, two situations were examined, adjusting PS^*_c while holding V'_i / V'_c at the true value, or adjusting PS^*_c and V^*_i. The latter gave slightly better fits, as expected, but again, the best values of PS_c were little affected by freezing up V_i'. The interesting feature is the constancy of the underestimating of PS_C, about 23% over the range from 0.3 to 2.0 mℓ g^{-1} min^{-1}.

4. Estimation of Flow from Deposited Tracers
a. Flow Estimation from Outflow, C(t), or Residue Function, R(t)

The estimation of cardiac output or of organ blood flow or of regional blood flows within an organ are all based on the principle of conservation of mass. The technique described by Fick[29] for measuring cardiac output by A-V oxygen differences was generalized in an important way by Stewart[98,101] to show that flow can be measured at a relevant point or points in the circulation. By using a bolus (pulse) injection, the resultant indicator dilution curve can, in many circumstances, be obtained without any contamination due to recirculation, in which case the flow can be calculated by measuring the area under the recorded indicator dilution curve:

$$F = q_0 / \int_0^\infty C_o(t)\,dt \qquad (52)$$

where F is the flow in milliliters per second, q_0 is the injected mass of indicator, and $C_0(t)$ is the concentration, gram per milliliter recorded at a representative outflow point, and time, t, is in seconds.

In 1929, Hamilton et al.[42] refined this technique so that it could be applied for the measurement of cardiac output in an intact animal. Their technique, which was supported by experiments in hydraulic recirculating models, was to assume that the downslope of the indicator dilution curve had a monoexponential form. Recirculated tracer, which was masking the later part of the tail of the curve, was excluded by plotting the early part of the downslope on semilogarithmic paper, and extrapolating it linearly to later times. This identified the primary, or first pass, indicator. The relevant area to be used in the equation above is therefore the area underneath the primary curve. This approach, with the monoexponential extrapolation, is known as the Stewart-Hamilton indicator dilution technique for estimating flow.

The general theory for indicator dilution was outlined by Stephenson[97] and then described explicitly for the measurement of cardiac output by Meier and Zierler.[73] In these papers, some theoretical considerations were given for unsteady flow and for recirculation, and in both the conditions under which the specific theory held true was carefully outlined.

The theory has been substantially extended. In 1965, Zierler[121] showed the use of the same principle for measuring flow by external detection. The problems related to unsteady flow in the circulation for the Fick technique were identified in principle and with some special examples by Visscher and Johnson.[109] Cropp and Burton[24] identified the problems in the constant rate indicator dilution technique that occurred when the flow was unsteady. Bassingthwaighte et al.[10] showed the influences of the phase at which injection is made during unsteady sinusoidal flow, and of the frequency of the sinusoidal variation in flow on the estimation of flow, mean transit time, and of mean transit time volume from the observable indicator dilution curves. All of the above authors observed, as was predicted by Zierler,[119] that at very high frequencies of flow variation there was little error in the estimates, but at low frequencies the variation causes systematic errors in the estimates.

Washout methods of estimating flow per unit volume of tissue were established by Kety.[55] Kety's technique was based on the assumption that the indicator was wholly and completely mixed within the organ at all moments (as for lumped compartmental analysis), and that washout was proportional to the flow through the organ, the classic flow-limited case. The method was perhaps too well accepted initially, but there is no doubt that it made a very substantial contribution, providing estimates of flows from organs that had been hitherto unavailable. Zierler[121] generalized the methods showing that the residue function gave the flow per unit volume as discussed in an earlier section, which removed the need for the assumption that the uniform was wholly and instantaneously mixed throughout. Zierler's technique was to compute the area under the residue function curve to infinity giving an estimate of the plasma flow per gram of tissue F_p,

$$F_p = \frac{\lambda_p \text{ Height}}{\rho \text{ Area}} = \frac{\lambda_p}{\rho} R(0)/\int_0^\infty R(t)dt \qquad (53)$$

where λ_p is the tissue-plasma partition coefficient, the ratio at equilibrium of the concentration in the tissue to that in the plasma, and ϱ is the tissue specific gravity. Hoedt-Rasmussen et al.[47] and Bassingthwaighte, Strandell, and Donald[12] provided modifications of the height over area technique which accounted for prolonged and unmeasurable tails or recirculation. This was done by stopping the integration at a time, T, and assuming that the rest of the curve beyond T was monoexponential. This approach is strictly analogous to that used by Hamilton et al.[42] in finding a correction for recirculation of the bolus injection technique. The formula most commonly used is

$$F_p = \frac{\lambda_p[R(0) - R(T)]}{\rho \int_0^T R(t)dt} \qquad (54)$$

b. Deposition and Uptake Techniques

Kety, with Schmidt,[56] pioneered again with a technique for measuring flow per unit volume from the integral of the amount of tracer extracted during passage through the capillary bed of an organ. This Kety-Schmidt technique was demonstrated to be of value for cerebral blood flow, and has since been applied to many organs. The technique was to integrate the arteriovenous difference as a function of time after changing the concentration in the inflowing arterial blood until equilibrium was reached. The calculation for the blood flow per gram of tissue, F_B, is

$$F_b = \frac{\lambda_b C_A(\infty)}{\rho \int_0^\infty [C_A(t) - C_V(t)] \, dt} \qquad (55)$$

where λ_b is the tissue-blood partition coefficient, $C_A(\infty)$ is the equilibrium concentration during a steady-state with no A-V difference, and C_A and C_V are the inflowing arterial and outflowing venous blood concentrations. The idea is essentially similar to that of the residue function analysis, but is more general in that it allows for a gradual change in inflowing concentration, whereas in Equation 53, the idea is that the material or tracer be introduced into the inflow suddenly at time zero, the pulse injection technique.

In such an experiment it is clear that when the blood-tissue exchange is purely flow-limited, and not impeded by a capillary or other barrier, then regions with higher flow will approach equilibrium more rapidly than those with lower flow. This idea was used by Oldendorf,[76] who measured the uptake of tritiated water in the various regions of the brain in order to estimate regional blood flows. Reivich et al.[79] used antipyrine and iodo-antipyrine with the same goal in mind. Both studies neglected the possibility

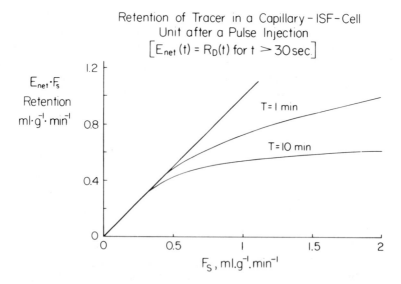

Retention of Tracer in a Capillary – ISF – Cell
Unit after a Pulse Injection
$$\left[E_{net}(t) = R_D(t) \text{ for } t > 30 \text{ sec}\right]$$

FIGURE 18.   Effect of flow on the blood-to-tissue-clearance or tissue retention of thallium, $F_S \cdot R_D(T)$ or $F_S \cdot E_{NET}(T)$, when there are capillary and cell membrane barriers to traverse. Values for capillary PS_C, 2 mℓ g^{-1} min^{-1}, and cell membrane PS_M, 12 mℓ g^{-1} min^{-1}, are typical for dog heart. The large volume of distribution for thallium ($\theta = 400$, $\gamma = 3$), aids in retaining a linear relationship, but the slope is governed mainly by the extraction and is less than unity. E_{net}, given by Equation 21, is the same as $R_D(t)$ for times after the reference tracer has washed out, which is the case for the times illustrated.

that antipyrine is probably barrier-limited or diffusion-limited in its exchange with the brain. There is little question that Reivich's estimates show more antipyrine deposition of regions of higher flow than of lower flow. This should be true even in strongly barrier-limited situations, since the amount escaping from the blood is proportional to $E \cdot F_B$, the extraction times the blood flow. However, the errors in absolute amount and in proportionality are not readily calculable.

c. Influence of Capillary and Cell Membrane Barriers on Estimation of Flow from Deposition

This topic has not been well explored, probably mainly because of the lack of available mathematical models which must be used to make the computations on a theoretical basis, and of the intensive experimentation and analysis that would be required to make comparisons with other standard techniques, such as microsphere deposition. A theoretical approach will tend to overestimate the error, because the effect of increasing flow is to open up new portions of the capillary bed, thereby increasing PS_c and perhaps PS_M. With the advent of scintiscanning techniques and image reconstruction, particularly from deposited positron emitters, the question has become much more important. In Figure 18 is shown the graph of the expected deposition at the end of 1 and 10 min after the injection of a bolus of thallium into the inflow of a typically dimensioned heart. The values for PS_C and PS_M of, 2 and 12 mℓ g^{-1} min^{-1} were similar to those obtained experimentally, and the graph shows the mathematical solution for Equations 38 through 40. For potassium with a slightly smaller PS_C and a clearly smaller PS_M, the deposition-flow relationship is more curvilinear.

In a recirculating system, the initial rate of tracer washout from high flow regions is greater than that from the lower regions, and the re-uptake of recirculated tracer occurs preferentially in regions with lower than average tracer concentrations. This combination results in the concentrations in the low flow regions increasing and those in the high flow regions decreasing compared to the concentrations at the end of the first pass. This effectively causes a relative uniformity of deposition and "apparent flow" within the organ. This subject has been treated on an interorgan basis by Downey[26] and Mitchell et al.,[75] but considerably more work needs to be done on each of the useful tracers in order to ascertain the magnitude of the problem.

5. Limitations to Compartmental Analysis

The basic assumptions of compartmental modeling are

1. Each compartment is wholly and instantaneously mixed so that the concentration within it is uniform at all times.
2. The system is in a steady-state with respect to mother substance (the tracer) so that tracer exchange rates are first order.
3. The volumes and exchange rates between compartments are constant.

The main problem with compartmental analysis is failure to meet the first condition. For example, it is obvious from observing indicator dilution curves in the circulation (e.g., Figure 1 or 6) that the plasma is not an instantaneously mixed compartment, and yet this is commonly assumed in pharmacokinetic modeling. A further condition therefore merits listing:

4. When the time required for complete mixing in a volume is very short compared to the time constant of the fastest exchange process, then condition (1) is reasonably well fulfilled.

How to calculate "very short" is the next question. Perhaps a safe rule of thumb might be defined: (a) Let the time required for concentration differences in different parts of a system to become less than 1% be t_{mix}. (b) The time constant for the fastest process shall be τ, which is the reciprocal of the rate constant, and which is equivalent to the volume, V, divided by the conductance for efflux, PS or F_s. Thus, $\tau = V/PS$ or V/F_s. (c) The rule of thumb is $t_{mix} < 0.1\tau$.

Whether this is too "safe" or not depends on the accuracy needed. We can state categorically that the estimation of capillary PS_c for small solutes is far too high to permit reasonable use of compartmental analysis. For example, for glucose with myocardial PS_c of 0.3 mℓ g^{-1} min^{-1} and capillary volume V_c = 0.03 mℓ g^{-1}, V_c/PS_c = 0.1 min = 6 sec; diffusional mixing for glucose would take 4 time constants or $4L^2/D$ = $4 \times (0.1$ cm$)^2/(0.5 \times 10^{-5}$ cm^2/sec) = 8×10^3 sec. Thus, t_{mix} is greater than 1000, which demonstrates that the requirements for compartmental analysis are not satisfied.

a. Misuse of Compartmental Models for Capillary-Tissue Exchange

In Figure 19, the response to a pulse input is shown for a traditional 2-compartment system. Consider the flowing compartment to be the capillary blood, and the second compartment to be the interstitial space. The response for the intravascular tracer is a monoexponential indicator dilution curve, but that for the permeating tracer has a sharper earlier phase and a much slower late washout phase. The extraction calculated from such a pair of curves, E(t), has a gradually rising value initially, and a well-defined peak. These curves differ from experimental dilution curves in their shapes, in contrast to those from distributed models which fitted experimental curves well, as discussed earlier.

A similar sort of problem occurs for the fractional escape rates or emergence func-

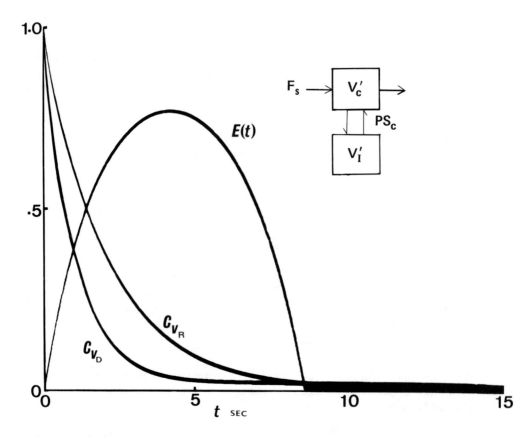

FIGURE 19.   Impulse response of a two-compartmental "capillary-tissue" unit, $C_{V_R} = h_R(t)$, is the outflow concentration-time curve for the reference tracer which remains confined to the flowing compartment. The vascular time constant is V_c/F_s, the "capillary" compartment volume is divided by the flow. C_{V_D} is the outflow concentration-time curve for the permeating tracer, which enters an adjacent "extravascular" compartment. The extraction $E(t)$, as defined in Equation 19, $= 1 - C_{V_D}(t)/C_{V_R}(t)$; the early values are steeply rising, the peak is at nearly 80%, and is very late relative to the main components of C_{V_R} and C_{V_D}.

tions, Equations 8 and 9. For the reference tracer following an impulse injection into a first order mixing chamber, the escape rate $\eta_R(t)$ is the flow divided by the capillary volume. Because the impulse response for the permeating tracer has at least two exponential components, therefore η_D declines from a high initial rate of escape to a tail portion which shows a constant rate of escape (see Figure 20). The final emergence rate is, however, not $F_s/(V_c' + V_i')$, but, being limited by the permeability is close to PS_c/V_i' as Perl showed from his model in which axial diffusion was infinitely rapid. If the capillary permeability were higher in this situation, then the fractional escape rate, $\eta(t)$, would be closer to the $F_s/(V_c' + V_i')$ as expected from the Kety washout expression. In general, one may say that the maximum rate of washout is either $F_s/(V_c' + V_i')$ or PS_c/V_i', but at intermediate values will be lower than the lesser of these. The Krogh cylinder (distributed) models, described above in Section A.2, give the same extreme limitations to the washout rate from the extravascular region, but give intermediate cases which are quite different from the compartmental models because fastest transit time from inflow to outflow is V_c'/F_s, not instantaneous, and the intravascular and extravascular dispersion is smaller.

b. Errors in Estimate of PS_M Using a Three-Compartment Organ Model

Conn and Robertson[21] and Sheehan and Renkin[91] used a three-compartment capillary-ISF-cell model to estimate PS_M. By analogy to Figure 19, one can readily surmise that the three-compartmental system could not be fitted to the observed transient

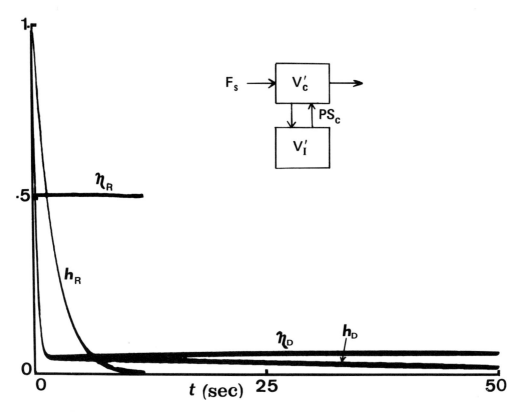

FIGURE 20. Impulse responses and emergence functions, $\eta(t)$, for a two-compartment "capillary-tissue" unit. The rate of washout of the vascular component is the same as in Figure 19, and is $F/V_c' = 0.5 \text{ sec}^{-1}$, (which is $1/\tau$, where τ is the time constant). The initial rate of diminution of $h_D(t)$ is much faster due to uptake of tracer into the vascular region, and the early values of $\eta_D(t)$ are almost superimposed since $\eta(t) = h(t)/R(t)$ and $R_D(t)$ is close to 1.0. Later values of $\eta_D(t)$ are 10% of $\eta_R(t)$, indicating that tracer in the extravascular compartment is limited in its washout almost solely by the capillary membrane, i.e., the rate is close to PS_c/V_i'.

responses and that its value for interpreting the near steady-state observations should be reexamined. However, when there is a large cellular sink, so that the flux is dominantly a unidirectional influx, then apparently reasonable values might be obtained.

c. Compartmental Models Can Be Useful

Several general statements that may be of value in helping to determine when compartmental models may be used are given with the idea in mind that it is commonly helpful to be able to use very simple, easily manipulated models even when they are not necessarily completely correct. The general categories of usefulness are

1. When the exchange rate is low. When a single process dominates, then a consortium of processes tends to become monoexponential, and therefore this limiting rate constant can be estimated. A case in point is the washout of a substance from the interstitial space when its permeability is low, when the washout rate is PS_c/V_i'. This washout rate constant is seen to occur as the final value for washout from distributed capillary-ISF models for larger molecules or low values of PS_c. The implication is clear, namely that the flow does not influence the washout. Thus, an experimental test for the adequacy of the approach is to increase the flow, and if the washout does not increase, then one can be assured that it is barrier-limited. There is a problem, however, with using this test in an organ such as the heart, for increasing the flow may make more capillaries functional,

increasing the functional surface area S_c, thus making the test appear invalid when in fact it may be valid.

2.   When rate constants differ by an order of magnitude. The separation of exponential time constants when the observed curve contains a set of exponentials is mathematically reasonable when the data are virtually noiseless, and when the time constants differ by at least a factor of 4. When there is any significant noise in the data, even if the data have been obtained over extended periods of time with many observations, then the rate constants should differ by a larger factor, more nearly a factor of 10. An example of an application of this is given by Rogus and Zierler[84] in which they observed washout of ^{24}Na over a period of many hours from rat skeletal muscle. Three time constants were clearly distinguishable and led to the development of a model of sodium in the sarcoplasm, the sarcoplasmic reticulum, and the extracellular space. The rate constants for exchange were so different that there seemed to be little problem in concluding that specific barriers were providing the limitation to washout and that these were mathematically distinguishable from each other.

3.   As descriptors of data. Most washout processes show continuous curvature on semilogarithmic plots, and thus lend themselves to being described by sums of exponentials, as if they were made up of an aggregate of first order washout processes in parallel. In testing different methods of estimating coronary blood flow by the washout of diffusable indicators, Bassingthwaighte, Strandell, and Donald[12] fitted washout curves with one or two exponentials, finding that xenon and antipyrine washout almost never required three exponentials to obtain very good fits. The descriptions with two exponentials gave estimates of the areas of the curves, and therefore approximated the "height-over-area" technique, Equation 53, reasonably well. Use of the steepest exponential flow, fitting by replotting on semilog paper and fitting the best straight line through the curve at about 30% of the peak height gave acceptable estimates of flow for both antipyrine and xenon except when the curves were obtained for xenon by residue detection over the whole heart, in which situation a substantial amount of xenon enters into the fatty regions of the myocardium and wash out more slowly. As another example, Langer[60] used multiple exponential equations to describe Ca^{2+} washout from embryo heart cells employing five exponential components in parallel to fit the data. However, they interpreted each of these components as intracellular regions of interest; since washout from an intracellular site involves traversal of at least two barriers in series, their use of compartmental analysis was most unpersuasive and seriously detracted from the presentation of the data. (It should be noted that these authors have not persisted in this approach to the analysis.)

Equations for simple compartmental systems were provided by Solomon.[95] An extensive and powerful capability for analyzing complex compartmental systems has been built up by Berman and his colleagues during the past 2 decades and is available on many computers as SAAM (Systems Analysis and Applied Mathematics). His general approach has been well described, although the details of the methodology are not readily available.[15] Excellent reference works on compartmental analysis are those of Sheppard[93] and Jacquez.[51]

B. Whole Body Kinetics of Tracers Taken Up into Cells
1. Observations on Dispersion and Disappearance
a. Plasma Proteins

Disappearance of plasma proteins from the circulation has been studied extensively over the years because of their use in the estimation of blood volume. Mixing of tracer-labeled proteins throughout the plasma space in the body has been a major feature of the reviews on blood volume estimation by Lawson[63] and Sjostrand.[94] [131]I and Evans blue dye (T-1824) have been excellent markers with which to label albumin since they bind firmly to the protein. On the other hand, indocyanine green is stripped from the albumin relatively readily during its passage through the liver, so much so that the rate of disappearance of indocyanine green from the plasma has been used as a method of estimating hepatic blood flow.[28]

Plasma proteins escape slowly from the vascular bed or organs with closed capillary endothelium such as heart, brain, and skeletal muscle, and faster in those organs with open capillaries, such as the liver, the gut, and the spleen. They recirculate through the lymph. The extravascular space for plasma proteins is smaller than the space for sulfate or inulin in the ISF because the interstitial matrix excludes molecules of the size of albumin to a substantial extent. The combination of volume exclusion in the interstitium and the filtration of fluid into the lymph leads to the lymphatic concentrations of albumin being lower than those in the plasma.[59]

b. Sucrose and Other Extracellular Markers

One would expect that when such markers are injected into the plasma they would have a slow rate of equilibration with the total body extravascular, extracellular space, compared to dispersion in the plasma, but this does not appear to be a particularly big problem for [24]Na (and presumably other small molecules such as sucrose, and Co-EDTA as suggested by Figure 21). The figure shows the time course of diminution of concentrations of an intravascular tracer, ^{99m}Tc-albumin, an extracellular tracer, [24]Na, and a body water tracer, ^{125}I-antipyrine. It may be seen that all the tracers approach an equilibrium plateau within about 50 min, and that the plasma protein curve is not very much faster than the others. A commonly used marker for extracellular space is inulin, which has been measured chemically or with ^{3}H or [14]C. There have been significant problems with this marker since the molecular weight (nominally 5,000) is not discrete, and the apparent molecular diameters range from 10 to 15 Å.[107]

c. Water and Similar Tracers Taken Up into Large Volumes of Distribution

In general, these are tracers which penetrate cell walls fairly quickly, insuring their distribution throughout body water space. The commonly used ones, [3]HHO and D_2O, suffer only minor isotope effects when used in tracer level concentrations. (D_2O has significant physiological effects when used in high concentrations to replace H_2O.) Markers such as mannitol and urea probably enter all body cells, but are much slower to do so than are water molecules. Although urea can enter red blood cells faster than water, having a negative reflection coefficient,[66] it enters the brain very slowly, and has been used clinically as an agent for reducing cerebral edema by infusing it in hypersomatic solutions.[68,77]

Tracers like potassium, rubidium, and thallium, for which there are large intracellular volumes of distribution and some significant renal clearance, demonstrate rapid disappearance from the plasma. The high rate of cellular uptake of these tracers contributes to the initial disappearance rate, and this is followed by cellular retention for several hours time with very low plasma concentrations. Since the half-lives of these tracers are short, the biological risk due to the radioactivity is small in spite of the long retention.

d. Influences of Rapid Clearance on the Estimates of Spaces

The usual technique for estimating the volume of distribution of Evans blue-labeled albumin in the plasma is to take a few samples over the first hours, to plot the concentrations on semilogarithmic paper, and to extrapolate linearly back to time zero. The use of the linear extrapolation is based on the assumption that the clearance from the

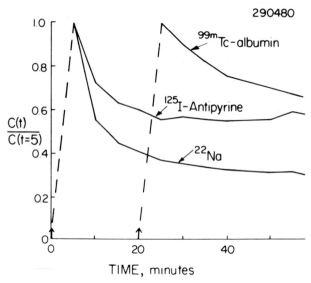

Plasma Concentrations of Tracers
Following Intravenous Injection
(3.2 kg hepatectomized, nephrectomized rabbit)

FIGURE 21.   Time course of equilibration of ^{99m}Tc-labeled albumin, [22]Na, and ^{125}I-antipyrine in a hepatectomized, nephrectomized rabbit. The data were obtained by Dr. F. Gonzalez in our laboratory; the tracers were injected at t = 0 and at t = 20 min, and blood samples taken at 5-min intervals.

body is a first order of washout process, namely renal clearance divided by the plasma volume. Knowing the amount injected, q_0, the plasma volume is calculated from the concentration estimated at time zero:

$$V_p = \frac{q_0}{C_p(t = 0)} \qquad (56)$$

This technique works quite well when the clearance rate is low.

However, when the clearance is high, as it is for indocyanine green, there is a problem. The half time of disappearance of indocyanine green in humans is about 3 or 4 min, and in dogs about 7 min. When one uses the technique of semilogarithmic extrapolation back to time zero, then the apparent initial concentration in the plasma is an overestimate, and Equation 56 gives an underestimate of V_p. The reason for this is that circulatory mixing takes several minutes and that the plasma is not a uniformly mixed pool from time zero onward. In the dog, to estimate V_p using indocyanine green, one should not extrapolate back to time zero, but to 1 to 2 min after the injection. The overestimates obtained by using C(t = 0) are on the order of 10%, and may be expected to be somewhat larger in humans than in dogs because of the faster clearance. The explanation for this is provided in more detail by an examination of the distribution of plasma labels throughout the circulation.

2. Modeling of Whole Body Exchanges
a. Indicator Dispersion in the Circulating Blood

In general, dispersion in the circulation is due to four distinct types of processes:

1. Velocity profile produced by differences in the velocities of particles at different distances from the wall of the vessel
2. Mixing pool effects, such as occur in eddies or in cardiac chambers which exchange a portion of their volume with the blood flowing through or past them
3. Random movement of particles backward, forward, and across the stream as in disturbed or turbulent flow or by diffusion, and
4. Differences in lengths or transit times of parallel pathways through the capillary matrix of an organ or through different organs of the body in parallel

Of all of these, the most important dispersing mechanism in whole body distribution is the differences in path lengths or transit times through different vessels of an organ, and particularly through different organs in parallel. The great dispersion of the cardiothoracic circulation is due to the differences in lengths of, and the velocities in, different pathways through the capillary bed of the lungs, and to the mixing pool effects of the cardiac chambers. However, dispersion of intravascular indicator during passage through even such compact organs as the heart and the kidney is still large, having a relative dispersion of about 35%.[7] Even so, this is small compared with the dispersion occurring during traversal of a limb: the transit time between femoral artery and femoral vein across a contracting skeletal muscle in the upper thigh might be only a few seconds, whereas transit through a leg at rest, down to the toes and back up to the femoral vein, may take 2 to 5 min. This wide range of transit times causes great dispersion. This is obviously also the major cause for slow equilibration throughout the plasma space.

b. Models for Whole Body Distribution of Excreted Tracers

Whole body models were considered by Jacquez et al.[52] Models of chemotherapy have been substantially extended in recent years by Himmelblau and Bischoff,[46] Lightfoot,[67] and by Dedrick and his co-workers.[25] Such modeling forms the formal basis for pharmacokinetic analysis, which is really an area of application of the kinetics presented in some detail in this chapter. For computational reasons, most of these models have been fairly simple, and do not take into account the known transport functions across each of the individual organs. This will be a new approach to pharmacokinetics, providing higher accuracy in the descriptions of the kinetics of substances which have fast actions or rapid clearance.

An example of a model of a closed recirculating system with one excretory outlet is that for indocyanine green shown in Figure 22.

This model was used for the analysis of indocyanine green dilution curves in human subjects, and for obtaining estimates of their hepatic clearance of the dye over a range of plasma concentrations. The latter was accomplished using a servo-controlled pump to infuse the dye at a variable rate, with the goal of governing the concentrations at chosen levels. When the concentration was constant long enough for mixing throughout plasma space, then the rate of infusion via the pump was equal to the hepatic excretion rate, giving the clearance estimate directly from the pump rate. The results are shown in Figure 23.

The response to a single bolus injection into venous circulation of 5 mg of indocyanine green is shown in the upper panel. The model is fitted to this dilution curve accounting for recirculation and for loss during trans-hepatic passage. The hepatic clearance would give a half time for loss from the plasma of about 3 min. In the lower panel is shown the fit of the same model with the identical parameters to the variable rate infusion begun a few minutes later in the same subject. Indocyanine green was infused via a variable rate pump so that the input rate was I(t) milligram per minute into the venous system. This resulted in the observed rising concentration-time curve,

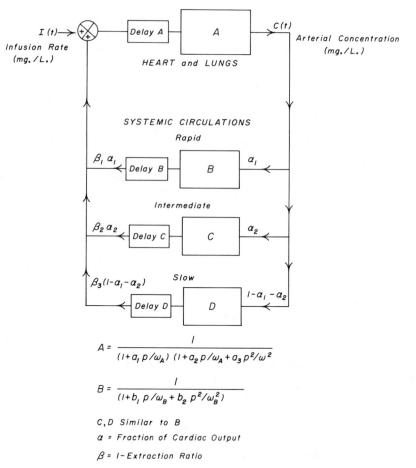

$$A = \frac{1}{(1+a_1\, p/\omega_A)\,(1+a_2\, p/\omega_A + a_3\, p^2/\omega^2}$$

$$B = \frac{1}{(1+b_1\, p/\omega_B + b_2\, p^2/\omega_B^2)}$$

C, D Similar to B

α = Fraction of Cardiac Output

β = 1 – Extraction Ratio

FIGURE 22.   Whole body circulation model using dispersive linear differential operators to represent groups of organs. Although the model is very simple, the dispersive nature of each of the operators makes their impulse responses similar to those in true life and rather different from first order mixing chambers. The combination of linear operator and delay line is to give the correct ratio of standard deviation mean transit time, that is, relative dispersion. These operators are easily made flow dependent.[10] The excretory loss was from compartment B at a rate K·C(t).

C(t). The desired concentration level used as the set point for the servo-controller was changed at t = 8 min. in order to achieve a higher plasma concentration, and was turned off at t = 16 min. The model fitted to the observed data can be seen to be fairly close. The differences between the model and the experiment probably are due to the rate of clearance of indocyanine green by the liver being reduced as a function of the load of dye excreted. This was seen in each of several subjects, and was also observed in the earlier studies of Edwards et al.[28] on the dogs.

The principle illustrated in this figure is that if the system is stable and correctly described, then two or more different experiments should be describable by the same system of equations even though the input or driving functions are of quite different form. If two different experiments done on the same system near the same time give strongly different parameter estimations for the best fits to the data, then one can be reasonably certain that the model used for the analysis is wrong.

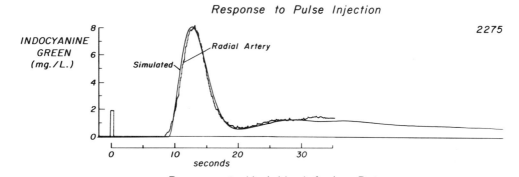

SIMULATION OF INDOCYANINE GREEN TRANSPORT

Response to Pulse Injection

2275

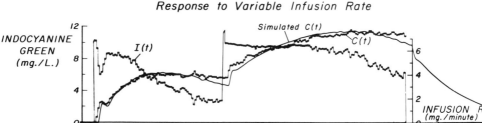

Response to Variable Infusion Rate

FIGURE 23. Indocyanine green dilution curves in a human subject fitted to the mathematical model of the circulation shown in Figure 22. Upper panel: Arterial indicator dilution curve following 5 mg dye injection into superior vena cava. Lower panel: Dye concentration, C(t) in response to pump infusion at rate I(t).

This approach, to incorporate correct descriptions of individual organ intravascular transport functions into whole body models, will be extended in the future to the distribution of indicators traversing the capillary and cell membranes.

c. Recirculation and Redistribution of Deposited Tracers

This is an area of clinical importance in the use of gamma and positron emitting tracers for examining body distributions at different times after injection. The studies of Downey and Bashour[26] and Mitchell et al,[75] utilize a conceptual approach similar to that of the model shown in Figure 22, but are more complex, since the extravascular regions of each organ must be included in the model. The models of the Krogh cylinder type shown in Section A.2 appear to be the appropriate ones to use for this kind of analysis. With respect to the use of thallium for examining regional flows in an organ such as the heart, the initial distribution will represent the delivery to the organ by the flow, modified by the somewhat variable extraction through regions of different flow. At much later times the distribution will represent only the volume of distribution of the tracer in the tissue and will have no meaning with respect to flow. For thallium in the heart, it may turn out that these two items of information have some similarity: regions deprived of flow, and therefore of the initial deposition, may be the same regions which have lost cellular potassium because of cell damage and which may not retain thallium as well. Although it would certainly be convenient for clinical users if this were true, there is no direct evidence on whether or not the volume of distribution for thallium is reduced when potassium is lost from myocardial cells.

C. Summary

It has not been the authors' intention to review all of the techniques or data on the cellular uptake of radio-tracers, but to present those aspects of the field which are new, and which therefore may merit special attention. For such reasons, we have emphasized the use of distributed models as opposed to lumped, compartmental models, and have been careful to look at the influence of both the capillary and the cell membrane on the transport of tracers from the blood to the cell, and in the opposite direction as well. Because the heterogeneity of flows within organs has been virtually totally neglected in the past, we have made a special emphasis on various ways to approach the ideas of heterogeneity and how to account for them. This section of the work in the field is really only at a beginning, so that we emphasize that one should consider the effects of heterogeneity rather than to depend upon the specific methods which we have suggested.

We have only given a few hints with respect to the whole body kinetics since this is really another topic in itself. What we believe is that the approach and techniques provided in Section A are the basis of exploring whole body kinetics and pharmacokinetics in general, and we have attempted to only give an example of this in Section B.

ACKNOWLEDGMENT

The authors express their appreciation to Wilma Dlouhy for her help in the preparation of this manuscript and to Hedi Nurk for the preparation of the illustrations.

REFERENCES

1. Alvarez, O. A. and Yudilevich, D. L., Heart capillary permeability to lipid insoluble molecules, *J. Physiol.*, 202, 45, 1969.
2. *American Institute of Physics Handbook*, McGraw-Hill, New York, 1957.
3. Anderson, D. U., Knopp, T. J., and Bassingthwaighte, J. B., SIMCON-Simulation control to optimize man-machine interaction, *Simulation*, 14, 81, 1970.
4. Bassingthwaighte, J. B., Plasma indicator dispersion in arteries of the human leg, *Circ. Res.*, 19, 332, 1966.
5. Bassingthwaighte, J. B., Blood flow and diffusion through mammalian organs, *Science*, 167, 1347, 1970.
6. Bassingthwaighte, J. B., A concurrent flow model for extraction during transcapillary passage, *Circ. Res.*, 35, 483, 1974.
7. Bassingthwaighte, J. B., Physiology and theory of tracer washout techniques for the estimation of myocardial blood flow: flow estimation from tracer washout, *Prog. Cardiovasc. Dis.*, 20, 165, 1977.
8. Bassingthwaighte, J. B., Ackerman, F. H., and Wood, E. H., Applications of the lagged normal density curve as a model for arterial dilution curves, *Circ. Res.*, 18, 398, 1966.
9. Bassingthwaighte, J. B., Chinard, F. P., Crone, C., Lassen, N. A., and Perl, W., Definitions and terminology for indicator dilution methods, in *Capillary Permeability (Alfred Benzon Symp. II)*, Crone, C. and Lassen, N. A., Eds., Munksgaard, Copenhagen, 1970, 665.
10. Bassingthwaighte, J. B., Knopp, T. J., and Anderson, D. U., Flow estimation by indicator dilution (bolus injection): reduction of errors due to time-averaged sampling during unsteady flow, *Circ. Res.*, 27, 277, 1970.
11. Bassingthwaighte, J. B., Knopp, T. J., and Hazelrig, J. B., A concurrent flow model for capillary-tissue exchanges, in *Capillary Permeability (Alfred Benzon Symp. II)*, Crone, C. and Lassen, N. A., Eds., Munksgaard, Copenhagen, 1970, 60.
12. Bassingthwaighte, J. B., Strandell, T., and Donald, D. E., Estimation of coronary blood flow by washout of diffusible indicators, *Circ. Res.*, 23, 259, 1968.
13. Bassingthwaighte, J. B., Yipintsoi, T., and Harvey, R. B., Microvasculature of the dog left ventricular myocardium, *Microvasc. Res.*, 7, 229, 1974.
14. Bellman, R., Jacquez, J. S., and Kalaba, R., Some mathematical aspects of chemotherapy. I. One-organ models, *Bull. Math. Biophys.*, 22, 181, 1960.

15. **Berman, M.,** Compartmental anaylsis in kinetics, in *Computers in Biomedical Research II,* Stacy, R. W. and Waxman, B., Eds., Academic Press, New York, 1965, 173.

16. **Bohr, C.,** Uber die spezifische Tatigkeit der Lungen bei der respiratorischen Gasaufnahme und ihr Verhalten zu der durch die Alveolarwand stattfindenden Gasdiffusion, *Skand. Arch. Physiol.,* 22, 221, 1909.

17. **Bustamente, J. C., Mann, G. E., and Yudilevich, D. L.,** Characterization of neutral amino acid carriers at the basal side of salivary epithelium by paired-tracer single circulation, *J. Physiol. (London),* 291, 26, 1979.

18. **Chinard, F. P. and Enns, T.,** Transcapillary pulmonary exchange of water in the dog, *Am. J. Physiol.,* 178, 197, 1954.

19. **Chinard, F. P. and Flexner, L. B.,** Mechanism of passage of substances across capillary walls: the diffusion hypothesis, *Proc. 19th Internat. Cong. Physiol. Sci.,* The Canadian Physiology Society, Montreal, 1953, 267.

20. **Chinard, F. P., Vosburgh, G. J., and Enns, T.,** Transcapillary exchange of water and of other substances in certain organs of the dog, *Am. J. Physiol.,* 183, 221, 1955.

21. **Conn, H. L. and Robertson, J. S.,** Kinetics of potassium transfer in the left ventricle of the intact dog, *Am. J. Physiol.,* 181, 319, 1955.

22. **Crone, C.,** The permeability of capillaries in various organs as determined by use of the "indicator diffusion" method, *Acta Physiol. Scand.,* 58, 292, 1963.

23. **Crone, C.,** Facilitated transfer of glucose from blood into brain tissue, *J. Physiol.,* 181, 103, 1965.

24. **Cropp, G. J. A. and Burton, A. C.,** Theoretical considerations and model experiments on the validity of indicator dilution methods for measurements of variable flow, *Circ. Res.,* 18, 26, 1966.

25. **Dedrick, R. L.,** Animal scale-up, in *Pharmacokinetics,* Teorell, T., Dedrick, R. L., and Condlife, P. G., Eds., Plenum Press, New York, 1975, 117.

26. **Downey, H. F. and Bashour, F. A.,** Dynamics of tissue distribution of radio-potassium as affected by simulated differences in regional extractions, *Cardiovasc. Res.,* 9, 607, 1975.

27. **Duran, W. N., Alvarez, O. A., and Yudilevich, D. L.,** Influence of maximal vasodilatation on glucose and sodium blood-tissue transport in canine heart, *Microvasc. Res.,* 6, 347, 1973.

28. **Edwards, A. W. T., Bassingthwaighte, J. B., Sutterer, W. F., and Wood, E. H.,** Blood level of indocyanine green in the dog during multiple dye curves and its effect on instrument calibration, *Proc. Staff Meet. Mayo Clin.,* 35, 745, 1960.

29. **Fick, A.,** Ueber die messung des Blutquantums in den Herzventrikeln. Sitzungsb. der phys.-med. Ges. zu Wurzburg. 1870. p. 36. (Quoted in its entirety by Hoff, H. E. and Scott, H. J., *N. Engl. J. Med.,* 239, 122, 1948.)

30. **Flexner, L. B., Cowie, D. B., and Vosburgh, G. J.,** Studies on capillary permeability with tracer substances, *Cold Spring Harbor Symp. Quant. Biol.,* 13, 88, 1948.

31. **Goresky, C. A.,** A linear method for determining liver sinusoidal and extravascular volumes, *Am. J. Physiol.,* 204, 626, 1963.

32. **Goresky, C. A. and Bach, G. G.,** Monohydric alcohols: the demonstration of a shared hepatocyte enzymic space, *Am. J. Physiol.,* (submitted).

33. **Goresky, C. A., Bach, G. G., and Nadeau, B. E.,** On the uptake of materials by the intact liver - The concentrative transport of rubidium-86, *J. Clin. Invest.,* 52, 975, 1973a.

34. **Goresky, C. A., Bach, G. G., and Nadeau, B. E.,** On the uptake of materials by the intact liver - The transport and net removal of galactose, *J. Clin. Invest.,* 52, 991, 1973b.

35. **Goresky, C. A., Bach, C. G., and Nadeau, B. E.,** Red cell carriage of label: its limiting effects on the exchange of materials in the liver, *Circ. Res.,* 36, 328, 1975.

36. **Goresky, C. A., Daly, D. S., Mishkin, S., and Arias, I. A.,** Uptake of labeled palmitate by the intact liver: role of intracellular binding sites, *Am. J. Physiol.,* 234, E542, 1978.

37. **Goresky, C. A., Ziegler, W. H., and Bach, G. G.,** Capillary exchange modeling: barrier-limited and flow-limited distribution, *Circ. Res.,* 27, 739, 1970.

38. **Gosselin, R. E.,** The tissue tracer injection method for assessing capillary permeability, in *Capillary Permeability (Alfred Benzon Symp. II),* Crone, C. and Lassen, N. A., Eds., Munksgaard, Copenhagen, 1970, 218.

39. **Gray, S. D. and Renkin, E. M.,** Microvascular supply in relation to fiber metabolic type in mixed skeletal muscles of rabbits, *Microvasc. Res.,* 16, 406, 1978.

40. **Grunewald, W.,** The influence of the three-dimensional capillary pattern on the intercapillary oxygen diffusion - A new composed model for comparison of calculated and measured oxygen distribution, in *Oxygen Supply,* Urban and Schwarzenburg, Munich, 1973.

41. **Guller, B., Yipintsoi, T., Orvis, A. L., and Bassingthwaighte, J. B.,** Myocardial sodium extraction at varied coronary flows in the dog: estimation of capillary permeability by residue and outflow detection, *Circ. Res.,* 37, 359, 1975.

42. Hamilton, W. F., Moore, J. W., Kinsman, J. M., and Spurling, R. G., Studies on the circulation. IV. Further analysis of the injection method, and of changes in hemodynamics under physiological and pathological conditions, *Am. J. Physiol.*, 990, 534, 1931.

43. Harris, T. R. and Newman, E. V., An analysis of mathematical models of circulatory indicator-dilution curves, *J. Appl. Physiol.*, 28, 840, 1970.

44. Harris, T. R., Gervin, C. A., Burks, D., and Custer, P. L., Effects of coronary flow reduction on capillary-myocardial exchange in dogs, *Am. J. Physiol.*, 3, H679, 1979.

45. Heppner, R. L., Harvey, R. B., and Bassingthwaighte, J. B., Creatinine distribution dynamics in the dog, *J. Appl. Physiol.*, 32, 495, 1972.

46. Himmelblau, D. M. and Bischoff, K. B., *Chemical Process Analysis,* John Wiley & Sons, New York, 1965.

47. Hoedt-Rasmussen, K., Sveinsdottir, E., and Lassen, N. A., Regional cerebral blood flow in man determined by intra-arterial injection of radioactive inert gas, *Circ. Res.*, 18, 237, 1966.

48. Holloway, G. A., Jr., Williams, D. W., and Levin, M., Thallium and potassium uptake kinetics in the dog heart, *Fed. Proc., Fed. Am. Soc. Exp. Biol.*, 37, 1095, 1978.

49. Hughes, S. P. F., Lemon, G. J., Davies, D. R., Bassingthwaighte, J. B., and Kelly, P. J., Extraction of minerals after experimental fractures of the tibia in dogs, *J. Bone Joint Surg.*, 61-A, 857, 1979.

50. Inesi, G., Active transport of calcium ion in sarcoplasmic membranes, *Ann. Rev. Biophys. Bioeng.*, 1, 191, 1972.

51. Jacquez, J. A., *Compartmental Analysis in Biology and Medicine,* Elsevier, New York, 1972.

52. Jacquez, J. A., Bellman, R., and Kalaba, R., Some mathematical aspects of chemotherapy. II. The distribution of a drug in the body, *Bull. Math. Biophys.*, 22, 309, 1960.

53. Kelly, P. J. and Bassingthwaighte, J. B., Studies on bone ion exchanges using multiple-tracer indicator-dilution techniques, *Fed. Proc., Fed. Am. Soc. Exp. Biol.*, 36, 2634, 1977.

54. Kelly, P. J., Yipintsoi, T., and Bassingthwaighte, J. B., Estimation of canine tibial diaphyseal collateral blood flow by ^{125}I-antipyrine washout, *J. Lab. Clin. Med.*, 74, 889, 1969.

55. Kety, S. S., Measurement of regional circulation by local clearance of radioactive sodium, *Am. Heart. J.*, 38, 321, 1949.

56. Kety, S. S. and Schmidt, C. F., The nitrous oxide method for the quantitive determination of cerebral blood flow in man: theory, procedure, and normal values, *J. Clin. Invest.*, 27, 476, 1948.

57. Krambeck, F. J., Shinnar, R., and Katz, S., Stochastic mixing models for chemical reactors, *Ind. Eng. Chem. Fundamentals*, 6, 276, 1967.

58. Kuikka, J., Bouskela, E., and Bassingthwaighte, J. B., D-, L-, and 2-deoxy-D-glucose uptakes in the isolated blood perfused dog hearts, *Bibl. Anat.*, 18, 239, 1979.

59. Landis, E. M. and Pappenheimer, J. R., Exchange of substances through capillary walls, in *Handbook of Physiology*, 2, 961, 1963.

60. Langer, G. A., Kinetic studies of calcium distribution in ventricular muscle of the dog, *Circ. Res.*, 15, 393, 1964.

61. Lassen, N. A. and Crone, C., The extraction fraction of a capillary bed to hydrophilic molecules: theoretical considerations regarding the single injection technique with a discussion of the role of diffusion between laminar streams (Taylor's effect), in *Capillary Permeability,* Crone, C. and Lassen, N. A., Eds., Munksgaard, Copenhagen, 1970, 48.

62. Lassen, N. A. and Perl, W., *Tracer Kinetic Methods in Medical Physiology,* Raven Press, New York, 1979.

63. Lawson, J. C., The volume of blood - a critical examination of methods for its measurement, in *Handbook of Physiology*, 1, 23, 1962.

64. Levin, M., Kuikka, J., and Bassingthwaighte, J. B., Sensitivity analysis in optimization of time-distributed parameters for a coronary circulation model, *Med. Prog. Technol.*, 7, 119, 1980.

65. Levin, M., Kuikka, J., and Bassingthwaighte, J. B., Estimation of myocardial capillary and cellular permeability-surface area products with heterogeneity of regional flows, *Circ. Res.* (submitted).

66. Lifson, N., Grim, E., and Johnson, J. A., Osmosis and water transport, in *Medical Physics,* Glasser, O., Ed., Vol. III, Year Book Medical, Chicago, 1960, 410.

67. Lightfoot, E. N., *Transport Phenomena and Living Systems,* John Wiley & Sons, New York, 1974.

68. Livingstone, A. S., Potvin, M., Goresky, C. A., Finlayson, M. H., and Hinchey, E. J., Changes in the blood-brain barrier in hepatic coma after hepatectomy in the rat, *Gastroenterology,* 73, 697, 1977.

69. Mann, G. E., Smaje, L. H., and Yudilevich, D. L., Permeability of the fenestrated capillaries in the cat submandibular gland to lipid-insoluble molecules, *J. Physiol. (London),* 297, 335, 1979a.

70. Mann, G. E., Smaje, L. H., and Yudilevich, D. L., Transcapillary exchange in the cat salivary gland during secretion, bradykinin infusion and after chronic duct ligation, *J. Physiol. (London),* 297, 355, 1979b.

71. Martin, P. and Yudilevich, D., A theory for the quantification of transcapillary exchange by tracer-dilution curves, *Am. J. Physiol.*, 207, 162, 1964.

72. Maseri, A., Myocardial flow by precordial residue detection following intracoronary slug injection of radioactive diffusible indicators, in *Myocardial Blood Flow in Man,* Maseri, A., Ed., Minerva Medica, Torino, 1972.

73. Meier, P. and Zierler, K. L., On the theory of the indicator-dilution method for measurement of the blood flow and volume, *J. Appl. Physiol.*, 6, 731, 1954.

74. Metzger, H., Po_2 histograms of three dimensional systems with homogeneous and inhomogeneous microcirculation - a digital computer study, in *Oxygen Supply,* Urban and Schwarzenburg, Munich, 1973.

75. Mitchell, R., Gupta, N. K., Keltz, P. D., and Gertz, E. W., Regional myocardial blood flow from dynamic analysis of thallium-201, *Computers in Cardiology,* Sept., 205, 1978.

76. Oldendorf, W. H., Measurements of brain uptake of radio labeled substances using a tritiated water internal standard, *Br. Res.*, 24, 373, 1970.

77. Rapaport, S. I., *Blood-brain Barrier in Physiology and Medicine,* Raven Press, New York, 1976.

78. Rasio, E. A., Bendayan, M., and Goresky, C. A., Diffusion permeability of an isolated rete mirabile, *Circ. Res.*, 41, 791, 1977.

79. Reivich, M., Jehle, J., Sokoloff, L., and Kety, S., Measurement of regional cerebral blood flows using C^{14} antipyrine, *J. Appl. Physiol.*, 27, 296, 1969.

80. Renkin, E. M., Capillary and cellular permeability to some compounds related to antipyrine, *Am. J. Physiol.*, 173, 125, 1953.

81. Renkin, E. M., Transport of potassium-42 from blood to tissue in isolated mammalian skeletal muscles, *Am. J. Physiol.*, 197, 1205, 1959a.

82. Renkin, E. M., Exchangeability of tissue potassium in skeletal muscle, *Am. J. Physiol.*, 197, 1211, 1959b.

83. Robinson, R. A. and Stokes, R. H., *Electrolyte Solutions,* Butterworth, London, 1959.

84. Rogus, E. and Zierler, K. L., Sodium and water contents of sarcoplasm and sarcoplasmic reticulum in rat skeletal muscle: effects of anisotonic media, ouabain and external sodium, *J. Physiol.*, 233, 227, 1973.

85. Rose, C. P. and Goresky, C. A., Vasomotor control of capillary transit time heterogeneity in the canine coronary circulation, *Circ. Res.*, 39, 541, 1976.

86. Rose, C. P. and Goresky, C. A., Constraints on the uptake of labeled palmitate by the heart: the barriers at the capillary and sarcolemmal surfaces and the control of intracellular sequestration, *Circ. Res.*, 41, 534, 1977.

87. Rose, C. P., Goresky, C. A., and Bach, G. G., The capillary and sarcolemmal barriers in the heart: an exploration of labeled water permeability, *Circ. Res.*, 41, 515, 1977.

88. Roselli, R. J. and Harris, T. R., A four phase model of capillary tracer exchange, *Ann. Biomed. Eng.*, 7, 203, 1980.

89. Sangren, W. C. and Sheppard, C. W., A mathematical derivation of the exchange of a labeled substance between a liquid flowing in a vessel and an external compartment, *Bull. Math. Biophys.*, 15, 387, 1953.

90. Schlossmacher, E. J., Weinstein, H., Lochaya, S., and Shaffer, A. B., Perfect mixers in series model for fitting venoarterial indicator-dilution curves, *J. Appl. Physiol.*, 22, 327, 1967.

91. Sheehan, R. M. and Renkin, E. M., Capillary, interstitial, and cell membrane barriers to blood-tissue transport of potassium and rubidium in mammalian skeletal muscle, *Circ. Res.*, 30, 568, 1972.

92. Sheppard, C. W., Mathematical consideration of indicator-dilution techniques, *Minn. Med.*, 37, 93, 1954.

93. Sheppard, C. W., *Basic Principles of the Tracer Method,* John Wiley & Sons, New York, 1962, 219.

94. Sjostrand, T., Blood volume, in *Handbook of Physiology,* 1, 51, 1962.

95. Solomon, A. K., Equations for tracer experiments, *Clin. Invest.*, 28, 1297, 1979.

96. Staub, W. M., Flanagan, D. F., Aaron, R., and Rose, J. C., Fate of injected radioiodinated 4-iodoantipyrine in the dog and rat, *Proc. Soc. Exp. Biol. Med.*, 116, 1119, 1964.

97. Stephenson, J. L., Theory of the measurement of blood flow by the dilution of an indicator, *Bull. Math. Biophys.*, 10, 117, 1948.

98. Stewart, G. N., Researches on the circulation time in organs and on the influences which affect it. I. Preliminary paper, *J. Physiol. (London),* 15, 1, 1894.

99. Stewart, G. N., Researches on the circulation time in organs and on the influences which affect it. II. The time of the lesser circulation, *J. Physiol. (London),* 15, 31, 1894.

100. Stewart, G. N., The circulation time in organs and the influences which affect it. III. The circulation time in the thyroid gland, and the effects of section and stimulation of nerves upon it, *J. Physiol. (London),* 15, 73, 1894.

101. **Stewart, G. N.**, Researches on the circulation time and on the influences which affect it. IV. The output of the heart, *J. Physiol. (London)*, 22, 159, 1897.
102. **Stow, R. W. and Hetzel, P. S.**, An empirical formula for indicator-dilution curves as obtained in human beings, *J. Appl. Physiol.*, 7, 161, 1954.
103. **Strandell, T. and Shepherd, J. T.**, The effect in humans of exercise on relationship between simultaneously measured ^{133}Xe and ^{24}Na clearances, *Scand. J. Clin. Lab. Invest.*, 21, 99, 1968.
104. **Strauss, H. W., Harrison, K., Langan, G. K., Lebowitz, E., and Pitt, B.**, Tl-201 for myocardial imaging: relation of thallium-201 to regional myocardial perfusion, *Circulation*, 51, 641, 1975.
105. **Tancredi, R. G., Yipintsoi, T., and Bassingthwaighte, J. B.**, Capillary and cell wall permeability to potassium in isolated dog hearts, *Am. J. Physiol.*, 229, 537, 1975.
106. **Thompson, H. K., Starmer, G. F., Whalen, R. E., and McIntosh, H. D.**, Indicator transit time considered as a gamma variate, *Circ. Res.*, 14, 502, 1964.
107. **Vargas, R. and Johnson, J. A.**, Permeability of rabbit heart capillaries to nonelectrolytes, *Am. J. Physiol.*, 213, 87, 1967.
108. **Verjovski-Almeida, S. and Inesi, G.**, Rapid kinetics of calcium ion transport and ATPase activity in the sarcoplasmic reticulum of dystrophic muscle, *Biochim. Biophys. Acta*, 558, 119, 1979.
109. **Visscher, M. B. and Johnson, J. A.**, The Fick Principle: analysis of potential errors in its conventional application, *J. Appl. Physiol.*, 5, 635, 1953.
110. **Winkler, B. and Schaper, W.**, Tracer kinetics of thallium, a radionuclide used for cardiac imaging, in *The Pathophysiology of Myocardial Perfusion*, Schaper, W., Ed., Elsevier/North Holland Biomedical Press, New York, 1979, 102.
111. **Winkler, B., Mueller, K. D., Carl, H., Stemmler, G., and Schaper, W.**, Multiple indicator dilution experiments using thallium in the isolated dog heart, *Bibl. Anat.*, 18, 246, 1978.
112. **Yipintsoi, T. and Bassingthwaighte, J. B.**, Circulatory transport of iodoantipyrine and water in the isolated dog heart, *Circ. Res.*, 27, 461, 1970.
113. **Yudilevich, D. L. and Alvarez, O. A.**, Water, sodium, and thiourea transcapillary diffusion in the dog heart, *Am. J. Physiol.*, 213, 308, 1967.
114. **Yudilevich, D. L. and De Rose, N.**, Blood-brain transfer of glucose and other molecules measured by rapid indicator dilution, *Am. J. Physiol.*, 220, 841, 1971.
115. **Yudilevich, D. L., De Rose, N., and Sepulveda, F. V.**, Facilitated transport of amino acids through the blood-brain barrier of the dog studied in a single capillary circulation, *Brain Res.*, 44, 569, 1972.
116. **Yudilevich, D. L., Renkin, E. M., Alvarez, O. A., and Bravo, I.**, Fractional extraction and transcapillary exchange during continuous instantaneous tracer administration, *Circ. Res.*, 23, 325, 1968.
117. **Ziegler, W. H. and Goresky, C. A.**, Transcapillary exchange in the working left ventricle of the dog, *Circ. Res.*, 29, 181, 1971a.
118. **Ziegler, W. H. and Goresky, C. A.**, Kinetics of rubidium uptake in the working dog heart, *Circ. Res.*, 29, 208, 1971b.
119. **Zierler, K. L.**, Theoretical basis of indicator-dilution methods for measuring flow and volume, *Circ. Res.*, 10, 393, 1962.
120. **Zierler, K. L.**, Theory of use of indicators to measure blood flow and extracellular volume and calculation of transcapillary movement of tracers, *Circ. Res.*, 12, 464, 1963.
121. **Zierler, K. L.**, Equations for measuring blood flow by external monitoring of radioisotopes, *Circ. Res.*, 16, 309, 1965.

Chapter 8

EFFECT OF SOLUTE STRUCTURE ON TRANSPORT OF RADIOTRACERS

Yukio Yano

TABLE OF CONTENTS

I. INTRODUCTION

Most radiotracers are administered intravenously and first enter the vascular compartment. The radiotracer then enters various tissues through the capillaries. Finally, the intracellular uptake of the radiotracer occurs by transport across the cell membrane. This movement of small ions or hydrophilic substrates across the membrane can occur by facilitated diffusion or by mediated transport.

Mediated transport is not necessarily related to the "barrier nature" of the biological membrane, but it is determined by the interaction of a large number of specific transport systems located in the membrane and acting independently.[1] These transport systems can be working simultaneously to transport sugars, amino acids, or alkali metal ions into the cell. There could be separate transport systems for each substrate; however, it is more likely that one transport system would move analogous solutes.

A number of transport mediators somewhat similar to enzymes acting as catalytic activators could be characterized by sensitive recognition sites whose specificity is dependent on protein structure.[1] Cells and organelles carry a wide range of recognition sites for occupation by substrates; unlike enzymes, however, they do not cause chemical reaction of the substrate.

The localization of radiotracers within the body is determined by the size and shape of the substrate, protein binding to blood and tissue, lipid solubility, and specific cellular transport mechanisms.[2]

Protein binding can be influenced by a variety of factors. Some of these include metal ions such as Zn^{+2} and Sn^{+2}, pH, nature of the protein which determines the number of NH^+_3 groups relative to the number of OH^- and COO^- groups, intramolecular distance between NH^+_3 and COO^- groups, anion concentration, and buffer anions. Low concentrations of 10^{-3} M and pH of about 5 increases the protein binding by serving as a bridge in the radiotracer-protein chelate.[2]

Diffusion across the lipid membranes can play an important part in the distribution of radiotracers. A few freely diffusible substances such as ^{133}Xe and radioiodinated antipyrine have been used in nuclear medicine. More of these lipid-soluble compounds will be synthesized and used in the future as dynamic studies are done to measure the rates of change in concentration through lipid membranes.[2]

II. GENERAL PRINCIPLES OF SOLUTE STRUCTURE AND TRANSPORT

A. Diffusion and Lipid Solubility[3]

In simple diffusion it is not structure but size which determines the diffusion rate. The diffusion coefficient is inversely proportional to the radius of the diffusing molecule, or approximately to the cube root of the molecular weight. For larger molecules, the diffusion coefficient is dependent upon the movement of the solvent molecules and is more closely related to the square root of the molecular weight.

Since nonspecific migration across cellular membranes depends more on the lipid solubility of the solute than on simple diffusion, there is relatively good correlation between permeability and the partition coefficient of the solute distribution between olive oil and water. Apolar bonding of the molecule assists the entry of the molecule into the apolar environment of the cell membrane.

Certain hydrophilic molecules such as water and urea move faster through plasma membrane than other molecules of similar size which show very slow permeation. There is slower permeation for D-leucine than for L-leucine, for L-glucose than D-glucose, and for β-alanine than α-alanine. This shows that a simple view of the cell membrane as a lipid barrier or in combination with the idea of water-filled channels does not provide sufficient explanation for the permeability of biological membranes. Some explanation can be derived from the concept of specific mediated transport through a protein type membrane rather than a lipid membrane.

B. Cell Membranes[3-7]

Cell membranes are dynamic changing structures composed of a basal membrane made up of glycoproteins and collagens as well as other proteins such as lipoproteins. The type of protein in the membrane varies from cell to cell and within the cell itself. The plasma membrane is high in ATP-ase and Mg^{++}. The outer surface of the mito-chondrion membrane is high in monoamine oxidase, while the inner mitochondrion contains enzymes involved in the citric acid cycle that leads to the oxidation of two carbon fragments to CO_2. In this process electrons are transferred along the respiratory chain enzymes. This is coupled to oxidative phosphorylation which leads to the pro-duction of the high energy phosphate compound ATP.

The difference in the ionic composition of the intracellular environment and the interstitial fluid leads to a potential difference across the cell membrane with the inside of the cell negative to the outside in the range of -10 to -100 mV in the resting cell.

The cell membrane is practically impermeable to intracellular proteins and organic anions. It is moderately permeable to Na^+, and readily permeable to K^+ and Cl^- ions.

1. Mediated (Facilitated) Diffusion Across the Cell Membrane[7]

Interaction of the solute molecule with the membrane can enhance or restrict move-ment across the cell membrane. When the translocation is enhanced, it is facilitated diffusion. Membrane mediation may also couple the penetration to other processes such as active transport. Mediated transport is a transient binding of a penetrating molecule to a specific site of a mobile or fixed site on the membrane. The mediator or translocator behaves in a manner analogous to enzymes; that is, it (1) is substrate-specific, (2) follows saturation kinetics, (3) undergoes competitive inhibition by sub-strate analogues and enzyme poisons, (4) undergoes activation by cofactors, and (5) is controlled by genetic and feedback regulators.

Mediators are substrate-specific and they initiate or accelerate translocation of the substrate across the membrane barrier. However, these transport systems are not as specific as enzymes in that they will handle more glucose analogues than will hexoki-nase. Also, they are not as stereospecific as enzymes in the recognition of optical iso-mers because they will transport both the L and D isomers of some amino acids.

C. Structural Specificity in Transport[3]

Amino acids are only slightly lipid soluble and are relatively unreactive to nonspe-cific transport. Furthermore, the amino acid molecule usually contains three or more sharply different chemical groups: the amino group, the carboxyl group; and a side-chain which varies as to geometry, separation, dissociation, etc. Amino acids are there-fore extremely useful in investigating features of membrane transport. In addition, the amino acids are of great biological importance.

1. Structural Features That Determine the Reactivity of the Substrate with the Trans-port System

The structural features of amino acids which are recognized by the transport system are (1) the α-carboxyl group and the α-amino group which must be at prescribed dis-tances, (2) sidechain apolarity and stereospecificity, and (3) receptor sites that permit wide variations in substrate structure. Great latitude is permitted by some of the trans-port systems, especially the L-system, for structure in the sidechain region. This latitude has been utilized pharmacologically to transport active agents to the desired site of

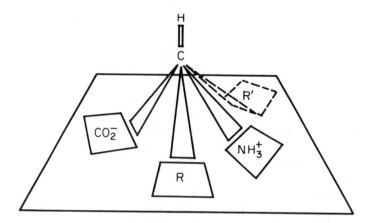

FIGURE 1.   Complete stereospecificity if the side chain R (L-form) is required for receptor binding of the amino acid, incomplete stereospecificity if binding can also occur with R′ (D-form) as the side chain. The side chain binding to the receptor site is required in addition to binding at the CO_2^- and NH_3^+ sites.

action, such as introducing α-methyldopamine into the central nervous system as α-methyldopa.[3]

Figure 1 shows the effect of either complete or incomplete stereospecificity where R and R′ represent the sidechain of the amino acid and its binding site on the cell membrane. If R is the L form and R′ the D form, and only the L form is utilized, then complete stereospecificity prevails; however, if the D form can be utilized as well, then incomplete stereospecificity prevails.

2. Co-Substrate Action of Na^+

Another important consideration is the generation of a recognition site for Na^+. Certain Na^+-dependent amino acid transport systems require Na^+ as a co-substrate. In general, there is an alkali metal dependence for the uphill transport of amino acids and monosaccharides.

The use of various sidechains containing hydroxyl, sulfhydryl, and amino groups on the sidechain of amino acids as sensors for the position of sodium has led to the study of sodium as a possible co-substrate also for the transport of sugar. The sodium-dependent transport of glucose appears to be dependent on the 2-hydroxyl group as shown by the work of Kleinzeller who demonstrated an exclusive sodium-independent transport for 2-deoxy sugars.[8]

3. Possibility of Making Structural Changes in the Substrate Which Effect Transport[3]

Some analogues of substrates are able to inhibit transport but are not themselves transported. Some examples of such cases are arginine, methionine, or norleucine without Na^+; and fructose or phlorizin in the Na^+-dependent transport of sugar. Another important effect in substrate structure is the slowing down of transport rather than complete stoppage. An N-methyl group on alanine or the α-aminoisobutyric acid reduces the V_{max} by about one third the rate for all other substrates of the same system. The opposite effect of accelerating the rate limiting step by alterations in the structure of the substrate was seen in two systems for neutral amino acids. The presence of distal amino groups with a pK′ of about 8.4 have given them greatly increased maximal velocities for the neutral system.

Several of these are α,γ-diaminobutyric acid (for system A), and S-2-amino-ethylcysteine for both systems (A and L), and 4-amino-l-methyl-piperdine-4-carboxylic acid (for System L). For these amino acids the uptake rates are fast compared to their exit.

III. SOLUTE STRUCTURE IN RADIOTRACER DESIGN

Recent developments in radiotracer design have made significant progress in utilizing substrate structure to investigate various aspects of transport and metabolism. Included among these radiotracers are [^{18}F]-2-fluoro-2-deoxy-d-glucose, radiolabeled fatty acids, iodinated phenyl-alkyl amines, [^{111}In]-oxine, and ^{99m}Tc-labeled agents.

A. Metabolic Trapping and Biodistribution of [^{18}F]-2-Fluoro-2-Deoxy-D-Glucose (^{18}FDG)[9]

The use of ^{18}FDG as in vivo method for measuring regional glucose metabolism, especially in the brain, was stimulated by the work of Sokoloff and Reivich who used ^{14}C 2-deoxy-glucose and quantitative autoradiography to measure glucose metabolism in the brain.[10] When the hydroxyl group at C-2 of the glucose molecule is replaced by hydrogen, the deoxyglucose serves as a substrate to measure the hexokinase reaction because the 2-deoxy-D-glucose-6-phosphate (^{14}C-DG-6-P) does not undergo further steps in the glycolysis cycle, but is metabolically trapped.[11] The same principle of metabolic trapping applies to ^{18}FDG-6-P.[12,13] The FDG is readily transported across the cell membrane, but ^{18}FDG-6-P is not transported back across the cell membrane, nor is it utilized in glucose metabolism beyond the phosphorylation step. Further, no detectable glucose-6-phosphatase activity was present in the heart or brain when hexokinase activity was high and at pH 6.5[9] The ^{18}FDG-6-P remains trapped in the heart and brain, but ^{18}FDG is rapidly removed from the other organs by excretion into the urine.

Figure 2 is the proposed mechanism for ^{18}FDG accumulation in the heart and brain.

Reivich, Kuhl, Wolf, et al. utilized ^{18}FDG for the measurement of local cerebral glucose metabolic rate (LCMRgl) in man.[14] The determination of LCMRgl requires information about the arterial blood plasma glucose concentration and ^{18}FDG concentration as a function of time after intravenous infusion of ^{18}FDG until the time the brain concentration of ^{18}FDG is determined by tomographic scans of the brain. The concentrations of glucose and ^{18}FDG were determined by periodic sampling, analysis, and counting of arterial blood.

The use of ^{18}FDG for calculating glucose metabolic rates in different areas of the brain during various conditions of brain activity demonstrates the importance of the structure of the molecule and its subsequent metabolic fate. A simple modification at the C-2 position of glucose by exchanging the OH$^-$ group with H and labeling with ^{18}F has provided a valuable radiotracer for quantitating metabolic processes during changing experimental conditions.

The same principle of ^{18}FDG trapping appears to be a very useful method for determining regional glucose metabolism in the myocardium.[15,16] This approach is potentially of great importance in the diagnosis and treatment of heart disease.

Another variation in the structure of the glucose molecule is the 3-deoxy-3-fluoro-D-glucose (3-FDG) synthesized by Tewson, Welch, and Raichle.[17]

There is evidence to indicate that glucose transport across the blood-brain barrier (BBB) resembles that in human erythrocytes. Facilitated diffusion appears to be the process involved; both systems are sodium-independent and not sensitive to insulin and behave like transport inhibitors.[18]

To study active transport in organs other than the brain, the 3-FDG molecule appears to be the desired structure because in experiments using the hamster's small intestines as a model, a hydroxyl group is necessary at C-2 while a hydrogen bond acceptor is necessary at C-3.[19] This is the case when fluorine is substituted for the 3-β-hydroxyl group. The 2-FDG is not actively transported while the 3-deoxy-D-glucose is transported poorly, and only the 3-deoxy-3-fluoro-glucose has a K_i and V_{max} reflecting active transport similar to that for glucose.[19]

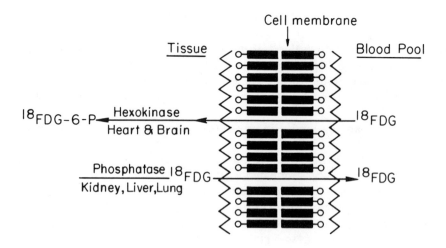

FIGURE 2.   Probable action of ¹⁸FDG in vivo. Mediated diffusion across cell membrane, hexokinase phosphorylation and trapping in heart and brain cells as a measure of glucose metabolism. In kidney, liver, and lungs the activity diffuses back across the cell membrane as ¹⁸FDG into the blood pool.

In animal experiments using [¹⁸F]-3-FDG, Tewson et al. determined its extraction fraction, and from the calculated cerebral blood flow and arterial plasma glucose concentration, an estimate of the ratio of glucose flow across the BBB was found to be 1.55,[17] which is in good agreement with the ratio of 1.37 as determined by Raichle et al., with [¹¹C]-glucose.[20] From these results it is concluded that [¹⁸F]-3-FDG behaves in a manner similar to glucose in passage across the BBB.[17]

B. Radiolabeled Fatty Acids

Long-chain ¹⁸F fatty acids have been studied by Knust et al. for study of regional metabolism in the heart.[21] The ¹⁸F-fluoro fatty acids 9-10-[¹⁸F] stearic, 2-[¹⁸F] hexadecanoic, and 17-[¹⁸F] heptadecanoic showed varied uptake. The 2-[¹⁸F] stearic had little uptake in the myocardium but had increased uptake in the liver. On the other hand, the ¹⁸F label in the middle or at the end of the carbon chain showed uptake and clearance similar to the ¹¹C-labeled fatty acid palmitic acid in which there is rapid concentration within 1 min and clearance by a slow and a fast component. The 16-[¹⁸] hexadecanoic acid and the 17-[¹⁸F] heptadecanoic have different turnover pools and different rates. Nearly all the ¹⁸F in the heart from 17-[¹⁸F] heptadecanoic was recovered as ¹⁸F fluoride, while practically no fluoride ¹⁸F was found for 16-[¹⁸F] hexadecanoic acid. These results were interpreted on the basis of the odd-even rule in which β oxidation of even numbered fatty acids produces [¹⁸F] fluoroacetic acid while odd-numbered fatty acids result in β-[¹⁸F] fluoroproprionic acid. The latter compound undergoes dehalogenation to produce free fluoride, but the fluoroacetic acid undergoes further metabolism in the citric acid cycle.[21]

C. Structure and Localization of [¹²³I]-Iodophenylalkyl Amines[22]

The uptake of iodinated phenylalkylamines in the rat brain was investigated by Winchell et al.[22] They found the following relationship for highest activity in brain and the brain-to-blood activity ratios for the iodine position on the benzene ring and for the alkyl groups attached to the ring; p>m>o and α methylethyl>ethyl>methyl>no alkyl group. For N additions a single lipophilic group >H> two lipophilic groups. Of these agents, the N-isopropyl-p-iodoamphetamine was chosen for further study in rats because it showed the highest brain activity and brain-to-blood ratio. The brain activity was 1.57%/g at 5 min and 2.14%/g at 60 min with a brain-to-blood ratio of 12.6 and 20.7, respectively.[22]

Amines are chemical mediators of brain function; however, some pharmacologically active amines can alter brain function by altering transport and uptake. From the data reported in this work and the work of Sargent et al., for 2,5-dimethoxy-*p*-bromoamphetamine,[23] halogenation gives greater uptake and psychotomimetic activity than the unhalogenated compound.

D. Other Radiotracers

1. *[111]In-oxine*

[111]In-oxine is lipid soluble and passively penetrates the cell membrane. The ^{111}In binds to cytoplasmic components of 540,000; 80,000; and 3,600 mol wt by exchange. Only a small part of ^{111}In-oxine binds to DNA and a large part of the oxine is released from the cell.[24,25] The neutral ^{111}In oxine complex diffuses rapidly across the cell membrane and then dissociates. Some of the oxine diffuses out of the cell while the ^{111}In changes its chemical form and binds to various intracellular components to form a stable bond.

2. *[99mTc]-Glucoheptonate*

(^{99m}Tc-GH) compared to ^{99m}TcO$_4$ as a brain scanning agent indicates that ^{99m}Tc-GH is a superior tumor imaging agent, especially for primary and metastic lesions of the posterior fossa.[26] There is no advantage of ^{99m}Tc-GH over ^{99m}TcO$_4^-$ in infarcts or ischemic lesions. The improved uptake especially in metastic lesions with time of ^{99m}Tc-GH compared to ^{99m}TcO$_4$ indicates other than increased vascularity and permeability due to the breakdown of the blood-brain barrier.[26] An alternative explanation utilizes the glucoheptonate analogue of glucose as a substrate for energy by the brain tumor. The low blood level of GH after 1 hour and the subsequent gradual increase in accumulation in the brain tumor indicates an active transport mechanism rather than passive diffusion.

3. *Other ^{99m}Tc Radiotracers*

Loberg et al. studied the membrane transport of ^{99m}Tc-labeled radiotracers and their uptake in brain by passive transport.[27] The chelating agents used were *N*-substituted carbamoylmethyliminodiacetates, substituted oxines, *N,N'*-diesters of EDTA or *N*-substituted derivatives of DTPA. These ^{99m}Tc complexes were able to cross the blood-brain barrier in proportion to lipophilicity as determined by their partition coefficient in octanol-saline. Of these compounds, the substituted oxines appear to be suitable compounds for diffusible brain tracers. The substituted oxines were of the structure

where (a) R = H, (b) R = I, (c) R = SO$_3$H, and (d) R = CHOHCH$_2$NHCH(CH$_3$)$_2$. The case of R being (a) or (b) gave a high extraction by the brain, but in the case of R being (c) or (d) there was lower extraction into the brain.

This work demonstrates the relationship between lipophilicity and permeability across the blood-brain barrier. The compounds reported here can cross the lipophilic barriers but high uptake by protein binding preclude their use as diffusible tracers.[27]

New compounds need to be developed which are lipophilic, but are minimally protein bound to study transport across lipid barriers.

IV. CONCLUSION

Significant progress has been made in the design of substrate structure to study specific transport mechanisms and metabolic pathways. The work with [18]FDG utilizing positron emission tomography is an excellent example of what can be accomplished with modifications to normally utilized substrate structure. Other studies with radiotracers structurally designed for lipophilicity and uptake in specific receptor binding sites are providing greater insight into the transport process as it relates to cell membrane permeability as opposed to the undesirable binding to blood proteins.

Further studies on the effect of substrate structure on transport can be accomplished by the following investigational protocol suggested by Christensen:[3]

1. Design of system-specific substrates for investigation of distinct transport systems
2. Separation of molecular transport from unrelated metabolic events; design of substrates resistant to metabolism
3. Description of geometric relations to receptor sites
4. Study of distinct events in transport
   a. Substrates not entering steps subsequent to binding
   b. Substrates that slow or accelerate a subsequent step through either a modification of their charge state or state of protonation during transport
   c. Identification of proton-receiving and proton-donating structures at the receptor site
   d. Eliminate trans-stimulation or trans-inhibition by structural modification

REFERENCES

1. Christensen, H, N., *Biological Transport,* W. A. Benjamin, London, 1975, chap. 1.
2. McAfee, J. G. and Subramanian, G., Radioactive agents for imaging, in *Clinical Scintillation Imaging,* Freeman, L. M. and Johnson, P. M., Eds., Grune & Stratton, New York, 1975, 13.
3. Christensen, H. N., *Biological Transport,* W. A. Benjamin, London, 1975, chap. 5.
4. Ganong, W. F., *Review of Medical Physiology,* Lange, Los Altos, Calif., 1977, chap. 1.
5. Fini, A., Effect of solute structure in the transport of radiotracers, in *Principles of Radiopharmacology,* Vol. II, Colombetti, L. G., Ed., CRC Press, Boca Raton, Fla., 1979, 241.
6. Heinz, E., *Mechanics and Energetics of Biological Transport,* Springer-Verlag, Berlin, 1978, chap. 3.
7. Medzihradsky, F., Structure and function of cell membranes and cellular transport of drugs, in *Principles of Radiopharmacology,* Vol. II, Colombetti, L. G., Ed., CRC Press, Boca Raton, Fla., 1979, 197.
8. Kleinzeller, A., The specificity of the active sugar transport in kidney cortex cells, *Biochim. Biophys. Acta,* 211, 264, 1970.
9. Gallagher, B. M., Fowler, J. S., Gutterson, N. I., MacGregor, R. R., Wan, C. N., and Wolf, A. P., Metabolic trapping as a principle of radiopharmaceutical design: some factors responsible for the biodistribution of [^{18}F] 2-deoxy-2-fluoro-D-glucose, *J. Nucl. Med.,* 19, 1154, 1978.
10. Sokoloff, L., Reivich, M., Kennedy, C., Des Rosiers, M. H., Patlak, C. S., Pettigrew, K. D., Sakurada, O., and Shinohara, M., The [^{14}C] deoxyglucose method for the measurement of local cerebral glucose utilization: theory, procedure, and normal values in the conscious and anesthetized albino rat, *J. Neurochem.,* 28, 897, 1977.
11. Sols, A. and Crane, R. K., Substrate specificity of brain hexokinase, *J. Biol. Chem.,* 210, 581, 1954.
12. Bessell, E. M., Foster, A. B., and Westwood, J. H., The use of deoxy-D-glucopyranoses and related compounds in a study of yeast hexokinase specificity, *Biochem. J.,* 128, 199, 1972.
13. Bessell, E. M. and Thomas, P., The effect of substitution at C-2 of D-glucose 6-phosphate on the rate of dehydrogenation by glucose 6-phosphate dehydrogenase (from yeast and rat liver), *Biochem. J.,* 131, 83, 1973.

14. Reivich, M., Kuhl, D., Wolf, A., Greenberg, J., Phelps, M., Ido, T., Casella, V., Fowler, J., Hoffman, E., Alavi, A., Som, P., and Sokoloff, L., The [^{18}F] fluorodeoxyglucose method for the measurement of local cerebral glucose utilization in man, *Circ. Res.*, 44, 127, 1979.

15. Gallagher, B. M., Ansari, A., Atkins, H., Casella, V., Christman, D. R., Fowler, J. S., Ido, T., MacGregor, R. R., Som, P., Wan, C. N., Wolf, A. P., Kuhl, D. E., and Reivich, M., Radiopharmaceuticals XXVI. ^{18}F-labeled 2-deoxy-2-fluoro-D-glucose as a radiopharmaceutical for measuring regional myocardial glucose metabolism in vivo: tissue distribution and imaging studies in animals, *J. Nucl. Med.*, 18, 990, 1977.

16. Phelps, M. E., Hoffman, E. J., Selin, C., Huang, S. C., Robinson, G., MacDonald, N., Schelbert, H., and Kuhl, D. E., Investigation of [^{18}F]-2-fluoro-2-deoxyglucose for the measure of myocardial glucose metabolism, *J. Nucl. Med.*, 19, 1311, 1978.

17. Tewson, T. J., Welch, M. J., and Raichle, M. E., [^{18}F]-labeled 3-deoxy-3-fluoro-D-glucose: synthesis and preliminary biodistribution data, *J. Nucl. Med.*, 19, 1339, 1978.

18. Betz, A. L., Gilboe, D. D., and Drewes, L. R., The characteristics of glucose transport across the blood brain barrier and its relation to cerebral glucose metabolism, *Adv. Exp. Med. Biol.*, 69, 133, 1976.

19. Barnett, J. E. J., Fluorine as a substituent for oxygen in biological systems: examples in mammalian membrane transport and glucosidase action, in *CIBA Found. Symp., Carbon-Fluorine Compounds: Chemistry, Biochemistry and Biological Activities*, Associated Scientific Publishers, Amsterdam, 1972, 95.

20. Raichle, M. E., Larson, K. B., Phelps, M. E., Grubb, R. L., Jr., Welch, M. J., and Ter-Pogossian, M. M., In vivo measurement of brain glucose transport and metabolism employing glucose-^{11}C, *Am. J. Physiol.*, 228, 1936, 1975.

21. Knust, E. J., Kupfernagel, Ch., and Stöcklin, G., Long-chain F-18 fatty acids for the study of regional metabolism in heart and liver: odd-even effects of metabolism in mice, *J. Nucl. Med.*, 20, 1170, 1979.

22. Winchell, H. S., Baldwin, R. M., and Lin, T. H., Development of I-123 labeled amines for brain studies: localization of I-123 iodophenylalkyl amines in rat brain, *J. Nucl. Med.*, 21, 940, 1980.

23. Sargent, T., Braun, G., Braun, U., Budinger, T. F., and Shulgin, A. T., Brain and retina uptake of a radio-iodine labeled psychotomimetic in dog and monkey, *Commun. Psychopharmacol.*, 2, 1, 1978.

24. Thakur, M. L., Segal, A. W., Welch, M. J., Hopkins, J., and Peters, T. J., Indium-111-labeled cellular blood components: mechanism of labeling and intracellular location in human neutrophils, *J. Nucl. Med.*, 18, 1020, 1977.

25. Thakur, M. L. and Gottschalk, A., Role of radiopharmaceuticals in nuclear hematology, in *Proc. 2nd Int. Symp. Radiopharmaceuticals II*, Sorenson, J. A., Coordinator, Society of Nuclear Medicine, New York, 1979, 341.

26. Léviellé, J., Pison, C., Karakand, Y., Lemieux, and Vallieres, B. J., Technetium-99m glucoheptonate in brain tumor detection: an important advance in radiotracer techniques, *J. Nucl. Med.*, 18, 957, 1977.

27. Loberg, M. D., Corder, E. H., Fields, A. T., and Callery, P. S., Membrane transport of Tc-99m-labeled radiopharmaceuticals. I. Brain uptake by passive transport, *J. Nucl. Med.*, 20, 1181, 1979.

Chapter 9

EFFECT OF TRANSPORT ON DISTRIBUTION OF RADIOIONS AND RADIOMETABOLITES

Yukio Yano

TABLE OF CONTENTS

I. INTRODUCTION

Many factors can influence the transport and thus the biodistribution of the radiotracers (radioions or radiometabolites); some of the interrelated factors are (1) route of administration, (2) carrier concentrations and complexed or ionic species, (3) cell-membrane permeability (extracellular or intracellular accumulation) by a passive or active process, and (4) enzyme and hormonal stimulation or depression and the metabolic state, i.e., fasting, etc.[1] An understanding of the transport process could provide greater insight into the development of radiotracers for selective and enhanced movement of the agent into cells of specific tissue such as bone, brain, kidneys, liver, marrow, myocardium, pancreas, prostate, and tumors. An earlier publication covered the basic aspects of the effect of transport on the distribution of radiotracers.[1] The present chapter presents information about the effects of transport on the distribution of radiotracers currently in clinical use or under development. In the latter group are positron-emitting radionuclides such as ^{11}C, ^{13}N, or ^{18}F, which are useful tracers for imaging and quantitation studies with recently developed positron imaging systems. These systems can be used to perform biochemistry in vivo. Quantitative time-course changes of radiotracer concentrations can be determined for specifically labeled amino acids, sugar, or fatty acids. In addition, the uptake and clearance of ions or gaseous radiotracers can be utilized to determine blood flow (perfusion) or ventilation.

II. BASIS OF TRANSPORT

In general, most radiotracers are administered by intravenous injection. Thus, the first consideration in transport is the binding of radiotracers to blood proteins such as serum albumin, gamma globulin or transferrin. In most cases the binding to the blood elements is relatively weak, which allows the radiotracer to be carried to a specific site which binds the tracer more strongly and clears it from the blood.

A. Nature of Radiotracers and Selective In Vivo Distribution[2]
1. Ionic Radiotracers

Many radiotracers are injected as simple ions such as $^{99m}TcO_4^-$, $^{18}F^-$, $^{113m}In^{+3}$, $^{111}In^{+3}$, $^{67}Ga^{+3}$, $^{43}K^{+1}$, $^{201}Tl^{+1}$, $^{131}I^-$, and $^{123}I^-$. When ions are injected intravenously, their localization in the body is determined by their valence state at blood pH (7.41), their solubility, their tendency to incorporate into organic compounds, their ability to enter into exchange reactions with body ions, and their protein-binding characteristics.[2,3] Ionic indium, for example, will bind to the plasma protein transferrin and remain in the plasma with a half-life of 8 to 10 hr, which makes it useful as a blood pool scanning agent. Pertechnetate, on the other hand, is loosely bound to plasma proteins and rapidly leaves the plasma compartment. This allows pertechnetate to cross the endothelium and to penetrate the tumor in brain scanning. Ion exchange is important in the trapping of TcO_4^- or I^- by the thyroid gland and in the exchange of ^{18}F with hydroxyapatite in bone crystals.

2. Colloids and Particles

Colloids, particles in suspension ranging in size from 1 mμ to 1 μ, are used in controlled particle size range to select the site of biologic distribution. The chemical and physical properties of the colloid are determined by charge-mediated interactions at the surface of the particles.[4] The biologic distribution of a colloid is determined by size and surface charge of the particles, the dispersity of the colloid, and the polarity of the dispersion medium.[3] The colloids which are foreign to the body are recognized by the plasma protein, opsonin, and phagocytized by macrophages in the reticuloendothelial (R.E.) system. Colloids are useful to image organs with a large number of R.E. cells. The liver, spleen, and bone marrow are dominant sites of deposition for radiocolloids. The relative distribution can be altered by changing the size of the particles. Particles less than 100 mμ are phagocytized to a greater extent in the marrow than in liver and spleen. Intermediate particles, 300 to 1000 mμ, are localized more in the liver, whereas particles in the 1 to 5 μ range are deposited more in the spleen.[5] Particles larger than 5 μ are not true colloids and will settle out on standing. The size of the pulmonary capillary bed is about 8 μ. Thus, particles of 10 to 75 μ of labeled macroaggregates of albumin are trapped in the capillary bed and used for perfusion lung scans. Other particles used for lung scanning are iron hydroxide particles and albumin microspheres.

3. Chemical Compounds

The distribution of useful radiotracers can be significantly altered by binding the radiotracer to a chemical compound which is relatively specific and predictable in distribution.

Radionuclides, which are usually ionic, are complexed or synthesized into biochemically differentiated compounds.

Chemical compounds can be formed by analogue substitution such as ^{75}Se for S in methionine, or by binding a normal substituent such as ^{131}I for I in labeled tyrosine.

Generator-produced tracers such as $^{99m}TcO_4$ or ^{113m}In are complexed to compounds which permit exchange into binding sites of specific areas of interest such as bone, bone marrow, tumors, kidneys, or blood pool.

The use of ^{99m}Tc is facilitated by its reactivity in the reduced valence states of Tc^{+3}, Tc^{+4}, or Tc^{+5} to form complexes of diethylenetriamine pentaacetic acid (DTPA), dimercapto succinic acid (DMSA), hydroxyethylene diphosphonate (HEDP), methylene diphosphonate (MDP), human serum albumin (HSA), red blood cell (RBC), and hepatobiliary agents such as substituted iminodiacetates (IDA).

Other radionuclides such as ^{11}C, ^{11}N, ^{15}O, or ^{18}F are synthesized into biochemically significant compounds such as amino acids, sugars, fatty acids, nucleic acids, proteins, enzymes, and chemical inhibitors of metabolic pathways. Others are used as radioactive gases such as $^{13}N_2$, $^{13}NO_2$, $C^{15}O_2$, $C^{15}O$, or $^{15}O_2$.

III. TRANSPORT AND DISTRIBUTION OF RADIOTRACERS

A. Technetium-99m

This 6 hr generator-produced radionuclide, which decays by isomeric transition and emission of 140 keV gamma rays, is the most useful imaging agent in nuclear medicine. Elution of the ^{99m}Tc generator yields anionic $^{99m}TcO_4^-$.

1. Pertechnetate Anion

Intravenously administered $^{99m}TcO_4^-$ is loosely bound to protein and moves rapidly out of the blood plasma compartment. A three-phase compartmental analysis gives 50 to 60% of $^{99m}TcO_4^-$ with a $T_{1/2}$ of 1 to 2 min in the plasma, 15% with a $T_{1/2}$ of 5 to 7.5 min, and 20 to 30% with a $T_{1/2}$ of 100 to 300 min.[6] Its distribution in the body is reflected by early concentration in salivary gland, gastric mucosa, choroid plexus, and thyroid gland where significant quantities of ^{99m}Tc are found at 1 hr after injection. Pertechnetate will also cross the placenta and deliver radiation to the fetus. The pertechnetate ion is excreted primarily by the gastrointestinal tract and kidneys. Excretion is by filtration with about 85% of the filtered ^{99m}Tc reabsorbed by the renal tubules. About 30% of the injected dose is excreted in urine during the first 24 hr. Fecal excretion is slower with about 40% recovered by 4 days.[6] Technetium activity appears in left colon as early as 1 hr after injection with suggestion that a portion of this activity is transported and secreted from the bloodstream.[7] Once the technetium has been secreted into the colon it is not reabsorbed and is dependent on fecal excretion for removal. The colon is the critical organ in terms of radiation exposure, and receives 1 to 2 rads/10 mCi of $^{99m}TcO_4^-$.

The biological distribution of $^{99m}TcO_4^-$ can be altered by pretreatment of the patient with perchlorate (ClO_4^-),[8] a monovalent anion of approximately the same size as TcO_4^-. Perchlorate blocks the uptake of TcO_4^- in the thyroid gland, salivary gland, choroid plexus, and gastric mucosa by competitive inhibition. Table 1 shows this effect on the uptake of $^{99m}TcO_4^-$ in thyroid, blood, and stomach.

Sodium pertechnetate is a useful agent for brain scanning because of its rapid clearance from the plasma compartment and its accessibility to breakdown in the blood-brain barrier.

The structure and size of the TcO_4^- anion is similar to the iodide ion which allows it to be trapped by the thyroid gland.[9,10]

2. ^{99m}Tc-Labeled Human Serum Albumin (HSA) and Red Blood Cells

^{99m}Tc bound to a carrier such as human serum albumin with a long residence time in the intravascular compartment can be used as a tracer for the intravascular space.[11,12]

Pertechnetate can also be bound to red blood cells by in vitro or in vivo methods using stannous ion as a pretreatment before labeling with TcO_4^-.[12-16,16a] The reduced ^{99m}Tc binds to the globin portion of the red cell hemoglobin with preferential binding to the β-chain.[17] Using ^{99m}Tc-labeled red cells, one can visualize major blood pools and large peripheral vessels.[13] Of the administered activity, 10 to 20% is found in the spleen at 3 hr.

3. ^{99m}Tc-Colloids

Technetium-99m sulfur colloids probably existing as $^{99m}Tc_2S_7$ coprecipitated with colloidal sulfur is stabilized with gelatin. After intravenous injection, the Tc_2S_7 is rapidly cleared from the blood with a half-time of 3 min. The colloid is phagocytized by the cells of the reticuloendothelial system. In normal subjects about 90% of the activity localizes in the liver and about 5% in the spleen.[18]

4. ^{99m}Tc-Phosphates and Phosphonates for Bone Scanning

The distribution of ^{99m}Tc-polyphosphate or phosphonates is dependent upon the pharmacodynamics of the chemical moiety to which ^{99m}Tc is attached. The ^{99m}Tc radiotracers depend on the polyanionic phosphate portion to allow entry into the bone structure. Bone is composed of a tightly bound inner ionic layer and a loosely bound outer hydration shell which is in rapid exchange with the plasma environment. This exchange

Table 1
EFFECT OF NaCℓO₄ ON ^{99m}Tc UPTAKE IN
MOUSE *

	Per cent injected ^{99m}Tc/g 90 min after injection		
	Blood	Thyroid	Stomach
I.V. NaTcO₄	1.1	100	20.0
I.V. NaTcO₄, NaCℓO₄			
15 min before	3.2	0	1.2

Note: Values are per cent of thyroid concentration.

From Lathrop, K. A. and Harper, P. V., *Progr. Nucl. Med.*, 1, 145, 1972. With permission.

primarily involves the ions which are found in the hydroxyapatite crystal (Ca^{++}, $PO_4\equiv$ and OH^-).[2] However, other monovalent and divalent cations, as well as polyvalent ionic complexes, may substitute in surface reactions. This exchange reaction takes only minutes. Both [18]F^- and ^{99m}Tc-polyphosphates are taken up on the bone surface as the result of increased bone reactivity or increased blood flow. Regional bone blood flow appears to be the rate limiting step.[19] For ^{18}F there is a rapid two-phase exponential clearance of ^{18}F from the blood. Phase I has a 24-min half-time that reflects bone uptake, while phase II with a half-time of 198 min represents renal clearance.[20] Figure 1 shows 3.8% of injected dose of ^{18}F/ℓ blood at 10 min and 0.73% ℓ of blood at 30 hr.[20] By comparison for ^{99m}Tc-polyphosphate (PP), phase I has a 30 min half-time and phase II has a 264 min half-time with 5.7% injected dose per liter of blood at 10 min and 2.4% at 3 hr.[20] Thus for ^{18}F the 10 min to 4 hr drop of ^{18}F blood activity was 85%. From 1 to 3 hr, 14 to 16% of the ^{18}F plasma radioactivity was protein-bound while the remaining 84 to 86% was free in plasma.[20] There was no significant RBC binding of [18]F. For ^{99m}Tc-PP, the 10 min to 4 hr drop in blood activity was 63%. Between 10 min and 4 hr post-injection, 68 to 84% of the plasma activity was protein-bound.[20] For ^{99m}Tc-PP, 21.7%, 16.7%, 18.5%, 21.4%, 15.5%, and 6.2% of plasma-protein activity was bound, respectively, to albumin, alpha-1, alpha-2, beta-globulins, fibrinogen, and gamma-globulin fractions.[20]

a. ^{99m}Tc-Methylene Diphosphonate (MDP)[21]

The physiological distribution of MDP is determined in a large part by its protein binding in plasma. The greater the protein-binding, the less the plasma clearance, urinary excretion, and tissue uptake.

The extent of plasma protein binding of ^{99m}Tc-MDP at 10 min; 1, 2, and 4 hr after intravenous injections into patients was determined by trichloroacetic acid and ammonium sulfate precipitation, dialysis, and Sephadex® gel chromatography. The percent administered dose bound to plasma proteins decreases with time, whereas the fraction of the plasma activity bound to plasma proteins increases with time after injection, Figure 2. The ratio of the plasma activity to the RBC activity is about 10. About 10% of the ^{99m}Tc-MDP is in 1 ℓ of plasma at 10 min. By 4 hr, the activity in the plasma has decreased to about 1% of ^{99m}Tc-MDP injected per liter of plasma. Somewhat similar results were reported by Subramanian et al.[22] There was 38% of the tracer removed by urinary excretion at 2 hr and 62% at 24 hr. This suggests that the rate of removal of ^{99m}Tc-MDP by bone uptake and urinary excretion is much faster than the rate of disappearance of the protein-bound tracer.

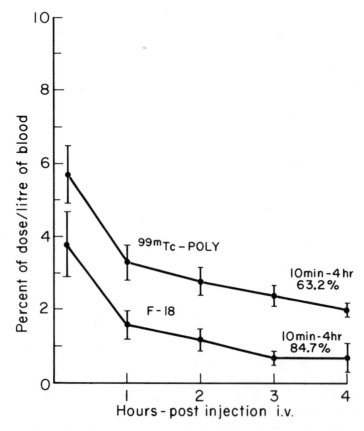

FIGURE 1.   Clearance of i.v. injected ^{18}F and ^{99m}Tc polyphosphate from blood (mean of 10 patients). (From Krishnamurthy, G. T., Thomas, P. B., Tubis, M., Endow, J. S., Pritchard, J. H., and Blahd, W. H., *J. Nucl. Med.,* 15, 832, 1974. With permission.)

The decrease in activities in plasma and whole blood reflects the removal of ^{99m}Tc-MDP by urinary excretion and bone uptake. The plasma clearance of ^{99m}Tc-MDP is biphasic, indicating a short and long exponential component. About 10% of the administered dose of ^{99m}Tc-MDP is protein bound at 2 to 3 hr after injection.[21] Low plasma protein binding enhances urinary excretion and bone uptake, which facilitates earlier bone imaging than bone agents having higher plasma protein binding. The in vivo kinetics of ^{99m}Tc-MDP and other technetium complexes in humans were compared and referenced to [18]F (the standard for bone scanning) by Subramanian et al.[22] These results are shown in Figure 3. The most rapid blood clearance of ^{99m}Tc-labeled complexes was obtained with MDP, which was nearly identical with [18]F. The blood clearance of PPi was much slower than either EHDP or MDP, and the clearance of polyp was the slowest of the four complexes. The diffusion of labeled diphosphonate into the circulating red cells was negligible. For polyphosphates, from 10 to 15% of the remaining blood activity was localized in the red cell fraction between 1 and 3 hr, increasing to 22% at 24 hr. Pyrophosphate showed greater cell diffusion; from 10 to 30% of the remaining blood activity was contained within the red cell fraction between 1 and 3 hr, increasing to 60% at 24 hr.[22] However, for all of these agents the total fraction of the activity in the bloodstream at 24 hr is very small.

The ^{99m}Tc complexes developed for bone scanning have been widely used, and of these ^{99m}Tc-MDP appears to be the most satisfactory agent because of its faster clearance from soft tissue and blood, whereas the "long-chain" polyphosphates are the least satisfactory because of slower clearance from the background tissues.[22]

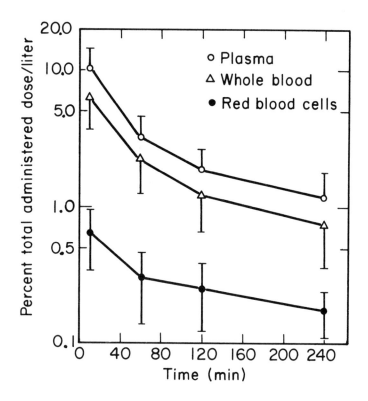

FIGURE 2. Percent of administered dose of ^{99m}Tc-MDP/ℓ of plasma, whole blood, and red blood cells with time after injection. (From Saha, G. B. and Boyd, C. M., *Int. J. Nucl. Med. Biol.* 6, 201, 1979. With permission.)

b. ^{99m}Tc-Pyrophosphate (PYP)

The short-chain polyphosphate, (n = 2) pyrophosphate is useful for bone imaging. ^{99m}Tc-pyrophosphate (PYP) is also useful for myocardial infarct imaging.

The observation that calcium is deposited in crystalline and subcrystalline form in irreversibly damaged myocardial cells,[24,25] led Bonte et al. to believe that the bone agent technetium-99m pyrophosphate (^{99m}Tc-PYP) could provide a means of identifying irreversibly damaged myocardial cells.[26] Subsequent clinical studies have confirmed that ^{99m}Tc-PYP does concentrate in myocardial damage.[27]

In most experimental models of myocardial ischemia and in patients, the cellular alterations occur initially in subendocardial tissue with subsequent spread to epicardial regions.[28] The alterations take place in cell membrane integrity and in mitochondrial calcification. The number of cells showing such changes increases with duration and severity of the ischemic insult.[28] There was a close temporal and topographical relationship between calcium accumulation in acute myocardial infarcts and ^{99m}Tc-PYP uptake.[29]

A study to understand the binding of ^{99m}Tc-chelates with serum proteins in relationship to the uptake of the agent in infarcted myocardium was conducted by Dewanjee and Kahn.[30] Gel filtration and dialysis experiments indicated the enhanced protein-binding affinity of ^{99m}Tc-pyrophosphate $(P_2O_7)_n$ compared to ^{45}Ca or ^{99m}Tc-DTPA as shown in Figure 4A and Table 2, respectively.[30] These studies with chelation of metal ions indicate an enhanced protein-binding affinity as well as localization in damaged myocardium. A possible mechanism for the localization of metal chelates of ^{99m}Tc, ^{113m}In, etc., in dead cells of myocardial infarcts, and facilitated by membrane damage,

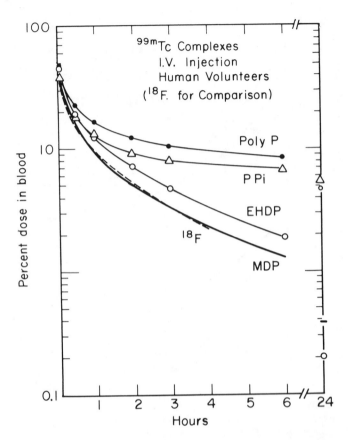

FIGURE 3. Blood clearance of ^{99m}Tc-MDP, PPI, PolyP, EHDP, and ^{18}F in humans after i.v. injections. (From Subramanian, G., McAfee, J. G., Blair, R. J., Kallfelz, F. A., and Thomas, F. D., *J. Nucl. Med.*, 16, 744, 1975. With permission.)

is shown in Figure 4B. The strength of the bond between ^{99m}Tc chelate and macromolecules depends on the number of receptor sites on the macromolecule, the orientation of the ^{99m}Tc chelate during attachment, and the number of available chelating atoms in the ^{99m}Tc chelate. The flexibility of denatured macromolecules helps them fit in a complete octahedral ^{99m}Tc complex.[30]

It was concluded by Willerson et al.[28] that:

1. ^{99m}Tc-PYP concentrates selectively in regions of necrosis and in severely injured myocardial cells
2.   Concentration of ^{99m}Tc-PYP results from selective adsorption of this agent to various forms of tissue calcium stores, including amorphous calcium phosphate, crystalline hydroxyapatite, and calcium complexed with myofibrils and other macromolecules
3.   The lack of a linear relationship between ^{99m}Tc-PYP concentration and tissue calcium levels was probably the result of local differences in composition and physiochemical properties of tissue calcium stores as well as local variations in blood flow which are responsible for the delivery of ^{9}Tc-PYP.[29] The schema shown in Figures 5 and 6 were proposed to explain the concentration of ^{99m}Tc-P in necrotic myocardium.

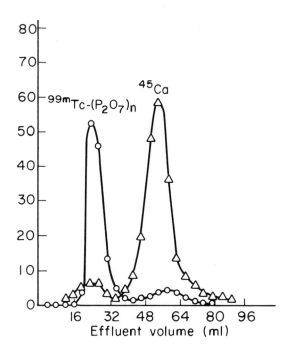

A

B

FIGURE 4(A). Sephadexe gel filtration of serum of rabbit injected 3 hr earlier with ^{99m}Tc-pyrophosphate and ^{47}Ca. (B) Possible mode of binding of ^{99m}Tc-HEDP to calcium ion on hydroxyapatite crystals or macromolecules. (From Dewanjee, M. K. and Kahn, P. C., *J. Nucl. Med.*, 17, 639, 1976. With permission.)

Table 2
DIALYSIS OF ^{99m}Tc-DTPA AND ^{99m}Tc-(PYROPHOSPHATE)$_n$ IN PRESENCE OF HUMAN SERUM ALBUMIN

	^{99m}Tc-DTPA (%)	^{99m}Tc-pyrophosphate(%)
Control:		
Retentate	2.7 ± 0.1	3.2 ± 0.1
Container	5.7 ± 0.9	7.1 ± 0.85
Albumin:		
Retentate	21.7 ± 1.1	55.7 ± 5.4
Container	2.8 ± 0.1	6.9 ± 1.0

From Dewanjee, M. K. and Kahn, P. C., *J. Nucl. Med.*, 17, 639, 1976. With permission.

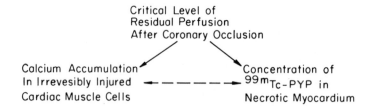

FIGURE 5. Relationship between collateral blood flow, pathological calcification and concentration of ^{99m}Tc-PYP in necrotic myocardium. (Adapted from Willerson, J. T., Parkey, R. W., Bonte, F. J., Lewis, S. E., Corbett, J., and Buja, L. M., *Semin. Nucl. Med.*, 10, 54, 1980. With permission.)

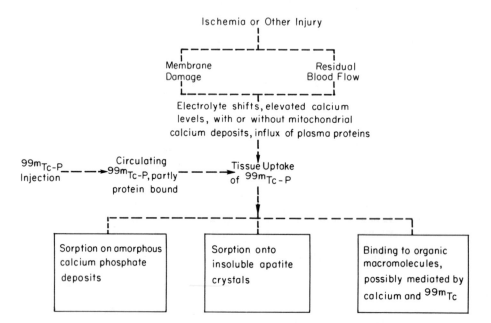

FIGURE 6. Proposed pathophysiologic basis for detection of tissue damage with ^{99m}Tc-P radiopharmaceuticals. (From Buja, L. M., Tofe, A. J., Kulharni, P. V., Mukherjee, A., Parkey, R. W., Francis, M. D., Bonte, F. J., and Willerson, J. T., *J. Clin. Invest.*, 60, 724, 1977. With permission.)

5. ^{99m}Tc-Hepatobiliary Agents
a. Anatomy and Physiology[31]

The liver is the largest organ in the body, averaging 2% of the body weight. It performs a complex variety of metabolic functions which occur primarily in the parenchymal cells or hepatocytes. This system of well-developed organelles is richly perfused by a vast network of hepatic sinusoids (Figure 7).[31] The products of hepatocyte metabolism are secreted into either the plasma or bile or stored within the cells.

An active transport process exists at the hepatocytes which selectively removes compounds from the blood and concentrates them in the bile.[32-34] As shown in Figure 7, four carrier-mediated transport pathways have been identified in the hepatocyte, each with separate sites of uptake at the cell membrane. These pathways accommodate either organic anions, organic cations, neutral compounds, or conjugated bile salts. In the transport processes, there may be intermediate storage sites such as ligand in Y protein and Z protein, which bind bilirubin and other organic anions; and metabolic processing may be required prior to secretion. Many of the compounds utilizing these

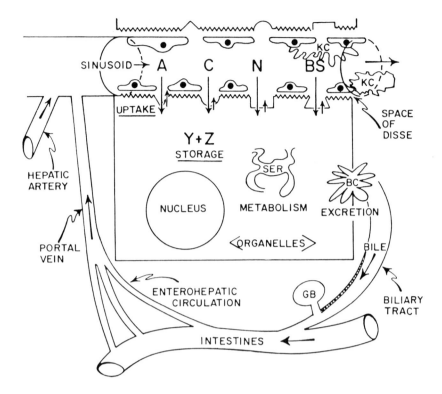

FIGURE 7. Schematic representation of an hepatocyte. Substrates in the blood diffuse through pores in the endothelial lining of the sinusoids and bind to the hepatocyte at one of four membrane-bound carriers: anionic (A), cationic (C), nonionic (N), bile salt (BS). Inside the hepatocyte, the substrate my be stored at specific binding sites such as Y and Z proteins, and it also may undergo metabolic conversion at other sites including the smooth endoplasmic reticulum (SER). Biliary excretion occurs at a biliary canaliculus (BC). Subsequently the substrate in the bile may be stored and concentrated in the gall bladder (GB) or excreted into the intestines. Some biliary components are reabsorbed from the intestines into the portal vein and reextracted by the hepatocyte ("enterohepatic circulation"). The sinusoids are lined by Kupffer cells (KC) which are a part of the reticuloendothelial system. (From Loberg, M. D., Porter, D. W., and Ryan, J. W., *Proc. 2nd Int. Symp. Radiopharmaceuticals II,* Sorenson, J. A., Coordinator, Society of Nuclear Medicine, New York, 1979, 519. With permission.)

uptake and metabolic pathways are secreted into the bile at a bile canaliculus. While the exact mechanisms of transport and bile secretion are not well understood, it is agreed that the rate-limiting step for the overall transport of compounds from the blood into the bile is the excretory process at the bile canaliculus.[31] Bile flow is a function of osmotic forces, and two processes which actively transport solutes into the bile canaliculus have been reasonably well identified. They are the system for bile salt transport ("bile acid dependent flow") and the sodium pump ("bile acid independent flow"). After leaving the liver, bile may enter the duodenum directly or it may flow into the gallbladder where it is concentrated, stored, and subsequently passed into the intestines during gallbladder contractions. Bile is important for the efficient digestion and absorption of ingested fats. Some bile components may be resorbed from the intestines and returned to the liver via the portal circulation, a cyclic process that has been termed the enterohepatic circulation.[31]

b. Hepatobiliary Agents[31]

The clinical usefulness of hepatobiliary (HB) agents is based upon their ability to produce liver images reflecting the distribution of hepatocytes, to outline the biliary tract, and to trace the pathway of bile flow. To accomplish these goals, a radiotracer must be capable of binding to receptors in membranes, concentrating within hepatocytes, and undergoing biliary excretion. There are several hepatocyte cell membrane receptors and a variety of intrahepatic transport pathways available for radiotracer uptake and transit to the excretory sites at the bile canaliculus. Both the nature of the physiological function to be measured and the underlying mechanisms of the HB diseases to be evaluated by these agents are important factors which must be considered in the design of clinically useful cholescintigraphic agents.

The development of HB imaging agents began in 1955 when the known specific hepatic uptake and subsequent biliary clearance of the dye, rose bengal, led Taplin to synthesize ^{131}I-rose bengal (RB).[35] This agent achieved widespread clinical usage and prompted the development of other dye type compounds labeled with ^{131}I and [123]I. Some of these compounds included bromosulfthalein,[36,37] indocyanine green,[38,39] and ^{123}I rose bengal.[40]

Recently, many ^{99m}Tc-labeled hepatobiliary agents have been developed. The first agent labeled was ^{99m}Tc-pencillamine by Tubis et al.[41] Subsequently, other ^{99m}Tc-labeled hepatobiliary agents such as ^{99m}Tc-labeled glutamate esters, ^{99m}Tc-pyridoxylideneglutamate (^{99m}Tc-PYG), and ^{99m}Tc-N(2,6 dimethylacetanilido) imino-diacetate (HIDA) were developed.[42,42a,42b,43] Various derivatives of ^{99m}Tc-HIDA have been prepared by altering the substituents on the aromatic ring.[44,45] In general, ^{99m}Tc-HIDA derivatives possess greater hepatobiliary specificity than do ^{99m}Tc-PYG derivatives.[31]

The characteristics of an effective cholescintigraphic agent were examined by Firnau.[46] He found that all ^{99m}Tc hepatobiliary agents had molecular weights between 300 and 1000, existed as organic anions, contained at least 2 aromatic ring systems in the molecule, and were all bound to human serum albumin.

Insight into the importance of radiochemical structure in determining in vivo distribution was provided by a comparative distribution study using ^{99m}Tc-HIDA, ^{14}C-HIDA, and [113]Sn-HIDA.[47] These results are shown in Table 3. These data indicate that the ^{99m}Tc complex, and not the complexing agent, was the main compound undergoing hepatobiliary clearance. ^{99m}Tc-HIDA has a higher molecular weight than HIDA (782 compared to 294), but because of the bis structure of the ^{99m}Tc complex, it was also more lipophilic than HIDA as demonstrated by HPLC on reversed phase column.[48]

A systematic study of nine different aromatically substituted derivatives of ^{99m}Tc-HIDA in mice by Burns et al.[49] established a linear relationship between the percent biliary excretion and the natural log of the molecular weight divided by the charge, which is a most significant relationship between distribution and structure for a hepatobiliary agent. When ^{51}Cr, which is known to form biocomplexes with iminodiacetate, was substituted for ^{99m}Tc, the biliary excretion of ^{51}Cr-HIDA was similar to the ^{99m}Tc-HIDA. The role of ^{99m}Tc is that of a metal ion which shapes the structure of the complex for ^{99m}Tc-HIDA hepatobiliary agents.[49] The structure of the Tc bis compound is shown in Figure 8.[48] The anionic charge on the complex indicates that ^{99m}Tc-HIDA is transported by the anionic pathway shown in Figure 7. Inhibition studies with the anionic compound bromosulfthalein demonstrated a marked decrease in the liver's anionic clearance of ^{131}I-rose bengal and ^{99m}Tc-HIDA from 20% to 6% and 55% to 1.5%, respectively.[50] Saturation levels of cationic oxyphenonium, however, did not affect the hepatobiliary clearance of these agents.[31]

The development of ^{99m}Tc hepatobiliary agents has created new interest in cholescintigraphy. Excellent images are obtained in studies of biliary physiology and bile flow in nonjaundiced patients. New radiopharmaceuticals should be developed for studies of biliary flow in jaundiced patients. These new agents should either displace bilirubin from binding sites or utilize separate and distinct carrier-mediated processes.[31]

Table 3
HEPATOBILIARY
EXCRETION OF Tc-99m HIDA,
[^{14}C] HIDA, AND Sn-113 HIDA

Time (min)	Percent injected dose in bile		
	Tc-99m HIDA[a]	Sn-113 HIDA[b]	[^{14}C] HIDA[c]
0—15	3.5	0.006	0.004
15—30	18.4	0.005	0.010
30—45	17.3	0.002	0.047
45—60	16.1	0.002	0.061
60—90	15.7	—	0.031
TOTAL	71.0	0.015	0.153

[a] Mean of three dogs.
[b] Mean of two dogs.
[c] Mean of two dogs.

From Ryan, J., Cooper, M., Loberg, M., Harvey, E., and Sikorski, S., *J. Nucl. Med.*, 18, 997, 1977. With permission.

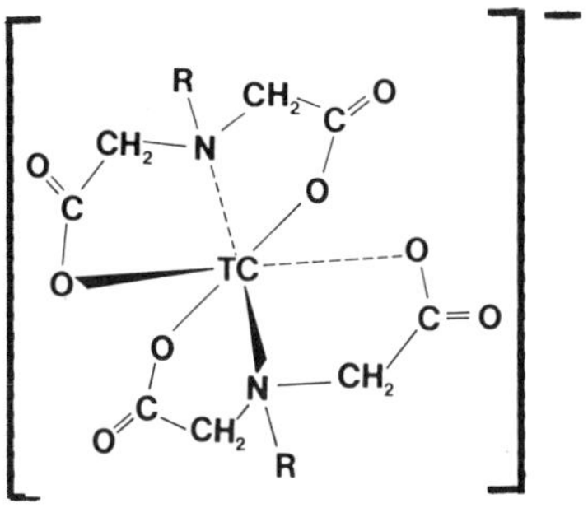

FIGURE 8. Bis complex of N-substituted ^{99m}Tc-iminodiacetate. (From Loberg, M. D., Porter, D. W., and Ryan, J. W., *Proc. 2nd Int. Symp. Radiopharmaceuticals II,* Sorenson, J. A., Coordinator, Society of Nuclear Medicine, New York, 1979, 519. With permission.)

B. Radioiodine: ^{131}I, ^{125}I, ^{123}I

The radionuclides of iodine have been used extensively since the early days of nuclear medicine; first as 8.0-day ^{131}I (364 keV gamma rays), next as 60-day ^{125}I (35 keV X-rays) mostly for radioimmunoassay, and more recently as 13-hr ^{123}I (159 keV gamma rays) for scintigraphy. A comparison of these radionuclides by Myers presents the progress of radioiodine developed for nuclear medicine applications.[51]

1. Radioiodide

Radioiodide was first used to investigate the biochemistry of iodine in the thyroid.[52] Iodide is concentrated in the thyroid by active transport to levels 20 times the plasma concentration. Oxidation of iodide to iodine in the thyroid leads to incorporation into tyrosine of thyroglobulin. The iodinated tyrosyl molecules are coupled to give iodothyronines; thyroxine (T$_4$) or triiodothyronine (T$_3$).[53]

Thyroid hormones secreted by the thyroid enter the bloodstream and bind to the thyroid-binding proteins in the plasma which are thyroid-binding globulin (TBG), thyroid binding prealbumin (TBPA), and thyroid-binding albumin (TBA). Combined binding of T_4 is 99.95% by TBG, TBPA, and TBA.[54,55]

Radioiodine has been useful in scintigraphy of functioning thyroid or for therapeutic application to thyroid disease.

2. Radioiodination of Proteins

Radioiodination of proteins is accomplished by several methods: (1) iodine monochloride, (2) chloramine T, (3) enzymatic, and (4) electrolytic.

A number of proteins have been radioiodinated including plasma proteins, colloidal proteins, enzymes, hormones, antigens, antibodies, and bacterial toxins.[3]

a. ^{131}I-Albumin (^{131}I-HSA)

[131]I-albumin has many applications in scintigraphy. It has been used for delineation of brain tumors, blood pool, and active synovitis. ^{131}I-HSA has shown a relatively high tumor to normal brain uptake ratio of 33:1. Radioactive substances bound to serum proteins penetrate the damaged blood-brain barrier more readily than ionic substances. The normal blood-brain barrier (BBB) physiologically limits the exchange of substances between the blood in the cerebral capillary lumen and the neurone.

Chemicals not required for brain metabolism are excluded from brain tissue despite a rich blood supply. However, fat-soluble substances such as O_2, CO, and noble gases readily cross into the brain cells.

Mediated transport mechanisms must be present for glucose and amino acids to cross the BBB. Limited transport is provided for ions such as K^+, Na^+, and Mg^{++} and water molecules.

b. ^{131}I-Macroaggregated Albumin (^{131}I-MAA)

^{131}I-MAA was first developed by Taplan and used by Wagner and others to visualize lung perfusion.[56,57] Macroaggregated albumin particles which are 1000 times larger than colloids are taken out in the first capillary bed seen by the particles. In normal perfusion, both lungs are evenly visualized, while reduced perfusion will give reduced uptake compared to the normal lung.

c. ^{131}I-Orthoiodohippurate (^{131}I-OIH)

^{131}I-OIH is the only suitable agent for estimation of effective renal plasma flow (ERPF). This can be accomplished by single injection clearance techniques. ^{131}I-orthoiodohippurate or ^{18}F clears rapidly through the kidneys without retention, although in the first pass there is retention in the cortex which clears within 30 sec.[3] They then become localized in the inner medulla and in the urine within the pelvocalyceal system. Radiorenography is usually accomplished with dual probe counting and development of the clearance curve over each kidney.

Serial imaging of the kidneys with ^{131}I-OIH will provide information on patency of vascular supply, function, size, and location of the kidney and the patency of the urinary outflow tract.[58,59]

C. Other Kidney Agents

Other renal agents in addition to those previously mentioned in the radioiodine section include radio mercury chlormerodrin and [131]pertechnetate chelates or saccharides.[59a] Of these agents, radiochlormerodrin is extracted by the renal tubules from the plasma with increasing concentration in the cortex from 1 to 3 hr post-injection.[60,61] Most of the radioactivity is intracellular in the proximal and distal tubules. The rate of urinary excretion is slow and the medullary concentration remains low. After the urinary activity has cleared the kidney, the activity remaining is that trapped in the cortical tubules.

^{99m}Tc-Pertechnetate appears rapidly in the cortex and medulla with little cortical trapping and thus provides a good assessment of renal perfusion.[62,63] ^{99m}Tc-Iron ascorbate complex moves rapidly through the kidney; however about 10% is retained in cortex after the medulla has cleared.[64-68]

A comparison of a number of ^{99m}Tc complexes for renal imaging was reported by Arnold et al.[69] Renal agents covered in this report were ^{99m}Tc-labeled iron ascorbate (Fe-Asc), 2,3-dimercaptosuccinic acid (DMS), and glucoheptonate (GHA). The results of the blood clearance of these agents in humans are seen in Table 4.[69] The blood clearance of DMS is relatively slow even after 6 hr. GHA has a relatively rapid blood clearance, identical to that of gluconate,[70] and similar to that of ^{113m}In-DTPA for the first 2 hr, but slower thereafter. Fe-Asc clears rapidly for the first 6 hr, but then slows markedly. For both DMS and GHA, nearly all of the activity is in the plasma with little diffusion into the red cells. About 50% of the plasma activity GHA is loosely bound to proteins initially and then increases to about 75% after 6 hr. For DMS, about 75% of the plasma activity is loosely bound to proteins in the first 6 hr and increases to 90% by 24 hr. For Fe-Asc, about 80% of the total activity is in the plasma fraction and the remaining 20% reversibly diffuses into the red cell volume. About 50 to 70% of the plasma activity is loosely bound to plasma proteins.

Routine renal imaging for visualizing abnormalities of both the pelvocalyceal collecting system and the renal parenchyma can be accomplished with ^{99m}Tc-gluconate or GHA.[69,70]

The urinary excretion of ^{99m}Tc complexes of GHA and DMS in humans as 24 hr cumulative urinary clearance is shown in Figure 9.[69] The clearance of DMS is very slow while the initial clearance of GHA is faster. Images with ^{99m}Tc-DMS showed progressive accumulation in the renal parenchyma up to 6 hr without accumulation in the renal collecting system.[69] ^{99m}Tc-DMS was designed to replace mercury-labeled chlormerodrin.[71] The absolute renal concentration is about twice that of other ^{99m}Tc complexes in man, approaching that of chlormerodrin.[69] The plasma clearance of DMS is similar to that of chlormerodrin,[72] but its blood clearance is slower. The urinary excretion of DMS is extremely slow which gives a poor image of the pelvocalyceal system.

D. Heart and Brain Agents for Flow and Metabolic Studies

1. The Control of Metabolism by Ion Transport Across Membranes[73]

Translocation of certain ions can greatly increase metabolic rates within the cell. Thus, there is an important interaction of transport of ions across the membranes with metabolic pathways.

Transport in general is the means for bringing into or out of the cells the necessary materials for metabolic pathways. Many of these materials are coincidentally ions. The transport system requires energy to work so that the cells utilize much of their metabolism to drive the transport system.

The effects of ion transport on metabolism can be either direct or indirect.

a. Direct Effects of Ions on Enzyme Systems

Ions can either be stimulatory or inhibitory on enzyme action. Enzyme action is favored by the presence of certain ions such as K^+ and Mg^{2+} which are specific on pyruvate kinase. On the other hand, pyruvate kinase is inhibited by low concentrations of Ca^{2+}. Another effect is caused by H^+ transport which can change the pH of the medium containing different enzymes.

Table 4

BLOOD CLEARANCE OF ^{99m}Tc RENAL COMPLEXES IN HUMANS

Time	Percent dose technetium-iron-ascorbate complex (n = 12)			Percent dose technetium-glucoheptonate (n = 9)			Percent dose technetium-dimercaptosuccinic acid (n = 7)		
	Blood volume	Plasma volume	Plasma protein fraction	Blood volume	Plasma volume	Plasma protein fraction	Blood volume	Plasma volume	Plasma protein fraction
5 min	42.7 ± 12.0	34.6 ± 13.3	23.3 ± 9.2	32.9 ± 4.00	32.7 ± 3.90	15.4 ± 2.30	69.2 ± 6.90	69.2 ± 6.90	52.8 ± 3.30
15 min	28.9 ± 7.7	23.5 ± 10.3	14.9 ± 5.6	21.3 ± 3.50	21.1 ± 3.30	10.5 ± 2.50	55.6 ± 5.80	55.6 ± 6.40	44.4 ± 9.40
30 min	21.9 ± 5.6	18.6 ± 6.0	11.1 ± 4.4	15.2 ± 2.70	15.1 ± 2.60	7.9 ± 1.70	43.0 ± 4.60	43.0 ± 5.10	33.3 ± 6.50
60 min	17.7 ± 5.3	13.1 ± 4.6	9.6 ± 3.3	11.4 ± 2.00	11.2 ± 2.10	6.1 ± 1.00	29.8 ± 3.90	29.8 ± 3.90	22.7 ± 4.70
90 min		—	—	9.2 ± 1.30	8.9 ± 1.10	5.2 ± 0.94	23.9 ± 2.30	23.8 ± 2.80	18.1 ± 3.90
3 hr	10.1 ± 3.5	8.6 ± 3.4	6.3 ± 2.2	6.6 ± 1.10	6.3 ± 1.20	4.5 ± 1.20	14.4 ± 1.20	13.8 ± 1.30	10.5 ± 1.60
6 hr	7.5 ± 2.9	6.1 ± 2.7	5.1 ± 2.8	5.1 ± 1.00	4.9 ± 1.00	3.8 ± 0.96	9.5 ± 1.00	9.4 ± 1.30	7.2 ± 1.30
24 hr	4.2 ± 1.9	4.0 ± 1.8	3.9 ± 1.1	3.1 ± 0.55	3.1 ± 0.57	2.7 ± 0.41	4.4 ± 0.54	4.3 ± 0.64	4.0 ± 0.65

From Arnold, R. W., Subramanian, G., McAfee, J. G., Blair, R. J., and Thomas, F. D., *J. Nucl. Med.*, 16, 357, 1975. With permission.

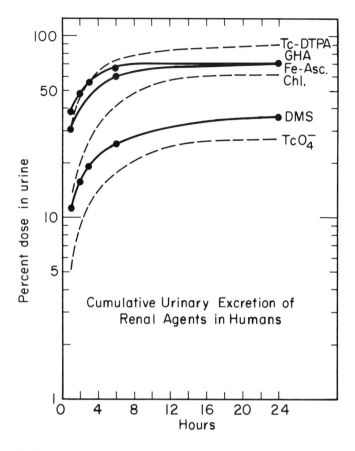

FIGURE 9. Mean cumulative urinary excretion curves up to 24 hr: ^{99m}Tc-DMS, ^{99m}Tc-GHA, and ^{99m}Tc-Fe Asc in volunteers and patients. (From Arnold, R. W., Subramanian, G., McAfee, J. G., Blair, R. J., and Thomas, F. D., *J. Nucl. Med.*, 16, 357, 1975. With permission.)

b. Some Ions Which Must Be Transported

Ion transport systems sometimes indirectly regulate the function of metabolic pathways, because they carry through the membrane organic ions which are the substrate of some enzymes. Such is the case with the substrates of the tricarboxylic acid cycle. All of the enzymes are located within the mitochondria, and the substrates, when present outside, need to be transported to the inside of the mitochondria. This represents the clearest example of the dependence of metabolism on transport. Two classes of transport of this type are (1) ionic substrates which are transferred across the membrane, and (2) substrates which are not ions, but whose transport is dependent on ions. Examples of the former are members of the tricarboxylic acid cycle: phosphate, adenine nucleotides, and amino acids. Some transport systems of nonionic substrates seem to be linked to the transport of ions. Two such examples are the transport of glucose linked to the sodium ions and the coupling of proton transport to the transport of galactose.[74,75] Ion transport systems are capable of stimulating metabolism to satisfy their energy requirement. Some important facts related to energy requirements for ion transport are (1) materials transported into or out of cell membranes that are utilized in metabolic pathways or degradation products, and (2) transport of K^+ which increases glycolysis by a factor of two and provides the energy required.

It has been shown that K^+ accumulation is necessary for providing electrical energy to drive the transport of neutral amino acids.[76]

This diagram from Pena shows two facts:[73]

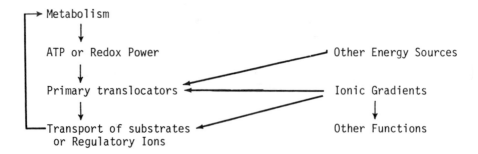

(1) One of the main roles of ion-transport systems is that of feeding and regulating metabolism, and (2) that ion transport, through establishment of ionic gradients, can be directly utilized to drive other transport systems.[73]

2. Transport of Thallium[77,78]

Thallium is transported from the extracellular fluid across the cell membrane to a preferred intracellular location. The transport kinetics is similar to potassium and is facilitated by depolarization and repolarization of the myocardial cell membrane. About 3% of the intracellular K^+ is exchanged with extracellular K^+ and Tl^+ with each beat when aerobic metabolism and glucose fuel the Na-K ATP-ase pump. The Tl^+ uptake is dependent on membrane transport and flow in the early clearance of ^{201}Tl. With anaerobic metabolism, little or no Tl is incorporated into the cell even under high flow conditions.

Although $^{201}Tl^+$ is a transitional metallic element of Group III-A of the periodic table, it has biological properties similar to potassium. Like K, Tl^+ can activate the Na/K ATP-ase system.[79]

The initial distribution of ^{201}Tl is related to: (1) regional perfusion and (2) cellular extraction efficiency. After intravenous injection, the blood levels of Tl^+ reach a peak rapidly and then drop to a low level within 10 to 15 min. Initial $^{201}Tl^+$ distribution has been shown to be closely related to regional blood flow as defined by microspheres.[80]

Extraction of Tl^+ from the blood by the myocardium may be reduced by acidosis, hypercapnea, digitalis, and propranolol. Extraction may be increased by insulin, glucose, and isoproternol.[81] The myocardial extraction efficiency for ^{201}Tl is about 85% under basal conditions. This extraction efficiency causes the initial distribution of ^{201}Tl to be related to blood flow. The myocardial kinetics of thallium-201 and potassium-42 in patients with normal coronary angiography were studied to determine the effect of myocardial blood flow (MBF) and coronary output (CO) on the extraction of ^{201}Tl and ^{42}K by the myocardium.[82] Iodine-125 radioiodinated human serum albumin (^{125}I RIHSA) was used as the intravascular tracer and tritiated water (THO) was the extravascular tracer. Some of these results are shown in Figure 10.[82] Small but consistent differences were present in arterial concentration of the four isotopes during first passage, resulting from their different space of distribution in the lungs. Immediately after initial dilution, ^{201}Tl and ^{42}K concentration showed a progressive and rapid fall relative to the reference tracers, indicating a retention in extravascular space. ^{201}Tl and ^{42}K activity in the arterial blood averaged, respectively, 2.5% and 2.5% of the injected dose per liter of blood at 2 min, 0.8% and 0.7% at 10 min, and 0.4% and 0.3% at 30 min. The time course of the arterial curves of ^{201}Tl and ^{42}K was similar in all patients only during the first minute; after 1 min there was individual variability,[82] indicating individual differences in total body extraction of the two tracers.

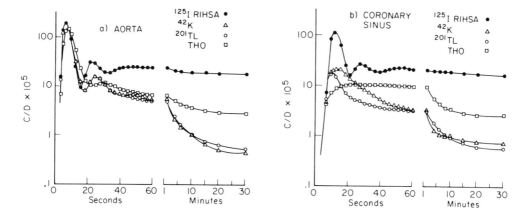

FIGURE 10.   Time-concentration curves of ^{125}I radioiodinated human serum albumin (^{125}I RIHSA), potassium-42 (^{42}K), thallium-201 (^{201}Tl) and tritiated water (THO) of patient 2: (a) in the aorta, and (b) in the coronary sinus. The concentration (C) is expressed as a fraction of the injectate (D). The arterial concentration of ^{125}I RIHSA, ^{42}K, and ^{201}Tl are similar during the first pass, while that of THO is more dispersed. Obvious differences are also present during the first minute in the coronary sinus, indicating wide differences in the accessible space. (From L'Abbate, A., Biagini, A., Michelassi, C., and Maseri, A., *Circulation*, 60, 776, 1979. With permission.)

3. Fluorodeoxyglucose or Deoxyglucose (^{18}F-FDG or ^{11}C-Methyl DG)

^{18}F-FDG or ^{11}C-DG are useful as tracers for regional glucose consumption in cerebral structures.[83] FDG behaves like DG with essential properties such that: (1) it is transported and competes with glucose for phosphorylation by cerebral hexokinases to their respective hexose-phosphates; and (2) FDG-phosphate, once formed, is sufficiently slowly degraded that it can be considered essentially trapped. In two patients studied with ^{14}F-FDG, the following conditions were used:

1.   5.3 mCi FDG (8.9 mCi/mg)
2.   8.2 mCi FDG (8.8 mCi/mg)

The following equation and assumption were made to calculate glucose consumption:[83]

$$R = \frac{C_T{}^*(T) - k_1{}^* e^{-(k_2{}^*+k_3{}^*)T} \int_0^T C_p{}^* e^{(k_2{}^*+k_3{}^*)t}\, dt}{\left[\dfrac{\lambda \cdot V_{max}{}^* \cdot K_m}{\phi \cdot V_{max} \cdot K_m{}^*}\right]\left[\int_0^T (C_p{}^*/C_p)\, dt - e^{-(k_2{}^*+k_3{}^*)T} \int_0^T (C_p{}^*/C_p) e^{(k_2{}^*+k_3{}^*)t} dt\right]}$$

where

R	=	calculated rate of glucose consumption per gram tissue
$^*C_T$	=	concentration of DG + DG − 6 − PO$_4$ in tissue
$^*C_p$ and C_p	=	arterial plasma concentration of DG and glucose
$k_1{}^*, k_2{}^*, K_3{}^*$	=	rate constant (transport plasma to precursor pool, transport back to plasma from tissue, and phosphorylation of DG in tissue)
λ	=	ratio of distribution volume of DG in tissue to that of glucose
ϕ	=	fraction of glucose, once phosphorylated continues down glycolytic pathway

$k_m{}^*$, $V_{max}{}^*$, and k_m and V_{max} are kinetic constants of hexokinase for DG and glucose respectively. Six constants lumped together,

$$(\lambda \cdot V_{max}^* \cdot k_m / \phi \cdot V_{max} \cdot k_m^*) = k$$

Requirements or assumed conditions for calculations and use in studies of metabolism per gram tissue are

1. Taken up by brain at rate proportional to glucose, metabolic products must remain within tissue in known form, i.e., as DG
2. γ-Emitting radionuclide
3. Low radiation exposure

The use of ^{18}F-FDG for determination of local cerebral glucose metabolism requires knowledge of both arterial blood plasma glucose and ^{18}F-FDG concentration as a function of time following i.v. bolus injection. Both DG and FDG are transported from blood into the brain by the same saturable carrier mechanism that transports glucose.[84,85]

Once phosphorylated to DG-6-PO$_4$ it remains in the tissue in that form. It is essentially trapped since the half-life of DG-6-PO$_4$ in gray matter is 8 hr and 10 hr in white matter.[86] Note that, in sufficiently high concentration, DG inhibits the transport and utilization of glucose,[87] possibly by depletion of available ATP, but mainly by competitive inhibition of phosphohexokinase isomerase by DG-6-PO$_4$. Therefore DG must be used in trace amounts so as to have no effect on glucose metabolism.

The substitution of a fluorine atom for hydrogen on C-2 of DG does not alter its metabolic fate. It has been shown that FDG is phosphorylated by hexokinase to 2-deoxy-2-fluoro-D-glucose phosphate.[88] The modification of glucose at C-2 to 2-DG or 2-FDG does interfere with its ability to undergo active transport,[89] but since brain glucose transport is carrier-mediated, it is not necessary for the substrate to possess the structure needed for active transport. It has been shown that glucose and DG share the same transport systems facilitating entry across the blood-brain barrier,[90] thus demonstrating that structural modification at C-2 does not interfere with carrier-mediated transport,[84] although it does interfere with active transport.

Evidence indicates that FDG is a nonreversible inhibitor of glucose metabolism,[90] but this is not a factor when FDG is used in tracer amounts.

The transport of glucose across cell membranes is thought to occur via a saturable process called facilitated diffusion.[91] Studies have shown that binding of hexose to the membrane carrier involves hydrogen bonding of the pyranose form at several sites, notably C-1, C-2, C-3, and C-6. Substitution of the C-6 hydroxyl by a lipophilic iodine atom caused no change in the binding affinity of 6-iodo-6-deoxygalactose when compared with D-glucose.[92]

The biodistribution of ^{18}F-FDG in mice was investigated by Gallagher et al.[93] It was found that the ^{18}F-FDG initially distributes to all the organs and then rapidly clears, except from the brain and heart. This metabolic trapping of ^{18}F-FDG-6-P results from high hexokinase activity and low or absent glucose-6-phosphatase activity.[93] The ^{18}F-FDG that clears from lungs, liver, and kidneys is excreted into urine as unchanged ^{18}F-FDG. Apparently the kidney tubules cannot reabsorb FDG. Thus, virtually all of the ^{18}F-FDG that is transported through the heart and brain is rapidly phosphorylated by hexokinase. The potential clinical utility of [18]FDG for measuring the ability of the brain and heart to transport, phosphorylate, and utilize glucose in vivo depends upon an understanding of the mechanism which relates [18]FDG metabolism to glucose metabolism.[93]

Emission computed tomography (ECT) can provide in vivo quantitative concentrations of radiotracers over selected time frames to measure physiologic functions of flow and metabolic rates. The use of ^{18}F-labeled deoxyglucose or ^{11}C-labeled fatty acids in conjunction with ECT can be useful in studies of ischemic heart disease for diagnosis and therapy.[94] In the normal heart perfused with free fatty acids (FFA) and glucose, FFAs are the primary substrate for oxidative metabolism. The amount of FFA uptake depends on FFA concentration and rate of oxidative respiration.

The metabolism of glucose in the aerobic heart depends upon the plasma concentration of glucose and insulin, availability of other substrates (FFA), workload, and rate of oxidative metabolism.[95-98] Under anaerobic conditions, the rate of glucose metabolism appears to be primarily flow related.[94]

The uptake and long retention of [18]FDG in the myocardium are consistent with the hypothesis that in the myocardium FDG competes for transport sites and hexokinase in the same way as has been determined in the brain for ^{14}C-deoxyglucose and ^{18}F-FDG.[86,99] The FDG-6-PO$_4$ appears to be formed and trapped in the myocardium as in brain because of low cellular membrane permeability as shown in Figure 11.[94] The low activity of glucose-6-phosphatase prevents the conversion back to FDG which could diffuse out of the tissue into blood. In the work of Phelps et al.[94] there was low uptake in liver at 40 min. This, coupled with the rapid liver clearance found by Gallagher et al.,[100] suggests that FDG is not converted to glycogen in liver as seen in Figure 11 for glucose.[94] If FDG is specific for myocardial glycolysis from glucose in the blood, but not from intracellular glycogen, then FDG would not reflect the amount coming from glycogen stores as shown in Figure 11. However, this is not a significant difference since the amount of glycogen in the myocardial cells is small and can provide glucose for only a short time.

FDG can be used as a tracer for in vivo studies of myocardial metabolic rates for exogenous glucose in various metabolic states.[94] FDG in combination with a FFA, such as ^{11}C-palmitic acid, will permit a measure of regional anaerobic and aerobic myocardial metabolic rates and a measure of the working state of the myocardium.

a. Fatty Acids

Nonesterified fatty acids are transported in the blood as a soluble complex with plasma albumin.[101] Free fatty acids are mobilized from adipose tissue by several hormones including norepinephrine, adrenal corticotropic hormone, insulin, and thyroid hormone.[102]

Free fatty acids are rapidly removed from the circulation with a half-life of about 2 min when injected intravenously in dogs.[101] The rate of passage of the fatty acid molecule across the cell membrane is many times greater than the passage of the albumin molecules with which the fatty acids are associated. The fatty acid is kept in solution until the fatty acid-albumin complex dissociates at the surface of the endothelial cell in blood.[103]

Oxidation of fatty acids, which is the primary myocardial energy source, is dependent upon the length of the fatty acid chain.[104] From 25 to 75% of myocardial oxygen use can be accounted for by uptake of nonesterified fatty acids.[105]

In circulating blood, oleic acid is the largest component of free fatty acids, and the myocardial uptake rate is the highest for oleic acid in both man and dogs.[106,107] Long-chain fatty acids of greater than 16 carbons are dependent upon the enzyme carnitine acyl-COA transferase for their translocation from the extramitochondrial to the intramitochondrial sites. Under aerobic conditions, myocardial fatty acid beta oxidation yields intracellular accumulation of citrate and isocitrate. It has been demonstrated that beta oxidation of fatty acid is dependent upon the chain length of fatty acid when palmitate was metabolized at a rate greater than octanoate.[104]

In the isolated heart, nonesterified fatty acids are rapidly extracted by the heart muscle and a portion of the uptake is temporarily stored as tissue triglyceride and phospholipid.[108] Infusion of glucose and insulin and radioiodinated oleic acid in-

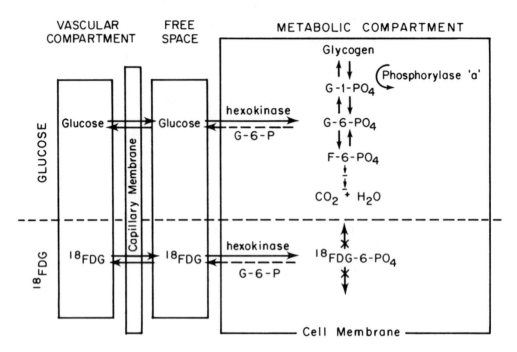

FIGURE 11.   Simplified schematic representation of myocardial utilization of glucose and a physiologic analogue, 2-deoxyglucose labeled with ^{18}F (FDG). G-6-PO$_4$ is a glucose-6-PO$_4$; G-1-PO$_4$ is glucose-1-PO$_4$; F-6-PO$_4$ is fructose-6-PO$_4$. FDG competes with glucose for transport sites in the capillary and cell membrane and for hexokinase, the enzyme for converting glucose to glucose-6-PO$_4$. FDG is trapped in myocardial cells as FDG-6-PO$_4$, since the enzymatic conversion to G-1-PO$_4$ and F-6-PO$_4$ is inhibited by the 2-deoxy analogue of glucose and low membrane permeability to DG-6-PO$_4$. Slow tissue clearance of FDG-6-PO$_4$ shown in this work indicates that cellular concentration of glucose-6-phosphatase (G-6-P), which converts FDG-6-PO$_4$ back to FDG, must be low. Note that glycolysis can occur from both exogenous (cellular glycogen) sources, whereas FDG is specific to the exogenous route. (From Phelps, M. E., Hoffman, E. J., Selin, C., Huang, S. C., Robinson, G., MacDonald, N., Schelbert, H., and Kuhl, D. E., *J. Nucl. Med.*, 19, 1311, 1978. With permission.)

creased the ratio of radioactivity in heart muscle to blood by enhancing storage of the fatty acid as a myocardial triglyceride and decreasing oxidation of the fatty acid in heart and other tissues.

4. Coronary Flow Measurements with ^{133}Xe, ^{127}Xe, or ^{81m}Kr

The measurement of actual myocardial cell perfusion is possible with continuous perfusion of ^{81m}Kr,[109] or washout of ^{133}Xe or ^{127}Xe. In comparison, coronary arteriography permits only a two-dimensional representation of large vessel coronary anatomy. Flowthat is determined by the resistance in the microarteriolar bed rather than by the caliber of the main vessels is best determined by the use of gas flow measurements which provide a physiologic measurement of flow.

More useful than a single static flow measurement is the application of "maximum dilation" stimuli which increases flow 2.5- to 4-fold in 10 to 30 sec after injection in normal regions.[110] This coronary reserve is reduced by critically narrowed proximal vessels or by proximal coronary spasms.

E. ^{67}Ga-Tumor Imaging

Human melanoma cells were incubated with ^{67}Ga-citrate, a mixture of ^{67}Ga-citrate and transferrin, ^{67}Ga-transferrin, and ^{67}Ga-transferrin-^{125}I.[111] It was found that there was a greater and more rapid uptake of ^{67}Ga by the tumor cell when the gallium was complexed to transferrin. It was further found that when melanoma cells were incubated with ^{67}Ga-transferrin-^{125}I, the ^{125}I associated with the cell fraction remained constant after 15 min of incubation, while the ^{67}Ga continued to increase beyond this point.

Indications point to both a passive and active mechanism for the uptake of radiogallium by the human tumor cells. However, it appears that passive diffusion did not play a major role in the uptake of ^{67}Ga. The transport of ^{67}Ga into the tumor cells was mediated through transferrin of the serum proteins studied. It is suggested that ^{67}Ga enters the cell after the gallium-transferrin complex combines with a cell surface receptor.

It is known that once ^{67}Ga-citrate is injected intravenously it is bound to plasma proteins and particularly to transferrin.[112,113] Transferrin not only plays an important role as a carrier of gallium in the bloodstream, but also appears to be essential for the incorporation of ^{67}Ga into human tumor cells.

While there is some support for the idea that transferrin enters the cell by endocytosis, very good evidence supports the concept of the existence of cell surface receptors which specifically bind transferrin.[114,115] Gallium-67, as the cation, enters the cell from the cell surface receptors where it can be stored by lysosomes bound to ferritin or lactoferritin.[116-119]

Results with ^{67}Ga-transferrin-^{125}I confirm the existence of cell membrane receptors which bind transferrin, allowing for the transport of gallium into the cells and subsequently releasing the transferrin.[111] The rapid continuing increase of ^{67}Ga activity in conjunction with the constant ^{125}I activity implies that a rapid turnover of the protein exists at the tumor cell surface membrane.

The exact mechanism facilitating the transfer of ^{67}Ga from the plasma to the cell is still unknown.[120] However, the association of ^{67}Ga with transferrin is known.[112,121,122] Tissue-bound ^{67}Ga is also associated with the iron-binding proteins ferritin and transferrin,[112,118,123] and ^{67}Ga is found primarily in microvesicles of tumor cells and lysosomes of normal liver cells.[116]

Gallium-67, a Group III-b transition metal, resembles ferric ion in atomic radius, charge, and in the type of inorganic complexes formed.[124,125] A major difference between gallium and iron is the inability of gallium to be reduced in vivo, whereas ferric ion is easily reduced and interacts with protoporphyrin to form heme,[119] but gallium remains bound to ion-transport proteins and carrier molecules. This difference in a large part explains why the biologic distribution of iron and gallium are different in spite of similar physical properties.

Gallium binds to at least four iron-binding molecules: transferrin (TF); lactoferrin (LF); ferritin; and siderophores, which are low molecular weight compounds facilitating iron uptake by microorganisms.[120] The dissociation constants for gallium-macromolecular complexes vary with pH and concentration. The relative affinity of gallium for ferritin is unknown, but the relative affinity for the other iron-binding molecules are as follows: siderophore > LF > TF.[127] This order of affinity is similar to ferric iron although the magnitude is considerably different.

Ferric ion easily displaces gallium from TF and, to a lesser extent, from LF.[120] When a large excess of ferric ion is administered before or coincident with ^{67}Ga, tumor and tissue localization of ^{67}Ga is inhibited, and urinary excretion is enhanced.[128]

F. Radionuclides of Indium

1. Indium-113m

Indium-113m decays with a half-life of 1.7 hr by isomeric transition and emission of 390 keV gamma rays. The ^{113m}In is obtained by elution with hydrochloric acid from its 118-day ^{113}Sn parent. When ^{113m}In is administered intravenously at a pH < 4, ^{113m}In binds to the plasma globulin transferrin to serve as a blood pool label.[128a] The removal of [113m]In from the transferrin into the bone marrow and liver is a slow process with a half-time of 8 to 10 hr.[2,129,130]

Indium-113m transferrin can be used to determine cardiac dynamics such as cardiac output and, because of its short half-life, repeated measurements can be made without undue radiation dose to the patient.[131]

2. Indium-111

Indium-111, $T_{1/2}$ 2.8 days, decays by electron capture with 173 and 247 keV γ-emissions.[132] Ionic ^{111}In binds to transferrin and its pharmacologic fate is similar to [113]In. The longer half-life of ^{111}In makes it suitable for slow biologic processes such as cisternography which require 48 to 72 hr images.[133,134] Indium-111 bound to DTPA chelate is injected intrathecally for these studies.

Indium-111 has been used as a tumor scanning agent as ^{111}In-transferrin or as ^{111}In-bleomycin.[135,136] However, there is conflicting evidence as to the in vivo stability of ^{111}In-bleomycin. It appears that the in vivo distribution of ^{111}In-bleomycin and ^{111}In-transferrin is similar, which points to an in vivo conversion from ^{111}In-bleomycin to ^{111}In-transferrin because of the stronger binding to transferrin relative to bleomycin.

Ionic ^{111}In-transferrin has been suggested as a bone marrow scanning agent. In vitro similarities between ^{59}Fe and ^{111}In with localization in red cells and reticulocytes indicated uptake in hematopoietic marrow.[137] However, there appear to be significant differences in ^{59}Fe and ^{111}In red cell binding and metabolism to create uncertainty for the use of ^{111}In in bone marrow imaging.[138-140]

[111]In-oxine has been used as a nonspecific label of blood elements such as platelets[141] and leukocytes.[142] Oxine is dissolved in ethanol and added to carrier-free ^{111}In to form a neutral lipophilic complex.[142] To this is added the separated blood elements in plasma free medium to give efficient labeling.

The location of the ^{111}In tracer within the cell has been studied in the case of neutrophils.[143] It was concluded that the lipid-soluble ^{111}In-oxine complex passively penetrates the cell membrane, where the vast majority of ^{111}In binds to three cytoplasmic components of apparent molecular weights 540,000, 80,000, and 3600. Only a small part of the ^{111}In binds to DNA, and a large part of the oxine is released from the cell.[143,144]

Since ^{111}In-oxine is a nonspecific label, selective cell labeling requires pure cell type suspensions which can cause cell damage. Thus there is a need for a radionuclide which will label cells in a nutrient medium and which will label only specific types of cohort cells.[144]

IV. CONCLUSION

The in vivo distribution of commonly used radiotracers has been discussed with emphasis upon the transport of various radiotracers when they are administered intravenously or intrathecally. In most cases, an important consideration has been the interaction of the radiotracer with the blood elements such as plasma proteins or cells. Another consideration has been the mechanism of uptake, whether by specific binding sites or cell membrane permeability.

The scope of this chapter has been relatively wide ranging to touch upon a number of radionuclides and radiotracers with the purpose of presenting a general overview of transport and radiotracer distribution for imaging in nuclear medicine.

Except for [11]C- and ^{18}F-labeled deoxyglucose and ^{11}C-palmitic acid, it has not been possible to cover many of the newer and promising positron emitting radiotracers for quantitative in vivo studies with [11]C-, [13]N-, or ^{15}O-labeled biochemical compounds and flow tracers. All of these agents, in conjunction with positron-emission computed tomography, are useful for quantitative perfusion and metabolic studies to determine variations between normal and diseased states.

Recent work has been reported on the use of ^{18}F-fluorodeoxyglucose and ^{13}N-ammonia in partial epilepsy,[145] and on the use of ^{18}F-deoxyglucose for determination of cerebral metabolism in senile dementia.[146] Other work has been reported on the use of ^{15}O-labeled O_2 and CO_2 for the measurement of oxygen utilization and cerebral blood flow in the brain of man.[147,148]

Another area not covered but certainly of growing importance is the use of radiolabeled enzyme inhibitors and radiotracers for uptake in specific binding sites as scanning agents with greater specificity for understanding in vivo biochemistry.

Recent work has been reported on ^{11}C-steroids for potential receptor binding,[148] and on cell-specific hepatic binding protein ligands.[149,150] In addition, studies have been done with receptor binding of radiolabeled estrogen.[151] Other studies used radioiodinated beta adrenoceptor blockers for in vivo receptor binding,[152] and cardioselective radiolabeled beta adrenergic antagonists for myocardial imaging.[153]

The instrumentation and radiotracers now under development will be powerful tools to study and quantitate the in vivo dynamic processes of transport and biochemistry as they relate to normal vs. diseased states.

REFERENCES

1. **Yano, Y.**, Effects of transport on distribution of radioions and radiometabolites, in *Principles of Radiopharmacology*, Vol. II, Colombetti, L. G., Ed., CRC Press, Boca Raton, Fla., 1979, 225.
2. **Alderson, P. O., Krohn, K. A., and Welch, M. J.**, Radiopharmaceuticals, in *Diagnostic Nuclear Medicine*, Gottschalk, A., Ed., Williams & Wilkins, Baltimore, 1976, chap. 6.
3. **McAfee, J. G. and Subramanian, G.**, Radioactive agents for imaging, in *Clinical Scintillation Scanning*, Freeman, L. M. and Johnson, P. M., Eds., Grune & Stratton, New York, 1975, 13.
4. **Bell, E. G. and McAfee, J. G.**, Concepts of colloid chemistry, in *Hematopoietic and Gastrointestinal Investigations with Radionuclides*, Charles C Thomas, Springfield, Ill., 1972, 59.
5. **Taplin, G. V.**, The scintillation image, in *Clinical Scintillation Scanning*, Freeman, L. M. and Johnson, P. M., Eds., Grune & Stratton, New York, 1975, 147.
6. **Lathrop, K. A. and Harper, P. V.**, Biological behavior of ^{99m}Tc and ^{99m}Tc-pertechnetate ion, *Progr. Nucl. Med.* 1, 145, 1972.
7. **Patton, D. D. and Crenshaw, R. T.**, Colon scanning with technetium-99m pertechnetate, *J. Nucl. Med.*, 8, 394, 1967.
8. **Welch, M. J., Adatepe, M., and Potchen, E. J.**, An analysis of technetium kinetics; the effect of perchlorate and iodide pretreatment, *Int. J. Appl. Radiat. Isot.*, 20, 437, 1969.
9. **Beierwaltes, W. H.**, Physiology of the thyroid gland, in *Principles of Nuclear Medicine*, Wagner, H. N., Jr., Ed., W. B. Saunders, Philadelphia, 1968, 308.
10. **Keys, J. W., Jr., Thrall, F. H., and Carey, J. H.**, Technical considerations in in vivo thyroid studies, *Semin. Nucl. Med.*, 8, 43, 1978.
11. **Rhodes, B. A.**, Considerations in the radiolabelling of albumin, *Semin. Nucl. Med.*, 4, 281, 1974.
12. **Atkins, H. L., Eckelman, W. C., Hauser, W., Klopfer, J. G., and Richards, P.**, Splenic sequestration of ^{99m}Tc-labeled red blood cells, *J. Nucl. Med.*, 13, 811, 1972.
13. **Atkins, H. L., Eckelman, W. C., Klopfer, J. G., and Richards, P.**, Vascular imaging with ^{99m}Tc red blood cells, *Radiology*, 106, 357, 1973.
14. **Kato, M.**, In vivo labeling of red blood cells with Tc-99m with stannous pyridoxylideneaminates, *J. Nucl. Med.*, 20, 1071, 1979.
15. **Pavel, D. G., Zimmer, A. M., and Patterson, V. N.**, In vivo labeling of red blood cells with ^{99m}Tc: a new approach to blood pool visualization, *J. Nucl. Med.*, 18, 305, 1977.
16. **Hamilton, R. G. and Alderson, P. D.**, A comparative evaluation of techniques for rapid and efficient in vivo labeling of red blood cells with ^{99m}Tc pertechnetate, *J. Nucl. Med.*, 18, 1010, 1977.
16a. **Colombetti, L. G. and Siddiqui, A.**, Efficiency of in vivo labeling of red blood cells with ^{99m}Tc, *Nuklearmedizin*, 15(5), 211, 1976.

17. Dewanjee, M. K., Binding of ^{99m}Tc to hemoglobin, *J. Nucl. Med.,* 15, 703, 1974.
18. Smith, E. M., Internal dose calculations for ^{99m}Tc, *J. Nucl. Med.,* 6, 231, 1965.
19. Blau, M., Ganatra, R., and Bender, M. A., ^{18}F-fluorine for bone-imaging, *Semin. Nucl. Med.,* 2, 31, 1972.
20. Krishnamurthy, G. T., Thomas, P. B., Tubis, M., Endow, J. S., Pritchard, J. H., and Blahd, W. H., Comparison of ^{99m}Tc-polyphosphate and ^{18}F. I. Kinetics, *J. Nucl. Med.,* 15, 832, 1974.
21. Saha, G. B. and Boyd, C. M., A study of protein-binding of ^{99m}Tc-methylene diphosphonate in plasma, *Int. J. Nucl. Med. Biol.,* 6, 201, 1979.
22. Subramanian, G., McAfee, J. G., Blair, R. J., Kallfelz, F. A., and Thomas, F. D., Technetium-99m-methylene diphosphonate - a superior agent for skeletal imaging: comparison with other technetium complexes, *J. Nucl. Med.,* 16, 744, 1975.
23. Krishnamurthy, G. T., Tubis, M., Endow, J. S., Singhi, V., Walsh, C. F., and Blahd, W. H., Clinical comparison of the kinetics of ^{99m}Tc-labeled polyphosphate and diphosphonate, *J. Nucl. Med.,* 15, 848, 1974.
24. Shen, A. C. and Jennings, R. B., Myocardial calcium and magnesium in acute ischemic injury, *Am. J. Pathol.,* 67, 417, 1972.
25. D'Agostino, A. N., An electron microscopic study of cardiac necrosis produced by 9 α-fluoro-cortisol and sodium phosphate, *Am. J. Pathol.,* 45, 633, 1964.
26. Bonte, F. J., Parkey, R. W., Graham, K. D., and Moore, J., A new method for radionuclide imaging of acute myocardial infarction, *Radiology,* 110, 473, 1974.
27. Parkey, R. W., Bonte, F. J., Meyer, S. L., Atkins, J. M., Curry, G. L., Stokely, E. M., and Willerson, J. T., A new method for radionuclide imaging of acute myocardial infarction in humans, *Circulation,* 50, 540, 1974.
28. Willerson, J. T., Parkey, R. W., Bonte, F. J., Lewis, S. E., Corbett, J., and Buja, L. M., Pathophysiologic considerations and clinicopathological correlates of technetium-99m stannous pyrophosphate myocardial scintigraphy, *Semin. Nucl. Med.,* 10, 54, 1980.
29. Buja, L. M., Tofe, A. J., Kulkarni, P. V., Mukherjee, A., Parkey, R. W., Francis, M. D., Bonte, F. J., and Willerson, J. T., Sites and mechanisms of localization of technetium-99m phosphorus radiopharmaceuticals in acute myocardial infarcts and other tissues, *J. Clin. Invest.,* 60, 724, 1977.
30. Dewanjee, M. K. and Kahn, P. C., Mechanism of localization of ^{99m}Tc-labeled pyrophosphate and tetracycline in infarcted myocardium, *J. Nucl. Med.,* 17, 639, 1976.
31. Loberg, M. D., Porter, D. W., and Ryan, J. W., Review and current status of hepatobiliary imaging agents, in, *Proc. 2nd Int. Symp. Radiopharmaceuticals II,* Sorenson, J. A., Coordinator, Society of Nuclear Medicine, New York, 1979, 519.
32. Javitt, N. B., Hepatic bile formation, *N. Engl. J. Med.,* 295, 1464, 1976.
33. Fortner, E. L., Mechanisms of hepatic bile formation, *Annu. Rev. Physiol.,* 39, 323, 1977.
34. Berk, P. D. and Berlin, N. I., Eds., *International Symposium on Chemistry and Physiology of Bile Pigments,* Publ. No. (NIH) 77-1100, U.S. Department of Health, Education and Welfare, Bethesda, Md., 1977.
35. Taplin, G. V., Meredith, O. M., and Kade, H., The radioactive I-131 tagged rose bengal uptake excretion test for liver function using external gamma ray scintillation counting techniques, *J. Lab. Clin. Med.,* 45, 665, 1955.
36. Nomoto, H., Kato, T., and Aoyama, B., Clinical studies on the visualization of the common bile duct in the sequential scanning with I-131 BSP, in *Recent Advances in Nuclear Medicine,* Lawrence, J. H., Ed., Grune & Stratton, New York, 1974, 457.
37. Goris, M. L., ^{123}I-iodo-bromsulphthalein as a liver and biliary scanning agent, *J. Nucl. Med.,* 14, 820, 1973.
38. Prokopowicz, D., Uber die Brauchbarkeit der Indocyaninprobe zur Beurteilung der Leberfunktion bei Infektionskrankheiten, *Dtsch. Gesundheitswes.,* 46, 2188, 1973.
39. Ansari, A. N., Atkins, H. L., and Lambrecht, R. M., ^{123}I-indocyanine green (^{123}I-ICG) as an agent for dynamic studies of the hepatobiliary system, in *Dynamic Studies with Radioisotopes in Medicine,* Vol. 1, International Atomic Energy Agency, Vienna, 1975, 111.
40. Christy, B., King, G., and Smook, W. M., Preparation of iodine-123 labeled rose bengal and its distribution in animals, *J. Nucl. Med.,* 15, 484, 1974.
41. Tubis, M., Krishnamurthy, G. T., and Endow, J. W., ^{99m}Tc-penicillamine a new cholescintigraphic agent, *J. Nucl. Med.,* 13, 652, 1972.
42. Baker, R. J., Bellen, J. C., and Ronai, P. M., ^{99m}Tc-pyridoxylideneglutamate: a new rapid choleoscintigraphic agent, *J. Nucl. Med.,* 15, 476, 1974.
42a. Barnes, W. E. and Colombetti, L. G., ^{99m}Tc labeled complexes of aldehydes and glutamic acid as cholescintigraphic agents, *Nuklearmedizin,* 14(4), 350, 1975.
42b. Colombetti, L. G., Glutamate esters as agents for cholescintigraphy, *Radiobiol. Radiother.,* 16(1), 101, 1976.

43. Loberg, M. D., Cooper, M., Harvey, E., Callery, P., and Faith, W., Development of new radiopharmaceuticals based on N-substitution of iminodiacetic acid, *J. Nucl. Med.*, 17, 633, 1976.
44. Wistow, B. W., Subramanian, G., and McAfee, J. G., An evaluation of ^{99m}Tc-labeled hepatobiliary agents in experimental animals, *J. Nucl. Med.*, 17, 545, 1976.
45. Wistow, B. W., Subramanian, G., and Heertum, R. L., An evaluation of ^{99m}Tc-labeled hepatobiliary agents, *J. Nucl. Med.*, 18, 455, 1977.
46. Firnau, G., Why do ^{99m}Tc-chelates work for cholescintigraphy, *Eur. J. Nucl. Med.*, 1, 137, 1976.
47. Ryan, J., Cooper, M., Loberg, M., Harvey, E., and Sikorski, S., Technetium-99m-labeled N-(2,6-dimethylphenylcarbamoylmethyl) iminodiacetic acid (Tc-99m HIDA): a new radiopharmaceutical for hepatobiliary imaging studies, *J. Nucl. Med.*, 18, 997, 1977.
48. Fields, A. T., Porter, D. W., Callery, P. S., Harvey, E. B., and Loberg, M. D., Synthesis and radiolabeling of technetium radiopharmaceuticals based on N-substituted iminodiacetic acid: effect of radiolabeling conditions on radiochemical purity, *J. Labelled Compds. Radiopharm.*, 15, 387, 1978.
49. Burns, H. D., Worley, P., and Wagner, H. N., Design of technetium radiopharmaceuticals, in *The Chemistry of Radiopharmaceuticals*, Masson, New York, 1977, 269.
50. Harvey, E., Loberg, M. D., and Ryan, J., Hepatic clearance mechanism of ^{99m}Tc-HIDA and its effect on quantitation of hepatobiliary function, *J. Nucl. Med.*, 20, 310, 1979.
51. Myers, W. G., Comparisons of ^{131}I, ^{125}I, ^{123}I for in vivo and in vitro applications in diagnosis, in *Transactions of the VIIth International Congress of Internal Medicine*, Vol. 2, Wollheim, E. and Schlegel, B., Eds., Georg Thieme Verlag, Stuttgart, 1968, 858.
52. Owens, A. O. and Flock, E. V., Synthesis, transport, and degradation of thyroid hormones, in *The Thyroid*, Hazard, J. B. and Smith, D. E., Eds., William & Wilkins, Baltimore, 1964, chap. 3.
53. Yano, Y., Trapping and metabolism of radioions by the thyroid, in *Mechanisms of Localization of Radiotracers*, Billinghurst, M. W., Ed., CRC Press, Boca Raton, 1982, chap. 9.
54. Rapoport, B. and DeGroot, L. J., Current concepts of thyroid physiology, *Semin. Nucl. Med.*, 1, 265, 1971.
55. Lutz, J. H. and Gregerman, R. I., pH dependent of the binding of thyroxine to prealbumin in human serum, *J. Clin. Endocrinol.*, 29, 487, 1969.
56. Taplin, G. V., Johnson, D. E., Dore, E. L., and Kaplan, H. S., Suspensions of radioalbumin aggregates for photoscanning the liver, spleen, lung, and other organs, *J. Nucl. Med.*, 5, 259, 1964.
57. Wagner, H. N., Sabiston, D. C., McAfee, J. G., Tow, D., and Stern, H. S., Diagnosis of massive pulmonary embolism in man by radioisotope scanning, *N. Engl. J. Med.*, 271, 377, 1964.
58. Hayes, M., Swanson, L. A., and Taplin, G. V., Rapid sequential imaging renal scanning, *Radiology*, 91, 984, 1968.
59. Rosenthal, L., Greyson, D., and Martin, R. H., Serial radiohippurate renal scintigraphy, *Can. Med. Assoc. J.*, 103, 1266, 1970.
59a. Colombetti, L. G., A cold kit for the preparation of a ^{99m}Tc(Sn) mannonate renal scintigraphic agent, *J. Nucl. Biol. Med.*, 20(2), 55, 1976.
60. McAfee, J. G. and Wagner, H. N., Jr., Visualization of renal parenchyma by scintiscanning with Hg-203 neohydrin, *Radiology*, 75, 820, 1960.
61. Reba, R. C., McAfee, J. G., and Wagner, H. N., Jr., Radiomercury labeled chlormerodrin for in vivo uptake studies and scintillation scanning of unilateral renal lesions associated with hypertension, *Medicine*, 42, 269, 1963.
62. Hiramatou, Y., O'Mara, R. E., McAfee, J. G., and Markarian, B., Intrarenal distribution of diagnostic agents, *Invest. Radiol.*, 5, 295, 1970.
63. Dayton, D. A., Maher, F. T., and Elvebach, L. R., Renal clearance of technetium (Tc-99m) as pertechnetate, *Mayo Clin. Proc.*, 44, 549, 1969.
64. Aquino, J. A. and Cunningham, R. M., Tc-iron complex: radiopharmaceutical for renal scanning and function studies, in *Medical Radioisotope Scintigraphy*, Vol. II, International Atomic Energy Agency, Vienna, 1969, 255.
65. Gottschalk, A., Renal scanning, *JAMA*, 202, 221, 1967.
66. Harper, P. V., Lathrop, K. A., Jiminez, F., Fink, R., and Gottschalk, A., Tc-99m as a scanning agent, *Radiology*, 85, 101, 1965.
67. Schmidt, K. J., Brod, K. H., Wolf, R., and Haas, J. P., Gundlagen und technik der nierenszintrgraphie mit einem Tc-99m eisen complex, *Röontgenfortschritte*, 107, 713, 1967.
68. Winston, M. A., Halpern, S., Weiss, E. R., Endow, J., and Blahd, W. H., Critical evaluation of Tc-99m-Fe ascorbic acid complex as a renal scanning agent, *J. Nucl. Med.*, 12, 171, 1971.
69. Arnold, R. W., Subramanian, G., McAfee, J. G., Blair, R. J., and Thomas, F. D., Comparison of ^{99m}Tc complexes for renal imaging, *J. Nucl. Med.*, 16, 357, 1975.
70. Boyd, R. E., Robson, J., Hunt, F. C., Sorby, P. J., Murray, I. P. C., and MacKay, W. J., ^{99m}Tc-gluconate complexes for renal scintigraphy, *Br. J. Radiol.*, 46, 604, 1973.

71. Lin, T. H., Kentigan, A., and Winchell, H. S., A ^{99m}Tc chelate substitute for organoradiomercurial renal agents, *J. Nucl. Med.,* 15, 34, 1974.

72. Reba, R. C., McAfee, J. G., and Wagner, H. N., Radiomercury-labeled chlormerodrin for in vivo uptake studies and scintillation scanning of unilateral renal lesions associated with hypertension, *Medicine (Balt.),* 42, 269, 1963.

73. Pena, A., The control of metabolism by ion transport across membrane, in *Perspectives in Membrane Biology,* Estrada, D. S. and Gitler, C., Eds., Academic Press, New York, 1974, 195.

74. Crane, R. K., Uphill out flow of sugar from intestinal epithelial cells induced by reversal of the Na$^+$ gradient: its significance for the mechanism of Na$^+$-dependent active transport, *Biochem. Biophys. Res. Commun.,* 17, 481, 1964.

75. West, I. C. and Mitchell, P., Stoichiometry of lactose-protein transport across the plasma membrane of *Escherichia coli, Biochem. J.,* 132, 587, 1973.

76. Asghar, S. S., Levin, E., and Harold, F. M., Accumulation of neutral amino acids by *Streptococcus faecalis* energy coupling by a proton-motive force, *J. Biol. Chem.,* 248, 5225, 1973.

77. Pierson, R. N., Jr., Fiedman, M. I., Tansay, W. A., Castellana, F. S., Enlander, D., and Huang, P. J., Cardiovascular nuclear medicine: an overview, *Semin. Nucl. Med.,* 9, 224, 1979.

78. Pohost, G. M., Alpert, N. M., Ingwall, J. S., and Strauss, H. W., Thallium redistribution: mechanisms and clinical utility, *Semin. Nucl. Med.,* 10, 70, 1980.

79. Britten, J. S. and Blank, M., Thallium activation of the (Na$^+$-K$^+$) activated ATPase of rabbit kidney, *Biochem. Biophys. Acta,* 159, 160, 1968.

80. Strauss, H. W., Harrison, K., Langan, J. K., Lebowitz, E., and Pitt, B., Thallium-201 for myocardial imaging. Relation of thallium-201 to myocardial perfusion, *Circulation,* 51, 641, 1975.

81. Schelbert, H., Ingwall, J., Watson, R., and Ashburn, W., Factors influencing the myocardial uptake of thallium-201, *J. Nucl. Med.,* 18, 598, 1977.

82. L'Abbate, A., Biagini, A., Michelassi, C., and Maseri, A., Myocardial kinetics of thallium and potassium in man, *Circulation,* 60, 776, 1979.

83. Reivich, M., Kuhl, D., Wolf, A. P., Greenberg, J., Phelps, M., Ido, T., Casella, V., Fowler, J., Hoffman, E., Alavi, A., Som, P., and Sokoloff, L., The [^{18}F] fluorodeoxyglucose method for the measurement of local cerebal glucose utilization in man, *Circ. Res.,* 44, 127, 1979.

84. Bachelard, H. S., Specificity and kinetic properties of monosaccharide uptake into guinea pig cerebral cortex in vitro, *J. Neurochem.,* 18, 213, 1971.

85. Horton, R. W., Meldrun, B. S., and Bachelard, H. S., Enzymic and cerebral metabolic effects of 2-deoxy-D-glucose, *J. Neurochem.,* 21, 507, 1973.

86. Sokoloff, L., Reivich, M., Kennedy, C., Des Rosiers, M. H., Patlah, C. S., Pettigrew, K. D., Sakurada, D., and Shinohara, M., The [^{14}C] deoxyglucose method for the measurement of local cerebral glucose utilization: theory, procedure, and normal values in the conscious and anesthetized albino rat, *J. Neurochem.,* 28, 897, 1977.

87. Tower, D. B., The effects of 2-deoxy-D-glucose on metabolism of slices of cerebral cortex incubated in vitro, *J. Neurochem.,* 3, 185, 1958.

88. Bessell, E. M., Foster, A. B., and Westwood, J. H., The use of deoxyfluoro-D-glucopyranoses and related compounds in a study of yeast hexokinase specificity, *Biochem. J.,* 128, 199, 1972.

89. Barnett, J. E. G. and Munday, K. A., Structural requirements for active intestinal sugar transport in the hamster, in *Transport Across the Intestines,* Burland, W. L. and Samuel, P. D., Eds., Churchill Livingstone, London, 1972, 110.

90. Coe, E. L., Inhibition of glycolysis in ascites tumor cells preincubated with 2-deoxy-2-fluoro-D-glucose, *Biochem. Biophys. Acta,* 264, 319, 1972.

91. Barnett, J. E. G., Holman, G. D., Chalkley, R. A., and Munday, K. A., Evidence for two assymetric conformational states in the human erythrocyte sugar-transport system, *Biochem. J.,* 145, 417, 1975.

92. Barnett, J. E. G., Holman, G. D., and Munday, K. A., Structural requirements for binding to the sugar-transport system of the human erythrocytes, *Biochem. J.,* 131, 211, 1973.

93. Gallagher, B. M., Fowler, J. S., Gutterson, N. I., MacGregor, R. R., Chung-Nan, W., and Wolf, A. P., Metabolic trapping as a principle of radiopharmaceutical design: some factors responsible for the biodistribution of [^{18}F] 2-deoxy-2-fluoro-D-glucose, *J. Nucl. Med.,* 19, 1154, 1978.

94. Phelps, M. E., Hoffman, E. J., Selin, C., Huang, S. C., Robinson, G., MacDonald, N., Schelbert, H., and Kuhl, D. E., Investigation of [^{18}F] 2-fluoro-2-deoxy-glucose for the measure of myocardial glucose metabolism, *J. Nucl. Med.,* 19, 1311, 1978.

95. Neely, J. R. and Morgan, H. E., Relationship between carbohydrate and lipid metabolism and the energy balance of heart muscle, *Annu. Rev. Physiol.,* 36, 413, 1974.

96. Opie, L. H., Owen, P., and Riemersma, R. A., Relative rates of oxidation of glucose and free fatty acids by ischemic and non-ischemic myocardium after coronary artery ligation in the dog, *Eur. J. Clin. Invest.,* 3, 419, 1973.

97. Rovetto, M. J., Lamberton, W. F., and Neely, J. R., Mechanisms of glycolytic inhibition in ischemic rat hearts, *Circ. Res.,* 37, 742, 1975.

185

98. Hillis, L. D. and Braunwald, E., Myocardial ischemia, *N. Engl. J. Med.*, 296, 971, 1034, 1093, 1977.

99. Reivich, M., Kuhl, D. E., and Wolf, A., Measurement of local cerebral glucose metabolism in man with ^{18}F-2-fluoro-2-deoxy-D-glucose, in *Cerebral Function, Metabolism and Circulation,* Ingavar, D. H. and Lassen, N. A., Eds., Munksgaard, Copenhagen, 1977, 190.

100. Gallagher, B. M., Ansari, A., Atkins, H., Casella, V., Christman, D. R., Fowler, J. S., Ido, T., MacGregor, R. R., Som, P., Wan, C. N., Wolf, A. P., Kuhl, D. E., and Reivich, M., Radiopharmaceuticals. XXVII. ^{18}F-labeled 2-deoxy-2-fluoro-D-glucose as a radiopharmaceutical for measuring regional myocardial glucose metabolism in vivo: tissue distribution and imaging in animals, *J. Nucl. Med.*, 18, 990, 1977.

101. French, J. E., Morris, B., and Robinson, D. S., Removal of lipids from the bloodstream, *Br. Med. Bull.*, 14, 234, 1958.

102. Oram, J. F., Bennetch, S. L., and Neely, J. R., Regulation of fatty acid utilization in isolated perfused rat hearts, *J. Biol. Chem.*, 248, 5299, 5309, 1973.

103. Hoogland, D. R., Weichert, J. P., Sirr, S. A., Frick, M. P., Forstrom, L. A., and Loken, M. K., Effect of solubility on the biodistribution and evaluation of 16-[^{123}I]-9-hexadecenoic acid as a myocardial imaging agent, in *Radiopharmaceuticals II,* Sorenson, J. A., Ed., Society of Nuclear Medicine, New York, 1979, 55.

104. Weiss, E. S., Hoffman, E. J., Phelps, M. E., Welch, M. J., Henry, P. D., Ter-Pogossian, M. M., and Sobel, B. E., External detection and visualization of myocardial ischemia with ^{11}C-substrates in vitro and in vivo, *Circ. Res.*, 39, 24, 1976.

105. Gordon, R. S. and Cherkes, A., Unesterified fatty acids in human blood plasma, *J. Clin. Invest.*, 35, 206, 1956.

106. Rothlin, M. E. and Bing, R. J., Extraction and release of individual fatty acids by the heart and fat deposits, *J. Clin. Invest.*, 40, 1380, 1961.

107. Bing, R. J., Metabolic activity of the intact heart, *Am. Med.*, 30, 679, 1961.

108. Evans, J. R., Gunton, R. W., Baker, R. G., Beanlands, D. S., and Spears, J. C., Use of radioiodinated fatty acid for photoscans of the heart, *Circ. Res.*, 16, 1, 1965.

109. Selwyn, A. P., Jones, T., Turner, J. H., Pratt, T., Clark, J., and Lavender, P., Continuous assessment of regional myocardial perfusion in dogs using krypton-81m, *Circ. Res.*, 42, 771, 1978.

110. Gould, K. L., Hamilton, G. S., Lipscomb, K., Ritchie, J. L., and Kennedy, J. W., Method for assessing stress induced regional malperfusion during coronary arteriography, *Am. J. Cardiol.*, 34, 557, 1974.

111. Noujaim, A. A., Lentle, B. C., Hill, J. R., Ferner, U. K., and Wong, H., On the role of transferrin in the uptake of gallium by tumor cells, *Int. J. Nucl. Med. Biology*, 6, 193, 1979.

112. Clausen, J., Edeling, C. J., and Fogh, J., ^{67}Ga binding to human serum proteins and tumor components, *Cancer Res.*, 34, 1931, 1974.

113. Gunasekara, S., King, L. J., and Lavendar, D. J., The behavior of tracer gallium-67 toward serum proteins, *Clin. Chim. Acta*, 39, 401, 1972.

114. Loh, T. T., Yeung, Y. G., and Yeung, D., Transferrin and iron uptake by rabbit reticulocytes, *Biochem. Biophys. Acta*, 471, 118, 1977.

115. Verhoef, N. J. and Noordeloos, P. J., Binding of transferrin and uptake of iron by rat erythroid cells in vitro, *Clin. Sci. Mol. Med.*, 52, 87, 1977.

116. Brown, D. H., Byrd, B. L., Carlton, J. E., Swartzendruber, D. C., and Hayes, R. L., A quantitative study of the subcellular localization of ^{67}Ga, *Cancer Res.*, 36, 959, 1976.

117. Swartzendruber, D. C., Nelson, B., and Hayes, R. L., Gallium-67 localization in lysosomal-like granules of leukemic and nonleukemic murine tissues, *J. Natl. Cancer Inst.*, 46, 941, 1971.

118. Hegge, F. N., Mahler, D. J., and Larson, S. M., The incorporation of Ga-67 into the ferritin fraction of rabbit hepatocytes in vivo, *J. Nucl. Med.*, 18, 937, 1977.

119. Hoffer, P. B., Huberty, J., and Khayam-Bashi, H. J., The association of Ga-67 and lactoferrin, *J. Nucl. Med.*, 18, 713, 1977.

120. Hoffer, P. B., Gallium: mechanisms, *J. Nucl. Med.*, 21, 282, 1980.

121. Hartman, R. E. and Hayes, R. L., Gallium binding by blood serum, *Fed. Proc., Fed. Am. Soc. Exp. Biol.*, 26, 780, 1967.

122. Hara, T., On the binding of gallium to transferrin, *Int. J. Nucl. Med. Biol.*, 1, 152, 1974.

123. Aulbert, E., Gebhardt, A., Schulz, E., and Haubold, U., Mechanism of ^{67}Ga accumulation in normal rat liver lysosomes, *Nucl. Med.*, 15, 185, 1976.

124. Cotton, F. A. and Wilkinson, G., in *Advanced Inorganic Chemistry,* 3rd ed., Interscience, New York, 1972, 260.

125. Latimer, W. M., in *The Oxidation States of the Elements and Their Potentials in Aqueous Solutions,* Prentice-Hall, Englewood Cliffs, N.J., 1952, 158.

126. Maines, M. D. and Kappas, A., Metals as regulators of heme metabolism, *Science*, 198, 1215, 1971.

127. Weiner, R. E., Thakur, M. D., Goodman, M. M., and Hoffer, P. B., Relative stabilities of In-III and Ga-67 desferrioxime and transferrin complexes, *Am. J. Roentgenol.*, 132, 489, 1979.

128. Oster, Z. H., Larson, S. M., and Wagner, H. N., Jr., Possible enhancement of ⁶⁷Ga-citrate imaging by iron dextran, *J. Nucl. Med.,* 17, 356, 1976.

128a. Goodwin, D. A., Colombetti, L. G., De Nardo, G. L., and Jacobson, S., ¹¹³ᵐIn Labeled Transferrin for Blood Pool Imaging, San Francisco State University, November, 1967.

129. Alvarez, J., Preparation of In-113-m radiopharmaceuticals, in *Radiopharmaceuticals,* Subramanian, G., Rhodes, B. A., Cooper, J. F., and Sodd, V. J., Eds., Society of Nuclear Medicine, New York, 1975, 102.

130. Hosain, F., Iqbal, H. M., Carulli, N., and Wagner, H. N., Measurement of plasma volume using ⁹⁹ᵐTc and ¹¹³In-labeled proteins, *Br. J. Radiol.,* 42, 627, 1969.

131. Hosain, P., Som, P., Iqbal, Q. M., and Hosain, F., Measurement of cardiac output with indium-113m labeled transferrin, *Br. J. Radiol.,* 42, 931, 1969.

132. Finston, R., Goodwin, D., Beaver, J., and Hupf, H., Indium-111: production radionuclide purity, and dosimetry of a new radiopharmaceutical for lymphatic scanning, *Phys. Med. Biol.,* 15, 173, 1970.

133. Goodwin, D., Finston, R., Colombetti, L., Beaver, J., and Hupf, H., ¹¹¹In for imaging; lymph node visualization, *Radiology,* 94, 175, 1970.

134. Main, P. and Goodwin, D. A., Cerebrospinal fluid scanning with ¹¹¹In, *J. Nucl. Med.,* 12, 668, 1971.

135. Goodwin, D. A., Goode, R., Brown, L., and Imbornone, G. J., ¹¹¹In labeled transferrin for detection of tumors, *Radiology,* 100, 175, 1971.

136. Thakur, M. L., The preparation for indium-111 labeled bleomycin for tumor localization, *Int. J. Appl. Radiat. Isot.,* 24, 357, 1973.

137. Lillien, D. L., Berger, H. G., Anderson, D. P., and Bennett, L. R., ¹¹¹In-chloride; a new agent for bone marrow imaging, *J. Nucl. Med.,* 14, 184, 1973.

138. Beamish, M. R. and Brown, E. B., The metabolism of transferrin-bound ¹¹¹In and ⁵⁹Fe in the rat, *Blood,* 43, 693, 1974.

139. Beamish, M. R. and Brown, E. B., A comparison of the behavior of ¹¹¹In and ⁵⁹Fe-labeled transferrin on incubation with human and rat reticulocytes, *Blood,* 43, 703, 1974.

140. McIntyre, P. A., Larson, S. M., Eikman, E. A., Colman, M., Scheffel, V., and Hodkinson, B. A., Comparison of the metabolism of iron-labeled transferrin (Fe · T_f) and indium-labeled transferrin (In · T_f) by the erythropoietic marrow, *J. Nucl. Med.,* 15, 856, 1974.

141. Scheffel, U., McIntyre, P. A., Evatt, B., Dvornicky, T. K., Natarajan, D. R., Bolling, D. R., and Murphy, E. A., Evaluation of indium-111 as a new high photon yield gamma-emitting "physiological" platelet label, *Johns Hopkins Med. J.,* 140, 285, 1977.

142. Thakur, M. L., Coleman, R. E., and Welch, M. J., Indium-111 labeled leukocytes for the location of abscesses. Preparation, analysis, tissue distribution and comparison with gallium-67 citrate in dogs, *J. Lab. Clin. Med.,* 89, 217, 1977.

143. Thakur, M. L., Segal, A. W., Welch, M. J., Hopkins, J., and Peters, T. J., Indium-111-labeled cellular blood components: mechanism of labeling and intracellular location in human neutrophils, *J. Nucl. Med.,* 18, 1020, 1977.

144. Thakur, M. L. and Gottschalk, A., Role of radiopharmaceuticals in nuclear hematology, in *Proc. 2nd Intl. Symp. Radiopharmaceuticals II,* Sorenson, J. A., Coordinator, Society of Nuclear Medicine, New York, 1979, 341.

145. Kuhl, D. E., Engel, J., Jr., and Phelps, M. E., Emission computed tomography of ¹⁸F-fluorodeoxyglucose and ¹³N ammonia in partial epilepsy, *J. Nucl. Med.,* 21 (Abstr.), 21, 1980.

146. Alavi, A., Ferris, S., Wolf, A., Reivich, M., Farkas, T., Dann, R., Christman, D., MacGregor, R. R., and Fowler, J., Determination of cerebral metabolism in senile dementia using ¹⁸F-deoxyglucose and positron emission tomography, *J. Nucl. Med.,* 21 (Abstr.), 21, 1980.

147. Alpert, N. M., Ackerman, R. H., Correia, J. A., Finklestein, S., Buonanno, F. S., Brownell, G. L., and Taveras, J., Transverse section measurements of oxygen utilization in the brain of man, *J. Nucl. Med.,* 21 (Abstr.), 22, 1980.

148. Alpert, N. M., Correia, J. A., Ackerman, R. H., Finklestein, S., Buonanno, F. S., Brownell, G. L., and Traveras, J. M., Transverse section measurements of cerebral blood flow in man, *J. Nucl. Med.,* 21 (Abstr.), 22, 1980.

149. Feenstra, A., Vaalburg, W., Piers, D. A., Reiffers, S., Woldring, M. G., and Doorenbos, H., Carbon-11 labeled steroids as potential receptor binding radiopharmaceuticals, *J. Nucl. Med.,* 21 (Abstr.), 21, 1980.

150. Vera, D. R., Krohn, K. A., and Steffen, S. M., Synthesis and testing of labeled glycoconjugates as cell-specific receptor radiopharmaceuticals, *J. Nucl. Med.,* 21 (Abstr.), 12, 1980.

151. Vera, D. R., Krohn, K. A., and Stadalnik, R. C., Radioligands that bind to cell-specific receptors: hepatic binding protein ligands for hepatic scintigraphy, in *Radiopharmaceuticals II,* Sorensen, J. A., Coordinator, Society of Nuclear Medicine, New York, 1979, 565.

152. Gibson, R. E., Mazaitis, A., Francis, B., Patt, R., Eckelman, W. C., and Reba, R. C., In vivo receptor binding of radiolabeled estrogens, *J. Nucl. Med.*, 21 (Abstr.), 36, 1980.
153. Eckelman, W. C., Gibson, R. E., Vieras, F., Rzeszotarski, W. J., Francis, B., and Reba, R. C., In vivo receptor binding of iodinated beta adrenoceptor blockers, *J. Nucl. Med.*, 21 (Abstr.), 57, 1980.
154. Hanson, R. N., Davis, M. A., and Cohen, Z., Cardio-selective radiolabeled beta adrenergic antagonists as potential myocardial imaging agents, *J. Nucl. Med.*, 21 (Abstr.), 59, 1980.

Chapter 10

TRANSPORT OF PROTEIN-BOUND RADIOTRACERS INTO TISSUES*

William M. Pardridge

TABLE OF CONTENTS

*   Supported by the National Science Foundation (BNS 78-05500), the Basil O'Connor Fund of the March
    of Dimes-Birth Defects Foundation, and the National Institutes of Health (AM-25744).

I. INTRODUCTION

Substances such as hormones, metabolic substrates, vitamins, drugs, or electrolytes exist at equilibrium in two physical states when placed in a test tube with a plasma protein that has a measurable affinity for the ligand. These two states are the protein-bound and the free, e.g., dialyzable or filtratable. Over many years the concept has evolved that the fraction of hormone or drug that is free in vitro at equilibrium is also free in vivo. That is, the effects of plasma protein binding on ligand distribution in the living state may be quantitated simply by measuring the free fraction in vitro. For example, if the latter falls due to increased protein binding, then the hormone or drug will enter tissues less readily. Conversely, if the free fraction in vitro rises due to decreased protein binding, then ligand transport into tissue from the plasma will be enhanced. The main objective of this review is to illustrate the shortcomings of the equilibrium hypothesis in adequately describing the transport into tissue of substances bound by plasma proteins. The view will be advanced that is illusory to equate the fraction of ligand that is free in a test tube at equilibrium with the fraction that is free in a capillary of a living organism. The free fraction in vitro is a simple (and absolute) function of the total number of binding sites and the equilibrium constant of ligand binding to the protein. Conversely, the free fraction in vivo is an intricate (and relativistic) function of three kinetic parameters: the unidirectional ligand debinding rate ($t_{1/2}$ = millisecond to second), the capillary transit time (1 to 10 sec) and the ligand flux through the biological membrane ($t_{1/2}$ = millisecond to second). If the $t_{1/2}$ of ligand debinding and ligand diffusion through the membrane is fast relative to the capillary transit time, then the free ligand fraction may become large as the protein-bound moiety is effectively transported into the tissue. Conversely, if the debinding $t_{1/2}$ or the membrane diffusion $t_{1/2}$ is long relative to the capillary transit time, then free fraction in vivo will be equal to the free fraction in vitro. Under these latter conditions, the only mechanism by which protein-bound ligand may be transported into the tissue is via a collision mechanism. That is, the plasma protein-ligand complex binds to a cell membrane receptor and the ligand is subsequently transported into the cell.

To summarize the above discussion, there are three possible modes of ligand transport: (1) influx of the free (dialyzable) moiety, (2) transport of the protein-bound fraction via a free intermediate mechanism, and (3) transport of the protein-bound moiety via a collision mechanism. As will be discussed in subsequent sections, the collision mechanism is applicable to the transport of cholesterol, vitamins A and D, iron, and vitamin B_{12}. Conversely, the transport of tryptophan and other indole compounds, thyroid and steroid hormones, free fatty acid, drugs, and albumin-bound electrolytes, occurs via the free intermediate mechanism. In virtually all cases, the protein-bound moiety is the major fraction available for transport, while the free (dialyzable) moiety represents a trivial component of the plasma ligand available for transport. Prior to discussing the transport of various substances, two introductory sections will be presented. First, the Oldendorf technique or tissue sampling-single injection methodology will be reviewed. The significance of this method is derived from the fact that the Oldendorf technique provides a fast, simple, and highly reproducible way to study in vivo the trans-capillary passage of protein-bound substances. Secondly, the theoretical principles underlying the transport of protein-bound ligands via the free intermediate mechanism will be discussed.

II. THE OLDENDORF METHODOLOGY

In 1970, Oldendorf[1] published the details of a simple and novel technique for the in vivo study of transport phenomena at the brain capillary wall, i.e., the blood-brain barrier (BBB). The Oldendorf technique laid the foundation for tissue sampling-single injection methodology, an approach to capillary permeability studies which is much simpler and faster than a venous sampling-single injection methodology.[2] Application of the Oldendorf technique to the study of BBB transport of metabolic substrates has permitted the in vivo description of the Michaelis-Menten kinetics of nearly 50 compounds which traverse the BBB by 1 of 8 different carrier systems.[3] In terms of in vivo quantitation, the BBB is one of the most well-characterized membranes in biology, due simply to the availability of a technique which permits the rapid and simple determination of the parameters of biological transport. Briefly, the Oldendorf technique involves the use of anesthetized small animals, e.g., the adult rat, the suckling rat, or the newborn rabbit. A common carotid artery is exposed and a 100 to 200 $\mu\ell$ bolus is rapidly (less than 1 sec) injected. The bolus of buffered Ringer's solution contains labeled test compound, e.g., ^{3}H-steroid hormone, ^{14}C-amino acid, or ^{125}I-thyroid hormone; labeled diffusible reference, e.g., ^{3}H water, or ^{14}C-butanol; and an optional third isotope, e.g., ^{113m}In-EDTA, which serves as an extravascular reference.[1,4,5] At 5 to 15 sec after injection, the animal is decapitated; this time interval is long enough for the bolus to make a single pass of brain, but short enough to minimize efflux back to blood of isotope taken up by brain. Samples of brain and injection mixture are taken for double (triple) isotope liquid scintillation counting, and a brain uptake index (BUI) is calculated,

$$ \text{BUI} = \frac{\dfrac{\text{test dpm}}{\text{reference dpm}} \text{(brain)}}{\dfrac{\text{test dpm}}{\text{reference dpm}} \text{(injectate)}} \times 100 \qquad (1) $$

The BUI $= E_T/E_R$, where E is the extraction of unidirectional influx of test or reference isotope through the BBB.[6] Given E_R, then $E_T = (\text{BUI})(E_R)$. If cerebral blood flow (F, mℓ/min/g) is known, then E_T may be converted into a permeability-surface product (PS, mℓ/min/g) by Crone's equation[7]

$$ E_T = 1 - e^{-PS/F} \qquad (2) $$

Therefore, quantitative estimates of BBB permeability may be obtained with the Oldendorf technique.

The major advantage of the method, however, is the fact that by virtue of the bolus injection, the concentration of substrates or proteins at the capillary transport sites may be controlled by simply adjusting the composition of the injection bolus. This is because, contrary to what one might expect, there is no significant mixing of the bolus with the circulating plasma. Since the rate of carotid injection greatly exceeds the rate of common carotid blood flow, the injection solution traverses the cerebral capillary circulation as a discrete bolus. Therefore, the kinetics of carrier-mediated transport may be studied by adding unlabeled substrate to the injection solution.[3] In addition, and more pertinent to the present discussion, various concentrations of a plasma protein, which binds the test compound, may be added to the injection solution. The plasma protein may be added as a purified protein or as a constituent of a serum sample obtained from essentially any source. Since the plasma protein inhibits ligand transport into brain by virtue of the protein binding the ligand, then the in vivo free fraction of ligand may be computed from the fractional inhibition of ligand transport that is caused by the protein, e.g.,

$$ \text{free fraction in vivo} = \frac{E_p - E_{ns}}{E_O - E_{ns}} \qquad (3) $$

where E_O = the extraction after injection of the compound in Ringer's solution, E_P = the extraction after injection of the compound in the protein solution, and E_{NS} = the extraction due to nonspecific, extracellular uptake. After determining the free fraction in vivo, this value may be compared to the free ligand fraction in vitro at equilibrium; the two estimates should be comparable if predictions made by the equilibrium hypothesis are correct. Conversely, if protein-bound ligand is transported into tissues, then the apparent free fraction in vivo will exceed the free fraction in vitro.

In addition to brain, the Oldendorf method has been adapted to liver with a portal injection technique,[8,9] and it is probable that the method could be used to study transport phenomena in vivo for a number of other tissues.

III. THEORETICAL CONSIDERATIONS

As noted in the Introduction, there are two possible mechanisms by which protein-bound ligands may be transported into tissues: free intermediate vs. collision mechanism. A collision mechanism involves the precise interaction of the plasma protein with a specific cell membrane receptor in such a way that the ligand is directly transferred from the plasma binding site to the membrane binding site. Conversely, the free intermediate mechanism requires no collision between the plasma protein and a membrane macromolecule. Rather, the ligand undergoes debinding into the free state during the course of the capillary transit time and, once in the free state, the ligand may either reassociate with the plasma protein or diffuse through the membrane. The membrane diffusion step may occur via either lipid-mediation (free diffusion) or carrier-mediation. Therefore, in the case of a highly lipid soluble compound, e.g., steroid hormones or free fatty acids, no membrane macromolecule need be postulated to mediate the trans-membrane movement of the ligand.

The major factor determining whether a protein-bound ligand traverses a cell membrane via either a collision mechanism or a free intermediate mechanism is the rate of ligand debinding relative to the capillary transit time. If debinding is slow relative to the transit time, then either a collision mechanism must be operative or no ligand transport will occur, aside from the trivial free (dialyzable) fraction. A few systems fall into the collision model, e.g., retinol-[10] or cholesterol-[11] binding systems. The unidirectional dissociation of retinol or cholesterol from the respective binding protein, e.g., retinol-binding protein (RBP) or lipoproteins, is very slow relative to even the slowest of capillary transit times. Moreover, it is known that RBP-bound retinol or low density lipoprotein-bound cholesterol enters tissues via receptor-mediated, i.e., collision, mechanisms (see later section on lipids and vitamins).

The majority of ligand binding systems, however, are characterized by a fast debinding rate relative to capillary transit time (Figure 1). Moreover, both fast and slow debinding systems have evolved to accommodate tissues with fast and slow capillary transit times. For example, the capillary transit time in brain,[12] skeletal muscle,[13] or placenta,[14] $\sim$1 sec, is fast compared to the transit time in liver $\sim$5 sec.[15] Moreover, the debinding of hormones from albumin, $t_{1/2} \ll 1$ sec,[16] is fast relative to tissue transit times. Conversely, the $t_{1/2}$ of hormone debinding from globulin binding systems ($\sim$1 to 10 sec), is slow relative to the brain transit time, but is fast relative to the liver transit time.[17]* Given these observations, the design principle underlying the evolution of hormone-binding globulins becomes apparent. The addition of a globulin to the system keeps hormone off of albumin and thereby limits distribution to peripheral

---

* The transit time in liver is long owing to the unique anatomy of the hepatic microcirculation. Transit time = capillary volume/blood flow. Since all proteins the size of albumin or less distribute instantaneously into the liver interstitial space, the capillary plasma volume is large and results in a prolonged transit time.[41]

TRANSPORT OF PLASMA PROTEIN-BOUND
LIGANDS INTO TISSUES

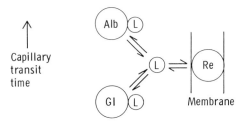

FIGURE 1.   The "free intermediate" model for the transport of protein-bound substances into tissues emphasizes the three major determinants underlying the transport process: (i) the capillary transit time (0.5 to 5 sec), (ii) the rate of unidirectional debinding of ligand from the plasma protein, and (iii) the rate of ligand diffusion through the membrane, which may occur via either a lipid-mediated or a receptor (carrier)-mediated mechanism. Abbreviations: Alb, albumin; Gl, globulin; L, ligand; Re, receptor.

tissues such as brain. However, both albumin-bound and globulin-bound hormone are available to tissues such as liver.[17] Therefore, the globulin amplifies the amount of hormone entering the metabolically active hepatocyte relative to the less metabolically active peripheral tissues.*

The above discussion has emphasized the importance of two factors, debinding rates and capillary transit times, which determine whether a protein-bound ligand enters tissues. A third factor, membrane permeability, is of equal importance. A ligand may unidirectionally dissociate well within a capillary transit time; however, if the tendency for the ligand to diffuse through the membrane is slow relative to the transit time, then the ligand will simply reassociate with the plasma protein. Under these conditions, no protein-bound hormone will enter the tissue and the availability of hormone will be accurately reflected by in vitro measurements of free hormone. Membrane permeability is a function of (1) the free diffusion of the ligand owing to lipid-mediation, or (2) the facilitated diffusion of the compound due to carrier-mediation.

The previous discussion has emphasized the view that the free ligand in vivo is a dynamic parameter that is transit time-dependent and permeability-dependent. Moreover, explicit relationships may be derived which predict the change in free ligand with fluctuations in transit time or modulations in membrane permeability. Two equations have been derived depending on whether the ligand diffuses through the membrane via (1) lipid-mediation, i.e., free diffusion which does not involve a cell membrane binding system, and (2) carrier-mediation, which does require a prerequisite binding of the ligand by a cell membrane transport system.

In the case of lipid-mediation, e.g., steroid hormones,[16,17] the following mechanism occurs,

---

*   Metabolic activity in this context refers to protein synthesis, e.g., protein synthesis rates in liver are about 10-fold rates in brain and 20-fold rates in heart or muscle.[112-114] The steroid and thyroid hormones modulate protein synthesis;[115-116] therefore, it is reasonable to suggest that liver cells should take up more hormone than peripheral tissues.

$$AL \underset{k_2}{\overset{k_1}{\rightleftharpoons}} A_F + L_F \qquad (4)$$

$$\xrightarrow{k_3} L_M$$

where AL is albumin-bound ligand, A_F is free albumin, L_F and L_M are free and membrane-transported ligand, k_1 (sec^{-1}) and k_2 (M^{-1} sec^{-1}) are the dissociation and association rate constants, and k_3 (sec^{-1}) is the rate constant of ligand flux through the membrane. The model assumes that $k_1 > 1/t$, where t = the capillary transit time. Since d(AL)dt $= k_2 A_F L_F - k_1$ (AL) and $A_F = A_T - AL$, then

$$(AL) = \frac{k_2 A_T L_F - d(AL)/dt}{k_2 L_F + k_1} \qquad (5)$$

Assuming the steady-state condition, i.e., $d(AL)/dt \ll k_2 A_T L_F$, then

$$(AL) = \frac{A_T L_F}{K_D + L_F} \qquad (6)$$

where $K_D = k_1/k_2$. The above definitions of (AL) indicate the steady-state assumption is not, as is commonly believed, that $d(AL)/dt = 0$, but only that $d(AL)/dt$ is small compared to $k_2 A_T L_F$.[16,18] Since $d(AL)/dt$ in vivo is proportional to $k_3 L_F$, i.e., loss of ligand from the plasma space due to trans-membrane transport, then the steady-state approximation for in vivo ligand protein interactions requires that $k_3 L_F \ll k_2 A_T L_F$, or $k_3 \ll k_2 A_T$.[16] That is, if the free ligand is more likely to reassociate with albumin ($k_2 A_T$), rather than diffuse through the membrane (k_3), then the steady-state assumption holds. However, if ligand dissociates and reassociates many, many times per transit time, then extensive transport of albumin-bound ligand may eventually occur causing a substantial fall in the capillary AL concentration with time.[16] That is, a bolus of plasma passes through a continuous succession of steady-states, and although $d(AL)/dt \gg 0$, the magnitude of $d(AL)/dt$ is still small compared to $k_2 A_T$. The quantity, $k_2 A_T$, is of very large magnitude, e.g., a typical k_2 is 10^6 to 10^8 M^{-1} sec^{-1},[19] and a physiological A_T is 0.5×10^{-3} M; therefore, $k_2 A_T$ ranges from 500 to 50,000 sec^{-1}, which is log orders greater than k_3 (see section on steroid hormones, Table 6).

Estimates of k_3 may be obtained as follows. The ligand conservation equation is $L_T = L_F + AL + L_M$. The expressions for L_M and L_F may be obtained by integrating $d(L_M)/dt = k_3 L_F$, and $d(L_F)/dt = k_1$ (AL) $- k_2 A_F L_F - k_3 L_F$. Given AL $= (A_F) (L_F) / K_D$, then integration of $d(L_F)/dt$ results in $L_F = e^{-k_3 t}$. Therefore, $L_M = 1 - e^{-k_3 t}$. Substituting AL and L_M into the ligand conservation equation, and assuming $A_F \simeq A_T$ (because $K_D \gg L_F$), then the in vivo bound fraction of ligand (B) is given by

$$B = \frac{A_T}{K_D(e^{k_3 t}) + A_T} \qquad (7)$$

and the double reciprocal plot is $1/B = 1 + K_D$ (app) $1/A_T$, where

$$K_D \text{ (app)} = K_D (e^{k_3 t}) \qquad (8)$$

That is, the apparent (app) K_D in vivo deviates exponentially from the K_D in vitro in proportion to membrane permeability (k_3) or capillary transit time (t). Stated differently, the apparent free fraction in vivo deviates exponentially from the free fraction in vitro if $k_3 \geq t$. Rearrangement of Equation 7, given $B = 1 - F$, where $F = $ free, then

$$\text{app F in vivo} = \frac{K_D(e^{k_3 t})}{K_D(e^{k_3 t}) + A_T} \qquad (9)$$

If $k_3 \ll t$, then K_D (app) $= K_D$ (Equation 8) and the apparent free ligand in vivo $= $ the free (dialyzable) fraction in vitro.

In the case where the ligand traverses the cell membrane via carrier-mediation, e.g., tryptophan[20] or thyroid hormone[21] flux through the BBB, then a cell membrane binding system competes with the plasma protein for binding of the ligand, e.g.,

$$AL \underset{k_2}{\overset{k_1}{\rightleftharpoons}} A_F + L_F$$
$$+$$
$$C_F \underset{k_4}{\overset{k_3}{\rightleftharpoons}} CL \overset{k_5}{\longrightarrow} C_F + L_M$$

where CL is the carrier-ligand complex, C_F is free carrier, and k_5 is the rate constant of CL movement through the membrane. Assuming the steady-state conditions for both binding systems, then $(AL) = A_T L_F/(K_D + L_F)$ and $(CL) = (C_T)(L_F)/(K_M + L_F)$, where $K_D = k_1/k_2$ and $K_M = (k_4 + k_5)/k_3 \simeq k_4/k_3$ (see below). The ligand conservation equation is $L_T = L_F + AL + CL + L_M$. Substitution of the relationships for AL and CL into the equation for L_T, and assuming $L_F \ll K_M$ or K_D, results in,

$$\frac{1}{B} = \frac{L_T}{AL} = 1 + \frac{K_D}{A_T} + \frac{C_T K_D}{A_T K_M} + \frac{L_M K_D}{L_F A_T} \qquad (10)$$

The relationship for L_M is obtained by integrating $d(L_M)/dt = k_5 C_T L_F/K_M$. The value for L_F is obtained via integration of $d(L_F)/dt = k_1(AL) - k_2 A_F L_F + k_4(CL) - k_3 C_F L_F$; substituting the above relationships for AL and CL and given $A_F \simeq A_T$ and $C_F \simeq C_T$, then $d(L_F)/dt = 0$. Given $L_F = $ a constant, integration of $d(L_M)/dt$ results in $L_M = (k_5 C_T/K_M)L_F t$.[20] Substitution of this relationship for L_M into Equation 10 results in,

$$\frac{1}{B} = 1 + K_D(\text{app})(1/A_T) \qquad (11)$$

$$K_D(\text{app}) = K_D\{1 + C(\text{app})/K_M\} \qquad (12)$$

$$C(\text{app}) = C_T(1 + k_5 t) \qquad (13)$$

Therefore, in the case of carrier-mediation of ligand transport, the plasma protein binding of the ligand in vivo is also a transit time- and permeability-dependent parameter. For example, increases in transit time (t), carrier affinity (K_M), carrier concentration (C_T), or carrier mobility (k_5), will all cause K_D (app) to deviate from the K_D in vitro. Conversely, if carrier mobility (k_5) is slow relative to the transit time, then the apparent binding capacity of the carrier, C(app), will approximate C_T, which is invariably small relative to K_M; under these circumstances, K_D (app) $= K_D$, and the carrier will not effectively strip ligand off the plasma protein. The above relationship for C(app) illustrates the relativistic nature of the apparent binding capacity of a carrier, e.g., the apparent capacity expands with increases in k_5 relative to t.[20]

Rearrangement of the 1/B equation, given $B = 1 - F$, where $F =$ the free fraction of ligand in vivo, results in,

$$\text{App F in vivo} = \frac{1 + C(\text{app})/K_M}{1 + A_T/K_D + C(\text{app})/K_M} \tag{14}$$

Therefore, if $C(\text{app}) > K_M$, then the apparent free fraction in vivo will deviate from the free fraction in vitro, which is given by,

$$\text{F in vitro} = \frac{1}{1 + A_T/K_D} \tag{15}$$

The model for app F (Equation 14) is dependent on three assumptions:[20] (1) ligand dissociation (k_1) is rapid relative to the transit time (t); (2) both binding systems are in a steady-state, i.e., $d(AL)/dt$ and $d(CL)/dt$ are small relative to $k_2 A_F L_F$ and $k_3 C_F L_F$, respectively, and (3) the transport K_M represents a true affinity constant, i.e., $K_M = k_4/k_3$, because $k_4 > k_5$. Rates of tryptophan debinding from albumin have not been measured, but the rate of triiodothyronine (T_3) dissociation from albumin (k_1) is characterized by a $t_{1/2} < 1$ sec.[22] Since the K_D of T_3 binding to albumin, $4 \mu M$,[23] is manyfold less than the K_D of tryptophan binding to albumin, $130 \mu M$,[20] and since $K_D = k_1/k_2$, it is probable the k_1 for tryptophan is $\ll 1$ sec, i.e., fast relative to the brain capillary transit time, ~ 1 sec. With regard to the second assumption, changes in $d(AL)/dt$, $d(CL)/dt$, or dL_F/dt are all >0 during the course of a bolus of plasma through tissues; however, these rates are still small compared to $k_2 A_F L_F$ and $k_3 C_F L_F$; therefore, the steady-state approximation, i.e., $d(AL)/dt \simeq 0$ and $d(CL)/dt \simeq 0$, may be made, even for a single injection methodology such as the Oldendorf technique. In addition to these theoretical considerations, there is firm experimental evidence in support of the steady-state assumption for the single injection technique. Substrate transport rates predicted on the basis of kinetic constants obtained with the single injection technique correlate highly ($r = 0.8$ to 0.9) with experimentally observed rates obtained with a constant infusion method.[24] Finally, the assumption that the K_M of tryptophan or T_3 transport is a true affinity constant requires that $k_4 > k_5$.[20] Clearly, the debinding of ligand from the carrier (k_4) cannot be substantially greater than the rate of CL movement through the membrane; otherwise, ligand transport through the membrane would not take place. However, it is assumed that k_4 is sufficiently greater than k_5 such that the major factor determining K_M is k_4, not k_5. Evidence in support of this assumption comes from the observation that the maximal transport rate, V_{max}, for a number of neutral amino acids is relatively constant.[20,25] V_{max} constancy suggests the slow step in transport is relatively independent of substrate structure; since k_4 is more likely to be a function of ligand structure than is k_5, it is probable k_5 is the rate-limiting step in the transport reaction, i.e., $k_4 > k_5$.[20]

The theoretical section has attempted to emphasize the following points:

1. Relatively simple and explicit relationships may be derived for the apparent free ligand in vivo, for either free diffusion or facilitated mechanisms of transport
2. The steady-state approximation does not require that $d(AL)/dt = 0$ exactly, but only that the change in AL or L_F with time is small relative to the $k_2 A_F L_F$ product
3. The app free fraction in vivo, like the definition of a steady-state, is a relativistic parameter, e.g., the free ligand is a transit time- and permeability-dependent parameter, and
4. Since capillary transit times and membrane permeabilities are not considered in

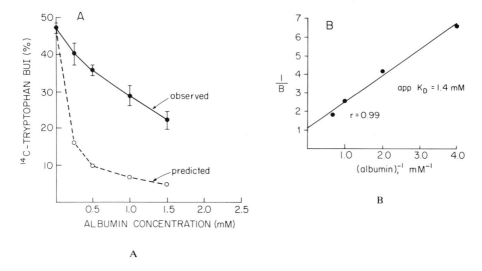

A

FIGURE 2. The comparison of experimentally observed rates of blood-brain barrier (BBB) transport of tryptophan in vivo vs. rates predicted on the basis of the assumption that only the tryptophan fraction that is free (dialyzable) in vitro is free and available for transport in vivo. The gross disparity between predicted and observed results indicates albumin-bound tryptophan is transported in vivo or, stated differently, the fraction of ligand that is free in vivo is much greater than the fraction that is free in vitro (Table 1). The BUI is defined in Equation 1 and is approximately equal to the first pass extraction of tryptophan by the rat brain after a carotid injection of a solution containing various concentrations of bovine albumin. The apparent K_D of albumin binding in vivo, 1.4 mM, is obtained from the slope of the double reciprocal plot (inset), and this value is more than 10-fold the K_D of albumin binding of tryptophan in vitro, 0.13 mM. The bound (B) tryptophan in vivo was calculated according to Equation 3. The predicted BUI = (BUI$_o$) × (% free in vitro), where BUI$_o$ = the BUI at zero albumin concentration (i.e., 47%) and the percent free tryptophan in vitro was calculated according to Equation 15, given K_D = 0.13 mM. Data from Reference 20.

in vitro measurements of free ligand, it should not be surprising that in vitro estimates of free ligand grossly underestimate the free fraction in vivo

IV. TRANSPORT OF TRYPTOPHAN

Unlike other circulating amino acids, tryptophan is bound by albumin.[26] Under normal conditions the K_D of albumin binding of tryptophan is about 0.15 mM;[20,26] therefore, at an albumin (A_T) level of 0.5 mM (3.4 g/100 mℓ) the percent free tryptophan in vitro is 23% (Equation 15). The K_D is directly proportional to the existing free fatty acid level, i.e., albumin binding of free fatty acid lowers the affinity for tryptophan.[27] While it is commonly believed that only the free (dialyzable) fraction of tryptophan is available for transport into tissues, e.g., brain;[28,29] studies by Madras et al.,[27] Fernstrom et al.,[30] and Yuwiler et al.[31] have shown that protein-bound amino acid is readily transported into brain. Stated differently, the free fraction of tryptophan in vivo greatly exceeds the free fraction in vitro. Moreover, Equation 14 predicts that the deviation of the free tryptophan in vivo from the in vitro free amino acid should increased in proportion to (1) increases in the capacity (increased V_{max}) or affinity (decreased K_M) of the neutral amino acid transport system in the BBB, (2) decreases in albumin concentration or affinity, or (3) increases in brain capillary transit time (decreased cerebral blood flow). Assuming little change in carrier capacity, albumin concentration, or brain blood flow, the free fraction in vivo of tryptophan rises in proportion to the K_D/K_M ratio. As noted above, K_D is directly related to changes in plasma free fatty acid. Conversely, K_M is directly related to changes in plasma large neutral amino acids.

The effect of competition by other neutral amino acids (AA) on the apparent (app) K_M of BBB tryptophan transport may be quantitated by the following relationship,[24]

$$K_M(app)^{trp} = K_M^{trp} \left\{ 1 + \Sigma \frac{AA}{K_M}AA \right\} \tag{16}$$

where $\Sigma\, AA/K_M^{AA}$ is the sum of the ratio of plasma amino acid concentration to transport K_M for each respective competing amino acid. Inspection of Equation 16 yields a fundamental insight into the role of competition in vivo. If the $K_M \ll (AA)$, then K_M (app) $= K_M$, i.e., no effective competition occurs unless the K_M of the transport process approximates (AA).

While amino acid competition is frequently shown to occur in vitro, the level of amino acid needed in vitro for the large neutral amino acids is invariably severalfold greater than the plasma level in vivo, i.e., 0.1 to 0.5 mM. The K_M of BBB neutral amino acid transport is in the 0.1 to 0.5 mM range, but the K_M in other tissues is 1 to 10 mM or greater.[32] Therefore, in vivo competition selectively affects amino acid transport into brain, and not other tissues. Owing to the approximation of the K_M of BBB amino acid transport by plasma amino acid concentration, the brain is uniquely sensitive to competition effects caused by physiological changes in plasma amino acids.[24] Therefore, a high fat diet, by raising K_D, or a diet low in large neutral amino acid, by lowering K_M, will lend to raise the K_D/K_M ratio. That is, the magnitude of the change in the K_D/K_M ratio will vary according to the ingested diet (Table 1).

The failure to recognize that the free tryptophan in vivo is a function of the competition between albumin and the BBB carrier, and is not a simple function of albumin binding in vitro, has led to much confusion in the literature. While some investigators showed a correlation between brain tryptophan and free tryptophan in vitro,[28,29] other studies clearly documented situations in which these two parameters were not linked.[20,27,30,31] For example, switching animals from a protein diet without fat to a protein - 40% fat diet resulted in a 5-fold increase in free serum tryptophan, yet brain tryptophan increased only 20%;[30] the hyperaminoacidemia of the protein diet resulted in a high K_M which blunted the increased K_D caused by the addition of fat to the diet. Conversely, changing rats from a protein - 40% fat diet to a carbohydrate - 40% fat diet results in no change in free tryptophan in vitro but causes a doubling of brain tryptophan;[30] the K_M falls precipitously with the induction of a carbohydrate (insulin)-mediated hypoaminoacidemia (Table 1).

Finally, it must be emphasized that increases in the free tryptophan in vivo may occur irrespective of the more common changes in K_M or K_D. Decreases in albumin binding site concentration, e.g., the newborn;[33] increases in capillary transit time owing to decreased cerebral blood flow, e.g., the newborn;[34] or increases in carrier capacity, e.g., hepatic encephalopathy or ammonia administration,[35] will all tend to elevate the apparent free tryptophan and cause this parameter to more closely approximate the total plasma tryptophan rather than the free tryptophan in vitro (see Equation 14).

Two other indole compounds related to tryptophan, melatonin (*N*-acetyl-5-methox-ytryptamine) and tryptophol (3-indole ethanol), are also bound by albumin. Melatonin is about 60% albumin-bound and 40% free (dialyzable),[36] and tryptophol is about 90% albumin-bound and 10% free in vitro.[37] However, both the BBB and the liver cell membrane are highly permeable to the lipid-soluble indole compounds. Moreover, virtually all of albumin-bound melatonin is transported into brain or liver and albumin-bound tryptophol freely enters brain.[36,37] These results indicate albumin-binding

Table 1
FREE TRYPTOPHAN IN VITRO VS. FREE TRYPTOPHAN IN VIVO IN BRAIN CAPILLARIES

Condition or diet	K_M (app)[a] (μM)	K_D[b] (μM)	Free[c] in vitro (%)	Free[d] in vivo (%)
Carbohydrate/fat	400	300	38	77
Basal	700	300	38	69
Carbohydrate	400	100	17	53
Protein	900	100	17	38
Phenylketonuria	5000	100	17	21

[a] Directly related to the sum of competing neutral amino acids (Equation 16).
[b] Directly related to the free fatty acid level.
[c] Calculated from K_D and given albumin = 500 μM (Equation 15).
[d] Calculated from K_M (app) and given C (app) = 1900 μM (Equation 14).

of melatonin or tryptophol has no effect on the in vivo distribution of these compounds.

V. TRANSPORT OF THYROID HORMONES

Similar to tryptophan, the thyroid hormones, T_3 and T_4 (thyroxine), traverse the BBB via a specific transport system that is independent of the tryptophan-neutral amino acid carrier.[21] The diffusibility of the thyroid hormones through biological membranes is somewhat of an anomaly. The 3 to 4 iodine moieties of T_3, or T_4 render the molecules highly lipid-soluble, e.g., the 1-octanol/Ringer's partition coefficients are 100 to 200.[38] Similarly, iodinated contrast agents are highly lipid soluble.[39] Yet, were it not for the T_3/T_4 carrier in the BBB, little plasma hormone would diffuse through the barrier into brain. (Moreover, the low diffusibility of the lipid soluble iodinated contrast agents is precisely the reason these agents are employed to visualize cerebral vessels in angiography.) The low inherent diffusibility of the thyroid hormones may explain why these compounds do not freely diffuse through the placenta.[40] Owing to the apparent lack of thyroid hormone carrier in the placenta, these hormones do not freely exchange between the maternal and fetal circulation.[40] Finally, the hepatocyte cell membrane is readily permeable to T_3 and T_4.[38,41] However, T_3 or T_4 transport into liver is nonsaturable,[38] which suggests (but does not prove) that the hormones traverse the hepatocyte plasma membrane via free diffusion. Owing to the profusely mammillated surface of the liver cell membrane,[15] the surface area is enormous and this factor may explain the rapid transport of T_3 or T_4 into liver, despite the apparent absence of a T_3 or T_4 transport system at the liver cell membrane.[38]

The moderate permeability of the BBB or the liver cell membrane to thyroid hormone provides a setting in which the transport of protein-bound thyroid hormone may occur for these two tissues. As noted in previous sections of this review, a second prerequisite to the transport of protein-bound ligand is a rapid rate of unidirectional debinding *relative* to the capillary transit time of the organ in question. In an important series of experiments, Hillier measured the rates of T_3 and T_4 debinding from the three thyroid-binding proteins of human serum.[22,42] As shown in Table 2, the rate of hormone debinding from albumin is fast relative to the capillary transit time in either brain ($\sim$1 sec) or liver ($\sim$5 sec). Moreover, the rate of T_3 debinding from thyroid-

Table 2
RATES OF
THYROID
HORMONE
DEBINDING
FROM PLASMA
PROTEINS AT
$37°C^{22,42}$

Plasma protein	Half-time (sec)	
	T_4	T_3
TBG	39	4
TBPA	8	—
Albumin	—	<1

binding globulin (TBG) is fast relative to the transit time in liver. On the other hand, T_4 debinding from either TBG or thyroid-binding prealbumin (TBPA) is slow relative to the capillary transit times in either brain or liver. These considerations lead to the predictions, which have been experimentally supported,[38] that (1) albumin-bound T_3 or T_4 is transported into brain or liver, (2) TBG-bound T_3 is transported into liver, but not brain, and (3) TBPA-bound T_4 is not transported into liver.

The transport of albumin-bound T_3 through the BBB has been documented for both the adult rat[21] and the newborn (6- to 24-hr-old) rabbit.[43] The data for either animal are comparable and the results obtained for the newborn rabbit are shown in Figure 3. The unidirectional extraction of labeled T_3 by the newborn brain is 22% after carotid injection of the isotope in Ringer's solution containing 0.025 g/100 mℓ albumin, i.e., conditions under which the great majority of T_3 is free in vitro. The addition of albumin, which is the T_3-binding protein of rabbit serum,[44] to the carotid injection solution should result in a progressive inhibition of T_3 transport. Moreover, the percent inhibition by albumin of T_3 transport in vivo should equal the percent binding of T_3 in vitro if the equilibrium free hormone hypothesis is correct. When neonatal rabbit serum is progressively diluted, the free fraction in vitro of T_3 increases, e.g., 0.5% of total T_3 is free at 100% serum and 50% is free at a 0.5% serum dilution. Since the albumin concentration of newborn rabbit serum is 335 μM, the K_D of newborn rabbit albumin binding of $T_3 = (0.5\%) \times (335 \mu M) = 1.6 \mu M$[43] (see Equation 15), a figure which correlates well with the reported K_D of albumin binding of T_3.[23] However, the apparent K_D of albumin binding of the hormone at the capillary level of the newborn rabbit brain is 13.7% serum or 46 μM albumin (Figure 3). That is, the BBB T_3 transport system competes with albumin at the capillary level and this competition results in the transport of albumin-bound T_3 into brain. Stated differently, the apparent binding of T_3 by albumin in vivo is inhibited and this inhibition is reflected by the higher app K_D in vivo. On the basis of Equation 12, the apparent binding index of the BBB carrier may be calculated from the K_D (1.6 μM) and app K_D (46 μM) values, e.g., app C/K_M = 28. Substitution of app C/K_M = 28 and A_T/K_D = (335 μM) ÷ (1.6 μM) = 209 into Equation 14 indicates the app free T_3 in vivo at the BBB is 12.2% or 25-fold greater than the free T_3 in vitro, 0.5%.

The longer capillary transit time and the greater cell membrane permeability in liver, relative to brain, provides the setting for an even greater degree of transport of albumin-bound T_3 into liver. As shown in Figure 4, the unidirectional extraction of T_3 and T_4 is 77% and 43%, respectively, after rapid portal injection of Ringer's solution con-

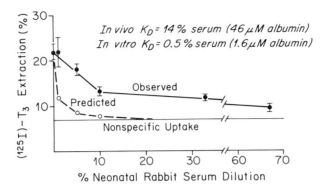

FIGURE 3. The first pass extraction of triiodothyronine (T_3) by the newborn (6 to 24 hr old) rabbit brain after carotid injection of various concentrations of newborn rabbit serum (predicted line) is compared to the extraction that would be expected if only the T_3 that was free (dialyzable) in vitro was also free and available for transport in vivo. The concentrations of serum resulting in 50% binding of T_3 in vivo, 14%, or in vitro, 0.5%, were determined by double reciprocal plots (see Figure 2). Since the concentration of albumin, which is the T_3 binding protein of rabbit serum, is 335 μM, then the app K_D of T_3 binding in vivo = (14%) × (335 μM) = 47 μM, and the in vitro K_D = (0.5%) × (335 μM) = 1.6 μM. Data from Reference 43.

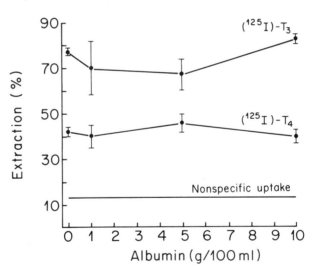

FIGURE 4. The first pass extraction of T_3 or T_4 by rat liver in vivo is unaffected by the concentration of bovine albumin in the portal injection solution, despite the fact that these levels of albumin bind 98 to 99% of thyroid hormone in vitro. The nonspecific uptake represents the extraction obtained after injection of hormone mixed in a 10% T_4- or T_3-specific rabbit antiserum. These results indicate albumin-bound hormone is freely cleared by liver cells, but antibody-bound hormone is not transported at all, e.g., the 13% nonspecific extraction is equal to the uptake of extracellular space compounds such as sucrose or iodide. Data from Reference 38.

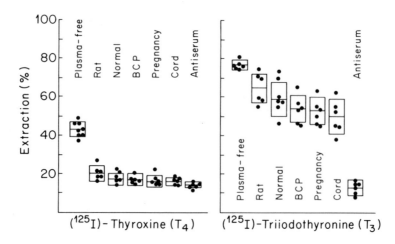

FIGURE 5. The first pass extraction for T_4 and T_3 by rat liver after a single portal injection of isotope mixed in various human or rat sera. Plasma-free solutions = Ringer's solution (0.1 g/100 mℓ albumin). Each point represents a different patient, volunteer, or animal. The boxes represent the mean ± SD. BCP = birth control pills. (Data from Reference 38.) These results are used to calculate the percent free T_4 and free T_3 in liver sinusoids in vivo (see Table 3).

taining 0.1 g/100 mℓ albumin. Liver transport of T_3 or T_4 is unaffected by concentrations of albumin, 1 to 10 g/100 mℓ, that bind more than 99% of hormone in vitro, i.e., <1% is free in vitro, but ~100% is free in vivo.[38] Rat serum lacks TBG, but contains TBPA,[44] which binds approximately 80% and 10% of total T_4 and T_3, respectively; about 20% and 90% of T_4 and T_3 in rat serum is bound by albumin. The addition of rat serum to the bolus portal injection solution results in a 19% and an 82% inhibition of T_3 and T_4 transport, respectively (Figure 5). Since the percent inhibition of T_4 transport correlates with the distribution of the hormone to TBPA, it is concluded that TBPA-bound T_4 is not transported into liver.[38] The addition of normal human serum, which contains TBG,[23] to the bolus portal injection solution results in a 28% and an 89% inhibition of T_3 and T_4 transport. Since about 70% of circulating T_3 or T_4 is bound to TBG in human serum,[45] the observation that T_3 transport is inhibited only 28% by human serum indicates most of TBG-bound T_3 is transported into liver. Moreover, the addition to the portal injection solution of human serum containing elevated concentrations of TBG, e.g., serum obtained from pregnant or estrogen-treated patients, results in no significant changes in T_3 transport into liver (Figure 5). However, the free T_3 fraction in vitro is markedly reduced in serum obtained from pregnant patients.[22,38] Therefore, in vitro measurements of free T_3 do not reliably predict what is free in vivo in liver sinusoids, because TBG-bound T_3 is readily transported into liver. Conversely, only albumin-bound T_4[21] is transported into peripheral tissues such as brain, and only albumin-bound T_4 is transported into liver.[38] Since both the albumin-bound and free (dialyzable) fractions are inversely related to the existing TBG or TBPA levels, the free (dialyzable) fraction will, under most circumstances, parallel the albumin-bound fraction and thereby reliably predict the free T_4 in vivo. However, it must be emphasized that the albumin-bound fraction is log orders greater than the free (dialyzable) fraction.

Finally, the use of T_3- or T_4-specific rabbit antisera as portal injection vehicles provides a useful model system.[38] Owing to the slow debinding of thyroid hormones from antibodies,[46] antibody-bound hormone does not dissociate into the free state, even within the liver transit time. Therefore, the extraction of antibody-bound T_3 or T_4,

Table 3
TRANSPORT OF T₃ AND T₄ INTO RAT LIVER IN VIVO

Portal vein injection vehicle	T₃		T₄	
	E^a	Free[b] in vivo (%)	E	Free in vivo (%)
Ringer's solution	77 ± 2	100	43 ± 2	100
Rat serum	65 ± 4	81	20 ± 2	18
Normal human	59 ± 5	72	18 ± 2	11
Birth control pill-treated	54 ± 4	64	16 ± 2	4
Pregnancy	53 ± 3	62	16 ± 2	4
Cord	50 ± 5	58	16 ± 1	4
Antiserum	13 ± 2	0	14 ± 1	0

[a]   First pass extraction (from Reference 38).
[b]   Calculated from Equation 3.

14% (Figure 5), is equal to the extraction of hepatic extracellular space markers, e.g., iodide or sucrose. In the presence of a specific antibody, only the minute fraction of free (dialyzable) hormone is available for transport into cells. The comparison of liver transport of thyroid hormone bound to antibodies vs. the normal plasma proteins illustrates an important point. Hormone-binding plasma proteins with debinding rates similar to antibodies did not evolve; rather the debinding kinetics of thyroid-binding proteins (Table 2) have adapted to the time frame of tissue capillary transit times.

VI. TRANSPORT OF STEROID HORMONES

The gonadal and adrenal steroid hormones are bound by albumin and specific globulins.[19,47,48] In man, testosterone and estradiol are bound by sex hormone-binding globulin (SHBG) and cortisol is bound by corticosteroid-binding globulin (CBG). There are numerous species differences in the distribution of the binding globulins. For example, CBG is present in virtually all vertebrates except amphibians and fish; SHBG is present in primates and ruminants, but is absent in rodents.[49] Pregnant guinea pigs have an unusual gestational sex hormone-binding globulin, progesterone-binding globulin (PBG), which also binds androgens, but not estrogens.[19] Fetal and neonatal rats possess an estradiol-binding protein (EBP), which binds estrogens, but not androgens.[50] Progesterone is bound by orosomucoid, an acute phase reactant, and is also bound by CBG.[19,51] Aldosterone is also bound actively in vitro by CBG.[52] However, owing to the excess concentration of corticosteroids in plasma, e.g., cortisol in man or corticosterone in rats, the apparent affinity of CBG for progesterone or aldosterone in vivo is low and only ∿10% of plasma progesterone or aldosterone circulates bound to CBG.[51]

As noted in previous sections, the distribution of steroid hormones to either albumin- or globulin-binding sites may be predicted from the law of mass action, e.g.,

$$\text{albumin fraction} \quad = \quad \frac{BI_A}{1 + BI_A + BI_G} \tag{17}$$

$$\text{globulin fraction} \quad = \quad \frac{BI_G}{1 + BI_A + BI_G} \tag{18}$$

$$\text{free (dialyzable) fraction} \quad = \quad \frac{1}{1 + BI_A + BI_G} \tag{19}$$

Table 4

HORMONE DISTRIBUTION TO PLASMA PROTEINS[a]

Binding globulin	Hormone	Globulin-bound (%)	Albumin-bound (%)	Free-dialyzable (%)
TBG	T_4[b]	70	10	0.03
	T_3	70	30	0.3
SHBG	Dihydrotestosterone	80	20	2
	Testosterone	60	40	2
	Estradiol	40	60	2
CBG	Cortisol	75	15	10
	Progesterone	10	90[c]	2
	Aldosterone	10	50	40

[a]   Data compiled from References 19, 23, 45, and 51.
[b]   About 20% T_4 circulates bound to TBPA and less than 5% of T_3 is bound by TBPA.
[c]   Includes binding to orosomucoid.

Table 5

RATES OF STEROID HORMONE
DEBINDING FROM PLASMA PROTEIN
AT 37°C

Plasma protein	Hormone	Half-time (sec)
CBG	Cortisol	≤8
PBG	Progesterone	1.8
SHBG	Dihydrotestosterone	100
	Testosterone	22
	Estradiol	≤7
Albumin	Testosterone	<1

Data from References 19, 53, 54, and 55.

where BI = the binding index of albumin (A) or globulin (G); the binding index is the concentration of binding sites ÷ the K_D of the binding site. The distribution of the steroid hormones to the above three states is shown in Table 4.

While it is generally regarded that only the free (dialyzable) fraction is available for transport in vivo, one might expect on theoretical grounds that the transport of protein-bound steroid hormones into tissues is extensive. The unidirectional debinding rates of steroid hormones from albumin are extremely fast with a $t_{1/2}$ <1 sec.[16,53] The debinding rates of steroid hormones from globulin binding sites are on the order of 5 to 10 sec (Table 5). Therefore, steroids readily dissociate from albumin binding sites within brief capillary transit times, e.g., brain (∼1 sec), and these hormones may even dissociate from globulin-binding sites within long capillary transit times, e.g., liver (∼5 sec). Given a sufficient membrane permeability to the steroid hormones, one would expect rapid transport of protein-bound ligand.

The selective permeability properties of the BBB to the major steroid hormones has been measured[16] (Figure 6). Barrier transport of the steroid hormones is nonsaturable and is believed to occur via a noncarrier-mediated mechanism, e.g., free diffusion.[16] The permeability of the BBB to the steroid hormones is directly related to the lipid solubility of the compound (Figure 7). The major structural feature which determines the lipid solubility of the steroid hormones is the number (N) of hydrogen bonds which are formed in aqueous solution by polar functional groups.[56] As shown in Figure 8, the N value can be easily determined by inspection of the steroid structure. As shown

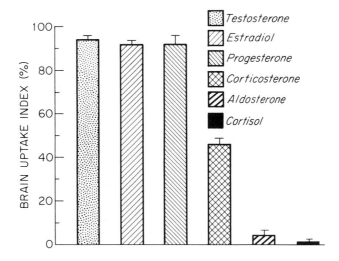

FIGURE 6. The BUI or first pass extraction by rat brain of steroid hormones after carotid injection of isotope in Ringer's solution (0.1 g/100 mℓ albumin). The selective permeability properties of the BBB to the steroid hormones are a function of the lipid solubility and hydrogen bond forming properties of the steroids (see Figure 7). Data from Reference 16.

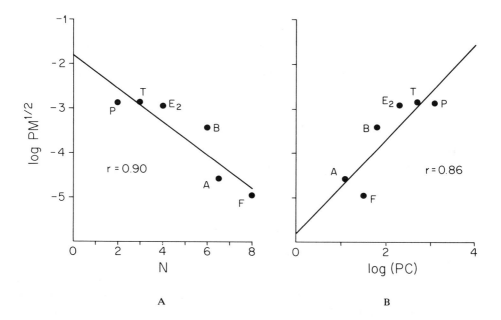

FIGURE 7. The log P (mol wt)$^{1/2}$ for the steroid hormone is plotted vs. the N number (A) or vs. the log of the 1-octanol/Ringer's partition coefficient or PC (B). The P (mol wt)$^{1/2}$ = the product of the BBB permeability constant (centimeter per second) times the square root of the molecular weight for each steroid. The N value is assigned according to the rules of Stein:[56] 2 for hydroxyl groups, 1 for carbonyls of aldehydes or ketones, 0 for ether moieties. See Figure 8 for steroid structures. Abbreviations: P-progesterone, T-testosterone, E$_2$-estradiol, B-corticosterone, A-aldosterone, F-cortisol. Data from Reference 16.

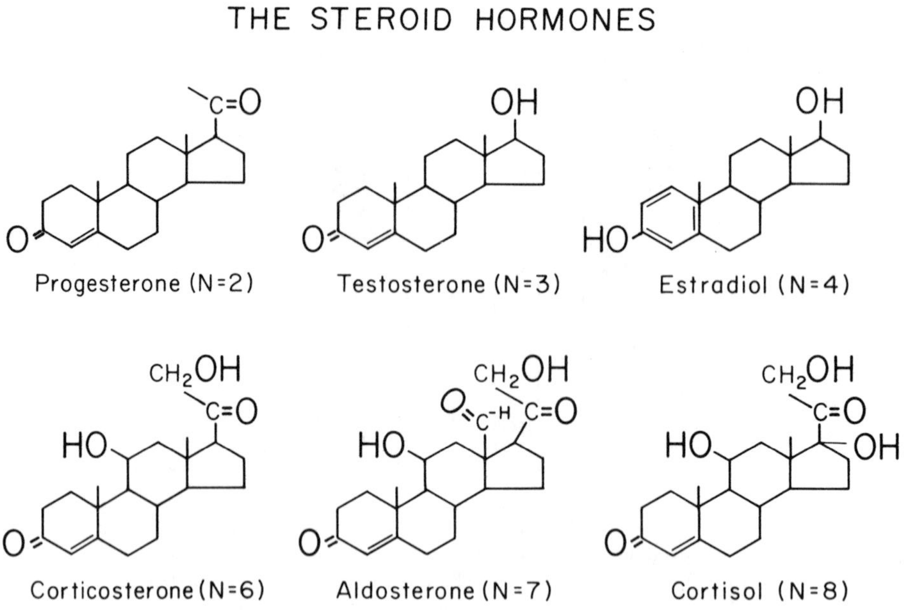

THE STEROID HORMONES

FIGURE 8.   Molecular structures for steroid hormones with emphasis placed on hydrogen bond forming functional groups. The addition of one hydroxyl group to corticosterone results in the formation of cortisol and a log order drop in BBB permeability (see Figure 7A).

in Figures 6 and 7, there is a log order drop in BBB permeability for each pair of hydrogen bonds added to the steroid.[16] For example, the addition of one hydroxyl group ($N = 2$) to corticosterone yields cortisol, and the latter penetrates the BBB a log order slower than corticosterone.

The higher the permeability of the BBB to the steroid hormones, the greater the ability of the membrane to compete with albumin for the circulating steroid.[16] Stated differently, the greater the rate of diffusion of the steroid through the membrane, the less likely the ligand is going to reassociate with albumin subsequent to an intra-capillary debinding event. These considerations are illustrated in Figures 9 through 12, which show the spectrum of the ability of albumin to compete with the BBB for the steroids. As the N value increases from 2 (progesterone) to 6 (corticosterone), the in vivo binding of the steroid by albumin increases. This is reflected in the ratio of app K_D/K_D (Table 6); the in vivo K_D (app) is $\geqslant$200-fold the in vitro K_D of albumin binding of progesterone, but the K_D (app) is only 8-fold greater than the in vitro K_D for corticosterone.

As discussed earlier (Equation 8), the K_D (app) $= K_D$ $(e^{k_3 t})$, where $K_3 =$ the rate constant of ligand flux through the membrane and $t =$ capillary transit time. If $k_3 \ll t$, then K_D (app) $= K_D$, i.e., the free fraction in vivo $=$ the free fraction in vitro. However, if $k_3 \simeq t$, then K_D (app) deviates exponentially from K_D. The K_D (app)/K_D ratio may be used to calculate the $k_3 t$ product for brain (Table 6). Since $t \simeq 1$ sec for brain, the data in Table 6 provide approximate estimates of k_3. Therefore, the $t_{1/2}$ of steroid diffusion through the BBB is on the order of 100 to 400 msec.

The rapid transport of albumin-bound steroid hormone through the BBB is due to the rapid debinding of steroid relative to the capillary transit time and to the high k_3 relative to the transit time. Steroid hormones are also bound to globulins (Table 4) and the globulin debinding rates are slow relative to the brain transit time (Table 5). Therefore, it is to be expected that globulin-bound hormone may not enter brain as readily as does albumin-bound hormone. The effects of BBB testosterone or estradiol

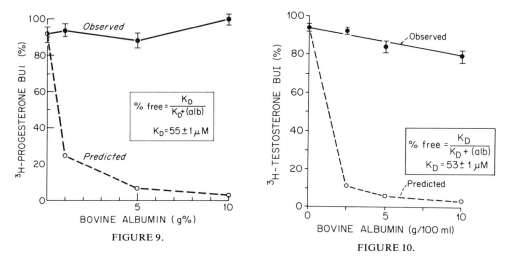

FIGURE 9. The BUI or first pass extraction by rat brain of progesterone after rapid carotid injection of hormone mixed in various concentrations of albumin. The predicted line represents the product of the BUI at zero albumin × the free (dialyzable) progesterone level in vitro at each albumin concentration. Essentially all of albumin-bound progesterone is transported into brain. Data from Reference 16. FIGURE 10. The BUI or first pass extraction by rat brain of testosterone after rapid carotid injection of hormone mixed in various concentrations of albumin. See Figure 9 for explanation of predicted line. Data from Reference 16.

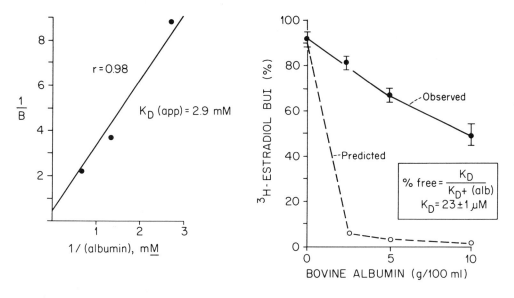

FIGURE 11. The BUI or first pass extraction by rat brain of estradiol after rapid carotid injection of hormone mixed in albumin solutions. See Figure 9 for details of predicted line. See Figure 2 for details of double reciprocal plot. See Table 6 for comparison of K_D in vitro, 23 μM, vs. app K_D in vivo, 2900 μM. Data from Reference 16.

transport of human serum containing widely varying levels of SHBG are shown in Figure 13. As the level of SHBG decreased, the transport of testosterone or estradiol increased. The relationship between transport rate and SHBG level may be quantitated by the following model,[57] which assumes that no globulin-bound hormone enters, but that albumin-bound hormone enters brain freely. Rearrangement of Equation 17 results in

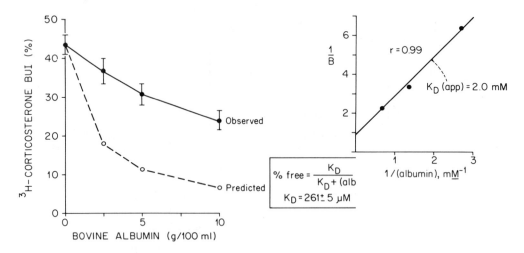

FIGURE 12.   The BUI or first pass extraction by rat brain of corticosterone after rapid carotid injection of steroid in various albumin solutions. See legend to Figure 11 for detail. Data from Reference 16.

Table 6
COMPARISON OF ALBUMIN BINDING OF STEROID HORMONES IN VITRO VS. IN VIVO[a]

Steroid	$K_D{}^b$ in vitro	K_D (app)[c] in vivo	$\dfrac{K_D \text{ (app)}}{K_D}$	$k_3\, t^d$
Progesterone	$55\mu M$	$\geqslant 10\ mM$	$\geqslant 200$	>5.3
Testosterone	53	>10	>200	>5.3
Estradiol	23	2.9	120	4.8
Dihydrotestosterone	53	3.1	60	4.1
Corticosterone	261	2.0	8	2.0

[a]   Data from Reference 16 and unpublished data of W. M. Pardridge.
[b]   Determined by equilibrium dialysis at 37°C.
[c]   From Figures 9 to 12.
[d]   Calculated from Equation 8, where t = the brain capillary transit time ($\sim$1 sec) and k_3 = the rate constant of steroid transport through the blood-brain barrier ($t\frac{1}{2}$ = 100-400 msec).

$$\frac{1}{\text{albumin-bound fraction}} = 1 + \left(\frac{K_A}{A_T K_G}\right)(\text{SHBG}) \qquad (20)$$

where K_A and K_G are the dissociation constants of albumin and SHBG, respectively, A_T = the total albumin concentration. Based on Figures 10 and 11, it may be assumed that at physiological concentrations of albumin, e.g., 3.4 g/100 mℓ, nearly all of the albumin-bound testosterone or estradiol enters brain; therefore 1/albumin-bound fraction = 1/BUI. A plot of 1/BUI vs. SHBG is shown in Figure 14; the plot is highly linear (r = 0.98 to 0.99) and has an intercept of $\sim$1, as predicted from Equation 20. The slope = K_A/ ($A_T \times K_G$); therefore, the ratio of the testosterone slope/estradiol slope, which is 5.4, is equal to the K_A/K_G ratio for testosterone divided by the K_A/K_G ratio for estradiol. Since the affinity of albumin for estradiol is 2.3-fold the affinity of testosterone (Figures 10, 11), these data indicate the affinity of SHBG in vivo is (5.4) $\div$ (2.3) = 2.4-fold greater for testosterone relative to estradiol. These predictions

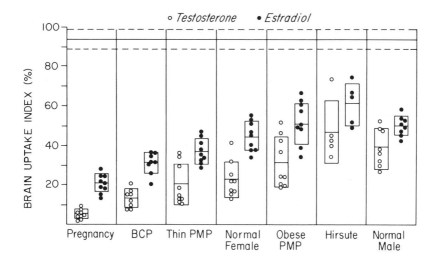

FIGURE 13. The brain uptake index (BUI) or first pass extraction of testosterone and estradiol by rat brain after rapid carotid injection of hormone mixed in either Ringer's solution (horizontal line, mean ± SD), or in patient serum (boxes are mean ± SD). Abbreviations used: BCP, birth control pills; PMP, post-menopausal. The level of sex hormone binding globulin (SHBG) in each patient group varied in an inverse relationship to the extraction for either hormone, e.g., SHBG = 323 ± 83nM, 126 ± 41 nM, 74 ± 27 nM, 65 ± 26 nM, 43 ± 13 nM, 28 ± 8 nM, and 17 ± 5 nM, in pregnancy, BCP-treated, thin PMP, normal female, obese PMP, normal male, and hirsute female, respectively. Data from Reference 57.

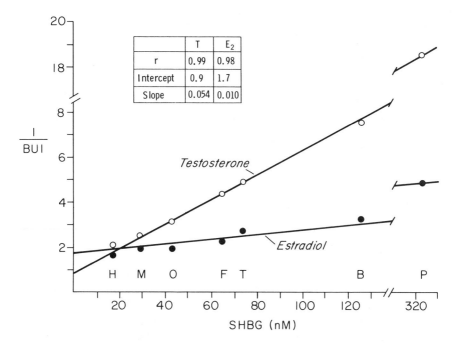

FIGURE 14. The reciprocal of the mean BUI for testosterone or estradiol is plotted vs. the SHBG level in each of the 7 groups of patients studied in Figure 13. Abbreviations: P, pregnancy; B, birth control pills; T, thin post-menopausal; F, normal female; O, obese post menopausal; M, normal male; and H, hirsute. Data obtained by linear regression are shown in the inset. A model based on the free transport of albumin-bound hormone and the absence of transport of globulin-bound steroid forms the basis of this plot (see Equation 20). Data from Reference 57.

correlate with in vitro measurements, e.g., $K_G = 2$ nM for testosterone and $K_G = 5$ nM for estradiol.[58] In addition, the high degree of correlation between the BUI and SHBG level supports the validity of the model that no SHBG-bound sex steroid enters brain.[57]

The concentration of SHBG in human serum is relatively low, e.g., 20 to 300 nM (Figure 13). Consequently, albumin is able to compete with the globulin and, as a result, steroid is distributed to both binding sites. The use of sera containing μM concentrations of high-affinity binding globulins, however, eliminates the problem of multiple plasma protein-binding sites.[59] For example, the PBG of pregnant guinea pig serum,[19] the EBP of neonatal rat serum,[50] or a steroid-specific antibody of a rabbit antiserum all exist in plasma at a concentration of 5 to 20 μM. All three globulins are high-affinity binding proteins, e.g., $K_D \simeq 5$ nM; therefore, the binding index = (5000 to 20,000 nM) $\div$ 5 nM = 1000 to 4000. In contrast, the binding index of albumin = 500 $\mu M \div 25 \mu M = 20$ for most of the sex steroids.[51] Consequently, $\sim$99% of the steroid is globulin-bound and $\sim$1% is albumin-bound (Equations 17 and 18).

A progesterone-specific rabbit antiserum has been used to investigate whether antibody-bound steroid is transported into brain.[59] As shown in Figure 15, increasing concentrations of the antibody results in increased binding of progesterone and decreased transport through the BBB. Moreover, the bound fraction in vitro, as determined by a charcoal separation technique, corresponds to the bound fraction in vivo, as determined by the blood-brain barrier method. Therefore, antibody-bound steroid like SHBG-bound steroid, is not transported through the BBB. However, the lack of transport into brain of globulin-bound steriod is not a fixed rule. As shown in Figure 16, progesterone, 17-hydroxyprogesterone, or androgen, bound to PBG, is readily transported into brain. As in the case of the transport of albumin-bound hormone, the basis to the rapid transport of PBG-bound steroid is the rapid rate of steroid debinding. As shown in Table 5, the $t_{1/2}$ at 37°C of progesterone debinding from PBG is 1.8 sec,[19] which is considerably faster dissociation than steroid debinding from SHBG. Since the K_{off} is generally directly related to the K_D,[19] and since the K_D of PBG for testosterone ($K_D = 5.6$ nM) binding is 8-fold greater than the K_D for progesterone ($K_D = 0.7$ nM), it is probable the greater rate of transport of PBG-bound testosterone (Figure 16) is due to a faster debinding process, relative to PBG-bound progesterone.

Although the debinding rates of estradiol dissociation from the EBP of neonatal rat serum have apparently not been measured, it is probable the K_{off} for estradiol is about the same as that observed for progesterone dissociation from PBG. As in the case of PBG-bound progesterone (Figure 17), about 10% of EBP-bound estradiol is transported into brain. That is, both PBG and EBP reduce progesterone or estradiol clearance by brain by about tenfold, but the presence of these globulins does not completely abolish brain uptake of the steroids. Indeed, if the function of PBG or EBP were to completely restrict steroid clearance by peripheral tissues such as brain, the proteins would have evolved with debinding processes more on the order of SHBG.

The preceding discussion has emphasized the view that the transport of protein-bound steroid hormones into brain may be described by a spectrum: albumin-bound > PBG- or EBP-bound $\geqslant$ SHBG or antibody-bound. The basis to the spectrum is the differential rate of steroid debinding from plasma proteins. In all sera samples tested thus far, except for specific antisera, the free fraction in vivo $\geqslant$ free (dialyzable) fraction in vitro.

As noted above, one way to bring about transport of globulin-bound steroid into a tissue is to increase the debinding $t_{1/2}$ so that this process approximates the capillary transit time, e.g., PBG (fast debinding) vs. SHBG (slow debinding). The other way to cause transport of globulin-bound steroid is to increase the transit time, e.g., brain (brief transit time, $\sim$1 sec) vs. liver (long transit time, $\sim$5 sec). As shown in Figures

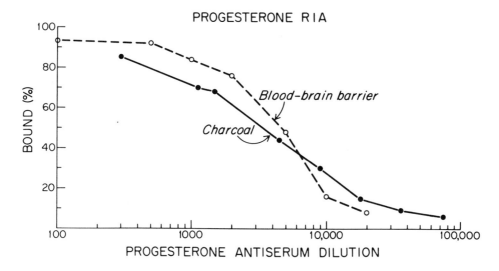

FIGURE 15. In vivo (blood-brain barrier) and in vitro (charcoal) techniques are compared for the separation of antibody-bound and free progesterone. The percent bound progesterone in vivo was calculated from the percent inhibition of BBB transport by various dilutions of antiserum (Equation 3). The good correlation between the in vivo and in vitro techniques indicates only the fraction of progesterone that is free in vitro is free and available for transport in vivo. These observations underscore the general principle that if plasma transport proteins exhibited the binding kinetics of antibodies, then the free ligand fraction at equilibrium in vitro would represent the free ligand in vivo. Data from Reference 59.

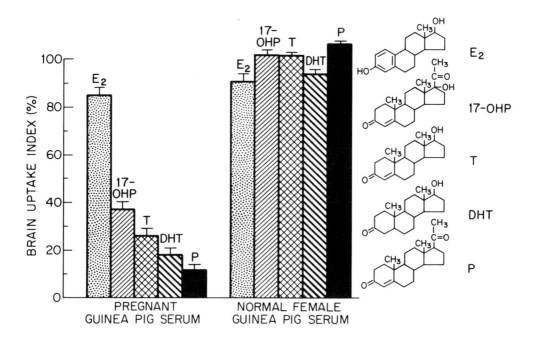

FIGURE 16. The brain uptake index or first pass extraction of five steroid compounds by rat brain after rapid carotid injection of steroid mixed in either pregnant or normal female guinea pig serum. Abbreviations: E_2, estradiol; 17-hydroxyprogesterone, 17-OHP; T, testosterone; DHT, dihydrotestosterone; P, progesterone. The presence of progesterone-binding globulin (PBG), which also binds androgens, in serum of the pregnant guinea pig accounts for the differences. Data from Reference 59.

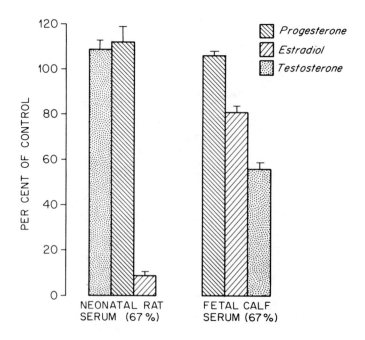

FIGURE 17.   The percent free hormone in vivo in rat brain capillaries is shown for different sera used as the carotid injection solution. Since the steroids were all cleared by brain ∿90% after injection of hormone in Ringer's solution (which served as the control), the percent of control shown here is essentially equal to the percent free hormone in vivo. Data from Reference 16.

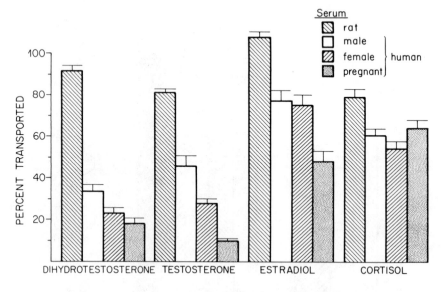

FIGURE 18.   The percent transported or percent free hormone (Equation 3) in vivo in liver capillaries is shown after rapid portal injection of hormone mixed in the sera samples shown. Data from Reference 17.

18-21, the transport of protein-bound steroid hormones into liver is extensive. With regard to corticosteroids, CBG is present in high concentrations (∿500 nM) in rat serum;[60] however, cortisol is nearly freely transported into liver (Figure 18). These results confirm the work of Yates[61] or Rosner[62] and their associates, which indicate

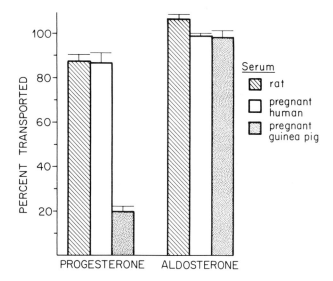

FIGURE 19. The percent transported or percent free in vivo (Equation 3) of progesterone or aldosterone in liver capillaries after portal injection of various serum samples. Data from Reference 17.

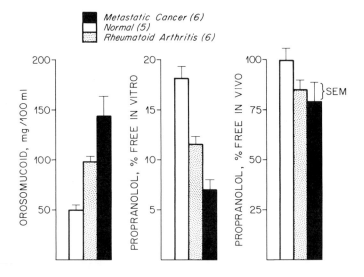

FIGURE 20. The orosomucoid level, the percent free propranolol in vitro and the percent free propranolol in vivo are shown for three different patient groups. Orosomucoid, a propranolol-binding protein, and an acute phase reactant, rises with inflammation, and this is associated with a parallel drop in the in vitro free fraction of drug. However, the free propranolol fraction in rat brain capillaries in vivo (from Equation 3) is relatively unaffected by high serum orosomucoid levels. Unpublished data of R. Sakiyama and W. M. Pardridge.

CBG-bound corticosteroid is readily transported into liver. Comparison between between brain and liver transport of protein-bound cortisol cannot be made, owing to the low permeability of the BBB to cortisol (Figure 6). However, corticosterone, which is the major corticosteroid in the rat, is readily transported into brain (Figure 6), and

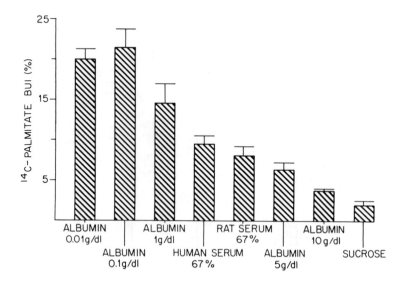

FIGURE 21.   The brain uptake index (BUI) of ^{14}C-palmitate is inhibited by increasing concentrations of albumin added to the carotid injection serum. The bar marked sucrose represents the uptake of substances by the extracellular space of brain. Data from Reference 70.

Table 7
COMPARISON OF IN VIVO FREE CORTICOSTERONE IN BRAIN AND LIVER CAPILLARIES[a]

Serum source[b]	Brain	Liver
Rat, male	31 ± 6	77 ± 8
Human, male	15 ± 1	74 ± 7
Human, pregnant	23 ± 3	51 ± 3

[a]   Data from References 17 and 57 and unpublished data of W. M. Pardridge. Data are mean ± SE.

[b]   Carotid artery or portal vein injection vehicle.

studies of protein-bound corticosterone transport into brain have been reported.[16] A comparison of corticosterone clearance by brain and liver is shown in Table 7. The data indicate only the free (dialyzable) and albumin-bound fractions of corticosterone are transported into brain, but these moieties plus the majority of the CBG-bound fraction are available for entry into liver.[17] The transport of CBG-bound corticosteroid into liver may be attributed to the longer transit time in liver, which approximates the $t_{1/2}$ of corticosteroid debinding from CBG (Table 5). In addition, the transport of protein-bound corticosteroids into liver is facilitated by the much higher permeability of the hepatocyte cell membrane to the adrenal steroids relative to the permeability of the BBB (Table 8). Steroids traverse both membranes, the BBB and the hepatocyte cell membrane, by a nonsaturable mechanism, which is probably free diffusion.[16,17] Therefore, the differences in membrane permeability between the two tissues cannot be attributed to a greater abundancy in the liver cell membrane of a corticosteroid transport system. The higher permeability in liver is probably due to a much greater cell membrane surface area (square centimeter per gram) in liver related to brain.

Table 8
COMPARISON OF FIRST PASS EXTRACTION OF STEROID HORMONES BY THE BRAIN AND LIVER[a]

	Unidirectional extraction (%)	
Steroid	Brain	Liver
Dihydrotestosterone	93 ± 3	107 ± 6
Testosterone	85 ± 1	92 ± 2
Progesterone	83 ± 4	85 ± 2
Estradiol	85 ± 3	85 ± 2
Corticosterone	39 ± 2	70 ± 2
Aldosterone	4 ± 1	83 ± 5
Cortisol	1 ± 0.3	73 ± 2

Note: Hormones were administered to brain or liver via rapid injection of Ringer's solution; therefore, the extractions are independent of plasma protein binding and the differences in extraction reflect only differences in membrane permeability in brain and liver.

[a] From References 16 and 17 and unpublished data of W. M. Pardridge.

Table 9
COMPARISON OF IN VIVO FREE ESTRADIOL AND TESTOSTERONE IN BRAIN AND LIVER CAPILLARIES[a]

Hormone	Serum source[b]	Brain	Liver
Estradiol	Rat, male	87 ± 4	108 ± 3
	Human, male	55 ± 2	77 ± 8
	Human, female	49 ± 3	75 ± 7
	Human, pregnant	23 ± 2	48 ± 8
Testosterone	Rat, male	88 ± 2	81 ± 1
	Human, male	42 ± 4	46 ± 7
	Human, female	24 ± 4	28 ± 3
	Human, pregnant	5 ± 1	10 ± 1
Estradiol/testosterone ratio	Rat, male	1.0	1.3
	Human, male	1.3	1.7
	Human, female	2.1	2.7
	Human, pregnant	3.9	4.8

[a] Data compiled from References 17 and 57. Mean ± SE.
[b] Carotid artery or portal vein injection vehicle.

The data in Table 7 suggest the design principle underlying the evolution of CBG. The globulin selectively amplifies the amount of corticosteroid cleared by the metabolically active liver[b] relative to the less active peripheral tissues.

With regard to testosterone and estradiol, the clearance data for liver (Figure 18), and brain (Figure 13) are compared in Table 9. Owing to the slow debinding of testosterone from SHBG, only albumin-bound hormone is available for entry in liver or brain (Table 9). Consequently, as SHBG increases, the albumin-bound fraction decreases and proportionate decreases in testosterone clearance by liver ensue. However, due to the more rapid debinding of estradiol from SHBG,[55] globulin-bound estrogen is selectively transported into liver, but not into brain. Therefore, as SHBG increases, the estradiol/testosterone (E_2/T) clearance ratio in liver rises faster than the E_2/T clearance ratio in brain. That is, the estradiol amplifier function of SHBG[63] is even more pronounced in liver (Table 9) than it is in brain (Figure 14).

The lack of significant binding of progesterone or aldosterone to a slowly dissociating globulin in rat or human plasma results in the nearly free transport of these two steroids into liver (Figure 19). As in brain (Figure 16), the presence of PBG in pregnant guinea pig serum greatly retards, but does not abolish, progesterone transport into liver (Figure 19). However, the amount of PBG-bound progesterone available for transport into liver is about twofold the PBG-bound hormone in brain. The greater rate of transport of globulin-bound progesterone in liver, relative to brain, may be attributed to the longer hepatic capillary transit time.

VII. TRANSPORT OF DRUGS

Similar to the widespread acceptance of the free hormone hypothesis in endocrinology and physiology, it is an often-stated principle in pharmacology that only the free (dialyzable) drug is available for transport into tissue. However, the recognition that a drug such as propranolol, which is only 10% free in vitro but is 90% cleared by liver on single pass, has led to a revision of the free drug hypothesis.[64] Drugs are now classified according to restrictive (free only) vs. nonrestrictive (free plus protein-bound) transport into liver. For example, propranolol and warfarin are characterized by nonrestrictive and restrictive transport, respectively.[64]

Although protein-bound propranolol is recognized to be freely available for transport into liver, it is generally regarded that only the free (dialyzable) fraction is transported into peripheral tissues.[65] Moreover, changes in the free (dialyzable) fraction of propranolol associated with alterations in propranolol binding proteins in diseased states is believed to be predictive of the availability of the drug to tissues.[66] Propranolol is primarily bound to orosomucoid or α_1-acid glycoprotein, an acute phase reactant.[67] This globulin, which actively binds a number of basic drugs in addition to propranolol, rises markedly in inflammatory conditions[66] such as rheumatoid arthritis or metastatic cancer. Moreover, the free (dialyzable) drug fraction decreases substantially in association with increases in orosomucoid and it has been suggested that more drug should be administered to patients to compensate for the increased protein binding.[66]

In addition to orosomucoid, propranolol is also bound by albumin.[68] However, the binding index of orosomucoid is much greater than the binding index of albumin and most of the drug is globulin-bound. Therefore, the plasma protein transport characteristics are analogous to the thyroid or steroid hormones. Based on studies with these hormones, we expected *a priori* that albumin-bound propranolol would freely cross the BBB, but orosomucoid-bound drug would not. However, the experimental results indicate exactly the opposite occurs. In the presence of albumin, the free (dialyzable) propranolol faction in vitro is essentially equal to the free drug fraction in brain capillaries.[117] The lack of transport of albumin-bound drug into brain suggests the rate of propranolol debinding from albumin is slow relative to the brain capillary transit time, $\sim$1 sec. Yet albumin-bound propranolol is known to freely enter liver.[64] These results suggest, but do not prove, the $t_{1/2}$ of propranolol debinding from albumin is greater than the brain transit time ($\sim$1 sec), but less than the liver capillary transit time ($\sim$5 sec). Given the albumin K_D for propranolol, $K_D = K_{off}/K_{on} = 2.8 \times 10^{-4} M$,[117] and $K_{off} = 0.2$ sec^{-1} (ln 2/$t_{1/2}$ of 3 sec), then $K_{on} = 0.8 \times 10^3 M^{-1}$ sec^{-1}. This estimate of

K_{on} is 10^3 to 10^5-fold lower than the K_{on} of most ligand-protein interactions,[19] which suggests the kinetics of propranolol binding to albumin may be very unusual. Moreover, given an albumin concentration of $0.5 \times 10^{-4}M$, the rate of propranolol association with albumin would only be $(0.5 \times 10^{-4}M) \times (0.8 \times 10^3 M^{-1} sec^{-1}) = 0.04 sec^{-1}$ or $t_{1/2} = 17$ sec. This estimate is considerably slower than the estimated rate of steroid association with albumin, $t_{1/2} < 1$ msec.[16] Since the kinetics of unidirectional dissociation and association of albumin binding of propranolol have apparently not been measured, the above considerations are largely hypothetical. However, the propranolol data[117] vs. that in Figures 9 through 12, underscore the fundamental difference between the rates of albumin debinding for the steroid hormones vs. propranolol.

Unlike the hormone-binding globulins, orosomucoid is commercially available in pure form. The effects of physiological concentrations of orosomucoid on BBB propranolol transport have been studied.[117] The apparent free fraction in vivo is greater than the free fraction in vitro, e.g., the concentration of orosomucoid which inhibits BBB transport of propranolol 50% is $\sim$25 μM vs. the level of orosomucoid which binds 50% of the drug in vitro, 3.3 μM.[117] Given ln K_D (app)/K_D = k_3t (Equation 8), and K_D (app) = 25 μM and K_D = 3.3 μM, then k_3t = 2.0. This estimate of k_3t is comparable to that of corticosterone (Table 6), which is to be expected since the permeability of the BBB to propranolol and corticosterone is comparable.

Given that most of plasma propranolol is orosomucoid-bound and that most of orosomucoid-bound propranolol is transported through the BBB, it is to be expected that the relationship between the free fraction in vivo of propranolol and the existing orosomucoid level is blunted. Moreover, in vitro measurements of free propranolol, being inversely related to orosomucoid levels, will grossly underestimate the free drug in vivo. These principles are illustrated in Figure 20. In inflammatory illness, e.g., rheumatoid arthritis or metastatic cancer, the plasma orosomucoid is markedly elevated in association with proportionate decreases in the free (dialyzable) propranolol level (Figure 20). On the basis of the in vitro data, a nearly threefold increase in propranolol dosage would be recommended for patients with metastatic cancer, since the free (dialyzable) fraction falls to 33% of controls (Figure 20). However, the free drug level in brain capillaries is only decreased to 80% of normal in conditions such as metastatic cancer; therefore, based on in vivo measurements of free propranolol levels (Figure 20), the drug dosage should be increased by $\leq$20% in conditions associated with threefold elevations in plasma orosomucoid. Moreover, increases in propranolol levels in proportion to decreases in the free (dialyzable) concentration in vitro may possibly lead to drug toxicity.

VIII. TRANSPORT OF LIPIDS: FREE FATTY ACIDS AND CHOLESTEROL

Long-chain free fatty acids are tightly bound to albumin; the fatty acids are distributed over multiple binding sites of both high and low affinity.[69] The function of the nonlinear relationship of albumin binding of free fatty acids, i.e., the multiple sites of varying affinity, is probably aimed at a selective transport of free fatty acids to different tissues. That is, it is probable that the debinding of free fatty acids from high affinity sites is slow relative to the fast capillary transit time in brain. Conversely, a fast debinding of free fatty acid from low affinity sites provides a mechanism by which free fatty acid may be delivered to brain. As shown in Figure 21, about 5% of plasma palmitate, which is log orders greater than the free (dialyzable) fatty acid in vitro, is available for transport into brain at physiologic concentrations of albumin.[70] Moreover, as the albumin concentration decreases, the transport of palmitate into brain increases. These results are consistent with the model (Theory Section) that the transport of protein-bound ligands is a function of the $k_3/(k_2A_T)$ product. That is, a drop in albumin concentration, i.e., A_T, will favor transport of a ligand that debinds within a capillary transit time.

In addition, the data in Figure 21 indicate that a dilution of albumin beyond 0.1 g/ 100 mℓ fails to further enhance brain palmitate transport beyond an extraction of 15 to 20%. These results suggest that only about 15% of plasma palmitate is bound to a binding site that is characterized by a debinding rate that is fast relative to the brain capillary transit time.

In contrast to brain, the unidirectional extraction of free fatty acid in other organs may be as high as 25% (liver)[71] or 60% (heart).[72] There is little evidence that free fatty acids traverse endothelial membranes via a collision mechanism.[69] Therefore, the selective transport of free fatty acid into tissues such as heart or liver, relative to brain, cannot be ascribed to an increased amount of free fatty acid carrier in cardiac endothelia or hepatocyte cell membranes. Rather, the selective transport of free fatty acids via the free intermediate mechanism occurs via tissue differences in capillary transit time and capillary (or hepatocyte) surface area. That is, the longer transit time and greater transport surface area in heart and liver, relative to brain, account for the faster transport of albumin-bound free fatty acid into heart and liver.

Unlike free fatty acids, cholesterol does not normally circulate bound to albumin. Cholesterol and cholesterol-free fatty acid esters are bound by plasma lipoproteins,[73] e.g., high density lipoprotein (HDL), low density lipoprotein (LDL), very low density lipoprotein (VLDL), and chylomicrons (CM). Since cholesterol is extremely lipid soluble, any lipoprotein-bound cholesterol that undergoes debinding within a tissue transit time would readily escape through the capillary wall and enter the tissue. As shown in Figure 22, the BBB is readily permeable to albumin-bound cholesterol.[70] Moreover, when ^{3}H-cholesterol was mixed with human serum, cholesterol transport through the BBB was also rapid (Figure 22), which at first glance would seem to indicate lipoprotein-bound cholesterol is readily transported into brain. However, reports in the literature have emphasized that simply mixing ^{3}H-cholesterol with serum does not lead to lipoprotein-bound ^{3}H-cholesterol,[74] because the association is not spontaneous. However, incubation of serum overnight at 37°C leads to the formation of lipoprotein-bound cholesterol and, under these conditions, cholesterol transport through the BBB does not occur.[70] These results are consistent with the model that lipoprotein-bound cholesterol does not debind within tissue transit times. Therefore, if cholesterol is to enter cells, a collision mechanism must be operative.

Evidence in favor of a collision transport mechanism for LDL-bound cholesterol has been reported by Goldstein and Brown.[11] The LDL cell membrane receptor is present in liver and tissues of active steroidogenesis, e.g., adrenal cortex or the ovarian corpus luteum.[75] The LDL receptor is low in tissues such as brain, red cell, muscle, lung, fat, intestine, or testis.[75] Moreover, cholesterol is known not to cross the blood-testis barrier, i.e., the Sertoli cell.[76] With regard to brain, cholesterol is known to slowly enter brain from blood over a time period of several months.[77] Since it is unlikely such blood-to-brain cholesterol transport occurs at the BBB, the slow rate of cholesterol uptake may occur via transport through the blood-cerebrospinal fluid-barrier, e.g., the choroid plexes.

IX. TRANSPORT OF VITAMINS

A. Lipid Soluble

The fat-soluble vitamins are A, D, E, K. Apparently, no specific transport proteins exist in plasma for vitamins E or K, and these substances will not be reviewed.

Specific transport globulins do exist for vitamin A (retinol), e.g., retinol-binding

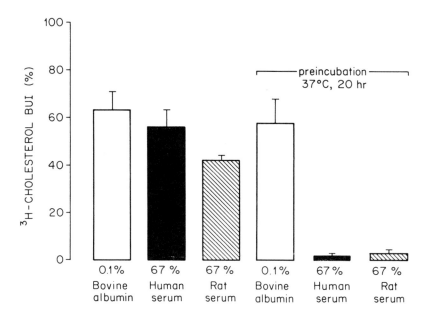

FIGURE 22. The brain uptake index (BUI) or first pass extraction of cholesterol by rat brain after carotid injection of isotope mixed in various serum solutions with or without preincubation. The clearance of cholesterol by brain from incubated serum was not different from the clearance for sucrose, an extracellular space marker. Data from Reference 70.

protein (RBP),[10] and vitamin D derivatives (25-hydroxy cholecalciferol, 25-D; and 1,25-dihydroxy vitamin D, 1,25-D), e.g., vitamin-D-binding protein (DBP).[78] In addition, albumin actively binds vitamins A and D in vitro.[10,79] Therefore, at first glance, the characteristics of vitamin A and D transport in plasma would appear to be quite similar to the steroid and thyroid hormones and, indeed, this generalization is frequently made in the literature. However, several fundamental differences exist between the plasma protein transport of vitamins A and D vs. the steroid or thyroid hormones (see below).

Retinol-binding protein is a 14,000 mol wt protein secreted by the liver and transported in the circulation bound to TBPA.[80] The K_D of TBPA-binding of RBP is about 5 μM,[80] a figure which approximates the normal plasma level of TBPA.[81] The function of TBPA binding of RBP is believed to be the restriction of RBP clearance by glomerular capillaries, which are fenestrated and are permeable to small proteins such as RBP. However, the question then arises as to how RBP dissociates from TBPA to traverse the fenestrated choroidal capillaries of the eye. The choroidal capillaries are permeable to proteins such as myoglobulin (extraction = 8%, mol wt − 18,000) and presumably, RBP, but not to albumin (extraction = 0%, mol wt 68,000) or presumably, TBPA (mol wt 50,000).[82] However, if the K_D in vivo of TBPA binding of RBP is comparable to the in vitro K_D of 5 μM, then given Equation 15 and TBPA = 7 μM, then the percent free RBP = 42%. Therefore, free RBP would normally represent a large part of the total plasma RBP pool and would be cleared in part by choroidal and, presumably, glomerular capillaries.

In addition to the binding of RBP to TBPA, a second major difference between retinol transport and steroid or thyroid hormone transport is that RBP-bound retinol is transported into target organs such as the eye[10] or gut epithelia[83] via a collision mechanism. That is, a RBP receptor on the choroidal aspect of the pigment epithelia of the eye, and on the serosal aspect of gut epithelia, mediates the trans-membrane transport of retinol.

The third important difference between the transport of retinol vs. the steroid or thyroid hormones is the nature of the kinetics of the RBP-retinol-binding reaction. The debinding of retinol from RBP is unusually slow. Consequently the molecule appears to be secreted by liver attached to RBP and to enter cells via the RBP receptor without ever entering the "free" state in vivo. Therefore, albumin, which actively binds retinol in vitro,[10] and which has a binding index for retinol that is equal to or even greater than the binding index of RBP for retinol,[84] is probably never able to "compete" with RBP and thereby bind a fraction of plasma retinol. Indeed, albumin is believed not to transport any of retinol in vivo.[10] Conversely, retinoic acid in vivo is bound entirely by albumin,[85] although RBP has a measurable affinity for the compound.[86] However, given a reasonable rate of debinding of retinoic acid from RBP, the relative binding indexes of albumin vs. RBP will determine which protein is the primary transport protein (see Equations 17 and 18).

Similar to retinol and in contrast to the steroid or thyroid hormones, DBP-bound 25-D is believed to enter target tissues via a collision mechanism.[87] Moreover, recent evidence indicates the DBP enters the cell, which is in contrast to results with RBP. The latter is believed to bind a membrane receptor, transfer retinol to the cell, and then return to the circulation for subsequent degradation. The DBP receptor-mediated mechanism for 25-D clearance is unlikely to be a generalized phenomenon, since many vertebrates lack DBP.[79] For example, albumin is the sole vitamin D transport protein in the Pacific dolphin, the killer whale, the elephant, and the New World monkey.

The fact that albumin actively binds vitamin D derivatives may explain one puzzling aspect in regard to DBP physiology. The concentration of DBP is quite high ($\sim$4 μM); this protein comprises 6% of serum α-globulin and the concentration of DBP is 25 to 50-fold the concentration of 25-D.[88] The function of the large excess of DBP is unknown, but may be to keep the vitamin off of albumin. Since albumin is 550 μM, this protein can compete on an equal basis with DBP for vitamin D derivatives if the affinity of albumin for the ligand is at least 1% of the DBP affinity. The K_D of purified human DBP for 25-D, 1,25-D, and cholecalciferol is 64 nM, 240 nM, and 430 nM, respectively at 4°C.[89] However, these values may represent minimum estimates; the K_D of nonpurified DBP for 25-D in human serum at 0°C is 0.8 nM;[90] given the concentration of DBP = 1800 nM the binding index = 1800/0.8 = 2250. In addition, the affinity of nonpurified DBP in rat serum is high, e.g., K_3 = 3.3 nM at 37°C.[91]

Since 25-D is highly lipid soluble and therefore would be expected to readily distribute to tissues, the debinding of 25-D from DBP must be slow relative to tissue transit times. This is because the plasma $t_{1/2}$ of 25-D is quite long, e.g., $t_{1/2}$ = 21 days.[92] In contrast, 1,25-D or vitamin D (cholecaliferol) are rapidly cleared from plasma in a few hours.[92,93] These results suggest the kinetics of the binding reaction of DBP with 25-D differs substantially from that of 1,25-D or cholecalciferol.

B. Vitamin B_{12}

Transcobalamin II (Tc-II) and R-protein (transcobalamin I) are two plasma proteins which transport vitamin B_{12}.[95] About 85% of B_{12} is transported by R protein (mol wt 60,000) which is a glycoprotein, and about 15% of B_{12} is transported by Tc-II (mol wt 53,000), which is not a glycoprotein.[95] Serum B_{12} bound to R protein has a long halftime, e.g., $t_{1/2} \simeq$ 10 days, and B_{12} bound to Tc-II is rapidly cleared, e.g., $t_{1/2}$ <1 hr. The R-protein is 80 to 100% saturated by serum B_{12} and constitutes the major plasma moiety, whereas Tc-II is largely unsaturated by serum B_{12}. Patients with a congenital deficiency of R protein have decreased plasma B_{12} values, but have normal red cells. Conversely patients with a congenital deficiency of Tc-II have normal plasma B_{12} levels but develop severe megaloblastic anemia.[95] Moreover, it is known that Tc-II-bound B_{12} is transported into red cell precursors or into liver by a cell membrane collision mechanism that is specific for Tc-II and not free B_{12} or B_{12}-bound to R protein.[94,95]

X. TRANSPORT OF ELECTROLYTES

Several divalent cations, e.g., calcium (Ca^{++}), copper (Cu^{++}), zinc (Zn^{++}), and iron (Fe^{++}), are bound by albumin or specific globulins, e.g., ceruloplasmin (Cu) or transferrin (Fe). About 50% of plasma calcium is free (dialyzable) and about 50% is protein-bound. While it is generally regarded that only the free (dialyzable) calcium is free in vivo, this may not be the case. Similar to the nonlinear binding of free fatty acid to albumin, calcium binding to this protein is also nonlinear.[96] Therefore, both the rapidly dissociating albumin fraction and the free (dialyzable) moiety of plasma calcium may comprise the free fraction in vivo. Moreover, the permeability of cell membranes to calcium differs widely. For example, the extraction of calcium by bone is 53%[97] as opposed to that of brain, $\sim$1%.[98] Therefore, in tissues such as bone which have a high membrane permeability to calcium, the apparent free calcium in vivo is probably much greater than the free fraction in vitro.

Copper is bound both by albumin and by ceruloplasmin.[99] The kinetics of copper binding to albumin are of interest; the $K_D = 10^{-16}M$ and the $K_{off} = 0.1\ sec^{-1}$,[99] which indicates the $K_{on} = 10^{15}\ M^{-1}\ sec^{-1}$, a value that is 10^6 to 10^8-fold faster than the usual rate of ligand protein association. Given the $t_{1/2} \simeq 7\ sec$ (ln 2/0.1 sec) of copper debinding from albumin, albumin-bound copper would be expected to readily enter a tissue such as liver with a capillary transit time of $\sim$5 sec. In fact, the estimated extraction by liver of albumin-bound copper is 23%,[99] although the free (dialyzable) fraction is $\ll 1\%$.

Globulin-bound cations, e.g., ceruloplasmin-bound copper or transferrin-bound iron, probably enter tissues via a collision mechanism. In fact, evidence has been reported that transferrin-bound iron is transferred to intracellular ferritin stores via a collision mechanism at the cell membrane.[100] Moreover, it is believed transferrin enters the cell, releases the iron, and then returns to the plasma via efflux across the cell membrane.[101]

XI. TRANSPORT OF BILIRUBIN

Unconjugated bilirubin is a highly lipid-soluble compound[102] that is not only neurotoxic in high doses,[103] but can, under pathologic conditions, achieve high levels in plasma. Therefore, a functional plasma protein transport system for bilirubin must prevent bilirubin entry into brain, but allow for transport of the compound into liver for conjugation. The available evidence indicates the tissue transport of albumin-bound unconjugated bilirubin is analogous to that of CBG-corticosteroid (Figure 19) or SHBG-bound estradiol (Figure 20). Albumin binds bilirubin with a $K_D = 10^{-9}\ M$[104] and a $K_{off} = 0.10\ sec^{-1}$[99] or $t_{1/2} = 7$ sec. Therefore, the debinding of bilirubin from albumin is slow relative to the brain transit time ($\sim$1 sec), but approximates the hepatic capillary transit time ($\sim$5 sec). Moreover, bilirubin is known to rapidly enter liver cells via a nonsaturable mechanism, e.g., lipid mediation or free diffusion.[102]

It is apparent that in order for albumin-bound bilirubin to selectively debind within the liver transit time, but not within the brain transit time, the margin of safety is not particularly wide. Therefore, a drop in albumin affinity due to an increased K_{off} will result in bilirubin debinding within the brain transit time and result in transport of bilirubin through the BBB. Competing anions, e.g., free fatty acids or salicylate, or acidosis[105] enhance brain uptake of bilirubin in the newborn brain. Since the BBB is highly developed at birth,[106] the susceptibility of the newborn to the neurotoxic effect of hyperbilirubinemia, e.g., kernicterus, cannot be ascribed to an immaturity of the BBB. The brain blood flow is reduced,[34] i.e., the transit time is increased in the newborn, and this factor, as well as changes in the K_{off} of albumin-bound bilirubin, appear to account for the development of bilirubin encephalopathy in the newborn.

BRAIN TRANSPORT AND METABOLISM:
TWO-COMPARTMENT MODEL

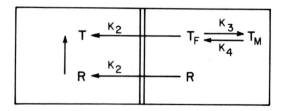

$$\frac{dT_F}{dt} = -(K_2 + K_3)T_F + K_4 T_M \qquad \frac{dR}{dt} = -K_2 R \qquad \frac{dT_M}{dt} = K_3 T_F - K_4 T_M$$

$$\frac{T}{R} = (0.5 + D)e^{(S_1 + K_2)t} + (0.5 - D)e^{(S_2 + K_2)t}$$

FIGURE 23.   A two-compartment model of brain transport (efflux) and sequestration (binding or metabolism) of radiolabeled test (T) and reference (R) compounds during a brief period (up to 4 min) after carotid injection. Since $T = (T_F + T_M)$, where T_F is free test compound and T_M is sequestered test compound, then T/R may be obtained by integrating the three rate equations for dT_F/dt, dT_M/dt, and dR/dt. The T/R ratio is the BUI (Equation 1), which normalizes the brain T/R ratio for differences in amount of radiolabeled T and R injected. See Reference 109 for definitions of the parameters, D, S_1, and S_2, which comprise the constants, k_2, k_3, and k_4.

XII. TISSUE-BINDING PROTEINS

The widely held view that the distribution of a hormone, substrate, or drug into tissues may be predicted on the basis of the free (dialyzable) ligand level in vitro is erroneous for two reasons. The first reason, which has been discussed extensively in previous sections of this review, is that the apparent binding power of plasma protein may decrease exponentially from what occurs in vitro, depending on the relative relationships of debinding rates, membrane permeabilities, and capillary transit times. The second reason that the free (dialyzable) ligand level is not necessarily predictive of ligand distribution relates to the presence of tissue-binding proteins. The net distribution of the ligand is a function of the tissue-binding index divided by the in vivo apparent binding index of the plasma protein, where binding index = the concentration of binding sites ÷ the apparent K_D of either the plasma or tissue-binding protein. Many lipid-soluble compounds are actively bound by cytoplasmic proteins. Ligandin is a 46,000 mol wt protein which exists in liver in 100 μM concentrations.[107] Ligandin binds glutathione, free fatty acids, bile salts, estradiol, testosterone, bilirubin, T_3, and T_4.[107] Protein A (aminoazodye-binding protein) which is also called Z-protein or fatty acid-binding protein is a 14,000 mol wt protein in liver which binds many of the same ligands as does ligandin.[107] The function of ligandin or Z-protein binding of lipid-soluble compounds is to "solubilize" these substances in aqueous cytoplasm, and thereby inhibit the sequestration of the compound within the membrane lipid. As pointed out by Ketterer and associates,[107] without cytoplasmic binding proteins, the aqueous cytoplasm acts effectively as a diffusional block to the compounds reaching cytoplasmic enzymes or receptors. There are both organ and developmental differences to the distribution of the cytoplasmic binding proteins. For example, the Z-protein is high in liver, intermediate in kidney or bowel, and low in testis or ovary.[108] Moreover, the level of Z-protein in liver of the newborn is only 1% of that of adult liver.[108]

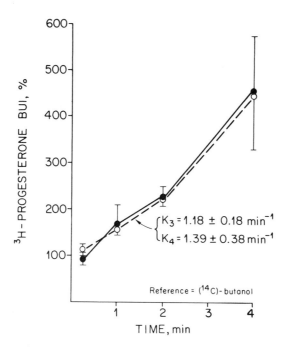

FIGURE 24. The brain uptake index (BUI) (mean ± SD, n = 3 to 4 rats per point) for ³H-progesterone, relative to ¹⁴C-butanol, is plotted vs. circulation time after bolus carotid injection (solid line). The k_3 and k_4 estimates (mean ± SD) are the rate constants of progesterone sequestration by brain, and are computed by fitting the experimental data to the equation for T/R (Figure 23), given $k_2 = 0.67$ min⁻¹ (Reference 109); the predicted curve, obtained by fitting the observed data to the model, is shown by the dashed line. Data from Reference 109.

Recently, the Oldendorf technique has been adapted to study the kinetics of steroid hormone binding to proteins in brain cells in vivo.[109] Based on a two-compartment model (Figure 23) the kinetics of tissue binding of ligands may be studied in vivo. The results for progesterone sequestration by brain are shown in Figure 24 and the data for a number of steroids are shown in Table 10. The nature of the brain steroid hormone binding protein is not known, but it is of interest that neither hepatic Z-protein[110] nor the brain steroid hormone binding protein (Table 10) binds corticosteroids. Moreover, both the hepatic Z-protein and the brain steroid hormone-binding proteins are absent in the newborn period.[108,109]

The debinding of steroids from the brain steroid binding protein is slow, $t_{1/2} \simeq 0.5$ min (Table 10), relative to the rate of steroid debinding from plasma protein (Table 5). Moreover, the rate of estradiol debinding from the brain protein, $t_{1/2} = 0.4$ min, approximates the rate of estradiol debinding from the uterine 4S cytoplasmic estradiol receptor, e.g., $t_{1/2} = 2.3$ min at 35°C in vitro.[111] These debinding rates are fast relative to the debinding of steroids from the 5S nuclear receptor, e.g., $t_{1/2} = 23$ min, for estradiol debinding at 35°C in uterine tissue.[111] Therefore, a spectrum exists for steroid debinding rates from various binding proteins: albumin > PBG > SHBG > cytoplasmic-binding proteins > nuclear-binding proteins. Therefore, the rate of ligand debinding from plasma transport proteins and tissue sequestration proteins is fast and slow, respectively.[19]

Table 10
RATE CONSTANTS OF STEROID ASSOCIATION
(K_3) AND DISSOCIATION (K_4) WITH THE
GONADAL STEROID BINDING PROTEIN OF
RAT BRAIN[a]

Steroid	K_3 (min⁻¹)	K_4 (min⁻¹)	$\frac{K_3}{K_4}$
Dihydrotestosterone	1.23 ± 0.09	1.28 ± 0.17	0.96
Progesterone	1.18 ± 0.18	1.39 ± 0.38	0.85
Testosterone	1.17 ± 0.26	1.57 ± 0.61	0.75
17-β-Estradiol	1.15 ± 0.31	1.58 ± 0.77	0.73
17-α-Estradiol	1.04 ± 0.35	1.95 ± 1.22	0.53
17-Hydroxyprogesterone	0.59 ± 0.02	1.79 ± 0.16	0.33
Corticosterone	<0.05	—	—

[a] From Reference 109. Details of calculations in Figures 23 and 24. Data are mean ± SD.

XIII. CONCLUSIONS

1. This review has presented the view that it is illusory to equate the fraction of ligand that is free (dialyzable) in vitro with the fraction of ligand that is free in vivo. The basis of the illusion is apparent on inspection of Equations 9 and 14. If membrane permeability is such that the rate of ligand diffusion through the membrane (k_3 in Equation 9 and k_s in Equation 14) is slow relative to the capillary transit time (t), then the apparent free fraction in vivo is equal to the free fraction in vitro (given by Equation 15). Conversely, if the rate of ligand flux through the membrane is fast relative to the transit time, then part or all of the protein-bound ligand is available for transport.

2. Even though the exchange of protein-bound substances across capillary walls is characterized by a dynamic, nonequilibrium state, the quantitative analysis of transport data may still assume the steady-state condition. As discussed in Equations 4 through 6, d (AL)/dt may be >0, but since $k_3 \ll k_2 A_T$, the magnitude of d(AL)/dt is small compared to $k_2 A_T L_F$. Consequently, the fact that the concentration of the protein ligand complex falls during the capillary transit does not, in most circumstances, restrict the use of a steady-state analysis. It is an unfortunate but widespread misconception in the transport literature that the steady-state condition necessitates d(AL)/dt be exactly equal to zero.

3. Although the free (dialyzable) hormone level is trivial compared to the amount of protein-bound hormone transported into liver or brain, there are many circumstances under which the in vitro free hormone level is still predictive of tissue transport in vivo. Since both the albumin-bound fraction and the free (dialyzable) fraction are inversely related to the existing level of binding globulin, e.g., TBG, CBG, or SHBG, the free (dialyzable) hormone level will accurately predict the free fraction in vivo if only albumin-bound hormone is transported. For example, only albumin-bound thyroid or steroid hormone is available for transport into brain and only albumin-bound T_4 or testosterone is free in liver capillaries. However, if globulin-bound hormone is transported into the tissue, then the free (dialyzable) hormone level will not reliably predict the free fraction in vivo. For example, TBG-bound T_3, SHBG-bound estradiol and CBG-bound corticosteroid are all transported into liver.

4. The function of the hormone-binding globulins appears to be the selective trans-

port of hormone to tissues. Since globulin-bound T_3, estradiol, or corticosteroid is transported into liver, but not peripheral tissues such as brain, the globulin acts as a hormone amplifier for liver. That is, liver cells are exposed to nearly the total plasma estradiol, corticosteroid, or T_3 level, as opposed to peripheral tissues such as brain, in which the free hormone level is restricted to the albumin-bound moiety. The binding of hormones to rapidly dissociating sites (e.g., albumin) and to slowly dissociating sites (e.g., globulins) is analogous to the nonlinear binding of free fatty acids to multiple albumin binding sites of varying debinding rates. The design principle of either system is the selective transport of protein-bound ligands to different tissues.

5. The net distribution of a protein-bound ligand to tissues is a function of the ratio of the binding index of tissue-binding proteins relative to the in vivo apparent binding index of plasma proteins. Therefore, in vivo measurements of free ligand, while superior to in vitro measurements, are predictive of ligand distribution in vivo only if the activity of tissue-binding proteins remains relatively constant.

ACKNOWLEDGMENTS

The author is indebted to Lawrence J. Mietus for his superior technical assistance and to Charlotte Limberg for preparing the manuscript.

REFERENCES

1. **Oldendorf, W. H.**, Measurement of brain uptake of radiolabeled substances using a tritiated water internal standard, *Brain Res.*, 24, 372, 1970.
2. **Chinard, F. P., Vosburgh, G. J., and Enns, T.**, Transcapillary exchange of water and of other substances in certain organs of the dog, *Am. J. Physiol.*, 178, 221, 1955.
3. **Pardridge, W. M. and Oldendorf, W. J.**, Transport of metabolic substrates through the blood-brain barrier, *J. Neurochem.*, 28, 5, 1977.
4. **Oldendorf, W. H. and Szabo, J.**, Amino acid assignment to one of three blood-brain barrier amino acid carriers, *Am. J. Physiol.*, 230, 94, 1976.
5. **Oldendorf, W. H. and Braun, L. D.**, (^{3}H) Tryptamine and ^{3}H-water as diffusible internal standards for measuring brain extraction of radio-labeled substances following carotid injection, *Brain Res.*, 113, 219, 1976.
6. **Pardridge, W. M. and Oldendorf, W. H.**, Kinetics of blood-brain barrier transport of hexoses, *Biochim. Biophys. Acta*, 382, 377, 1975.
7. **Crone, C.**, The permeability of capillaries in various organs as determined by use of the 'indicator diffusion' method, *Acta Physiol. Scand.*, 58, 292, 1963.
8. **Pardridge, W. M. and Jefferson, L. S.**, Liver uptake of amino acids and carbohydrates during a single circulatory passage, *Am. J. Physiol.*, 228, 1155, 1975.
9. **Pardridge, W. M.**, Unidirectional influx of glutamine and other neutral amino acids into liver of fed and fasted rat in vivo, *Am. J. Physiol.*, 232, E492, 1977.
10. **Futterman, S. and Heller, J.**, The enhancement of fluorescence and the decreased susceptibility to enzymatic oxidation of retinol complexed with bovine serum albumin, β-Lactoglobulin, and the retinol-binding protein of human plasma, *J. Biol. Chem.*, 247, 5168, 1972.
11. **Brown, M. S. and Goldstein, J. L.**, Familial hypercholesterolemia: a genetic defect in the low-density lipoprotein receptor, *N. Engl. J. Med.*, 294, 1386, 1976.
12. **Furlow, T. W. and Bass, N. H.**, Cerebral hemodynamics in the rat assessed by a non-diffusible indicator-dilution technique, *Brain Res.*, 110, 366, 1976.
13. **Honig, C. R., Odoroff, C. L., and Frierson, J. L.**, Capillary recruitment in exercise: rate, extent, uniformity, and relation to blood flow, *Am. J. Physiol.*, 238, H31, 1980.
14. **Hill, E. P. and Longo, L. D.**, Dynamics of maternal-fetal nutrient transfer, *Fed. Proc., Fed. Am. Soc. Exp. Biol.*, 39, 239, 1980.

15. Goresky, C. A. and Rose, C. P., Blood-tissue exchange in liver and heart: the influence of heterogeneity of capillary transit times, *Fed. Proc., Fed. Am. Soc. Exp. Biol.,* 36, 2629, 1977.
16. Pardridge, W. M. and Mietus, L. J., Transport of steroid hormones through the rat blood-brain barrier, primary role of albumin-bound hormone, *J. Clin. Invest.,* 64, 145, 1979.
17. Pardridge, W. M. and Mietus, L. J., Transport of protein-bound steroid hormones into liver in vivo, *Am. J. Physiol.,* 237, E367, 1979.
18. Wong, J. T., *Kinetics of Enzyme Mechanisms,* Academic Press, New York, 1975, 10.
19. Westphal, U., Steroid-binding serum globulins; recent results, in *Receptor and Hormone Action,* Vol. 2, O'Malley, B. W. and Birnbaum, L., Eds., Academic Press, New York, 1978.
20. Pardridge, W. M., Tryptophan transport through the blood-brain barrier: in vivo measurement of free and albumin-bound amino acid, *Life Sci.,* 25, 1519, 1979.
21. Pardridge, W. M., Carrier-mediated transport of thyroid hormones through the rat blood-brain barrier: primary role of albumin-bound hormone, *Endocrinology,* 105, 605, 1979.
22. Hillier, A. P., The rate of triiodothyronine dissociation from binding sites in human plasma, *Acta Endocrinol.,* 80, 49, 1975.
23. Robbins, J., Rall, J. E., and Gorden, P., *Duncan's Disease of Metabolism,* Bondy, P. K. and Rosenberg, L. E., Eds., W. B. Saunders, Philadelphia, 1974, 1023.
24. Pardridge, W. M., Kinetics of competitive inhibition of neutral amino acid transport across the blood-brain barrier, *J. Neurochem.,* 28, 103, 1977.
25. Pardridge, W. M. and Oldendorf, W. H., Kinetic analysis of blood-brain barrier transport of amino acids, *Biochim. Biophys. Acta,* 401, 128, 1975.
26. McMenamy, R. H., Lund, C. C., Van Marcke, J., and Oncley, J. L., The binding of L-tryptophan in human plasma at 37°C, *Arch. Biochem. Biophys.,* 93, 135, 1961.
27. Madras, B. K., Cohen, E. L., Messing, R., Munro, H. N., and Wurtman, R. J., Relevance of free tryptophan in serum to tissue tryptophan concentrations, *Metabolism,* 23, 1107, 1974.
28. Fernando, J. C. R., Knott, P. J., and Curzon, G., The relevance of both plasma free tryptophan and insulin to rat brain tryptophan concentration, *J. Neurochem.,* 27, 343, 1976.
29. Biggio, G., Fadda, F., Fanni, P., Tagliamonte, A., and Gessa, G. L., Rapid depletion of serum tryptophan, brain tryptophan, serotonin and 5-hydroxyindoleacetic acid by a tryptophan-free diet, *Life Sci.,* 14, 1321, 1974.
30. Fernstrom, J. D., Hirsch, M. J., and Faller, D. V., Tryptophan concentrations in rat brain: failure to correlate with free serum tryptophan or its ratio to the sum of other serum neutral amino acids, *Biochem. J.,* 160, 589, 1976.
31. Yuwiler, A., Oldendorf, W. H., Geller, E., and Braun, L., Effect of albumin binding and amino acid competition on tryptophan uptake into brain, *J. Neurochem.,* 28, 1015, 1977.
32. Pardridge, W. M., The role of blood-brain barrier transport of tryptophan and other neutral amino acids in the regulation of substrate-limited pathways of brain amino acid metabolism, *J. Neur. Trans. Suppl.,* 15, 42, 1979.
33. Hamon, M. and Bourgoin, S., Ontogenesis of tryptophan transport in the rat brain, *J. Neur. Trans. Suppl.,* 15, 93, 1979.
34. Hernandez, M. J., Brennan, R. W., Vannucci, R. C., and Bowman, G. S., Cerebral blood flow and oxygen consumption in the newborn dog, *Am. J. Physiol.,* 234, R209, 1978.
35. James, J. H., Ziparo, V., Jeppsson, B., and Fischer, J. E., Hyperammonaemia plasma aminoacid inbalance, and blood-brain amino acid transport: a unified theory of portal-systemic encephalopathy, *Lancet,* II, 772, 1979.
36. Pardridge, W. M. and Mietus, L. J., Transport of albumin-bound melatonin through the blood-brain barrier, *J. Neurochem.,* 34, in press, 1980.
37. Cornford, E. M., Bocash, W. D., Braun, L. D., Crane, P. D., and Oldendorf, W. H., Rapid distribution of tryptophol (3-Indole Ethanol) to the brain and other tissues, *J. Clin. Invest.,* 63, 1242, 1979.
38. Pardridge, W. M. and Mietus, L. J., Influx of thryoid hormones into rat liver in vivo: differential availability of T_4 and T_3 bound by plasma proteins, *J. Clin. Invest.,* 66, in press, 1980.
39. Rapoport, S. I., Blood-brain barrier, in *Physiology and Medicine,* Raven Press, New York, 1976, 166.
40. Fisher, D. A., Thyroid function in the fetus, in *Perinatal Thyroid Physiology and Disease,* Fisher, D. A. and Burrow, G. N., Eds., Raven Press, New York, 1975.
41. Hasen, G., Bernstein, G., Volpert, E., and Oppenheimer, J. H., Analysis of the rapid interchange of thyroxine between plasma and liver and plasma and kidney in the intact rat, *Endocrinology,* 82, 37, 1968.
42. Hillier, A. P., Human thyroxine-binding globulin and thyroxine-binding pre-albumin: dissociation rates, *J. Physiol. (London),* 217, 625, 1971.
43. Pardridge, W. M. and Mietus, L. J., Transport of thyroid and steroid hormones through the blood-brain barrier of the newborn rabbit; primary role of protein-bound hormone, *Endocrinology,* 108, in press, 1981.

44. Sutherland, R. L. and Brandon, M. R., The thyroxine-binding properties of rat and rabbit serum proteins, *Endocrinology*, 98, 91, 1976.

45. Hagen, G. A. and Elliott, W. J., Transport of thyroid hormones in serum and cerebrospinal fluid, *J. Clin. Endocrinol. Metab.*, 37, 415, 1973.

46. Premachandra, B. N. and Ibrahim, I. I., Thyroxine antibody vs. serum protein binding of T_4 in the cold; differential charcoal adsorption of T_4 from immuno and conventional T_4 binding sites, in *Thyroid Hormone Metabolism*, Harland, W. A. and Orr, J. S., Eds., Academic Press, New York, 1975, 281.

47. Vermeulen, A., Transport and distribution of androgens at different ages, in *Androgens and Antiandrogens*, Martini, L. and Motta, M., Eds., Raven Press, New York, 1977.

48. Rosenthal, H. E., Slaunwhite, W. R., Jr., and Sandberg, A. A., Transcortin: a corticosteroid-binding protein of plasma. X. Cortisol and progesterone interplay and unbound levels of these steroids in pregnancy, *J. Clin. Endocrinol.*, 29, 352, 1969.

49. Corvol, P. and Bardin, C. W., Species distribution of testosterone-binding globulin, *Biol. Reprod.*, 8, 277, 1973.

50. Payne, D. W. and Katzenellenbogen, J. A., Binding specificity of rat α-fetoprotein for a series of estrogen derivatives: studies using equilibrium and nonequilibrium binding techniques, *Endocrinology*, 105, 743, 1979.

51. Westphal, U., *Steroid-Protein Interactions*, Springer-Verlag, New York, 1971.

52. Zipser, R. D., Speckart, P. F., Zia, P. K., Edmiston, W. A., Lau, F. Y. K., and Horton, R., The effect of ACTH and cortisol on aldosterone and cortisol clearance and distribution in plasma and whole blood, *J. Clin. Endocrinol. Metab.*, 43, 1101, 1976.

53. Baird, D. T., Horton, R., Longcope, C., and Tait, J. F., Steroid dynamics under steady-state conditions, *Recent Prog. Horm. Res.*, 25, 611, 1969.

54. Dixon, P. F., The kinetics of the exchange between transcortin-bound and unbound cortisol in plasma, *J. Endocrinol.*, 40, 457, 1967.

55. Heyns, W. and De Moor, P., Kinetics of dissociation of 17 β-hydroxysteroids from the steroid binding β-globulin of human plasma, *J. Clin. Endocrinol.*, 32, 147, 1971.

56. Stein, W. D., *The Molecular Basis of Diffusion across Cell Membranes*, Academic Press, New York, 65, 124, 1967.

57. Pardridge, W. M., Mietus, L. J., Frumar, A. M., Davidson, B. J., and Judd, H. L., Effects of human serum on the transport of testosterone and estradiol into rat brain, *Am. J. Physiol.*, 239, in press, 1980.

58. Mickelson, K. E. and Petra, P. H., Purification and characterization of the sex steroid-binding protein of rabbit serum, *J. Biol. Chem.*, 253, 5293, 1978.

59. Pardridge, W. M. and Mietus, L. J., Effects of progesterone-binding globulin versus a progesterone antiserum on steroid hormone transport through the blood-brain barrier, *Endocrinology*, 106, 1137, 1980.

60. Jobin, M. and Perrin, F., Evaluation of three constants involved in the binding of corticosterone to plasma proteins in the rat, *Can. J. Biochem.*, 52, 101, 1973.

61. Keller, N., Richardson, U. I., and Yates, F. E., Protein binding and the biological activity of corticosteroids: in vivo induction of hepatic and pancreatic alanine aminotransferases by corticosteroids in normal and estrogen-treated rats, *Endocrinology*, 84, 49, 1969.

62. Rosner, W. and Hochberg, R., Corticosteroid-binding globulin in the rat: isolation and studies of its influence on cortisol action in vivo, *Endocrinology*, 91, 626, 1972.

63. Anderson, D. C., Sex-hormone-binding globulin, *Clin. Endocrinol.*, 3, 69, 1974.

64. Shand, D. G., Cotham, R. H., and Wilkinson, G. R., Perfusion-limited effects of plasma drug binding on hepatic drug extraction, *Life Sci.*, 19, 125, 1976.

65. Wood, A. J. J., Kornhauser, D. M., Wilkinson, G. R., Shand, D. G., and Branch, R. A., The influence of cirrhosis on steady-state blood concentrations of unbound propranolol after oral administration, *Clin. Pharmacol.*, 3, 478, 1978.

66. Piafsky, K. M., Borga, O., Odar-Cederlof, I., Johansson, C., and Sjoqvist, F., Increased plasma protein binding of propranolol and chlorpromazine mediated by disease-induced elevations of plasma α_1 acid glycoprotein, *N. Engl. J. Med.*, 299, 1435, 1978.

67. Cooper, E. H. and Stone, J., Acute phase reactant proteins in cancer, *Adv. Cancer Res.*, 30, 1, 1979.

68. Evans, G. H., Nies, A. S., and Shand, D. G., The disposition of propranolol. III. Decreased half-life and volume of distribution as a result of plasma binding in man, monkey, dog and rat, *J. Pharmacol. Exp. Ther.*, 186, 114, 1973.

69. Spector, A. A. and Fletcher, J. E., Transport of fatty acid in the circulation, *in Disturbances in Lipid and Lipoprotein Metabolism*, Dietschy, J. M., Gotto, A. M., Jr., and Ontko, J. A., Eds., American Physiological Society, Bethesda, 1978.

70. Pardridge, W. M. and Mietus, L. J., Palmitate and cholesterol transport through the blood-brain barrier, *J. Neurochem.*, 34, 463, 1980.

71. Goresky, C. A., Daly, D. S., Mishkin, S., and Arias, I. M., Uptake of labeled palmitate by the intact liver: role of intracellular binding sites, *Am. J. Physiol.*, 234, E542, 1978.

72. Rose, C. P. and Goresky, C. A., Constraints on the uptake of labeled palmitate by the heart: the barriers at the capillary and sarcolemmal surfaces and the control of intracellular sequestration, *Circ. Res.*, 41, 534, 1977.

73. Brunzell, J. D., Chait, A., and Bierman, E. L., Pathophysiology of lipoprotein transport, *Metabolism*, 27, 1109, 1978.

74. Sodhi, H. S. and Kudchodkar, B. J., A physiological method for labelling plasma lipoproteins with radioactive cholesterol, *Clin. Chim. Acta*, 51, 291, 1974.

75. Kovanen, P. T., Basu, S. K., Goldstein, J. L., and Brown, M. S., Low density lipoprotein receptors in bovine adrenal cortex. II. Low density lipoprotein binding to membranes prepared from fresh tissue, *Endocrinology*, 104, 610, 1979.

76. Setchel, B. P. and Waites, G. M. H., The blood-testis barrier, in *Handbook of Physiology — Endocrinology V*, Greep, R. O. and Astwood, E. B., Eds., American Physiological Society, Washington, D.C., 1975.

77. Serougne, C., Lefevre, C., and Chevallier, F., Cholesterol transfer between brain and plasma in the rat: a model for the turnover of cerebral cholesterol, *Exp. Neurol.*, 51, 229, 1976.

78. Haddad, J. G. and Chyu, K. J., 25-Hydroxycholecalciferol-binding globulin in human plasma, *Biochim. Biophys. Acta*, 248, 471, 1971.

79. Hay, A. W. M. and Watson, G., The plasma transport proteins of 25-hydroxydholecalciferol in mammals, *Comp. Biochem. Physiol.*, 53B, 163, 1976.

80. Raz, A., Shiratori, T., and Goodman, D. S., Studies on the protein-protein and protein-ligand interactions involved in retinol transport in plasma, *J. Biol. Chem.*, 245, 1903, 1970.

81. Navab, M., Smith, J. E., and Goodman, D. S., Rat plasma prealbumin-metaboli studies on effects of Vitamin A status and on tissue distribution, *J. Biol. Chem.*, 252, 5107, 1977.

82. Tornquist, P., Capillary permeability in cat choroid, studied with the single injection technique (II), *Acta Physiol. Scand.*, 106, 425, 1979.

83. Rask, L. and Peterson, P. A., In vitro uptake of Vitamin A from the retinol-binding plasma protein to mucosal epithelial cells from the monkey's small intestine, *J. Biol. Chem.*, 251, 6360, 1976.

84. Sreekrishna, K., Bhat, M. K., Podder, S. K., and Cama, H. R., Vitamin A transporting system in plasma, *World Rev. Nutr. Diet*, 31, 52, 1978.

85. Smith, J. E., Milch, P. O., Muto, Y., and Goodman, D. S., The plasma transport and metabolism of retinoic acid in the rat, *Biochem. J.*, 132, 821, 1973.

86. Chen, C. C. and Hellen, J., Transport and utilization of retinoic acid by the retina: intravascular injection of retinoic acid as a complex with retinol binding protein, *Exp. Eye Res.*, 26, 561, 1978.

87. Cooke, N. E., Walgate, J., and Haddad, J. G., Jr., Human serum binding protein for Vitamin D and its metabolites. I. Physicochemical and immunological identification in human tissues, *J. Biol. Chem.*, 254, 5958, 1979.

88. Haddad, J. G., Jr. and Walgate, J., Radioimmunoassay of the binding protein for Vitamin D and its metabolites in human serum — Concentrations in normal subjects and patients with disorders of mineral homeostasis, *J. Clin. Invest.*, 58, 1217, 1976.

89. Haddad, J. G., Jr. and Walgate, J., 25-Hydroxyvitamin D transport in human plasma — Isolation and partial characterization of calcifidiol-binding protein, *J. Biol. Chem.*, 251, 4803, 1976.

90. Haddad, J. G., Hillman, L., and Rohanasathit, S., Human serum binding capacity and affinity for 25-hydroxyergocalciferol and 25-hydroxycholecalciferol, *J. Clin. Endocrinol. Metab.*, 43, 86, 1976.

91. Rohanasathit, S. and Haddad, J. G., Ontogeny and effect of Vitamin D deprivation on rat serum 25-hydroxyvitamin D binding protein, *Endocrinology*, 100, 642, 1977.

92. Smith, J. E. and Goodman, D. S., The turnover and transport of Vitamin D and of a polar metabolite with the properties of 25-hydroxycholecalciferol in human plasma, *J. Clin. Invest.*, 50, 2159, 1971.

93. Gray, R. W., Wilz, D. R., Caldas, A. E., Lemann, J., Jr., and DeLuca, H. F., Disappearance from plasma of injected ^{3}H-1,25-(OH)$_2$-D$_3$ in healthy humans, in *Vitamin D — Biochemical, Chemical and Clinical Aspects Related to Calcium Metabolism*, Norman, A. W., Schaefer, K., Coburn, J. W., DeLuca, H. F., Fraser, D., Grigoleit, H. G., and Herrath, D. V., Eds., W. de Gruyter, New York, 1977.

94. Rappazzo, M. E. and Hall, C. A., Transport function of transcobalamin II, *J. Clin. Invest.*, 51, 1915, 1972.

95. Allen, R. H., Human vitamin B$_{12}$ transport proteins, *Prog. Hematol.*, 9, 57, 1975.

96. Wortsman, J. and Traycoff, R. B., Biological activity of protein-bound calcium in serum, *Am. J. Physiol*, 238, E104, 1980.

97. Schoutens, A., Bergmann, P., and Verhas, M., Bone blood flow measured by ^{85}Sr microspheres and bone seeker clearances in the rat, *Am. J. Physiol.*, 236, H1, 1979.

98. Katzman, R., Ion movement, in *Handbook of Neurochemistry*, Vol. 4, Lajtha, A., Ed., Plenum Press, New York, 1979, 313.

99. **Peters, T., Jr., and Reed, R. G.**, Serum albumin as a transport protein, in *Transport by Proteins,* Blauer, G. and Sund, H., Eds., W. de Gruyter, New York, 1978.

100. **Batey, R. G., Williams, K., and Milsom, J. P.**, A physiological model for hepatic metabolism of transferrin-bound iron, *Am. J. Physiol.,* 238, G30, 1980.

101. **Neville, D. M., Jr. and Chang, T. M.**, Receptor-mediated protein transport into cells. Entry mechanisms for toxins, hormones, antibodies, viruses, lysosomal hydrolases, asialoglycoproteins, and carrier proteins, *Curr. Top. Membr. Trans.,* 9, 65, 1978.

102. **Iga, T., Eaton, D. L., and Klaassen, C. D.**, Uptake of unconjugated bilirubin by isolated rat hepatocytes, *Am. J. Physiol.,* 236, C9, 1979.

103. **Walters, W. J., Richert, D. A., and Rawson, H. H.**, Bilirubin encephalopathy, *Pediatrics,* 13, 319, 1954.

104. **Odell, G. B.**, Influence of binding on the toxicity of bilirubin, *Ann. N.Y. Acad. Sci.,* 226, 225, 1973.

105. **Diamond, I. and Schmid, R.**, Experimental bilirubin encephalopathy. The mode of entry of bilirubin-^{14}C into the central nervous system, *J. Clin. Invest.,* 45, 678, 1966.

106. **Braun, L. D., Cornford, E. M., and Oldendorf, W. H.**, Newborn rabbit blood-brain barrier is selectively permeable and differs substantially from the adult, *J. Neurochem.,* 34, 147, 1980.

107. **Ketterer, B., Carne, T., and Tipping, E.**, Ligandin and Protein A: intracellular binding proteins, in *Transport by Proteins,* Blauer, G. and Sund, H., Eds., W. de Gruyter, New York, 1978.

108. **Bannikov, G. A., Guelstein, V. I., and Tchipsheva, T. A.**, Distribution of basic azo-dye-binding protein in normal rat tissues and carcinogen-induced liver tumors, *Int. J. Cancer,* 11, 398, 1973.

109. **Pardridge, W. M., Moeller, T. L., Mietus, L. J., and Oldendorf, W. H.**, Blood-brain barrier transport and brain sequestration of the steroid hormones, *Am. J. Physiol.,* 239, in press, 1980.

110. **Ketterer, B., Tipping, E., and Hackney, J. F.**, A low-molecular weight protein from rat liver that resembles ligandin in its binding properties, *Biochem. J.,* 155, 511, 1976.

111. **Weichman, B. M. and Notides, A. C.**, Estrogen receptor activation and the dissociation kinetics of estradiol, estriol, and estrone, *Endocrinology,* 106, 434, 1980.

112. **Mortimore, G. E., Woodside, K., and Henry, J. E.**, Compartmentation of free valine and its relation to protein turnover in perfused rat liver, *J. Biol. Chem.,* 247, 2776, 1972.

113. **McKee, E. E., Cheung, J. Y., Rannels, D. E., and Morgan, H. E.**, Measurement of the rate of protein synthesis and compartmentation of heart phenylalanine, *J. Biol. Chem.,* 253, 1030, 1978.

114. **Lajtha, A. and Dunlop, D.**, Protein metabolism in neuroendocrine tissues, in *Subcellular Mechanisms in Reproductive Neuroendocrinology,* Naftolin, F., Ryan, K. J., and Davies, J., Eds., Elsevier, Amsterdam, 1976, chap. 4.

115. **Oppenheimer, J. H., Dillmann, W. H., Schwartz, H. L., and Towle, H. C.**, Nuclear receptors and thyroid hormone action: a progress report, *Fed. Proc., Fed. Am. Soc. Exp. Biol.,* 38, 2154, 1979.

116. **Vuller, R. E. and O'Malley, B. W.**, The biology and mechanism of steroid hormone receptor interaction with the eukaryotic nucleus, *Biochem. Pharmacol.,* 25, 1, 1976.

117. **Sakiyama, R. and Pardridge, W. M.**, Propranolol transport through the rat blood-brain barrier. Primary role of globulin-bound drug. In preparation, 1981.

Chapter 11

TRANSPORT OF RADIOLABELED ENZYMES

René M. Babin and Paul Blanquet

TABLE OF CONTENTS

I. INTRODUCTION

Radiolabeled enzymes will remain an important topic of future studies in areas such as the following:

1.   The use of scintigraphic agents in vivo
2.   The development of possible therapeutic agents with beta-emitting radiotracers
3.   The development of radioimmunoassays with organic fluids or tissue extracts
4.   Studies of the localization of enzymes in animal tissues in vitro and occasionally in human anatomopathological slides

As Thomas observed in the early 1970s,[1] "descriptions of the preparation of labeled drugs are few and, to some extent, hidden in the recent periodical literature." Unfortunately, the situation for the labeling of enzymes is even worse, primarily because of the difficulties encountered in the labeling of such complex and often poorly characterized molecules. Reports of experiments often are incomplete, a circumstance that makes it difficult to judge whether the work was conceptually weak, erroneously performed, or simply obsolete. Commenting on this matter, Beinert[2] notes that "no single investigator can be expected to have the experience..." to foresee and accommodate all possible developments.

II. THE LABELING OF ENZYMES

Enzymes may be radiolabeled *directly* by introducing a radionuclide into the protein molecule or into its cofactors, coenzyme or metal (when these constituents are present)—or *indirectly*, by coupling the enzyme with already labeled molecules.

A. The Direct Radiolabeling of Enzymes
1. Enzymes That Do Not Require Coenzymes
Many enzymes belonging to this category are purely protein, composed entirely of amino acids; others contain glycosidic or lipid constituents that are important in their biological transport. Most such enzymes can be radiolabeled by techniques similar to those used for other proteins. New enzymes — particularly in the class of bacterial nucleases — are discovered daily and therefore the list remains far from complete; each biological reaction is mediated by its own specific enzyme, which alone is able to transform the appropriate substrate. Of this group, only well-defined examples will be mentioned here.

At one time, the criterion of purity for an enzyme was crystallinity.[3] Nowadays it is recognized that a crystallized enzyme may not be really pure because of the likelihood of coacervation or syncrystallization with other proteins, as in the case of muramidase.[4] Ruyssen and Lauwers[5] have pointed out that the crystalline state is not synonymous with the fully active state. Several investigators have described the problems involved in the purification of enzymes that are to be labeled,[6-9] while Harwig et al.[10] suggested that, because of the problem of denaturation, the "labeling of proteins requires the individual evaluation of each system by analytical methods." In comparing the biological activities of labeled and unlabeled enzymes, the techniques employed must be carefully described in the fullest detail to facilitate proper evaluation of the results obtained from experiments conducted with the enzyme in its two states. The significance of experiments with labeled enzymes strongly depends upon their purity, which is best assured through the use of precise, modern physicochemical procedures such as high-pressure liquid chromatography (HPLC), gas chromatography coupled with mass spectrometry (GC-MS), nuclear magnetic resonance (NMR), and so on.

a. Tritiation of Enzymes

The most convenient procedure for protein/enzyme tritiation is the exchange of a hydrogen-3 ion supplied by tritiated water that is diluted in an organic solvent in the presence of a catalyst. The risk of protein denaturation seems very small. Evans et al.,[11] Wilzbach,[12] Means,[13] and Bailey and Knowles[14] described labeling procedures. Endert[15] suggested the use of HPLC techniques for the separation of radiochemical impurities.

b. Radiolabeling with Carbon-13 and Carbon-14

Shindo et al.[16] labeled muramidase with ^{13}C and studied the product by means of NMR. Jaeck and Benz[17] have synthesized ribonuclease radiolabeled with ^{14}C on methionine-29; Noyer et al.[18] have also labeled ribonuclease with ^{14}C, but only on the "saccharidic structure." Since the entire ribonuclease molecule — of 124 amino acids — has been synthesized, it appears that it will be possible to synthesize other enzymes containing amino acids labeled with ^{14}C.

c. Enzymes Labeled with Sulfur-35 and Selenium-75

According to Thomas,[1] sulfur-35 and tritium are the tracers most easily incorporated in enzymes without impairing their specific activity. Despite the availability of (^{35}S)-L-cysteine, thiol enzymes, such as papain, do not appear to have been labeled with it. (^{75}Se)-L-*selenomethionine* has been used in scintigraphic studies of the pancreas and parathyroid. Since 1978, Tappel[19] has used (^{75}Se)-selenite for the determination of glutathione peroxidases in rat liver and in human erythrocytes in vivo.

d. Iodination of Enzymes with ^{123}I, ^{125}I, and ^{131}I

The binding of iodine depends upon the nature and number of amino acids in the molecule of the enzyme to be labeled. By using the technique of Hunter and Greenwood,[20] Matthews[21] was able to label several plasma proteins, and Cohen et al.[22] labeled hyaluronidase and streptokinase. Meyniel and Veyre[23] have carried out a study upon the choice of labeling agents, and Parsons et al.[24] have labeled proteinases with ^{125}I to demonstrate their binding to plasma proteins. Bolton and Hunter[25] have perfected their iodination process by the addition of acylating agents, Aprotinin (the pancreatic trypsin inhibitor of Kunitz) has been labeled with ^{125}I and ^{99m}Tc by Kutas et al.,[26] and recently Baret et al.[27,28] have labeled cupro-zinc and manganese superoxide dismutase (Mn S.O.D.) from human erythrocytes, human crude extracts, and blood mitochondrial fractions.

e. Labeling of Enzymes with ^{99m}Tc

Proteins are quite commonly labeled with ^{99m}Tc. Because of its short half-life, the use of ^{99m}Tc makes possible scintigraphic studies in living human patients. Heparin, gelatin, fibrinogen, human serum albumin, and immunogammaglobulin, for example, have all been labeled by Benjamin,[29] Wong,[30-33] Dworkin,[34] Jonckheer et al.,[35] and Colombetti et al.[36]

Yet it seems that only a few enzymes have been labeled with ^{99m}Tc. Persson and Kempi[37] used ^{99m}Tc-labeled streptokinase to study the action of the enzyme in venous thromboses; Ramos et al.[38] also labeled streptokinase and urokinase with ^{99m}Tc; and Som and Rhodes[39] compared urokinases labeled with ^{125}I and ^{99m}Tc. Walter and Greengard[40] also utilized the tracer ^{99m}Tc in their work on AMP-dependent protein kinases.

2. Enzymes Dependent Upon a Coenzyme That Can Be Labeled

Some enzymes are separable by ultrafiltration or dialysis into a protein part, the apoenzyme, and an aproteinic part, the coenzyme or prosthetic part. Enzymes that belong to this category may be labeled by introducing a radionuclide in the coenzyme portion, which ordinarily is a small, more easily managed molecule. This subject has been adequately described by McCormick and Wright.[41]

B. The Indirect Radiolabeling of Enzymes

Certain antibiotics (notably sulfanilamide and its derivatives) and alkaloids bind strongly to some enzymes. The resulting complexes can be made radioactive by labeling the binding agent and then used to study the biological transport of the enzymes in vivo. The value of this technique may be illustrated by the following examples. Bleomycin has been labeled with ^{57}Co by Cohen et al.[42] and with ^{99m}Tc by Plagne et al.[43] Müller and Zahn[44] have shown that the enzymatic incorporation of thymine in nucleic acids is inhibited if the enzyme is complexed with a labeled antibiotic. Cohen's results[45] indicate that chloramphenicol inhibits the fixation of mRNA on bacterial ribosomes and blocks the inducing β-galactoside permease. The biological transport of this permease may be studied in vitro by using chloramphenicol labeled with ^{15}N. Benzyl penicillin labeled with ^{14}C can be used to label mucopeptidases involved in the synthesis of bacterial cell walls.

Among the alkaloids used are tritiated vinca derivatives, which exert a carcinostatic action because they block nucleases involved in the replication of nucleic acids in cancerous cells.

Tritiated digoxin, a cardiac glycoside, is useful because of its ability to bind to plasma proteins.

III. RESULTS OF ENZYME RADIOLABELING

The radiolabeling of enzymes is subject to several influences, both favorable and unfavorable. Among the advantages are, of course, those inherent in radiotracer properties; among the disadvantages are the instability of these compounds and their potential for inflicting radiation damage. Other unfavorable aspects are treated in the following sections.

A. The Lack of Specificity in Radiolabeling Enzymes

There is no general method for directing a radionuclide to a selected point of covalent attachment in a molecule having as many similar target sites as a protein. In the present state of the art of studying biological transport of enzymes, this kind of nonspecificity is not a drawback: what is essential is that the radionuclide be firmly bound to one or another of the susceptible amino acid residues in such a way as not to alter the biological properties of the enzyme (in particular, those associated with substrate binding and catalytic action). A labeled enzyme can be subjected to several steps of purification to ensure that it is homogeneous and that the radionuclide is covalently bound; since a single atom of the radionuclide is sufficient to label the whole protein molecule, a highly purified, singly labeled enzyme can usually be considered to have the same biological specificity as the unlabeled substance. It must be remembered that the substitution of one metal for another, such as copper for cobalt, may lead to an inactive enzyme.

B. Perturbations Resulting From β or γ Emissions

Around 1950, Lefort[46] published his results concerning the effects of radiation on aqueous solutions. Babin[47] found that 10^{-7} M hydrogen peroxide was produced by exposure to highly active sources (18 mCi of $^{60}CoCl_2$ and 2 mCi of $^{203}HgCl_2$). In 1962, Augenstine[48] investigated the effects of radiation from intense sources upon amylase, trypsin, hyaluronidase, invertase, myosin, papain, catalase, urease, ribonuclease, and xanthine oxidase. Wacker[49] and Weiss[50] explained the mechanism by which ionizing radiation affects nucleic acids. Kanazir's work[51] also dealt with radiation-induced alterations of DNA. In all these studies, little has been said about the possible inactivation of the enzyme bound to the radionuclide. Rosselin[52] found that 10^{-12} M protein is affected by labeling. To determine whether labeling perturbs the active site of the enzyme, a biochemical assay must be performed in vitro before and immediately after labeling.

C. The Risk of Loss of Enzymatic Activity Upon Labeling

Tritiated enzymes — It has been said that tritiation is the least hazardous technique for labeling enzyme proteins, because the risk of denaturation is slight and stereochemical integrity is maintained.

Iodinated enzymes — The oxidative properties of iodine and of agents, such as chloramine-T, iodine chloride, or lactoperoxidase, used in iodinating enzymes must be kept in mind. The number of atoms of iodine introduced must be kept as low as possible to prevent loss of activity. Oxidoreductases, thiol enzymes, catalases, etc., are the enzymes most susceptible to oxidative altteration. In general, enzymes labeled with ^{125}I or ^{131}I are useful for only 10 to 15 days; the more sensitive types mentioned have even briefer useful lifetimes.

Technetated enzymes — The reduced species obtained from ^{99m}Tc-pertechnetate by the action of Sn^{2+}, $Na_2S_2O_3$, ascorbic acid, or electrolysis have been widely described, but the effect of these reducing systems on the physiological properties of enzymes in vivo is unknown. Molybdenum-containing enzymes are very important in life processes, but the role of the electron-carrier system $Mo^{VII} \rightleftharpoons Mo^{V}$ is not yet fully understood. It should also be noted that ^{99}Mo is a precursor of ^{99m}Tc, which may be freed from its label.

IV. THE TRANSPORT OF RADIOLABELED ENZYMES

A. General Physicochemical Influences

The transport of a radiolabeled enzyme, or of any other compound used for studies in vivo, is dependent upon certain general conditions, which vary widely according to the nature of the enzyme and the medium in which it is present. To illustrate the role of the physiological and pathological conditions that are involved in the transport of radiolabeled enzymes and that have a bearing on the stability of the radiolabeled molecules, the following sections deal with some of the principal factors of this kind, in the contexts of studies in vitro as well as in vivo.

1. The Role of pH

Hydrogen ion activity is one of the dominant influences on the biological transport of radiolabeled enzymes absorbed from the intestine or administered intravenously. Babin et al.[53] have published measurements of blood pH in neonatal humans and animals. In healthy humans, the pH is normally stable at 7.37 at 37° C; in the newborn and in numerous pathological conditions, however, the pH may fall below 7.0, increasing the possibility of liberating metallic radionuclides in ionic forms. One should also consider that in the digestive tract of humans, the pH varies from 6 to 7 in saliva, from 1 to 2 in gastric juice, and from 5 to 8 in different regions of the intestine. The pH also depends strongly on dietary habits and the actions of normal bacterial flora. Within the range of acidity or basicity encountered in most tissues, acidification generally raises the proportion of uncomplexed metal ions. Liberation of the radionuclide caused by variations in acidity constitutes a risk that must be minimized by carefully controlling the pH. (In blood serum, the pH_i of an enzyme, radiolabeled or not, generally differs from the normal total pH_i.)

2. Redox Potentials

The optimum redox potentials of enzymes are seldom know accurately because these potentials are measured, ordinarily, in experimental mediums formulated for observation of the activity of an enzyme toward a specific substrate or for use of the enzyme as a pharmaceutical (e.g., as a reagent for reducing sugars). Peroxidase, flavine enzymes, cytochrome oxidase, S.O.D., and catalase are most active at high redox potentials — about 400 to 700 mV at 37°C. NADP enzymes, some dehydrogenases, and thiol enzymes, on the other hand, are active at low potentials. Sometimes the presence of reducers, such as cysteine, is required for optimal activity; such is the case with papain.

In the microbiological area, bacterial enzymes "work" from O_2, sometimes in hyperbar oxybiosis, to H_2 (anoxybiotic enzymes of some *Clostridia*). To appreciate what may happen when enzymes or radiolabeled enzymes are joined to a bacterial medium, the r H_2 scale of Clark and Wurmser is an aid to be kept in mind.

In many instances, the E_o of an enzyme is very far from the E_o of the transporting fluid. While ^3H lowers the redox potential, the iodine tracers and ^{99m}Tc raise it; in other words, the introduction of a tracer atom may perturb the E_o of the enzyme. Even with short-lived ^{99m}Tc, the determination of the oxidation state of the unbound radionuclide in radiotracers is of prime importance.

Colombetti et al.[54] gave a detailed account of various techniques for the determination of free pertechnetate in radiopharmaceuticals and supplied a comparison among them, giving the limits of confidence in their use. Jones[55] has demonstrated that the deiodination of the labeled protein [^{125}I] diiodotyrosine during intestinal transmission in rats modifies the redox potential. Witt[56] has studied the variations of electrical potentials and currents across biomembranes as well as the velocity of reactions in the binding steps between enzyme and hemoglobin allosteric systems. It should be noted that the normal redox potential of well-oxygenated, circulating blood in adult humans is about 320 mV for a pH $= 7.37$ at 37°C.

3. Hydrophilic and Lipophilic Balance

The ratio W/O or O/W, which depends upon the respective concentrations of water and lipids in the heterogenous medium, determines the facility and velocity of transport of all biological constituents; thus the transport of hydrophilic enzymes will differ from that of lipophilic enzymes.

4. Interfacial Tension

The transport of radiolabeled enzymes also depends upon the tensio-activity at the surfaces that they encounter: the walls of the vessels containing the blood, cerebrospinal fluid, and bile, the tubules of the kidney, and other biomembranes, including the envelopes of the organelles and ribosomes in cells. Similarly, interfacial tensio-activity will influence the interactions between enzymes and kinetic constituents, such as red blood cells, leukocytes, lymphocytes, platelets, etc. It must also be borne in mind that the presence of biliary salts affects the transport of radiolabeled digestive enzymes, raises the concentration of lipids in emulsions, and — in the presence of Mg^{2+} — activates enterokinase. Microbial enzymes of the normal intestinal flora also conform to the rules of interfacial activity.

5. Osmotic Pressure

According to Cohen and Monod,[57] osmolarity plays a major role in the permeability of cellular barriers. This phenomenon is controlled by the Donnan membrane principle: the passage of ions depends on their diameter, their electric charge, and their hydrophilic attraction to water dipoles. The normal osmotic pressure of blood in adult humans is 303 μosmol, but it can be changed greatly by numerous agencies, including the intravenous injection of sugars, amino acids, vitamins, and salts. The work of Ussing[58] on membrane permeability is worth noting: he showed the influx of $^{22}Na^+$, the efflux of $^{24}Na^+$, and the transport of $^{35}Cl^-$ and $^{38}Cl^-$ ions.

6. Allosteric Sites in Enzymes

This section deals mainly with enzymes composed solely of protein whose catalytic sites and binding sites are defined by the sequence of amino acids in the native molecular structure.

Koshland[59] has demonstrated the roles of individual amino acid residues at the active sites of enzymes (histidine in cytochrome C oxidase, serine in phosphorylases) and the method of locating the disulfide bridges in ribonuclease. In order to explain some enzyme activities, the concept of a double-active site has been advanced: one site is responsible for the catalytic action of the enzyme upon its substrate, and the other — distinct but nearby — is involved in binding another molecule, not an isostere of the substrate, as an effector. This theory explains the functioning of activators and inhibitors, either competitive or noncompetitive, reversible or irreversible.

Keech and Barritt[60] have demonstrated the activation of the pyruvate carboxylase from sheep kidney by Mg^{2+} and adenosine triphosphate ion; Cohen[45] has found that acetyl coenzyme A acts at the same site of this enzyme. In 1966, Stadtman[61] worked on the allosteric regulation of enzyme activities and on the allosteric effects resulting from ligands that are either identical or different. More recently Wold[62] has provided some definitions and an overview of labeling affinity. The distinct activity of the two active sites can be explained by the existence of transition states in allosteric enzymes, in their tertiary or quaternary structures. Thermodynamic studies can account for the distinct activity of the two sites by differences between binding forces. In 1980, Lindquist[63] proved that a molecule will bind many orders of magnitude more tightly (10^8 to 10^{10} times) to a given enzyme than the substrate will bind to that enzyme. Tetrahedral transition states and multisubstrate analogues, as well as tetrahedral intermediates may explain the binding of some molecules in the neighborhood and beyond the active site of allosteric enzymes. Wolfenden[64] has also compared the differences in the binding between effector and substrate.

The allosteric sites seem to play a fundamental role in the biological transport of the protein fraction of all enzymes, whether radiolabeled or not. To maintain their catalytic activity during transport, the enzymes are probably bound at their allosteric sites by Van der Waals ligands to other proteins, such as those of serum globulins. In conclusion, it can be seen that the allosteric theory in the enzymatic structure remains a matter open to further investigations.

7. Enzymes Linked to Radiolabeled Coenzymes or Radioactive Metal Ions

As mentioned in Section II.A.2, a few enzymes have been labeled in their coenzymes or metal ligands, but no specific studies of the transport of such enzymes seem to have been published.

B. Specific Biological Influences

It should be noted that there exists a great difference between the molecular weight of the protein enzyme, always greater than 13,000, and the low molecular weight of coenzymes or the atomic weight of the radionuclide involved. The patterns observed for proteins in electrophoresis and the results of chromatographic studies of enzymes are almost identical to those of their respective pure protein-enzymes. In radiolabeled enzymes, the tracer is covalently bound to the whole molecule, and the protein, with its radioisotope well-linked, will differ only slightly from the nonlabeled enzyme. Some examples of the transport of enzymes and radiolabeled enzymes and possible resulting interferences will be elucidated next.

1. Oral Transport; the Problem of Enzymes Crossing the Intestinal Barrier

Pepsin, pancreatic enzymes, enterokinase, cellulase, papain, and bromelain are all widely used in therapeutics for the normalization of the gastrointestinal transit. Arginase and glucuronidase have also been added to this list recently. Other enzymes such as chymotrypsin, α-amylase, catalase and mucopolysaccharidases are used as anti-inflammatory agents. Lysozyme acts perhaps as an antiviral agent, while hyaluronidase is used to promote absorption in subcutaneous or intramuscular injections and in surgery.[5]

The majority of autbors believe that enzymes administered orally do not cross the intestinal barrier without undergoing some denaturation, and that their pharmacokinetics depends on their metabolites or on other products resulting from their catalytic action on their substrates. This view explains the allergic reactions sometimes caused by oral administration of pharmaceutical enzymes.

Martin et al.[65] administered [^{131}I]trypsin to rats by buccal and intestinal routes and observed its absorption through the intestine. They could not define the exact nature of the mechanism responsible for the level of radioactivity produced in the blood. Working with bromelain in 1961, Smyth et al.[66] suggested that orally administered enzymes could produce their clinical effects by causing the creation of a secondary enzyme or another biochemical in the intestine. Miller[67] and Miller and Opher[68] demonstrated the absorption of orally administered [^{131}I]trypsin by the gastrointestinal tract in humans; they also demonstrated the intestinal absorption of orally administered bromelain and papain and of orally or rectally administered streptokinase.

Moriya et al.[69,70] studied the passage of ^{131}I-labeled hog pancreatic kallikrein, or kininogenase, across the rat intestinal wall and showed the distribution of orally administered [^{131}I]α-chymotrypsin in the liver, kidney, spleen, thyroid, and serum. Isaka et al.[71] studied the gastrointestinal absorption of [^{125}I]bromelain administered to dogs by intragastric or intraduodenal routes; they observed the production of an anti-inflammatory effect. Warshaw et al.[72] noted the uptake of tritiated bovine serum albumin in the intestine of rats and provided evidence for the absorption of intact macromolecules. After administering [^{125}I]bromelain gastrointestinally to rats, Seifert et al.[73] studied the resorption of this proteolytic enzyme and its passage into the blood and lymph.

The results of this recent work support the position of those who advocate the oral administration of enzymes intended for absorption. There are conflicting data concerning the percentage of radiolabeled enzyme that is absorbed, perhaps because of variations among different animal species (dogs, rabbits, rats, or mice) and also because of differences in the techniques used to measure enzymatic activities. The latter problem arises from the choice of different substrates (casein, hemoglobin, BAEE, BCEE, or BTEE) and different analytical reagents (biuret or phenolic reactions used for the dosages).

2. Intravenous or Parenteral Administration

Ribonuclease and urokinase have been labeled for use in studies of the absorption of enzymes to intact animals. Davidson[74,75] published his results on the cell metabolism of bovine [^{125}I] ribonuclease injected intravenously into mice and rats. The observation of the rapid decrease of radioactivity in kidney homogenates supplies proof of an existing proteolytic activity of lysosomes after the incubation and digestion of the absorbed ribonuclease by pinocytosis at 37°C. When the digestive activity measured by the percentage of released tracer increases, the exogenous ribonuclease content of the kidney diminishes, demonstrating the degradation of the injected enzyme. Variations in the pH of the tissues seem to be important in the release of iodine-125: 76 percent is liberated at pH 7.0, and 100 percent at pH 5.5.

Woodard et al.[76] injected [^{125}I]urokinase into the femoral vein of rats anesthetized with pentothal to study the fate of the enzyme at various times after administration. Fifty percent of the infused radioenzyme was found in the liver and kidney 15 min post administration, and less than 5% could be detected after 4 hr. The metabolic fate of [^{131}I]urokinase in dogs and rats was studied by Tajima et al.,[77] and the results were compared to those obtained with [^{131}I]plasminogen. In the same year, Som and Rhodes[40] published an abstract on the comparative biological behavior of [^{99m}Tc]- and [^{125}I]-labeled urokinase in mice and dogs, and on the use of streptokinase as a clot-localizing agent.

3. The Transport of Radiolabeled Enzymes by Blood Cells

The molecular weight of the enzyme, its shape, its ampholytic state in circulating blood, and the adsorption capacity of the surfaces of red blood cells, leukocytes, and platelets play an important role in transport. Flowers and Sharon[78] have noted the importance of carbohydrate complexes and lipoproteins in biological transport. They also studied sialidase, which catalyzes the hydrolysis of certain mucopolysaccharides present in the walls of cells. Frazier and Glaser[79] used trypsin, which modifies the cell surface without actually penetrating it, to probe the existence of specific sites involved in transport.

Chan and Schatz[80] prepared ^{125}I-labeled gamma globulin antibodies to aid in their study of membrane components. Baron[81] similarly used inhibiting antibodies to determine the role of specific enzymes on cell surfaces. Ryo et al.[82] noted that the classical chelator EDTA changes the properties of red blood cell membranes, while Colombetti and Siddiqui[83] noted that phospholipids found in these membranes could bind ^{99m}Tc trapped by the pyrophosphate-tin complex.

4. Hepatocytes, Bacterial Cells, and the Permease System

The biological transport of the enzymes of hepatocytes and bacterial cells is perhaps best understood by linking it to the presence of a particular system of permeases that are involved in the transport of simple molecules. (The term permease was introduced by Cohen and Monod.[84]) Cohen-Bazire and Jolit,[85] as well as Cohen and Jacob,[86] studied the properties of β-galactoside permease and the thiol enzyme of the *Escherichia coli* membrane. Halvorson[87] observed the synthesis of proteins in cells and studied their kinetics. Cohen[45] discovered numerous permeases capable of biosynthesis in bacterial cells; among them were maltose permeases; amino acid permeases (capable of concentrating L-valine, L-leucine, L-isoleucine, and L-norleucine in bacterial cells); permeases for aromatic amino acids and for arginine and proline; sulfate permeases; phosphate permeases; etc. Glycuronide permease should also be mentioned because of its importance in the detoxification of hepatocytes and other cells damaged by various pharmaceutical phenolic products.

V. DISCUSSION AND CONCLUSION

The discussion here will be limited to the fundamentals concerning the structure and the radiolabeling of enzymes. Because the absolute configuration of enzymes and their stereochemistry are known from their amino acid sequences, the possibility of radiolabeling enzymes can be predicted. These amino acid sequences can be determined for low molecular weight enzymes, such as ribonuclease, muramidase, papain, and bromelain, by using an autoanalyzer. Results for 13 glucose-6-phosphate dehydrogenases have been reported by Levy.[88] The absolute configuration of enzymes may be obtained by a comparison with the absolute configuration of the same enzyme synthesized from crystalline amino acids. This was foreseen in 1974 by Colombetti,[89] who stated — concerning pancreatic enzymes — that "labeled amino acids will be used during synthesis and will be incorporated into the new enzymes being produced."

Despite our advances, we still are unable to tell exactly where the radioisotope is bound to the enzyme, because of the many groups that could be labeled in compounds of more than 100 amino acids. The binding force of the tracer to different aminoacids may vary according to the location of the amino acid in the chain sequence of the protein enzyme. The risk of competition with another serum protein or enzyme may also depend upon the actual amino acid labeled.

Labeling, as described in the first part of this chapter, is considered very elementary by chemists today. However, for radiolabeled enzymes, as well as for nonradiolabeled enzymes, the biological ratio E/S remains of primary importance as it signifies the theoretical ratio (kinetic agent)/(static agent) and influences the optimization of life. Enzymopathies, for instance, so important in medicine, will be much better understood once a good approach to the quantification of E/S in living beings is worked out. Although in vitro determination of E/S is sometimes difficult, Babin and Babin[90] have arrived at a value for E/S, but one which is still far from the [E]/[S] that can be determined for well-defined crystallized enzymes and substrates.

VI. PROSPECTS FOR THE FUTURE

Compared to the numerous radiolabeled proteins such as hormones, fibrinogen, and gamma globulins used for in vivo studies in man, the use of radiolabeled enzymes is not very significant. Nonetheless, the high specificity of enzymes and the sensitivity of radioanalytical techniques used in their examination remain to tempt the researcher. It is hoped that organic complexes of radioisotopes in radiotracers, which are selective for cells or tissues, will be discovered so that their selective and sensitive properties can be used to advantage in the investigation of enzyme catalysis. Already, promising results have been obtained in the use of [^{99m}Tc]streptokinase and urokinase for scintigraphy in man, and radiolabeled enzyme immunoassay in vitro work is rapidly approaching the femtomole (10^{-15}) and soon the attomole (10^{-18}) scale, thus converging upon the physicochemist's dream of investigating actual molecules one at a time.

ACKNOWLEDGMENTS

The authors would like to thank Prof. E. Jouzier of the University of Bordeaux; Dr. M. Thely of the Institut Choay, Paris; Dr. R. B. Christie of Armour, Eastbourne; Dr. A. Baret of CERB Toulon Naval; M. S. Vitellio, Research Associate INSERM - U.53, Bordeaux.

REFERENCES

1. **Thomas, R. C.**, Preparation of radioisotope labeled drug, *Annu. Rep. Med. Chem.,* 7, 296, 1972.
2. **Beinert, H.**, Micromethods for the quantitative determination of iron and copper in biological material, *Methods Enzymol.,* 54, 435, 1978.
3. **Northrop, J. H., Kunitz, M., and Herriott, R. M.,** *Crystalline Enzymes,* 2nd ed., Columbia University Press, New York, 1955.

4. Hannouz, M., Antigénicité et pureté d'une préparation de lysozyme, *Path. Microbiol.*, 28, 1, 139, 1965.

5. Ruyssen, R. and Lauwers, A., *Pharmaceutical Enzymes*, Story, E., Ed., Scientia, Ghent, Belgium, 1978, 4.

6. Stoclet, J. C., Les inhibiteurs de nucleotides cycliques phosphodiestérasiques, in *Actualités de Chimie Thérapeutique*, Vol. 7, Société Francaise de Chimie Therapeutique, Paris, 1980, 213.

7. Silipo, C. and Vittoria, A., Relations structure-activite et recherche d'inhibiteurs d'enzymes, in *Actualites de Chimie Therapeutique*, Vol. 7, Societe Francaise de Chimie Thérapeutique, Paris, 1980, 147.

8. Hansch, C., The interaction of ligands with enzymes. A starting point in drug design, *Il Farmaco, Ed. Sc.*, 34, 729, 1979.

9. Monks, R., Oldham, G., and Tovey, K. C., Labelled Nucleotides in Biochemistry, Review 12, *The Radiochemical Center Ltd.*, Amersham, England, 1971, 18.

10. Harwig, J. F., Harwig, S. L., Wells, L. D., and Welch, M. J., In vitro studies of ^{99m}Tc, labeled proteins, *J. Nucl. Med.*, 16, 6, 534, 1975.

11. Evans, E. A., Sheppard, H. C., Turner, J. C., and Warrel, D. C., New approach to specific labeling of organic compounds with tritium. Catalyzed exchange in solution with tritium gas, *J. Labelled Compd.*, 10(4), 569, 1974.

12. Wilzbach, K. E., Tritium labeling by exposure of organic compounds to tritium gas, *J. Am. Chem. Soc.*, 79, 1013, 1957.

13. Means, G. F., Reductive Alkylation of amino groups. Radioactive labeling, *Methods Enzymol.*, 47, 476, 1977.

14. Bailey, H. and Knowles, J. R., Photoaffinity labeling. Radioactive labeling, *Methods Enzymol.*, 46, 69, 1977.

15. Endert, E., Determination of noradrenaline and adrenaline in plasma by a radio enzymatic assay using HPLC for the separation of the radiochemical products, *Clin. Chim. Acta*, 96, 3, 233, 1979.

16. Shindo, H., Egan, W., and Cohen, J. S., Studies of individual carboxyl groups in protein by carbon 13 nuclear magnetic resonance spectroscopy, *J. Biol. Chem.*, 253, 19, 6751, 1978.

17. Jaeck, G. and Benz, F. W., Synthesis of ribonuclease labeled with ^{14}C on methionine 29, *Biochem. Biophys. Res. Commun.*, 86, 3, 885, 1979.

18. Noyer, M., De Vries-Petiau, G. M., Dolmans, M., and Leonis, J., Preparation of ribonuclease labelled on the saccharidic structure, *Arch. Int. Physiol. Biochem.*, 80, 4, 953, 1978.

19. Tappel, A. L., Glutathione peroxidase and hydroperoxides, *Methods Enzymol.*, 52, 504, 1978.

20. Hunter, W. M. and Greenwood, M. C., Preparation of iodine 131 labelled human growth hormone of high specific activity, *Nature (London)*, 194, 2, 495, 1962.

21. Matthews, C. M. E., The theory of tracer experiments with ^{131}I labeled plasma protein, *Phys. Med. Biol.*, 2, 36, 1957.

22. Cohen, Y., Berger, J. A., Gaillard, G., and Hegesippe, M., Radiopharmacologie, in *Pharmacologie Clinique*, Vol. 1, Giroud, J. P., Mathé, G. and Meyniel, G., Eds., Expansion Scientifique, Paris, 1978, 231.

23. Meyniel, G. and Veyre, A., in *Pharmacologie Clinique*, Vol. 1, Giroud, J. P., Mathé, G., and Meyniel, G., Eds., Expansion Scientifique, Paris, 1978, 98.

24. Parsons, M., Bossen, A., Blessingmoore, J., and Cavallisforza, L. L., Binding of ^{125}I labeled proteinases to plasma proteins in cystic fibrosis, *Pediatr. Res.*, 13, 9, 1030, 1979.

25. Bolton, A. E. and Hunter, W. M., The labelling of proteins to high specific activity by conjugation to a ^{125}I containing acylating agent, *Biochem. J.*, 130, 529, 1973.

26. Kutas, V., Mohari, K., Szekerke, M., and Hudecz, F., Organ distribution of polypeptides searching for an ideal agent for renal scintigraphy, *Eur. J. Nucl. Med.*, 4, 2, 128, 1979.

27. Baret, A., Michel, P., Imbert, M. R., and Morcellet, J. L., A radioimmunoassay for copper containing superoxide dismutase, *Biochem. Biophys. Res. Commun.*, 88, 2, 357, 1979.

28. Baret, A., Schiavi, P., Michelson, A. M., and Puget, K., A radioimmunoassay for manganese containing superoxide dismutase, *FEBS Lett.*, 1980.

29. Benjamin, P. P., A rapid and efficient method of preparing ^{99m}Tc human serum albumin. Its clinical application, *Int. J. Appl. Radiat. Isot.*, 20, 187, 1969.

30. Wong, D. W. and Mishkin, F. S., Technetium 99m human fibrinogen, *J. Nucl. Med.*, 16, 5, 343, 1975.

31. Wong, D. W. and Huang, J. T., Labeling of human immuno-gamma-globulin with ^{99m}Tc, *Int. J. Appl. Radiat. Isot.*, 28, 8, 719, 1977.

32. Wong, D. W., Mishkin, F. S., and Lee, T., A rapid chemical method of labeling human plasma protein with ^{99m}Tc pertechnetate at pH = 7,4, *Int. J. Appl. Radiat. Isot.*, 29, 4-5, 251, 1978.

33. Wong, D. W., Tanaka, T., Mishkin, F. S., and Lee, T., In vitro assessment of ^{99m}Tc labeled bovine thrombine and streptokinase activated human plasmin concentration, *J. Nucl. Med.*, 20, 967, 1979.

34. Dworkin, H. J. and Gutkowski, R. F., Rapid closed system production of ^{99m}Tc albumin using electrolysis, *J. Nucl. Med.*, 12, 8, 562, 1971.

35. Jonckheer, M. H., Abramovici, J., Jeghers, O., Dereume, J. P., and Goldstein, M., The interpretation of phlebograms using fibrinogen labeled with ^{99m}Tc, *Eur. J. Nucl. Med.*, 3, 4, 233, 1978.

36. Colombetti, L. G., Goldman, J., Patel, G. C., et al., A rapid method for labeling IgG with ^{99m}Tc, *J. Nucl. Med.*, 20(6), 652, 1979.

37. Persson, B. R. R. and Kempi, V., Preparation and testing of ^{99m}Tc labelled streptokinase for scintigraphic imaging of thrombi, *J. Nucl. Med.*, 16, 6, 557, 1975.

38. Ramos, J., Calistro, W., Castejon, J., Rodriguez, U., Abascal, J., Schapira, A., Chamorro, J. L., and Ortiz-Berrocal, J., Early diagnosis of thrombosis with ^{99m}Tc radiotracers, *Eur. J. Nucl. Med.*, 4.2. 132, 1979.

39. Som, P. and Rhodes, B. A., Comparative biologically behaviour of ^{99m}Tc and ^{125}I labeled urokinase, *J. Nucl. Med.*, 15 (Abstr.), 534, 1974.

40. Walter, U. and Greengard, P., Quantitative labeling type II c AMP dependent protein kinase, *J. Cyclic Nucleotide Res.*, 4, 6, 437, 1978.

41. McCormick, D. B. and Wright, L. D., Eds., Vitamins and coenzymes, *Methods in Enzymology*, Vol. 66 and Vol. 67, Academic Press, New York, 1980.

42. Cohen, Y., Berger, J. M., Gaillard, G., and Hegesippe, M., Radiopharmacologie, in *Pharmacologie Clinique*, Vol. 1, Giroud, J. P., Mathé, G., and Meyniel, G., Expansion Scientifique, Paris, 1978, 232.

43. Plagne, R., Meyniel, G., and Robert, J., Detection selective des tumeurs malignes, in *Pharmacologie Clinique*, Vol. 1, Giroud, J. P., Mathé, G. and Meyniel, G., Expansion Scientifique, Paris, 1978, 408.

44. Müller, W. E. G. and Zahn, R. K., Bleomycin an antibiotic that removes thymine from double stranded DNA, in *Progr. Nucleic Acid Res. Mol. Biol.*, 20, 22, 1977.

45. Cohen, G., Le Métabolisme Cellulaire et sa Régulation, Hermann, Paris, 1967.

46. Lefort, M., Chimie des radiations des solutions aqueuses. Aspects actuels des résultats expérimentaux, *Actions Chim. Biol. Radiat.*, 1, 1955.

47. Babin, R. M., Quelques Actions Biochimiques des Radiations X et gamma, Sc. D. Thesis, Université de Bordeaux, Baillet, 1955.

48. Augenstine, L. G., The effects of ionizing radiations on enzymes, *Adv. Enzymol. Relat. Areas Mol. Biol.*, 24, 359, 1962.

49. Wacker, A., Molecular mechanism of radiation effects, *Progr. Nucleic Acid Res. Mol. Biol.*, 1, 360, 1963.

50. Weiss, J. J., Chemical effects of ionizing radiation on nucleic acid and related compounds, *Progr. Nucleic Acid Res. Mol. Biol.*, 3, 103, 1964.

51. Kanazir, D. T., Radiation induced alterations on the structure of deoxyribonucleic acid and their biological consequences, *Progr. Nucleic Acid Res. Mol. Biol.*, 9, 117, 1969.

52. Rosselin, G., Radioanalyse specifique des milieux biologiques, in *Pharmacologie Clinique*, Vol. 1, Giroud, J. P., Mathé, G., and Meyniel, G., Eds., Expansion Scientifique, Paris, 1978, 202.

53. Babin, J. P., Bilstein, G., and Martin, Cl., Physiopathogénie de l'acidose néo-natale (formes courantes), *Méd. Infant.*, 84, 6, 681, 1977.

54. Colombetti, L. G., Moerlien, S., Patel, G. C., and Pinsky, S. M., Rapid determination of oxidation state of unbound ^{99m}Tc and labeling yield in ^{99m}Tc radiopharmaceuticals, *J. Nucl. Med.*, 17, 9, 805, 1976.

55. Jones, R. E., De-iodination of labelled protein during intestinal transmission in the suckling rat, *Proc. R. Soc. London Ser. B*, 199, 279, 1977.

56. Witt, H. T., Measurement of the change of electrical potentials and currents across biomembranes in the range of nanoseconds to seconds, *Methods Enzymol.*, 53, 61, 1978.

57. Cohen, G. N. and Monod, J., Bacterial permeases, *Bacteriol Rev.*, 21, 169, 1957.

58. Ussing, H. H., Some aspects of the application of tracers in permeability studies, *Adv. Enzymol. Relat. Areas Mol. Biol.*, 13, 21, 1952.

59. Koshland, D. E., Jr., The active site and enzyme action, *Adv. Enzymol.*, 22, 45, 1960.

60. Keech, B. and Barritt, G., Allosteric activation of sheep kidney pyruvate carboxylase by Mg^{2+} and the magnesium triphosphate ion (Mg ATP^{2-}), *J. Biol. Chem.*, 242, 1983, 1967.

61. Stadtman, E. R., Allosteric regulation of enzyme activity, in *Adv. Enzymol. Relat. Areas Mol. Biol.*, 28, 41, 1966.

62. Wold, F., Affinity labeling. An overview, *Methods Enzymol.*, 46, 3, 1977.

63. Lindquist, R. N., Transition state analogs in basis for the design of enzyme inhibitors, in *Actualités de Chimie Thérapeutique*, Vol. 7, Société Francaise de Chimie Thérapeutique, Paris, 1980, 67.

64. Wolfenden, R., Transition state analogs as potential affinity labeling reagents, *Methods Enzymol.*, 46, 15, 1977.

65. Martin, G. J., Bogner, R. L., and Edelman, A., Further in vivo observations with radioactive trypsin, *Am. J. Pharm.,* 11, 386, 1957.

66. Smyth, R. D., Brennan, R. M., and Martin, G. J., The systemic absorption of an orally administered proteolytic enzyme : bromelain, *Am. J. Pharm.,* 133, 294, 1961.

67. Miller, J. M., Objective criteria of efficacy in clinical enzymology, *Exp. Med. Surg. (Suppl.),* 23, 26, 1965.

68. Miller, J. M. and Opher, A. W., The increased proteolytic activity of human blood serum after the oral administration of bromelain, *Exp. Med. Surg.,* 22, 277, 1964.

69. Moriya, H., Moriwaki, C., and Akimoto, S., Studies on kallikreins. II. Passage of ¹³¹I labelled hog pancreatic kallikrein across the rat intestine, *Chem. Pharm. Bull.,* 15, 4, 403, 1967.

70. Moriya, H., Moriwaki, C., Akimoto, S., Yamaguchi, K., and Iwadare, M., Studies on the passage of alpha chymotrypsin across the intestine, *Chem. Pharm. Bull.,* 15, 11, 1662, 1967.

71. Isaka, K., Yamada, M., Kawano, T., and Suyama, T., Gastro intestinal absorption and anti-inflammatory effect of bromelain, *Jpn. J. Pharmacol.,* 22, 519, 1972.

72. Warshaw, A. L., Walker, W. A., and Isselbacher, K. J., Protein uptake by the intestine : evidence for absorption of intact macromolecules, *Gastroenterology,* 66, 987, 1974.

73. Seifert, von J., Ganser, R., and Brendel, W., Die resorption eines proteolytischen enzyme pflanzlichen ursprunges aus dem Magen-Darm-Trakt in das Blut und die Lymph von erwachsenen Ratten, *Z. Gastroenterologie,* 17, 1, 8, 1979.

74. Davidson, S. J., Proteolytic activity within lysosomes and turnover of pinocytic vesicles. A kinetic analysis, *Biochim. Biophys. Acta,* 411, 2, 282, 1975.

75. Davidson, S. J., Protein absorption by renal cells. II. Very rapid lysosomal digestion of exogenous ribonuclease in vitro, *J. Cell Biol.,* 59, 213, 1973.

76. Woodard, W. T., Day, E. D. and Silver, D., The fate of infused urokinase, *Surgery,* 68, 4, 692, 1970.

77. Tajima, J., Ishiguro, J., and Nonaka, R., Metabolic fate of urokinase, *Chem. Pharm. Bull. Jpn.,* 22, 4, 727, 1974.

78. Flowers, H. M. and Sharon, N., *Glycosidases,* Properties and application to the study of complex carbohydrates and cell surfaces, *Adv. Enzymol. Relat. Areas Mol. Biol.,* 48, 29, 1979.

79. Frazier, W. and Glaser, L., Surface components and cell recognition, *Annu. Rev. Biochem.,* 48, 1979.

80. Chan, S. H. P. and Schatz, G., Use of antibodies for studying the sidedness of membrane components, *Methods Enzymol.,* 56, 286, 1979.

81. Baron, J., Use of inhibitory antibodies to determine the role of the specific enzyme in a metabolic pathway, *Arch. Biochem. Biophys.,* 174, 226, 1976.

82. Ryo, U. Y., Mohammadzadeh, A. A., Siddiqui, A., Colombetti, L. G., and Pinsky, S. M., Reply on R.B.C.s. , *J. Nucl. Med.,* 17, 12, 1114, 1976.

83. Colombetti, L. G. and Siddiqui, A., Efficiency of in vivo labelling of R.B.C.s with ⁹⁹ᵐTc, *Nucl. Med.,* 15, 5, 211, 1976.

84. Monod, J. and Cohn, M., La biosynthèse induite des enzymes, adaptation enzymatique, *Adv. Enzymol. Relat. Areas Mol. Biol.,* 13, 67, 1952.

85. Cohen-Bazire, G. and Jolit, M., Isòlement par selection de mutants d'Escherichia Coli synthetisant spontanément l'amylomaltase et la beta galactosidase, *Ann. Inst. Pasteur, Paris,* 84, 937, 1953.

86. Cohen, G. and Jacob, F., Sur la repression de la synthese des enzymes intervenant dans la formation du tryptophane chez *Escherichia coli, C. R. Acad. Sci. Paris,* 248, 3490, 1959.

87. Halvorson, H. O., The induced synthesis of proteins. The inducer transport system: permeases, *Adv. Enzymol. Relat. Areas Mol. Biol.,* 22, 99, 1960.

88. Levy, H. R., Glucose 6 phosphate dehydrogenases, *Adv. Enzymol. Relat. Areas Mol. Biol.,* 48, 97, 1979.

89. Colombetti, L. G. and Pinsky, S., The potential use of gastro intestinal hormones and enzymes for pancreatic scanning, *Proc. 1st World Cong. Nucl. Med. Tokyo,* 9/10, 1974.

90. Babin, R. and Babin, Ph., L'importance du rapport$^E/_S$ dans les titrages enzymatiques, *Bull. Soc. Pharm. Bordeaux,* 112, 144, 1973.

Chapter 12

TRANSPORT OF RADIOLABELED ANTIBODIES

Robert E. Belliveau

TABLE OF CONTENTS

I. INTRODUCTION

The ultimate goal of administered radiolabeled antibodies has been the achievement of tumor localization which might be utilized in the detection and treatment of tumors. The labeling of nontumor proteins, particularly albumin,[1,2] with isotopes has been conducted for many years in order to measure the blood pool and its kinetics. The addition of label to nontumor and tumor tissue antibodies was first reported in the 1950s with developments leading to studies in nonhuman and human tumor systems for tumor detection and therapy.[3,4] The greatest impetus for the development of these antibodies has come from the more recent isolation and detection of tumor-associated antigens, such as CEA,[5,6] which have specific relationships to tumors. Their use in immunization of xenogeneic species has resulted in the production of specific antibodies to these antigens. Routes of administration have been primarily intravenous, including some selective catheterization of blood vessels, and more recently lymphatic following cannulation or subcutaneous administration.

The utilization of immune therapy to supplement chemo- and radiotherapeutic modalities has concentrated primarily on cellular immunity.[7-9] However, the development of specific antibodies has led to extensive study of radiolabeled antibodies and humoral systems for tumor detection and therapy.[10] Both in vitro and in vivo studies of tumor systems have shown definitive cytostasis with tumor cell death[11-13] and failure to alter tumor cell growth.[14,15] Because of these conflicting studies, the present review will highlight these as well as present a conceptual model of the transport of radiolabeled antibodies, their historical development, characteristics, advantages and disadvantages, and suggestions for their future development.

II. TRANSPORT MODEL

The major routes of distribution of radiolabeled tumor antibodies can be considered vascular and lymphatic. The conceptual model provided in Figure 1 integrates these routes with the methods of administration and localization. The ultimate goal of administered radiolabeled tumor antibody is binding to specific tumor antigens with resultant destruction of tumor cells.

Intravenously administered radiolabeled antibodies distribute themselves in proportion to the circulation. Those organs receiving greater perfusion will receive greater exposure to circulating antibodies. Proper mixing of radiolabeled antibody within the circulation prior to arrival at the capillary level is desirable. At the capillary level, immunoglobulins diffuse through endothelial pores and into the extracellular space at the $T_{1/2}$ rate of 18 to 24 hr.[16] Radiolabeled antibodies must pass through these pores since they are lipid-insoluble materials and consequently cannot pass directly through the lipoprotein barrier of the capillary endothelial membrane. Capillaries developing within neoplasms and inflammatory sites have a greater porosity with facilitation of immunoglobulin transport into the extracellular space and localization at tumors. In addition, molecular size and shape determine the transcapillary kinetics with electrostatic charge having little importance.

Possible mechanisms interfering with this localization in tumors include nonselective binding to nontumor antigens and development of antigen-antibody complexes in the circulation. Tumor cell antigens, in addition to being chemically unique, also share some chemical features with nontumor cells. For instance, carcinoembryonic antigen (CEA) shares chemical and cross-reactive features with normal blood group substances.[17] Also, individuals with CEA-bearing tumors often have circulating blood levels of CEA which may combine with administered anti-CEA resulting in complexes which are phagocytized and cleared by the reticuloendothelial system, particularly in

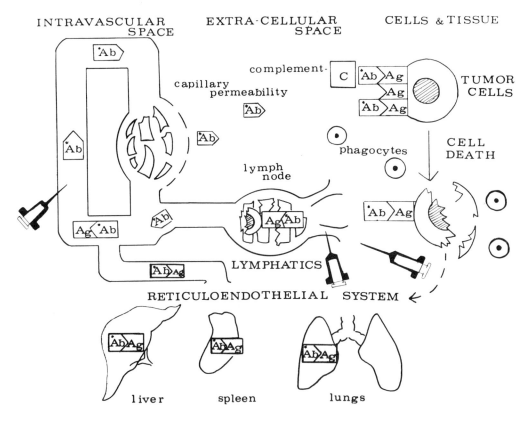

INTRAVASCULAR   EXTRA-CELLULAR   CELLS & TISSUE
        SPACE   SPACE

FIGURE 1. Schematic representation of the sites of administration (syringes), transport, localization, and
metabolism of radiolabeled antibody (*Ab) and relationships to tumor antigen (Ag.)

liver, spleen, and lungs.[18,19] Thus, these factors can diminish the effective delivery of
high tumor levels of radiolabeled antibody and result in high background radioactivity.
Also, radiolabel may be translocated to another molecular species and localize in normal tissue.

Radiolabeled antibodies within the extracellular space return to the circulation
through the lymphatics, including lymph nodes, via direct cannulation of lymphatic
channels or absorption and diffusion from the extracellular space following subcutaneous injection. Lymphatics are slow to develop in tumor and inflammatory sites with
consequent retardation of antibody egress.[16,18] Once within the lymphatics, the radiolabeled antibodies can bind to trapped tumor cells bearing antigens, tumor antigens
alone, or return to the vascular circulation for redistribution. Usual sites of localization
of radiolabeled antibodies are within lymph nodes bearing tumor cells with corresponding antigens.

Once the radiolabeled tumor antibodies are bound to tumor cell antigens, cell destruction and death may ensue as a consequence of radiation effect or altered cell
permeability following the binding of complement. If tissue necrosis at a tumor or
nontumor site is active, ingestion of radiolabeled immunoglobulin may occur due to
the increased pinocytosis exhibited by macrophages and necrotic cells. The products
of these reactions are then bound and cleared by the reticuloendothelial system with
potential localization of label within nontumor tissues. For instance, liberated iodine
can concentrate within the thyroid or be excreted via the urinary tract.

The model presented is rather "idealized" since many of the cellular changes, tissue
reactions, and extracellular processes are shared by nontumor and inflammatory proc-

esses.[19] Capillary and lymphatic proliferation can occur during the organization phase of inflammation. Therefore, nonselective localization may occur in nontumor conditions. The data presented and reviewed in Table 1 have not compared tumor and nontumor systems.

III. LITERATURE REVIEW

A listing of relevant studies is presented chronologically in Table 1 with highlights emphasized in the following discussion. The ability of radiolabeled antibodies to localize in nontumor and tumor tissues in vivo following intravenous administration were first reported in the 1950s by Pressman and Korngold.[3,4] Tumor-associated antibodies were identified with attempts at greater specificity and less cross-reactivity developed using absorption and elution techniques.[20] However, continued but lesser accumulation of labeled antibodies occurred in nontumor tissues, particularly liver, spleen, lungs, and kidneys. This was attributed to the technical difficulty of preparing a pure antigen for immunization. Further studies of the transport of radiolabeled antibodies were somewhat refined and accomplished using a double antibody system in which two isotopes, ^{131}I and ^{133}I were each conjugated with tumor-localizing and normal serum antibodies and injected simultaneously in vivo.[21] Thus, each animal served as its own control. After measurement of nonspecific binding of normal antibody, quantitation of tumor antibody binding could be assessed. The differences in tumor localization of radiolabeled antibody were considered primarily related to local changes in tumor perfusion.

To evaluate the importance of perfusion and the known tumor localization by proteins,[22-25] Day and Bale studied the kinetics of radiolabeled fibrinogen and anti-fibrinogen within tumor models.[26,27] Preferential tumor uptake was found along with lengthened survival of tumor-bearing rats. The kinetics of radiolabeled fibrinogen following intravenous administration was studied and showed preferential accumulation in tumors following transplantation and during the rapid growth stage.[28] In the absence of tumor binding, fibrinogen was cleared rapidly from the circulation. In studies of ^{131}I antifibrin in dogs having spontaneous tumors, which eliminated the possible transplantation artifact, Spar et al. found that preferential uptake did occur in some dogs and that the level was satisfactory for therapy.[29] Studies were then conducted in humans having disseminated tumors. Radioiodinated antifibrin doses (400 to 1000 μCi) were administered with unequivocal detection of tumors in 75% of the patients studied.[30,31] Spar postulated that tumor growth produced an inflammatory reaction as a consequence of injury to blood vessels and stroma. This in turn resulted in deposition of fibrin and later, antifibrin. Peterson et al. attributed the higher uptake in tumors to passive leakage of fibrinogen through the highly permeable tumor capillaries.[32]

The efforts of the 1960s were directed toward a more specific identification of tumor antigen and antibody as well as a better characterization of each component. The work of Ghose with Ehrlich ascites tumor (EAC) and a lymphoma (EL-4) combining in vitro and in vivo techniques resulted in the preparation of tumor-associated antibodies which were conjugated with either radiolabel or chemotherapeutic agents. The administration of these resulted in partial or complete suppression of the respective tumors and prolonged survival.[33,34] Ghose also noted that the actual amount of radiolabeled tumor-specific antibody usually amounted to only 1% of the total administered, and that better purification and isolation should result in more efficacious results. Less nonselective accumulation within the liver, spleen, and lungs might also be expected. He also added that freely circulating tumor cells, such as occur in hematopoietic tumors, would be more amenable to therapy since the agent was more freely accessible than in the presence of solid tumor.[36]

Application of radiolabeled antibodies to a hematopoietic tumor model, a mouse

Table 1

CHRONOLOGICAL LISTING OF RADIOLABELED ANTIBODIES IN HUMAN AND NONHUMAN TISSUE LOCALIZATION AND THERAPY

Investigator (year)	Tumor type	Host	Tumor site[a]	Agent (isotope)	Species producing Ab	Tumor blood ratio[b]	Survival[c]	Critical organ[d]	Comment	Ref.
Pressman and Korngold (1953)	Wagner osteogenic sarcoma	Mouse (Akm)	S.C.	131I-anti WOS Ig	Rabbit	U	U	Kidney/liver	Purification of Ab by absorption techniques	3
	Adenocarcinoma E0771	Mouse (C57)	S.C.	131I-anti EO771	Rabbit	U	U	Kidney/liver		
Korngold and Pressman (1954)	Lymposarcoma-Murphy-Strum	Sherman rat	S.C.	131I-antilymphosarcoma Ig	Rabbit	U	U	Spleen	Normal tissue Ab not in tumor	4
Day et al. (1956)	Lymphosarcoma-Murphy-Strum	Wistar rat	S.C.	131I-antilymphosarcoma Ig	Rabbit	U	U	Liver	Double fractional absorption; normal tissue then tumor Ag	20
Pressman et al. (1957)	Lymphosarcoma-Murphy-Strum	Wistar rat	S.C.	131I-antilymphosarcoma Ig 123I-NRS Ig	Rabbit	U	U	Liver	Internal control system in each animal (double isotope)	21
Day et al. (1959)	Lymphosarcoma-Murphy-Strum	Wistar rat	S.C.	131I-antifibrin Ig	Rabbit	U	U	U	Antifibrin and fibrinogen localize in tumors	26
Bale et al. (1960)	Lymphosarcoma-Murphy-Strum	Sprague-Dawley rat	S.C.	131I-antifibrin Ig	Rabbit	≃3.5	+	Blood	Increased survival and cure after radiolabeled antifibrin therapy	27
Spar et al. (1960)	Various tumors (spontaneous)	Dog	X	131I-antifibrin Ig	Rabbit	U	U	U	Suggest antifibrin use in man	29
Ghose et al. (1967)	Ehrlich ascites carcinoma	Mouse (BALB/ c)	I.P.	131I-anti Ehrlich ascites Ig	Rabbit	U	+	U	In vitro incubation with in vitro transfer	33
Spar et al. (1967)	Various tumors	Human	X	131I-antifibrin Ig	Rabbit	U	U	U	First human administration of radiolabeled antifibrin	31
Reif (1971)	Myeloma MOPC-21A	Mouse (BALB/ c)	S.C.	125,131I-anti-myeloma & NRS Ig	Rabbit	U	+	U	Complexes interfere with Ag Ab reactions	37
Izzo et al. (1971)	Fischer MC tumor	Fischer rat	S.C.	125I-antiFischer 344 transpl. Ig	Buffalo rat	≃3.7	U	Blood		39
Quinones et al. (1971)	Human choriocarcinoma	Syrian hamsters	C.P.	125I-anti-HCG Ig 131I-NRG Ig	Rabbit	≃0.5	U	Ovary, liver, uterus	Scintillation imaging and localization of tumor	57

Table 1 (continued)
CHRONOLOGICAL LISTING OF RADIOLABELED ANTIBODIES IN HUMAN AND NONHUMAN TISSUE LOCALIZATION AND THERAPY

Investigator (year)	Tumor type	Host	Tumor site[a]	Agent (isotope)	Species producing Ab	Tumor blood ratio[b]	Survival[c]	Critical organ[d]	Comment	Ref.
Kellen and Lo (1973)(14)	Mammary tumor R35,R3230OAC	Sprague-Dawley rat	S.C.	^{125}I-antitumor assoc. Ig	Rabbit	U	U	Kidney/liver		40
Primus et al. (1973)	Human colonic carcinoma, GW39	Syrian hamster	C.P.	^{125,131}I-anti CEA Ig ^{125,131}I-NRS Ig	Goat	≃2.0	U	Lungs	Clearance of radiolabeled anti-CEA studied	42
Goldenberg et al. (1974)	Human colonic carcinoma, GW39	Hamster	C.P.	^{125}I-anti-CEA and ^{125}I-NRS Ig	Goat	5.06±0.74	U	Lungs, heart, U. bladder	Scintillation imaging of tumor with ^{125}I-anti-CEA	43
	Sarcoma, HS-1	Syrian hamster	C.P.	^{125}I-anti-CEA and ^{125}I-NRS Ig	Syrian hamster	≃0.7	U	Lungs, U. bladder		
	Amelanotic melanoma-3	Hamster	C.P.	^{125}I-anti-CEA and ^{125}I-NRS Ig		U	U	Lungs, U. bladder		
Hoffer et al. (1974)	Colonic tumor GW-39	Hamster	S.C.	^{125}I-anti-CEA Ig	Goat	0.81	U	Blood	^{125}I-anti-CEA better localizing agent than tumor-avid isotopes	44
Reif et al. (1974)	Carcinoma colon	Human	X	^{131}I-anti-CEA Ig	Rabbit	U	U	Liver, lungs	First human administration	45
Ghose and Guclu (1974)	EL-4 lymphoma	Mouse (C57BL)	I.P.	^{131}I-anti-EL4 Ig	Rabbit	U	+	U	In vitro incubation	36
Pressman and Watanabe (1975)	Myeloma MOPC-104E	Mouse	S.C.	^{131}I-antimyeloma Ig ^{131}I-NRS Ig	Rabbit	U	U	Liver	Microsome localization of Ab	38
Terman et al. (1975)	Neuroblastoma C-1300	Mouse	S.C.	^{125}I-anti-C1300 Ig	Rabbit	U	U	U	Scintillation imaging for localization possible	41
Order et al. (1975)	Hodgkin's disease	Human	X	^{131}I-anti-F antigen Ig	Rabbit	U	U	U	First lymphangiographic application of radio-antibodies	60
Ghose et al. (1975,1976)	Lymphoma EL4	Mouse (C57/BLO)	I.P.	^{131}I-anti-EL4 and ^{131}I-NRS Ig	Rabbit	U	+	Heart, liver, spleen, lungs		51-53
	Ehrlich ascites carcinoma	Mouse (BALB/c)	I.P.	^{131}I-anti-EAC NRS Ig	Rabbit	U	+	Liver, spleen, lungs		

Belliveau (1976)	Various tumors	Human	X	^{131}I-antitumor Ig	Rabbit	U	U	Liver, spleen, lungs	First non-CEA antibody administered in man	58
	Neuroblastoma C-1300	Mouse (A/J)	S.C.	^{125}I-anti-PGE Ig ^{126}I-NRS Ig	Rabbit	≈ 7.0	U	Lung		
Primus et al. (1977)	Human colonic carcinoma, GW-39	Syrian hamster	C.P.	$^{125,131}I$-anti-CEA Ig	Goat	= 3.0	U	Blood	Greater tumor localization by affinity purified Ab	48
Beliksky et al. (1978)	Renal cell carcinoma	Human	X	^{131}I-antitumor Ig	Goat	U	U	Liver, spleen, lungs	Use of pooled antitumor globulin	54,55
Goldenberg et al. (1978)	Various tumors	Human	X	^{131}I-anti-CEA Ig	Goat	U	U	U	Affinity purified Ab, blood pool and computer subtraction techniques	49
DeLand et al. (1979)	Breast, GI, and GU cancers	Human	X	^{131}I-anti-CEA Ig	Goat	U	U	U	Lymph node lymphoscintigraphy using radiolabeled anti-CEA	51

[a] Abbreviations for tumor sites: S.C., subcutaneous; X, multiple sites; auto, spontaneous; I.P., intraperitoneal; C.P., cheek pouch.

[b] Ratio expressed on basis of % injected dose/g tissue studied; U, unknown.

[c] Survival abbreviations: U, unknown; +, improved or lengthened.

[d] Critical organ refers to organ or organs having highest levels of radiolabeled antibody compared to tumor.

bearing plasma cell tumor, was undertaken by Pressman and Watanabe and Reif.[37,38] Prolongation of mice survival was only observed under very specific circumstances with the bulk of information failing to show any effect due to exposure of this agent.[37] Accentuated localization was again noted in nontumor tissues, particularly those of the reticuloendothelial system. Other efforts utilizing solid tumors,[39] including mammary neoplasms and neuroblastomas[40,41] and their respective radiolabeled antibodies, continued to show nontumor uptake. However, scintillation imaging and detection of tumor was demonstrated by Terman.[41]

The work of Gold in the 1960s, in which he isolated and identified a tumor-specific antigen, a carcinoembryonic antigen (CEA), provided a new impetus to the development of radiolabeled antibodies.[5,6] Prior to this, antibodies were generated in xenogeneic and allogeneic animals from homogenates of tumor cells which also included many nontumor antigens. Primus et al. found that radioiodinated heterospecific anti-CEA localized significantly in hamsters bearing human colonic tumors (GW-39 tumors).[40] The greatest localization occurred in the 5 g size tumor with diminution on increasing tumor size. This phenomenon was attributed to lessened availability of CEA to anti-CEA, depressed CEA synthesis, and increased clearance of CEA and anti-CEA complexes in larger tumors. Using radiolabeled anti-CEA, these GW-39 tumors less than 200 mg were visualized by photoscanning.[43] Of interest, blood clearance of radioiodinated anti-CEA was slower than that of radioiodinated normal immunoglobulin due to tumor binding, formation of CEA and anti-CEA complexes, and phagocytosis. In hamsters bearing larger GW-39 tumors, radiolabeled normal immunoglobulin was as effective as radiolabeled anti-CEA.

Hoffer undertook comparison of ^{131}I anti-CEA to other tumor-scanning agents, including ^{111}In-bleomycin, ^{67}Ga-citrate, and ^{131}I-normal immunoglobulin, and found ^{131}I-anti-CEA best for photoscanning.[44] He suggested the use of affinity chromatography as a method of producing a purer and better localizing anti-CEA fraction. The possibility of circulating CEA competing with tumor-bound CEA for radiolabeled anti-CEA was noted as diminishing the effective delivery of radiolabeled antibody to the tumor.

The applicability of ^{131}I-anti-CEA to human tumor detection was first reported in 1974.[45] Prior concern for pyrogenicity and toxicity had precluded its use. However, in this first case report, intravenous and hepatic artery infusions of ^{131}I-anti-CEA were performed in a patient with known metastatic adenocarcinoma of the colon and elevated blood CEA levels. These procedures failed to demonstrate localization within known hepatic metastases, but did show marked uptake in the entire liver and lungs. A slight, but medically controlled, allergic reaction was noted. The apparent failure of ^{131}I-anti-CEA to localize in the tumor was attributed to cross-reactivity with normal blood group substances,[17] since CEA and these share chemical identity, binding to circulating CEA with complex clearance by the reticuloendothelial system,[46,47] and lack of accessibility to the tumor. The possibility of tumor enhancement or rejection secondary to the administration of antibody was also raised. Some studies showed that tumor antibody alone without label could suppress tumor growth in small tumors, but that this effect was lost in larger tumors.

Better tumor localization and imaging of GW-39 human colonic cancer in hamsters was achieved following affinity chromatography techniques of purifying antibody.[46] Up to 90% of primary human CEA-producing tumors and their metastases were detected following this same technique.[49,50] Background subtraction of radioactivity by combining a blood pool agent and computer-assisted subtraction techniques were also essential. Circulating CEA and ^{131}I-anti-CEA complexes were identified in the presence of high blood CEA levels, but without interference or impairment in tumor visualization.

Other trials in human tumors were reported in 1976 by Ghose, in which xenogeneic antibodies to different tumors, including renal and lung carcinomas and melanomas, were intravenously administered following radioiodination.[51-53] Good tumor localization was accomplished without adverse reactions. Another report utilizing a pool of ^{131}I-antitumor immunoglobulin prepared from a pool of renal cell carcinomata antigens revealed good imaging of the neoplasm.[54,55] Subsequently, the pooled antigen has been identified as reacting exclusively with proximal convoluted tubules.[56] The sensitivity and specificity of this pool has not been completely studied. However, the availability of such a pool may provide for its general use in the staging of patients with renal cell carcinoma without the need to prepare an antibody to each neoplasm.

Most efforts had been directed toward the production of antibodies to specific tumor antigens. However, some attempts had been directed to the use of radiolabeled antibodies to hormones produced by tumors. In 1971, Quinones reported that radiolabeled antibody to human chorionic gonadotropic hormone (UCG) could be used to detect choriocarcinomas transplanted in hamsters' cheek pouches.[57] UCG is specifically produced by this tumor. The sites of localization of this antibody were on the cell membrane and within its cytoplasm. The latter localization was attributed to cellular pinocytosis. Another study in 1976 using mice bearing neuroblastomas,[58] a tumor known to contain and produce very high levels of prostaglandins,[59] showed that radiolabeled antibodies to specific prostaglandins failed to localize in the tumors to any greater degree than similarly administered pooled and radiolabeled nontumor immunoglobulin. No other reports or follow-up studies of similar attempts using radiolabeled antibodies to hormones have appeared. The isolation and identification of specific tumor antigens rather than hormones appear to offer greater potential for success.

More recently, a modification of intravenous radiolabeled antibody has been reported with application to lymphangiography.[60] Pelvic and inguinal lymph nodes having Hodgkin's disease were identified following cannulation of the lower extremity lymphatics and administration of radiolabeled antibody to the F antigen, a Hodgkin's disease-associated antigen. These findings correlated well with those documented by lymphangiography and surgery. DeLand et al.[61] combined radionuclide lymphoscintigraphic techniques as developed by Ege[62] with the use of a radiolabeled antibody, ^{131}I-anti-CEA. Radionuclide lymphoscintigraphy technique involves the subcutaneous administration of radiolabeled colloid, such as ^{99m}Tc-antimony colloid, with subsequent scintillation imaging to evaluate lymphatic channel patency and anatomic variation, either primary or secondary. This technique alone does not allow for the detection of tumor involvement. However, by combining this technique with an agent which is tumor avid and specific, ^{131}I-anti-CEA, DeLand et al. found that axillary and inguinal lymph node involvement by metastatic breast, gastrointestinal, or urogenital carcinomata could be detected.[61] A few instances of false positives were attributed to scarred lymph nodes or entrapment of tumor antigen alone within the lymph nodes. In addition to detecting suspected and proven metastatic carcinoma, instances of unsuspected contralateral metastatic breast carcinomata and retrograde abdominal carcinomata were detected. Perhaps the greatest tumor staging information might be obtained by a combination and correlation of results obtained from both colloid and radioantibody lymphoscintigraphy.

IV. PROPERTIES OF TUMOR ANTIGENS

The isolation of specific antigens to tumors with minimal cross-reactivity to normal tissues has been the priority and essential step toward the development of effective radiolabeled tumor antibodies. The usual characterization of an antigen involves a definition of its structural, affinitive, and compartmental (organism, organ, cellular,

Table 2
PROPERTIES OF TUMOR ANTIGENS AND THEIR CORRESPONDING TUMORS

1.   Tumor antigens accessible along cellular surface of tumor.
2.   Tumor antigen distinctly different identity from normal cellular antigens.
3.   Tumor antigens must demonstrate a long $T_{1/2}$ at the cellular surface.
4.   Unique tumor antigens with each type of tumor.
5.   Development of pooled tumor antigens to specific tumors.
6.   Tumor antigens should be present in circulation at very low or negligible levels.
7.   Tumor antigen binding sites many times greater than number of radioantibodies needed to deliver tumoricidal dose.
8.   Tumor mass limiting factor — circulating tumor cellular elements more responsive than solid tumor.
9.   Tumor antigens amenable to storage with retention of immunological integrity for immunization.

Table 3
PROPERTIES OF RADIOLABELED TUMOR ANTIBODIES

1.   Tumor antibody must demonstrate specificity for tumor antigen without significant cross-reactivity to normal cellular membrane antigens.
2.   Tumor antibody capable of binding isotope with maintenance of specificity and biologic activity (with ^{131}I, 2 molecules ^{131}I/molecule Ab).
3.   The use of ^{131}I as isotope is capable of delivering therapeutic and cytocidal dose of 500 rads (beta radiation).
4.   Radiolabeled tumor antibody reaction with tissue-bound antigen resulting in cellular destruction.
5.   Preferential localization of radiolabeled tumor antibody in tumor with rapid clearance of blood and nontumor levels with time.
6.   Minimal translocation of isotope from radiolabeled tumor antibody.
7.   Short-lived isotopes advantageous since less opportunity for free isotope formation and effects on nontumor tissues (thyroid).

and subcellular distribution) specificities and cross-reactivity relative to identifiable antibodies.[63,64]

The properties of tumor antigens and their corresponding tumors are listed in Table 2. The desirable features of a tumor antigen include localization along the cell membrane surface for extended lengths of time to allow access of binding antibody and ample time for isotope and cellular interaction. The number of binding sites should far exceed the number of radiolabeled antibodies needed for a tumoricidal dose.[65,66] The tumor-associated antigens should be distinctly different from normal tissue antigens as well as unique to a specific tumor type. The levels of circulating tumor antigens should be low or diminished by prior administration of unlabeled tumor antibody since complexes may form and result in lessened availability of radioantibody for tumor binding. Tumor antigens should also be amenable to storage with possible pooling of antigens from similar tumors for subsequent immunization.[55]

V. PROPERTIES OF RADIOLABELED TUMOR ANTIBODIES

Following the isolation of a specific tumor antigen, immunization of xenogeneic animals with this antigen results in the production of antibodies having varying degrees of specificity. Given an immunoglobulin pool from an immunized animal, a tumor-related fraction of 5 to 10% is considered quite an effective yield.[66] Purification of this fraction with increased specificity can be obtained through affinity chromatography and isoelectric focusing techniques prior to radiolabeling. However, radiolabeling itself can further reduce the effective and specific tumor related fraction due to antibody denaturation. Thus the effective tumor-specific antibody represents a small fraction of the total immunoglobulin pool.

Table 4

PHYSICAL CHARACTERISTICS OF RADIONUCLIDE USED IN
RADIOLABELED ANTIBODIES

Radionuclide	Half-life	Type of radiation	Principal energy	
[131]I	8.05 days	β	E^Bmax	= 0.188 MeV
		γ		0.364 MeV
[133]I	20.8 hours	β	E^Bmax	= 1.27 MeV
		γ		0.529 MeV
[32]P	14.3 days	β	E^Bmax	= 1.71 MeV
[10]Bo + neutron capture	—	α		2 MeV

After labeling, immunological distribution analysis techniques can be applied to measure the in vivo localization and its kinetics.[63] The rates of localization or disappearance of radioantibody can be measured and compared to control situations. From this, the optimum time for imaging or treating tumors using radiolabeled antibodies can be obtained. The tumor radioantibody must demonstrate significant specificity for the tumor without reacting to normal cellular antigens.

Besides depending upon the development of specific tumor antibodies and the maintenance of their integrity by proper labeling, the localization of radioantibodies within tumors depends upon the delivery of an adequate dose via the circulation and the lymphatic system.[67] In addition, tumor cells exhibit increased affinity to bind proteins, including immunoglobulins, and increased pinocytosis or liposomotropic activity.[66] The results of this localization within tumors should result in a rapid clearance of circulating unbound radioantibody as well as nonselective and nonreactive bound fractions with better discrimination of tumors.[63]

The choice of radiolabel for antibody binding has been primarily ^{131}I, since it binds efficiently to immunoglobulin, provides gamma radiation for external detection, and delivers adequate and tumoricidal beta radiation for tumor cell destruction.[65] Damage to the radiolabeled antibody can alter its reactivity, solubility, and biologic half-life. Chromatographic techniques before and after radioiodination may isolate the present tumor-related radioantibody. Labeling of antibody while it is bound to tumor antigens in order to protect these sites may also increase the effective yield.[69] Subsequent elution of tagged antibody thus provides free antibody-binding sites. Short-lived isotopes are preferable since they maximize the delivery of radiation and minimize the potential toxicity to normal and surrounding tissue following the liberation of isotope. Table 4 lists the physical characteristics of ^{131}I as well as other isotopes, including [133]I, [10]B, and [32]P.[65,70,71]

An adequate tumoricidal radiation dose of 500 rad/cell can be achieved in the form of [131]I. Day and McGaughey determined that the number of radiolabeled antibodies necessary to deliver this dose is far less than the total number of available antigen sites.[64,65] The binding of two ^{131}I molecules per antibody can provide the necessary dose as well as preserve the functional integrity of the antibody. Consideration of shorter-lived isotopes, such as [133]I, could provide a higher cell kill with less chance for free isotope formation and translocation to normal tissues. However, the ultimate choice of iodine isotope has resulted in the practical preference for ^{131}I since it is readily available at a modest cost.

The actual mode of action of radiolabeled antibodies and their interaction with tumor cells is considered a synergistic reaction of antibody and radiation effect in the destruction of tumor cells.[72] The role of antibody alone in tumor destruction is unsettled with different tumor studies showing both favorable and unfavorable results. However, the addition of label to antibody has been found more effective and additive

Table 5

PROBLEMS OF TRANSPORT AND LOCALIZATION OF RADIOLABELED
TUMOR ANTIBODIES

1. Tumor antibody purification efficiency is very low (5 to 10%).
2. Tumor antibody can bind circulating tumor antigens.
3. Complexes of tumor antigen-antibody taken up by RE system with concentration in liver and spleen.
4. Tumor antibody specificity quite variable with potential binding to nontumor tissue.
5. Tumor antibody may localize in sites of inflammation.
6. Antigenic sites on tumor cells may be covered by blocking antibodies with loss of effective antigen-antibody binding.
7. Tumor antibody administration may blunt host's own immune response — immunologic enhancement.
8. Isotope liberated from tumor antibody may translocate to other organs (thyroid).
9. Antibodies to other substances, such as brain gangliosides, known to cause epileptiform activity.
10. Xenogeneic antisera may cause serum sickness or anaphylaxis upon repeated exposure.

in its tumoricidal action. Similarly, the addition of chemotherapeutic agents to tumor antibodies has shown results analogous to those obtained with radiolabeled antibodies.[72]

VI. PROBLEMS OF TRANSPORT AND LOCALIZATION OF RADIOLABELED TUMOR ANTIBODIES

The preparation, radioiodination, and isolation of specific tumor radioantibodies to tumor-associated antigens present many problems (Table 5). The isolation of specific tumor-associated antigens for immunization is difficult since many tumor antigens share chemical identities with normal tissue antigens. For instance, CEA shares common chemical composition with normal blood group substances.[17] As a result, radiolabeled antibodies produced to these antigens will show cross-reactivity with normal tissue antigens when administered. Consequently, this will reduce the effectiveness of tumor localization and discrimination. In addition, if antibodies to normal tissue antigens are produced during immunization and purified for administration, these may have adverse effects on nontumor tissues. For instance, if antibodies to brain antigens are produced, toxicity may result since antibodies to brain gangliosides have been reported to cause epileptiform activity.[75]

Following tumor antigen isolation, animal immunization with ultimate isolation and radioiodination of antibody results in a very low yield of effective tumor radioantibody.[66] The process of radioiodination itself can damage or alter the molecular configuration and reactivity of the antibody with resultant nonselective localization of radiolabeled antibody. In order to minimize this problem, administration of radioantibody in proximity to suspected tumor sites as performed during lymphangiography may be preferred to reduce the potential for nonselective binding. Radiolabeled antibody can be preferentially bound and sequestered in tumor tissue during first-pass following injection.[60,61] Consequently, there is less radioantibody available for generalized nonselective binding.

The binding of tumor radioantibody to circulating tumor antigens has been observed, but even in the presence of very high antigen blood levels, tumor localization has been achieved.[47] Administration of nonlabeled antibody prior to the introduction of radiolabeled tumor antibody has been considered as a means of removing circulating tumor antigens and achieving greater tumor localization of label with lessened background radioactivity. The clearance and sequestration of tagged complexes by the reticuloendothelial system might also contribute to the high background radioactivity with consequent problems of tumor detection and treatment.[66]

Nonselective localization of radiolabeled antibody in nontumor tissues, including inflammatory sites, continues to present problems with consequent difficulties in detecting and discriminating tumor from nontumor sites.[66] Inflammatory sites have a great propensity to sequester proteins, including radioantibodies.[16] In addition to binding radiolabeled antibody, inflammatory sites can metabolize the radioantibody with the liberation of tag and antibody fragments. The translocated isotope can localize in other nontumor tissues and contribute to background radioactivity. Misleading information, as well as exposure of nontumor sites to radiation toxicity, is likely.

The interactions of radiolabeled antibody with the host's normal immune response have not been fully evaluated. The theoretical possibility of blunting the host's own immune response by administering radioantibodies with consequent tumor enhancement is still unsettled.[14,15,74] Likewise, the host's own antibodies, blocking antibodies, may interfere with the localization by radiolabeled antibodies.[66]

Another possibility is that radioantibodies may suppress tumor cell antigenicity and preferentially select-out antigen-negative tumor cells for continued growth. The results of these processes would be continued tumor growth without effective response to radioantibodies.

Thus to date, the use of radiolabeled antibodies in tumor therapy cannot be considered alone, but as an adjunctive modality to surgery, chemotherapy, and radiotherapy.[72] Improved means of purifying and providing more effective pools of radioantibodies must be evaluated. The use of autologous antibodies for radiolabeling is theoretically preferable, but practically impossible. Ethical considerations of such human immunization preclude this approach.[72] Therefore, xenogeneic antibodies must be utilized, but these are potentially harmful and may cause serum sickness with possible anaphylaxis upon repeated usage.

REFERENCES

1. Eckleman, W. C., Technical considerations in labeling of blood elements, *Semin. Nucl. Med.*, 5, 3, 1975.
2. Wright, R. R., Tono, M., and Pollycove, M., Blood volume, *Semin. Nucl. Med.*, 5, 63, 1975.
3. Pressman, D. and Korngold, L., The *in vivo* localization of anti-Wagner osteogenic sarcoma antibodies, *Cancer (Philadelphia)*, 6, 619, 1953.
4. Korngold, L. and Pressman, D., The localization of antilymphosarcoma antibodies in the Murphy lymphosarcoma of the rat, *Cancer Res.*, 14, 96, 1954.
5. Gold, P. and Freedman, S. O., Demonstration of tumor-specific antigens in human colonic carcinomata by immunological tolerance absorption techniques, *J. Exp. Med.*, 121, 439, 1965.
6. Krupey, J., Gold, P., and Freedman, S. O., Physiochemical studies of the carcinoembryonic antigens of the human digestive system, *J. Exp. Med.*, 128, 387, 1968.
7. Wright, P. W., Hellström, K. E., Hellström, I. E., and Bernstein, I. D., Serotherapy in malignant disease, *Med. Clin. N. Am.*, 60, 607, 1976.
8. McKhann, C. F. and Gunnarsson, A., Approaches to immunotherapy, *Cancer (Philadelphia)*, 34, 1521, 1974.
9. Smith, R. T., Possibilities and problems of immunologic intervention in cancer, *N. Engl. J. Med.*, 287, 439, 1972.
10. Rubens, R. D., Antibodies as carriers of anticancer agents, *Lancet*, 498, 1974.
11. Shin, H. D., Pasternack, G. R., Economou, J. S., Johnson, R. J., and Hayden, M. L., Immunotherapy of cancer with antibody, *Science*, 194, 327, 1976.
12. Segerling, M., Ohanian, S. H., and Borsos, T., Chemotherapeutic drugs increase killing of tumor cells by antibody and complement, *Science*, 188, 55, 1975.
13. Order, S. E., Donahue, V., and Knapp, R., Immunotherapy of ovarian carcinoma — an experimental model, *Cancer (Philadelphia)*, 32, 573, 1973.
14. Kalis, N., Dynamics of immunologic enhancement, *Transplant Proc.*, 2, 59, 1970.

15. Hellström, K. E. and Hellström, I., Immunological enhancement as studied by cell culture techniques, *Annu. Rev. Microbiol.*, 24, 373, 1970.
16. Winchell, H. S., Mechanisms for localization of radiopharmaceuticals in neoplasms, *Semin. Nucl. Med.*, 6, 371, 1976.
17. Alastair, D., Simmons, R., and Perlmann, P., Carcinoembryonic antigen and blood group substances, *Cancer Res.*, 33, 313, 1973.
18. Spar, I. L., An immunologic approach to tumor imaging, *Semin. Nucl. Med.*, 6, 379, 1976.
19. Haynie, T. P., Konikowski, T., and Glenn, H. F., Experimental models for evaluation of radioactive tumor localizing agents, *Semin. Nucl. Med.*, 6, 347, 1976.
20. Day, E. D., Planinsek, J., Korngold, L., and Pressman, D., Tumor-localizing antibodies purified from antisera against Murphy rat lymphosarcoma, *J. Natl. Cancer Inst.*, 17, 517, 1956.
21. Pressman, D., Day, E. D., and Blau, M., The use of paired labeling in the determination of tumor-localizing antibodies, *Cancer Res.*, 17, 845, 1957.
22. Duran-Reynals, F., Studies on the localization of dyes and foreign proteins in normal and malignant tissues, *Am. J. Cancer*, 35, 98, 1939.
23. Bauer, F. K., Tubis, M., and Thomas, H. B., Accumulation of homologous radioiodinated albumin in experimental tumors, *Proc. Soc. Exp. Biol. Med.*, 90, 140, 1955.
24. Busch, H., Fujiwara, E., and Firszt, D. C., Studies on the metabolism of radioactive albumin in tumor-bearing rats, *Cancer Res.*, 21, 371, 1961.
25. Ghose, T., Nairn, R. C., and Fothergill, J. E., Uptake of proteins by malignant cells, *Nature (London)*, 1, 109, 1962.
26. Day, E. D., Planinsek, J. A., and Pressman, D., Localization *in vivo* of radioiodinated anti-rat-fibrin antibodies and radioiodinated rat fibrinogen in the Murphy rat lymphosarcoma and in other transplantable rat tumors, *J. Natl. Cancer Inst.*, 22, 413, 1959.
27. Bale, W. F., Spar, I. L., and Goodland, R. L., Experimental radiation therapy of tumors with ^{131}I-carrying antibodies to fibrin, *Cancer Res.*, 20, 1488, 1960.
28. Day, E. D., Planinsek, J. A., and Pressman, D., Localization of radioiodinated rat fibrinogen in transplanted rat tumors, *J. Natl. Cancer Inst.*, 23, 799, 1959.
29. Spar, I. L., Bale, W. F., Goodland, R. L., Casarett, G. W., and Michaelson, S. M., Distribution of injected I^{131}-labeled antibody to dog fibrin in tumor-bearing dogs, *Cancer Res.*, 20, 1501, 1960.
30. Spar, I. L., Bale, W. F., Goodland, R. L., and Izzo, M. J., Preparation of purified I^{131}-labeled antibody which reacts with human fibrin. Preliminary tracer studies on tumor patients, *Cancer Res.*, 24, 286, 1964.
31. Spar, I. L., Bale, W. F., Marrack, D., Dewey, W. C., McCardle, R. J., and Harper, P. V., ^{131}I-labeled antibodies to human fibrinogen, *Cancer (Philadelphia)*, 20, 865, 1967.
32. Peterson, H. I., Appelgren, K. L., and Rosengren, B. H. O., Experimental studies on the mechanism of fibrinogen uptake in a rat tumor, *Eur. J. Cancer*, 8, 677, 1972.
33. Ghose, T., Cerini, M., Carter, M., and Nairn, R. C., Immunoradioactive agent against cancer, *Br. Med. J.*, 1, 90, 1967.
34. Ghose, T. and Cerini, M., Radiosensitization of Ehrlich ascites tumor cells by a specific antibody, *Nature (London)*, 222, 993, 1969.
35. Ghose, T. and Nigam, S. P., Antibody as carrier of chlorambucil, *Cancer (Philadelphia)*, 29, 1398, 1972.
36. Ghose, T. and Guclu, A., Cure of a mouse lymphoma with radioiodinated antibody, *Eur. J. Cancer*, 10, 787, 1974.
37. Reif, A. E., Studies on the localization of radiolabeled antibodies to a mouse myeloma protein, *Cancer (Philadelphia)*, 27, 1433, 1971.
38. Pressman, D. and Watanabe, T., Tumor localization of radiolabeled antibodies raised by a mouse plasma cell tumor, *Immunochemistry*, 12, 581, 1975.
39. Izzo, M. J., Buchsbaum, D. J., and Bale, W. F., Localization of an I^{125}-labeled rat transplantation antibody in tumors carrying the corresponding antigen, *Proc. Soc. Exp. Biol. Med.*, 139, 1185, 1972.
40. Kellen, J. A. and Lo, J. S., Localization of ^{125}I-labeled antibodies against tumor-associated proteins from experimental rat mammary neoplasms, *Res. Commun. Chem. Pathol. Pharmacol.*, 5, 411, 1973.
41. Terman, D. S., Stewart, I., Tavel, A., and Kirch, D., Localization of neuroblastoma *in vivo* with tumor-specific antibodies, *Cancer Res.*, 35, 1761, 1975.
42. Primus, F. J., Wang, R. H., Goldenberg, D. M., and Hansen, H. J., Localization of human GW-39 tumors in hamsters by radiolabeled heterospecific antibody to carcinoembryonic antigen, *Cancer Res.*, 33, 2977, 1973.
43. Goldenberg, D. M., Preston, D. F., Primus, F. J., and Hansen, J. H., Photoscan localization of GW-39 tumors in hamsters using radiolabeled anticarcinoembryonic antigen immunoglobulin G., *Cancer Res.*, 34, 1, 1974.

44. Hoffer, P. B., Lathrop, K., Bekerman, C., Fang, V. S., and Refetoff, S., Use of ^{131}I-CEA antibody as a tumor scanning agent, *J. Nucl. Med.,* 15, 323, 1974.
45. Reif, A. E., Curtis, L. E., Duffield, R., and Shauffer, I. A., Trial of radiolabeled antibody localization in metastases of a patient with a tumor containing carcinoembryonic antigen (CEA), *J. Surg. Oncol.,* 133, 1974.
46. Primus, F. J., Wang, R. H., Cohen, E., Hansen, J. H., and Goldenberg, D. M., Antibody to carcinoembryonic antigen in hamsters bearing GW-39 human tumors, *Cancer Res.,* 36, 2176, 1976.
47. Primus, J., Bennett, S., Schmidt, D., Casper, S., and Goldenberg, D. M., Evidence for immune complexes in cancer patients receiving radioantibodies to carcinoembryonic antigen (CEA), in *American Association for Cancer Research Abstracts,* New York, 1979, 95.
48. Primus, F. J., MacDonald, R., Goldenberg, D. M., and Hansen, H. J., Localization of GW-39 human tumors in hamsters by affinity purified antibody to carcinoembryonic antigen, *Cancer Res.,* 37, 1544, 1977.
49. Goldenberg, D. M., DeLand, F., Kim, E., Bennett, S., Primus, F. J., vanNagell, J. F., Estes, N., DeSimone, P., and Rayburn, P., Use of radiolabeled antibodies to carcinoembryonic antigen for the detection and localization of diverse cancers by external photoscanning, *N. Engl. J. Med.,* 298, 1384, 1978.
50. DeLand, F. H., Kim, E. E., Primus, F. J., Casper, S., and Goldenberg, D. M., *In vivo* radioimmunodetection of neoplasms, *Cancer (Philadelphia),* 31, 1978.
51. Ghose, T., Guclu, A., Tai, J., MacDonald, A. S., Norvell, S. T., and Aquino, J., Antibody as carrier of ^{131}I in cancer diagnosis and treatment, *Cancer (Philadelphia),* 36, 1646, 1975.
52. Ghose, T., Tai, J., Aquino, J., Guclu, A., Norvell, S., and MacDonald, A., Tumor localization of ^{131}I-labeled antibodies by radionuclide imaging, *Radiology,* 116, 445, 1975.
53. Ghose, T., Tai, J., Guclu, A., Norvell, S. T., Bodurtha, A., Aquino, J., and MacDonald, A. S., Antibodies as carriers of radionuclides and cytotoxic drugs in the treatment and diagnosis of cancer, *Ann. N.Y. Acad. Sci.,* 277, 671, 1976.
54. Belitsky, P., Ghose, T., Aquino, J., Tai, J., and MacDonald, A. S., Radionuclide imaging of metastases from renal cell carcinoma by ^{131}I-labeled antitumor antibody, *Radiology,* 126, 515, 1978.
55. Belitsky, P., Ghose, T., Aquino, J., Norvell, S. T., and Blair, A. H., Radionuclide imaging of primary renal cell carcinoma by I[131]-labeled antitumor antibody, *J. Nucl. Med.,* 19, 427, 1978.
56. Ghose, T., Belitsky, P., Tai, J., and Janigan, D. T., Production and characterization of xenogeneic antisera to a human renal cell carcinoma associated antigen, *J. Natl. Cancer Inst.,* 63, 301, 1979.
57. Quinones, J., Mizejewski, G., and Beierwaltes, W. H., Choriocarcinoma scanning using radiolabeled antibody to chorionic gonadotrophin, *J. Nucl. Med.,* 12, 69.
58. Belliveau, R. E., Unpublished data, 1976.
59. Puri, S., Belliveau, R. E., Spencer, R. P., and Bachur, N. R., Prostaglandins in mice with neuroblastoma, *J. Nucl. Med.,* 16, 83, 1975.
60. Order, S. E., Blomer, W. D., Jones, A. G., Kaplan, W. D., Davis, M. A., Adelstein, S. J., and Hellman, S., Radionuclide immunoglobulin lymphangiography: a case report, *Cancer (Philadelphia),* 35, 1487, 1975.
61. DeLand, F. H., Kim, E. E., Corgan, R. L., Casper, S., Primus, F. J., Spremulli, E., Estes, N., and Goldenberg, D. M., Axillary lymphoscintigraphy by radioimmunodetection of carcinoembryonic antigen in breast cancer, *J. Nucl. Med.,* 20, 1243, 1979.
62. Ege, G. M., Internal mammary lymphoscintigraphy, *Radiology,* 118, 101, 2976.
63. Day, E. D., Immunological distribution analysis, *Res. Immunochem. Immunobiol.,* 3, 41, 1973.
64. Day, E. D. and Bigner, D. D., Specificity, cross-reactivity, and affinity of ^{125}I-labeled antiglioma antibodies for monolayers of cultured glioma cells, *Cancer Res.,* 33, 2362, 1973.
65. McGaughey, C., Feasibility of tumor immunoradiotherapy using radio-iodinated antibodies to tumor-specific cell membrane antigens with emphasis on leukemias and early metastases, *Oncology,* 29, 302, 1974.
66. Belliveau, R. E. and Witek, J. T., Possible therapeutic use of radiolabeled antibodies: a review, in *Therapy in Nuclear Medicine,* Spencer, R. P., Ed., Grune & Stratton, New York, 1978, 295.
67. Potchen, E. J., Elliott, A. J., Siegal, B. A., Studer, R., and Evens, R. G., Pathophysiologic basis of soft tissue tumor scanning, *J. Surg. Oncol.,* 3, 593, 1971.
68. DeDuve, C., DeBarsy, T., Poole, B., Trouet, A., Tulkens, P., and VanHoof, F., Lysosomotropic agents, *Biochem. Pharmacol.,* 23, 2495, 1974.
69. Day, E. D., Lassiter, S., and Fritz, R. B., Radioiodination of antibodies absorbed to insoluble antigens, *J. Immunol.,* 98, 67, 1967.
70. Mallinger, A. G., Jozwiak, E. L., and Carter, J. C., Preparation of Boron-containing bovine γ-globulin as a model compound for a new approach to slow neutron therapy of tumors, *Cancer Res.,* 32, 1947, 1972.

71. Spencer, R. A., Swan, J. M., DeBoer, W. G. R. M., Ghose, T., Nairn, R. C., Rolland, J. M., Ward, H. A., and Wright, S. H. B., A new immunoradioactive agent: ^{32}P-conjugated antibody, *Clin. Exp. Immunol.*, 3, 865, 1968.

72. Ghose, T. and Blair, A. H., Antibody-linked cytotoxic agents in the treatment of cancer: current status and future prospects, *J. Natl. Cancer Inst.*, 61, 657, 1978.

73. Hunter, W. M., Preparation and assessment of radioactive tracers, *Br. Med. Bull.*, 30, 18, 1974.

74. Carter, S. K., Immunotherapy of cancer in man, *Am. Sci.*, 64, 418, 1976.

75. Karpiak, S. E., Graf, L., and Rapport, M. M., Antiserum to brain gangliosides produces recurrent epileptiform activity, *Science*, 194, 735, 1976.

Chapter 13

CLINICAL CONSIDERATIONS
IN RADIOTRACER
BIODISTRIBUTION STUDIES

Robert Hodges

The use of radioisotope tracers in biological systems led to an understanding of the dynamic state of body constituents. The concept that chemical constituents in body fluids are usually within a narrow range suggested that deviation from these norms is indicative of a disease process. In addition to detecting variations in biological homeostasis in a wide variety of disease states, tracers allow the elucidation of complex metabolic and biosynthetic pathways and focus attention on concepts not previously considered.[1]

In a clinical situation, it is important to be aware of drug effects on the distribution of diagnostic tracers if any unusual behavior of the tracer is to be construed to be due to disease-induced effects. The intent of this paper is to address the potential for altered distribution of radiotracers due to the presence of pharmacologic agents.

A wide range of drug classes exert their pharmacological effect on the cell membrane. Groups such as neurohumors and their antagonists, local and general anesthetics, diuretics, antibiotics, steroids, fat-soluble vitamins, and many cations have supposed sites of action on the cell membrane. It is thought that many drugs can cause relatively major changes in the properties of cell membranes. It is likely that the large membrane permeability changes that occur with some drugs represent upheaval of the membrane ultrastructure such as the creation or enlargement of pores through which lipid-insoluble ions can pass.[2]

Concern about alterations to transport of tracers must not only consider effects on membrane permeability but also interactions of the tracer while it exists in particular compartments. For instance, many molecules and blood components found in the circulatory system can interact with tracers. Not only can plasma proteins bind with the tracer, but body tissue may produce antibodies to the tracer. The tracer may also interact with red blood cells, platelets, or neutrophils. The fate of the tracer is then dependent on the destiny of the blood component. For example, tracers that bind to serum may be faced with fewer available binding sites on plasma protein molecules if therapeutic doses of drugs which are highly protein bound are present in the blood pool. This could be expected to alter the biologic half-life of the tracer as larger numbers of the tracer molecules are free of binding and are available for interacting with cell membranes or to other agents in the bloodstream. Thus, consideration of drug effects on biodistribution of tracers must not only consider the direct effects on the tracer, but also the effect on biologic molecules, membranes, and cells that may interact with the tracer.

Tracer distribution may also be altered if molecules or ions are present which affect membrane permeability to the tracer. This may occur through a direct interaction between the pharmacologic agent and a particular cell membrane by creation of a channel of sufficient size and ionic charge to allow passage of the tracer. The pharmacologic agent can also enhance cellular expulsion of membrane-altering lysosomal enzymes, cause release of histamines, prostaglandins, or their precursors, or they may initiate chaotic activation of the complement cascade with intense ramifications for membrane function.

During phagocytosis, neutrophil membranes invaginate forming a vacuole where superoxide radical (O_2^-) is produced, however, much of the superoxide (SO) is produced on regions of the plasma membrane that remain on the exterior of the cell. These neutrophils release SO into extracellular fluid surrounding the cell. It is believed that cytotoxicity of SO plays a significant role in the inflammatory process.[3]

Superoxide is a product of biological reduction of oxygen. Xanthine oxidase produces superoxide as does aldehyde oxidase. Flavoenzyme dehydrogenases produce lesser amounts of superoxides.[3]

Free radicals are also produced after exposure to hyperoxia, ionizing radiation, during phagocytosis, and after administration of certain drugs and chemicals. When free radicals go unchecked, they can damage membrane lipids and even denature DNA.[4] Metals at active sites of enzymes are reduced by SO, suggesting that it may also reduce metallic tracers.[3]

Current concepts of cellular membranes include a general structure of a quasi-fluid, hydrated, phospholipid bilayer in which proteins have varying degrees of mobility. The bulk of membrane phospholipids are zwitterionic and are anionic at physiological pH. Anionic lipids bind divalent cations avidly, but without great specificity for individual ionic species. They also interact strongly with a variety of amphiphilic cationic species such as alkylamines, local anesthetics, and phenothiazine tranquilizers. The interactions of anionic lipids with divalent cations including Ca^{+2} and with amphiphilic cations are mutually competitive.[5]

The fundamental processes characteristic of the living state are all dependent at some critical stage on selective permeation at a membranous site. Selective permeation of cell membranes appears to depend upon selective movement of ions across the lipid barrier. There is a direct coupling of solute movement utilizing established ionic gradients.[6]

The most essential active function of membranes includes selective control of the movements of ions and other solutes, packaging and translocation of macromolecules, grouping and orientation of enzyme systems, and transmission of extracellular information to the cell interior.[5] Seventeen glycoenzymes have been identified on cell surfaces. Some are involved directly in transport across membranes and some prepare their substrates for transport by converting them to products which can be handled by other transport systems.[7]

While membranes are much less permeable to cations than to anions, it is known that immunological reactions alter the low cation permeability of membranes. In intact cells, cation permeability is a function of membrane structure and is interdependent with cellular metabolism. Membrane cation permeability may be modified by lectins or antibodies, by activation or inactivation of transport sites, or changes in kinetic parameters of transport processes.[8]

Because most neurotransmitters and drug molecules are cationic at physiologic pH, acidic lipids are likely candidates to serve in transport mechanisms, or to serve as binding sites themselves. Three roles for lipids have been described: (1) direct involvement in ligand binding, (2) serving as cofactors for the receptor, and (3) as regulators for the receptor-effector system, i.e., lipids that surround receptor molecules modulate the three-dimensional structure and regulate ligand affinity for the receptor or regulate the lateral mobility of the receptor and thus control the ligand-receptor complex interaction with an effector (second messenger) such as adenylate cyclase.[9]

Lipid bilayer membranes are highly impermeable to small inorganic ions. A variety of molecules, including the antibiotics valinomycin and nonactin, interact with lipid bilayer membranes and increase their permeability to small ions via a carrier mechanism comparable to the highly ion-permeable nerve membranes. Other membrane-modifying molecules, such as gramicidin A and alamethicin, facilitate the passive diffusion of ions by creating a pathway through the membrane through which ions can move down an electrochemical gradient. Other pore-forming antibiotics are nystatin and amphotericin B.[10]

There is extensive literature on the effects of anesthetics on the transmembrane flow of ions and neutral solutes. It appears that the anesthetics can increase or decrease passive and active flows. Facilitated diffusion or carrier-mediated translocation of glucose is inhibited by halothane, methoxyfluorane, ether, and various alcohols and detergents. Facilitated transfer of amino acids is inhibited by ethanol. It appears that neutral anesthetics increase passive cation diffusion, while positive anesthetics decrease it.[11]

A large variety of organic molecules show local anesthetic activity, suggesting that local anesthesia must result from a relatively nonspecific interaction rather than from a specific binding of the drug to a receptor in the membrane.[12] This is compatible with more recent concepts of receptors. The traditional "lock and key" model of membrane receptors has given way to the view that both the drug and receptor have three-dimensional flexibility and the surface topography of both can be varied by mutual inductive forces or by other chemical species in the vicinity. Current concepts of molecule-receptor interaction conform to usual chemical bonding phenomena, i.e., covalent, ionic, ion-dipole, hydrogen, and van der Waal bonding forces.[13]

Many, if not most, of the membrane actions of anesthetics and tranquilizers occur in both excitable and nonexcitable membranes. It is generally assumed that the primary actions of anesthetics are on the cell membrane rather than on intracellular processes.[11]

A relationship between local anesthetic potency and lipid solubility suggests that the primary effect of local anesthetics is on the lipid component of the cell membrane.[12] If the membrane contains lipids in both the gel and liquid-crystalline phases, the addition of anesthetic could, by lowering the lipid phase transition temperatures, trigger a change from the gel phase to the liquid-crystalline state resulting in an increase in fluidity of the membrane.[12]

When a lipid undergoes a phase transition, in addition to the fluidity, other physical parameters change, i.e., both lipid packing density and polar head groups are altered.[9] Membranes undergoing a phase transition have shown increased binding of proteins and fluorescent probes, as well as enhanced membrane transport of dyes and increased enzymatic activity.[14] The degree of membrane fluidity affects enzyme activity such as Ca^{+2}-ATPase, Na^+-K^+ ATPase and the B-galactoside transport system.[15] The resultant effect on the transport of tracers is open to speculation.

Following the discovery that cationic, amphiphilic drugs such as chlorpromazine (CPZ) enhance ^{32}P incorporation into phosphatidic acid and phosphatidylinositol, subsequent studies led to the realization that CPZ and other drugs such as local anesthetics, imipramine, amphetamines, and levorphanol act on phosphatidate phosphohydrolase in intact cells. These agents modify the pattern of incorporation of labeled glycerin into glycerolipids of liver lymphocytes. The ultimate effect is an increased cellular phosphatidylinositol content.

Phosphatidylinositol, a membrane phospholipid, binds divalent cations avidly, but without great specificity for individual ionic species. Affinity for monovalent cations is much lower.[5]

Great strides are being made in the understanding of the multiple roles that the Ca^{+2} ion plays in the regulation of cell function and membrane fluidity. Ionized calcium may be a mediator for a number of cell functions such as cellular and organellar motility or microtubule fluxes and may reflect surface membrane changes or other events which are closely related to cell function.[16]

Calcium plays a critical role in control of intracellular cyclic nucleotide concentrations through its ability to inhibit adenylcyclase, stimulate guanylcyclase, and regulate the phosphodiesterase regulator protein.[17]

Calcium and acidic phospholipids are intimately involved in excitatory mechanisms of biological membranes, and the displacement of membranous calcium leads to a functional instability of the membrane.[18]

It is likely that in biological membranes, Ca^{+2} control of permeability involves specific interactions of Ca^{+2} with proteins. Conformational changes in the protein by itself or in concert with surrounding lipids could be responsible for permeability changes.[19]

The di- and trivalent cations Mn^{+2}, Mg^{+2}, Co^{+2}, La^{+3}, and the organic molecules, methoxyverapamil and nifedipine, are calcium channel antagonists. Some data suggest that the calcium channels may possess gating mechanisms involving phosphatidylinositol breakdown as the initial event required to open calcium channels following agonist-receptor interactions.[17]

The organic calcium antagonists which have been developed may block entry of calcium ions from the outside to the inside of the cell and modify the effects of various calcium-dependent agonists. Quercitin and dantrolene are also Ca^{+2} antagonists.[17]

In the Ca^{+2} channel, divalent cations with ionic radii similar to Ca^{+2} may be expected to substitute for or act as antagonists of Ca^{+2} permeation. Both Sr^{+2} and Ba^{+2} can substitute for Ca^{+2}.[17]

Hormone-receptor interactions may lead to direct changes in the physical, electrical, and biological properties of the cell membrane. These alterations in membrane structure may have implications in the transport of other molecules.[20]

Liposome-cell interactions have induced changes in cell membrane composition and a variety of cellular activities. Charged liposomes alter the carrier-medicated transport of divalent anions. Data indicated a specific effect on the carrier and not a nonspecific increase in membrane permeability. Such properties as osmotic fragility, glycerol, and K^+ permeability and membrane microviscosity have been altered by liposome interactions with erythrocytes, platelets, normal lymphocytes, and leukemic cells. Liposome studies also show that the presence of acidic groups within the bilayer increase permeability to cations and decrease permeability to anions. The interactions between liposomes and cells can have profound effects on the properties of cell membranes.[21]

It is not yet possible to document the precise effect that the previously discussed factors may play in membrane transport, especially in regard to tracers; however, technological advances are making possible a much more detailed understanding of membrane permeability and transport of a variety of charged and neutral molecules and particulates. A few suspected drug interactions with radiotracers will be considered in light of the previous discussion of membrane transport, and factors sited as being important in biodistribution of drugs such as: (1) molecular size, (2) lipid solubility, (3) plasma protein binding, and (4) specific receptors. Changes in any of these factors may result in significant modifications of biochemical, biochemical precursor, and other small molecules which may be labeled with radioactive tracers.[22] Consideration of these factors will begin with brain imaging agents.

The effectiveness of most brain imaging agents depends upon distribution in extracellular spaces and exclusion from normal brain tissue.[23] It is believed that it is the blood-brain barrier (BBB) which protects the brain from unwanted molecules. This protection is lost when tumors, CVAs, abscesses, and other abnormalities destroy the integrity of the BBB resulting in unusual distribution of the labeled tracer.[24] This may be due to any of a number of resultant biochemical disturbances induced by ischemia, neovascularization, abnormal ion fluxes, pH gradients, altered membrane potentials, or infiltration by neutrophils which are capable of generating numerous powerful enzymes and peroxide radicals.

Pharmacological agents such as the anti-inflammatory steroids or agents which promote formation of cAMP can reduce the membrane reaction to pathological abnormalities. This may in turn reduce the degree of localization of tracers in the affected area. One example of this is the effect of dexamethasone which reduces the accumulation of some tracers in brain pathology.[25,26] Such steroids have well-known stabilizing effects on biological membranes.

Perchlorate has been used extensively to alter the uptake of pertechnetate in the choroid plexus. The ability of sodium perchlorate to attenuate or block the uptake of pertechnetate at its usual uptake sites has been advantageous, however, by blocking several secretion routes; concentrations in blood, tumor, and brain are generally increased. These levels decline more slowly and this leads to prolonged tissue concentrations.[27] This tissue redistribution of pertechnetate probably results, in part, from release of pertechnetate from plasma into red cells within 2 to 3 min after perchlorate administration.[28] Sodium periodate oxidation of membrane carbohydrates in intact cells seems to affect membrane permeability and induce cellular transformation.[8] Perchlorate would be expected to have similar effects on cell membranes.

More recently, a group of imaging agents has been developed to study glucose metabolism and oxygen utilization in the brain. This required tracers capable of crossing the BBB.[29] Such transport appears to be dependent on lipid/water partition coefficients based on a pH gradient. These agents are neutral and lipid soluble at blood pH. Because they are weak bases, they diffuse easily into brain cells where the lower pH results in the molecule picking up a hydrogen ion. This acquisition of a charge leaves the molecule no longer lipid soluble and thus cannot diffuse out of the cell. Many tissues have low intracellular pH, including metabolically active tissues such as brain, heart, and tumors. The unusually low pH associated with ischemic heart muscle suggests an important application in cardiology for these agents.[30] It would not be surprising if some of the agents capable of altering membrane fluidity or lipid content could affect the biodistribution of these unique agents.

A frequently used class of radiotracers may be classified as reticuloendothelial (RES) scanning agents. This class consists of a variety of labeled particulates. Localization of these agents depends on a functional RES. A number of pharmacological agents and other factors can affect the integrity of the RES.

Heparin may theoretically affect the RES function according to at least four mechanisms: (1) interaction with the surface of the particle directly, (2) interaction with plasma opsonins, (3) binding to the cell surface of macrophages, and (4) influencing the lysosomal enzyme activity of the macrophage. Heparin, injected i.v., has been shown to accumulate mainly in the RES, suggesting that it may affect phagocytic activity at the cellular level. Heparin depressed the internalization of microaggregated albumin particles by the RES which could be attributed to an increase in the negative charge density of the macrophage cell surface resulting in an impaired attachment of the negatively charged albumin particles.[31]

Injection of endotoxin which is a known RES stimulator causes a 20-fold increase in the deposition of ^{99m}Tc-SC in the lungs relative to the liver. Bone marrow deposition is also enhanced.[32] The effect of Gram-negative endotoxin on capillary permeability is complex and involves antigen-antibody reactions, the participation of platelets and polymorphonuclear leukocytes, as well as the release of various permeability altering substances such as lysosomal enzymes and histamines.[33]

Animal studies have shown that macrophages normally migrate from the liver, spleen, and bone marrow to the lungs, where some of them pass through the capillary walls and provide a source of alveolar macrophages. In animals, macrophages migrate to the lungs in unusually large numbers in response to certain types of stress and continue to phagocytize colloid after reaching pulmonary capillaries.[34]

One of the complement components is thought to activate granulocytes to produce microbicidal oxygen radicals (superoxide and hydrogen peroxide). It is believed that these radicals may act as attractants for other phagocytes in the area. A serious complication of shock is thought to be due to prolonged activation of complement. One of the features of shock is a unique plugging of the lung microvasculature by granulocytes and monocytes. Pulmonary abnormalities occurring in hemodialyzed patients produced similar, but less pronounced, pulmonary abnormalities. It is possible that complement activation occurs as plasma flows over the cellophane dialyzer coils of the hemodialysis apparatus.[35] Such a phenomenon is not surprising when it is realized that dialyzer cellophane is a polysaccharide like zymosan, inulin, and endotoxin, all of which are capable of activating complement.[36]

Free radicals of oxygen are generated by granulocytes during complement interaction. These radicals are responsible for the endothelial damage. Although endotoxin has no deleterious effects alone, significant damage occurs when it is added with granulocytes, especially in the presence of complement fresh serum.[35]

One possible interference in phagocytosis is the altered state of microtubules that develops between phagocytic vacuoles and lysosomes. Drugs with this capability are colchicine and vinblastin. These drugs have been shown to inhibit urate crystal phagocytosis, intracellular digestion, redistribution of granule associated hydrolases, and antigen-induced release of histamines.[37]

Renal accumulation of SC has been reported in renal transplant patients during rejection and during episodes of acute tubular necrosis.[38] Several of the commonly used antibiotics, especially kanamycin, are known to cause acute tubular necrosis.[39]

Increasing velocity of blood flow is without significant effect on tracer deposition on osteoid surfaces; however, if sympathetic nervous control of microvasculature is blocked, vessels that are normally closed now open up and areas of osteoid not normally exposed to tracer are now able to participate in tracer uptake. Studies show that bone is highly sensitive to changes in extraction efficiency resulting from hormonal alterations. Both hyperparathyroidism and hyperthyroidism give "superscans" of high contrast.[40]

Unusual renal parenchymal concentrations of ^{99m}Tc PPi have been observed in children being treated with cyclophosphamide, vincristine, and doxorubicin. Within hours of i.v. injection, about 50% of the tracer is excreted in the urine. Because of the high urinary radioactivity, renal, urinary tract, and bladder abnormalities are sometimes observed during bone imaging in patients taking drugs which may damage renal tubules.[41]

Calcitonin is a hormone which inhibits bone resorption and is known to cause suppression of elevated urinary hydroxyproline excretion. Kinetic studies indicate that calcitonin may have a significant effect on ^{99m}Tc diphosphonate (DP) clearance from blood. This would give rise to an increased rapidity of blood clearance of the tracer. At the same time, bladder activity was observed earlier in the calcitonin-treated patients, possibly due to a decrease in the proximal renal tubular reabsorption of electrolytes in patients with Paget's disease.[42]

The administration of 1.25 mg of vitamin D_3 intravenously in rats caused a significant decrease in the uptake of ^{99m}Tc PPi and ^{99m}TcDP by bone. Administration of 1.25 mg of dihydrotachysterol by stomach tube caused a significant increase in the ratio: uptake of ^{99m}Tc PPi by myocardial infarct/uptake by bone.[43]

Parathyroid hormone (PTH) elevation in serum has been observed to increase urinary excretion of ^{99m}Tc PPi.[44] This suggests at least a potential that drugs which influence PTH levels may have some effect on excretion of ^{99m}Tc PPi.

Altered distribution of the bone agents DP and PPi has been observed in the presence of Ca^{+2} and Fe (II). These metal ions may facilitate the dissociation of the ^{99m}Tc from the carrier ligand, producing both ^{99m}Tc deposition at the reaction site as well as translocation to other tissues, possibly with the migrant ^{99m}Tc bound to another ligand. The formation of CaEHDP complexes in the presence of calcium gluconate could release ^{99m}Tc followed by scavenging of the liberated ^{99m}Tc by gluconate to form a ligand with renal imaging properties. In the absence of gluconate, the CaEHDP reaction produced a significant amount of liver agent, possibly colloidal ^{99m}TcO$_2$. Such transchelation may account for the fact that PPi and DP are effective imaging agents for myocardial infarction. Other potential drug interactions are suggested by the fact that ^{99m}Tc (Sn) at high pH in the presence of appropriate dihydroxyglycols other than gluconate, such as glucoheptonate, mannitol, ethylene glycol, and glycerol all give essentially the same tissue distribution as observed with ^{99m}Tc gluconate.[45] Numerous glycols are present in pharmaceuticals.

Additional reports of the effect of iron on tissue distribution of phosphorus-containing bone agents suggests a relationship between the degree of iron overload and the decrease in skeletal uptake. Patients with a history of transfusion and hemochromatosis showed reduced skeletal uptake of bone agent which correlated with the degree of expected iron overload in these patients.[46]

Liver uptake of ^{99m}Tc-Sn-EHDP has been demonstrated in the presence of Al^{+3} ions possibly leached from the technetium generator. This was believed to be due to the formation of a colloidal complex, although no particles were visible under light microscopy.[47] Plasma aluminum levels have been reported to rise markedly during ingestion of aluminum hydroxide, carbonate, and aminoacetate.[48]

When tin complex (DP or PPi) is administered prior to pertechnetate, the distribution of the tracer is altered, the concentration in cerebral pathology is reduced, the concentration in mucus cells by stomach, thyroid, and salivary glands and the choroid plexus is increased, and there is a shift of pertechnetate from plasma to the red blood cells.[49]

An atypical bone scan was reported with ^{99m}Tc DP on a patient receiving phosphosoda. The scan was characterized by poor skeletal uptake with increased tracer activity in the stomach, thyroid, and lungs. It is possible that the poor bone uptake of the tracer might result from saturation of bone binding sites by phosphate ions from the phospho-soda preparation.[50]

Oily lymphangiographic contrast material preceding total-body ^{67}Ga citrate scanning has resulted in radionuclide accumulation in the lungs. This may be due to an irritant effect of contrast material on pulmonary parenchyma.[51] Another example of ^{67}Ga uptake due to irritant effects of drugs is the production of pseudomembranous colitis by drugs such as clindamycin. This syndrome is known to accumulate ^{67}Ga.[52]

There has been a reported case of diethylstilbestrol (DES) induced gynecomastia with resultant breast uptake of ^{99m}Tc DP which could lead to misinterpretation as rib metastasis.[63] Methylprednisolone has been shown to accelerate PPi blood clearance, lowering blood, and normal myocardial PPi levels.[54]

The anthracycline antibiotics, such as doxorubicin, are widely used as anticancer agents. These agents are known for their tendency to produce serious myocardial damage. Abnormal ^{99m}Tc PPi accumulation has been observed in patients undergoing treatment for neoplasia with this drug.[55]

There is a definite association between therapeutic irradiation of the left hemithorax and increased localization of ^{99m}Tc PPi in the cardiac region. This is consistent with the known pathological effects of radiation of the great and major arteries.[56]

It is of interest to note that doxorubicin is known to induce peroxidation of cardiac lipids by the formation of free radicals.[57] Free radical-lipid peroxidation occurs under a variety of circumstances, including vitamin E deficiency, intoxication with carbon tetrachloride, exposure to ionizing radiation, carcinogenesis, the aging process, and possibly hyperlipidemia accompanying atherosclerosis.[58] Peroxidation is also observed during degranulation of leukocytes and platelets. As noted earlier, free radicals can have intense effects on cell membranes.

Attack by oxidants on a relatively small number of critical features of membranes such as thiols and amines could result in secondary effects, for example, membrane enzyme inhibition due to structural rearrangement near active sites.[59]

Lipid peroxides formed by radiation exposure have been reported to have effects on nucleic acids and biological membranes.[60]

Insulin and 20% glucose given with K, Rb, and Cs leads to a significant increase in myocardial uptake of these radionuclides and also prolongs the myocardial half-life of ^{131}I oleic acid.[61]

The combination of insulin in hypertonic glucose has been used clinically to alter the extra-to-intracellular potassium distribution in patients and also has been used to ameliorate the effects of ischemic myocardium. Rapid injection of 20% glucose can quickly lower circulating K levels and has a direct effect on transmembrane potential. Insulin may alter myocardial ion transport and enhance inorganic phosphate uptake in the liver, which may be accompanied by intracellular K migration.[62]

The following effects of insulin on the cell membrane have been reported:

1.   Stimulation of transport of sugar, amino acids, fatty acids, ions, and nucleic acid precursors
2.   Activation and inhibition of enzymes
3.   Change of membrane potential, and
4.   Alterations of cell surface morphology

Similar alterations have been reported in the cytosol, endoplasmic reticulum, ribosomes, mitochondria, lysosomes, and nucleus.[63]

Researchers are making dramatic discoveries about drug action mechanisms and are rapidly developing the expertise and technology to modify naturally occurring and synthetic biologically active molecules, and it is likely that entirely new classes of pharmacologic agents are on the horizon.

Medical practice in the computer age will leave little to chance, and subjective evaluation of patient progress will bow to evaluations based upon monitoring of predetermined biological parameters which will be subjected to a detailed computer analysis.

It is likely that radionuclides will play an ever-expanding role in medicine of the future. Because of the increasing use of cyclotron-produced, ultra-short-lived radionuclides involving great expense, there is a heightened importance for an awareness of all variables which have a potential for influencing or invalidating test results. The burden for evaluating the potential interferences not only of existing, but also of new generations of pharmaceuticals with nuclear medicine procedures, logically belongs to the nuclear medicine practitioner. A simple recognition of the need to consider the possible interferences of drugs with the localization of radiotracers is inadequate. Concrete efforts must be made to identify the cause of the occasional aberrant scan. Such as effort will require a systematic effort to correlate medications received by a large number of patients with the quality of scan results. When studies of this type become commonplace, rapid strides will be made in understanding mechanisms of tracer uptake, as well as drugs and other influences which may alter tracer behavior.

REFERENCES

1. **Wagner, H. N.**, Outline of the past and future of nuclear medicine, in *The Chemistry of Radiopharmaceuticals*, Masson Publishing, New York, 1978, chap. 1.

2. **Cuthbert, A. W.**, Membrane lipids and drug action, *Pharmacol. Rev.*, 19, 59, 1967.

3. **McCord, J. M. and Fridovich, I.**, The biology and pathology of oxygen radicals, *Ann. Int. Med.*, 89, 122, 1978.

4. **Oski, F.**, Vitamin E — a radical defense, *N. Engl. J. Med.*, Aug., 454, 1980.

5. **Michell, R. H.**, Inositol phosphopipids and cell surface receptor function, *Biochem. Biophys. Acta*, 415, 81, 1975.

6. **Urry, D. W.**, Basic aspects of calcium chemistry and membrane interaction; on the messenger role of calcium, *Ann. N. Y. Acad. Sci.*, 307, 3, 1978.

7. **Riordan, J. R. and Forstner, G. C.**, Glycoprotein membrane enzymes, *Current Topics in Membranes and Transport, Vol. II, Cell Surface Glycoproteins; Structure, Biosynthesis and Biological Functions*, Academic Press, New York, 1978, 146.

8. **Lauf, P. K.**, Antigen-antibody reactions and cation transport in biomembranes; immunophysiological aspects, *Biochem. Biophys. Acta*, 415, 173, 1975.

9. **Loh, H. H. and Law, P. Y.**, The role of membrane lipids in receptor mechanisms, *Ann. Rev. Pharmacol. Toxicol.*, 20, 201, 1980.

10. **Eisenberg, N., Kleinberg, M. E., and Shaper, J. H.**, Channels across black lipid membranes, *Electrical Properties of Biological Polymers, Water and Membranes*, 303, 281, 1977.

11. **Seeman, P.**, The membrane actions of anesthetics and tranquilizers, *Pharmacol. Rev.*, 24, 583, 1972.

12. **Lee, A. G.**, Local anesthesia; the interaction between phospholipids and chlorpromazine, propranolol and practolol, *Mol. Pharmacol.*, 13, 474, 1977.

13. **Gringauz, A.**, Selected classes of drugs — how do they work?, *U. S. Pharmacist*, 4, 55, 1979.

14. **Papahadjopoulos, D., Vail, W. J., Newton, C., Nir, S., Jacobson, K., Poste, G., and Lazo, R.**, Studies on membrane fusion. III. The role of calcium-induced phase changes, *Biochem. Biophys. Acta*, 465, 579, 1977.

15. **Rimon, G., Hanski, E., Braun, S., and Levitzki, A.**, Mode of coupling between hormone receptors and adenylate cyclase elucidated by modulation of membrane fluidity, *Nature (London)*, 276, 394, 1978.

16. **O'Flaherty, J. T., Showell, H. J., Becker, E. L., and Ward, P. A.**, Substances which aggregate neutrophils, *Am. J. Pathol.*, 92, 155, 1978.

17. **Middleton, E.**, Antiasthmatic drug therapy and calcium ions; review of pathogenesis and role of calcium, *J. Pharm. Sci.*, 69, 243, 1980.

18. **Rubin, R. P. and Laychock, S. G.**, Prostaglandins and calcium-membrane interactions in secretory glands, *Ann. N. Y. Acad. Sci.*, 307, 377, 1978.

19. **Schulz, I. and Heil, K.**, Ca^{+2} control of electrolyte permeability in plasma membrane vesicles from cat pancreas, *J. Membr. Biol.*, 46, 41, 1979.

20. **Pollet, R. J. and Levey, G. S.**, Principles of membrane receptor physiology and their application to clinical medicine, *Ann. Int. Med.*, 92, 663, 1980.

21. **Fry, D. W., White, J. C., and Goldman, I. D.**, Alterations of the carrier-mediated transport of an anionic solute, methotrexate, by charged liposomes in Ehrlich ascites tumor cells, *J. Membr. Biol.*, 50, 123, 1979.

22. **Burns, H. D., Worley, P., Wagner, H. N., Jr., Marzilli, L., and Risch, V.**, Design of technetium radiopharmaceuticals, *The Chemistry of Radiopharmaceuticals*, Masson Publishing, New York, 1978, 269.

23. **Harper, P. V., Lathrop, K. A., and Gottschalk, A.**, Pharmacodynamics of some technetium-99m preparations, *Radio-active Pharmaceuticals*, Symposium, Oak Ridge Institute of Nuclear Study, Oak Ridge, Tenn., 1965.

24. **Matin, P.**, *Handbook of Clinical Nuclear Medicine*, Medical Examination Publishing Company, Garden City, N.Y., 1977.

25. **Marty, R. and Cain, M. L.**, Effects of corticosteroid (dexamethasone) administration on the brain scan, *Radiology*, 107, 117, 1973.

26. **Stebner, F. C.**, Steroid effect on the brain scan in a patient with cerebral metastases, *J. Nucl. Med.*, 16, 320, 1975.

27. **Konikowski, T. and Haynie, T. P.**, The effect of perchlorate on the localization of 99mTc-pertechnetate in a mouse brain sarcoma, *J. Nucl. Med.*, 11, 443, 1970.

28. **Oldendorf, W. H., Sisson, W. B., and Iisaka, Y.**, Affect of perchlorate ion on distribution of $99mTcO_4$ to plasma protein binding, *J. Nucl. Med.*, 11, 85, 1970.

29. **Loberg, M. D.**, Radiotracers for cerebral function imaging; a new class, *J. Nucl. Med.*, 21, 183, 1980.

30. Kung, H. F. and Blau, M., Regional intracellular pH shift; a proposed new mechanism for radio-pharmaceutical uptake in brain and other tissue, *J. Nucl. Med.*, 21, 147, 1980.

31. Berghem, L. E., Ahlgren, L. T., Grundfeldt, M.-B., Lahnborg, G., and Schildt, B. E., Heparin-induced impairment of phagocytic and catabolic functions of the reticuloendothelial system in rats, *J. Reticuloendothel. Soc.*, 23, 21, 1978.

32. Keyes, J. W., Jr., Wilson, G. A., and Quinonest, J. D., An evaluation of lung uptake of colloid during liver imaging, *J. Nucl. Med.*, 14, 687, 1973.

33. Clawson, C. C., Hartmann, J. F., and Vernier, R. L., Electron microscopy of the effect of gram-negative endotoxin on the blood-brain barrier, *J. Comp. Neurol.*, 127, 183.

34. Klingensmith, W. C., III, Ryerson, T. W., and Corman, J. L., Lung uptake of 99mTc-sulfur colloid in organ transplantation, *J. Nucl. Med.*, 14, 757, 1973.

35. Jacob, H. S., *The Role of Complement and Granulocytes in Septic Shock*, Upjohn, Kalamazoo, Mich., 1978.

36. Craddock, P. R., Fehir, J., Dalmasso, A. P., Brigham, K. L., and Jacob, H. S., Pulmonary vascular leukostasis resulting from complement activation by dialyzer cellophane membranes, *J. Clin. Invest.*, 59, 879, 1977.

37. Weissman, G., Dukor, P., and Zurier, R. B., Effect of cyclic AMP on release of lysosomal enzymes from phagocytes, *Nature (London) New Biol.*, 231, 131, 1971.

38. Kim, Y. C., Massari, P. U., Brown, M. L., Thrall, J. H., Chang, B., and Keyes, J. W., Clinical significance of 99mTc technetium sulfur colloid accumulation in renal transplant patients, *Radiology*, 124, 745, 1977.

39. Goodman, L. S. and Gilman, A., *The Pharmacological Basis of Therapeutics*, 4th ed., MacMillan, New York, 1970, 1287.

40. Harkes, C., Mechanisms of skeletal tracer uptake, *J. Nucl. Med.*, 20, 794, 1979.

41. Lutrin, C. L., McDougall, I. R., and Goris, M. L., Intense concentration of technetium-99m pyro-phosphate in the kidneys of children treated with chemotherapeutic drugs for malignant disease, *Radiology*, 128, 165, 1978.

42. Waxman, A. D., Ducker, S., McKee, D., Slemsen, J. K., and Singer, F. R., Evaluation of 99mTc diphosphonate kinetics and bone scans in patients with Paget's disease before and after calcitonin treatment, *Radiology*, 125, 761, 1977.

43. Carr, E. A., Jr., Carroll, M., and Montes, M., The use of adjunctive drugs to alter uptake of 99mTc-Sn-pyrophosphate by myocardial lesions and bone, *Life Sci.*, 22, 1261, 1978.

44. Krishnamurthy, G. T., Bland, W. H., and Brickman, A. S., Technetium-99mTc-Sn-pyrophosphate pharmacokinetics and bone image changes in parathyroid disease, *J. Nucl. Med.*, 18, 236, 1977.

45. McRae, J., Hambright, P., and Bearden, A. J., Chemistry of Tc99m tracers; II. In vitro conversion of tagged HEDP and pyrophosphate (bone seekers) into gluconate (renal agent). Effects of Ca and Fe(II) on in vivo distribution, *J. Nucl. Med.*, 17, 208, 1976.

46. Parker, J. A., Jones, A. G., Davis, M. A., McIlmoyle, G., and Tow, D. E., Reduced uptake of bone-seeking radiopharmaceuticals related to iron excess, *Clin. Nucl. Med.*, 1, 267, 1976.

47. Chaudhuri, T. K., Liver uptake of 99mTc-diphosphonate, *Radiology*, 119, 485, 1976.

48. Kaehny, W. D., Hegg, A. P., and Alfrey, A. C., Gastrointestinal absorption of aluminum from aluminum-containing antacids, *N. Engl. J. Med.*, 296, 1389, 1977.

49. Ancri, D., Lonchampt, M., and Basset, J., The effect of tin on the tissue distribution of 99mTc-sodium pertechnetate, *Radiology*, 124, 445, 1977.

50. Saha, G. B., Herzberg, D. L., and Boyd, C. M., Unusual in vivo distribution of 99mTc-diphosphon-ate, *Clin. Nucl. Med.*, 2, 303, 1977.

51. Lentle, B. C., Castor, W. R., Khaliq, A., and Dierich H., The effect of contrast lymphangiography on localization of 67Ga-citrate, *J. Nucl. Med.*, 16, 374, 1975.

52. Tedesco, F. J., Coleman, R. E., and Siegel, B. A., Gallium citrate Ga67 accumulation in pseudomem-branous colitis, *JAMA*, 235, 59, 1976.

53. Brill, D. P., Gynecomastia demonstrated on the bone scan, *J. Urol.*, 118, 62, 1977.

54. Schneider, R. M., Downing, S. E., Berger, H. J., Donabedian, H. K., and Zaret, B. L., Effect of methyl prednisolone upon abnormal 99mTc pyrophosphate myocardial uptake following transtho-racic DC countershock, *Circulation*, 53, 54, (Suppl. II,) 218, 1976.

55. Chacko, A. K., Gordon, D. H., Bennett, J. M., O'Mara, R. E., and Wilson, G. A., Myocardial imaging with Tc-99m pyrophosphate in patients on adriamycin treatment for neoplasia, *J. Nucl. Med.*, 18, 680, 1977.

56. Soin, J. S., Cox, J. D., Youker, J. E., and Swartz, H. M., Cardiac localization of 99mTc(Sn) pyro-phosphate following irradiation of the chest, *Radiology*, 124, 165, 1977.

57. Henderson, I. C. and Frey, E., III, Adriamycin and the heart, *N. Engl. J. Med.*, 300, 310, 1979.

58. Moncada, S. and Vane, J. R., Arachidonic acid metabolites and the interaction between platelets and blood-vessel walls, *N. Engl. J. Med.*, 300, 1142, 1979.

59. Koontz, A. E. and Heath, R. L., Ozone alteration of transport of cations and the Na + /K + -ATPase in human erythrocytes, *Arch. Biochem. Biophys.*, 198, 493, 1979.

60. Inouye, B., Aono, K., Iida, S., and Utsumi, K., Influence of superoxide generating system, Vitamin E and superoxide dismutase on radiation consequences, *Physiol. Chem. Phys.*, 11, 151, 1979.

61. Schelbert, H. R., Ashburn, W. L., Depew, M. C., and Halpren, S. E., Comparative myocardial uptake of intravenously administered radionuclides, *J. Nucl. Med.*, 15, 1092, 1974.

62. Olefsky, J. M., *The Relationship Between Receptor Sites, Insulin Resistance and the Treatment of Diabetes Mellitus*, Upjohn, Kalamazoo, Mich., 1980.

Chapter 14

THE MEASUREMENT OF TRANSPORT IN VIVO USING RADIOTRACERS

Brian M. Gallagher

TABLE OF CONTENTS

I. INTRODUCTION

The primary challenge in attempting to measure transport across a particular cell membrane from the circulating fluid is in the design of a suitable radiotracer. This design problem has been largely circumvented by employing naturally occurring substrates of known endogenous biomolecules. Labeling is achieved without the destruction of the biological activity by employing the various positron-emitting isotopes of the elements carbon-11, nitrogen-13, oxygen-15, or analogues of naturally occurring substrates labeled with fluorine-18, such as 2-deoxy-2-fluoro-D-glucose.[1-5] The activity distribution within discrete tissue volumes can be precisely determined using positron emission transaxial tomography in vivo and related to the transport properties of the substrate being studied.[6] Since these compounds are usually of known biological function with well-defined metabolic and transport properties, the primary focus of these studies has involved observations of the changes in the spatial distribution of the radiotracer as a function of time. This can be applied to both normal and abnormal states in humans and the rates of accumulation related to transport and metabolic functions. These types of studies permit truly in vivo biochemical measurements in a wide variety of disease states. Of greater difficulty, however, is the design of new radiotracers which may mimic naturally occurring biomolecules in their transport properties or display unique localization properties, but employ the more widely available nuclides.

II. RADIOTRACER TRANSPORT

The distribution of any drug introduced into an organism depends upon a complex series of physical and chemical processes which are often interrelated. These processes remove and dilute the substance from its point of entry, carry it to the various body tissues, permit it to diffuse or be actively transported across several membranes, and determine its accumulation, disposition, and excretion by the organism. The concentration of a substance within an organ with time depends upon the integrated arterial blood concentration, the proportion of cardiac output perfusing the tissue, the physical processes occurring at the capillary endothelium (e.g., solubility and diffusion), and the chemical processes which may involve active or facilitated transport, receptor binding, and metabolism. Several of these processes are determined in part by the nature of the capillary endothelium within a given tissue. Although the capillary blood volume represents less than 5% of the volume of most tissues,[7] the large surface area provided by this tissue determines the uptake of many drugs. The capillary endothelium of most vertebrate tissues and organs consists of a single layer of flattened cells bound together with an acellular basal lamina.[8] Materials may penetrate this structure by passing directly through the cells, that is, through two thicknesses of cell membrane and a layer of cytoplasm; or they may penetrate without entering the cells, by extracellular channels which extend through the cells; or lastly, through the junctions between them (fenestrated capillaries). Most compounds leave the blood by a combination of these pathways and the exact mechanism varies within a given tissue.[8]

A. pH Partitioning of Se Diamines

The rate at which a drug leaves the bloodstream will depend also upon its lipid solubility (partition coefficient), its molecular weight, and the physical state of association with plasma proteins. If it is bound to macromolecules, its rate of transcapillary passage will be determined either by that of the protein and/or the dynamic equilibrium which may exist between bound and free drug in the plasma. Most drugs contain acidic or basic groups. The position of equilibrium between the neutral and anionic or cationic species is mainly a function of the local pH, since shifts in the position of

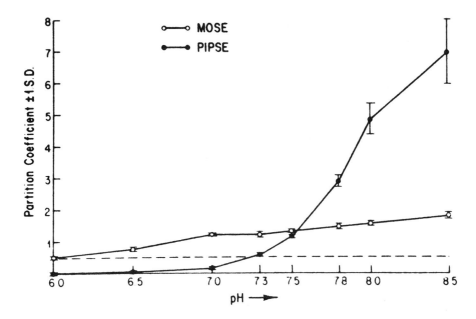

FIGURE 1. Partition coefficients for Se-diamines as a function of pH in an *n*-octanol/water system. Compounds showing values above the dotted line (0.5) generally cross the blood-brain barrier, whereas those below cannot. (From Kung, H. F. and Blau, M., *J. Nucl. Med.*, 21, 147, 1980. With permission.)

equilibrium due to proton transfer are usually very rapid. Dipolar ions (e.g., amino acids) present a separate problem. Thus, interaction with receptor sites is partly a function of pH, pK_a, or pK_b. These ionized groups interact strongly with water dipoles and charged plasma proteins and consequently penetrate lipid cell membranes poorly or not at all. Thus, drugs that are partially ionized at body pH enter cells at rates that are strongly pH dependent.[9] When diffusion is the most significant factor governing transport, the concentration gradient of the neutral form almost solely determines the rate of penetration.[10] This well-known concept, termed the pH partition hypothesis,[11] has been recently exploited to design radiotracers to permeate the intact blood-brain barrier (BBB).[12,13] These compounds include PIPSE and MOSE,

PIPSE

MOSE

which are diamines that incorporate the bases piperidine and morpholine, respectively, and contain two N-substituted amines attached via ethyl groups to a central selenium atom. Since many tissues, such as the highly metabolic tissues of the brain, heart, and tumors, have a relatively lower intracellular pH compared to the plasma,[14] these compounds were designed to exist largely in the neutral form at plasma pH 7.4. In the case of PIPSE, the conversion of the neutral to the charged species between pH 7.5 and 7.0 is quite great (Figure 1). Thus, there exists a pH gradient between the brain at pH 7.0 to 7.1 and the blood at ∼pH 7.4, and PIPSE should diffuse into the brain and remain trapped intracellularly through rapid protonation. MOSE, on the other hand, is much less subject to protonation over this pH range, and since it is quite lipophilic, should also diffuse into the brain but would back diffuse relatively faster than PIPSE. This can be expressed diagrammatically:

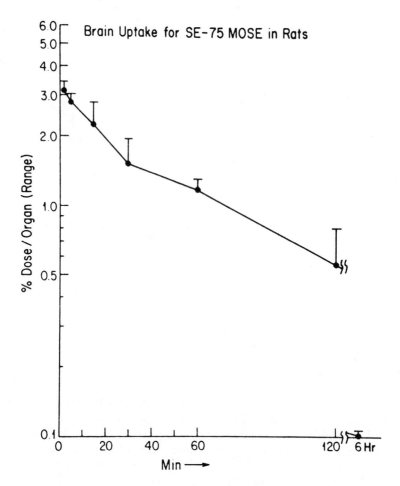

FIGURE 2.   The uptake and clearance of radioactivity in rat brain following the injection of ⁷⁵Se-MOSE. (From Kung, H. F. and Blau, M., *J. Nucl. Med.*, 21, 147, 1980. With permission.)

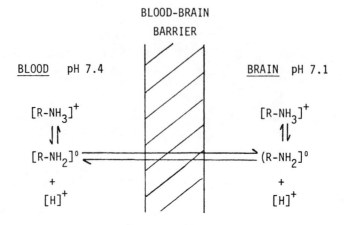

These two radiotracers have been studied in mice and rats and the initial brain uptake is quite high (Figures 2 and 3), with MOSE showing ∼3% of the injected dose initially and the less lipophilic PIPSE showing a slower accumulation which reaches a maximum of ∼1.5% of the dose at about 2 hr.[12,13] MOSE clears from the brain much more

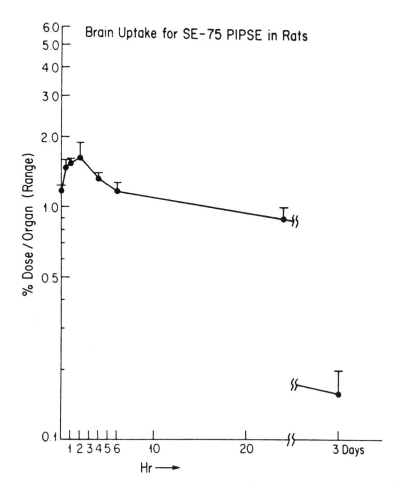

FIGURE 3. The uptake and clearance of radioactivity in rat brain following the injection of ^{75}Se-PIPSE. Note the much slower clearance compared to MOSE. (From Kung, H. F. and Blau, M., *J. Nucl. Med.*, 21, 147, 1980. With permission.)

rapidly, with a $t_{1/2}$ of $\sim$30 min, whereas PIPSE clears over a period of days. This very slow clearance of PIPSE exceeds the rates predicted on the basis of the pH partition hypothesis, however, and suggests possible intracellular binding and/or metabolism to be involved.[15] It does appear that these two radiotracers do initially distribute into the brain in accord with the pH partition hypothesis and, in principle, could be utilized for the differential measurement of regional intracellular pH in the brain. This should employ single photon transaxial tomographic instrumentation and more suitable isotopes such as ^{99m}Tc and [123]I. It is necessary for future studies to vary intracellular pH through experimental intervention and determine the effect on regional PIPSE distribution to demonstrate the utility of agents which localize via this mechanism.

B. [81m]Kr

Tomographic reconstruction methods are particularly important for the functional assessment of transport in a heterogeneous organ such as the brain, since conventional two-dimensional imaging methods frequently show a uniform distribution of activity due to superimposition of information above and below the plane of interest. The use of [81m]Kr for the tomographic assessment of cerebral perfusion in humans has been recently demonstrated.[16] The technique involves the continuous infusion of ^{81m}Kr via the internal carotid artery and images of the head are collected by means of a commercial imaging system designed for single-photon computerized tomography. The 13-sec $t_{1/2}$ of ^{81m}Kr is ideal for such studies because the short physical half-life prohibits equilibration of the highly diffusible tracer within the brain. Thus the tissue distribution of this tracer reflects regional perfusion. Using this technique, it has been possible to demonstrate the elevation in cerebral blood flow to the motor cortex of the brain relative to the other neural centers following hand movement.[16] These results are most exciting, and the extension of similar methods using other radiotracers labeled with single-photon nuclides provides a powerful tool for the measurement of transport in vivo.

C. Brain Uptake Index

The net transport of a solute from the blood to an organ such as the brain is the result of serial kinetic steps involving its initial transfer across the capillaries, uptake by the cells, and subsequent metabolic steps. Two methods which have been used to discriminate between the capillary transfer step and the slower steps include the indicator dilution technique and the brain uptake index (BUI).[11] With each technique, an experimental compound and a reference compound are mixed and then co-injected into the carotid artery of an animal. The indicator dilution method measures the loss of the test compound from samples of the venous blood, whereas the BUI technique measures the relative brain uptake. The application of the BUI to brain glucose metabolism has been recently reviewed elsewhere in this series.[17]

D. Indicator Dilution Techniques

In the indicator dilution method, the concentrations of test and reference compounds are measured in serial sagittal sinus blood samples. In this case, the reference compound is a nondiffusible substance such as labeled albumin, ^{99m}Tc-RBC, ^{22}Na, etc. The brain extraction (E) is calculated from the sagittal sinus blood concentration C′, where C′ = C plasma/C injectate:

$$E = 1 - \frac{C' \text{ Test Compound}}{C' \text{ Reference Compound}}$$

E is taken from average ratios of samples collected on the steeply rising part of the indicator dilution curve or by extrapolating concentrations back to the time of injection (Figure 4). Capillary permeability (P) can be estimated from E according to the following equation:

$$P = \frac{-\overset{\circ}{Q}}{A} \ln (1 - E) \text{ cm} \cdot \text{sec}^{-1}$$

where $\overset{\circ}{Q}$ is the cerebral blood flow and A is the capillary surface area.[11] Values of E < 0.04 depend on the choice of reference compound, which may partially diffuse out of the vascular space, and are not reliable. Values of E > 0.80 give permeability coefficients that are too low because brain extraction is more "flow limited" than "diffusion limited". That is, with highly diffusible tracers such as ethanol, the solute is extracted completely within the capillaries with little or no barriers to diffusion. Thus, small errors in E obtained with flow-dependent solutes are amplified by its logarithmic relationship.[11]

The uses of indicator dilution techniques are not restricted to use in the brain, and can be applied to measure the capillary extraction across most vascular beds in vivo.

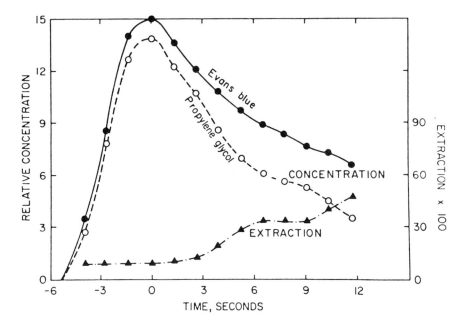

FIGURE 4.   Relative concentrations of propylene glycol and Evans blue-albumin in samples of sagittal sinus blood following their simultaneous injection into the internal carotid artery of the dog. Concentrations refer to concentrations of the injectate and zero time is defined at the time of peak concentration in blood. Extraction (E) of propylene glycol is defined E = 1 − C′ Test/C′ Reference. (From Rapoport, S. I., *Blood-Brain Barrier in Physiology and Medicine,* Raven Press, New York, 1976, chap. VI. With permission.)

This can be illustrated by studies carried out to measure the pulmonary extraction of the biogenic amines norepinephrine and serotonin.

The lungs are in an excellent strategic position for cleansing the blood since the entire cardiac output passes through them several times a minute and they provide an immense endothelial surface area. Apart from their respiratory function, work from several laboratories has highlighted a less widely appreciated, but perhaps equally important function of the lungs, the removal of vasoactive amines from the blood and their metabolism.[18-30] Amine regulation is also accomplished by enzymatic degradation by monoamine oxidase (MAO) in the lungs and other organs. It was of interest to develop an in vivo method to detect biogenic amine transport by the human lung, so that the physiological and pathophysiological implications of this process could be evaluated. The methods used are based on the multiple indicator dilution technique.[31] One method[30] employs the use of a vascular indicator such as [³H]-dextran or indocyanine green dye (ICG) and a suitably labeled test compound. The two indicators are mixed, injected via a catheter inserted into the right atrium, and blood samples are rapidly collected from the ascending aorta through a densitometer to measure the ICG time/concentration curve (Figure 5). Samples of arterial blood are collected and counted for radioactivity of the test amine. The differences in the integrated time-activity (or concentration) curves compared to the injectate represent the fractional extraction of the test compound. This technique has been extended to a less invasive closed-chest dog model and indicator dilution techniques to measure the first pass extraction of ¹¹C-norepinephrine (¹¹C-NE) and ¹¹C-5-hydroxytryptamine, or serotonin (¹¹C-5HT).[32]

The experimental model employs the positioning of a Swan-Ganz catheter into the pulmonary artery via a jugular vein. This catheter is used to monitor pulmonary arte-

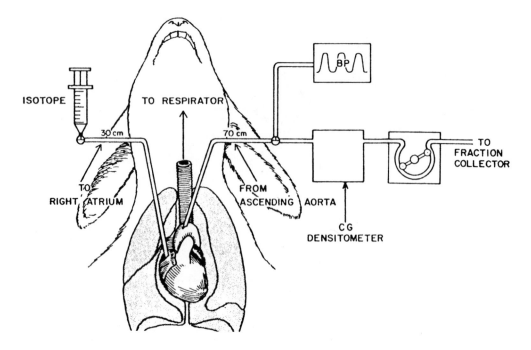

FIGURE 5.   Schematic diagram of the experimental model used for the measurement of amine clearance by the rabbit lung in vivo using the single injection of double or triple indicators. (From Catravas, J. D. and Gillis, C. N., *J. Pharmacol. Exp. Ther.*, 213, 120, 1980. With permission.)

rial and capillary wedge pressures and for the injection of the ^{11}C-amine. A sample collection catheter is placed in the descending aorta via a femoral artery and a rapid sampling pump and fraction collector attached to provide rapid serial samples of blood.

The vascular indicator is the dye indocyanine green (ICG), which is confined to the vascular space over the time course of the measurement, and the diffusible tracer is either ^{11}C-NE or ^{11}C-5HT. The two tracers are co-injected into the pulmonary artery and the rapid serial samples of systemic blood are collected simultaneously and analyzed for both ^{11}C-amine content by counting and ICG concentration spectrophotometrically. The cardiac output is calculated for both tracers using the following equation:

$$\text{Cardiac Output} = \text{CO} = \frac{I}{\int_0^\infty C\, dt}$$

where: I = quantity of tracer injected, C = concentration of tracer in arterial blood, and t = time, or alternatively:

$$\text{CO (}\ell/\text{min)} \frac{60I}{\overline{C}T}$$

where: $\overline{C}$ = mean concentration (mg/ℓ) or (μCi/ℓ) of the tracer and T = duration of the curve.

The activity and ICG levels can be plotted semilogarithmically and the area under the curve (shaded) determined following extrapolation of the downslope to zero (Fig-

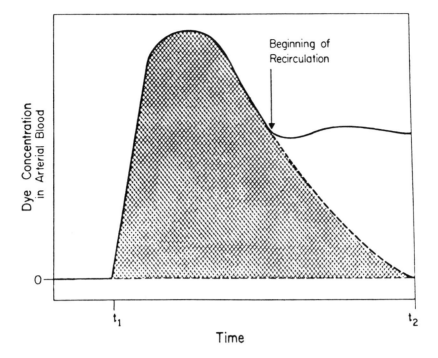

FIGURE 6. Typical dye concentration curve recorded following bolus injection. Because of recirculation of the dye, semilogarithmic extrapolation of the descending slope is necessary.

ure 6). This latter step is necessary due to recirculation (second pass) of the tracer over the course of the measurement. The transport of the amine can then be calculated by the following equation:

$$\% \text{ Amine Removal } = 100 \cdot 1 - \frac{\text{Cardiac Output ICG}}{\text{Cardiac Output } {}^{11}\text{C-amine}}$$

As more amine is extracted, the cardiac output calculation will be disproportionate to that measured for ICG. Using this technique it has been shown (see Table 1) that both ^{11}C-NE and ^{11}C-5HT are rapidly removed from the pulmonary circulation, but to a different extent. 5HT removal averages around 60% of the first pass dose and the lung transporting capacity for this compound is unchanged from subphysiological (carrier free) levels up to 25 μg/kg. The carrier doses of 5HT produced significant increases in pulmonary arterial and systemic blood pressures due to its potent vasoconstrictive influence, but amine extraction was unaffected. The duration of the pressor response was directly related to the dose of the administered amine. The absolute removal of ^{11}C-NE was significantly lower and averaged $\sim$28% of the first pass dose at carrier-free levels. The capacity of the norepinephrine transporting system was shown to be much lower than that for serotonin, since doses of 10 μg/kg produced significantly lower lung uptake. The extension of these invasive in vivo measurements of amine transport in experimental animals to humans using the gamma camera has been reported using ^{11}C-octylamine.[25]

More recently, a quantitative extension of these earlier studies has been developed for measurement of the pulmonary extraction of ^{11}C-chlorpromazine.[33] The ^{11}C-chlorpromazine is mixed with ^{113m}In-transferrin and injected intravenously into patients positioned under a scintillation camera. Acquisition of the counting data over the lung

Table 1
REMOVAL OF BIOGENIC AMINES BY DOG LUNG IN VIVO

Compound	Concentration (μg/kg)	(n)	Removal ± SDM	P[a]
^{11}C-5HT	Carrier-free	3	61.8 ± 1.49	
	0.4-25	4	60.9 ± 1.80	NS
^{11}C-NE	Carrier-free	4	28.6 ± 2.0	
	1-10	3	16.2 ± 2.2	<0.05

[a]   Values determined using the Student's "t" test.

^{11}C-5HT vs. ^{11}C-NE: $p < 0.001$

field as a function of time was made using two separate energy windows for ^{11}C and ^{113m}In. The counts recorded in each 250-msec interval are plotted against time, and the ^{113m}In curve is corrected for Compton scatter from ^{11}C activity using a phantom. Both curves are normalized so that their peak values are set to 1 in order to represent residue functions, R(t). R(t) is the ratio of the counts in the area of interest at time t divided by the maximum number of counts corresponding to time 0. The assumption is made that at time 0, all the tracer is within the lungs. Using conventional outflow detection, the extraction is calculated[31] by:

$$E(t) = \frac{\int_0^t C_R(t) - C_T \, dt}{\int_0^t C_R(t) \, dt}$$

where: C_R = the radioactive concentration of the ^{113}In-transferrin, and C_T = the radioactive concentration of the ^{11}C-chlorpromazine. Each value of C_R and C_T is normalized by dividing the concentration at time t by the amount of tracers injected and expressed as $m\ell^{-1}$. This formula was modified to calculate extraction from the residual lung radioactivity content for both tracers. For each tracer, the amount of radioactivity at any time is equal to the difference between the quantity injected at time 0 and the quantity that has exited from the lungs between time 0 and time t. This can be expressed as follows:

$$R(t) = 1 - F \int_0^t C(t) \, dt$$

where F = pulmonary blood flow. The extraction formula is obtained from the residue functions:

$$E(t) = \frac{[R_T(t) - R_R(t)]}{[1 - R_R(t)]}$$

Thus, the extraction E at time t is equal to the difference between the ^{11}C-chlorpromazine content at time t, $[R_T(t)]$ minus the ^{113m}In-transferrin content, $[R_R(t)]$. Graphically, the counting data in a normal subject is shown in Figure 7. Lung activity increases rapidly as the bolus enters the lung field. The washout of ^{11}C-chlorpromazine was much slower than that of the vascular indicator, transferrin. Using this technique, it was shown that the mean initial extraction of chlorpromazine was $\sim$90% in normal

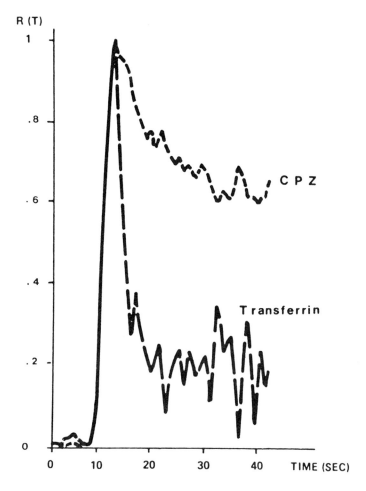

FIGURE 7. Curves of residue function against time for ^{11}C-chlorprom-
azine and [113m]In-transferrin recorded in an area of interest over the right
lung. Ordinate shows the normalized activity recorded every 250 msec.
(From Syrota, A., Pascal, O., Crouzel, M., and Kellershohn, C., *J. Nucl.
Med.*, 22, 145, 1981. With permission.)

patients vs. ∿64% in patients with chronic obstructive pulmonary disease ($p < 0.001$).
This difference was attributed to possible differences in the qualitative or quantitative
alterations of lung disease. The significance of these preliminary studies is that a quantitative and noninvasive technique is now available to assess the significance of the
pulmonary extraction of suitably labeled compounds in both normal and disease states
in humans. Such studies should permit a better understanding of the role of the lungs
in regulating various endogenous and xenobiotic compounds.

E. Use of External Detectors

The in vivo blood-brain barrier permeability of suitable labeled metabolic substrate
analogues has been recently demonstrated using external collimated NaI(Tl) detectors
positioned on the skull.[34] The uptake of 3-deoxy-3-fluoro-D-glucose (3-FDG) was assessed in rhesus monkeys by the bolus injection of 3-FDG into the internal carotid
artery.[34] This measurement was made with the simultaneous measurements of cerebral
blood flow (CBF) and cerebral metabolic rate (CMR) for glucose, determined by detection of the washout of $H_2[15]O$ injected into the right internal carotid artery and the

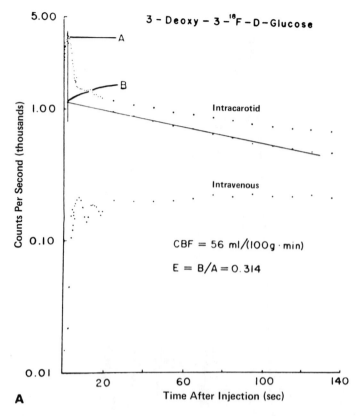

A

FIGURE 8. Behavior of [¹⁸F]-3-FDG during single capillary (upper curve, intracarotid) transit through the brain of rhesus monkeys as measured with a single, externally placed NaI scintillation probe. The extraction (E) of 3-FDG by the brain is computed from such data after correction is made for recirculating tracer by a second injection of tracer into the venous effluent of the brain (lower curve, intravenous) and subtraction of these two curves. Extraction (E) is computed from the ratio of B to A as shown. Cerebral blood flow (CBF) is determined from the clearance of H₂¹⁵O following intracarotid injection. (From Tewson, T. J., Welch, M. J., and Raichle, M. E., *J. Nucl. Med.*, 19, 1339, 1978. With permission.)

brain arteriovenous difference for plasma glucose concentration. A second catheter is positioned in the right jugular bulb for collection of cerebral venous blood. The time course of 3-FDG and ¹⁵O-labeled blood through the brain is detected continuously (Figure 8). The extraction (E) of 3-FDG by the brain is computed from the ratio of the back-extrapolated value of (B) determined by the slope of the slow component of the washout of 3-FDG from the brain and the peak count rate achieved as the bolus passes through the detector field (A). The magnitude of A is therefore a function of the injected dose for a given probe configuration, and the B/A ratio at the peak is a direct measure of the brain extraction of the compound.

This initial estimate of the extraction fraction is somewhat high due to the presence of recirculating tracer in the detector field. To correct for this, a second injection of 3-FDG into the venous outflow from the brain into the right jugular bulb is made. The tracer curve generated from this injection is then used to subtract the amount of tracer presented to the detector due to recirculation. From the computed fractional extraction of 3-FDG, the forward flux of glucose across the blood-brain barrier can be made. This is done by combining the arterial plasma glucose concentration, the fractional extraction of 3-FDG, and the computed cerebral blood flow.[35]

Another application of an external probe to measure brain transport has employed ^{18}F-3,4,dihydroxy-5-fluorophenylalanine (^{18}F-fluorodopa).[36,37] In order to monitor changes in intracerebral ^{18}F-content resulting only from ^{18}F-fluorodopa, it was necessary to subtract the contribution of ^{18}F activity in the cerebral blood volume from the total radioactivity recorded. The intracranial blood volume was estimated by injecting ^{113m}In-labeled transferrin intravenously and recording the radioactivity with the head probe and the concentration of indium radioactivity in a peripheral blood sample. The ^{18}F content of the intracranial blood pool could then be calculated at any time after the injection of ^{18}F-fluorodopa by multiplying the concentration of ^{18}F in the peripheral blood by the estimated intracranial blood volume and subtracting this value from the total ^{18}F detected in the head.[34]

This technique has permitted the atraumatic measurement of the intracerebral transport and metabolism of a neurotransmitter analogue in fully conscious primates.[37] The changes in the accumulation of intracerebral ^{18}F in response to various drug interventions were consistent with the known action of these compounds. For example, α-methyldopa, a competitive inhibitor of dopa transport and decarboxylation,[38] prevented the accumulation of ^{18}F. Reserpine, which releases stored intracerebral dopamine,[39] decreased ^{18}F counts; pargyline, a monoamine oxidase inhibitor,[40] and haloperidol, a known augmentor of intracerebral dopamine turnover,[41] both increased the net brain counting rates.

The simplicity of such techniques when applied to humans may permit data on the role of catecholamines in schizophrenia and depression and provide a means to study therapeutic efficacy of new drugs. One obvious advantage of using probe techniques is the low cost of the required instrumentation. In addition, virtually any suitably labeled radiotracer which can be detected externally can be used.

III. SUMMARY

With the appropriate choice of the radiotracer based on the application of the well-known principles of drug design, it is possible to measure transport across various vascular beds in vivo. The application of the Se diamines illustrates the pH partition hypothesis in the brain. The use of multiple indicator dilution techniques to measure transport into the intact brain and the lung illustrates a second approach to this problem, either invasively by serial sampling or noninvasively with the gamma camera. Lastly, the use of collimated external probes allows the measurement of the brain extraction of 3-fluorodeoxyglucose and fluorodopa. All of these techniques are relatively simple to apply to experimental studies on the design of new and better radiotracers for the measurement of transport in vivo.

REFERENCES

1. **Wolf, A. P., Christman, D. R., Fowler, J. S., and Lambrecht, R. M.**, Synthesis of radiopharmaceuticals and labeled compounds using short-lived isotopes, in *Radiopharmaceuticals and Labeled Compounds,* Vol. 2, International Atomic Energy Agency, Vienna, 1974, 345.
2. **Wolf, A. P. and Redvanly, C. S.**, Carbon-11 and radiopharmaceuticals, *Int. J. Appl. Rad. Isot.,* 28, 29, 1977.
3. **Fowler, J. S.**, Positron-emitting nuclides and their synthetic incorporation into radiopharmaceuticals, in *The Chemistry of Radiopharmaceuticals,* Brady, L. W., Croll, M. N., Honda, T., Burns, H. D., and Heindell, N. D., Eds., Masson, New York, 1978.
4. **Gallagher, B. M., Fowler, J. S., Gutterson, N. I., MacGregor, R. R., Wan, C. N., and Wolf, A. P.**, Metabolic trapping as a principle of radiopharmaceutical design: some factors responsible for the biodistribution of [¹⁸F]-2-deoxy-2-fluoro-D-glucose, *J. Nucl. Med.,* 19, 1154, 1978.
5. **Gallagher, B. M., Fowler, J. S., MacGregor, R. R., Lambrecht, R. M., Wolf, A. P., Crawford, E. J., and Friedkein, M. E.**, *In vivo* measurement of transport and metabolic processes using radiotracers, in *Principles of Radiopharmacology,* Vol. III, Colombetti, L. G., Ed., CRC Press, Boca Raton, Fla., 1979, 135.
6. **Kuhl, D. E., Hoffman, E. J., Phelps, M. E., Ricci, A. R., and Reivich, M.**, Design and application of the Mark IV Scanning System for radionuclide computed tomography of the brain, in *Medical Radionuclide Imaging,* Vol. I, International Atomic Energy Agency Symposium on Medical Radionuclide Imaging, Los Angeles, Calif., 1977, 309.
7. **Kety, S. S.**, Physiological and physical factors governing the initial stages of drug distribution, in *Pharmacology and Pharmacokinetics,* Teorell, T., Dedrick, R. L., and Condliffe, P. G., Eds., Plenum Press, New York, 1974, 233.
8. **Renkin, E. M.**, Multiple pathways of capillary permeability, *Circ. Res.,* 41, 735, 1977.
9. **Goldstein, A., Aronow, L., and Kalman, S. M.**, The absorption, distribution and elimination of drugs, in *Principles of Drug Action: The Basis of Pharmacology,* John Wiley & Sons, New York, 1974, chap. 2.
10. **Manos, G. A. J., Ariëns, E. J., and Simonis, A. M.**, Drug transference: distribution of drugs in the organism, in *Molecular Pharmacology,* Vol. 1, Ariëns, E. J., Ed., Academic Press, New York, 1964, chap. 1.A.
11. **Rapoport, S. I.**, Regulation of drug entry into the nervous system, in *Blood-Brain Barrier in Physiology and Medicine,* Raven Press, New York, 1976, chap. VI.
12. **Kung, H. F. and Blau, M.**, Regional intracellular pH shift: a proposed new mechanism for radiopharmaceutical uptake in brain and other tissues, *J. Nucl. Med.,* 21, 147, 1980.
13. **Kung, H. and Bau, M.**, Synthesis of selenium-75 labeled tertiary diamines: new brain imaging agents, *J. Med. Chem.,* 23, 1127, 1980.
14. **Waddell, W. J. and Bates, R. G.**, Intracellular pH, *Physiol. Rev.,* 49, 285, 1969.
15. **Loberg, M. D.**, Radiotracers for cerebral functional imaging — a new class, *J. Nucl. Med.,* 21, 183, 1980.
16. **Fazio, F., Fieschi, C., and Collice, M.**, Tomographic assessment of cerebral perfusion using single-photon emitter krypton-81m and a rotating gamma camera, *J. Nucl. Med.,* 21, 1139, 1980.
17. **Gallagher, B. M.**, The measurement of brain glucose metabolism using radiotracers, in *Studies of Cellular Function Using Radiotracers,* Billinghurst, M. W., Ed., CRC Press, Boca Raton, Fla., 1982, chap. 1.
18. **Fishman, A. P. and Pietra, G. G.**, Handling of bioactive materials by the lung, *N. Engl. J. Med.,* 291, 884, 1974.
19. **Gillis, C. N.**, Metabolism of vasoactive hormones by the lung, *Anesthesiology,* 39, 626, 1973.
20. **Gillis, C. N., Cronau, L. H., Greene, N. M., and Hammond, G. S.**, Removal of 5-hydroxytryptamine and norepinephrine from the pulmonary vascular space of man: influence of cardiopulmonary bypass and pulmonary arterial pressure on these processes, *Surgery,* 76, 608, 1974.
21. **Tierney, D. F.**, Lung metabolism and biochemistry, *Ann. Rev. Physiol.,* 36, 209, 1974.
22. **Junod, A. F.**, Metabolism, production and release of hormones and mediators in the lung, *Ann. Rev. Respir. Dis.,* 112, 93, 1975.
23. **Fowler, J. S., Gallagher, B. M., MacGregor, R. R., and Wolf, A. P.**, Carbon-11 labeled aliphatic amines in lung uptake and metabolism studies: potential for dynamic measurements *in vivo, J. Pharmacol. Exp. Ther.,* 198, 133, 1976.
24. **Fowler, J. S., Gallagher, B. M., MacGregor, R. R., and Wolf, A. P.**, Radiopharmaceuticals. XIX. ¹¹C-labeled octylamine, a potential diagnostic agent for lung structure and functions, *J. Nucl. Med.,* 17, 752, 1976.

25. Gallagher, B. M., Christman, D., Fowler, J., MacGregor, R., Wolf, A., Som, P., Ansari, A., and Atkins, H., Radioisotope scintigraphy for the study of the dynamics of amine regulations by the human lung, *Chest*, 71, 2825, 1977.

26. Gallagher, B. M., Fowler, J. S., MacGregor, R. R., and Wolf, A. P., Evaluation of radiorespirometry for the determination of monoamine oxidase activity *in vivo* utilizing [¹¹C]-octylamine as a substrate, *Biochem. Pharmacol.*, 26, 1917, 1977.

27. Gillis, C. N. and Greene, N. M., Possible clinical implications of metabolism of bloodborne substances by the human lung, in *Metabolic Functions of the Lung*, Bakhle, Y. S. and Vane, J. R., Eds., Marcel Dekker, New York, 1977, 173.

28. Gillis, C. N., Huxtable, R. J., and Roth, R. A., Effect of monocrotaline pretreatment of rats on removal of 5-hydroxytryptamine and norepinephrine by perfused lung, *Br. J. Pharmacol.*, 63, 435, 1978.

29. Gillis, C. N., Cronau, L. H., Mandel, S., and Hammond, G. L., Indicator dilution measurement of 5-hydroxytryptamine clearance by human lung, *J. Appl. Physiol.*, 46, 1178, 1979.

30. Catravas, J. D. and Gillis, C. N., Pulmonary clearance of [¹⁴C]-5-hydroxytryptamine and [³H]-norepinephrine *in vivo*: effects of pretreatment with imipramine or cocaine, *J. Pharmacol. Exp. Ther.*, 213, 120, 1980.

31. Crone, C., The permeability of capillaries in various organs as determined by the use of the indicator diffusion method, *Acta Physiol. Scand.*, 58, 292, 1963.

32. Gallagher, B. M., Hara, T., Fowler, J. S., McGregor, R. R., and Wolf, A. P., unpublished results.

33. Syrota, A., Pascal, O., Crouzel, M., and Kellershohn, C., Pulmonary extraction of C-11 chlorpromazine, measured by residue detection in man, *J. Nucl. Med.*, 22, 145, 1981.

34. Tewson, T. J., Welch, M. J., and Raichle, M. E., [¹⁸F]-labeled 3-deoxy-3-fluoro-D-glucose: synthesis and preliminary biodistribution data, *J. Nucl. Med.*, 19, 1339, 1978.

35. Raichle, M. E., Eichling J. O., and Straatmann, M. G., Blood-brain barrier permeability of ¹¹C-labeled alcohols and ¹⁵O-labeled water, *Am. J. Physiol.*, 230, 543, 1976.

36. Firnau, G., Garnett, E. S., Chan, P. K. H., and Belbeck, L. W., Intracerebral dopamine metabolism studied by a novel radioisotope technique, *J. Pharm. Pharmacol.*, 28, 584, 1976.

37. Garnett, E. S., Firnau, G., Chan, P. K. H., Good, S., and Belbeck, L. W., [¹⁸F]-fluoro-dopa, an analog of dopa, and its use in external measurements of storage, degradation and turnover of intracerebral dopamine, *Proc. Natl. Acad. Sci. U.S.A.*, 75, 464, 1978.

38. Sourkes, T. L., Murphy, G. F., Chavez, B., and Zielinska, M., The action of some α-methyl and other amino acids on cerebral catecholamines, *J. Neurochem.*, 8, 109, 1961.

39. Carlsson, A., Pharmacological depletion of catecholamine stores, *Pharmacol. Rev.*, 18, 541, 1966.

40. Tozer, T. N., Neff, N. H., and Brodie, B. B., Application of steady state kinetics to the synthesis rate and turnover time of serotonin in the brain of normal and reserpine treated rats, *J. Pharmacol. Exp. Ther.*, 153, 177, 1966.

41. Andén, N. E., Ross, B. E., and Werdinius, B., Effects of chlorpromazine, haloperidal and reserpine on the levels of phenolic acids in rat corpus striatum, *Life Sci.*, 3, 149, 1964.

Chapter 15

IN VITRO TECHNIQUES TO STUDY THE TRANSPORT OF RADIOTRACERS

Marco Salvatore, Luigi Mansi, Gianni Morrone, Rosa Ferraiuolo,
and Salvatore Venuta

TABLE OF CONTENTS

I. INTRODUCTION

The in vivo study of transport of radiotracers is hindered by many variables, such as hormonal, immunological, nervous, vascular factors, and by the presence of different cell types in the tissue studied.[1] Using in vitro techniques, the factors that can regulate the transport can be tested individually.

A very interesting approach is that of the cell culture system, where the radiotracer is taken up by a homogeneous cell population under controlled growth conditions.

In this paper, some examples of transport studies of radiotracers will be illustrated making special reference to our experience with in vitro grown chick embryo fibroblasts and thyroid carcinoma cells.

II. MECHANISM OF TRANSPORT

The transport across the cell membrane depends on the magnitude of the molecules considered. Small molecules cross the membrane by the following mechanisms[2-5] which are described in other chapters of this book:

1. Simple diffusion
2. Facilitated diffusion
3. Active transport

It is important to remember that the distribution and/or accumulation of radiotracers in tissue or organs is affected by factors that do not necessarily relate to the uptake by parenchymal cells, but rather to the presence of other components or factors such as hematic cells or alteration of the vascular permeability.

III. IN VITRO SYSTEMS

A. General Features

The use of an in vitro system has the advantage of analyzing single parameters involved in the radiotracers transport mechanism.[6-10] In this respect, such a methodological approach that must always be associated to and complemented with in vivo experiments, may play an extremely important role both in identifying new radiotracers and in a more correct understanding of the biochemical mechanism that governs their transport and accumulation. Such an understanding is essential for explaining the behavior of radiotracers in clinical practice. The main features of in vitro techniques are the following:

1. Their low cost
2. The possibility of rapidly obtaining a high number of statistically significant experimental data
3. Their better reproducibility as compared with animal studies

The in vitro study of radiotracers begins with the use of techniques which, in absence of biological structures, analyze the relations of the radiotracers with the chemical and physical environment (such as variations of pH, ionic force, influence of other molecules, etc.).

We are interested in the possibility of studying transport of radiotracers in living cell systems.

B. Biological Systems

Systems derived from pluricellular animal structures are numerous.[11-15] These systems can be studied with various techniques: histological (extremely interesting information is provided by electron microscopy), histochemical, autoradiographic, and biochemical.

Among the in vitro systems, we wish to mention perfused organs, tissue slices, homogenates, isolated cells, cell organelles and the tissue cultures.[16] As far as the first system, perfused organs, is concerned, there is a more immediate correlation between in vivo and in vitro studies. The system analyzes an isolated organ (in the absence, for example, of other compartments of radiotracer distribution) which involves a complex anatomohistological structure with vascular, parenchymal, and stromal components. Therefore, because of the many variables involved in such systems, an analysis of the experimental findings is complex.

Isolated biological membranes have an important role in the study of the mechanism of transport. The use of this system allows the identification of the function the plasma membrane performs in regulating the accumulation of radiotracers.[17] Many studies were already made with cell cultures[18-21] using different systems.

A distinction should be made[22] between primary cultures and cell lines. The term "primary cultures" refers to cells freshly derived from tissue explants and therefore characterized by their close relationship with cells present in vivo. However, a drawback of this system is represented by the lack of homogeneity in the cell population. An example of this type is represented by chicken embryo fibroblasts (CEF).

Cell lines, on the contrary, consist of cells selected because of their capability to grow "endlessly". These cells allow study of cellular clones, e.g., populations derived from one single cell. Establishing a cell line is not always easy and straightforward. There are animal species from which it is relatively common to obtain long-term in vitro growth of cells, e.g., rodents; while human and chicken fibroblasts, for example, do not divide in vitro more than 100 or 40 times, respectively.[7]

Cell lines tend to show alterations in their characteristics, e.g., of the karyotype, and thus differ from the cells of the tissue from which they originate. This is particularly true for specialized functions. The improvement in the tissue culture techniques has, however, been continuous. The identification of regulatory molecules as well as of appropriate cellular microenvironments has permitted the establishment of in vitro systems in which a differentiation pathway can be studied from its early in differentiated precursor cell to its final differentiation step.

Another advantage which the cell culture system offers is the possibility of modifying the culture media by adding or subtracting those molecules whose regulatory role needs to be studied.

The possibility of in vitro transformation is still another advantage of using cell culture systems.[10] This occurs in CEF infected by Rous sarcoma virus (RSV) and allows the comparison between neoplastic (CEF [RSV]) and normal (CEF) cells that grow at the same rate, and the evaluation of the "transformation" effect in genotypically identical normal and transformed cells. These two cell populations are also grown in the same culture conditions. Incidentally, another approach to the study of tumors is that of animal tumor models.[23,24] An example is represented by the EMT-6 system utilized by Larson. As an example of cell culture systems we shall briefly consider both the normal and RSV-transformed CEF and the normal and tumor-derived rat thyroid cells.

1. Chick Embryo Fibroblasts

CEF can be infected by the Rous sarcoma virus, RSV. This virus was isolated in 1911 owing to its capability of inducing sarcoma in chickens,[25] and thus provided the unequivocal evidence that viruses can cause cancer. RSV replicates in in vitro-grown CEF and gives rise to the malignant transformation of cells. Two important features of the transformed cells are the capability of growing in agar suspension and that of growing in liquid culture under conditions in which normal cells would arrest their multiplication. Furthermore, rounded and refractile morphology is a characteristic of transformed cells that distinguishes them from normal cells.

The advantages offered by the CEF (RSV) system are the following:

1.   CEF and CEF (RSV) can be easily cultivated in vitro.
2.   It is possible to obtain a large number of cells rapidly and at very low cost.
3.   Since they are primary cultures, the problem of contamination control is futile.
4.   The virus induces a complete transformation in 2 days.[9,26,27]

Because of these advantages, this system has been the favorite of many investigators and has allowed the study of many factors such as the effect of cell density, serum concentrations, and pH on the cell growth rate of normal cells.[28,29]

Extremely important studies are those which are concerned with the analysis of the transport mechanism, in particular of glucose and amino acids, and the effects that transformation may have on transport. In this system, our research group has analyzed the transport of radiotracers and in particular of ^{67}Ga-citrate (^{67}Ga) and of Tl-201 chloride (^{201}Tl). Primary cultures of CEF are prepared according to published methods.[26] Briefly, body walls of 10-day-old embryos are trypsinized and the cells obtained are plated and incubated in an atmosphere of 5% CO_2 at 30°C. All the experiments reported are usually performed with secondary or tertiary cultures obtained by trypsinization of 3- to 6-day-old primaries or secondaries.

2. Thyroid Carcinoma Cells

Starting with Carrell's pioneering works, thyroid studies employing tissue cultures have steadily increased[16,31,32] and several cell lines have been obtained.[30,33,34]

Our experience has been with rat thyroid cells obtained by the Ambesi-Impiombato and Coon technique.[30] The interest of this system consists of the opportunity of comparing the transport pattern of epithelial cell lines from normal thyroids (FRT), and that of cell lines from thyroid tumors at different stage of differentiation (FRA, 1-5G).

The isolation and characterization of these cell lines and the culture conditions have been described.[30] Briefly, three lines have been used: FR-A 22-1, 1-5G Cl_1 and FR-T Cl_1. The FR-A line has been derived from a differentiated rat tumor and tends to form three-dimensional pseudofollicular structures containing PAS-positive material; it produces thyroglobulin and injected into adult rat produces a tumor of 2 to 3 cm in diameter in 1 month.

The 1-5G Cl_1 line has been derived from a poorly differentiated rat thyroid tumor; it forms dome-like structures containing PAS-negative liquid, does not produce thyroglobulin, and causes the formation of a tumor of 1 to 2 cm in diameter 2 months after the injection into the animal.

FR-T is a normal epithelial thyroid cell line derived from normal rat thyroid; it forms follicular structures in vitro and does not develop into tumor if injected in animals.

IV. ^{67}GA CITRATE UPTAKE

From 1969, the clinical experience concerning the use of Ga-67 citrate in oncology and in the study of inflammatory pathology has developed enormously.[35-37]

From the standpoint of biological behavior, the existence of analogies between gallium and Fe (mainly), Ca, and — less likely — Mg has been suggested.[38-41]

Gallium, injected intravenously in the form of citrate to facilitate solubilization, binds with proteins, especially with transferrin (TF).[42-43] Evidence also exists that Ga can bind with lactoferrin (LF), ferritin, and the siderophores.[44-46] In fact a relationship has been noted in clinical practice between Ga accumulation and values of sideremia and ferritinemia.[47,48] The importance of Ga binding with TF and the interference with the Fe transport mechanism have led various authors to suggest the use of substances that interfere at such a level as a means of improving scintigraphic imaging.[49,50]

The subcellular distribution of Ga is debatable. Most experimental evidence focuses the attention on the role played by lysosomes;[51-53] however, some authors have reported the presence of the largest amount of gallium in the soluble fraction and/or associated to other submicroscopic particles.[54,55] In the cell, gallium is bound with proteins,[56,57] and Hayes has identified two of these proteins, one with 120,000 mol wt, the other with 45,000 mol wt. The latter is present in huge quantities in tumor cells.[58]

In the accumulation mechanism of Ga in cells or tissues, relevance has also been given to polymorphonuclear cell (PMN), to vascularization, to variations in the membrane permeability, and to cellular multiplication rate.[54,59,60-65] In the inflammatory tissue, the accumulation of Ga seems to depend on many factors. First of all the enhanced capillary permeability associated with the inflammatory process facilitates the passage of protein-bound Ga[60] into the interstitial space; however, the protein-free gallium also accumulates in the inflammatory tissue.[66] In such a tissue, the presence of PMN contribute to the accumulation of Ga;[59] PMN are rich in LF, which strongly binds the Ga.[59,67] Another factor which favors the accumulation of Ga in the inflammatory tissue is represented by the gallium that penetrates into bacteria either through simple or facilitated diffusion;[68] in particular an important role in the Ga-uptake is played by bacterial siderophores.[46] It should be noted, however, that in experimentally induced abscesses, 24 hr after the injection of Ga, only 20% is found in PMN or bacteria with the remainder being in the noncellular soluble fraction.[69]

Several studies have reported the role of TF in the Ga uptake of tumor cell. Larson[70] reports that the presence of TF gives rise to an accumulation of Ga in the EMT-6 sarcoma cells and that this accumulation is proportional to the TF quantity in the culture medium. Larson suggests that the uptake of the Ga-TF complex is mediated by a receptor present in the plasma membrane of the cell, and that the uptake of the Ga-TF complex occurs through endocytosis, according to the mechanism already demonstrated for the transport of Fe in erythrocytes.[71,72] A protein of 250,000 mol wt that binds TF has been isolated from EMT cells.[73] Furthermore, in vivo studies in the mouse are consistent with a role of TF in the uptake of Ga.[23] Studies by Harris[74] in mouse myeloma cells indicate that the uptake of Fe and Ga is stimulated by the addition of TF to the culture medium. It has also been reported that factors such as PO_4^{3-} and $FeCl_3$ which interfere with the binding between Ga and TF reduce the uptake of Ga.[75] Similar results can be attained in other experimental systems such as human fibroblasts,[76] thymic lymphomas, and mastocytomas.[77] The gallium taken up by the cell strongly binds with intracellular components that delay its efflux from the cell. This intracellular binding is particularly strong in tumor cells.[78] However, the study of the inhibition by nonradioactive Fe[74] suggests that the Fe inhibition of Ga takes place with Fe concentrations that are higher than that necessary for saturating TF. This phenomenon could denote the presence of mechanisms different from those involving TF and that could account for Ga uptake.

Another line of research suggests, in fact, that Fe can enter tumor cells by a mechanism different from that requiring an initial binding to protein such as TF. Studies by Gams[61] report that the release of Ga bound to serum components facilitates its intracellular accumulation; for example scandium, which competes with Ga for protein binding, enhances the uptake of Ga.[79]

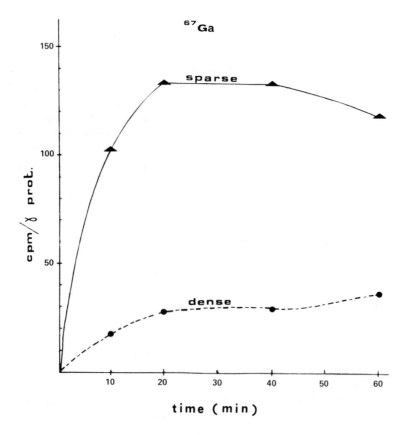

FIGURE 1.   Uptake of ^{67}Ga in sparse vs. dense cultures of CEF. During this experiment, the 1-hr incorporation of (^{3}H)-TdR was 89 cpm/μg of proteins in sparse cultures and 50 cpm/μg in dense cultures; the (^{3}H)-2dGlc uptake was 37 cpm/μg in sparse and 16 cpm/μg in dense CEF. Each point is the average of three measurements.

The latter mechanism of Ga uptake seems to be particularly important in tumors.[80,81] Works giving evidence that lowering of pH increases the transport of Ga into tumor cells seem to support this mechanism of uptake,[66,82] since the dissociation of the Ga-TF complex is favored at low pH.

The effect of growth rate on the uptake of Ga has been investigated using hamster embryo cells. These studies indicate that growing cells take up more Ga compared with resting cells.[61] It should be noted that in NKR cells the increase in cell density and the accompanying decrease in multiplication rate are associated with a decrease in the uptake of ^{125}I marked TF[83] (see the above-mentioned mechanism of uptake of Ga in transformed cells). Such increase of Ga uptake in fast-growing cells has been also detected under other experimental conditions as well.[61-63] At any rate there are systems, such as the regenerating liver, where an enhancement in cell proliferation[64,65] does not appear to affect Ga accumulation.

Our chicken embryo fibroblasts system permits an easy and efficient control of changes in growth rate which can be measured by the incorporation of (^{3}H) thymidine (^{3}H-TdR) and the uptake of (^{3}H)-2-deoxy-glucose, (^{3}H-2dGlc). It has been demonstrated that 2dGlc uptake increases in fast-growing cells.[15] Of course the incorporation of TdR in DNA is due to the chromosome duplication which procedes cell division.

We have studied the uptake of gallium in CEF at different growth rates.[84,85] Figure 1 shows a study of Ga uptake in sparse (fast growing) or dense (slow growing) cells.

The TdR incorporation and the 2dGlc uptake were two times higher in fast growing than in slow-growing CEF. Figure 1 shows an increased uptake of Ga in sparse CEF and suggests that the growth rate greatly contributes to Ga accumulation. Similar results have been obtained with a 4-hr incubation.

We have also studied whether the transformation, per se, independently of changes in growth rate, has an effect on the uptake of Ga in tumor cells.[84] The in vitro study of the effect of transformation is greatly advantaged by the availability of a control population of normal cells which is identical with regard to genetic characteristics and growth conditions to the transformed cells. This is true in the case of the chicken embryo fibroblasts system. In this system, the Rous sarcoma virus is able to cause a massive transformation of the cell population in 24 to 48 hr,[9] and the normal cells can be grown at a rate identical to that of transformed cells. Therefore, the effect of transformation can be studied without the interference of the change in growth rate which accompanies the malignant transformation of cells. Without the control of the cell growth rate, it is impossible to determine if the change of a parameter is transformation-specific or common to all the normal conditions in which there is a change of the cell doubling time. The growth rate of CEF and CEF(RSV) is measured by incorporation of thymidine in the DNA and uptake of 2-deoxy-D-glucose (2-dGlc), a glucose analogue.

One of us has shown that when CEF and CEF(RSV) have identical growth rates, as measured by thymidine incorporation and cell number doubling time, the transformed cells take up 2-dGlc at a rate that is about three times faster than that of normal cells.[26,80] Therefore we have an extremely controlled cell system in which transformed and normal cells growing at the same rate can be compared. In this system, we have studied the uptake of ^{67}Ga in order to understand if the uptake of this compound is altered by the malignant transformation of cells.

We have shown (Figure 2) that transformed fibroblasts take up ^{67}Ga at a slower rate than normal fibroblasts. This study was undertaken in conditions in which normal and transformed fibroblast had the same growth rate. We have also followed the kinetics of Ga uptake up to 4 hr and again found that the transformation does not stimulate the uptake of Ga (Table 1).

Gams et al. have studied the uptake of ^{67}Ga in hamster embryo cells transformed by adenovirus 7 and in fast-growing normal cells; they find that transformed cells take up ^{67}Ga at a slower rate than normal cells.[61] This is in apparent contrast with the in vivo studies which show an increased ^{67}Ga uptake in the tumor tissue.[37] Our results are in agreement with those of Gams, and, because of the characteristics of the system described above, appear to indicate that ^{67}Ga is not a specific marker of the malignant transformation.

Apparently the increased uptake of ^{67}Ga in the tumor tissue is not due to cell transformation per se, but to other factors such as changes in the cell growth rate induced by the transformation (Figure 1).

We should add that, in our in vitro system, other radioisotopic agents such as [57]Co-bleomycin are taken up by transformed cells at a higher rate than that observed in fast-growing normal cells (Figure 3). This result shows that [57]Co-bleomycin is a specific marker of cell transformation in contrast to [67]Ga. It also indicates that the poor uptake of Ga in transformed fibroblasts is not due to a generalized aspecific decrease in the uptake of these compounds in transformed CEF. A similar conclusion is derived from the study of ^{201}Tl uptake.

V. [201]TL-CHLORIDE UPTAKE

The utilization of thallium in nuclear medicine originates from Kawana's observa-

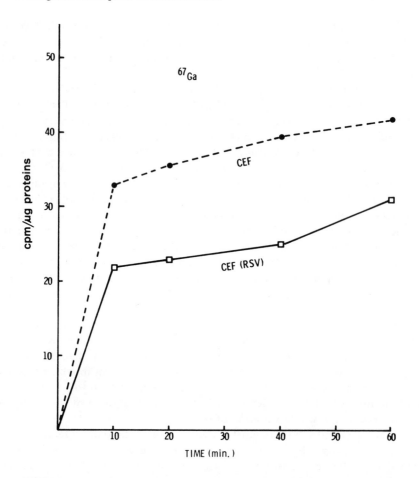

FIGURE 2.   Uptake of ^{67}GA in normal and transformed fibroblasts. 1×10^6 CEF and 1.5×10^6 CEF (RSV) were inoculated in 35 mm tissue culture dishes. During the uptake study, CEF and CEF (RSV) had identical growth rate: (^{3}H)-TdR incorporation was equal to 2700 cpm/μg of proteins in CEF and 2400 cpm/μg of proteins in CEF (RSV); (^{3}H)-2dGlc uptake was equal to 51 cpm/μg of proteins in CEF and 160 cpm/μg of proteins in CEF (RSV). Each point is the average of three measurements.

Table 1
^{67}GA UPTAKE IN NORMAL (CEF) AND TRANSFORMED (CEF RSV) FIBROBLASTS

Time (hr)	CEF (cpm/μg protein)	CEF (RSV) (cpm/μg protein)
2	43	25.1
4	41	34

tions[88] and from the production of the isotope ^{201}Tl made possible by Lebowitz and co-workers.[89]

The biological rationale for the utilization of the thallium derives from its analogy with potassium[90] at trace concentrations (at higher concentrations Tl appears to be an analogue of Pb, As, Hg[91]). This Tl-K analogy seems to depend on the similarity between the ionic radius of the two ions in the hydrated form.[93] Thallium, as an analog

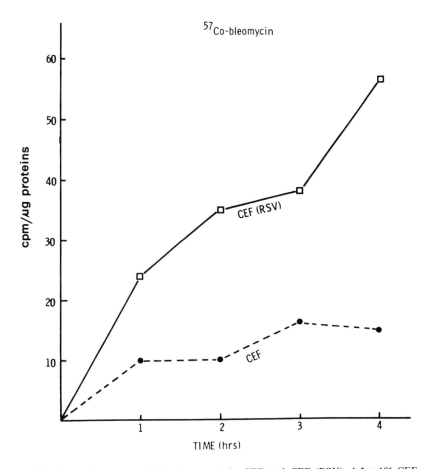

FIGURE 3. Transport of ^{57}Co-bleomycin in CEF and CEF (RSV). 1.5×10^6 CEF and 1.2×10^6 CEF (RSV) were inoculated in 35-mm dishes and, after 24 hr the transport of ^{57}Co-bleomycin was studied. Uptake of (^{3}H)-2dGlc and incorporation of (^{3}H)-TdR were also studied. It was found that while CEF incorporated 1/cpm of (^{3}H)-TdR per μg of proteins and transported 13.4 cpm of the glucose analogue per μg of proteins, CEF (RSV) had an incorporation of 0.8 cpm of (^{3}H)-TdR and an uptake of 38.6 cpm of (^{3}H)-2dGlc. Each point is the average of three measurements. We have also studied the incorporation in the acid-insoluble fraction and found that less than 10% of the total cellular radioactivity is present in this fraction.

of K, can substitute for K in the pyruvate-kinase activation[90] and requires Na-K AT-Pase for the intracellular transport.[92]

In clinical practice, thallium is mainly used for the study of myocardial pathology and the analysis of the uptake mechanism has developed mainly through kinetic studies of this tissue, where ^{201}Tl chloride accumulates.[89,94,94,101] Kidney is the other major site of Tl accumulation in the body.[89]

Studies of the transport in the erythrocyte have found that the uptake of Tl is mostly blocked by ouabain, which inhibits Na-K ATPase, and by sodium fluoride.[96] Therefore emphasis is placed on the importance of active transport and of Na-K ATPase in the transport of Tl. Potassium uptake mechanism has been described by few investigators.[97-100]

With regard to the myocardium uptake, kinetics of K and Tl are not completely identical. Thallium exhibits an initial uptake greater than that of potassium, a plateau starting at around 10 to 20 min and a fall in concentration which begins after about 60 min and becomes significant from approximately the 3rd hour.[90] The decrease in

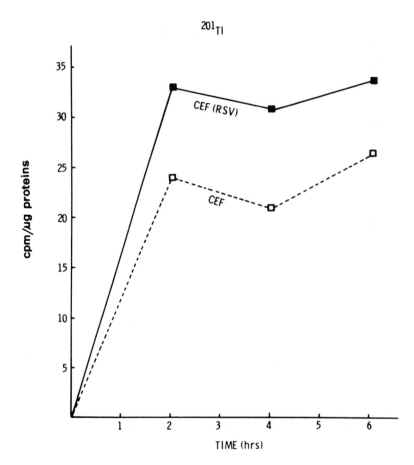

FIGURE 4.   Transport of ^{201}Tl in CEF and CEF(RSV). 1 × 10^6 CEF and 1 × 10^6 CEF (RSV) were plated in 35-mm dishes. The (^{3}H)-TdR incorporation was equal to 43 cpm/μg of protein in normal fibroblasts and 49 cpm/μg of protein in transformed cells. The (^{3}H)-2dGlc 15′ uptake was equal to 16 cpm/μg of proteins in CEF and 27 cpm/μg of proteins in CEF (RSV). Each point is the average of three measurements.

Tl concentration is slower than that of K and is ascribed to a stronger intracellular binding of Tl.[90]

The myocardial concentration of Tl is linearly correlated to the coronary flow at rest.[94] There is no proportionality, however, at high flow levels and the myocardial extraction of Tl decreases as the flow produced by vasodilators increases.[102] Other factors affecting the uptake are oxygenation and the metabolic activities necessary for the functioning of the Na-K-dependent ATPase.[103]

In addition to its use for the myocardium, thallium can be utilized for the study of skeletal muscle pathology[104] as well as in testicular[105] and renal pathology.[106]

In 1975, Salvatore[107,108] reported the possibility of using Tl in the study of pulmonary neoplasms, and subsequently for thyroid[109-111] and brain.[112] Since then there have been numerous reports dealing with the utilization of Tl for the study of human tumors.[113-116] An interesting feature which has stimulated this approach is the analogy between thallium and Cs-131 or K, already used as tumor-seeking indicator.[117,118]

Works by Potts[119] suggested that Tl could be used in melanomas. Ito and co-workers found a rapid accumulation of ^{201}Tl in rabbit tumors and a correlation between the accumulation of ^{201}Tl and ^{42}K, respectively.[120] Hudson and co-workers have confirmed these findings for the malignant melanoma in mice.[121]

Our results in CEF are in agreement with the hypothesis of a specific stimulation of ^{201}Tl uptake occurring after malignant transformation has taken place[84] (see Figure 4).

Table 2
UPTAKE OF [201] Tl IN
TRANSFORMED FIBROBLASTS

Time (Min)	Cpm/μg Protein
10	357
20	596
30	545
60	536
120	602

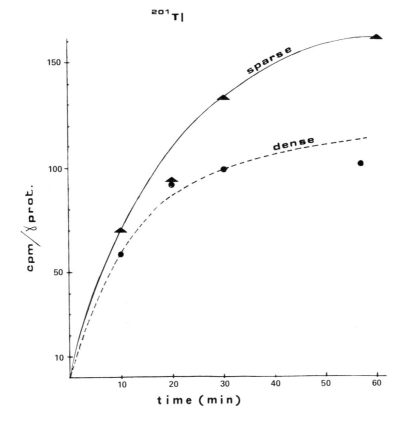

FIGURE 5. Uptake of ^{201}Tl in sparse, fast growing vs. dense, slow growing, CEF. The (^{3}H)-TdR incorporation was 5 cpm/μg of proteins in dense and 16 cpm/μg in sparse cultures; the (^{3}H)-2dGlc uptake was 5 cpm/μg of proteins in dense culture, while sparse CEF took up 11 cpm/μg.

Even though the extent of this stimulation is not great, it is reproducible. The kinetics of ^{201}Tl uptake is very rapid: in 20' a steady-state level is reached in transformed cells (Table 2) and a similar pattern is found in normal cells.

To determine the effects of growth rate, we have compared ^{201}Tl uptake in sparse vs. dense CEF and found that the uptake of ^{201}Tl is also stimulated by an increase in cell growth rate (Figure 5) which could obviously contribute to the accumulation of ^{201}Tl in the tumor tissue.

Recently, rat epithelial cell lines have been obtained from thyroid tumors.[30] These lines, as well as an epithelial line derived from normal thyroid, gave us the possibility of determining if the in vivo binding of Tl in thyroid tumors was due to a specific

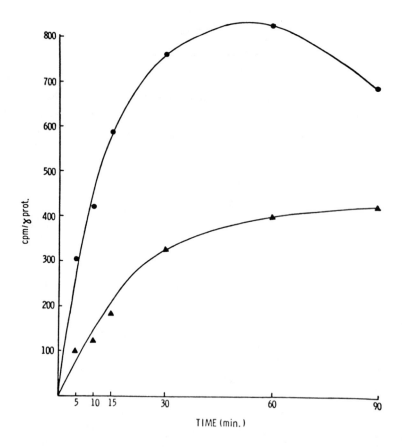

FIGURE 6. ^{201}Tl uptake in 1-5G and FR-T. 24 hr after plating the cells were washed with Hanks balanced salt solution (HBSS) and 1 m*l* of Coon's Modified Ham F-12M containing 5% of dialyzed calf serum and 2μ Ci of ^{201}Tl was added. The (^{3}H)-TdR incorporation per μg of proteins was 10 cpm and 12.5 cpm for 1-5G and FRT, respectively. The glucose uptake was 31 cpm/μg of proteins for the transformed clone 1-5G and 9 cpm/μg of proteins for the normal clone. Each point is the average of three cultures. 1-5G ●—●. FR-T ▲—▲.

increase in thallium uptake after malignant transformation. Our results[122] strongly support this possibility because the transformed epithelial clone 1-5G transports Tl at a faster rate and accumulates it to a higher equilibrium concentration than FR-T, a normal thyroid clone (Figure 6). This result was obtained in experimental conditions in which normal and transformed cells had the same growth rate.

FR-A, another cell line derived from rat thyroid tumors, transports Tl faster than FR-T (Figure 7). This again confirms the above conclusion. However FR-A has a multiplication rate higher than that of normal cells; therefore, part of the uptake difference shown in Figure 7 is due to the high growth rate of FR-A (see below and Figure 8 for the effect of growth on the uptake).

Finally, it should be noted that the kinetics of Tl uptake is very rapid; depending on the line used, the uptake is almost complete by 10 to 15 min.

The tumor cells very often have a higher growth rate than the surrounding normal tissue. In order to determine if changes in growth rate could contribute to the in vivo accumulation of Tl, we grew FR-T at different densities[122] and found that the sparse population grows at a faster rate and transports and accumulates Tl more than dense and slow-growing cells. The high growth rate is certainly not unique of transformed

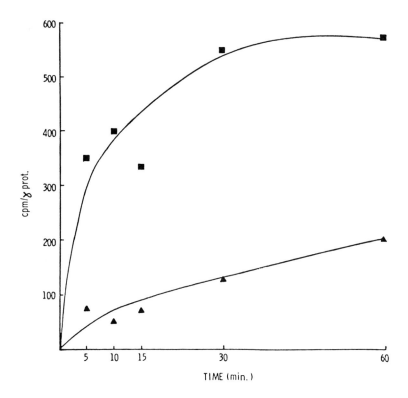

FIGURE 7. Uptake of ^{201}Tl in FR-A and FR-T. 2.2×10^6 FR-A and 1.8×10^6 FR-T cells were plated in 35-mm dishes. After 24 hr the plates were washed with HBSS and 2 μCi of ^{201}Tl were added. The (^{3}H)-TdR incorporation was 80 cpm/ μg of proteins in the FR-A cultures and 10 cpm/μg of proteins in the FR-T culture. Each point is the average of three cultures. FR-A ■—■. FR-T▲—▲.

cells, but is common to several normal cell compartments of the body; however, the above result suggests that this factor could contribute to the effect of the transformation "per se" and increase the in vivo accumulation of Tl in thyroid tumors. It should be pointed out that the effect of transformation (and growth) on Tl uptake is higher in thyroid lines than in the fibroblast system described above.[84] Nevertheless, the uptake shows the same qualitative changes in both systems.

The transport and accumulation mechanism of Tl in normal and transformed cells is not well known. However analogies with potassium, e.g., the capability of activating the Na-K-dependent ATPase, make us assume that a transport mechanism similar to that for potassium may be functioning. We will therefore present some data on the transport of K.

Perdue,[124] in a review on the transport of monovalent cations, reports that the transport of potassium is controlled by such factors as insulin, serum, phytohemagglutinin, and prostaglandins, all of which have a stimulating action on the uptake of K. On the contrary, an increase in cell density leads to a reduction in the activity of Na-K-dependent ATPase which results in a decrease uptake of K.[125] The concentration of potassium appears to increase in neoplastic tissues.[123] The transport of K has been studied in virus-transformed cells. The finding concerning the increase in K transport produced by transformation[127,128] is not confirmed by all the authors who have so far dealt with the subject.[126] In particular, it is stressed that transformation can give rise to a percentage variation of ouabain-sensitive and furosemide-sensitive transport as well as of the uptake due to passive diffusion. Experimental differences could be as-

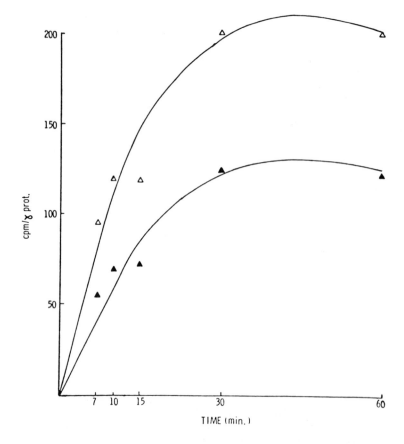

FIGURE 8.   ²⁰¹Tl uptake in sparse and dense culture of FR-T. 1 × 10⁵ or 1 ×
10⁶ FR-T cells were plated in 35-mm dishes and after 24 hr the ²⁰¹Tl transport
was studied. The sparse cultures incorporated 55 cpm of (³H)-TdR per μg of
proteins while the dense population incorporated 13 cpm/μg of proteins. Each
point is the average of three cultures. Sparse FR-T △—△. Dense FR-T ▲—▲.

cribed to lack of proper control in the systems employed. In this respect the CEF-
CEF(RSV) system, where a comparison is made of genotypically identical normal and
transformed populations, growing at the same rate and liable to internal control, appears to be extremely interesting for giving an answer to some of these questions.

VI. 2-DEOXY-D-GLUCOSE UPTAKE

The possibility of labeling biologically important compounds with positron emitters,
which can be used in vivo, has proved to be of extreme practical interest, in particular
for the use of radioactive glucose and glucose analogues in cerebral and cardiac ill-
nesses.[129,130]

Gallagher et al. studied the distribution of ¹⁸F-2-deoxy-2-fluoro-D glucose (2FDG)
in mouse and found that the heart contains about 3 to 4% of the radionuclide while
the brain accumulates about 2 to 3% of the injected isotope. These levels of radioactivity remained constant for about 2 hr after injection while liver, lungs, kidney, small
intestine, and blood showed a rapid clearance of the radioactivity.[130,131]

Larson[132] and Som[133] have shown that, in agreement with culture tissue studies, nonmetabolizable glucose analogues such as (¹⁴C)-2-deoxyglucose (2CDG) and 2FDG can
be used to visualize tumors. Larson has shown that 2CDG gives a tumor/blood ratio

at 1 hr from injection similar to that given with Ga at 48 hr, Som, using FDG, indicates that the tumor/blood ratio ranges between 2.1 and 17.8, while the tumor/normal tissue ratio ranges between 1.3 and 9.2. Among the suggested glucose tracers we should mention ^{11}C-glucose, ^{18}F-3-DG, and ^{18}F-2-D mannose;[134-136] however, ^{18}F-2-deoxy-2-fluoro-D-glucose (2FDG) is the most widely used at the present time. The choice of this compound is due to several reasons: (1) the substitution in C_2 does not affect the hexokinase reaction,[137] (2) the compound is nonmetabolizable and radiochemically stable,[131] (3) the product ^{18}F-2-deoxy-2-fluoro-D-glucose-6-phosphate (FDG-6P) has a low membrane permeability,[138] (4) the low affinity of 2DG for the glucose receptor at the renal level (importance of the hydroxil group in C_2) hinders the absorption by the renal proximal tubule with improvement of the tissue/blood ratio compared with glucose.[139]

The trapping of the 2FDG in brain and heart is due to its phosphorylation to FDG-6P by hexokinase present in these organs as well as to the absence or low activity of glucose-6-phosphatase;[131,140] the phosphorylated compound is unable to cross the plasma membrane and remains trapped inside the cells. The presence of phosphatase and/or the low hexokinase activity in other organs such as lung, kidney, and liver causes the release of the nonmetabolizable FDG from these organs and its excretion with urine.[131]

We will now briefly refer to a few studies on the mechanism of transport of glucose and its analogues.[15,141-145] Animal cells, in contrast to bacteria, use facilitated diffusion as the main sugar transport mechanism. However, in situations where sugar uptake is critical, such as absorption of nutrients from the intestinal lumen or recovery of otherwise lost nutrients from the kidney, the more flexible and efficient active transport is used. Therefore, as in bacteria, it seems that active transport systems are used preferentially on the membrane in contact with the variable environment.

Glucose is transported into fibroblasts by facilitated diffusion;[15] the glucose transport into the cell is a rate-limiting step of glucose metabolism.[15]

Many in vitro studies have revealed that glucose uptake is influenced by such different parameters as pH, cellular density serum, or trypsin, high concentrations of Zn^{++}, Mn^{++}, and Cd^{++}.[15]

Using (^3H) 2dGlc in CEF-CEF(RSV), we showed that glucose uptake can be used to evaluate the state of growth and the transformation of cells.[26,86] Indeed, when fibroblasts are grown at a high rate, they take up glucose at a faster rate than resting cells. Furthermore if the cells are transformed, e.g., by virus, and the rate of glucose uptake compared with that of normal cells growing at the same rate, it is found that transformed cells have a higher rate of uptake than normal cells. Other authors agree with these data.[141,142]

It has also been shown that neither hexokinase,[147] ATP concentration,[148] feedback inhibition of hexokinase by G-6-P, nor the glucose supply[15] is responsible for the increased rate of glucose accumulation inside the cells after viral transformation.

The increased rate of glucose transport in CEF(RSV) is not due to the appearance of new carrier species, but rather to an increase in either the number or the mobility of the carrier present in normal cells.[15] However, this increase appears to be specific for the glucose transport system since CEF(RSV) take up uridine and thymidine at the same rate as CEF under conditions in which infected and uninfected cells have identical growth rates.

The fast rate of glucose transport found in transformed cells is probably correlated to the high glycolytic rate of transformed cells.[149]

VII. CONCLUSIONS

Radioisotopic scanning agents are frequently used in clinical medicine. The study of the mechanism of action and the specificity of these agents is frequently hindered by the absence of appropriate test systems.

In vitro systems often are unable to distinguish between the tissue uptake due to factors such as increased vascularity and vessel permeability, necrosis, and phagocytosis, which are common to several pathological conditions, and the specific accumulation due, for example, to cell transformation.

For these reasons, a study performed using in vitro systems in which one can consider every single factor affecting the accumulation, e.g., the effect of cell transformation, is of great interest. We have shown that in highly controlled in vitro systems it is possible to identify radioisotopic scanning agents which are markers of the malignant transformation or useful for the study of specific organs (e.g., brain or heart).

This should be obviously useful for the choice of agents to be used in tumor diagnosis or study of organ functions.

These systems are ideal candidates for the identification and the study of the mechanism of action of scanning agents as well as examples of in vitro systems in which agents could be tested for their tumor specificity or uptake in differentiated tissues before they are used in nuclear medicine.

ACKNOWLEDGMENT

This work was supported by Progetto Finalizzato Virus, Sottoprogetto Virus Oncogeni, CNR, Italy.

REFERENCES

1. Winchell, H. S., Mechanisms for localization of radiopharmaceuticals in neoplasms, *Semin. Nucl. Med.*, 6, 371, 1976.
2. Stein, W. D., *The Movement of Molecules Across the Cell Membranes,* Academic Press, New York, 1967.
3. Roseman, S. J., The transport of carbohydrates by a bacterial phosphotransferase system, *J. Gen. Physiol.*, 54, 1385, 1969.
4. Schultz, S. and Curran, P. F., Coupled transport of sodium and organic solutes, *Physiol. Rev.*, 50, 637, 1970.
5. Wilson, D. B., Cellular transport mechanisms, *Ann. Rev. Biochem.*, 47, 934, 1978.
6. Haynie, T. P., Konikowski, T., and Glenn, H. J., Experimental models for evaluation of radioactive tumor localizing agents, *Semin. Nucl. Med.*, 6, 347, 1976.
7. Watson, J. D., *Molecular Biology of the Gene,* W. A. Benjamin, Menlo Park, Calif., 1976.
8. Dexter, T. M., Allen, T. D., and Lajtha, L. G., Conditions controlling the proliferation of haematopoietic stem cells *in vitro, J. Cell. Physiol.*, 91, 335, 1977.
9. Hanafusa, H., Cell transformation by RNA tumor viruses, *Compre. Virol.*, 10, 401, 1977.
10. Tooze, J., *Molecular Biology of Tumor Viruses,* Cold Spring Harbor Laboratory, Cold Spring Harbor, N.Y., 1973.
11. Larson, S. M., Mechanisms of localization of ^{67}Ga in tumors, *Semin. Nucl. Med.*, 8, 193, 1978.
12. Morris, H. P. and Wagner, B. P., Induction and transplantation of rat hepatomas with different growth rate (including "minimal deviation" hepatomas), in *Methods in Cancer Research,* Vol. IV, Busch, H., Ed., Academic Press, New York, 1968, 135.
13. Fogh, J., Ed., *Human Tumor Cells in Vitro,* Plenum Press, New York, 1975.
14. Martin, G. S., in *The Biology of Oncogenic Viruses,* Silvestri, L., Ed., North-Holland, Amsterdam, 1971.
15. Venuta, S., Relationship of Membrane Permeability to Growth and Viral Transformation of Chick Embryo Fibroblasts, Ph. D. thesis, University of California, Berkeley, 1974.
16. Siegel, E. and Siegel, E. P., In vitro experiments to demonstrate radiotracer metabolism, in *Principles of Radiopharmacology,* Vol. II, Colombetti, L., Ed., CRC Press, Boca Raton, Fla., 1979, 107.

17. Hochstadt, J., Quinlan, D. C., Rader, R. L., et al., Use of isolated membrane vesicles in transport studies, in *Methods in Membrane Biology,* Vol. V, Korn, W., Ed., Plenum Press, New York, 1974, 117.
18. Paul, J., *Cell and Tissue Culture,* Churchill Livingstone, Edinburgh, 1975.
19. Animal Cell Culture (a manual written by R. Pollack and S. Pfiffer for the 1971 Course and revised by R. Goldmann and H. Coon, for the 1973 Course), Cold Spring Harbor Laboratory, Cold Spring Harbor, N.Y., 1973.
20. Morgan, H., *Cell Culture and Somatic Variation,* Holt, Reinhart, & Winston, New York, 1964.
21. Pollack, R., Ed., *Readings in Mammalian Cell Culture,* Cold Spring Harbor Laboratory, Cold Spring Harbor, N.Y., 1975.
22. Elkind, M. M. and Whitmore, G. F., *The Radiobiology of Cultured Mammalian Cells,* Gordon & Breach, New York, 1967, 547.
23. Larson, S. M., Rasey, J. S., Allen, D. R., and Grunbaum, Z., A transferrin-mediated uptake of gallium-67 by EMT-6 sarcoma. II. Studies *in vivo* (BALB/c mice), concise communication, *J. Nucl. Med.,* 20, 843, 1979.
24. Rockwell, S., *In vivo-in vitro* tumor systems: new models for studying the response of tumors to therapy, *Lab. Anim. Sci.,* 27, 831, 1977.
25. Rous, P., A sarcoma of the fowl transmissible by an agent from the tumor cells, *J. Exp. Med.,* 13, 397, 1911.
26. Martin, G. S., Venuta, S., Weber, M., et al., Temperature-dependent alterations in sugar transport in cells infected by a temperature sensitive mutant of Rous Sarcoma Virus, *Proc. Natl. Acad. Sci. U.S.A.,* 68, 2739, 1971.
27. Temin, H. M. and Rubin, H., Characteristics of an assay for Rous Sarcoma Virus and Rous Sarcoma Cells in tissue culture, *Virology,* 6, 669, 1958.
28. Gurney, T., Local stimulation of growth in primary cultures of chick-embryo fibroblasts, *Proc. Natl. Acad. Sci. U.S.A.,* 62, 906, 1969.
29. Rubin, H., *Growth Control in Cell Cultures,* Wolstenholme, G. and Knight, J., Eds., Churchill-Livingstone, Edinburgh, 1971, 127.
30. Ambesi-Impiombato, F. S. and Coon, H. G., Thyroid cells in cultures, *Int. Rev. Cytol.,* in press.
31. Carrell, A., A method for the physiological study of tissues *in vitro, J. Exp. Med.,* 38, 407, 1923.
32. Tong, W., The isolation and culture of thyroid cells, in *Methods in Enzymology,* Vol. 32, Part B, Fleischer, S. and Packer, L., Eds., Academic Press, New York, 1974, 745.
33. Lissitzky, S., Fayet, G., and Verrier, B., in *Advances in Cyclic Nucleotide Research,* Vol. V, Drummond, G. I., Greengard, P., and Robison, J. A., Eds., Raven Press, New York, 1975, 183.
34. Siegel, E., The preservation of specialization by dispersed steer thyroidal Cells in lung. Term culture, *J. Cell. Sci.,* 9, 49, 1971.
35. Edwards, C. L. and Hayes, R. L., Tumor scanning with ^{67}Ga-Citrate, *J. Nucl. Med.,* 10, 103, 1965.
36. Lavender, J. P., Lowe, J., Barker, J. R., et al., Gallium-67 Citrate scanning in neoplastic and inflammatory lesions, *Br. J. Radiol.,* 44, 361, 1971.
37. Littemberg, R. L., Takata, R. M., Alaznaki, M. P., et al., Gallium-67 for the localization of septic lesions, *Ann. Int. Med.,* 79, 403, 1973.
38. Cotton, F. A. and Wilkinson, G., *Advanced Inorganic Chemistry,* 3rd ed., Interscience, New York, 1972, 260.
39. Latimer, W. M., The Oxidation States of the Elements and Their Potentials in Aqueous Solutions, Prentice-Hall, Englewood Cliffs, N.J., 1952, 158.
40. Anghileri, L. J., Mechanisms of localization of free radioions, in *Principles of Radiopharmacology,* Vol. III, Colombetti, L. G., Ed., CRC Press, Boca Raton, Fla., 1979, 243.
41. Higashi, T., Kanno, M., and Tomusa, K., Comparison of uptake of ^{67}Ga-Citrate and [57]Co-Bleomycin in tumor using a semiconductor detector, *J. Nucl. Med.,* 15, 1167, 1974.
42. Hartman, R. E. and Hayes, R. L., Gallium binding by blood serum, *Fed. Proc., Fed. Am. Soc. Exp. Biol.,* 26 (Abstr.), 780, 1967.
43. Gunasekera, S. W., King, L. J., and Lavender, P. J., The behavior of tracer Gallium-67 toward serum proteins, *Clin. Chim. Acta,* 39, 401, 1972.
44. Hoffer, P., Huberty, J., and Khajam-Bashi, II., The association of Ga-67 and lactoferrin, *J. Nucl. Med.,* 18, 713, 1977.
45. Hegge, F. M., Mahler, D. J., and Larson, S. M., The incorporation of Ga-67 into the ferritin fraction of rabbit hepatocytes *in vivo, J. Nucl. Med.,* 18, 937, 1977.
46. Emery, T., Siderophore mediated mechanism of Gallium uptake demonstrated in microorganisms, *J. Nucl. Med.,* 21 (Abstr.), P24, 1980.
47. Bradley, W. P., Anderson, P. O., and Weiss, J. F., Effect of iron deficiency on the biodistribution and tumor uptake of Ga-67 Citrate in animals, concise communication, *J. Nucl. Med.,* 20, 243, 1979.
48. Lentle, B. C., *Gallium-67 Citrate: Mechanisms of Localization and Clinical Applications,* 3rd Natl. Symp., Societa Italiana Di Radiologia Medica e Medicina Nucleare, Milan, Italy, 1979.

49. Hoffer, P. B., Samuel, A., Bushberg, T., et al. Effect of desferioxamine on tissue and tumor retention of Gallium-67: concise communication, *J. Nucl. Med.,* 20, 248, 1979.

50. Oster, Z. H., Som, P., Sacker, D. F., and Atkins, A., The effects of deferioxamine mesylate on Gallium-67 distribution in normal and abscess-bearing animals, concise communication, *J. Nucl. Med.,* 8, 21, 421, 1980.

51. Hayes, R. L., The tissue distribution of gallium radionuclides, *J. Nucl. Med.,* 18, 741, 1977.

52. Swartzendruber, D. C., Nelson, B., and Hayes, R. L., Ga-67 localization in lysosomial-like granules of leukemic and nonleukemic murine tissues, *J. Natl. Cancer Inst.,* 46, 941, 1971.

53. Haubold, U. and Aulbert, E., Ga-67 as a tumor scanning agent. Clinical and physiological aspects, in *Medical Radioisotope Scintigraphy,* Vol. 2, International Atomic Energy Agency, Vienna, 1973, 553.

54. Ito, Y., Okuyama, S., Sato, K., et al. ^{67}Ga tumor scanning and its mechanism studied in rabbits, *Radiology,* 100, 357, 1971.

55. Brown, D. H., Byrd, B. L., Carlton, J. E., et al., A quantitative study of the subcellular localization of ^{67}Ga, *Cancer Res.,* 36, 956, 1976.

56. Aulbert, E., Gebhardt, A., Schulz, E., et al., Mechanisms of ^{67}Ga accumulation in normal rat liver lysosomes, *J. Nucl. Med.,* 15, 185, 1976.

57. Clausen, J., Edeling, C. J., and Fogh,J., ^{67}Ga binding to human serum proteins and tumor components, *Cancer Res.,* 34, 1931, 1974.

58. Hayes, R. L. and Carlton, J. E., A study of the macromolecular binding of ^{67}Ga in normal and malignant animal tissues, *Cancer Res.,* 33, 3265, 1973.

59. Gelrud, L. G., Arsenau, J. C., Milder, H. S., et al., The kinetics of ^{67}Gallium incorporation into inflammatory lesions: experimental and clinical studies, *J. Lab. Clin. Med.,* 83, 489, 1974.

60. Tzen, K. J., Oster, Z. H., Wagner, H. N., Jr., and Tsan, M. F., Role of the iron-bindings proteins and enhanced capillary permeability on the accumulation of Gallium-67, *J. Nucl. Med.,* 21, 31, 1980.

61. Gams, R., Long, W., Alford, C., et al., Effect of growth rate and simian adenovirus-7 transformation on "in vitro" ^{67}Ga binding to hamster embryo cells, *J. Nucl. Med.,* 16, 231, 1975.

62. Bichel, P. and Hansen H. H., The incorporation of ^{67}Ga in normal and malignant cells and its dependence on growth rate, *Br. J. Radiol.,* 45, 182, 1972.

63. Farrer, P. and Saha, G., Studies on the mechanism of ^{67}Ga uptake by normal and malignant tissue and cell-system, *J. Nucl. Med.,* 14, 625, 1973.

64. Orii, H., Tumor scanning with Gallium (^{67}Ga) and its mechanism studied in rat, *Strahlentherapie,* 144, 192, 1972.

65. Hill, J. H. and Wagner, H. N., Jr., ^{67}Ga uptake in the regenerating rat liver, *J. Nucl. Med.,* 15, 818, 1974.

66. Glickson, J. D., Webb, J., and Gams, R. A., Effect of buffers and pH on *in vitro* binding of ^{67}Ga in L1210 leukemic cells, *Cancer Res.,* 34, 2957, 1974.

67. Weiner, R. E., Hoffer, P. B., and Thakur, H. L., Identification of Ga-67 binding components in human neutrophiles, *J. Nucl. Med.,* 19 (Abstr.), 732, 1978.

68. Menon, S., Wagner, H. N., Jr., and Tsan, M. F., Studies on Gallium accumulation in inflammatory lesions. II. Uptake by *Staphylococcus aureus:* concise communication, *J. Nucl. Med.,* 19, 44, 1978.

69. Tsan, M. F., Chen, W. J., Scheffel, U., and Wagner, H. N., Jr., Studies on Gallium accumulation in inflammatory lesions. I. Gallium uptake by human polymorphonuclear leukocytes, *J. Nucl. Med.,* 19, 36, 1978.

70. Larson, S. M., Rasey, G. S., Allen, D. R., and Nelson, N. J., A transferrin mediated uptake of Gallium-67 by EMT-6 sarcoma. I. Studies in tissue culture, *J. Nucl. Med.,* 20, 837, 1979.

71. Hemmaplardh, D. and Morgan, E. H., The role of endocytosis in transferrin uptake by reticulocytes and bone marrow cells, *Br. J. Haematol.,* 36, 85, 1977.

72. Bockxmeer, F. M. and Morgan, E. H., Identification of transferrin receptors in reticulocytes, *Biochim. Biophys. Acta,* 468, 437, 1977.

73. Larson, S. M., Grunbauer, Z., Rasey, J. S., et al., A transferrin binding macromolecular component of EMT-6 sarcoma (BALB/c mice), *J. Nucl. Med.,* 20 (Abstr.), 672, 1979.

74. Harris, A. W. and Sephton, R. G., Transferrin promotion of ^{67}Ga and ^{59}Fe uptake by cultured mouse myeloma cells, *Cancer Res.,* 37, 3634, 1977.

75. Terner, U. K., Wong, H., Noujaim, A. A., Lentle, B. C., and Hill, G. R., ^{67}Ga and ^{59}Fe uptake in human melanoma cells, *Int. J. Nucl. Med. Biol.,* 6, 23, 1979.

76. Sephton, R. G., Hodgson, G. S., De Abrew, S., and Harris, A. W., Ga-67 and Fe-59 distribution in mice, *J. Nucl. Med.,* 19, 930, 1978.

77. Sephton, R. G. and Harris, A. W., Gallium-67 citrate uptake by cultured tumor cells stimulated by serum transferrin, *J. Natl. Cancer Inst.,* 54, 1263, 1974.

78. Muranaka, A., Iasuhito, I., Michibuni, H., et al., Uptake and excretion of ^{67}Ga citrate in malignant tumors and normal cells, *Eur. J. Nucl. Med.,* 5, 31, 1980.

79. Hayes, R. L., Byrd, B. L., Carlton, J. E., et al., Effect of scandium on biodistribution of ⁶⁷Ga in tumor-bearing animals, *J. Nucl. Med.*, 12, 437, 1971.

80. Hayes, R. L., Byrd, B. L., Rafter, J. J., and Carlton, J. E., The effect of Scandium on the tissue distribution of Ga-67 in normal and tumor-bearing rodents, *J. Nucl. Med.*, 21, 361, 1980.

81. Bradley, W. P., Alderson, P. O., Eckelman, W. C., et al., Decreased tumor uptake of Gallium-67 in animals after whole-body irradiation, *J. Nucl. Med.*, 19, 204, 1978.

82. Vallabhayosula, S. R., Harwing, J. F., and Wolf, W., Mechanism of tumor localization of Gallium: effect of tumor pH, *J. Nucl. Med.*, 20 (Abstr.), 655, 1979.

83. Fernandez-Pol, J. A., Klos, D., Baer, K., and Donati, R. M., Transferrin receptors in normal and virus-transformed cells in culture, *J. Nucl. Med.*, 20 (Abstr.), 672, 1979.

84. Venuta, S., Morrone, G., Mansi, L., and Salvatore, M., Tissue Culture Study of Radiosotopic Scanning Agents, 1st Intl. Symp. Radiopharmacol., 1978, Innsbruck, Austria, Abstr.

85. Venuta, S., Morrone, G., Ferraiuolo, R., Mansi, L., and Salvatore, M., Meccanismo di azione di indicatori di neoplasie maligne e metodi di screening degli indicatori stessi, *Rass. Med. Sper.*, 26, 63, 1979.

86. Venuta, S. and Rubin, H., Sugar transport in normal and Rous Sarcoma Virus transformed chick embryo fibroblasts, *Proc. Natl. Acad. Sci. U.S.A.*, 70, 653, 1973.

87. Thesing, C. W., Driessen, O. M. J., Daems, W. T., et al., Accumulation and localization of gallium-67 in various types of primary lung carcinoma, *J. Nucl. Med.*, 19, 28, 1978.

88. Kawana, M., Krizeh, H., Porter, J., et al., Use of 199-Tl as a potassium analog in scanning, *J. Nucl. Med.*, 11, 333, 1970.

89. Lebowitz, E., Green, M. W., Bradley-Moore, P., et al., 201-Tl for medical use, *J. Nucl. Med.*, 14, 421, 1973.

90. Gehring, P. J. and Hammond, P. B., The interelationship between thallium and potassium in animals, *J. Pharmacol. Exp. Ther.*, 155, 187, 1967.

91. Negherbon, W. O., Ed., *Handbook of Toxicology*, Vol. III, W. B. Saunders, Philadelphia, 1959.

92. Britten, J. J. and Blank, M., Thallium activation of the (Na⁺-K⁺)-activated ATPase of rabbit kidney, *Biochim. Biophys. Acta*, 159, 160, 1968.

93. Körtum, F. A. and Bockris, J. O., *Textbook of Electrochemistry*, Vol. 2, Elsevier, Amsterdam, 1951.

94. Strauss, H. W., Harrison, K., Longan, J. K., et al., Thallium-201 for myocardial imaging: relation of thallium-201 to regional myocardial perfusion, *Circulation*, 51, 641, 1975.

95. Bailey, I. K., Griffith, L. S. C., Rouleau, J., et al., Thallium-201 myocardial perfusion imaging at rest and during exercise, *Circulation*, 55, 79, 1976.

96. Gehring, P. J. and Hammond, P. B., The uptake of thallium by rabbit erythrocytes, *J. Pharmacol. Exp. Ther.*, 145, 215, 1964.

97. Brierley, G. P., *The Molecular Biology of Membranes*, Fleischer, A., Hatefi, Y., MacLennan, H., and Tzagoloff, A., Eds., Plenum Press, New York, 1978.

98. Glynn, I. M. and Karlish, S. J. D., *Annual Review of Physiology*, Vol. XXXVII, Comroe, J. H., Jr., Ed., Annual Review, Inc., Palo Alto, Calif., 1975, 13.

99. Garrahan, P. J. and Garay, R. P., *Current Topics in Membrane and Transport*, Vol. VIII, Bronner, F. and Kleinzeller, A., Eds., Academic Press, New York, 1976, 29.

100. Katz, B., *Nerve, Muscle and Synapse*, McGraw-Hill, New York, 1966.

101. Pohost, G. M., Zir, L. M., Moore, R. H., et al., Differentiation of transiently ischemic from infarcted myocardium by serial imaging after a single dose of thallium-201, *Circulation*, 55, 294, 1977.

102. Welch, H. F., Strauss, H. W., and Pitt, B., The extraction of Thallium-201 by the myocardium, *Circulation*, 56, 188, 1977.

103. Hamilton, G. W., Narahara, K. A., Yee, H., et al., Myocardial imaging with Thallium-201: effect of cardiac drugs on myocardial images and absolute tissue distribution, *J. Nucl. Med.*, 19, 10, 1978.

104. Christenson, J., Larsson, I., Svensson, S. E., and Westling, L., Distribution of intravenously injected ²⁰¹Thallium in the legs during walking, *Eur. J. Nucl. Med.*, 2, 85, 1977.

105. Hosain, F., Hosain, P., and Spencer, R. P., Testicular imaging with Thallium-201 and comparison with other radionuclides, *J. Nucl. Med.*, 19 (Abstr.), 720, 1978.

106. Raynaud, C., Comar, D., and Brisson, M., Radioactive Tl: a new agent for scan of the renal medulla, in *Radionuclides in Nephrology*, Blaufox, M. D. and Funck-Brentano, J. L., Eds., Grune & Stratton, New York, 1970, 289.

107. Salvatore, M., Carratù, L., Malgieri, F., Bazzicalupo, L., and Muto, P., Use of Tl-201 (Thallium chloride) as a positive tumor indicator: preliminary experience, 15th Congr. of SIBMN, Turin, Italy, 1975, *J. Nucl. Med. Biol.*, 20 (Abstr.), 114, 1976.

108. Salvatore, M., Carratù, L., and Porta, E., Thallium-201 as a positive indicator: preliminary experiments, *Radiology*, 121, 487, 1976.

109. Salvatore, M., Tarallo, L., Lombardi, G., et al., La scintigrafia tiroidea, 27th Natl. Congr. SIRMN, Vol. 3, SIRMN, Bari, Italy, 1976, 29.

110. Salvatore, M., Carratù, L., Bazzicalupo, L., and Mansi, L., The use of Tl-201 Thallium Chloride as a positive tumor indicator, *Eur. J. Nucl. Med.*, 1 (Abstr.), 15, 1976.

111. Salvatore, M., Venuta, S., Bianco, A., and Mansi, L., Thallium-201 in thyroid tumors diagnosis, in *2nd Intl. Congr., World Fed. Nucl. Med. Biol.*, Washington, D.C., 1978, 31.

112. Salvatore, M., Bazzicalupo, L., Calabrò, A., et al., L'uso del ²⁰¹Tl cloruro quale indicatore positivo nella diagnostica delle neoplasie, in *27th Natl. Congr. SIRMN*, Vol. 3, SIRMN, Bari, Italy, 1976, 173.

113. Cox, P. H., Belfer, A. J., and van der Pompe, W. B., Thallium-201 chloride uptake in tumors. A possible complicator in heart scintigraphy, *Br. J. Radiol.*, 49, 767, 1976.

114. Harada, T., Ito, Y., Shimaoka, K., et al., Clinical evaluation of ²⁰¹Thallium chloride scan for thyroid nodule, *Eur. J. Nucl. Med.*, 5, 125, 1980.

115. Ancri, D. and Basset, J. Y., Diagnosis of cerebral metastases by Thallium-201, *Br. J. Radiol.*, 53, 443, 1980.

116. Tonami, N., Michigishi, T., Bunko, H., et al., Clinical tumor scanning with ²⁰¹Tl-chloride, *J. Nucl. Med.*, 18, 617, 1977.

117. Charkes, M. D., Sklaroff, D. M., Gershon-Cohen, J., et al., Tumor scanning with radioactive ¹³¹Cesium: *J. Nucl. Med.*, 6, 300, 1965.

118. Baker, W. H., Nathanson, I. T., and Seleverstone, B., Use of radioactive Potassium (K⁴²) in the study of benign and malignant breast tumors, *N. Engl. J. Med.*, 252, 612, 1955.

119. Potts, A. M. and Au, P. C., Thallous ion and eye, *Invest. Ophthal.*, 10, 925, 1971.

120. Ito, Y., Muranaka, A., Harada, T., et al., Experimental study on tumor affinity of ²⁰¹Tl Chloride, *Eur. J. Nucl. Med.*, 3, 81, 1978.

121. Hudson, F. R., Dewey, D. L., Galpine, A. R., and Whittingam, A. G., Tumor uptake of Thallium-201 Chloride, *Eur. J. Nucl. Med.*, 4, 283, 1978.

122. Venuta, S., Ferraiuolo, R., Ambesi-Impiombato, F. S., Mansi, L., and Salvatore, M., Uptake of ²⁰¹Tl in normal and transformed thyroid cell lines, *J. Nucl. Med. All. Sci.*, 23, 163, 1979.

123. De Long, R. P., Dale, R. C., and Zeidman, I., The significance of low calcium and high potassium content in neoplastic tissues, *Cancer (Philadelphia)*, 3, 718, 1950.

124. Perdue, J. F., *Virus Transformed Cell Membranes*, Nicolau, C., Ed., Academic Press, New York, 1978, 252.

125. Lelievre, L. and Paraf, A., Enzyme activities in membranes from three phenotypes of the murine plasmocytoma MOPC-173, activated in vitro, *Biochim Biophys. Acta*, 291, 671, 1973.

126. Spaggiare, S., Wallach, M. J., and Tupper, J. T., Potassium transport in normal and transformed mouse 3T3 cells, *J. Cell. Physiol.*, 89, 403, 1976.

127. Banerjee, S. P., Bosmann, H. B., and Morgan, H. R., Oncogenic transformation of chick embryo fibroblasts by Rous Sarcoma Virus alters rubidium uptake and ouabain binding, *Exp. Cell Res.*, 104, 111, 1977.

128. Kimelberg, H. K. and Mayhew, E., Increased Ouabain-sensitive ⁸¹Rb⁺ uptake and sodium and potassium ion-activated adenosine triphosphatase activity in transformed cell lines, *J. Biol. Chem.*, 250, 100, 1975.

129. Reivich, M., Kuhl, D., Wolf, A. P., et al., The (¹⁸F) Fluoro-Deoxy-Glucose method for the measurement of local cerebral glucose utilization in man, *Circ. Res.*, 44, 127, 1979.

130. Gallagher, B. M., Ansari, A., Atkins, H., et al., Radiopharmaceuticals. XXVII. ¹⁸F-labeled 2-Deoxy-2-Fluoro-D-Glucose as a radiopharmaceutical for measuring regional myocardial glucose metabolism *in vivo:* tissue distribution and imaging studies in animals, *J. Nucl. Med.*, 18, 990, 1977.

131. Gallagher, B. M., Fowler, J. S., Gutterson, M. I., et al., Metabolic trapping as a principle of radio-pharmaceutical design: some factors responsible for the biodistribution of (¹⁸F) 2-Deoxy-2-Fluoro-D-Glucose, *J. Nucl. Med.*, 19, 1154, 1978.

132. Larson, S. M., Grunbaum, Z., and Rasey, J. S., Positron imaging feasibility studies. I. Selective tumor concentration of ³H-thymidine, ³H-uridine and ¹⁴C-2-Deoxy-glucose, *J. Nucl. Med.*, P32, 21, 1980; abst.

133. Som, P., Atkins, H. L., Bandyopadhyay, D., et al., Early detection of neoplasms with radiolabeled sugar analogs, *J. Nucl. Med.*, 20, 662, 1979.

134. Raichle, M. E., Larson, K. B., Phelps, M. E., et al., *In vivo* measurement of brain glucose transport and metabolism employing ¹¹C-glucose, *Am. J. Physiol.*, 228, 1936, 1975.

135. Tewson, T. J., Welch, M. J., and Raichle, M. E., (¹⁸F)-Labeled 3-Deoxy-3-Fluoro-D-Glucose: synthesis and preliminary biodistribution data, *J. Nucl. Med.*, 19, 1339, 1978.

136. Robinson, G. D., Jr., Phelps, M. E., and Huang, S. C., F-18-2-Fluoro-D-Mannose: biological behavior compared with 2-Deoxy-2-Fluoro-D-glucose, *J. Nucl. Med.*, 20 (Abstr.), 672, 1979.

137. Coe, E. L., Inhibition of glycolysis in ascites tumor cells preincubated 2-Deoxy-2-Fluoro-D-glucose, *Biochim. Biophys. Acta*, 264, 319, 1972.

138. Bessell, E. M. and Thomas, P., The Deoxyfluoro-D-glucopyranose-6-phosphates and their effect on yeast glucose phosphate isomerase, *Biochem. J.*, 131, 77, 1973.

139. Turner, R. J. and Silverman, M., Sugar uptake into brush border vesicles from normal human kidney, *Proc. Natl. Acad. Sci. U.S.A.*, 74, 2825, 1977.

140. Long, C., Studies involving enzymic phosphorilation. 1. The hexokinase activity of rat tissues, *Biochem. J.*, 50, 407, 1952.

141. Singh, M., Singh, W. N., August, J. T. and Horecker, B. L., Transport and phosphorilation of hexoses in normal and Rous Sarcoma Virus-transformed chick embryo fibroblasts, *J. Cell. Physiol.*, 97, 285, 1978.

142. Lang, D. R. and Weber, M. J., Increased membrane transport of 2-Deoxy-Glucose and 3-O-Methylo Glucose is an early event in the transformation of chick embryo fibroblasts by Rous Sarcoma Virus, *J. Cell. Physiol.*, 94, 315, 1978.

143. Graff, J. C., Wohlveter, R. M., and Plagemann, P. G. W., Deoxyglucose and 3-O-Methyl-glucose transport in untreated and ATP-depleted Novikoff rat hepatoma cells. Analysis by a rapid kinetic technique. Relationship to phosphorilation and effects of inhibitors, *J. Cell. Physiol.*, 96, 171, 1978.

144. Lee, S. G. and Lipmann, F., Isolation from normal and Rous Sarcoma Virus-transformed chicken fibroblasts of a factor that binds glucose and stimulates its transport, *Proc. Natl. Acad. Sci. U.S.A.*, 74, 163, 1977.

145. Dubrov, R., Pardee, A. R., and Pollack, R., 2-amino-Isobutyric Acid and 3-O-Methyl-D-Glucose transport in 3-T-3, SV40-transformed 3T3 and revertant cell lines, *J. Cell Physiol.*, 95, 203, 1978.

146. Hatanaka, W. M., Huebner, R. J., and Gilden, R. V., Alterations in the characteristics of sugar uptake by mouse cells transformed by murine sarcoma viruses, *J. Natl. Cancer. Inst.*, 43, 1091, 1969.

147. Hatanaka, M., Angle, C., and Gilden, R. V., Evidence for a functional change in the plasma membrane of murine sarcoma virus-infected mouse embryo cells. Transport and transport associated phosphorilation of ^{14}C-2-Deoxy-D-glucose, *J. Biol. Chem.*, 245, 714, 1970.

148. Colby, C. and Edlin, G., Nucleotide pool levels in growing, inhibited and transformed chick fibroblast cells, *Biochemistry*, 9, 917, 1970.

149. Warburg, O., *The Metabolism of Tumors*, Arnold Constable, London, 1930.

INDEX

A

W

X

Z